T5-DHH-978

COST
ACCOUNTING

COST ACCOUNTING

James A. Cashin, M.B.A., C.P.A., C.I.A.

Emeritus Professor of Accounting
Hofstra University

Ralph S. Polimeni, Ph.D., C.P.A.

Chairman, Department of Accounting
Hofstra University

McGraw-Hill Book Company

New York   St. Louis   San Francisco   Auckland
Bogotá   Hamburg   Johannesburg   London
Madrid   Mexico   Montreal   New Delhi   Panama   Paris
São Paulo   Singapore   Sydney   Tokyo   Toronto

Library of Congress Cataloging in Publication Data

Cashin, James A
    Cost accounting.

    Includes bibliographical references and index.
    1. Cost accounting. I. Polimeni, Ralph S.,
joint author. II. Title.
HF5686.C8C2958   657'.42   80-16236
ISBN 0-07-010213-9

COST ACCOUNTING

234567890 DODO 8987654321

This book was set in Electra by Monotype Composition Company, Inc. The editors were Donald G. Mason and Elisa Adams; the designer was Rafael Hernandez; the production supervisor was Charles Hess. The drawings were done by J & R Services, Inc.
R. R. Donnelley & Sons Company was printer and binder.

ABOUT THE AUTHORS

JAMES A. CASHIN is Emeritus Professor of Accounting at Hofstra University, where he was formerly Chairman of the Accounting Department. His publishing credits include some 18 titles; he is author or coauthor of several accounting textbooks, including *Auditing* and *Modern Internal Accounting*, and coauthor of the entire Schaum's Outline Series in Accounting and is Editor-in-Chief of the Handbook for Auditors. Professor Cashin is a Certified Public Accountant and a Certified Internal Auditor. He holds a general degree (A.A.) from Augusta College, a B.S. degree in Accounting from the University of Georgia and an M.B.A. degree from New York University. He has had wide experience in business with large industrial companies, as chief cost accountant, then as chief accountant and general auditor with Bristol-Myers Company, and as chief internal auditor with St. Regis Paper Company. He has been a consultant for private firms and government agencies. He has also taught in the Graduate School of City University of New York and at New York University.

RALPH S. POLIMENI has been active in both business and academia. He was employed as an auditor for Deloitte Haskins & Sells and has served as a consultant to Cooper's and Lybrand, the City of New York, the New York State Special Prosecutor's Office, and several law firms.

Since 1974 Dr. Polimeni has been Chairman of the Accounting Department at Hofstra University and in 1978 received the Hofstra University Distinguished Teaching Award. He has also taught at City University of New York and the University of Arkansas and is the Director of Chaykin's CPA Review Program at Hofstra University.

Dr. Polimeni received a Ph.D. in accounting from the University of Arkansas in 1973 and holds a C.P.A. Certificate from New York State. He has written numerous articles (one of which won the Outstanding Contributor Award presented by the Institute of Internal Auditors) and has coauthored several books.

CONTENTS

PART 5 SPECIAL TOPICS

PREFACE

Our primary reason for writing this book is to provide a text that can be easily understood by students and still provide comprehensive coverage of the topics generally found in a cost accounting text. To achieve this goal, we have included extensive illustrations in each chapter and eliminated unnecessary words and details. Every chapter, except the first and last, includes the following additional sections to aid the student in understanding the subject matter: chapter review, glossary, comprehensive summary problems with solutions, and assignment materials in the form of questions, exercises, and problems. Wherever applicable, assignment material was adapted from C.P.A. and C.M.A. examinations.

Fundamental concepts and techniques are covered in depth before a student is exposed to the more complex areas of cost accounting. To ensure a solid foundation, the first half of this text (Chapters 1 through 12) presents a thorough coverage of product costing systems. The second half (Chapters 13 through 24) deals mainly with the concepts and techniques of cost analysis. We feel it is vital for students to have a thorough understanding of product costing before they can attempt to analyze the data produced from sophisticated cost accounting systems.

Another objective is to coordinate the assignment material at the end of each chapter with the concepts and techniques presented in the body of the chapter. Students have told us that nothing is more frustrating and nothing hinders their learning and motivation more than to find assignment material at the end of the chapter that cannot be answered by conscientiously studying the chapter. It is our belief that the learning process is fostered when students are able to apply their newfound skills to problem situations. Assignment material in each chapter covers a wide range, beginning with simple problems (to promote confidence) and gradually building up to complex problems at the end (to provide a challenge).

All the major areas of cost accounting and analysis are covered in detail, including the nature and concepts of cost accounting; the costing and control of materials, labor, and factory overhead; periodic cost accumulation procedures; job order costing; process costing (two chapters); standard costing (two chapters); direct costing; by-product and joint product costing; budgeting (three chapters); breakeven analysis, decentralized operations, and responsibility accounting; performance measurement; gross profit analysis; linear programming; transfer pricing; decision theory and techniques; and even a full chapter on human resource accounting. The primary emphasis of the text is on manufacturing organizations. However, cost accounting is equally applicable to nonmanufacturing enterprises such as banks, insurance companies, hotels and restaurants, churches, hospitals, schools, all levels of government, and specific activities such as marketing or distribution, and many types of administrative and clerical positions. Examples and end-of-chapter problems have thus been included from nonmanufacturing enterprises.

This text is designed primarily for a two-semester course, with the first semester devoted to product costing (Chapters 1 through 12) and the second semester emphasizing cost analysis (Chapters 13 through 24). However, it can also be used in a one-semester or a three-quarter course with the following format:

One Semester	Three Quarters
Chapters 1 to 5	First quarter 1 to 8
Chapters 7 to 8	Second quarter 9 to 16
Chapters 10 to 12	Third quarter 17 to 24
Chapters 13 to 15	
Chapter 17	
Chapter 22	
Chapter 23	

Two practice sets are available: job order costs (developed with the assistance of Carol Smith) and process costs (developed with the assistance of Kevin Fitzpatrick). These two practice sets provide a comprehensive review of the two major cost accounting systems used to compute product costs. A study guide is also available (developed with the assistance of Kevin Fitzpatrick, Andrew Rosman, and Carol Smith) that contains outlines of each chapter, objective questions (multiple choice, fill-in, and true-false), and short problems.

A solutions manual for assignment material and the practice sets are available for instructors.

The book was tested extensively by many undergraduate and graduate students at Hofstra University who reviewed the text and the related problem material. In some cases they had direct input into the initial preparation of the text and the problem material. We worked closely with students in order to develop a text that was student-oriented and directed at fulfilling students' needs. Chapters were revised a number of times until our student "judges" were satisfied that the material was presented in a simple, clear, and logical manner.

We wish to thank Dr. Thomas E. Johnson, Jr., Professor of Management, University of South Florida, who contributed the quantitative material relating to linear programming, decision theory, and certain break-even analysis data.

Our thanks go to the following students who made a significant impact on the text: Paula Calame, Raymond Calame, Fran Chimienti, Sheila Coates,

Gloria Duchene, Susan Greiser, Nellie Grimsley, Michael Nawrocki, Maureen O'Donnell, Kathleen Polimeni, and David Schector. Their comments and suggestions were an important contribution.

We also wish to thank the American Institute of Certified Public Accountants and the National Association of Accountants for their permission to use material adapted from C.P.A. and C.M.A. examinations.

Special thanks must also be given to Ninette Bertuglia, Maxine Elko, Emma McFarland, Lillian Palermi, Eva Stein, Rejeanne Vermeulen, and Sylvia Zaino, whose skill with the typewriter was essential to the project, and also to Michael Polimeni for his assistance in proofreading the text. Elisa Adams, Donald Chatham, and Donald Mason of McGraw-Hill were very supportive and helpful throughout the project.

We also wish to express our appreciation to the reviewers for their comments and suggestions, which were of great assistance in the preparation of this book: Donald Bostrom of the University of North Dakota, C. Willard Elliott, formerly of Louisiana State University, Frank Fabozzi of City University of New York, Howard Godfrey of the University of North Carolina, Joseph F. Goetz of Northern Arizona University, Merita Herbold of Hofstra University, Keith R. Leeseberg of Manatee Junior College, George Minmier of Memphis State University, Stanley E. Myers of Norwalk State Technical College, Nathan Slavin of Hofstra University, Ronald J. Thacker of the University of New Orleans. We would also like to express our special appreciation to Charles Brandon of Bernard Baruch College of the City University of New York for assisting us in the proof stages of the text by reviewing the end-of-chapter problem materials for accuracy.

**James A. Cashin
Ralph S. Polimeni**

COST
ACCOUNTING

PART ONE

COST ACCOUNTING PRINCIPLES

CHAPTER ONE

THE NATURE OF COST ACCOUNTING

The primary purpose of accounting is to provide financial information relating to an economic entity. Thus, accounting is concerned with measuring, recording, and reporting financial information to various groups of users. Financial information is required by management to plan and control the activities of a business. Financial information is also required by outsiders who provide funds or who have other interests requiring such material. As the needs of these users have grown, so have the concepts of accounting evolved to meet the needs of a changing society. Accounting is essential in every segment of our economy and is becoming even more important as computers and business technology become increasingly sophisticated. Individuals, hospitals, schools, churches, and government agencies, as well as those in business and industry, must account for all income and expenditures in accordance with accounting principles.

Nearly three hundred years ago a London merchant made the following observation:

> It is just as impossible for a Merchant to be prosperous in Trade without a knowledge of accounting as for a Mariner to sail a ship to all parts of the globe without a knowledge of navigation.

The same observation could well be made today about cost accounting.

FINANCIAL ACCOUNTING VERSUS COST ACCOUNTING

For our purposes, the field of accounting may be divided into *financial accounting* and *cost* or *managerial accounting*. Financial accounting is largely concerned with financial statements for external use by investors, creditors, labor unions, financial analysts, government agencies, and other interest groups. Cost or managerial accounting is primarily concerned with the accumulation and analysis of cost information for internal use by managers for planning, control, and decision making.

The principal contact that most people, other than accountants, have with accounting information is through published financial statements. These statements are generally the basis for investment decisions by stockholders, lending decisions by banks and credit institutions, and credit decisions by vendors. For this reason, financial accounting is concerned with proper recording, summarizing, and presenting of assets, liabilities, owners' equity, and profits and losses. Financial information prepared for external use is therefore closely regulated to protect the interests of these users.

All financial information published for external use must be presented in accordance with Generally Accepted Accounting Principles (GAAP). For example, fixed assets are recorded in historical dollars as required by GAAP. Thus a tract of land purchased for a plant site in 19X9 for $7,000 is recorded at its purchase price. That amount is maintained on the books until the property is resold.

For internal purposes, however, the current market value or replacement value may be more useful than the amount paid many years earlier. For example, the current market value or replacement value of a machine may be more helpful than its original price if management wishes to determine the rate of productivity of the machine or of a replacement. Thus management has great flexibility in using cost information for the wide variety of needs for planning and control of the company. We can see that cost accounting is far less restricted by outside influences than is financial accounting, and is more responsive to management needs.

Cost accounting is also more flexible with respect to the basis of measurement when used for internal operations. The basis of measurement for operations may be monetary (historical, present, or future dollars) or physical (labor hours, machine hours, or units produced). For example, management may wish to analyze the efficiency of workers in the factory. The cost data needed for this analysis may include the following:

1 A breakdown of hours worked by department, product, or process
2 Hourly rates by worker classification
3 Total labor hours and total labor dollars
4 Labor hours of idle time
5 Variances

The summarized cost information which will ultimately be used in external financial statements must adhere to generally accepted accounting principles.

Financial statements for external use generally must be prepared at least annually for stockholders, the Securities and Exchange Commission (SEC), the Internal Revenue Service (IRS), and to meet other requirements. Some companies are required by the SEC to report financial information quarterly.

TABLE 1-1
COMPARISON OF FINANCIAL ACCOUNTING AND COST ACCOUNTING

BASIS OF COMPARISON	FINANCIAL ACCOUNTING	COST ACCOUNTING
For whom prepared	External users	Internal users
Limitations	Direct regulation	Indirect regulation
Basis of valuation	Historical cost	Any form of monetary or physical measurement
When prepared	Periodically (as established by outside agencies)—at least once a year	Periodically (as determined by management)—when needed
Perspective	Entire company	Department, unit, or branch

Thus, such information for external use is reported at intervals established by outside agencies. Cost accounting reports are required at various intervals—weekly, biweekly, monthly—according to the needs of management. The nature of the reports and the content are determined by management. These monthly reports form the basis for annual reports. Furthermore, many studies and analyses are conducted for management on a one-time basis.

Financial statements published for external use include statements of financial position, results of operations, retained earnings, changes in financial position, and changes in stockholders' equity. While historical cost is still the basis for primary statements, certain large, publicly held enterprises must disclose supplementary information on both a constant dollar basis (adjusting accounting data for changes in the purchasing power of the dollar) and a current cost basis (current purchase price of an asset owned). Segmented information (operations in different industries, countries, and major customers) may also be required for certain enterprises.

Table 1-1 compares financial and cost accounting.

Operating Reports

In Figure 1-1 the reporting processes followed in the Coco Manufacturing Company are shown by division, broken down by weekly and monthly activities.

Table 1-2 is an *annual* income statement of Coco Manufacturing Company prepared for external use based on the monthly divisional income summaries. Table 1-3 is a summary of three divisional income reports prepared for the *month* of March for the Coco Manufacturing Company.

TABLE 1-2
COCO MANUFACTURING COMPANY
INCOME STATEMENT
FOR THE YEAR ENDED 12/31/X0

Sales	$275,670
Cost of sales	192,969
Gross profit	$ 82,701
Selling, general, and administrative expenses	55,134
Net income before taxes	$ 27,567
Taxes	13,784
Net income	$ 13,783

TABLE 1-3
COCO MANUFACTURING COMPANY
DIVISIONAL INCOME SUMMARY
FOR THE MONTH ENDED 3/31/X0

	DIVISION A		DIVISION B		DIVISION C		TOTAL	
	DOLLARS	PERCENT	DOLLARS	PERCENT	DOLLARS	PERCENT	DOLLARS	PERCENT
Sales	4,170	100	1,350	100	10,735	100	16,255	100
Cost of sales	2,500	60	800	59	8,300	77	11,600	71
Gross profit	1,670	40	550	41	2,435	23	4,655	29
SGA expenses:								
Sales expenses:								
Sales salaries	700	17	100	7	1,000	9	1,800	11
Other selling expenses	100	2	—	0	500	5	600	4
General and administrative (G & A) expenses:								
G & A salaries	100	2	50	4	700	7	850	5
Interest	50	1	20	2	20	—	90	1
Total SGA expenses	950	22	170	13	2,220	21	3,340	21
Net income before taxes	720	18	380	28	215	2	1,315	8

FIGURE 1-1   **Reporting Process, Coco Manufacturing Company**

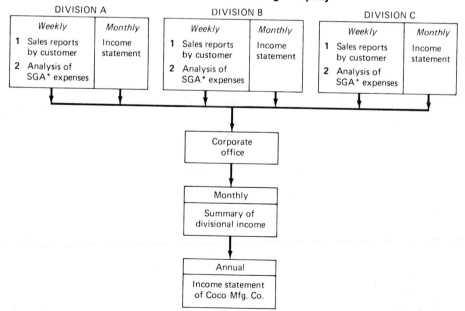

*SGA: Selling, General, and Administrative

6

COST ACCOUNTING
VERSUS MANAGERIAL ACCOUNTING

The National Association of Accountants (NAA) defined *cost accounting* as "a systematic set of procedures for recording and reporting measurements of the cost of manufacturing goods and performing services, in the aggregate and in detail. It includes methods for recognizing, classifying, allocating, aggregating, and reporting such costs and comparing them with standard costs." *Managerial accounting* is defined by the NAA as "that subset of the accounting process which provides planning and control information to the firm or components thereof." Though the preceding definition of cost accounting is specific, while that of managerial accounting is general, they are similar in meaning and therefore the terms are often used interchangeably in accounting literature. Some accountants feel that cost accounting refers primarily to the accumulation of cost data while managerial accounting refers primarily to the analysis of the cost data collected. In this text, the term "cost accounting" will refer to both cost accounting and managerial accounting.

PLANNING
AND CONTROL

Planning is defined as the formulation of objectives as well as programs of operation to achieve these objectives. Objectives and programs are prepared on a long- and short-range basis to provide guidelines for daily operations as well as future activities. The information provided by a cost accounting system is combined with other data and analyzed. Based on its findings, management makes decisions and formulates strategies for the future, affecting areas such as the following:

1. Sales prices and volume
2. Product profitability
3. Purchasing commitments
4. Capital expenditures
5. Plant expansion or contraction feasibility

x *Control* is defined as the continuous comparison of actual performance with programs, or budgets, prepared by the planning function. Budgets represent the standards of performance. By comparison with actual results, a judgment can be made as to the efficiency of operation, and the profitability of various products. Differences between budgeted (or standard cost) and actual cost, call for action on the part of management. Management must pinpoint the source of the problem. Is it incompetent workers or overpaid labor? Increased prices of raw materials or too much wasted material? Inefficient or obsolete manufacturing processes? Undersized plant? Oversized plant? Unrealistic budget? These are just some of the questions management must answer in order to achieve and maintain profitability. Success in today's highly complex

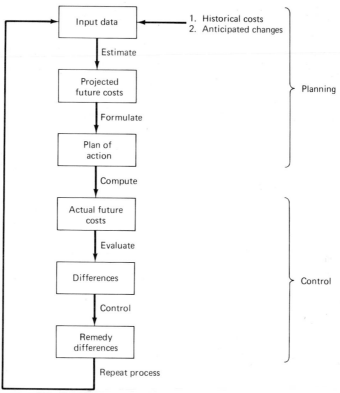

FIGURE 1-2 **Planning and Control Model**

and competitive business environment depends on management's ability to effectively plan and control operations.

Inherent in the planning and control functions of management is the determination of the most efficient methods of implementing an established course of action. Management must work within the restraints imposed by plant size, products manufactured, skills and education of its workers, and nature of the industry. An infinite number of detailed, theoretically perfect plans could be developed, but many are useless unless their implementation is both practical and possible within the existing restraints. In summary, planning is the formulation of objectives and the means to achieve these objectives, while control is the process of review, evaluation, and reporting which monitors the achievement, or lack of achievement, of objectives. Figure 1-2 shows how planning and control are interrelated.

INCOME MEASUREMENT

Another function of cost accounting is to provide cost data to be used in the periodic determination of income and reports of financial condition. Reports

8

generated by cost accounting may serve several purposes at once, as in our earlier illustration of the Coco Manufacturing Company. The divisional reports provide cost data for each division on a monthly basis. At the end of each period—month, quarter, or year—this cost data is used in the determination of net income. In addition to the routine cost information needed for financial statements, the cost accountant must provide a wide variety of studies and analyses needed for decisions by management.

As discussed earlier, cost data used in the preparation of financial statements for external use must adhere to generally accepted accounting principles applied on a consistent basis. For example, according to GAAP, the ending inventory must be costed under an acceptable method, such as fifo, lifo, or weighted average. A company cannot use standard costs for inventories in external financial statements, although these may be used for internal purposes.

In order to understand the objectives and techniques of cost accounting, one must be familiar with the organizational structure of a company, the functions of management, and the goals of the management team.

CORPORATE ORGANIZATION

Effective management requires a carefully defined organizational structure. It is the framework within which the company's activities will be performed and requires a delineation of the duties of each executive. Through the creation of a cohesive organization, the company is able to coordinate the activities of many departments and subdivisions, headed by individuals assigned varying degrees of authority and responsibility.

A major factor in developing an efficient organization is the breakdown of activities into clearly defined areas which can be easily managed, such as departments, divisions, branches, or sections. This allows for specialization of functions; in a manufacturing concern, these functions would be manufacturing, marketing, and administration. These may be subdivided further into many specialized departments, depending upon the size of the department, the scope of work, and the quantity of work involved.

Functions of Management

Managerial functions are generally performed by three levels of management— top, middle, and lower. Top-level management includes the president, vice presidents, and other key executives. Middle-level management includes division managers, branch managers, and department heads; lower-level management includes supervisors and section or unit heads.

The primary purpose of all levels of management is decision making: the careful consideration of alternative courses of action and selection of the best course to accomplish specific objectives. For management to be successful, comprehensive information regarding production and costs must be provided on a systematic and timely basis. This information is derived from accounting, more specifically cost accounting.

Within the corporate structure, all management positions can generally be

Chapter 1: The Nature of Cost Accounting

9

classified by function, and by the authority and responsibility necessary to perform that function. Most responsibility in a company can usually be broadly divided into either line or staff functions.

Line and Staff Functions

The line function is responsible for supervision, guidance, and decision making. In the line organization, a chain of command exists in which authority is traced in a direct line from the president to the lowest unit in the company. The president retains control over the entire company but delegates responsibilities to subordinates. The staff function provides advice and service to members in the line function but cannot require implementation of its ideas.

In other words, the staff members have no authority over the line personnel but provide specialized help to the various departments. For example, the controller, who is the chief accounting executive, fills a staff role in the company and also has line responsibility (for matters that concern his or her own department) as well as staff responsibility (for matters that concern other departments). The line and staff functions within the corporate organization can be clearly portrayed on an organization chart.

ORGANIZATION CHARTS

An organization chart indicates the responsibilities of the company's major management positions. At the same time, the chart is a diagram of the company's hierarchy; the flow of authority is clearly shown.

For cost accounting purposes, the following two organization charts should be considered.

Company Chart

This chart depicts the flow of authority from the stockholders to the corporate executives and on to the operating levels. (See Figure 1-3.)

Controller's Division Chart

As a member of the top management team, the controller is charged with providing accounting services to all the departments which need them. The technical and detailed activities for which the controller is responsible are carried out by a staff of accountants specializing in particular activities. The area of cost accounting is generally supervised by an accountant with the title of "cost supervisor" or, in a larger company, with the title of "chief cost accountant." (See Figure 1-4.)

FUNCTIONS OF THE CONTROLLER AND TREASURER

As the top accounting executive of the company, the controller is responsible for the collection, analysis, interpretation, and presentation of financial

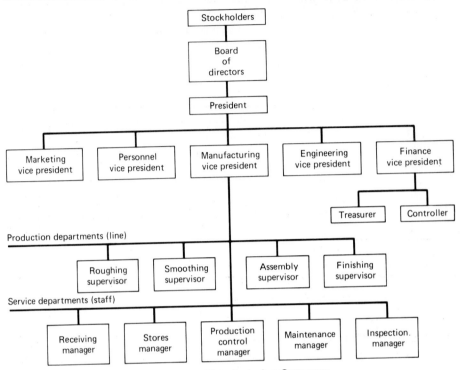

FIGURE 1-3 **Organization Chart for a Manufacturing Company**

information. This information varies from routine data for financial reports to complex analyses for management problem solving. The controller's functions have been broadly classified as (1) scorekeeping, (2) attention directing, and/ or (3) problem solving. The status of the controller in the company organization structure will generally depend on the priority given these functions. In the past, the controller's role was primarily scorekeeping, that is, preparing financial reports and tax returns according to accounting principles and government regulations. In recent years, the controller's reports have been more detailed and have gained the attention of managers by showing, for example, favorable and unfavorable variances for each section under the manager's jurisdiction. Gradually, the controller's importance earned recognition, and the function of controller expanded to include problem solving. The role of the modern-day controller now includes extensive input into top management's decision-making process, analysis of financial ratios and economic trends, deriving problem-solving data from the computer network, analysis of marketing trends, and evaluation of proposed acquisitions and dispositions.

The cost accountant has the same general functions as the controller but in a more specialized sense. Thus, for a supervisor of a manufacturing department or commercial office, the reporting of a total variance from standard or budget would be a scorekeeping item. For a plant manager or

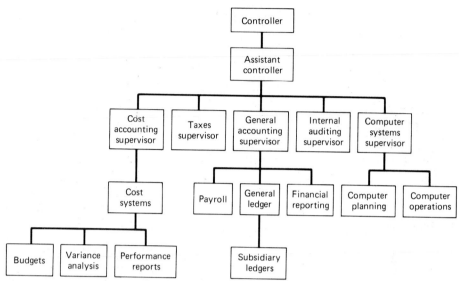

FIGURE 1-4 **Controller's Division Chart**

office manager, the reporting of cost variances for individual sections would be attention-directing items, focusing attention on units needing further review. For problem solving, management may use information from regular cost reports, or may ask the controller's department for a special cost study of the specific problem. Generally, a special studies unit can be established that can cross departmental lines and handle these studies on a "project" basis, that is, separate from the daily routine. In this way the regular work of the department will not be interrupted and preparation of periodic reports will not be affected.

The treasurer is responsible for custody of the corporate funds. Duties of the treasurer typically include the funding of operations, such as investments, capital requirements, and banking and credit policies.

The treasurer and controller are usually equal in authority and both report directly to the financial vice president.

APPLICATIONS OF COST ACCOUNTING

Cost accounting concepts and techniques were first applied to manufacturing operations many years ago. After cost accounting was firmly established in manufacturing, it was applied in various nonmanufacturing parts of the plant, such as the distribution, warehouse, and office sections. Standards were developed for operations such as processing orders from customers, order filling, packing, shipping, and billing. In the office, standards were developed for processing of customers' remittances, issuing of checks, and posting of various types of entries. Cost accounting was later applied to outside distribution costs, such as sales calls, traveling expenses, and other sales costs.

Unfortunately, even today many people think that cost accounting is applicable only to manufacturing. However, almost every type of financial activity can benefit from cost accounting.

In recent years, cost accounting concepts, standards, and cost control have been applied to a great many types of functions and individual operations in a wide variety of enterprises, including banks, finance companies, insurance companies, railroads, airlines, bus lines, shipping companies, hospitals, colleges, and federal, state, and local government agencies. Throughout the text, attention will be directed to various types of nonmanufacturing activities suitable for cost accounting applications.

PROFESSIONAL ASSOCIATIONS AND AGENCIES

Financial accounting has been subject to the regulations of professional associations and government agencies to a greater extent than has cost accounting. Investors, creditors, and other outsiders do not have access to as much information about the company as management does, and thus these outsiders' interests must be protected. Cost accounting has been influenced in varying degrees by professional associations and government agencies. In some cases the influence was direct; in other cases the influence was indirect.

Direct Influence

The following professional associations and government agencies are listed in descending order—in terms of the direct influence they have had on the field of cost accounting.

National Association of Accountants (NAA). This professional association, founded in 1919 (then called the National Association of Cost Accountants), has had the greatest impact to date on the field of cost accounting. NAA has played a leading role in developing new and sophisticated procedures in the cost and management accounting field. Its publications, which are practice-oriented, are the leading source of current information for cost and management accountants. The monthly magazine, *Management Accounting*, is written primarily by members who have practical experience and are affiliated with leading industrial and other business enterprises. The NAA Research Studies review current practice and analyze the factors that are considered and the approaches taken in arriving at the accepted solutions. An outstanding Continuing Education Program (CEP) is offered with short programs covering subjects ranging from direct costing to human resource accounting. A Self-Study Program (SSP) is also offered. An important development is the Institute of Management Accounting (IMA) (established in 1972), charged with developing the Self-Study Program and awarding the Certificate in Management Accounting. The program is described on page 15. For information or publications, write to 919 Third Avenue, New York, N.Y. 10022.

Cost Accounting Standards Board (CASB). The CASB is a congressional agency established in 1970 to "promulgate cost accounting standards designed to achieve uniformity and consistency in the cost accounting principles followed by defense contractors under federal contracts." Since that time, nondefense government contracts have been made subject to CASB standards in negotiated contracts exceeding $100,000. Negotiated contracts are those whose price is based on cost rather than on competitive bids. Potentially the CASB could be the most influential force in the cost accounting field if its standards were adopted by a significant number of companies for nongovernment work. The CASB standards are legally required in cost systems for government contracts, but not in the cost system of a government contractor for nongovernment work. Thus far, the accounting profession has not recognized the CASB as an accounting authority. For information or publications, write to 441 G Street N.W., Washington, D.C. 20548.

Financial Executives Institute (FEI). This professional association was established in 1931 as the Controller's Institute of America. It is a national organization whose members are the top financial officers in their companies. A financial executive, according to the FEI, is a person responsible for the administration of the assets of a firm. The actual title may be controller, treasurer, or vice president of finance, generally depending on the size of the company. The Institute's monthly magazine, the *Financial Executive*, presents authoritative views on the problems of business and financial management. Its research arm, the Financial Executives Research Foundation, publishes material relating to financial management and its evolving role in the management of business. To qualify for membership, an individual must be employed in a firm of specified size and be responsible for a major portion of the controllership or treasury function. The cost accountant generally reports to the financial executive through the controller. For information or publications, write to 633 Third Avenue, New York, N.Y. 10017.

Indirect Influence

The following professional associations and government agencies have had an important indirect influence on the field of cost accounting.

American Institute of Certified Public Accountants (AICPA). The AICPA is the national professional association of certified public accountants. State societies of CPAs, affiliated with the AICPA, are active in all states and territories. Until the establishment of the Financial Accounting Standards Board in 1973, the AICPA had long been the recognized authority for establishing accounting principles. It is still the authority for matters relating to certified public accounting and the auditor's report. The Institute's monthly magazine, the *Journal of Accountancy*, is the recognized authority for material in the area of public accounting. A wide range of research studies and technical practice aids are available to practitioners and others, as well as a large number of continuing education programs. The institute prepares and grades the uniform

CPA examinations given semiannually in all states and territories. The examination must be passed before an individual may use the title "certified public accountant." For information or publications, write to 1211 Avenue of the Americas, New York, N.Y. 10036.

Financial Accounting Standards Board (FASB). Since 1973, the FASB has established standards governing the preparation of financial reports in the private sector. The FASB, composed of seven members, is independent of all other business and professional organizations. The members are selected by nominees from six sponsoring organizations which have special knowledge and interest in financial reporting.

Before the present independent standard-setting structure was created, the financial and reporting standards were established by units of the American Institute of Certified Public Accountants. The first unit was the Committee on Accounting Procedure and later the Accounting Principles Board. The pronouncements of these two bodies remain in force unless amended or superseded by statements of the FASB. For information or publications, write to High Ridge Park, Stamford, Conn. 06905.

Internal Revenue Service (IRS). The Internal Revenue Service promulgates and issues regulations for determining tax liability, and examines the accounting records of individuals, partnerships, corporations, and other entities to determine their federal income tax liability. Although IRS regulations are for the purpose of determining one's tax liability, the regulations have a significant effect on financial accounting and cost accounting. For example, only certain methods of depreciation, inventory valuation, and costing are acceptable to the IRS. These regulations therefore directly affect the computation of cost of goods sold and, consequently, the amount of net income. For information or publications, write to your local Internal Revenue Service Center.

American Accounting Association (AAA). This professional association was founded in 1916 as the American Association of University Instructors in Accounting. While most members are college and university accounting teachers, membership was opened some years ago to all persons interested in accounting education and research. The present membership includes most accounting teachers of college rank as well as leading public, industrial, commercial, and government accountants. The association's quarterly publications, *The Accounting Review* and *Accounting Education News*, cover a broad range of topics, including accounting theory, cost and management accounting, auditing, taxes, and international and government accounting. For information or publications, write to 5717 Bessie Drive, Sarasota, Fla. 33583

Securities and Exchange Commission (SEC). The SEC is an independent regulatory government agency which exercises quasi-judicial, quasi-legislative, and administrative functions over securities and security exchanges. The commission is authorized to define specific accounting, technical, and trade terms and to prescribe the form in which information is to be reported and the details to be shown in financial statements. While the SEC has statutory authority to establish financial accounting and reporting standards under the Securities Act of 1934, it has relied generally on the private sector to carry out that task. The commission's primary responsibility is to protect the public— investors, creditors, and others—from misleading financial information. Generally, the SEC exercises control by requiring that all securities, whether they are additional securities of a company already registered, or new securities for a company "going public," be registered with the SEC before they are sold to the public. The commission can then examine the information to be submitted to prospective purchasers to determine that the requisite disclosure of financial information has been made.

Under the authority of various acts, the SEC issued Regulation S-X, the principal accounting regulation of the SEC, which governs the form and content of most required financial statements. From time to time, the Commission publishes *Accounting Series Releases*, which are opinions relating to major accounting, auditing, or administrative policies affecting financial statements. For information or publications, write to 500 North Capitol Street, Washington, D.C. 20549.

THE CERTIFICATE IN MANAGEMENT ACCOUNTING

Prior to 1972, the only recognized criterion for competence in accounting was the Certified Public Accountant (CPA) certification program of the AICPA, for competence in *public* accounting. In 1972, the National Association of Accountants established the Institute of Management Accounting and charged it with responsibility for developing and maintaining a program leading to a Certificate in Management Accounting (CMA).

The Certificate in Management Accounting was established to encourage high educational standards and provide an objective measure of an individual's proficiency and knowledge in the area. The program specifies a course of studies required of a management accountant. A management accountant must possess the knowledge to adequately formulate successful and timely plans and decisions in order to serve corporate management in today's complex business world.

To become a CMA, an individual must demonstrate certain levels of expertise in the following areas: (1) managerial economics and business finance; (2) organization and behavior; (3) public reporting standards, auditing, and taxes; (4) periodic reporting for internal and external purposes; and (5) decision analysis, including modeling and information systems analysis.

Requirements for Admission

In order to take the CMA examination, a candidate must (1) possess a baccalaureate degree from an accredited college or university, or (2) achieve a satisfactory score for the Credentials Committee of the IMA on either the

Graduate Record Examination (GRE) or the Graduate Management Admission Test (GMAT), or (3) be a certified public accountant or hold a comparable professional qualification outside of the United States that is approved by the Credentials Committee.

CHAPTER REVIEW

Financial accounting is primarily concerned with financial reports for external use by stockholders, creditors, and government agencies. Cost accounting is primarily concerned with cost information for internal use by management. Cost accounting greatly aids management in the formulation of objectives and programs of operation (planning), in the comparison of actual performance with expected performance (control), and in financial reporting (income measurement).

Cost accounting concepts and techniques can be used in practically every type of enterprise. Cost accounting is concerned mainly with the cost planning and control function and is essential in the decision-making process. It is much less restricted by external forces than is financial accounting. Reports are prepared when needed by management, and management may use any unit of measure deemed appropriate. Reports may use actual figures, estimates, or both, and are prepared for the various units within a company.

The management group of an organization can usually be divided into three levels: top, middle, and lower. The primary purpose of all levels of management is decision making—the careful selection among alternative courses of action to accomplish specific objectives.

An organization chart establishes the flow of authority and responsibility within an organization. The controller of a company is responsible for reviewing performance at varying levels of operation, reporting and interpreting financial data, tax planning, controlling asset levels, and preparing plans for operation. The treasurer of a company is responsible for the funding of operations, such as investments, capital requirements, and banking and credit policies.

The National Association of Accountants (NAA), the Cost Accounting Standards Board (CASB), the Financial Accounting Standards Board (FASB), the Securities and Exchange Commission (SEC), and the Internal Revenue Service (IRS) affect cost accounting in varying degrees. The Certificate in Management Accounting (CMA) program was established in 1972 by the National Association of Accountants (NAA) to certify candidates' knowledge of management accounting.

GLOSSARY

Accounting—the measuring, recording, and reporting of financial information.

Certificate in Management Accounting (CMA)—a certificate obtained upon passing the CMA examination, certifying a minimum degree of knowledge in management accounting.

Company Chart—a diagram that depicts the flow of authority in an organization from the stockholders to the corporate executives.

Control—the process of continuous comparison of actual performance with the programs established by the planning function.

Controller's Division Chart—an organization chart depicting the flow of authority in the controller's division.

Cost Accounting—concerned primarily with the accumulation and analysis of cost information for internal use to aid management in planning, control, and decision making.

Cost Accounting Standards Board (CASB)—a government agency which establishes rules, regulations, and standards of cost accounting for government contracts.

Financial Accounting—accounting concerned primarily with financial reports for external use.

Financial Accounting Standards Board (FASB)—establishes regulations and standards for financial reporting by companies.

Generally Accepted Accounting Principles (GAAP)—Current authoritative sources of GAAP are *Statements* issued by the FASB, *Opinions* issued by the Accounting Principles Board, *Accounting Research Bulletins*

issued by the American Institute of Certified Public Accountants Committee on Accounting Procedure, and *Accounting Series Releases* issued by the Securities and Exchange Commission.

Historical Dollars—reflect the fair value of an asset at the date of acquisition.

Internal Revenue Service (IRS)—a government agency that issues regulations to determine federal tax liability.

Line Function—deals with decision making, guidance, and supervision.

Managerial Accounting—accounting concerned primarily with the accumulation and analysis of cost and management information for planning and control.

Organization Chart—a diagram that depicts the flow of authority and responsibility of an organization by defining the duties of the management positions of a company.

Planning—the formulation of objectives and programs of operation to achieve management goals.

Securities and Exchange Commission (SEC)—establishes rules and standards for financial reporting by publicly held corporations.

Staff Function—advice and supervision provided by staff members to line members that is of a consulting nature (following their suggestions is not mandatory).

QUESTIONS

1 For whom are published financial accounting reports prepared? For whom are cost accounting reports prepared?
2 Discuss the planning, control, and income determination functions of cost accounting.

3   The Short Company has called in a management consulting firm for advice. The company officers are the president, factory manager, and supervisor. The supervisor reports to the factory manager, who in turn reports to the president. The cost accounting department forwards reports directly to the president, who then routes appropriate information back to the factory manager. The factory manager then informs the supervisor of any shortcomings. What recommendations would you make? Prepare an organization chart to reflect your suggestions.

4   In order for management to be successful, what factor is of major importance?

5   Distinguish between planning and setting objectives.

6   What is control, and how does a company control operations?

7   Distinguish between the terms "cost accounting" and "management accounting."

8   Contrast the terms "cost accounting" and "financial accounting."

9   The Burnt Corporation has called you in as a management consultant. You are given the following list of officers and department heads:

John Xavier	President
Mary Esposito	Controller
James Mitchell	Treasurer
Frank Kransky	Production Manager
Joan Lapatine	Vice President, Sales
Edward Gross	Finishing Department Supervisor
Ann Strindberg	Marketing Manager
Thomas Lind	Vice President, Personnel
Juanita Lopez	Vice President, Manufacturing
Lloyd Svensen	Vice President, Engineering
Ruth Janicek	Sales Manager, New Jersey
Andrew Chan	Vice President, Finance
Julie Drew	Production Control Chief
David Garcia	Production Planning Chief
Bette Herman	Production Supervisor
Kenneth Poe	Shipping Supervisor
Brian Poretsky	Assembly Supervisor
Fran Trusk	Internal Auditor
Greg Trent	Chief of Maintenance Department

Prepare an organization chart for the Burnt Corporation.

10   What is the function of the controller? Differentiate between the controller's functions and those of the treasurer.

11   Explain the function of the Cost Accounting Standards Board.

12   What are the five parts of the Certificate in Management Accounting Examination, and what are the requirements for taking the examination?

CHAPTER TWO

COST ACCOUNTING CONCEPTS, CLASSIFICATIONS, AND STATEMENTS

The initial phase in the study of any new area or subject involves familiarization with its unique concepts and terminology. This process of familiarization provides the student with a basic foundation on which to build an understanding of the procedures, issues, and applications that will be encountered in the study of a new area. Cost accounting is a distinct field of study and, therefore, we will present basic concepts, classifications, and financial statements to provide the foundation for a thorough understanding of the subject.

COST, EXPENSE, AND LOSS

As its name implies, cost accounting deals with cost—the use of, the control of, and the planning of cost. What is meant by cost and how is it used? *Cost is defined as the benefits given up to acquire goods or services.* The benefits (goods or services) given up are measured in dollars by the reduction of assets or incurrence of liabilities at the time the benefits are acquired. At the time of acquisition, the cost incurred is for present or future benefits. When these benefits are received, the cost becomes an expense. *An expense is defined as a cost that has given a benefit and is now expired.* Unexpired costs that can give future benefits are classified as assets.

Expenses are matched to revenues to determine net income or loss for a period. *Revenue is defined as the price of products sold or services rendered.* In certain instances, the goods or services purchased become valueless without having provided any benefit. These costs are called losses and appear on the income statement, as a deduction from revenues, in the period that the decrease in value occurred. Both expenses and losses have the same impact on net income—both are reductions. However, they are listed separately on an income statement in order to properly reflect the amounts associated with each.

For example, assume that on January 2 a company purchases two items of inventory at $1,000 each. On January 15, the company sells one of the items for $1,600. The remaining item of inventory is discarded as worthless on January 28 because it is found to be defective. The *cost* of buying the goods was $2,000 or $1,000 for each item. A $1,000 *expense* resulted on January 15 when the company sold one item and received *revenue* of $1,600. A *loss* of $1,000 resulted on January 28 when the remaining item in inventory was discarded.

COST CLASSIFICATIONS

Proper cost classification is essential for management to collect and use its information most effectively. Costs may be classified by the following:

1 Elements of a product
2 Relationship to production
3 Relationship to volume
4 Department where incurred
5 Functional areas
6 Period charged to income
7 Economic considerations—opportunity costs

Elements of a Product

The cost elements of a product, or its integral components, are materials, labor, and factory overhead. This classification provides management with information necessary for income measuring and product pricing. The elements of a product are defined as follows:

Materials. These are the principal substances used in production that are transformed into finished goods by the addition of labor and factory overhead. The cost of materials may be divided into direct and indirect materials as follows:

Direct Materials: All materials that can be identified with the production of a finished product; that can be easily traced to the product; and that represent a major material cost of producing that product. An example of a direct material is the lumber used to build a bunk bed.

Indirect Materials: All materials involved in the production of a product that are not direct materials. An example of an indirect material is the glue used to build a bunk bed.

Labor.   Labor is the physical or mental effort expended in the production of a product. Labor costs may be divided into direct and indirect labor as follows:

Direct Labor: All labor directly involved in the production of a finished product; that can be easily traced to the product; and that represents a major labor cost of producing that product. The work of machine operators in a manufacturing company would be considered direct labor.

Indirect Labor: All labor involved in the production of a product that is not considered direct labor. The work of a plant supervisor is an example of indirect labor.

Factory Overhead.   This is all the costs—other than direct materials and direct labor—of producing a product. Because the cost of any product equals the cost of direct materials, direct labor, and factory overhead, one might wonder how the cost of indirect materials and indirect labor are figured in the cost of an item. The answer is that they are included in factory overhead. Such costs are included in factory overhead because they cannot be identified with specific products. Examples of other factory overhead costs besides indirect materials and indirect labor, are rent, light, and heat for the factory, and depreciation of factory equipment. Factory overhead costs can be further classified as fixed, variable, and semivariable (definitions will be presented later in the chapter).

For example, assume a company incurs the following costs in manufacturing wood tables:

Materials:

Oak lumber	$150,000
Pine lumber	110,000
Glue	800
Screws	1,000
Total	$261,800

Labor:

Wood cutters	$180,000
Table assemblers	190,000
Sanders	170,000
Supervisor	20,000
Janitor	10,000
Total	$570,000

Other:

Factory rent	$70,000
Factory utilities	20,000
Office rent	16,000
Office salaries	80,000
Depreciation of factory equipment	21,000
Depreciation of office equipment	8,000
Total	$ 215,000
Grand total	$1,046,800

TABLE 2-1

ELEMENTS OF A PRODUCT

	DIRECT MATERIALS	DIRECT LABOR	FACTORY OVERHEAD	TOTAL COST
Oak lumber	$150,000			$150,000
Pine lumber	110,000			110,000
Glue			$ 800	800
Screws			1,000	1,000
Wood cutters		$180,000		180,000
Table assemblers		190,000		190,000
Sanders		170,000		170,000
Supervisor			20,000	20,000
Janitor			10,000	10,000
Factory rent			70,000	70,000
Factory utilities			20,000	20,000
Depreciation of factory equipment			21,000	21,000
Total	$260,000	$540,000	$142,800	$942,800

Based on the preceding figures, the cost of direct materials would be $260,000; direct labor, $540,000; and factory overhead, $142,800. These three figures represent the elements of the product, as broken down in Table 2-1. Not included as product costs are office rent ($16,000), office salaries ($80,000), and depreciation of office equipment ($8,000). These office costs are not elements of a product. They usually appear as deductions on the income statement under a caption such as "after operating costs" or "nonmanufacturing costs."

The classification of cost based on relationship to the product will change as the relationship changes. For example, lumber is a direct material cost when used in the manufacture of wood furniture. However, lumber is an indirect material cost when used for shipping crates for equipment. Maintenance personnel (janitors, custodians) in a manufacturing plant are an indirect cost; their function is not *directly* related to production. However, in a company which provides maintenance service to others, maintenance personnel would be considered a direct cost.

Relationship to Production

Costs may be classified according to their relationship to production. This classification is closely related to the cost elements of a product (materials, labor, and factory overhead) and the major objective of control.

The two categories, based on their relationship to production, are prime costs and conversion costs.

Prime Costs. Prime costs are direct materials and direct labor, costs directly related to production.

Conversion Costs. These are costs concerned with processing materials into finished products. Conversion costs are direct labor and factory overhead. Prime costs and conversion costs may be diagrammed as follows:

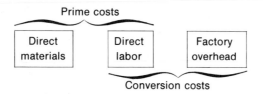

Note that direct labor is included under both categories. This does not result in double counting because this classification is used for purposes of analysis, not cost accumulation.

For example, assume the following costs:

Direct materials	$800,000
Direct labor	900,000
Factory overhead	300,000

Prime costs would equal $1,700,000 ($800,000 + $900,000); conversion costs would equal $1,200,000 ($900,000 + $300,000); and product costs would equal $2,000,000 ($800,000 + $900,000 + $300,000).

Relationship to Volume

Costs vary with changes in the volume of production. Understanding their behavior is vital to budget preparation and analysis of operations. Costs under this category are classified as variable, fixed, semivariable, or shutdown, and are defined as follows:

Variable. Variable costs are those in which the *total cost* tends to change in direct proportion to changes in volume, or output, while the *unit* cost remains constant. Variable costs are controlled by the department head responsible for incurring them. For example, if variable costs for direct materials are $100 per unit of output, each time output increases by one unit, the variable cost for direct material will increase by $100. Figure 2-1 presents the behavior pattern of variable direct material costs based on $100 per unit. The vertical line (axis) represents dollar cost while the horizontal line (axis) represents output. The slope line (labeled "variable costs" on the graph) can be drawn by selecting a level of output and computing the corresponding dollar cost for that output. In Figure 2-1, an output of 7 units was selected; the dollar cost for 7 units would be $700 ($100 per unit × 7 units). Point A on the graph represents the intersection of a horizontal line from $700 and a vertical line from 7 units. The slope indicating variable costs is drawn by connecting point A to the 0 point or origin (where the vertical and horizontal axes meet).

Fixed. Fixed costs are those in which *total cost* remains constant over a relevant range of output, while the cost per *unit* varies with output. *Relevant*

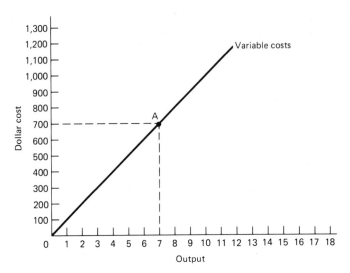

FIGURE 2-1　**Behavior Pattern of Variable Direct Material Costs**

range is defined as the various levels of production in which certain factory overhead costs tend to remain constant. It is a range of production level in which certain costs can be predicted with reasonable accuracy. Beyond the relevant range of output, fixed costs will vary. Top management controls the volume of production and is, therefore, responsible for fixed costs.

For example, the fixed cost for rent on a warehouse is $20,000 a year if production is between 5,000 and 15,000 units. If production is expected to be less than 5,000 units, a smaller warehouse can be rented at $15,000 a year. Therefore, two relevant ranges exist in this situation: relevant range A, covering from 1 to 4,999 units of output, and relevant range B, covering from 5,000 to 15,000 units of output. Figure 2-2 presents the behavior pattern of fixed warehouse costs based on the preceding figures.

Semivariable. These costs contain both fixed and variable characteristics; they are therefore often referred to as "mixed costs." Although semivariable costs are neither wholly fixed nor wholly variable in nature, they must ultimately be separated into fixed and variable components for purposes of planning and control. The fixed part of the semivariable cost usually represents a minimum fee for making a particular item or service available. The variable portion is the cost charged for actually using the service. For example, most telephone service charges are made up of two elements: a *fixed* charge for the privilege of being allowed to receive or make a phone call, plus an additional or *variable* charge for each phone call made. Telephone charges are relatively simple to separate into fixed and variable costs; however, in some situations, the variable and fixed components must be estimated.

Semivariable costs are shown graphically in Figure 2-3. Assume that a company rents a delivery truck at a flat fee of $2,000 per year plus $.15 for each mile driven. The fixed component is the $2,000 annual rental fee; the

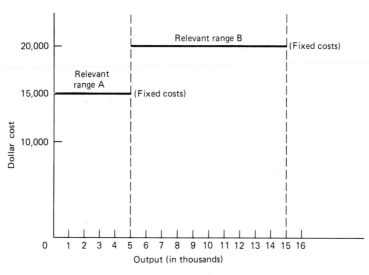

FIGURE 2-2 **Behavior Pattern of Fixed Warehouse Costs**

variable component is the $.15 for each mile driven. If 10,000 miles are driven during the year, the total annual cost of the delivery truck is $3,500, computed as follows:

Flat fee (fixed component)	$2,000
Mileage charge (variable component) (10,000 miles × $.15)	1,500
Total cost	$3,500

On Figure 2-3, the vertical axis represents total costs, and the horizontal axis represents mileage. The fixed portion, $2,000, is noted by a dashed horizontal

FIGURE 2-3 **Semivariable Costs**

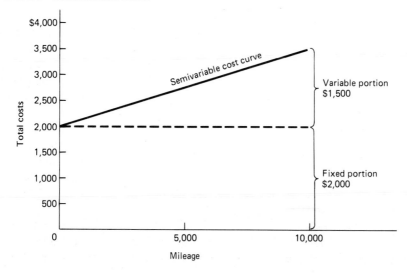

line from the vertical axis. The variable portion of $1,500 is represented by the space from $2,000 to $3,500.

In summary, as output changes, variable costs per unit remain constant while total variable costs change. And, as output changes, fixed costs per unit change while total fixed costs remain constant (within a relevant range). Semivariable costs contain elements of both variable and fixed costs, and must be separated into their components for purposes of planning and control. For example, Company X has two alternate levels of production under consideration, as follows:

```
Projected production level:
   Plan A .............................    50,000 units
   Plan B .............................    80,000 units
Fixed costs (relevant range is
   40,000 to 100,000 units) ..............  $200,000
Variable costs ........................    $1 per unit
```

Production costs under both plans are as follows:

	TOTAL	COST PER UNIT
Plan A:		
Variable costs (50,000 units × $1)	$ 50,000	$1.00
Fixed costs ($200,000 ÷ 50,000 units)	200,000	4.00
Total production costs	$250,000	$5.00
Plan B:		
Variable costs (80,000 units × $1)	$ 80,000	$1.00
Fixed costs ($200,000 ÷ 80,000 units)	200,000	2.50
Total production costs	$280,000	$3.50

Total production costs are lower for Plan A than Plan B, but the *cost per unit* under Plan A is higher than under Plan B. Note that total fixed costs remain the same under both plans while total variable costs change. Fixed costs per unit (and, therefore, total unit cost) are lower under Plan B because fixed costs are allocated over more units than under Plan A. Under both plans, variable costs per unit remain the same because they are not affected by changes in volume.

Table 2-2 shows some examples of variable, fixed, and semivariable costs.

Figure 2-4 presents the behavior patterns of variable, fixed, and semivariable costs.

Shutdown. Shutdown costs are those fixed costs that would be incurred even if there were no production. For example, a company had the following fixed costs for Plant 3:

TABLE 2-2
FACTORY COSTS

VARIABLE	FIXED	SEMIVARIABLE
Direct materials	Building maintenance	Truck rentals
Direct labor (piece rate)	Depreciation (except for	Equipment rentals
Electricity for machinery	units of production)	Utilities
	Plant taxes	Telephone service
	Plant insurance	
	Warehouse rent	

Equipment maintenance	$120,000
Taxes on factory building	80,000
Insurance on factory building	15,000
Production executives' salaries	90,000
Guards' salaries	18,000
Janitors' salaries	10,000
Total	$333,000

If Plant 3 were closed, the following *shutdown* costs would still be incurred:

Taxes on factory building	$ 80,000
Insurance on factory building	15,000
Guards' salaries	18,000
Total	$113,000

FIGURE 2-4   **Fixed, Variable, and Semivariable Costs**

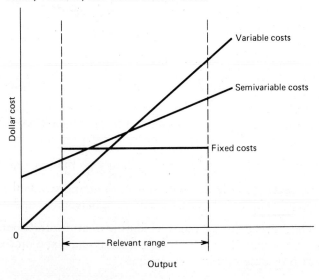

Department Where Incurred

A department is a major functional division of a business. Costing by departments helps management to control overhead cost and to measure income. The following types of departments are found in manufacturing companies:

Production Departments. These contribute *directly* to the production of the item and include departments in which conversion or production processes take place. They include manual and machine operations directly performed on the product manufactured.

Service Departments. These are departments which are not directly related to the production of an item. Their function is to provide services for other departments. Examples of these services are payroll, factory office, personnel, cafeteria, and plant security. The costs of the latter departments are usually allocated to production departments, since they benefit from the services provided.

For example, Company A has only one production department and all the machinery in that department is kept in operating condition by the maintenance department. The maintenance department is also required to provide janitorial and maintenance services to the rest of the company. Therefore, a portion of the maintenance department's cost should be allocated to the production department and will become part of product cost. The portion not allocated to the production department may be allocated to another service department or to a nonplant department, such as the sales department, and will be an expense for the current period. The basis for allocating service costs usually varies according to the nature of the service provided. Two common bases for allocating service department costs are square feet serviced and direct labor hours worked.

Functional Areas

Costs classified by function are accumulated according to activity performed. All costs of a manufacturing organization may be divided into manufacturing, marketing, administrative, and financing, and are defined as follows:

Manufacturing Costs. These are related to the production of an item. Manufacturing costs are the sum of direct materials, direct labor, and factory overhead costs.

Marketing Costs. These are incurred in selling a product or service.

Administrative Costs. These are incurred in directing, controlling, and operating a company and include salaries paid to management and clerical staff.

Financing Costs. These are related to obtaining funds for the operation of the company. This includes the interest the company must pay on loans, as well as the costs of providing credit to customers.

TABLE 2-3
ANALYSIS BY FUNCTION

	YEAR 1	YEAR 2	TOTAL CHANGE
Manufacturing costs	$250,000	$335,000	+ $ 85,000
Marketing costs	90,000	90,000	0
Administrative costs	50,000	70,000	+ 20,000
Financing costs	10,000	5,000	− 5,000
Total operating costs	$400,000	$500,000	+ $100,000

Analysis by Function. If the management of a company wants to analyze the current period's operation, one method would be to classify costs by functions and compare them to parallel costs for a previous year. Knowing that a company had $400,000 total operating costs for year 1 and $500,000 total operating costs for year 2 would not provide sufficient information for management to determine the cause(s) of the increase. A further detailed analysis by functions would be necessary in order to explain why total costs increased by $100,000. Assume that revenue was the same for both years. The analysis by function in Table 2-3 could be prepared.

The preceding analysis reveals that the increase in total operating costs resulted from manufacturing and administrative functions. These functions should be examined by management to determine if the increases were appropriate. The decrease in financing costs should also be analyzed to determine its cause.

Period Charged to Income

Costs may also be classified on the basis of when they are to be charged against revenues. Some costs are first recorded as assets and then expensed (charged as an expense) as they are used or expire. Other costs are initially recorded as expenses. The classification of costs into categories relating to the periods they benefit aids management in income measurement for the preparation of financial statements and is essential in matching expenses to revenues in the proper period. Two categories used are product costs and period costs, defined as follows:

X**Product Costs.** These are costs directly identifiable with the product. They are direct materials, direct labor, and factory overhead. These costs provide no benefit until the product is sold and are, therefore, inventoried upon completion of the product. When the products are sold, the total product costs are recorded as an expense. This expense is called the *cost of goods sold*. Cost of goods sold is matched against revenue for the period in which the products were sold.

X**Period Costs.** Those costs not directly related to the product are not inventoried. If the period cost benefits only one period, it is called a *revenue expenditure* because it is directly matched against revenue in the period in which the cost was incurred. An accountant's salary is an example of a revenue expenditure. If the period cost benefits more than one period, it is called a *capital expenditure*, is recorded as an asset, and is expensed when the asset is used or otherwise disposed of. For example, the purchase of equipment should be capitalized as an asset and then allocated as expense, through depreciation charges, to the periods that receive the benefit of its use.

For example, assume that during the first calendar year of operation, a company had the following revenues and costs:

Total revenues	$1,000,000
Total costs:	
Direct materials	$ 300,000
Direct labor	400,000
Factory overhead	200,000
Purchase of equipment—December 31	150,000
Office salaries	50,000
	$1,100,000

There were no units still in process at the end of the year, and 80% of the goods produced during the period were sold.

If no distinction is made between product and period costs, the total cost of $1,100,000 would either be expensed in the first year or inventoried and expensed when the inventory is sold. Obviously, both actions would lead to a distortion of the first year's net income or loss as follows:

	EXPENSE ALL COSTS WHEN INCURRED	CHARGE ALL COSTS TO INVENTORY	
Total revenue	$1,000,000	$1,000,000	
Total costs	1,100,000	880,000	($1,100,000 × 80% sold)
Net income (loss)	($ 100,000)	$ 120,000	

The following analysis should have been prepared.

	PROD-UCT COST	PERIOD COST CAPITAL EXPENDI-TURE	PERIOD COST REVENUE EXPENDI-TURE	TOTAL
Direct materials	$300,000			$ 300,000
Direct labor	400,000			400,000
Factory overhead	200,000			200,000
Purchase of equipment		$150,000		150,000
Office salaries			$50,000	50,000
Total	$900,000	$150,000	$50,000	$1,100,000

The correct first year's net income or loss can now be computed as follows:

Total revenue		$1,000,000
Product cost ($900,000 × 80% sold)	$720,000	
Period cost	50,000	770,000
Net income		$ 230,000

The purchase of equipment (capital expenditure) was made on December 31 and, therefore, no depreciation was charged for the first year of operation. (Assume that the equipment purchased will be used to automate certain production processes that were previously performed manually.)

Economic Considerations—Opportunity Cost

Since a firm's resources are often limited, proper planning is essential. The cost and expected benefits of decisions involving long-term investments should be carefully analyzed by management. Management should include in any analysis the opportunity cost of each major decision. *Opportunity cost* is defined as the measurable value of benefits that could be obtained by choosing an alternative course of action. For example, assume a company has $100,000 in excess cash available and can either put the cash in a savings account and earn $7,000 in interest a year, or purchase new equipment estimated to generate an extra $10,000 a year in profits (from increased efficiency and output). The $7,000 (interest foregone) is the opportunity cost of buying the equipment and the $10,000 (estimated extra profits) is the opportunity cost of depositing the excess cash in a savings account. For a single decision, numerous opportunity costs must be considered, and each one should be carefully analyzed before selecting the final course of action. Because opportunity costs are hypothetical, they do not represent cash receipts and disbursements, and therefore are not incorporated into formal accounting systems. However, opportunity costs should always be considered when investment decisions are made.

COST DATA
AND USES

Management is faced with a multitude of decisions: which products should be produced or discontinued, what quantity should be produced, how to plan and control product costs, and how to price goods to be sold. To be effective in making decisions, management must have a detailed knowledge of the cost activity within the company. Cost data is, therefore, a basic tool in the decision-making process. Cost data can be accumulated and presented in many different forms and in varying degrees of detail, depending upon the needs of management. The same data and format will not serve all purposes with equal efficiency, and how the data is used will vary with management's functions in different companies.

However, some of management's activities are common to most manufacturing companies. They are the following:

1 Planning
2 Controlling
3 Income measuring
   a   Cost of goods manufactured and computation of unit cost
   b   Determination of cost of goods sold
4 Decision making
   a   Product pricing policies
   b   Investment decisions

Planning

Planning involves the careful evaluation of alternative courses of action, the formulation of plans and objectives, and the adoption of programs for future operations. Planning can be long-range or short-range; it can be for specific projects or for specific periods. One of the basic tools in planning future costs is the budget. Through the forecast of levels of activity and resultant costs, management can spell out its alternatives and envision their consequences.

Controlling

Control involves the continuous comparison and evaluation of actual performance with the programs and budgets established by the planning function. This function is not only concerned with achieving the cost standards outlined in the budget but also with making adjustments in the budget when necessary. Inherent in the control function are the following three concepts:

Responsibility. All costs must be traced and assigned to one individual who is ultimately responsible for their incurrence and for explaining deviations from the standard.

Authority. Those persons charged with the responsibility for specific costs should have the authority to control their incurrence.

Periodic Reports. The performance of the individuals responsible for costs should be evaluated by comparison of actual results with budgets and the issuance of periodic reports covering the areas of their responsibility. These areas may be cost centers, departments, or divisions.

Income Measuring

Income measuring involves the accumulation and allocation of cost data to be used in the preparation of financial reports and the periodic determination of income. Inherent in the income measurement function are the following:

Cost of Goods Manufactured and Computation of Unit Cost. In a manufacturing concern, cost data is required in order to compute the cost of goods manufactured during a period. The cost of goods manufactured is equal to the sum of the materials, labor, and factory overhead incurred in the production process (assuming no beginning or ending units in process). When more than one unit is produced during a period, a cost per item produced, or unit cost, is also computed. Unit cost is equal to the total cost of goods manufactured divided by the number of units produced.

For example, assume a company produced 10,000 units and incurred the following costs:

Materials	$3,000
Labor	8,000
Factory overhead	4,000

There were no beginning and ending units in process. The cost of goods manufactured is $15,000 ($3,000 + $8,000 + $4,000) and the unit cost is $1.50 ($15,000 ÷ 10,000 units).

Determination of Cost of Goods Sold.   The cost of producing goods that are sold is the cost of goods sold and is treated as an *expense*. If, however, the goods produced did not result in revenue, and are discarded as worthless, the cost of producing these goods would be treated as a *loss* on the income statement. The cost of producing unsold goods that are not discarded as worthless (finished goods awaiting sale) is recorded as an *asset* (to be eventually charged as an expense or loss against the revenue of a future period). For example, assume during the year that a company produced 20,000 units (no units were in process at the beginning or end of the period) and the cost of goods manufactured was $120,000, resulting in a unit cost of $6 ($120,000 ÷ 20,000 units). During the period, 14,000 units were sold, 5,000 were still awaiting sale, and 1,000 were found defective and discarded as worthless. There was no beginning finished goods inventory. The *expense* for the period is $84,000 ($6 × 14,000 units), a *loss* of $6,000 ($6 × 1,000 units) resulted, and an *asset* of $30,000 ($6 × 5,000 units) is recorded as finished goods inventory.

Decision Making

Decision making involves a selection among alternative courses of action. In many business situations it is possible to quantify the alternative courses of action and analyze the consequences of each action. Two of the more common decision-making activities relating to cost accounting are the following:

Product Pricing Policies.   The development of pricing policies involves input from numerous sources and ultimately rests on the goals of management. Pricing policies may be concerned primarily with long-range profitability, short-range profitability, overcoming industry competition, or consideration of the environment. Whatever the objectives of a pricing policy, management requires data concerning the present and future costs of production, economic and industrial trends, forecast of product demand, and the availability of resources for present and future production.

Investment Decisions.   Management is often faced with the following non-recurring decisions: should new equipment be acquired, and if so, should it be purchased or leased; should a new product be added; should an existing product be discontinued. When decision making involves a new investment or a change in product line, a careful analysis must be made of the long-term effects on cash flows, revenues, and costs. Long-term planning involving financing and investment programs is commonly referred to as *capital budgeting*. The information received from cost accumulation procedures or systems is vital in making capital budgeting decisions.

COST OF GOODS MANUFACTURED STATEMENT

The most effective way of communicating accounting information for a fiscal period to external and internal users is through periodic reports. External users, such as creditors and investors, receive essential information in the company's annual report, which includes the balance sheet, the income statement, the statement of changes in financial position, and the statement of retained earnings. A manufacturing company will also usually prepare a cost of goods manufactured statement. The cost of goods manufactured statement shows the costs put into production during the period (direct materials + direct labor + factory overhead costs) plus the cost of work-in-process at the beginning of the period. Work-in-process represents the cost of incomplete goods still in production at the end of a period (which becomes beginning work-in-process for the next period). Work-in-process usually contains some portion of the three elements of a product: direct materials, direct labor, and factory overhead. The sum of costs put into production during the period plus beginning work-in-process equals the cost of goods in process during the year. In order to determine the cost of goods manufactured, the cost of ending work-in-process is subtracted from the cost of goods in process during the year.

In its basic form, a cost of goods manufactured statement may appear as in Table 2-4.

The cost of goods manufactured figure appearing at the bottom of the statement also appears on the income statement in the cost of goods sold

TABLE 2-4
PRODUCTION COMPANY
COST OF GOODS MANUFACTURED STATEMENT
FOR THE YEAR ENDED 12/31/X0

Costs put into production during the period:	
Direct materials	X
Direct labor	X
Factory overhead	X
Total cost put into production	X
Plus: Work-in-process at the beginning of the period	X
Cost of goods in process during the period	X
Less: Work-in-process at the end of the period	X
Cost of goods manufactured	X

TABLE 2-5
PRODUCTION COMPANY
INCOME STATEMENT
FOR THE YEAR ENDED 12/31/X0

Sales		X
Cost of goods sold:		
Opening finished goods inventory	X	
Plus: Cost of goods manufactured	X	
Goods available for sale	X	
Less: Closing finished goods inventory	X	X
Cost of goods sold		X
Gross profit		X
General, selling and administrative expenses		X
Net income		

section, as in Table 2-5. Note that the account called "cost of goods manufactured" is treated on the income statement of a manufacturing company the same way that the Purchases account is handled on the income statement of a merchandising company.

The interrelationship of the cost of goods manufactured statement, the income statement, the statement of retained earnings, and the balance sheet is presented in Table 2-6.

The statement of changes in financial position is based on the various

TABLE 2-6
TRIAL BALANCE

	DEBIT	CREDIT
Cash	$ 30,000	
Receivables	4,000	
Inventories (opening)*		
Work-in-process	10,000	
Finished goods	7,000	
Other assets (noncurrent)	10,000	
Total liabilities (current)		$ 22,000
Capital stock		4,000
Additional paid-in capital		6,000
Retained earnings (opening)		20,000
Direct materials	3,000	
Direct labor	2,000	
Factory overhead	4,000	
Sales		50,000
Marketing expenses	9,000	
Administrative expenses	6,000	
Other income		3,000
Other expenses	5,000	
Income taxes	9,000	
Dividends	6,000	
Total	$105,000	$105,000

*Note: For brevity, it is assumed there is no opening or closing materials inventory.

TABLE 2-6   Continued

Closing inventories:

Work-in-process	$ 7,000
Finished goods	6,000

COST OF GOODS MANUFACTURED STATEMENT

Costs put into production during the period:

Direct materials..	$ 3,000	
Direct labor	2,000	
Factory overhead	4,000	
Total costs put into production		$ 9,000
Plus: Work-in-process at the beginning of the period		10,000
Cost of goods in process during the year		$ 19,000
Less: Work-in-process at the end of the period		7,000
Cost of goods manufactured		$ 12,000

INCOME STATEMENT

Sales..		$ 50,000
Cost of goods sold:		
Opening finished goods inventory	$ 7,000	
Plus: Cost of goods manufactured	12,000	
Goods available for sale	$ 19,000	
Less: Closing finished goods inventory	6,000	
Cost of goods sold.....................................		13,000
Gross profit		$ 37,000
Less: Marketing and administrative expenses:		
Marketing expenses.....................................	$ 9,000	
Administrative expenses.................................	6,000	$ 15,000
Net income from operations		$ 22,000
Nonoperating income and expenses		
Other income...	$ 3,000	
Other expenses	5,000	$ 2,000
Net income before taxes		$ 20,000
Income taxes		9,000
Net income		$ 11,000

STATEMENT OF RETAINED EARNINGS

Retained earnings—opening...............................	$ 20,000
Plus: Net income	11,000
Total	$ 31,000
Less: Dividends..	6,000
Retained earnings—closing	$ 25,000

TABLE 2-6   Continued
BALANCE SHEET

Assets
Current:

Cash	$ 30,000	
Receivables	4,000	
Finished goods inventory..............................	6,000	
Work-in-process inventory	7,000	$ 47,000

Noncurrent:

Other assets		10,000
Total assets		$ 57,000

Liabilities and Stockholders' Equity

Total current liabilities		$ 22,000

Stockholders' Equity:

Capital stock	$ 4,000	
Additional paid-in capital	6,000	
Retained earnings—closing	25,000	35,000
Total liabilities and stockholders' equity		$ 57,000

financial statements discussed previously. It should be noted that the balance sheets of manufacturing companies and merchandising companies are different with respect to inventories. A manufacturing concern usually has three types of inventories—finished goods, work-in-process, and materials, while a merchandising concern has only an inventory of the goods purchased and held for resale. It was noted earlier that work-in-process inventory represents the costs of incomplete goods still on the production line at the end or beginning of a period. Finished goods inventory equals the cost of goods completed during a period that have not been sold at the end or beginning of a period. Materials (or stores) inventory refers to the cost of materials that have not yet been put into production and are still available for use at the end or beginning of a period.

A more detailed cost of goods manufactured statement for XYZ Manufacturing Company appears in Table 2-7.

CHAPTER REVIEW

The study of cost accounting requires a thorough understanding of certain basic concepts and definitions. Cost accounting deals with the use of, control of, and planning of cost. Cost is defined as the benefits given up to acquire goods or services. Cost benefits eventually expire and become expenses or losses.

TABLE 2-7
XYZ MANUFACTURING COMPANY
COST OF GOODS MANUFACTURED STATEMENT
FOR THE YEAR ENDED 12/31/X2

Costs put into production during the period:		
Direct materials:		
Materials inventory, January 1, 19X2	$700,000	
Purchases	42,000	
Materials available	$742,000	
Materials inventory, December 31, 19X2	34,000	
Direct materials used		$ 708,000
Direct labor		641,590
Factory overhead:		
Indirect materials	$ 34,650	
Indirect labor	59,217	
Heat	75,000	
Light	47,000	215,867
Total costs put into production		$1,565,457
Plus: Work in process at the beginning of the period		400,000
Cost of goods in process during the period		$1,965,457
Less: Work in process at the end of the period		200,000
Cost of goods manufactured		$1,765,457

In order to provide relevant, useful data to management, costs can be classified in the following manner:

1 Elements of a product
2 Relationship to production
3 Relationship to volume
4 Department where incurred
5 Functional areas
6 Period charged to income
7 Economic considerations—opportunity costs

Cost data is of value to both internal and external decision makers. Certain management activities common to most manufacturing companies are the following:

1 Planning
2 Controlling
3 Income measuring
   a Cost of goods manufactured and computation of unit cost
   b Determination of cost of goods sold
4 Decision making
   a Product pricing policies
   b Investment decisions

Planning involves the evaluation of alternative courses of action. Control involves the continuous comparison and evaluation of actual performance with the programs prepared by the planning function. Certain inherent aspects of the control function are responsibility, authority, and periodic reporting. Cost data provide the information necessary for the costing of goods manufactured and the allocation of these costs to ending inventory and cost of goods sold. Pricing policies depend on the information provided by cost data in addition to a multitude of external factors.

In addition to the reports prepared by nonmanufacturing concerns, a manufacturing company prepares a cost of goods manufactured statement. This statement shows total costs put into production, the cost of all goods in process during the year, and the cost of goods manufactured. The total cost of goods manufactured for the period can be found in the Cost of Goods Sold section of the income statement.

GLOSSARY

Capital Expenditures—costs that benefit more than one period.

Conversion Costs—those costs expended for the conversion of materials into finished products.

Cost—the benefits given up to acquire goods or services.

Cost of Goods Manufactured—equals materials, labor, and factory overhead incurred in the production process.

Cost of Goods Sold—represents that portion of the costs incurred in the production process that was sold during a period.

Direct Labor—all labor directly involved in the production of a finished product, that can be easily traced to the product, and that represents a major labor cost of producing that product.

Direct Materials—all materials used directly in the production of a finished product, that can be easily traced to the product, and that represent a major material cost of producing that product.

Expense—a cost that has given benefit and is now expired.

Factory Overhead—all the costs of producing a product other than direct materials and direct labor.

Fixed Costs—those costs which in total remain constant over a relevant range of output while the cost per unit varies with output.

Indirect Labor—in the production of a product, the labor involved that is not considered direct labor.

Indirect Materials—in the production of a product, all materials involved that are not considered direct materials.

Loss—the cost of goods or services that were purchased and became valueless without having provided any benefit.

Opportunity Cost—the measurable value of benefits that could be obtained by choosing an alternative course of action.

Period Costs—costs not related to the manufacture of a product.

Prime Costs—those costs directly related to the production of a product. **Product Costs**—production costs incurred in the manufacture of a product.

Relevant Range—the various levels of production in which certain factory overhead costs tend to remain constant.

Semivariable Costs—costs which pos-

sess characteristics of both fixed and variable overhead costs; a cost that varies with production but not in direct proportion to changes in the level of production.

Variable Costs—those costs where the total changes in direct proportion to changes in volume and the unit cost remains constant.

SUMMARY PROBLEMS

PROBLEM 1

Communications Manufacturing Company produces CB radios for cars. The following cost information is available for the period ended December 31, 19XX:

Materials put into production: $120,000, of which $80,000 was considered direct materials

Factory labor costs for the period: $90,000, of which $25,000 was for indirect labor

Factory overhead costs for utilities: $40,000

Beginning and ending work-in-process inventories: 0

Selling, general, and administrative expenses: $60,000

Units completed during the period: 10,000

REQUIRED:

Compute the following:

a Cost of goods manufactured
b Total cost of operation
c Prime costs
d Conversion costs

e Product costs
f Period costs
g Unit cost

PROBLEM 2

King Manufacturing Corporation has the following information relating to the period just ended:

Beginning work-in-process	$ 25,000
Ending work-in-process	10,000
Direct materials cost	95,000
Direct labor cost	110,000
Factory overhead costs	70,000
Beginning finished goods inventory	15,000
Ending finished goods inventory	45,000
Sales	300,000
Selling and general expenses	75,000

REQUIRED:

Based on the preceding information, compute the following:
- **a** Cost of goods manufactured
- **c** Net income or loss
- **b** Cost of goods sold

SOLUTIONS TO SUMMARY PROBLEMS

PROBLEM 1

a Cost of Goods Manufactured:

Direct materials cost		$ 80,000
Direct labor cost		65,000
Factory overhead costs:		
Indirect materials	$ 40,000	
Indirect labor	25,000	
Utilities	40,000	105,000
Cost of goods manufactured		$250,000

b Total Cost of Operation:

Cost of goods manufactured	$250,000
Selling, general, and administrative expenses	60,000
Total cost of operation	$310,000

c Prime Costs:

Direct materials	$ 80,000
Direct labor	65,000
Total prime costs	$145,000

d Conversion Costs:

Direct labor	$ 65,000
Factory overhead	105,000
Total conversion costs	$170,000

e Product Costs:

Equal to cost of goods manufactured	$250,000

f Period Costs:

Equal to selling, general and administrative expenses	$ 60,000

g Unit Cost:

$$\frac{\text{Total cost of goods manufactured}}{\text{Number of units produced}} = \frac{\$250,000}{10,000} = \$25 \text{ per unit}$$

PROBLEM 2

a Cost of Goods Manufactured:

Costs put into production during the period:	
Direct materials cost	$ 95,000
Direct labor cost	110,000
Factory overhead costs	70,000
Total costs of goods put into production	$275,000
Plus: Beginning work-in-process	25,000
Cost of goods in process during the period	$300,000
Less: Ending work-in-process	10,000
Cost of goods manufactured	$290,000

b Cost of Goods Sold:

Beginning finished goods inventory	$ 15,000
Plus: Cost of goods manufactured	290,000
Goods available for sale	$305,000
Less: Ending finished goods inventory	45,000
Cost of goods sold	$260,000

c Net Income or Loss:

Sales	$300,000
Less: Cost of goods sold	260,000
Gross profit	$ 40,000
Less: Selling and general expenses	75,000
Net loss	($ 35,000)

QUESTIONS

1 What does cost accounting deal with?
2 How are the benefits given up to acquire goods or services measured?
3 How are expenses and losses recorded on the income statement?
4 Discuss what is meant by the term "cost data."
5 What are the management activities common to most manufacturing companies?
6 What is one of the basic tools in the planning of future costs?
7 What three concepts are inherent in the control function?
8 How is the cost of goods manufactured computed?
9 What may the objectives in pricing policies be concerned with?
10 What does management require for an effective pricing policy?
11 Discuss what is meant by the term "capital budgeting."
12 How may costs be classified?

13 Where are the costs of indirect materials and indirect labor considered in the cost of the product?

14 How may costs be accumulated?

15 How do variable costs and fixed costs act as output changes?

16 Why is costing by departments an aid to management?

17 How may the costs of a manufacturing organization be divided?

18 Why is the classification of costs into categories relating to the periods they benefit important to management?

19 Differentiate between a revenue expenditure and a capital expenditure and state how they are shown on the financial statements.

20 Why is opportunity cost an important economic consideration?

21 How does the balance sheet of a manufacturing company differ from that of a merchandising company with respect to inventory?

EXERCISES

EXERCISE 1

Cost of Goods Manufactured and Cost of Operations

The Huffer Manufacturing Company manufactures rubber rafts. For the month of January, it incurred the following costs:

Materials	$10,000—80% for direct materials
Labor	5,000—70% for direct labor
Factory overhead	5,000—for heat, light, and power

In addition to the costs of production, the company incurred selling expenses of $7,500 and general administrative expenses of $8,500.

REQUIRED:

Compute the cost of goods manufactured and the total cost of operations.

EXERCISE 2

Prime Costs, Conversion Costs, and Product Costs

The following information relates to the Snowball Manufacturing Company:

Direct materials...	$25,000
Indirect materials	5,000
Direct labor	30,000
Indirect labor	4,500
Factory overhead (excluding indirect materials and indirect labor)	15,000

REQUIRED:

Compute the prime costs, conversion costs, and product costs.

EXERCISE 3

Revenue, Expense, and Loss Computation

The Lu-Lu Manufacturing Company purchased four identical items of inventory for a total cost of $20,000. On May 5, the company sold two of the items for $6,000 each and discarded as worthless the remaining two items of inventory on May 25, because they were found to be defective.

REQUIRED:

Compute the revenue, expense, and loss from these transactions.

EXERCISE 4

Cost of Goods Manufactured

The following information relates to the Comfy Water Bed Manufacturing Company: At the beginning of the period, there was $50,000 in work-in-process. During the year, they applied costs of $17,200 for direct materials, $15,700 for direct labor, and $32,100 for factory overhead (heat, light, and power). At the end of the period, there was work-in-process of $40,000.

REQUIRED

Compute the cost of goods manufactured for the Comfy Water Bed Manufacturing Company.

EXERCISE 5

Expense, Loss, and Asset Computation

The PITA Manufacturing Company produced 75,000 units for the year ending December 31, 19X1. No units were in process at the beginning or end of this period. The cost of goods manufactured was $300,000. During the year, the following occurred:

> 59,000 units were sold
> 14,000 units were still awaiting sale
> 2,000 units were found defective

There was no beginning finished goods inventory.

REQUIRED:

Compute:
   a   How much the *expense* was for the year
   b   How much *loss* was incurred for the year
   c   How much the *asset* to be recorded as finished goods inventory was for the year

EXERCISE 6

Relevant Range

The Chilly Air Conditioner Manufacturing Company stores its air conditioners in a warehouse. The rent for the warehouse is $37,000 a year if annual production is between 3,000 and 6,000 air conditioners. If production is expected to be less than 3,000 air conditioners, a smaller warehouse can be rented for $30,000 a year. If production is expected to be more than 6,000 air conditioners, a larger warehouse can be rented for $42,000 a year.

REQUIRED:

On a graph, show the relevant ranges that exist.

EXERCISE 7

Alternative Levels of Production

The Hi & Lo Zipper Manufacturing Company is considering two alternative levels of production as follows:

Projected production level:
Plan 1 .... 4,500 units
Plan 2 .... 7,200 units
Fixed costs: (relevant range is
3,000–8,000 units) $20,000
Variable costs .... $2.25 per unit

REQUIRED:

Compute the production costs under both plans.

EXERCISE 8

Product and Period Costs

The Gorilla Company manufactures small stuffed gorillas. The total revenue is $59,000. The company incurred the following costs:

Materials .... $ 5,200—10% is indirect materials
Labor .... 7,000—12% is indirect labor
Factory overhead .... 25,000—including indirect materials and indirect labor
General and administrative expenses 14,700
Office salaries 4,800
Equipment purchased at end of period
(ignore depreciation) 5,300
Total $62,000

There were no units still in process at the end of the year, and 92% of the goods produced during the year were sold.

REQUIRED:

a Compute what the net income or loss would be if there were no distinction between product and period costs, and Gorilla Company was on a cash basis.

b Show the analysis that should have been prepared.

c Compute the correct net income or loss.

EXERCISE 9

Cost of Goods Manufactured Statement

The Blimp Manufacturing Company produced 100,000 units during the year ending December 31, 19X1. It incurred the following costs for the year:

Materials .... $73,000—10% is indirect materials
Labor................................... $97,000—7% is indirect labor
Factory overhead .... 125% of direct labor
Work-in-process—January 1, 19X1 .... $35,250
Work-in-process—December 31, 19X1 .... $27,000

The factory overhead percentage includes indirect materials and indirect labor.

REQUIRED:

Prepare a cost of goods manufactured statement for the period.

EXERCISE 10

Cost of Goods Manufactured and Sold Statements

The Chippy Chocolate Cookie Company had for 19X2, raw materials on January 1 of $27,000 and raw materials on December 31 of $28,500. Work-in-process was $25,000 on January 1, 19X2 and $22,000 on December 31, 19X2. The balance in finished goods was $49,000 on January 1, 19X2 and $45,000 on December 31, 19X2. The company purchased materials for the year of $72,000. The direct labor and indirect labor were $32,000 and $9,000, respectively. Office salaries amounted to $12,000; electricity was $18,000. The selling, general, and administrative expenses were $37,000. The depreciation on office equipment was $6,000. Total factory overhead for the period was $73,500 including indirect materials and indirect labor.

REQUIRED:

Prepare a cost of goods manufactured statement and a cost of goods sold statement for the year 19X2.

PROBLEMS

PROBLEM 1

Computation of Various Costs

IOU Manufacturing Company produces wallets. The following cost information is available for the period ended December 31, 19X3:

Materials put into production: $82,000, of which $78,000 was considered direct materials

Factory labor costs for the period: $71,500, of which $12,000 was for indirect labor

Factory overhead costs for factory depreciation: $50,000

Beginning and ending work-in-process inventories: 0

Selling, general, and administrative expenses: $62,700

Units completed during the period: 18,000

REQUIRED:

Compute the following:

a	Cost of goods manufactured	e	Product costs
b	Total cost of operation	f	Period costs
c	Prime costs	g	Unit cost
d	Conversion costs		

PROBLEM 2

Cost of Goods Manufactured and Sold Statements and Net Income or Loss

The Nicole Manufacturing Company has the following information for the period just ended:

Beginning work-in-process	$ 5,000
Ending work-in-process	6,200
Direct materials	8,900
Direct labor	10,000
Factory overhead	15,000
Beginning finished goods inventory	12,000
Ending finished goods inventory	22,000
Sales	37,500
Selling and general expenses	17,000

REQUIRED:

From the above information, compute the following:

a Cost of goods manufactured   c Net income or loss
b Cost of goods sold

PROBLEM 3

Cost of Goods Manufactured and Sold Statement and Net Income or Loss

The Parrish Fertilizer Company produces various types of fertilizer. They had no beginning units in process or finished units on hand on January 1, 19X3 and 30,000 finished units on hand on December 31, 19X3, and had sold 95,000 units during the year. There were no units in work-in-process on December 31, 19X3. The materials put into production cost $300,000; 75% were direct materials. Labor costs were $350,000; 40% was for indirect labor. Factory overhead costs, other than indirect materials and indirect labor, were the following:

Heat, light, and power	$115,000
Depreciation	78,000
Property taxes	65,000
Repairs and maintenance	42,000

Selling expenses were $80,000; general and administrative expenses were $50,000.

REQUIRED:

Compute the following:

a	Cost of goods manufactured	e	Conversion costs
b	Total cost of operation	f	Period costs
c	Unit cost	g	Product costs
d	Prime costs		

PROBLEM 4

Cost of Goods Manufactured and Sold Statements and Net Income or Loss

The Blackwell Clock Company manufactures many types of clocks. They have just completed production for the current year. The sales for the year were $945,000 and inventories were as follows:

	Ending	Beginning
Work-in-process	$60,000	$75,000
Finished goods	54,000	35,000

Direct materials for the period cost $176,000, direct labor cost $250,000, and factory overhead was $237,500. Selling expenses were $55,000 and general and administrative expenses were $117,000.

REQUIRED:

a Prepare the following statements:
    1 Cost of goods manufactured
    2 Cost of goods sold
b Compute the net income or loss.

PROBLEM 5

Computation of Various Costs

Woody Lumber Manufacturing Company had no units in process on January 1. On December 31, there were 100,000 finished units on hand and no units in process. During the year, 250,000 units had been sold. Materials costing $375,000 had been put into process; 80% were direct materials. Labor costs were $400,000; 65% was direct labor. Additional factory overhead costs were the following:

Heat, light, and power	$160,000
Depreciation	45,000
Property taxes	85,000
Repairs and maintenance	20,000

Selling expenses were $125,000; general and administrative expenses were $80,000.

REQUIRED:

Compute the following:
- **a** Cost of goods manufactured
- **b** Total cost of operation
- **c** Prime costs
- **d** Conversion costs
- **e** Product costs
- **f** Period costs
- **g** Unit cost

PROBLEM 6

Cost of Goods Manufactured and Sold Statements and Net Income or Loss

The Stiff Shirt Company has just completed its third year of operation. Sales for the year were $1,300,000, and inventories were as follows:

	December 31	January 1
Work-in-process	$100,000	$95,000
Finished goods	64,000	76,000

Costs for the period were as follows:

Direct materials	$365,000
Direct labor	405,000
Factory overhead	445,500

Selling expenses were $26,000. General and administrative expenses were $82,000.

REQUIRED:

- **a** Prepare the following statements:
  - **1** Cost of goods manufactured
  - **2** Cost of goods sold
- **b** Compute the net income or loss.

PROBLEM 7

Preparation of Statements

The following are adjusted account balances for the Ralph Corporation on December 31, 19XX:

Cash	$ 20,350
Accounts receivable	29,600
Allowance for uncollectibles	1,450
Direct materials inventory, January 1	7,650
Work-in-process inventory, January 1	6,900
Finished goods inventory, January 1	3,750
Prepaid expenses	1,600
Factory equipment	121,500
Accumulated depreciation: factory equipment	36,400
Selling equipment	71,150
Accumulated depreciation: selling equipment	23,700
Patents	7,100
Accounts payable	15,300
Miscellaneous payables	2,850
Income taxes payable	23,272
Capital stock, $1 par value	100,000
Paid-in-capital in excess of par	25,000
Retained earnings, January 1	22,350
Dividends	11,000
Sales	396,200
Sales returns and allowances	2,850
Purchases of direct materials	83,350
Purchase returns and allowances	4,150
Freight-in	13,900
Direct labor	117,700
Factory overhead	60,750
Selling expenses	36,200
General and administrative expenses	32,050
Income tax expense	23,272

The inventories as of December 31 are as follows:

Direct materials	....	$8,050
Work-in-process	....	7,250
Finished goods	....	3,350

Additional Information

Assume that the depreciation expense on selling equipment is included in selling expense. Depreciation on factory equipment is included in factory overhead. Taxes are paid in January of the following year.

REQUIRED:

Prepare the following statements for the period ending December 31, 19XX:

a Cost of goods manufactured statement c Retained earnings statement
b Income statement   d Balance sheet

PROBLEM 8

Preparation of Financial Statements

Following is the adjusted trial balance of Mush's Marshmallow Company as of December 31, 19X9:

Cash	$ 81,000	
Accounts receivable...........................	187,800	
Allowance for uncollectible accounts		$ 9,000
Direct materials inventory, January 1	37,500	
Work-in-process, January 1	45,000	
Finished goods, January 1	33,300	
Prepaid expenses	5,400	
Factory equipment	588,000	
Accumulated depreciation: factory equipment		169,500
Office equipment	184,200	
Accumulated depreciation: office equipment		73,800
Accounts payable		111,300
Miscellaneous expenses payable..................		36,600
Capital stock, $5 par value		600,000
Retained earnings		116,700
Dividends.....................................	84,000	
Sales (net)		1,629,000
Purchases of direct materials	320,100	
Direct labor...................................	460,500	
Factory overhead	284,700	
Selling expenses	261,600	
Administrative expenses	97,800	
Income taxes	75,000	
	$2,745,900	$2,745,900

Inventories on December 31 were:

Direct materials	$45,300
Work-in-process	29,400
Finished goods	40,200

REQUIRED:

Prepare the following statements for the period ending December 31, 19X9:

a Cost of goods manufactured   c Retained earnings statement
b Income statement   d Balance sheet

CHAPTER THREE

COSTING AND CONTROL OF MATERIALS

Manufacturing is the process by which raw materials are converted into a finished product. Materials constitute an essential cost element of production. In this chapter, we will discuss the costing of materials and the methods by which costs are controlled.

DEFINITION AND CLASSIFICATION

Materials are the basic substances that are transformed into finished goods (through the use of labor and factory overhead) in the production process. Material costs can be either direct or indirect.

As discussed in Chapter 2, direct materials are those that can be identified with the production of a finished product, that can be easily traced to the product, and that represent a major material cost. An example is the steel used to build a car. Direct materials, along with direct labor, are classified as "prime costs."

Indirect materials are those that are not direct materials, although they are involved in the making of a product. Examples are glue used to put furniture together, and rivets used to assemble a car. Indirect materials are considered part of factory overhead costs.

ACCOUNTING FOR MATERIALS

Accounting for materials in a manufacturing company usually involves two activities: the purchase of materials and their issuance.

Purchase of Materials

Most manufacturing companies have a purchasing department whose function is to order the raw materials and supplies needed for production. The director of the purchasing department is responsible for making sure that the items ordered meet quality standards set by the company, and that the materials are acquired at the lowest possible price. Three forms are commonly used in purchasing goods: a purchase requisition, a purchase order, and a receiving report.

Purchase Requisition. This is a written order, usually sent by other employees to inform those in the purchasing department of a need for materials or supplies. For example, assume that on April 1, the materials storeroom clerk wishes to place an order for 20 widgets, Catalog Number 92, at an estimated unit price of $1.00. The goods are needed by May 1. The storeroom clerk would fill out a purchase requisition form and send it to the purchasing department to order the materials.

Although a purchase requisition is usually printed according to the specifications of a particular company, most forms include the following: the requisition number, name of department or individual making the request, quantity of items requested, identifying catalog number, description of the item, unit price, total price, total cost of entire requisition, order date, date delivery is required, and authorized signature.

Figure 3-1 shows a purchase requisition. Two copies are customarily made, the original going to the purchasing department (to place the order), and the copy remaining with the employee who made the order (to keep track of orders placed).

FIGURE 3-1 **Purchase Requisition**

LARGE MANUFACTURING COMPANY			No. 98	
PURCHASE REQUISITION				
DEPARTMENT OR INDIVIDUAL MAKING REQUEST _Store Room_				
ORDER DATE _4/1/X_ DELIVERY DATE REQUESTED _5/1/X_				
QUANTITY	CATALOG NUMBER	DESCRIPTION	UNIT PRICE	TOTAL
20	92	Widgets	$1.00	$20.00
APPROVED BY: _D. Donne_			TOTAL COST	$20.00

Purchase Order. If the purchase requisition is properly completed, the purchasing department will issue a purchase order (in this case, for 20 widgets). A purchase order is a written request to a supplier for specified goods at an agreed-upon price. The request also stipulates terms of delivery and terms of payment. The purchase order is the supplier's authorization to deliver goods and submit a bill. All items purchased by a company should be accompanied by purchase orders, which are serially numbered to provide control over their issuance. The following items are commonly included in a purchase order: preprinted name and address of company making the order, purchase order number, name and address of supplier, order date, date delivery is requested, delivery and payment terms, quantity of items ordered, catalog number, description, unit and total price, total cost of entire order, and authorized signature. Figure 3-2 shows a purchase order. The original is sent to the supplier (to place the order); copies usually go to the accounting department (to set up a file), to accounts payable (for future payment), and to the receiving department (to alert them to expect a delivery), and a copy is kept by the purchasing department (to maintain a file of all purchase orders issued).

Receiving Report. When the goods that were ordered are delivered, the receiving department will unpack and count them. (It is interesting to note that the quantity ordered is not shown on the copy of the purchase order sent to the receiving department. This omission ensures that the goods delivered are actually counted.) The goods are checked to be sure they are not damaged, and that they meet the specifications of the purchase order and the packing slip (a list, prepared by the supplier, that accompanies the order and details

FIGURE 3-2 **Purchase Order**

LARGE MANUFACTURING COMPANY   P.O. No. 086
18 SLATER ROW
NEW YORK, N.Y. 10022

PURCHASE ORDER

SUPPLIER _Widgets Inc._   ORDER DATE _4/2/X_

25 Stegdiw ln. N.Y. N.Y. DATE REQUESTED BY _5/11/X_

DELIVERY TERMS _FOB Destination_ PAYMENT TERMS _2/10 N 30_

QUANTITY	CATALOG NUMBER	DESCRIPTION	UNIT PRICE	TOTAL
20	92	widgets	$1.00	$20.00
			TOTAL COST	$20.00

APPROVED BY _K Palmer_

```
┌─────────────────────────────────────────────────────────┐
│         LARGE MANUFACTURING COMPANY    No. 109            │
│              RECEIVING REPORT                             │
│                                                           │
│   SUPPLIER ____ Widgets Inc. _____                 │
│                                                           │
│   PURCHASE ORDER NO. 086 _____                 │
│                                                           │
│   DATE RECEIVED ____ 5/1/X _____                 │
├──────────────┬──────────────────┬────────────────────────┤
│  QUANTITY    │                  │                        │
│  RECEIVED    │   DESCRIPTION    │    DISCREPANCIES        │
├──────────────┼──────────────────┼────────────────────────┤
│     20       │    Widgets       │       NONE              │
│              │                  │                        │
│              │                  │                        │
├──────────────┴──────────────────┴────────────────────────┤
│   AUTHORIZED SIGNATURE ___ Jack Doven ___                 │
└───────────────────────────────────────────────────────────┘
```

FIGURE 3-3 **Receiving Report**

what is in the shipment). Next, the receiving department issues a receiving report. This form includes the supplier's name, purchase order number, date delivery was received, quantity received, description of goods, discrepancies from the purchase order (or mention of damaged goods), and authorized signature. Figure 3-3 shows a receiving report for the 20 widgets. The original is kept by the receiving department. Copies of the receiving report are sent to the purchasing department (to indicate the order was received) and the accounts payable department (to be matched against the purchase order and the supplier's bill). If all three agree, payment is authorized. Copies are also sent to the accounting department (to journalize the purchase and record the payable), and to the employee originating the purchase requisition (to give notice that the goods arrived), and a copy accompanies the materials to the storeroom. Figure 3-4 (page 56) shows the use of the three forms. The vendor's invoice (supplier's bill) is included because the cycle is not complete until the invoice is paid in the proper amount.

For purposes of internal control, the three documents—the purchase order, receiving report, and vendor's invoice—should be matched and approved by someone who would not have a conflict of interest. For example, the purchasing agent who placed the order could approve the invoice at a higher price than the purchase order and perhaps receive a kickback from the supplier. It would be best for the people in the accounts payable section of the accounting department to be responsible for checking and approving since they would not have a conflict of interest.

Issuance of Materials

The person in charge of the storeroom is responsible for the proper storage and issuance of materials placed in his custody. The issuance must be

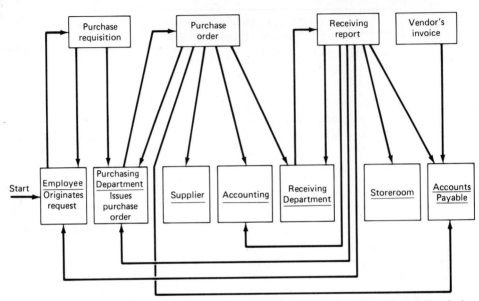

FIGURE 3-4 **Purchase Requisition, Purchase Order, Receiving Report, and Vendor's Invoice**

authorized by means of a materials requisition form prepared by the production manager or the department supervisor. Each materials requisition form shows the job number or department requesting the goods, the quantity and description of materials, and the unit cost and total cost of the goods issued. Figure 3-5 shows a materials requisition for 20 widgets requested by the assembly department.

The cost that is entered in the materials requisition is the amount charged to production for materials consumed. Computing the total cost of materials issued seems relatively simple: the unit cost of an item is multiplied by the quantity purchased. The quantity is readily determined from the materials requisition form; however, determining the unit cost of materials purchased is not that simple during periods of inflation (rising prices) or deflation (declining prices).

During a period of changing prices what price should be charged for materials placed into production during the period and what price should be charged for the materials still on hand at the end of a period (ending materials inventory)? Should the cost of materials issued be multiplied by the beginning unit price of materials, the average unit price for the period, or the ending unit price?

METHODS OF COSTING MATERIALS ISSUED TO PRODUCTION AND ENDING MATERIALS INVENTORY

In periods of fluctuating prices, the allocation of the cost of materials purchased to materials issued to production and to ending materials inventory can be

```
┌─────────────────────────────────────────────────────────────┐
│              MATERIALS REQUISITION FORM                       │
├─────────────────────────────────────────────────────────────┤
│                                                               │
│ DATE REQUESTED: __5/1/X__    DATE ISSUED: __5/1/X__           │
│                                                               │
│ DEPARTMENT REQUESTING: _Assembly_ APPROVED BY: _R. Slum_      │
│                                                               │
│ REQUISITION NO.: __98__        ISSUED TO: _M. Diaz_           │
├──────────┬────────────┬────────┬───────────┬─────────────────┤
│          │            │  JOB   │           │                 │
│ QUANTITY │DESCRIPTION │ NUMBER │ UNIT·COST │     TOTAL       │
├──────────┼────────────┼────────┼───────────┼─────────────────┤
│    20    │  Widgets   │  308   │  $1.00    │    $20.00       │
│          │            │        │           │                 │
│          │            │        │           │                 │
│          │            │        │           │                 │
├──────────┴────────────┴────────┴───────────┼─────────────────┤
│ RETURNED:                        SUBTOTAL   │    $20.00       │
│   NONE   │          │          │            │ ( −0− )         │
├─────────────────────────────────────────────┴─────────────────┤
│                                   TOTAL         $20.00         │
└───────────────────────────────────────────────────────────────┘
```

FIGURE 3-5   **Materials Requisition Form**

computed in a number of ways. Two systems cover the various measurement techniques: the periodic inventory system and the perpetual inventory system.

Costing by the Periodic Inventory System

Under a periodic inventory system, the purchase of materials is recorded in an account entitled "Purchases of Raw Materials." If a beginning materials inventory exists, it is recorded in a separate account entitled "Materials Inventory—Beginning." Purchases plus beginning inventory equal materials available for use during a period. To arrive at the ending materials inventory, a physical count must be made of the materials still on hand at the end of the period. The cost of materials issued for the period is determined by subtracting the ending materials inventory from the materials available for use during the period, as follows:

$$
\begin{array}{ll}
\text{Materials Inventory—Beginning} & X \\
\underline{+ \text{ Purchases}} & \underline{X} \\
= \text{Materials Available for Use} & X \\
- \text{ Materials Inventory—Ending} & \\
\underline{\quad\text{(based on a physical count)}} & \underline{X} \\
= \text{Cost of Materials Issued} & \underline{\underline{X}}
\end{array}
$$

Note that under this method the cost of materials issued is not directly determined; it is indirectly computed as a residual. In other words, the cost of materials issued equals what is left over after the ending inventory is subtracted from the materials available for use.

TABLE 3-1
MATERIALS PURCHASED AND USED

	DATE	UNITS PURCHASED	COST PER UNIT	UNITS USED	BALANCE OF UNITS AVAILABLE
Beginning inventory	1/1	20	$10	—	20
	1/5	50	11	—	70
	1/6	—	—	30	40
	1/9	40	12	—	80
	1/15	20	13	—	100
	1/20	—	—	60	40
	1/28	10	15	—	50
Total		140		90	

The following methods are commonly used to determine the value of an ending inventory under the periodic inventory system.

Specific Identification. Specific identification is the simplest but also the most time-consuming method of determining the cost of materials used and of the ending inventory. This method entails keeping a record of the purchase price of each specific unit and the quantity of specific units used. The cost of materials used is computed by multiplying the quantity used by the specific price of each material. In many cases, when materials are purchased, a tag showing the purchase price is attached in order to identify the item.

The information in Tables 3-1 and 3-2 is the basis for the following discussion of methods of costing materials.

For the specific identification method, assume that the 30 units issued on January 6 were taken from the lot purchased on January 5, and the 60 units issued on January 20 were taken from both the beginning inventory (20 units) and the lot purchased on January 9 (40 units). The computation of the ending materials inventory under the specific identification method would be as follows:

	PURCHASE DATE	UNITS PURCHASED	UNITS ISSUED FROM LOT	AMT. ON HAND		UNIT COST	ENDING INVENTORY
Beginning inventory	1/1	20	20	0	×	—	$ 0
	1/5	50	30	20	×	11	220
	1/9	40	40	0	×	—	0
	1/15	20	0	20	×	13	260
	1/28	10	0	10	×	15	150
						Total	$630

Therefore, the ending materials inventory is $630. The cost of materials issued is computed as follows:

Cost of materials available for use (Table 3-2)	$1,640
Less: Ending materials inventory	630
Cost of materials issued	$1,010

TABLE 3-2
MATERIALS AVAILABLE FOR USE

	DATE	UNITS PURCHASED		COST PER UNIT	TOTAL
Beginning inventory	1/1	20	×	$10	$ 200
	1/5	50	×	11	550
	1/9	40	×	12	480
	1/15	20	×	13	260
	1/28	10	×	15	150
		Cost of materials available for use			$1,640

The specific identification method is used when dealing with expensive materials which are unique—such as diamonds; it would not be economically feasible to use this method in keeping track of inexpensive materials. For example, a peanut processing company would not attach a price tag to each pound of peanuts purchased. Therefore, other methods must be employed when dealing with quantities of less expensive materials.

Average Cost. When an inventory contains many small, homogeneous materials (like peanuts), it is a fair assumption that the materials issued and on hand are likely to be a mixture of all the materials available for use. Consider a product like gasoline. When new supplies are added to the pumps, the new liquid will mix together with the existing gasoline, leaving no clear distinction between the purchases. There are two methods of computing average cost:

Simple Average. Under this method, the various purchase prices are added together and their sum is divided by the total number of purchases (beginning inventory is treated as a purchase) to arrive at the average cost per unit. The simple average price for our example is computed as follows:

	DATE	COST PER UNIT
Beginning inventory	1/1	$10
	1/5	11
	1/9	12
	1/15	13
	1/28	15
		$61 divided by 5 (beginning inventory plus four purchases) = $12.20

Therefore, the simple average is $12.20. Ending materials inventory is computed by multiplying the number of units on hand at the end of the period by the simple average:

$$\text{Ending materials inventory} = 50 \times \$12.20 = \underline{\$610}$$

However, if one were to compute the cost of materials issued in the same manner, the following error would result:

Cost of materials issued = 90 × $12.20 = $1,098
Plus the ending materials inventory 610
Cost of materials available for use $1,708

The computed cost of materials available for use would be $68 greater than the actual cost of materials available for use:

Actual cost of materials available for use (Table 3-2)	$1,640
Computed cost of materials available for use	1,708
Difference	$ 68

The discrepancy arises because a different quantity was purchased at each price. For example, on January 5, 50 units were purchased at $11 per unit; on January 15, 20 units were purchased at $13 per unit. Thus the simple average method only works when the same number of units is purchased at each price. When materials are purchased in varying quantities, another method of computing the average unit cost must be used.

Weighted Average. A weighted average is obtained by first multiplying each purchase price by the quantity of units in each purchase. The sum of the results are then divided by the total number of units available for use. The weighted average price for our example is computed as follows:

	PURCHASE DATE	UNITS PURCHASED		COST PER UNIT	TOTAL
Beginning inventory	1/1	20	×	$10	$ 200
	1/5	50	×	11	550
	1/9	40	×	12	480
	1/15	20	×	13	260
	1/28	10	×	15	150
Total		140			$1,640

Note: The total ($1,640) will always be the same figure as materials available for use.

$$\text{Weighted average} = \$1,640 \div 140 = \underline{\$11.71} \text{ (rounded off)}$$

The ending materials inventory is computed by multiplying the number of units on hand at the end of the period by the weighted average:

$$\text{Ending materials inventory} = 50 \times \$11.71 = \underline{\$586} \text{ (rounded off)}$$

The cost of materials issued may be computed in the same manner:

$$\text{Cost of materials issued} = 90 \times \$11.71 = \underline{\$1,054} \text{ (rounded off)}$$

Note that under the weighted average method, the ending inventory plus the cost of materials issued will equal the cost of materials available for use:

Ending inventory	$ 586
Cost of materials issued	1,054
Cost of materials available for use	$1,640

First-In, First-Out. In many situations, the materials that are received first are issued first. This is especially true when perishable items are involved. For example, in a milk processing plant, the manager would want to sell the oldest milk first. The fifo (initial letters of first-in, first-out) method of inventory costing is based on the premise that the first goods purchased are the first to be issued. Using the fifo method, the ending inventory would consist of materials received last, and prices would therefore closely reflect current costs.

The fifo method of inventory computation for our example is as follows: The 90 units issued are assumed to be from the following purchases:

	PURCHASE DATE	UNITS PURCHASED	COST PER UNIT	TOTAL
Beginning inventory	1/1	20	$10	$200
	1/5	50	11	550
	1/9	20	12	240
		Cost of materials issued		$990

The 50 units in ending inventory are computed from the last purchase price back as follows:

PURCHASE DATE	UNITS PURCHASED	COST PER UNIT	TOTAL
1/28	10	$15	$150
1/15	20	13	260
1/9	20	12	240
	Ending inventory		$650

Note that both the cost of materials issued and the ending materials inventory will include part of the purchase on January 9 of 40 units. Another way of looking at it is as follows:

```
PURCHASE
DATE        UNITS PURCHASED
1/1         | 20
1/5         | 50           Cost of materials issued
1/9         | 40               (90 units)
1/15        | 20
1/28        | 10           Ending materials inventory
                               (50 units)
```

To complete the cost of materials issued, work from the beginning materials inventory or earliest purchase and go forward in time. To compute the ending materials inventory, work from the most current purchase and go back in time.

Last-In, First-Out. The lifo (first initials of last-in, first-out) method of inventory pricing assumes that the materials received last are the first to be issued. Therefore, the ending inventory reflects the prices of the earliest materials received. Advocates of this method point out that it follows a flow of costs and provides a better matching of current costs with current revenue than does fifo. Under lifo, the cost of materials issued closely reflects current costs (during inflation); thus, the income determination should be more accurate because current costs are matched with current revenue. In some cases, this method may also adhere to the flow of materials concept. For example, when coal is poured down a chute into a bin, the last coal in will be the first coal out. However, this is the exception and not the rule.

The lifo method of computing inventory cost is the opposite of computing costs under fifo. The cost of materials issued is computed by taking the last purchase first and working backward. The ending materials inventory is computed by starting from the beginning materials inventory or earliest purchase and working forward.

The lifo method of inventory computation for our example is as follows: The 90 units issued are assumed to be from the following purchases:

PURCHASE DATE	UNITS PURCHASED	COST PER UNIT	TOTAL
1/28	10	$15	$ 150
1/15	20	13	260
1/9	40	12	480
1/5	20	11	220
		Cost of materials issued	$1,110

The 50 units in the ending inventory are computed from the earliest purchase price going forward:

PURCHASE DATE	UNITS PURCHASED	COST PER UNIT	TOTAL
1/1	20	$10	$200
1/5	30	11	330
		Ending materials inventory	$530

Note this time that both the cost of materials issued and the ending materials inventory include part of the purchase on January 5 of 50 units. Another way of looking at it is as follows:

PURCHASE DATE	UNITS PURCHASED		
1/1	20		
1/5	50	Ending materials inventory (50 units)	
1/9	40		
1/15	20	Cost of materials issued (90 units)	
1/28	10		

The major shortcoming of the periodic inventory method is that the cost of materials issued cannot be determined without a physical count of the ending materials inventory. Counting materials on hand can be very expensive and time-consuming. The periodic inventory techniques discussed would also be inadequate if information were continuously needed about the cost of materials issued and on hand. Because most sizable manufacturing companies need cost information continuously, they are likely to use a perpetual inventory system.

Costing by the Perpetual Inventory System

Under the perpetual inventory system, the purchase of materials is recorded in an account labeled "Materials Inventory," rather than a purchase account. If beginning materials inventory exists, it would also be recorded in the Materials Inventory account. When materials are issued, a credit is made to the Materials Inventory account for the cost of materials issued and a debit is made to a work-in-process materials account. The end result is that the cost of materials issued is allocated to production at the time when the materials are issued, and the balance in the Materials Inventory account shows the cost of materials still available for use. Thus, under the perpetual inventory method, both the cost of materials issued and the ending materials inventory are directly determined.

The use of the perpetual inventory method usually requires taking a physical count of materials on hand at least once a year in order to check for possible error or shrinkage due to theft or spoilage. If a physical count disagrees with the balances in the inventory account, the book figures are adjusted to reflect the actual count.

A detailed discussion of the periodic inventory system described various methods of assigning costs to the cost of materials issued and the ending materials inventory. Different inventory measurement methods were developed as a means of accounting for fluctuating prices. The use of the perpetual inventory system under fluctuating prices will now be illustrated.

Specific Identification. The cost of materials issued and the ending materials inventory are computed by multiplying the units issued or on hand by the specific cost of each unit issued or still on hand; therefore, the choice of either the perpetual or periodic inventory system will not affect the method of measurement.

Average Cost. Simple Average. Under the periodic inventory method, all the different purchase costs are added together at the end of each period. This sum is divided by the total number of purchases (beginning inventory is treated like a purchase) to arrive at the average cost per unit. When the perpetual inventory system is used, this computation must be performed *after each purchase*; this technique is usually referred to as the "simple moving average." Hence, many averages may be used in one period.

The same example used to illustrate the periodic inventory system will be used to demonstrate the perpetual inventory system (see page 58). The simple moving average cost for the cost of materials issued and the ending materials inventory is computed as in Table 3-3 (page 64).

TABLE 3-3
SIMPLE MOVING AVERAGE—PERPETUAL INVENTORY SYSTEM

DATE	PURCHASED UNITS	PURCHASED UNIT COST	COST OF MATERIALS AVAILABLE FOR USE	ISSUED UNITS	ISSUED UNIT COST	COST OF MATERIALS ISSUED	BALANCE UNITS	BALANCE UNIT COST	BALANCE TOTAL COST
Beginning inventory									
1/1			$ 200				20	$10.00	$ 200.00
1/5	50	$11.00	550				70	10.50 (a)	735.00
1/6				30	$10.50	$ 315.00	40	10.50	420.00
1/9	40	12.00	480				80	11.00 (b)	880.00
1/15	20	13.00	260				100	11.50 (c)	1,150.00
1/20				60	11.50	690.00	40	11.50	460.00
1/28	10	15.00	150				50	12.20 (d)	610.00
Total			$1,640		Total	$1,005.00		Ending balance	$ 610.00

(a) 1/1 $10.00
   1/5   11.00
       $21.00 ÷ 2 = $10.50

(b) 1/9 $21.00
        12.00
       $33.00 ÷ 3 = $11.00

(c) 1/15 $33.00
        13.00
       $46.00 ÷ 4 = $11.50

(d) 1/28 $46.00
        15.00
       $61.00 ÷ 5 = $12.20

Cost of materials issued $1,005.00
Ending inventory 610.00
Computed cost of materials available for use $1,615.00

Note: As recognized under the periodic inventory system, the *actual* cost of materials available for use ($1,640) will differ from the computed amount under the perpetual inventory system (the exception being when an equal number of units are purchased at each price). In all other instances, this problem is overcome by employing the weighted average cost method.

Weighted Average.   When the perpetual inventory system is used, the weighted average must be recomputed *after each purchase* instead of at the end of the period as with the periodic inventory system. The weighted average cost is computed after each purchase by dividing the *total cost* of materials on hand by the *total number* of *units* on hand. Under the perpetual inventory system, this technique is usually referred to as the "weighted moving average cost." The weighted moving average cost for the cost of materials issued and the ending materials inventory is computed as in Table 3-4.

Fifo.   Since the cost of materials issued is computed from the earliest materials purchased, and the ending material inventory consists of the most recent purchases, these two amounts will be identical under both the periodic and the perpetual inventory systems.

Lifo.   Here, the cost of materials issued and the ending materials inventory may differ under the periodic and perpetual inventory systems. The difference results from the cost to be assigned at the date that materials are issued. Under the perpetual inventory system, a cost must be assigned to each unit issued on the date of issue, whereas under the periodic inventory system, the cost is assigned at the *end* of the period.

Under the lifo perpetual cost inventory system, the cost of materials issued and the ending materials inventory are computed as in Table 3-5 (page 67).

Comparison of Inventory Methods

The method selected for valuing the ending materials inventory directly affects the allocation of the materials available for use between the cost of materials issued and the ending materials inventory. Table 3-6 (page 68) is a summary of the results of using the different methods and inventory systems in our example.

The largest gross profit results from computing inventory under the fifo method, while the lowest gross profit results when the lifo method is used. The fifo method results in the highest ending materials inventory (assuming inflation), while the lifo method results in the lowest ending materials inventory. The difference between the gross profit obtained under fifo versus lifo would be exactly equal to the difference between the two ending materials inventories and cost of materials issued.

In periods of rising prices, if a firm wishes to show a lower gross profit and therefore lower net income, it would use the lifo method. Imagine the amount of manipulation and confusion that would result if a firm were free to choose a different method of inventory valuation each period. To prevent this occurrence, generally accepted accounting principles state that once a method of valuing inventory has been selected, the same method must be used every

TABLE 3-4
WEIGHTED MOVING AVERAGE—PERPETUAL INVENTORY SYSTEM

DATE	PURCHASED UNITS	UNIT COST	COST OF MATERIALS AVAILABLE FOR USE	ISSUED UNITS	UNIT COST	COST OF MATERIALS ISSUED	BALANCE UNITS	UNIT COST	TOTAL COST
Beginning inventory									
1/1			$ 200				20	$10.000	$ 200.00
1/5	50	$11.00	550				70	10.714	750.00
1/6				30	$10.714	$ 321.42	40	(a) 10.714	428.56
1/9	40	12.00	480				80	(b) 11.357	908.56
1/15	20	13.00	260				100	(c) 11.686	1,168.60
1/20				60	11.686	701.16	40	11.686	467.44
1/28	10	15.00	150				50	(d) 12.349	617.45
Total			$1,640	Total		$1,022.58	Ending balance		$ 617.45

(a) 20 at $10.00 = $200.00
    50 at $11.00 = 550.00
    70           $750.00
    Average $10.714

(b) 40 at $10.714 = $428.56
    40 at 12.00 = 480.00
    80            $908.56
    Average $11.357

(c) 80 at $11.357 = $ 908.56
    20 at 13.00 = 260.00
    100          $1,168.56
    Average $11.686

(d) 40 at $11.686 = $467.44
    10 at 15.00 = 150.00
    50           $617.44
    Average $12.349

Cost of materials issued $1,023
Ending materials inventory 617
Cost of materials available for use $1,640

TABLE 3-5

LIFO—PERPETUAL INVENTORY SYSTEM

DATE	PURCHASED UNITS	PURCHASED UNIT COST	COST OF MATERIALS AVAILABLE FOR USE	ISSUED UNITS	ISSUED UNIT COST	COST OF MATERIALS ISSUED	BALANCE UNITS	BALANCE UNIT COST	BALANCE TOTAL COST
Beginning inventory									
1/1			$ 200				20	$10.00	$ 200.00
1/5	50	$11.00	550				20	10.00	750.00
							50	11.00	
1/6				30	11.00	$ 330.00	20	10.00	420.00
							20	11.00	
1/9	40	12.00	480				20	10.00	900.00
							20	11.00	
							40	12.00	
1/15	20	13.00	260				20	10.00	1,160.00
							20	11.00	
							40	12.00	
							20	13.00	
1/20				20	13.00	740.00	20	10.00	420.00
				40	12.00		20	11.00	
1/28	10	15.00	150				20	10.00	570.00
							20	11.00	
							10	15.00	
Total			$1,640	Total		$1,070.00	Ending balance		$ 570.00

Cost of materials issued $1,070
Ending inventory 570
Cost of materials available for use $1,640

TABLE 3-6
SUMMARY AND COMPARISON OF INVENTORY METHODS

	SPECIFIC IDENTIFI- CATION	WEIGHTED AVERAGE	FIFO	LIFO
Cost of materials issued:				
Periodic inventory system	$1,010	$1,054	$990	$1,110
Perpetual inventory system	1,010	1,023	990	1,070
Ending inventory:				
Periodic inventory system	630	586	650	530
Perpetual inventory system	630	617	650	570

year. This conforms to a major accounting concept; consistency. Once an acceptable method has been chosen, it must be used consistently, unless it is evident that changing to another method will improve the company's financial reporting. If the new method is an approved one, the prior year's financial statements must be adjusted when comparative financial statements are presented. The initial selection of a method should be based on which one results in the best approximation of periodic net income for a company. Since no two companies are identical, a firm's particular situation must be analyzed before the most appropriate valuation method can be selected.

JOURNALIZING OF MATERIALS

The method of journalizing materials will depend on whether materials inventory is based on the periodic or perpetual inventory system.

Under a periodic inventory system, when materials are purchased, a debit is made to an account entitled "Purchases of Raw Materials" (a credit is made to cash or vouchers payable). No entry is made during the period for materials placed into production. The cost of materials issued to production is computed at the end of the period by deducting the cost of materials on hand at the end of the period from the cost of materials available for use during the period.

Under a perpetual inventory system, when materials are purchased, a debit is made directly to the Materials Inventory account. When direct materials are put into production, a journal entry must be made to record the addition of materials to work-in-process.

For example, assume 10 units of materials are purchased for cash on 1/2/X0 at $5 each and that on 1/12/X0, 4 units of materials are placed into production (assume no previous purchases or beginning inventory). The journal entries under the periodic and perpetual inventory systems would appear as follows:

	Periodic			Perpetual		
1/2/X0—Purchase	Purchases of Raw Materials	50		Materials Inventory	50	
	Cash or A/P		50	Cash		50
	(10 units × $5)					
1/12/X0—Materials Placed into Production	No Entry			Work-in-Process	20	
				Materials Inventory		20
				(4 units × $5)		

LOWER OF COST OR MARKET (LCM)

Once an inventory method has been selected and used, the next step to consider is whether the "lower-of-cost-or-market" rule applies. This rule states that the ending materials inventory must be assigned either the *historical* cost (cost that the company paid and recorded on the books) or the current market value, whichever is lower. *Current market value* is defined as the replacement cost of an item, or how much it would cost the firm today to buy an item of inventory.

If replacement cost is greater than historical cost, no adjustment is necessary. However, if replacement cost is lower than historical cost, the ending materials inventory must be reduced and the cost of goods manufactured increased. Logically, it follows that if a raw material in inventory decreases in value, the selling price of the finished goods should also decrease; thus, an eventual loss of wealth will occur. The loss in wealth should be charged to the period in which the loss occurred. The LCM rule is supported by the doctrine of *conservatism*, which states that all potential losses should be accounted for in the period in which they occur.

Computation of LCM

The LCM rule may be applied to the total materials inventory figure or individually to various units of inventory. The method selected must be consistently applied.

The previous examples of inventory valuation assumed (for the sake of simplicity) that we had only one type of materials inventory. In a situation where only one type of inventory exists and where the replacement cost is lower than the actual unit cost, the replacement cost must be used instead of the actual cost. For example, refer back to our computation of materials inventory under lifo using the periodic inventory system. The following dollar amount of ending materials inventory resulted for the 50 units:

PURCHASE DATE	UNITS PURCHASED	COST PER UNIT	TOTAL
1/1	20	$10	$200
1/5	30	11	330
		Ending materials inventory	$530

No adjustment would be necessary if the replacement cost were greater than or equal to $11 per unit. However, assume that the replacement cost dropped to $8 per unit. Now the ending materials inventory would be computed as follows:

$$50 \text{ units} \times \$8 = \underline{\$400}$$

Materials inventory before LCM adjustment	$530
Materials inventory after LCM adjustment	400
Difference (to cost of goods manufactured)	$130

The resulting decrease of $130 in ending materials inventory would be added to the cost of goods manufactured because it represents a loss in inventory value.

Criticism of the LCM Rule

The LCM rule was introduced in a period when conservatism was considered to be extremely important. The LCM rule violates consistency, because in one period the ending materials inventory may be valued at cost, while in another period it is based on market value. It is also inconsistent to recognize a loss in inventory value before it is actually realized, while recognizing increases in replacement cost only when the finished inventory is sold.

CONTROL PROCEDURES

It is important that a company have a good system of materials inventory control. Achievement of good control keeps costs at a minimum level and plant production on a smooth schedule. The following concepts should be employed in an inventory-control system:

1 Inventory is the result of purchasing raw materials and parts. It is also the result of applying labor and factory overhead to the raw materials to create finished goods.
2 Reduction of inventory is the result of selling and/or scrapping.
3 Inventory investment is based on management's policies, which are designed to effectively balance size and variety of inventory with the cost of carrying that inventory.
4 Efficient purchasing, management, and investment in materials depend on an accurate forecast of sales and production schedules.
5 Forecasts help determine when to order materials. Controlling inventory is accomplished through scheduling production.
6 Inventory control is more than maintaining inventory records. Control is exercised by people who are using their personal judgments and experiences. Their decisions are made within the framework of stated rules and procedures. Control is relative, not absolute.
7 Methods of inventory control will vary depending on the materials. Basically, the differences involve the number of times the status of materials is reviewed and the amount of cost and effort used in conducting the review. Expensive materials, or those essential to production, will tend to be reviewed more frequently, and the review should be performed by an experienced supervisor.

Control procedures commonly used are (1) order cycling, (2) the Min-Max method, (3) the two-bin method, (4) the automatic order system, and (5) the ABC plan.

Order cycling is a method in which a review of materials on hand is made on a regular or periodic cycle. For example, materials inventory might be reviewed every 30 days. Cycle length will vary, depending on the type of materials being reviewed. Essential items have a shorter review cycle than less important items. At the time of the review, an order will be placed to bring the inventory to a desired level (e.g., a two-week supply).

A technique often used for small items is the 90-60-30 day method. When the inventory drops to a 60-day supply, an order is placed for a 30-day supply. Adjustments in the number of days' supply or the quantity ordered may be made during known periods of fluctuation.

The Min-Max method is based on the assumption that materials inventories have minimum and maximum levels. Once the specific minimum and maximum quantities are determined, the minimum quantity represents the order point. When the inventory reaches the minimum quantity, an order is placed to increase the inventory to the maximum quantity. Minimum quantities are usually based on the amount that will protect against stockouts.

The two-bin method is commonly used when materials are relatively inexpensive and/or nonessential. This system has the advantage of being simple and requiring a minimum of clerical work.

The materials inventory is divided and placed in two separate compartments or bins. The first bin contains the quantity of items that will be used between the time an order is received and the next order is placed. The second bin contains enough stock to cover the usage between ordering and delivery, plus additional units of safety stock. When the first bin is emptied, an order is placed. Items in the second bin are used until receipt of the shipment. An order is placed as soon as it is necessary to use items from the second bin.

The automatic order system is one under which orders are "automatically" placed as soon as the inventory reaches a predetermined order-point quantity. This system is particularly advantageous when a company uses data processing. Cards are maintained which record receipts and disbursements of the specific materials. When the order point is reached, the computer automatically sorts the material card. It is then processed by a clerk who places an order for the necessary quantity. With the use of a computer, it is possible to periodically recompute the economic-order quantity and thus revise order points, as well as print purchase orders.

The ABC plan is used when a company has a large number of individual items, each one having a different value. Materials control for a high-value item will be different from that for a low-value item. Thus, the ABC plan is a systematic way of grouping materials into separate classifications and determining the degree of control for each group.

The total cost of materials that will be used over a specific period is computed first. This amount is determined by multiplying the unit cost of each item by the estimated total usage for the period. Once total-usage costs for every item are tabulated, they are listed in descending order, the highest first and the lowest last. Two percentages are then computed: the percentage of each *item's cost* to *total cost* (total cost of each item is divided by the total cost of all items) and the percentage of each *item's units* to *total units* (total number of units of each item is divided by the total number of units for all items). Finally, the items are divided into three categories along the following general basis:

10% of the items = 70% of usage cost = A
30% of the items = 25% of usage cost = B
60% of the items = 5% of usage cost = C

Items under the A classification will have the following control characteristics:
(1) small quantity of safety stock, (2) frequent review, (3) frequent orders, (4) detailed records, and (5) most capable personnel.

In contrast, C items will have the following control characteristics: (1) large quantity of safety stock, (2) strict adherence to predetermined order points with little review, (3) only one or two orders a year, (4) no need for a perpetual inventory system, and (5) lower-echelon personnel.

Control characteristics of the B items generally fall between those applied to the A and C items. See Table 3-7 for an example of the ABC plan.

In conclusion, it should be noted that the ABC plan is a classification scheme for deciding what tools to use in inventory control. For example, B items can usually be analyzed on an end-of-quarter basis, A items need individual, more elaborate analysis; and an essentially loose, inexpensive control program can best be applied to C items.

CHAPTER REVIEW

Materials are the basic substances that are transformed into finished goods in the production process. *Materials costs* can be broken down into direct and indirect costs; this classification is usually based on the materials' relationship to the finished product.

Accounting for materials in a manufacturing company usually involves two activities: the purchase of materials (requiring a purchase requisition, purchase

TABLE 3-7
THE ABC PLAN

ITEM	PER UNIT COST (1)	YEARLY UNIT USAGE (2)	%	TOTAL USAGE COST (1) × (2)	%	
1	$10.00	2,600	5.2	$26,000	34.7	
2	20.00	800	1.6 } 10%	16,000	21.3 } 72% = A	
3	7.50	1,600	3.2	12,000	16.0	
4	2.00	4,500	9.0	9,000	12.0	
5	1.05	5,000	10.0 } 28%	5,250	7.0 } 25% = B	
6	1.00	4,500	9.0	4,500	6.0	
7	.10	14,000	28.0	1,400	1.9	
8	.05	12,000	24.0 } 62%	600	.8 } 3% = C	
9	.05	5,000	10.0	250	.3	
		50,000	100.0	$75,000	100.00	

order, and receiving report), and the issuance of materials (requiring a materials requisition form).

Materials may be entered in the books of record under either the periodic or perpetual system. The periodic system is relatively simple and does not maintain a continuous record of the large volume of materials issued. In contrast, under the perpetual system, the cost of materials issued is determined as the materials are placed in production.

Frequently, the unit cost of materials will vary during any one period. The following methods have been developed to determine the unit cost to be applied to the quantity on hand:

Specific Identification. The ending inventory is computed by multiplying the quantity on hand by the specific price of each unit on hand. The purchase price of each item of inventory must be known.

Simple Average. The different purchase prices are added together and the sum is divided by the total number of purchases (beginning inventory is treated like a purchase).

Weighted Average. Each purchase quantity and total price is added to inventory on hand. A weighted average is obtained by first multiplying each purchase price by the quantity of units in each purchase. The sum of the results is then divided by the total number of units available for use.

First-In, First-Out (fifo). Items issued are assumed to come from the earliest purchases. Therefore, ending inventory will include prices from the latest purchases.

Last-In, First-Out (lifo). The assumption is made that the latest materials received are the first to be issued. Therefore, the ending inventory will include prices from the earliest purchases.

The "lower-of-cost-or-market" rule (LCM) requires that the ending materials inventory be assigned historical cost or current value, whichever is lower. The LCM rule is applied after the materials inventory is computed under one of the previous methods discussed.

Efficient inventory control keeps costs down and helps production run smoothly. Control procedures commonly used are order cycling, the Min-Max method, the two-bin method, the automatic order system, and the ABC plan.

GLOSSARY

ABC Plan—a selective method of inventory control; attempts to segregate and group materials according to total value.

Automatic Order System—an inventory control method; uses economic-order quantity and order points to determine when an order should be placed.

Cost of Materials Available for Use—

the cost of materials available for use during the period is equal to beginning inventory plus purchases.

Cost of Materials Issued—the cost of materials that were issued to production.

First-In, First-Out—a method of inventory valuation where the ending inventory will reflect the prices from the *latest* purchase.

Last-In, First-Out—a method of inventory valuation where the ending inventory will reflect the prices from the *earliest* purchase.

Lower of Cost or Market—rule requiring that the ending inventory be assigned historical cost or current value, whichever is lower.

Materials Requisition Form—authorizes issuance of all materials or supplies from the materials storeroom.

Min-Max Method—an inventory control method based on the assumption that it is possible to determine minimum and maximum inventory quantities.

Order Cycling—an inventory control method in which materials are reviewed periodically, with orders placed at the time of review.

Periodic Inventory System—a system of determining inventory where a physical count of goods on hand is necessary in order to compute the ending materials inventory and cost of materials issued.

Perpetual Inventory System—a continuous recording of additions to and deductions from inventory. Both the cost of materials issued and the ending materials inventory are directly determined.

Purchase Order—a written request to a supplier for the purchase of specified goods, at an agreed price, noting terms of delivery and terms of payment.

Purchase Requisition—a form used to inform the purchasing department what materials or supplies are needed.

Receiving Report—a report issued by the receiving department of a company stating the quantity and condition of goods received.

Simple Average Cost—a method of valuing ending inventory by computing an average of the different purchase prices and multiplying this figure by the number of units in ending inventory.

Specific Identification—a method of valuing ending inventory by multiplying the quantity on hand by the unit cost of each item in the ending inventory.

Two-Bin Method—a method of control where the inventory items are divided into two bins. When the first bin becomes empty, an order is placed.

Weighted Average Cost—a method of valuing inventory on hand by multiplying each purchase price by the number of units purchased at this price. The resulting figure is then divided by the number of units available for use; this amount is multiplied by the number of units in ending inventory.

SUMMARY PROBLEMS

PROBLEM 1

The Villani Manufacturing Corporation made the following purchases of materials and put the following units of material into production:

	DATE	UNITS PURCHASED	COST PER UNIT	UNITS ISSUED
Beginning inventory	1/1	10	$25	—
	1/8	5	26	—
	1/9	—	—	3
	1/16	—	—	4
	1/22	6	28	—
	1/27	2	27	—
	1/30	—	—	6

Replacement cost of materials on January 31 is $27.

REQUIRED:

Compute the ending materials inventory and the cost of materials issued for January under the following methods, utilizing the *periodic inventory system:*

a   Specific identification (assume the materials issued on January 9 and January 16 came from the beginning inventory, and the materials issued on January 30 came from the lot purchased on January 22)

b   Weighted average cost

c   Fifo

d   Lifo

PROBLEM 2

Rework Problem 1, using the *perpetual inventory system.*

SOLUTIONS TO SUMMARY PROBLEMS

PROBLEM 1

a   Specific Identification

1   Ending materials inventory:

	PUR- CHASE DATE	UNITS PUR- CHASED	UNITS ISSUED FROM LOT	AMOUNT ON HAND	UNIT COST	ENDING INVEN- TORY
Beginning inventory	1/1	10	7	3	$25	$ 75
	1/8	5	0	5	26	130
	1/22	6	6	0	—	—
	1/27	2	0	2	27	54
			Ending materials inventory			$259

Note: The historical cost applies since the original value of the items in inventory is less than the replacement cost.

2 Cost of materials issued:

UNITS		COST	TOTAL
7	×	$25	$175
6	×	28	168
		Cost of materials issued	$343

b Weighted Average

1 Ending materials inventory:

	PURCHASE DATE	UNITS PURCHASED		COST PER UNIT	TOTAL
Beginning inventory	1/1	10	×	$25	$250
	1/8	5	×	26	130
	1/22	6	×	28	168
	1/27	2	×	27	54
		23		Cost of materials available for use	$602

Weighted average = $602 ÷ 23 = $26.17 (rounded)

Ending materials inventory = 10 × $26.17 = $262 (rounded)

2 Cost of materials issued = 13 × $26.17 = $340 (rounded)

Note: Since the weighted average unit cost ($26.17) is less than the replacement cost ($27), no adjustment is needed for the LCM rule.

c Fifo

1 Ending materials inventory:

PURCHASE DATE	UNITS PURCHASED	COST PER UNIT	TOTAL
1/27	2	$27	$ 54
1/22	6	28	168
1/8	2	26	52
	Ending materials inventory		$274

If the LCM rule is applied to each item, the purchase on January 22 must be reduced to $27 a unit (the replacement cost).

Actual cost..................	$28
Replacement cost	27
Difference	$ 1 × 6 units = $6 adjustment

Ending materials inventory (actual or historical cost) $274
Less: Adjustment for LCM rule 6
Adjusted ending materials inventory $268

2 Cost of materials issued:

Cost of materials available for use
    (beginning inventory plus purchases) $602
Less: Adjusted ending materials inventory 268
    Cost of materials issued $334

d Lifo

1 Ending materials inventory:

DATE	UNITS PURCHASED	COST PER UNIT	TOTAL
1/1	10	$25	$250

Note: Since the unit cost ($25) is less than the replacement cost ($27), no adjustment is needed for the LCM rule.

2 Cost of materials issued:

Cost of materials available for use
    (beginning inventory plus purchases) $602
Less: Ending materials inventory 250
    Cost of materials issued $352

PROBLEM 2

a Specific Identification—no change; same as for periodic inventory system.

b Weighted Moving Average Cost

DATE	PURCHASED UNITS	UNIT COST	COST OF MATERIALS AVAILABLE FOR USE	ISSUED UNITS	UNIT COST	COST OF MATERIALS ISSUED	BALANCE UNITS	UNIT COST	TOTAL COST
Beginning inventory 1/1			$250				10	$25.00	$250.00
1/8	5	$26.00	130				15	25.33 (a)	380.00
1/9				3	$25.33	$ 75.99	12	25.33	303.96
1/16				4	25.33	101.32	8	25.33	202.64
1/22	6	28.00	168				14	26.47 (b)	370.64
1/27	2	27.00	54				16	26.54 (c)	424.64
1/30				6	26.54	159.24	10	26.54	265.40
		Total	$602			$336.55		End balance	$265.45

(a)
$10 \times \$25 = \$250$
$\underline{5 \times 26} = \underline{130}$
$\underline{\underline{15}} \qquad \underline{\underline{\$380}}$
Average $25.33

(b)
$8 \times \$25.33 = \$202.64$
$\underline{6 \times 28.00} = \underline{168.00}$
$\underline{\underline{14}} \qquad \underline{\underline{\$370.64}}$
Average $26.47

(c)
$14 \times \$26.47 = \$370.64$
$\underline{2 \times 27.00} = \underline{54.00}$
$\underline{\underline{16}} \qquad \underline{\underline{\$424.64}}$
Average $26.54

Cost of materials issued $336.55
Ending materials inventory 265.40
Cost of materials available for use $601.95

Note: Since the weighted moving average unit cost ($26.54) is less than the replacement cost ($27.00), no adjustment is needed for the LCM rule.

c **Fifo**—no change, same as for periodic inventory system.
d **Lifo**

	PURCHASED		COST OF MATERIALS	ISSUED			BALANCE		
DATE	UNITS	UNIT COST	AVAILABLE FOR USE	UNITS	UNIT COST	COST OF MATERIALS ISSUED	UNITS	UNIT COST	TOTAL COST
Beginning inventory 1/1			$250				10	$25.00	$250.00
1/8	5	$26.00	130				10 5	25.00 26.00	380.00
1/9				3	$26.00	$ 78.00	10 2	25.00 26.00	302.00
1/16				2 2	26.00 25.00	102.00	8	25.00	200.00
1/22	6	28.00	168				8 6	25.00 28.00	368.00
1/27	2	27.00	54				8 6 2	25.00 28.00 27.00	422.00
1/30				2 4	27.00 28.00	166.00	8 2	25.00 28.00	256.00
		Total	$602			$346.00		Ending balance	$256.00

1 Ending Materials Inventory under Lifo:

DATE	UNITS		COST PER UNIT	
1/1	8	×	$25.00 =	$200.00
1/22	2	×	28.00 =	56.00
				$256.00

If the LCM rule is applied to each item, the purchase on 1/22 must be reduced to $27 a unit (the replacement cost).

Actual cost $28
Replacement cost 27
Difference .... $ 1 × 2 units = $2 adjustment

Ending materials inventory (actual or historical cost) $256
Less: Adjustment for LCM rule 2
Adjusted ending materials inventory $254

2 Cost of materials issued:

From chart $346
Plus: Adjustment for LCM rule 2
Cost of materials issued $348

QUESTIONS

1 What are the two classifications for materials costs? Explain the basis for each classification. What are prime costs?

2 Why may two companies in the same industry have different classifications for the same costs? Who has the final say when classifying these costs and determining their relationships to the product?

3 Describe the functions and responsibilities of the purchasing department. What are the responsibilities of the head of the materials storeroom?

4 Identify the three forms commonly used to purchase goods. What items are usually included in these forms? Where are copies of these forms usually sent?

5 What problems are associated with determining the unit cost of materials purchased?

6 How is the cost of materials issued determined when beginning and ending materials inventories are present?

7 Determine the ending materials inventory in units from the following information:

Beginning materials inventory .... 10,000 units
Purchases .... 55,000 units
Materials issued .... 40,000 units

8 Define the following terms as applied to materials inventory:
a Physical inventory
b Specific identification
c Simple average cost
d Weighted average cost

e   First-in, first-out
f   Last-in, first-out
g   Lower of cost or market

9 During a period of rising prices, will the fifo or lifo method of inventory valuation result in a higher reported net income? Explain.

10 Discuss the major differences between the periodic and perpetual inventory systems. When using the perpetual inventory system, is it still necessary to take a physical inventory?

11 It has been claimed that the lower-of-cost-or-market rule violates the concept of consistency. Do you agree? Explain.

12 Answer true or false for the following statements:
   a   Inventory control consists of only maintaining inventory records.
   b   Production scheduling involves making forecasts.
   c   Sales and scrapping reduce inventory.
   d   Inventory is based only on finished goods.
   e   People who exercise inventory control use personal judgment and experience instead of rules to make their decisions.

13 What is the 90-60-30 day method? Why do methods of materials control vary with different items?

14 For each of the following phrases, identify the control procedure that can be most closely associated with it, and briefly describe each procedure.
   a   "30% of the items = 25% of usage cost"
   b   "advantageous when a company uses data processing"
   c   "review at regular periods of time"
   d   "requires minimum of clerical work"
   e   "the order will increase the inventory to a maximum quantity"

15 Describe the control characteristics of the three classifications in the ABC plan.

EXERCISES

EXERCISE 1

Cost of Materials Issued

The beginning materials inventory and purchases of the Penny Company for the year are as follows:

	UNITS	TOTAL COST
January 1	65	$ 650.00
February 1	70	840.00
March 25	85	1,360.00
August 19	90	1,620.00
October 6	105	2,100.00
December 17	145	2,900.00
	560 units	$9,470.00

500 units were issued during the year. The fifo method of inventory valuation is used under a periodic inventory system.

REQUIRED:

Determine the cost of materials issued to obtain the ending materials inventory.

EXERCISE 2

Costing Methods under Periodic Inventory System

The beginning materials inventory and purchases for the Phaff Company for the year were as follows:

DATE			UNITS		TOTAL COST
January	1 —	Beginning inventory	50 at	$1.00 = $	50.00
January	20 —	Purchases	300 at	1.10 =	330.00
May	8 —	Purchases	1,000 at	.95 =	950.00
September	19 —	Purchases	700 at	1.20 =	840.00
December	19 —	Purchases	450 at	1.40 =	630.00
Total materials available for use			2,500		$2,800.00

On December 31, the ending materials inventory consisted of 500 units, including 300 units from the September 19 purchase and 200 units from the December 19 purchase.

REQUIRED:

Based on each of the following methods, determine the cost assigned to the ending materials inventory, using the periodic inventory system.

    a Specific identification   **c** Weighted average cost   **e** Lifo
    b Simple average cost   **d** Fifo

EXERCISE 3

Costing Methods under Perpetual Inventory System

Chaykin Corporation provided the following information relating to their inventory of material for the month of June:

	DATE	UNITS PURCHASED	COST PER UNIT	MATERIALS AVAILABLE FOR USE
Beginning inventory	6/1	20	$2.00	$ 40
	6/12	50	2.30	115
	6/23	40	2.40	96
	Total	110		$251

	DATE	UNITS ISSUED
	6/15	10 (from the 6/1 opening inventory)
	6/24	80 (40 from the 6/12 purchase and 40 from the 6/23
	Total	90 purchase)

REQUIRED:

Based on each of the following methods, determine the cost of materials issued and ending materials inventory, using the perpetual inventory system.

a Specific identification   d Fifo
b Simple moving average   e Lifo
c Weighted moving average

EXERCISE 4

Costing Methods under Periodic Inventory System

On January 1, the materials inventory of Mark's Manufacturing Corporation consisted of 10,000 units at a total cost of $150,000. During the month, Mark purchased materials in the following order: 10,000 units at $15.00 each, 30,000 units at $20.00, 5,000 units at $25.00, and 25,000 units at $30.00. 25% of the materials available for use were issued.

REQUIRED:

Based on each of the following methods, determine the cost assigned to the ending materials inventory for the month of January, using the periodic inventory system.

a Simple average cost   c Fifo
b Weighted average cost   d Lifo

EXERCISE 5

Lower of Cost or Market (LCM)

Assume the following information for the Klein Company's ending materials inventory on December 31:

MATERIALS	QUANTITY	COST PER UNIT	REPLACEMENT COST
A	10	$ 5	$ 8
B	5	2	2
C	20	8	10
D	25	10	6

REQUIRED:

Compute the ending materials at cost, before any LCM adjustment. Next, determing the total inventory value to appear on the Klein Company's balance sheet, using the LCM rule, assuming (a) that the rule is applied to inventory as a whole, and (b) that the rule is applied on an item-by-item basis.

EXERCISE 6

Lower of Cost or Market (LCM)

The London Company sells five materials which are included in their ending materials inventory. The following information is made available:

MATERIALS	QUANTITY	COST PER UNIT	REPLACEMENT COST
J	25	$ 5.00	$ 6.00
G	60	12.00	5.00
M	50	6.00	3.00
P	40	12.00	8.00
R	35	10.00	11.00

REQUIRED:

Compute the ending materials inventory of the London Company, assuming the following:

a   The LCM rule is applied to the inventory on an item-by-item basis.

b   The LCM rule is applied to inventory as a whole.

PROBLEMS

PROBLEM 1

Journal Entries—Perpetual and Periodic Inventory Systems

The president of Margo's Supply Company has supplied the following data concerning the company's wood pulp inventory for the month of January. (The company measures its ending inventory under the fifo method.)

January 1, Opening inventory: 1,000 lb of wood pulp costing $.50/lb
            10, Purchased: 300 lb at $.55/lb
            16, Issued: 300 lb
            26, Issued: 750 lb
            28, Purchased: 400 lb at $.60/lb
            31, Issued: 350 lb
All purchases are made by paying cash.

REQUIRED:

a   Journalize the above transactions under both the perpetual and the periodic inventory systems.

b   Compute the cost of materials issued and the ending materials inventory under each method.

PROBLEM 2

Journal Entries—Perpetual and Periodic Inventory Systems

The president of Sonny's Supply Company has provided the following data concerning the materials inventory for the month of September. (The company measures ending materials inventory under the fifo method.)

September 1, Opening materials inventory: 300 units costing $.75 each
                9, Purchased: 50 units at $.95 each
              16, Issued: 50 units
              20, Issued: 200 units

25, Purchased: 75 units at $1.00 each
30, Issued: 125 units
All purchases are made by paying cash.

REQUIRED:

a Journalize the above transactions under both the perpetual and the periodic inventory systems.

b Compute the cost of materials issued and the ending materials inventory under each system.

PROBLEM 3

Control Procedures—ABC Plan

The Ganite Manufacturing Company uses several raw materials in its production schedule. Management wishes to use a system of selective control. The following data has been compiled:

MATERIAL	YEARLY USAGE	UNIT COST	TOTAL COST
1 × 1	10,000	$ .50	$ 5,000
1 × 2	7,100	.65	4,615
1 × 3	2,000	2.50	5,000
1 × 4	5,250	2.00	10,500
1 × 5	6,000	1.75	10,500
1 × 6	2,750	.80	2,200
1 × 7	1,500	1.00	1,500
1 × 8	5,500	1.85	10,175
	40,100		$49,490

REQUIRED:

Assume that management adopts the ABC plan. Prepare the necessary chart.

PROBLEM 4

Control Procedures—ABC Plan

The Skinner Corporation groups its materials into separate classifications for purposes of stock control. The following data is to be analyzed by management:

STOCK NUMBER	YEARLY USAGE IN UNITS	UNIT COST
126	7,750	$ 3.00
241	10,900	.25
250	7,300	.90
333	4,500	30.00
401	3,500	6.00
560	13,500	.50
817	1,500	32.50
900	2,000	7.00

REQUIRED:

Using the ABC method of control, arrange the materials into the three classifications and prepare the chart that will be used in management's analysis.

PROBLEM 5

Costing Methods under Periodic Inventory System

The opening materials inventory and purchases of the Barbieri Corporation for the three months ending March 31 were as follows:

	UNITS	COST PER UNIT	TOTAL COST
1/1	100	$ 8.00	$ 800.00
1/26	200	12.00	2,400.00
2/6	500	15.00	7,500.00
2/23	200	16.00	3,200.00
3/11	100	17.00	1,700.00
3/27	200	20.00	4,000.00
	1,300 (units)		$19,600.00

The Barbieri Corporation takes a physical inventory quarterly and uses a periodic inventory system. Replacement cost per unit is determined to be $20.00 on March 31. LCM is applied on an individual basis. The Barbieri Corporation issued 900 units during the quarter.

REQUIRED:

Compute the ending materials inventory and determine the cost of materials issued, based on the following methods:
a   Weighted average cost
b   Fifo
c   Lifo

PROBLEM 6

Costing Methods under Periodic Inventory System

The Regal Corporation manufacturers and distributes various types of giftware. A schedule of opening raw materials inventory, purchases, and issuances for the current year is as follows:

	DATE	UNITS PURCHASED	COST PER UNIT	UNITS ISSUED
Opening inventory	1/1	2,500	$53.00	—
	3/2	3,275	54.50	—
	5/9	—	—	2,950
	7/11	2,320	57.00	—
	9/1	—	—	1,525
	10/6	1,905	56.00	—
	12/17	—	—	1,150

Additional information: The Regal Corporation uses a periodic inventory system. Replacement cost of each unit on December 31 is $56.00.

REQUIRED:

a Compute the ending materials inventory and cost of materials issued, based on the following methods:
1 Specific identification (assume that issues on May 9 came from the purchase of March 2); issues on September 1 came from the purchase of July 11; issues on December 17 came from the purchase of October 6)
2 Simple average cost
3 Weighted average cost
4 Fifo
5 Lifo
b Apply the LCM rule on an individual basis.

PROBLEM 7

Costing Methods under Perpetual Inventory System

The Chilly Air Conditioner Company sells one type of commercial air-conditioning unit. Each finished unit costs the company $130; the selling price per unit is $250, completely installed. The company had an opening inventory at January 1 of 130,000 units of material M. The total cost of the beginning materials inventory was $1,690,000. During the current year, the Chilly Company made purchases three times. On March 3, Chilly purchased 17,000 units of material M at a price of $14.50 each; on May 23, 13,000 units of material M at $15.25 each; and on November 2, 12,000 units of material M at $16.00 each. On February 5, 14,000 units of material M were issued; June 3, 12,000 units of material M were issued; and on August 19, 15,000 units of material M were issued. The Chilly Air Conditioner Company uses a perpetual inventory system, and the replacement cost for each unit of material M is $16.00 as of December 31.

REQUIRED:

Compute the ending materials inventory and cost of materials issued under the following methods:
a Specific identification, given that the materials issued on February 5 came from beginning materials inventory; June 3, from purchase of May 23; August 19, from purchase of March 3.
b Weighted average cost
c Fifo
d Lifo

PROBLEM 8

Costing Methods under Perpetual Inventory System

RRR (Ralph's Rolls Royce) Corporation sells one type of luxury car model, "The Executive Brougham." On January 1, at the corporation's warehouse in Great

Britain, the raw materials inventory was determined to be 320,000 units, with a cost of $4.50 per unit. During the year, purchases and issuances of RRR Corporation were as follows:

Purchases:

DATE	MATERIALS PURCHASED (UNITS)	COST PER UNIT
2/15	60,000	$4.85
4/30	20,000	4.90
9/19	10,000	5.00
10/25	10,000	5.05

Issuances:

DATE	MATERIALS ISSUED (UNITS)
3/15	80,000
6/9	60,000
11/6	100,000

RRR uses a perpetual inventory system. Replacement cost this year is $5.00 per unit.

REQUIRED:

a Compute the ending materials inventory and cost of materials issued under the following methods:
   1 Specific identification (assume that issuances on March 15 came from January 1; June 9 came from February 15; November 6 came from January 1)
   2 Simple average cost
   3 Weighted average cost
   4 Fifo
   5 Lifo
b Apply the LCM rule on an individual basis.

CHAPTER FOUR

COSTING AND CONTROL OF LABOR

After the raw materials are procured, the manufacturer proceeds to convert them into the finished product. Labor costs are an important element in the conversion process. This chapter will explore the costing and control of labor.

DEFINITION AND CLASSIFICATION

Labor is the physical or mental effort expended in manufacturing a product. Labor cost is the price paid for using human resources. The compensation to employees who work in production represents labor cost. As we discussed in Chapter 2, direct laborers are those who work on a product directly, either manually or by using machines. Direct labor was defined as all labor that is directly involved in the production of a finished product, that can be easily traced to the product, and that represents a major labor cost of producing that product. Examples are assembly-line workers in an automobile factory or knitting machine operators in a sweater factory. Direct labor is considered both a prime cost and a conversion cost.

Work referred to as indirect labor is not as readily traced to a product, and/or it is not considered worthwhile to determine the cost of the labor in relation to the product. Laborers whose services are indirectly related to production are job supervisors and product inspectors. Indirect labor is considered part of the total factory overhead cost.

COSTS INCLUDED IN LABOR

Gross earnings (or gross pay) equals regular earnings plus overtime premium, and applies to direct and indirect labor. Regular earnings represents the total hours worked, including overtime, multiplied by the regular pay rate. Overtime premium represents the overtime hours multiplied by the premium rate. The premium rate for overtime is usually one-half the regular rate. Overtime is therefore commonly referred to as time-and-a-half because the overtime hours worked are paid at the regular rate plus a premium of one-half the regular rate.

The principal labor costs are wages paid to production workers. *Wages* are payments made on an hourly, daily, or piecework basis. *Salaries* are fixed payments made regularly for managerial or clerical services. However, in practice, the terms "wages" and "salaries" are often used synonymously.

Total labor costs have been increasing rapidly in recent years, particularly in areas such as premiums, bonuses, vacation and holiday pay, pensions, hospitalization, life insurance, and other fringe benefits. In some cases these supplementary costs represent nearly 40% of regular earnings.

Overtime and Shift Premium

Overtime premium represents the one-half portion of time and a half. Overtime premium is preferably separated from straight-time earnings, since all manufactured units should be charged at the same rate. The overtime premium is charged to overhead, and spread over all production. Thus, if a production employee's wages are $4.00 per hour, the direct labor cost would be $4.00 per hour for all hours worked, and the overtime premium would be $2.00 per hour for only the overtime hours worked. Assuming the employee worked 50 hours in one week, the journal entry (assuming a perpetual cost accumulation system) would be as follows:

```
Work-in-process (50 × $4.00) .....................   200.00
Factory overhead control—
    Overtime premium (10 × $2.00) ...............    20.00
    Payroll ......................................           220.00
```

It is an accepted practice to pay shift premiums, or higher hourly rates, for the less desirable evening shift (3 to 11 P.M.) or night shift (11 P.M. to 7 A.M.). As with the overtime premium, the shift premium—or shift differential—should be charged to factory overhead rather than production, and spread over all units produced. For example, assume a company's day shift rate is $3.50 per hour, and the night shift rate for the same job is $3.75, or $.25 more per hour. The following entry (assuming a perpetual cost accumulation system) would be made for a production employee working a 40-hour week on the night shift.

```
Work-in-process (40 × $3.50) ...................    140.00
Factory overhead control—
    Shift premium (40 × $.25) ....................     10.00
        Payroll .......................................              150.00
```

Bonus

A bonus is a payment given in addition to an employee's usual compensation. A bonus may be given for a variety of reasons, but generally it is a reward for greater productivity or effort.

The amount of the bonus may be a set figure, a percentage of the profits, or a percentage of one's salary. A bonus given to a production worker is included directly in the cost of production. Theoretically, the bonus should be assigned to the Work-in-Process account where appropriate. However, it is usually simpler to include the total amount in factory overhead.

The bonus cost should be spread over the production period. If the bonus is paid at the year end, the entry to close out the Bonus Payroll account is made at that time. During the year, entries would be made periodically to charge production for the expense and to accrue the liability. For example during June, a worker earns $312 per week and is entitled to a bonus at the end of the year equal to one week's wages. The journal entry (assuming a perpetual cost accumulation system) reflecting the amount charged to production would be the following:

```
Work-in-process ...............................    312
Factory overhead control—
    Bonus pay ($312 ÷ 52 weeks) ................      6
        Payroll ......................................             312
        Bonus payable .............................               6
```

At the year end, when the bonus is paid, the bonus payable will be debited $312, and cash and appropriate withholdings will be credited $312.

Vacation and Holiday Pay

Factory employees are generally entitled to paid vacations after an initial period of employment. The amount of vacation time is usually based on length of employment. For example, an employee who has worked between one and five years may get two weeks vacation, while an employee who has worked more than five years may be entitled to three weeks.

Vacation pay should not be charged to Work-in-Process. An employee is contributing to production only while on the job. Therefore, only payroll costs for the weeks actually worked should be considered a direct labor cost. Vacation pay should be included in factory overhead costs, and accrued over the period of productive labor. For example, an employee earning $150 per week is entitled to a two-week paid vacation, or $300. In order to record the weekly labor cost to production, the entry (assuming a perpetual cost accumulation system) should show the following:

Work-in-process	150	
Factory overhead control—		
Vacation pay ($300 ÷ 50)	6	
Payroll		150
Vacation pay payable		6

This entry may be made for the 50 weeks that the employee is working. When it comes time for vacation, $300 will have accumulated in the Vacation Pay Payable account. Some companies, which have hundreds or even thousands of employees, may prefer to record the vacation pay as a separate monthly repetitive entry, based on one-twelfth of the annual estimated cost.

For holiday pay, the amount of the accrual will depend on provisions of the labor contract or on company personnel policies, with the number of paid holidays usually ranging from 8 to 11 during a year. Accounting for holiday pay is handled much the same as vacation pay; in fact, many companies combine the two costs into one account, Vacation and Holiday Pay, making one entry instead of two each time.

Actually in business these accruals are generally based on estimated annual totals. Thus the current total could be estimated from last year's totals, adjusted for any expected changes. Since most vacations are taken during July and August, any corrections in the accrual could be spread out over the last five or six months of the year and no costs would be unduly distorted. This same accrual procedure can be used for other paid absences, such as jury duty or sick leave. For a salaried employee, the vacation pay, holiday pay, or other paid leave will be charged to the period in which the absence occurs. It is assumed that the work will be done by another person during the absence or that the absent employee will take care of it upon returning. If a temporary worker is hired to handle the duties, the additional labor cost is charged to the departmental salary account.

Pensions

Under most pension plans, the employer and often the employee make contributions toward employee retirement benefits. Depending on the number of employees and terms of the plan, the company's costs can be substantial, and can have an important impact on net income, company financing, income tax expense, and employee relations. Pension costs should be considered in any labor cost computations. The total costs of a pension plan are based on the following factors:

1 Number of employees retiring each year
2 Amount of benefits paid to each retired employee
3 Length of time that benefits will be paid
4 Amount of income earned from pension fund investments
5 Amount of administrative expenses
6 Benefits for employees who leave before reaching retirement age

In the past, employers established and administered their own pension plans. However, efforts to protect the pension benefits of employees resulted in federal legislation, such as the Pension Reform Act (or the Employee Retirement Income Security Act) of 1974. This act sets specific standards for pension and other plans, assuring employees of the benefits to which they are entitled. For employers, the Pension Reform Act means increased pension costs because of the additional record keeping, disclosure, and reporting needed to comply with it.

Because of its legal and cost ramifications, the Pension Reform Act of 1974 should be carefully studied. Some of its major provisions dealing with labor-related costs are the following:

1 Minimum standards are set for the vesting of employee's rights. Vesting is a form of guarantee: benefits are assured an employee even if he or she leaves the company before retirement age. Upon retiring (possibly many years later), the employee will receive the vested benefits.

2 Participation in a pension plan cannot be denied an employee after one year of employment unless he or she is under 25 years of age, or if, at the end of a three-year waiting period, the benefits are fully vested.

3 Employers are required to make annual minimum payments into a pension fund.

4 Participants, beneficiaries, the Secretary of Labor, and the Secretary of the Treasury must be furnished with details of the plan and with all actuarial information.

Because of the complexity of most pension plans, actuaries are consulted to compute the costs, contributions, and benefits. *Actuaries* are experts in matters involving life expectancies implicit in pension plans and life insurance.

Once the pension-plan costs have been determined, they are allocated to factory overhead, marketing, or administrative costs, depending on the positions of the employees.

Fringe Costs

Paid vacations and pensions are only two of the fringe benefits frequently given to employees. Total payroll costs are now generally far above the cost of wages. Below are listed additional fringe costs that may be borne by the employer:

Social Security or FICA Taxes. The Federal Insurance Contributions Act (FICA) requires employers to match the employees' contribution to social security. To determine the amount of contribution, a fixed percentage is applied to gross earnings up to a maximum limit.

Federal Unemployment Taxes. Unlike FICA, this tax is levied on employers only. The funds collected by the federal government are divided among the states to administer their programs. To determine the amount of contribution, a fixed percentage is applied to gross earnings up to a maximum limit.

State Unemployment Taxes. In most states this tax is levied on employers only, but a few states also require employee contributions. To determine the amount of contribution, a fixed percentage is applied to gross earnings up to a maximum limit. The majority of states have some kind of merit rating plan that allows reduced rates for employers who maintain a low employee turnover rate.

State Workmen's Compensation Insurance (Tax). This insurance or tax is levied on employers and is based on earnings per employee. The rates vary according to degree of occupational hazards; the highest rates are paid for jobs having the greatest risks.

The preceding payroll taxes *must* be paid by the employer. Two optional benefits are contributions to health, life, or other insurance, and contributions to a guaranteed annual wage fund. It is very common today to have health and life insurance plans paid jointly by the employer and employee.

Because these additional payroll costs have increased appreciably, a number of companies treat fringe benefits as direct labor costs. However, most companies still include the costs of fringe benefits in factory overhead accounts.

Incentive Plans

A wage-incentive plan is a system employed by some companies as a means of minimizing and controlling labor cost. It involves the payment of additional compensation for greater productivity. The plan may apply to individuals, groups, or the entire plant. For the plan to be considered a success, increases in payroll must coincide with increases in production as well as reductions in labor cost per unit or with decreases in other factory costs.

Incentive plans vary in format and application. Two commonly used plans are the Gantt Task and Bonus Plan and the Taylor Differential Piece-Rate System. Under the Gantt Plan, a higher piece rate or a bonus is given for production above the standard number of units. Under the Taylor System, the bonus rate for all pieces is used as long as the standard is achieved. Another common incentive plan is a minimum hourly rate combined with a piecework rate. Employees receive the minimum wage, but they can earn more if they produce more. If the output multiplied by the piece rate results in less than the guaranteed wage, the difference is charged to factory overhead. An example of such a plan is shown in Table 4-1. Any employee who produces

TABLE 4-1
COMBINED MINIMUM RATE AND PIECEWORK RATE, DAILY SUMMARY

EMPLOYEE NAME	UNITS PRODUCED	PIECE RATE	PIECEWORK EARNINGS	DIFFER- ENCE*	TOTAL EARNINGS
H. Zaccaro	65	$ .60	$ 39	$6	$ 45
N. Frankel	75	.60	45	—	45
C. Lyle	80	.60	48	—	48
K. Mooney	70	.60	42	3	45
Totals	290	$2.40	$174	$9	$183

*Minimum guaranteed wage = $45.00

more than 75 units receives a bonus. Factory overhead is charged $9 ($6 + $3) because two employees did not produce the minimum guaranteed wage.

Before adopting an incentive plan, management must examine the possible negative effects. Incentive plans require additional record keeping, resulting in increased clerical costs. In addition, quantity may become the worker's main consideration, with the goal of extra units superseding that of quality.

ACCOUNTING FOR LABOR

Accounting for labor in a manufacturing company usually involves three activities: timekeeping, computation of total payroll, and allocation of payroll costs. These activities must be performed before the payroll is journalized.

Timekeeping

Most manufacturing companies have a separate timekeeping department whose function is to collect the time worked by employees. Two forms commonly used in timekeeping are the time card and the labor job ticket.

A *time card* is inserted in a time clock by the employee several times each day: upon arrival, going to lunch, taking a break, and when leaving for the day. By mechanically keeping a record of total hours worked each day by employees, this procedure provides a reliable source for computing and recording total payroll costs. Figure 4-1 shows a time card for Ray Villani (employee #22), who worked 35 hours on job #98, beginning April 10.

FIGURE 4-1 **Time Card**

EMPLOYEE NAME:	Ray Villani					
EMPLOYEE NUMBER:	22					
WEEK OF:	4/10/X					

	4/10	4/11	4/12	4/13	4/14	
SUN	MON	TUES	WED	THURS	FRI	SAT
___	9 AM	9 AM	9 AM	9 AM	9 AM	___
___	12 PM	12 PM	12 PM	12 PM	12 PM	___
___	1 PM	1 PM	1 PM	1 PM	1 PM	___
___	5 PM	5 PM	5 PM	5 PM	5 PM	___
	7	7	7	7	7	

REGULAR: 35

OVERTIME: 0

TOTAL: 35

```
┌─────────────────────────────────────────────────────────┐
│                    LABOR JOB TICKET                       │
│                                                           │
│   JOB No.:_____98_____      DEPT.:____Assembly_____     │
│                                                           │
│   DATE:_____4/10/X_____      EMPLOYEE:__R. Villani___    │
│                                                           │
│   START:____9:A.M._____      RATE:_____$ 7.50_____      │
│                                                           │
│   STOP:_____5:P.M._____                                  │
│                                                           │
│   TOTAL:___7 hours_____      TOTAL:____$52.50_____      │
│                                                           │
└─────────────────────────────────────────────────────────┘
```

FIGURE 4-2 **Labor Job Ticket**

Labor job tickets are prepared daily by employees for each job. Labor job tickets indicate the number of hours worked, a description of the work performed, and the employee's wage rate (inserted by the payroll department). Figure 4-2 shows a labor job ticket for Ray Villani for Monday, April 10. The sum of the labor cost and hours for different jobs (as shown on labor job tickets) should be equal to the total labor cost and labor hours for the period (as shown on time cards).

Computation of Total Payroll

Most manufacturing companies have a separate payroll department whose function is to compute the total payroll, including the gross amount earned and the net amount payable to employees after deductions (for federal withholding taxes, state withholding taxes, and so on). The payroll department also pays the employees and maintains records of their earnings, their wage rate, and job classification.

Allocation of Payroll Costs

Using time cards and labor job tickets as a guide, the cost accounting department must allocate the total payroll costs (including employer's portion of taxes and fringe costs) to individual jobs, departments, or products. Some companies have the payroll department prepare the allocation and send it to the cost accounting department where the appropriate journal entries are prepared. The total payroll cost for any one period must equal the sum of the labor costs allocated to the individual jobs, departments, or products. Figure 4-3 depicts the cycle for labor costs.

Journalizing Payroll

Payrolls are generally prepared weekly, semimonthly, or monthly. Gross wages for the individual are determined by multiplying the hours shown on time cards or other pay authorization by the rate per hour, plus any bonus or

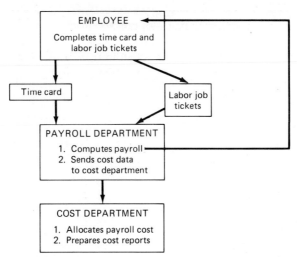

FIGURE 4-3 **Cycle for Labor Costs**

overtime. Journal entries to record the payroll and related liabilities for amounts withheld are made at each payroll period. Employer payroll expenses and payroll cost distributions are journalized at the end of the month.

Journal entries for both a limited cost accumulation system (periodic cost accumulation system) and an extensive cost accumulation system (perpetual cost accumulation system) are shown in Table 4-2 (page 98). A periodic cost accumulation system is a method of accumulating cost data which provides only limited information during a period and requires quarterly or year-end adjustments to arrive at the cost of goods manufactured. In most cases, cost accumulation ledger accounts are simply added to a financial accounting system and periodic physical inventories are taken, adjusting inventory accounts to arrive at the cost of goods manufactured. A perpetual cost accumulation system is a method of accumulating cost data through a work-in-process account, which provides continuous information about work-in-process, finished goods, and the costs of goods manufactured. The journal entries in Table 4-2 are based on the following costs:

Direct labor	$18,000
Indirect labor	17,000
Gross payroll	$35,000
FICA taxes payable (employee's portion)	$ 2,118
FICA taxes payable (employer's portion)	2,118
Federal income tax withheld	3,500
Federal Unemployment Taxes payable (FUT)	245
State Unemployment Taxes payable (SUT)	945

LEARNING CURVE

When a company introduces a new product or a new manufacturing process, the level of output will be influenced by a learning factor. As workers become

TABLE 4-2
JOURNAL ENTRIES FOR PAYROLL

	PERIODIC COST ACCUMULATION SYSTEM		PERPETUAL COST ACCUMULATION SYSTEM	
	DR.	CR.	DR.	CR.
1 *Recording Payroll*				
Payroll	35,000		35,000	
Accrued payroll payable		29,382		29,382
FICA tax payable		2,118		2,118
Federal income tax withheld		3,500		3,500
2 *Distributing Payroll Costs*				
Direct labor	18,000			
Indirect labor—factory overhead	17,000			
Payroll		35,000		
Work-in-process			18,000	
Factory overhead—Control			17,000	
Payroll				35,000
3 *Paying of Payroll*				
Accrued payroll payable	29,382		29,382	
Cash		29,382		29,382
4 *Employer's Payroll Taxes*				
Employer payroll expenses—				
Factory Overhead	3,308			
FICA payable		2,118		
FUT payable		245		
SUT payable		945		
Factory Overhead—Control			3,308	
FICA payable				2,118
FUT payable				245
SUT payable				945

more familiar with the process, output will increase. A learning curve is a visual representation showing how output is affected by the learning process. Studies have shown that the time required to complete one unit should decrease at a constant percentage rate from the first trial job until complete learning takes place.

When the cumulative number of units produced has doubled, the cost of producing the last unit that resulted in doubling the number of units produced will be a specified percentage less than the cost of producing the last unit before doubling took place. Thus, the cumulative average time required to produce one unit will decrease by a specified percentage after doubling takes place. The percentage decrease is usually between 60% and 85% (depending on the situation) of the cumulative average time or cost per unit before doubling took place. As the experience with a process increases, the average time per unit begins to stabilize. This is known as the "constant stage." This stage may be reached when a process becomes routine, when the life of the process is long, or when there is a large production output.

TABLE 4-3
COMPUTATIONS FOR 80 PERCENT LEARNING CURVE, LABOR HOURS

CUMULATIVE UNITS OF PRODUCTION	CUMULATIVE AVERAGE PER UNIT		TOTAL TIME NEEDED	OUTPUT PER HOUR
5	5	hr	25 hr	.20 (5 ÷ 25)
10	4	hr (5 × .80)	40	.25 (10 ÷ 40)
20	3.2	hr (4 × .80)	64	.31 (20 ÷ 64)
40	2.56	(3.2 × .80)	102.40	.39 (40 ÷ 102)
80	2.048	(2.56 × .80)	163.84	.49 (80 ÷ 164)

Table 4-3 shows the learning curve, assuming an 80% learning rate. Figure 4-4 is a graphic presentation of the learning curve. The points where output per hour (on the Y axis) intersects the corresponding cumulative units of production (on the X axis) are plotted on the graph and then connected. The learning curve is used appropriately in the beginning of a new process. The costs that are most affected by the learning process are labor and related overhead. As the workers increase their output per hour, the labor cost per unit will be decreasing. The learning process will be most noticeable where processes are complex or require dexterity. If a new process is fully automated, the learning curve will not be needed to determine estimated labor costs.

In determining standard costs or preparing budgets, unless there is complete automation, failure to take the learning process into consideration may result in large variances that could have adverse effects on managerial decisions.

FIGURE 4-4 **The Learning Curve**

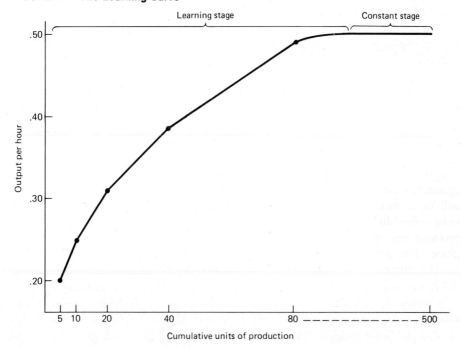

CHAPTER REVIEW

Labor is the physical or mental effort expended in the production of a product. Total labor costs are based on elements other than just gross wages. These additional costs include (1) bonus payments, 2) vacation pay, (3) pension costs, and (4) other fringe benefits, including employer payroll taxes and contributions to health, life, and other insurance.

Some companies have instituted incentive plans as a means of increasing productivity, minimizing costs, and improving cost control. Before an incentive plan is adopted, all factors, both positive and negative, should be carefully considered. The accounting for labor in a manufacturing company generally involves three activities: timekeeping, computation of total payroll, and allocation of payroll costs. Journal entries to record the payroll payments and associated liabilities for amounts withheld are made for each payroll period. The journal entries required will depend upon the cost accumulation system used by the firm.

When a company introduces a new process or product, the level of output per hour will be affected by the "learning process." As workers become more familiar with a procedure, output will increase with a resultant labor cost per unit decrease. Before determining standards, or evaluating present and future costs, management should compute the learning curve effect on labor cost.

GLOSSARY

Bonus Plans—incentive systems which award additional compensation for increased productivity.

Fringe Benefits—amounts paid by employers over and above gross wages, such as social security, pensions, and health and life insurance.

Incentive Plan—a system that provides for additional payment for productivity above the established standard.

Labor—the physical or mental effort expended in the manufacture of a product.

Labor Cost—the price paid for using human resources.

Labor Job Ticket—a form prepared daily by an employee for each job worked on, indicating hours worked,

job description. The wage rate will be inserted by the payroll department.

Learning Curve—the condition that occurs when a new process is introduced; cumulative average production time decreases at a constant rate as the cumulative quantity increases.

Pension Costs—amounts which the employer contributes toward retirement benefits for employees.

Periodic Cost Accumulation System—a method of accumulating cost data which provides only limited cost information during a period.

Perpetual Cost Accumulation System—a method of accumulating cost data, through a work-in-process account, that provides continuous information about work-in-process, finished goods, and the cost of goods manufactured.

Time Card—provides a record of total hours worked each day by an employee.

Vesting—guaranteeing benefits at retirement to employees even if they leave the company before retirement age.

SUMMARY PROBLEMS

PROBLEM 1

The A. B. Cody Company recently adopted an incentive plan. Factory workers are paid $.75 per unit with a guaranteed minimum wage of $200 per week. Following is a report on employees' productivity for the week ending May 19, 19XX. All employees had worked the full 40-hour week.

WEEKLY SUMMARY

NAME	UNITS PRODUCED
M. Akoto	240
J. Halstead	275
H. Glassman	250
A. Ianello	285
K. Rivera	225
V. Victor	265
Total	1,540

REQUIRED:

a Compute each employee's gross wages.
b What amount should be charged to work-in-process?
c What amount should be charged to factory overhead?

PROBLEM 2

Hammond Manufacturing Corporation has introduced a new product. It will be produced in a new department—Department 054. To produce the first unit will require 2 hours. Labor cost is $4.50 per hour.

REQUIRED:

a Assuming a learning curve of 85%, compute the cumulative average labor hour per unit through the sixteenth unit.
b Compute the total cumulative labor cost and the cumulative average cost per unit.

PROBLEM 3

Herman Highgear Manufacturing Corporation pays its employees weekly. Below is the payroll summary prepared by the payroll department for the week ending January 13, 19XX.

PAYROLL SUMMARY

NAME	HOURS	RATE	TOTAL GROSS PAY
J. Opoletto	40	$3.50	$140.00
T. Malmgren	35	2.75	96.25
K. Keller	40	3.00	120.00
A. McGahan	40	3.50	140.00
F. Polli	36	3.25	117.00
J. Montalban	40	3.00	120.00
B. Valli	40	3.50	140.00
Total			$873.25

Additional Information:

Total federal income tax withheld = $87.00
Total FICA tax withheld = $52.80

From the time cards, the following information was obtained:

NAME	TOTAL HOURS	DIRECT LABOR HOURS	INDIRECT LABOR HOURS
J. Opoletto	40	35	5
T. Malmgren	35	34	1
K. Keller	40	35	5
A. McGahan	40	30	10
F. Polli	36	30	6
J. Montalban	40	40	—
B. Valli	40	38	2
Totals	271	242	29

Assuming a perpetual cost accumulation system, show the entries to do the following:
a Record the payroll.
b Pay the payroll.
c Distribute the payroll cost.

PROBLEM 4

The H. B. Hayes Corporation vacation policy is as follows:
  1 to 2 years of service: 1 week paid vacation
  3 to 10 years of service: 2 weeks paid vacation
  Over 10 years: 3 weeks paid vacation
The payroll records show the following:

NAME	YEARS OF EMPLOYMENT	SALARY (WEEKLY)
K. Abby	3	$ 200
B. Caron	1½	153
S. O'Laughlin	7	300
L. Locklin	5	275
M. MacNamara	12	392
F. Stack	4	200
V. Tige	½	150
W. Brandy	1	153
K. Torres	5	275
T. Zello	15	441
		$2,539

REQUIRED:

a Determine the amount that should be accrued each week for each employee.
b Assuming no employee is on vacation, give the journal entry to distribute the weekly payroll.

PROBLEM 5

The Soapy Manufacturing Company awards a year-end bonus equal to two weeks salary to all employees who have been employed for at least one year. Following are the payroll records:

NAME	YEARS OF EMPLOYMENT	WEEKLY SALARY
J. J. Kosinsky	3	$ 208
F. B. Frome	10	286
H. H. Healy	½	198
K. L. Kim	4	182
A. C. Dorfman	4	234
C. I. Chu	5	260
		$1,368

REQUIRED:

a Compute each employee's bonus.
b Give the journal entry to distribute the weekly payroll, including the bonus accrual. (Assume perpetual cost accumulation system.)

SOLUTIONS TO SUMMARY PROBLEMS

PROBLEM 1

a

NAME	UNITS PRODUCED	PIECE RATE	PIECEWORK EARNINGS	BELOW MINIMUM	TOTAL EARNINGS
M. Akoto	240	$.75	$ 180.00	$20.00	$ 200.00
J. Halstead	275	.75	206.25	—	206.25
H. Glassman	250	.75	187.50	12.50	200.00
A. Ianello	285	.75	213.75	—	213.75
K. Rivera	225	.75	168.75	31.25	200.00
V. Victor	265	.75	198.75	1.25	200.00
Totals	1,540		$1,155.00	$65.00	$1,220.00

b $1,155

c $65

PROBLEM 2

a

CUMULATIVE UNITS OF PRODUCTION	CUMULATIVE AVERAGE LABOR HOURS PER UNIT	TOTAL LABOR HOURS REQUIRED
1	2 hr	2 hr
2	1.70 (2 × .85)	3.4
4	1.445 (1.70 × .85)	5.78
8	1.228 (1.445 × .85)	9.824
16	1.044 (1.228 × .85)	16.704

b

UNITS	TOTAL LABOR COST	LABOR COST PER UNIT
1	(2 hr × $4.50) = $ 9.00	$9.00
2	(3.4 hr × $4.50) = 15.30	7.65
4	(5.78 hr × $4.50) = 26.01	6.50
8	(9.824 hr × $4.50) = 44.21	5.53
16	(16.704 hr × $4.50) = 75.17	4.70

PROBLEM 3

a Payroll 873.25

    Payroll payable 733.45

    FICA payable 52.80

    Federal income tax payable 87.00

b Payroll payable 733.45

      Cash 733.45

c Work-in-process 776.50

      Factory overhead control—Indirect labor 96.75

            Payroll 873.25

Computations

	DIRECT LABOR	INDIRECT LABOR
J. Opoletto	35 × $3.50 = $122.50	5 × $3.50 = $17.50
T. Malmgren	34 × 2.75 = 93.50	1 × 2.75 = 2.75
K. Keller	35 × 3.00 = 105.00	5 × 3.00 = 15.00
A. McGahan	30 × 3.50 = 105.00	10 × 3.50 = 35.00
F. Polli	30 × 3.25 = 97.50	6 × 3.25 = 19.50
J. Montalban	40 × 3.00 = 120.00	— —
B. Valli	38 × 3.50 = 133.00	2 × 3.50 = 7.00
Totals	$776.50	$96.75

PROBLEM 4

a

NAME	VACATION WEEKS	VACATION SALARY	VACATION PAY ÷ WKS. ON JOB*	ACCRUAL
K. Abby	2	$200	$ 400 ÷ 50 =	$ 8
B. Caron	1	153	153 ÷ 51 =	3
S. O'Laughlin	2	300	600 ÷ 50 =	12
L. Locklin	2	275	550 ÷ 50 =	11
M. MacNamara	3	392	1,176 ÷ 49 =	24
F. Stack	2	200	400 ÷ 50 =	8
V. Tige	—	150	—	—
W. Brandy	1	153	153 ÷ 51 =	3
K. Torres	2	275	550 ÷ 50 =	11
T. Zello	3	441	1,323 ÷ 49 =	27
Total				$107

* 52 weeks less number of vacation weeks

b Work-in-process 2,539

      Factory overhead control—Vacation pay   107

            Payroll   2,539

            Liability for vacation pay   107

PROBLEM 5

a

NAME	WEEKLY SALARY × 2	BONUS
J. J. Kosinsky	$208 × 2	$ 416
F. B. Frome	286 × 2	־72
H. H. Healy	—	—
K. L. Kim	182 × 2	364
A. C. Dorfman	234 × 2	468
C. I. Chu	260 × 2	520
Total annual bonus payment		$2,340

b **Bonus Accrual:**

NAME	BONUS ÷ 52	AMOUNT
J. J. Kosinsky	$ 416	$ 8
F. B. Frome	572	11
H. H. Healy	—	—
K. L. Kim	364	7
A. C. Dorfman	468	9
C. I. Chu	520	10
	$2,340 ÷ 52 =	$45

Work-in-process	1,368	
Factory overhead control—Bonus pay	45	
Payroll		1,368
Bonus payable.....................................		45

QUESTIONS

1 What are total pension plan costs based on?
2 Why is the Pension Reform Act of 1974 important?
3 Describe the three types of incentive plans.
4 What are some of the pros and cons of an incentive plan?
5 Why does management use the learning curve?
6 What is meant by the *constant stage*, and when is this stage reached?
7 What may happen as a result of failing to take the learning process into consideration when determining standard costs or preparing budgets?
8 What are some other costs included in total labor costs besides gross wages?
9 State whether the following are true or false:

a Indirect labor costs are considered both a prime cost and a conversion cost.

b Vacation pay should be included in factory overhead costs, and it should be accrued over the period of productive labor.

c If the bonus is a predetermined figure, the cost should not be spread over the production period.

d Under a pension plan, both the employer and the employee make contributions to the plan.

e Fringe benefits may be treated as direct labor costs or as factory overhead costs.

f Studies have shown that the time required to complete one unit should decrease at an irregular percentage rate from the first trial job until complete learning takes place.

g The costs that are most affected by the learning process are labor and related overhead.

h The learning process will be most noticeable where processes are complex or require dexterity.

i Journal entries for payroll are the same for a limited cost accumulation system and an extensive cost accumulation system.

j When a company introduces a new process or product, the level of output per hour is unaffected by the "learning process."

10 a What is the basic cost included in labor cost determination?

b How may compensation be expressed?

11 How should a bonus paid to an employee be handled in the accounts?

12 How should vacation pay to an employee be handled?

13 What are four major provisions of the Pension Reform Act of 1974 that deal with labor-related costs?

EXERCISE

EXERCISE 1

Vacation Pay

The Tom Thumb Corporation follows this vacation policy for its factory workers:
   1 to 3 years of service: 1 week paid vacation
   4 to 12 years of service: 3 weeks paid vacation
   Over 12 years of service: 4 weeks paid vacation
   The payroll records show the following information pertaining to the next year (all employees work directly on the product):

NAME	YEARS OF EMPLOYMENT	SALARY (WEEKLY)
I. Gelati	5	$350
B. O'Hara	2	175
R. Reilly	6	370
F. Maestro	15	425
R. Auerbach	8	400
K. Sposare	5/12	125
T. Fyumo	3	390

REQUIRED:

a Determine the amount that should be accrued each week for each employee.

b Show next year's journal entry needed to distribute the weekly payroll. The Tom Thumb Corporation uses the perpetual cost accumulation system. To prepare the entry, assume that no employee would be on vacation.

EXERCISE 2

Incentive Plan

The O.T.R. Manufacturing Company adopted an incentive plan. Factory workers are paid $.48 per unit, with a guaranteed minimum wage of $2.60 per hour. The report on employees' productivity for the week ending June 21, 19XX follows. Each employee worked a total of 20 hours that week.

WEEKLY SUMMARY

EMPLOYEE'S NAME	UNITS PRODUCED
I. Phelps	110
G. Wong	116
T. Caine	106
K. Polli	108
R. Rochester	112
F. Chimmy	102
Total	654

REQUIRED:

a Compute each employee's gross wages.

b What amount should be charged to (**1**) Work-in-Process and (**2**) Factory Overhead?

EXERCISE 3

Incentive Plans

The Spring Trampoline Company has had an incentive plan for the past several years. The factory workers are paid $2.25 per unit with a minimum guaranteed wage of $175.00 per week. The report on employees' productivity for the week ending September 21, 1978 follows. All employees worked the full 40-hour week.

WEEKLY SUMMARY

EMPLOYEE'S NAME	UNITS PRODUCED
F. Chimienti	72
M. Donohue	80
G. Duchene	78
N. Grimsly	82
R. Strauss	68
S. Beeber	73
Total	453

REQUIRED:

a Compute each employee's gross wages.
b What amount should be charged to Work-in-Process?
c What amount should be charged to Factory Overhead?

EXERCISE 4

Payroll Entries

Charger Manufacturing Company pays its employees weekly. The payroll summary prepared by the payroll department for the week ending September 24, 19XX follows.

PAYROLL SUMMARY

NAME	DIRECT LABOR HOURS	INDIRECT LABOR HOURS	RATE	TOTAL GROSS PAY
A. Appel	30	5	$5.25	$ 183.75
B. Brandt	38	4	5.10	214.20
C. Farr	40	—	4.75	190.00
F. Salinger	28	10	5.10	193.80
G. Gasset	37	3	4.50	180.00
L. Morado	39	2	5.00	205.00
				$1,166.75

Additional Information:

Total federal and state income tax withheld $116.68
Total FICA withheld 70.55

REQUIRED:

Assuming periodic cost accumulation systems:
a Prepare the journal entry to record the payroll.
b Prepare the journal entry to distribute the payroll costs.
c Prepare the journal entry for the payment of payroll.

EXERCISE 5

Learning Curve

Tri-City Tile Company has introduced a new type of flooring called the "Durables." This flooring will be made in a new department, Department 36. To produce the first unit will require 3 hours. Labor cost is $3.25 per hour.

REQUIRED:

a   Assuming a learning rate of 92%, compute the cumulative average labor hours needed and the output per hour up to the sixteenth unit.

b   Draw a graph of the learning curve, assuming the 92% learning rate. Plot cumulative units of production on the X axis.

EXERCISE 6

Bonus Computation and Accrual

Snoopy's Manufacturers, Ltd., awards a bonus at the end of the year equal to three weeks salary to all employees who have been employed for more than one year. The payroll records show the following information pertaining to next year:

NAME	YEARS OF EMPLOYMENT	WEEKLY SALARY
B. Alexander	5	$ 225
M. Diskint	7	239
C. Ravel	2	150
P. Mahoney	3	200
S. Rapf	15	425
J. Terzella	10	375
N. Van Zandt	11/12	125
Total		$1,739

REQUIRED:

a   Compute each employee's bonus and the total annual bonus payment.

b   Show next year's entry made each week to distribute the payroll, including the bonus accrual (assume a perpetual cost accumulation system and that next year's bonus cost will be the same as this year's bonus cost).

EXERCISE 7

Learning Curve

Handy Harold's Hardware Supply Manufacturing Company has introduced a new product. Since it will be produced in a new department, the first unit will require 5 hours. Labor cost is $5.25 per hour.

REQUIRED:

a   Assuming a learning rate of 95%, compute the cumulative average labor hours needed and the output per hour up to the thirty-second unit.

b   Compute the labor cost and the labor cost per unit for each of the cumulative units of production.
c   Draw a graph of the learning curve, assuming the 95% learning rate. Plot cumulative units of production on the X axis.

EXERCISE 8

Payroll Entries

The Midget Manufacturing Company pays its employees weekly. Following is the payroll summary prepared by the payroll department for the week ending July 15, 19X8.

PAYROLL SUMMARY

NAME	DIRECT LABOR HOURS	INDIRECT LABOR HOURS	RATE
W. Bianco	39	1	$6.50
S. Cone	33	2	7.25
F. Giant	42	—	5.75
P. Malone	40	5	6.00
L. Palmeri	30	8	6.80
J. Teicher	36	3	7.10

Additional Information:

FICA taxes—employee	$ 95.00
FICA taxes—employer	95.00
Federal and state income taxes withheld	156.06
Federal unemployment taxes	10.92
State unemployment taxes	42.13

REQUIRED:

Assuming a perpetual cost accumulation system, prepare journal entries:
a   To record the payroll
b   To record the distribution of the payroll
c   For the payment of payroll
d   To record the employer's payroll taxes.

EXERCISE 9

Payroll Summary—Accruals

The following data pertains to the five weeks *beginning* Monday, September 30, 19X1 and *ending* Friday, November 1, 19X1.

	GROSS AMOUNT	FICA	FEDERAL WITHHOLDING TAX	STATE WITHHOLDING TAX
Direct labor	$16,000	$500	$2,000	$750
Indirect labor	2,000	100	400	100
Factory superintendents	650	50	160	40
Sales salaries	6,350	86	1,300	450
Office salaries	4,000	104	900	300

Additional Data:

	GROSS AMOUNT	FICA	FEDERAL WITHHOLDING TAX	STATE WITHHOLDING TAX
Payroll incurred on Sept. 30:				
Direct labor	$ 400	$ 35	$ 80	$ 30
Indirect labor	250	10	40	15
Factory superintendents	95	5	10	6
Sales salaries	300	16	40	10
Office salaries	275	14	25	5
Payroll incurred on Nov. 1:				
Direct labor	360	30	75	25
Indirect labor	200	10	30	10
Factory superintendents	100	6	12	8
Sales salaries	280	14	36	10
Office salaries	280	14	25	6

Assume the payroll for each week and its liabilities is recorded at the end of each week on Friday, and payroll is also paid each Friday.

REQUIRED:

a All payroll cost distributions for October are journalized at the end of the month. Assuming all payroll and associated liabilities are recorded for the month of October, prepare the entry to record the payroll cost distribution. Use the periodic cost accumulation procedures.

b Prepare the payroll entries for November 1, 19X1 (Do not include the entry to record payment of payroll.) Assume that there were no reversal entries at the beginning of November.

PROBLEMS

PROBLEM 1

Prime Costs and Conversion Costs

The following data were collected by Eileen's Rug Corporation in order to determine prime costs and conversion costs for the month ending July 31, 19X8:

Union dues	6.00%*	Direct labor	$30,100
FICA taxes paid by the employees and matched by employer	6.05%	Federal income taxes— employees	12.00%
		State unemployment taxes	2.70%
Amount contributed to the guaranteed annual wage fund—paid by corporation	.75%	Total contributions to the life insurance plan (50% paid by employer)	3.20%
Indirect materials	$15,500	Office salaries	$20,000
Sales salaries	$26,750	Direct materials	52,550
Federal unemployment taxes	.70%	Bonus accrual	1.07%
Other administrative expenses	$36,000	Other sales expenses	$10,500
Bonus given to factory supervisors	750	Health insurance contribution—paid by corporation	2.30%
Holiday pay accrual	.30%	Indirect labor	$11,900
State income taxes—employees	3.00%	Total contribution to the pension plan (75% paid by employer)	
Other factory overhead	$45,000		
Vacation pay accrual	4.60%		4.80%

* Each rate is a percentage of the employees' salaries.

REQUIRED:

a   Assuming that fringe benefits are treated as factory overhead, compute the (1) total conversion costs and (2) total prime costs using the information given in the problem.

b   Assuming that direct labor's fringe benefits are treated as direct labor, compute the (1) total conversion costs and (2) total prime costs.

PROBLEM 2

Vacation Pay and Bonus Accruals

The Sunnyside Rainwear Company gives a year-end bonus equal to 1½ weeks of salary to all employees who have been employed for at least two years. The company also has the following vacation policy:

   1 to 3 years of service: 1 week paid vacation
   4 to 9 years of service: 3½ weeks paid vacation
   Over 9 years of service: 4 weeks of paid vacation

The payroll records show the following:

NAME	YEARS OF EMPLOYMENT	WEEKLY SALARY
B. Milstein	7	$ 225
T. Boone	¼	125
A. Myoko	9	275
H. Kohl	12	350
M. Mooney	25	495
R. Ricardo	2	200
T. Sunker	1	175
S. Tarbet	6	210
		$2,055

REQUIRED:

a Determine the amount that should be accrued each week for each employee's vacation.

b Compute each employee's bonus and the total annual bonus payment.

c Give the journal entry to distribute the weekly payroll, including the bonus and vacation pay accruals. Assume a perpetual cost accumulation system.

PROBLEM 3

Journalizing Payroll

Assume the following data for the Grady Corporation for the month of June 19X0:

Factory wages	$105,000	Union dues	$1,420
Administrative		Federal and state	
salaries	56,750	income taxes	$32,143
Salespersons'		Life insurance	
salaries	20,750	plan (paid by	
FICA tax		employees)	$1,825
rate	6.05%		

(Assume no employee earned over $6,000 since the beginning of the year.)

REQUIRED:

a Prepare the journal entry to record the payroll liability for June 19X0. Assume that the Grady Corporation uses the periodic cost accumulation system of recording payroll.

b Prepare the necessary entries to record payment of the payroll and to allocate the payroll. Assume that 12% of the factory wages are indirect labor.

c Prepare the necessary entry to record the employer's payroll taxes. Assume that the state unemployment tax rate is 2.7%, and the federal unemployment tax rate is .7%.

PROBLEM 4

Payroll and Fringe Benefits

The Rich Shoglow Industries manufacture shoe boxes which they sell to retail stores throughout New York City. The following data concerning its payroll were collected by the company's accountants for the week of February 2, 19XX:

	GROSS SALARY	BONUS ACCRUAL	VACATION PAY ACCRUAL	PENSION PLAN COST
Salespersons	$ 5,600	$16	$150	$10
Materials inspectors	15,750	25	75	18
Machine operators	20,000	36	48	30
Office workers	3,760	—	60	15
Factory supervisors	1,250	12	40	6
Factory maintenance workers	7,400	18	100	20
Assembly line workers	25,400	25	78	10
Office managers	1,700	15	200	8
Factory craftspersons	9,600	30	65	—

Additional Data:

Social security taxes	6.05%
Federal income taxes—employees	.95%
State income taxes—employees	1.20%
Federal unemployment taxes	.70%
State unemployment taxes	2.70%

The pension plan is supported entirely by the Rich Shoglow Industries. The company uses the perpetual cost accumulation system.

REQUIRED:

Prepare journal entries to record the following for the week of February 2, 19XX:

a Payroll, pension, bonus, and vacation pay liabilities
b Payment of the payroll
c Allocation of the payroll to the appropriate expense accounts
d Employer tax liabilities and related expenses

PROBLEM 5

Journal Entries—Perpetual and Periodic Systems

The Ruby Company manufactures artificial jewels used to decorate Halloween and theatrical costumes. The company collected the following data on its four production departments during the month of October:

DEPARTMENT	NUMBER OF UNITS PRODUCED	DIRECT LABOR COST PER UNIT	
1	86,500	$.05	4325
2	100,000	.08	8000
3	54,000	.11	5940
4	50,500	.13	6565

24830

Additional information collected during October:

Indirect labor	$10,700
Salesperson salaries	25,600
Administrative salaries	17,050
FICA taxes	6.05%
FUT	.70%
SUT	2.70%
Federal and state income taxes..................................	16.00%
Guaranteed annual pension fund (% of each employee's salary)	.50%

REQUIRED;

a Assuming the company uses a periodic cost accumulation system, prepare the journal entries to record the:
1 Payroll
2 Pension fund
3 Distribution of the payroll
4 Payment of the payroll and the pension fund
5 Employer's payroll taxes

b Assuming the company uses a perpetual cost accumulation system, satisfy all five elements of the preceding requirement.

PROBLEM 6

Journal Entries—Perpetual and Periodic Systems

The Glatt Production Company manufactures vitamins that it sells throughout the United States. The following information was gathered concerning the employees of Production Department C for the week of December 18, 19XX:

	GROSS WAGE	FICA	FUT	SUT	FEDERAL WITH-HOLDING TAX	STATE WITH-HOLDING TAX
C. Hughes	$250	$15.00	$5.00	$12.50	$10.00	$8.20
N. Corona	235	14.10	4.70	11.75	9.75	6.00
S. Dunn	170	10.20	3.40	8.50	6.00	5.10
L. Hlawitschka	200	12.00	4.00	10.00	6.80	5.70
M. O'Shea	190	11.40	3.80	9.50	5.40	4.90
D. Oster	185	11.10	3.70	9.25	7.60	6.10
M. Petrossian	160	9.60	3.20	8.00	9.00	7.25
A. Rifkin	190	11.40	3.80	9.50	3.45	2.00
A. Rosman	210	12.60	4.20	10.50	7.90	5.30
A. Uscinski	170	10.20	3.40	8.50	5.70	4.10

The employees in Department C each received a surprise Christmas bonus equivalent to their current weekly salary. The company withheld 2% of each employee's salary for payment of union dues.

REQUIRED:

a Assuming the Glatt Production Company uses a perpetual cost accumulation system, prepare the journal entries to record the:
 1 Payroll
 2 Distribution of the payroll
 3 Bonus
 4 Payment of the payroll and the bonus
 5 Employer's payroll taxes
b Assuming the company uses the periodic cost accumulation system, satisfy all five elements of the preceding requirement.

PROBLEM 7

Journal Entries—Accruals

Mark Murphy's Manufacturing Corporation collected the following data pertaining to the excellent production record of its assembly line workers. Due to their unusual achievements, Murphy has decided to give them a bonus which will be equivalent to .5% of the profits during the month of January.
 The following data was collected during the month of January:

Monday–Friday	Payroll (Assembly line workers)
Jan 1.–Jan. 5	$1,320
Jan. 8–Jan. 12	1,260
Jan. 15–Jan. 19	1,420
Jan. 22–Jan. 26	1,280
Jan. 29–Feb. 2	1,250

Profits during January totaled $45,750.
Employee taxes payable:

FICA	6.05%
Federal withholding	2.30%
State withholding	1.20%

80% of the Feb. 2 payroll was incurred in January.
Employer taxes payable:

FICA	....	6.05%
FUT	....	.70%
SUT	....	2.70%

The payroll liability for each week and associated withholdings are recorded at the end of each week on Friday. The payroll liability is also paid on this day. The bonus is recorded and paid at the end of the month.

Employer payroll expenses and payroll cost distributions are journalized at the end of the month. The periodic cost accumulation system is used.

REQUIRED:

Make all the necessary journal entries for the following dates:
  a   January 5
  b   January 12
  c   January 31

PROBLEM 8

Payroll Entries—Accruals

The following calendar is used by Isaksen's Ink Manufacturing Company to determine the payroll expenses and liabilities for the month of April:

M	T	W	Th	F
		1	2	3
6	7	8	9	10
13	14	15	16	17
20	21	22	23	24
27	28	29	30	

There are 60 employees: 10 office workers, 30 machine operators, and 20 workers who are considered indirect labor.

All workers are paid the same rate of $5 per hour and work 8 hours a day, Monday through Friday. (Assume no one misses any work time.)

The payroll and associated liabilities for each week, which begins Monday and ends Friday, are normally recorded on the Monday immediately following that week. Payroll for the week is paid the following Monday also.

Employer expenses for each month and payroll cost distributions for the month are recorded the last day of each month.

Additional Payroll Data:

State and federal employee income taxes	15.60%
Social security (FICA) taxes	6.05%
Federal unemployment tax	.70%
State unemployment tax	2.70%
Health insurance—percentage taken out of employee's pay	.50%

(the employer contributes the same percentage as the employees)

REQUIRED;

    a   What is the amount in the Accrued Payroll Payable account on April 1?

    b   Assuming no reversing entries were made at the beginning of the month, record the entries made on April 6.

    c   Record the entries made on April 27.

    d   Record the entries made on April 30.

    e   What is the amount in the Accrued Payroll Payable account on April 30?

Use the perpetual cost accumulation system to record the entries.

CHAPTER FIVE

COSTING AND CONTROL OF FACTORY OVERHEAD

In Chapters 3 and 4, we discussed two of the three elements of product cost—materials and labor. In this chapter, we will discuss the costing and control of the third element—factory overhead.

FACTORY OVERHEAD COSTS

Factory overhead refers to all manufacturing costs other than direct materials and direct labor (selling, general, and administrative expenses are not manufacturing costs). Examples of factory overhead include the following:

> Indirect labor and indirect materials
> Heat, light, and power for the factory
> Rent on factory building
> Depreciation on factory building and equipment
> Maintenance of factory and equipment
> Taxes on factory building

Factory overhead costs are divided into three categories based on their behavior in relation to production. The categories are (1) variable, (2) fixed, and (3) semivariable.

Variable Factory Overhead Costs

Total variable factory overhead costs vary in direct proportion to the production of units; that is, the greater the number of units produced, the higher the total variable cost. However, variable cost *per unit* remains constant as production changes. Examples of variable factory overhead costs are indirect materials and indirect labor.

Fixed Factory Overhead Costs

Total fixed factory overhead costs remain constant within a relevant range of output, regardless of the varying levels of production within that range. (*Relevant range* was previously defined as the various levels of production in which certain total factory overhead costs remain constant.) Examples of fixed factory overhead costs are taxes on real estate and rent on the factory building.

Semivariable Overhead Costs

Semivariable overhead costs are neither wholly fixed nor wholly variable in nature but have characteristics of both. Semivariable overhead costs must ultimately be separated into fixed or variable components for purposes of planning and control. Examples of semivariable overhead costs are those for heat, light, and power.

Factory overhead costs are not incurred evenly throughout a period; therefore, an estimate can be made and a rate developed to apply factory overhead costs to jobs or departments as units are produced. The classification of a factory overhead cost as variable, fixed, or semivariable becomes important when the predetermined factory overhead rate is computed. In some manufacturing companies, however, the size of operations does not warrant the cost and the amount of work involved in applying factory overhead at predetermined rates. Rather, actual factory overhead costs are charged to operations as they are incurred.

Two key factors determine the factory overhead rate for a period:

1 Estimated factory overhead costs (numerator)
2 Estimated level of production (denominator)

ESTIMATED FACTORY OVERHEAD COSTS

A company must develop some means of arriving at a satisfactory estimate of factory overhead costs—the numerator of the predetermined rate. When the company budgets factory overhead for a period, each cost must be classified as either fixed or variable (semivariable costs have to be divided into their fixed and variable components). Fixed costs do not vary with changes in production levels (within a relevant range), and therefore the level of production is not a factor in determining fixed costs. For example, a company estimates fixed factory overhead for the next period as follows:

Rent for the facility	$250,000
Real estate taxes	50,000
Total fixed factory overhead costs	$300,000

These costs should remain constant unless some extreme variations in the level of production occurs.

Variable costs, on the other hand, vary in direct proportion to changes in the level of production or usage. Therefore, the variable costs require an estimate of variable cost per unit. To determine the total estimated variable overhead costs, the cost per unit must be multiplied by the estimated level of production or usage. Hence, the level of production or usage for the *next* period must also be determined in order to project the variable portion of factory overhead costs. For example, assume two components of variable cost exists, as follows:

Indirect Materials Cost
Estimated $.50 per unit produced with estimated production of 250,000 units:
Estimated production 250,000 units × $.50 estimated
cost per unit   = $125,000

Indirect Labor
Estimated $5.00 per hour with 15,000 hours of usage:
Estimated usage 15,000 hours × $5.00 estimated cost
per hour   = $ 75,000

Total factory overhead cost can now be summarized as follows:

Estimated fixed costs	$300,000
Estimated variable costs:	
Indirect materials	125,000
Indirect Labor	75,000
Total estimated factory overhead cost	$500,000

When preparing overhead estimates for the next period, assumptions must also be made about changes in costs due to inflation, technological advances, and policy decisions regarding production standards or objectives. Budgeting overhead costs requires careful analysis of past experiences, industry standards, and other concrete data, in order to arrive at the closest possible estimate for gauging actual production costs.

ESTIMATED LEVEL OF PRODUCTION

In computing the factory overhead rate for a period, the estimated level of production is an important consideration, because *total* factory overhead is a combination of variable, fixed, and semivariable costs (remember that fixed and semivariable costs per *unit* are affected by the volume of production).

What factors should be considered when estimating the number of units to be produced in a period? Should the figure be based on an estimate of plant and workers' *maximum* output under ideal conditions? Or should the figure allow for *practical considerations*, such as possible machinery breakdowns and absences? What about *marketing considerations?* Should estimates of production be tied into sales projections for the next period, or possibly the next few years? In reality, all the preceding factors and others must be considered when projections are made. The following are common bases for the determination of factory overhead:

Theoretical or Ideal Capacity

The maximum output that a department or factory is capable of producing under perfect conditions. In this model, the highest output physically possible is equal to 100%.

Practical or Realistic Capacity

Theoretical or ideal output, minus *external* contingencies such as supply shortages or power outages.

Normal or Long-Run Capacity

Practical output minus *internal* contingencies, such as slowdowns, machine breakdowns, or absenteeism. Normal capacity assumes an overhead rate in which projected expenses and production levels are based on an average utilization of plant and workers over a length of time sufficient to balance the high and low levels of production. The estimated normal capacity used each period to compute the overhead rate does not change. Normal capacity is based on projecting long-run demand (usually from three to five years) for the product, in conjunction with production considerations. Overhead costs will change only when certain expenses or fixed costs change. Normal capacity eliminates the premise that the overhead rate changes when production facilities are used at a higher or lower capacity.

Expected Actual or Short-Run Capacity

Anticipated real output for the *next* period may be used as a base to determine the expected actual output for subsequent periods. When using this basis, different rates are determined for each period according to estimated changes in factory overhead cost, short-run demand, and production considerations.

Comparison

The first two bases—theoretical and practical capacities—only take into consideration the *physical capacity* of a department or factory. Thus, if a company could sell everything it produced, these capacity levels would be used to compute the factory overhead rate. However, this is rarely the case; most companies produce only as much as they expect to sell. Therefore, sales projections are a vital factor in the planning process and must be considered when estimating production levels. For most companies, the normal capacity and expected actual capacity are used to compute factory overhead costs because these two bases include projected demand and real output in their estimates.

Assuming that all other factors remain constant, normal capacity results in

TABLE 5-1
FACTORY OVERHEAD RATES

	EXPECTED ACTUAL CAPACITY	NORMAL CAPACITY
Fixed expenses	$180,000	$180,000
Variable expenses:		
160,000 units × $1.15	184,000	—
200,000 units × $1.15		230,000
Total factory overhead costs........	$364,000	$410,000
Base for units of production	160,000	200,000
Factory overhead rate	$2.275	$2.05

uniform costs per unit for different periods. The use of normal capacity eliminates the possibility of manipulation of unit cost by changing production levels. The use of expected actual capacity may result in varying unit costs for different periods if output changes appreciably.

For example, a large automobile manufacturer used expected actual capacity as a basis for computing its factory overhead rate for a period. Since pricing was based on production costs, the expected actual capacity exaggerated the effect of business cycles. In years when demand was low, fewer cars would be produced, and this would cause the unit cost of production to increase, with a corresponding increase in price. The increase in price would lead to further decreases in the number of cars sold. To correct this situation, the company switched to normal capacity as a basis for computing its factory overhead rate and setting its prices.

Expected actual capacity is generally used only when normal production activity is difficult to determine. For example, assume a company has a normal capacity of 200,000 units. Expected actual capacity for the current year is 160,000 units. Management expects production of 205,000 units in the following year. Fixed expenses are $180,000; variable expenses are $1.15 per unit. The factory overhead rates computed for normal capacity and expected actual capacity are shown in Table 5-1. Different factory overhead rates result because the fixed overhead cost is spread over a greater number of units under normal capacity. The fixed rate is $.90 ($180,000 ÷ 200,000 units) under normal capacity, while it is $1.125 ($180,000 ÷ 160,000 units) under expected actual capacity.

DETERMINATION OF FACTORY OVERHEAD RATES

Once factory overhead *costs* are estimated and expected levels of production are determined, factory overhead *rates* can be computed. Factory overhead rates are generally stated in terms of dollars, or as a percentage of production. There are no fixed rules for determining which estimated activity to use as the denominator, or base, as it is often called. However, there must be a direct relationship between the base and factory overhead costs. Also, the method used to determine the rate should be simple to compute and apply, and should involve little, if any, additional costs to compute.

Once total factory overhead costs have been estimated and the base chosen, future activity levels must be estimated in order to compute the overhead rate. The formula for computing the factory overhead rate, which is the same regardless of the base chosen, is as follows:

$$\frac{\text{Estimated factory overhead}}{\text{Estimated base activity}} = \text{rate per unit, hour, or dollar}\,[1]$$

The following five bases are commonly used to compute the factory overhead rate:

1 Units of production
2 Direct materials cost
3 Direct labor cost
4 Direct labor hours
5 Machine hours

Note that in the following illustrations of the five commonly used bases, the difference will lie in the denominator (or base) used.

Units of Production

This method is very simple, since data on the units produced are readily available for applying factory overhead. The formula is as follows:

$$\frac{\text{Estimated factory overhead}}{\text{Estimated units of production}} = \text{rate per unit}$$

Assume, for example, estimated factory overhead expenses for the period are $500,000 and expected production is 250,000 units. The factory overhead rate would be computed as follows:

$$\frac{\$500,000}{250,000} = \$2.00 \text{ per unit}$$

This method applies factory overhead equally to each unit produced and is appropriate when a company or department manufactures only one product.

Direct Materials Cost

This method is appropriate when it can be determined that a direct relationship exists between factory overhead cost and direct materials cost. Generally, direct materials are a very large part of total cost. The formula is as follows:

$$\frac{\text{Estimated factory overhead}}{\text{Estimated direct materials cost}} \times 100$$

$$= \text{percentage of overhead per direct materials cost}$$

[1] For bases expressed in dollars, the rate is expressed as a percentage by multiplying the rate by 100.

For example, estimated factory overhead for the period is $500,000, and estimated direct materials cost is $100,000. Using direct materials cost as the base, the factory overhead rate is computed as follows:

$$\frac{\$500,000}{\$100,000} \times 100 = 500\% \text{ of direct materials cost}$$

One problem in using materials cost as a base where more than one product is manufactured is that different products require varying quantities and types of direct materials with different values. Therefore, overhead rates should be determined for each product. As can be seen, we are beginning to move away from one of our objectives—simplicity—with the use of two rates. This should indicate to management that perhaps another base would be more appropriate.

Direct Labor Cost

This is the most widely used base because direct labor costs are generally closely related to factory overhead cost, and payroll data is readily available. It therefore meets our objectives of having a direct relationship to factory overhead cost, being simple to compute and apply, and requiring little, if any, additional cost to compute. Thus this method is appropriate when a direct relationship exists between direct labor cost and factory overhead. (There are, however, situations where there is little relationship to factory overhead and this method would not be appropriate. For example, factory overhead may be composed largely of depreciation on expensive equipment, or wage rates may vary greatly within the department.) The formula is as follows:

$$\frac{\text{Estimated factory overhead}}{\text{Estimated direct labor cost}} \times 100$$

$$= \text{percentage of overhead per direct labor cost}$$

If estimated factory overhead costs were $500,000, and estimated direct labor costs were $1,000,000, the overhead rate would be computed as follows:

$$\frac{\$500,000}{\$1,000,000} \times 100 = 50\% \text{ of direct labor cost}$$

If there is little relationship to direct labor cost, the following base may be preferable.

Direct Labor Hours

This method is appropriate when there is a direct relationship between factory overhead costs and direct labor hours, and when there is a significant disparity in hourly wage rates. Timekeeping records must be accumulated to provide the data necessary for applying this rate. The formula is as follows:

$$\frac{\text{Estimated factory overhead}}{\text{Estimated direct labor hours}} = \text{rate per direct labor hour}$$

Assume that estimated factory overhead for the period is $500,000, and estimated direct labor hours are 100,000. The factory overhead rate, based on direct labor hours, would be computed as follows:

$$\frac{\$500,000}{100,000} = \$5.00 \text{ per direct labor hour}$$

This method, like the direct labor cost method, would be inappropriate if factory overhead were comprised of costs unrelated to the labor activity, as when depreciation is a major consideration.

Machine Hours

This method uses the time required for machines to perform similar operations as a base in computing the factory overhead rate. This method is appropriate when a direct relationship exists between factory overhead costs and machine hours. This generally occurs in companies or departments that are largely automated. The formula is as follows:

$$\frac{\text{Estimated factory overhead}}{\text{Estimated machine hours}} = \text{rate per machine hour}$$

Assume that estimated factory overhead costs for the period are $500,000 and estimated machine hours are 20,000. The factory overhead rate would be computed as follows:

$$\frac{\$500,000}{20,000} = \$25 \text{ per machine hour}$$

The disadvantages of this method are the additional cost and time involved in summarizing total machine hours per unit. Since every company is different, the decision regarding which base is appropriate for a particular manufacturing operation must be made by management after careful analysis.

APPLIED FACTORY OVERHEAD COST

After the factory overhead rate has been determined, it is used to apply (or match) estimated factory overhead costs to production. The estimated factory overhead costs are applied to production as goods are produced, according to the base used (that is, as a percentage of direct materials costs, direct labor hours, or dollars, or on the basis of units produced). For example, assume the factory overhead rate was determined to be $5.00, using direct labor hours as a base, and that 100,000 actual direct labor hours were worked. Then $500,000 (100,000 × $5.00) in estimated factory overhead would have been applied to production during the period as the direct labor hours were worked.

TABLE 5-2
CHART OF ACCOUNTS
FACTORY OVERHEAD

Indirect materials and indirect labor	Depreciation—factory building
Supervision	Depreciation—factory machinery
Light—factory	Factory rent
Electricity—factory	FICA tax—factory workers
Fuel—factory	Unemployment taxes—factory workers
Water—factory	Insurance—factory property
Small tools—factory	Compensation insurance—factory workers
Repairs and maintenance of factory equip-	Group insurance—factory employees
ment	Property taxes—factory

ACTUAL FACTORY OVERHEAD COSTS

Actual factory overhead costs are usually incurred daily and recorded periodically in the general and subsidiary ledgers. The use of subsidiary ledgers permits a greater degree of control over factory overhead costs by allowing related accounts to be grouped together, as well as by describing in detail the various expenses incurred by different departments.

Factory overhead encompasses many different items, and involves a variety of accounts. For this reason, many companies develop a chart of accounts, which indicates the account to which specific overhead costs are to be allocated. A sample chart of accounts relating only to factory overhead costs is shown in Table 5-2.

ACCOUNTING FOR FACTORY OVERHEAD

Factory overhead charges are gathered from many sources, such as the following:

1 Invoices—bills received from suppliers or service organizations
2 Vouchers—paid bills
3 Accruals—adjustments for items like accrued utilities payable
4 Year-end adjusting entries—adjustments for items like depreciation and amortization expense

Manufacturing companies commonly use one form for the computation of factory overhead costs—a departmental factory overhead cost sheet. Each department maintains a departmental factory overhead cost sheet which is a subsidiary ledger of the Factory Overhead Control account. These sheets are detailed records of the amount of total factory overhead actually incurred for each department. Reconciliation of the control and subsidiary ledgers should be performed at regular intervals.

Table 5-3 (page 130) is a departmental factory overhead cost sheet for a processing department, based on the following facts for the month of April:

DATE	ITEM	AMOUNT
4/3	Indirect materials requisitions	$ 800
4/3–4/20	Job tickets	1,200
4/10	Miscellaneous invoices	7,000
4/30	Utilities	1,500
4/30	Adjusting entries—Depreciation/Machinery	2,000
	Total	$12,500

JOURNALIZING
FACTORY OVERHEAD

The journal entries to record factory overhead costs will depend on the cost accumulation system used and the amount of information desired by management. When limited cost accumulation systems (referred to as periodic cost accumulation systems) are used, the factory overhead costs incurred during the period are charged to individual accounts, which are labeled to reflect the nature of the cost. For example, when rent of $10,000 for the factory is paid, the following entry would be made:

Factory rent....................	10,000	
Cash		10,000

The sum of all the individual accounts relating to factory overhead for the period should equal the total factory overhead cost incurred. Under periodic cost accumulation systems, only factory overhead costs are recorded and, therefore, no attempt is made to apply factory overhead during the period.

When an extensive cost accumulation system is used (referred to as a perpetual cost accumulation system), both actual and applied factory overhead costs are commonly recorded. The actual factory overhead costs are charged (debited) to a factory overhead control account when the costs are incurred. When factory overhead costs are applied to production, a work-in-process account is debited as production occurs. A predetermined factory overhead rate is used to apply factory overhead costs to the work-in-process account. The credit in this entry may be either to factory overhead control or to applied factory overhead (which must then be closed at the end of the period to factory overhead control). Journal entries to record both actual and applied factory overhead under a perpetual cost accumulation system are presented for two techniques, one using an applied factory overhead account and one using only the factory overhead control account.

Assume the following facts:

1 Applied factory overhead rates based on direct labor hours:

TABLE 5-3
DEPARTMENTAL FACTORY OVERHEAD COST SHEET
PROCESSING DEPARTMENT

DATE	SOURCE	INDIRECT MATERIALS	INDIRECT LABOR REGULAR	OVERTIME	OTHER DEPRECIATION MACHINERY	DEPRECIATION FACTORY	UTILITIES	MISCELLANEOUS	TOTAL OVERHEAD
4/3	Materials requisitions	$800							$ 800
4/3–4/20	Job tickets		$1,200						1,200
4/10	Miscellaneous invoices							$7,000	7,000
4/30	Utilities						$1,500		1,500
4/30	Adjusting entries				$2,000				2,000
	Total	$800	$1,200		$2,000		$1,500	$7,000	$12,500

DEPARTMENT	OVERHEAD RATE PER DIRECT LABOR HOUR	ACTUAL DIRECT LABOR HOURS
Processing	$5.00	2,500
Assembly	.50	1,000
Finishing	3.00	1,500

2 Actual factory overhead costs for the period were $17,500 (assume various credits).

The two sets of journal entries—one with and one without an applied factory overhead account—appear in Table 5-4 (page 132).

T accounts for the same data are shown in Table 5-5 (page 133). The end result will be the same whether or not an "applied factory overhead" account is used: the work-in-process account will have a balance of $17,500.

ACCOUNTING FOR THE DIFFERENCE BETWEEN APPLIED AND ACTUAL FACTORY OVERHEAD

The amount of factory overhead applied during a period will seldom equal the actual factory overhead incurred because the predetermined rate is based on *estimates*, not on actual results. Insignificant differences are usually treated as a period cost. The under- or overapplied balance is either charged (underapplied) or credited (overapplied) directly to cost of goods sold or to a temporary account called under- or overapplied factory overhead if the difference is to be highlighted. The balance in the under- or overapplied factory overhead account would eventually be closed to cost of goods sold.

Assume the following:

Factory overhead control $150,500
Applied factory overhead 151,000

Since the difference between factory overhead control and applied factory overhead is only $500 ($150,500 − $151,000), it is insignificant when compared to total factory overhead. Therefore, the following entries can be made:

1 Close factory overhead control and applied factory overhead:

Applied factory overhead 151,000
    Factory overhead control 150,500
    Overapplied factory overhead 500

2 Close overapplied factory overhead:

Overapplied factory overhead 500
    Cost of goods sold 500

When the difference between actual and applied factory overhead is considered significant, it may be either charged (or credited) directly to cost of goods sold or allocated to ending work-in-process inventory, ending finished goods inventory, and cost of goods sold, in proportion to the balances in these accounts. The allocation method is more accurate because it assigns the under- or overapplied overhead to those accounts that were distorted by using

TABLE 5-4
JOURNAL ENTRIES
WITH AND WITHOUT APPLIED FACTORY OVERHEAD ACCOUNT

USING APPLIED FACTORY OVERHEAD ACCOUNT	WITHOUT APPLIED FACTORY OVERHEAD ACCOUNT
1 *Applying factory overhead costs:*	
Work-in-process—Factory overhead 17,500	Work-in-process—Factory overhead 17,500
Applied factory overhead 17,500	Factory overhead control 17,500
Computed as follows:	
Department *Rate* × *Hours* = *Total*	
Processing $5.00 × 2,500 = $12,500	
Assembly .50 × 1,000 = 500	
Finishing 3.00 × 1,500 = 4,500	
Total to be applied $17,500	
2 *Record actual factory overhead costs:*	
Factory overhead control 17,500	Same Entry
Various credits 17,500	
3 *Closing applied factory overhead to factory overhead control*	
Applied factory overhead 17,500	No Entry
Factory overhead control 17,500	

TABLE 5-5
T ACCOUNTS WITH AND WITHOUT APPLIED FACTORY OVERHEAD ACCOUNT

USING APPLIED FACTORY OVERHEAD ACCOUNT	WITHOUT APPLIED FACTORY OVERHEAD ACCOUNT

USING APPLIED FACTORY OVERHEAD ACCOUNT

Applied Factory Overhead

Entry 3	17,500	Entry 1	17,500

WITHOUT APPLIED FACTORY OVERHEAD ACCOUNT

None

Factory Overhead Control (Using)

Entry 2	17,500	Enry 3	17,500

Factory Overhead Control (Without)

Entry 2	17,500	17,500	Entry 1

Work-in-Process—Factory Overhead (Using)

Entry 1	17,500	

Work-in-Process—Factory Overhead (Without)

Entry 1	17,500	

the incorrect rate, and adjusts their balances to approximately what they would have been if the correct rate had been used. However, if the under- or overapplied overhead was due to efficiency or insignificant errors in estimates, then only cost of goods sold should be adjusted.

Assume the following:

Factory overhead control	$24,500
Applied factory overhead	19,000
Cost of goods sold	20,000
Ending work-in-process inventory	2,000
Ending finished goods inventory	3,000

When applied factory overhead is closed to factory overhead control, a $5,500 debit balance ($24,500 − $19,000) remains in the Factory Overhead Control account. Since the amount is significant, and it is assumed it was not due to efficiency, it should be allocated as follows:

Balances before Allocation

Cost of goods sold	$20,000
Ending work-in-process inventory	2,000
Ending finished goods inventory	3,000
Total	$25,000

Underapplied overhead is allocated as follows:

1 To cost of goods sold $\frac{\$20,000}{\$25,000} \times \$5,500 = \$4,400$

2 To ending work-in-process inventory $\frac{\$2,000}{\$25,000} \times \$5,500 = 440$

3 To ending finished goods inventory $\frac{\$3,000}{\$25,000} \times \$5,500 = 660$

Total allocated $5,500

The journal entry to record the allocation is as follows:

Cost of goods sold	4,400	
Work-in-process inventory	440	
Finished goods inventory	660	
Factory overhead control		5,500

Any under- or overapplied factory overhead found at the end of a period should be analyzed by management to determine its cause.

ALLOCATION OF SERVICE DEPARTMENT COSTS TO PRODUCING DEPARTMENTS

Within a manufacturing company, there are two types of factory departments— producing and service. A producing department is one in which the conversion or production processes take place. A service department is one which provides benefits to the producing departments. Examples of service departments are the maintenance department, which is responsible for the upkeep of the machinery, building, and grounds; and the utility department, which is responsible for providing electricity for heating and lighting the factory, and use of electrical equipment. Since the producing departments are directly benefited by the service departments, a portion of the costs of operating the service departments should be allocated to the producing departments. The following methods are commonly used to allocate service department costs:

1   Direct method
2   Step method
3   Algebraic method

Direct Method

The direct method is the most commonly used one for allocating service department costs because of its mathematical simplicity and ease of application. Under the direct method, a specific allocation of service department cost is made to the producing departments. The basis for the allocation generally varies according to the nature of the service provided. For example, the cost of the building and grounds maintenance department may be allocated to the producing departments based on the number of square feet serviced.

   The following information illustrates how service costs are allocated in the Crane Manufacturing Company. The company has two service departments and two producing departments. The total overhead cost for the period for each department is shown in Table 5-6. Assume that the cost of the building and grounds maintenance department is allocated to the machinery and assembly departments, based on the number of square feet; the cost of the general factory administration department is allocated, based on estimated labor hours. The factory overhead rates for the producing departments are based on direct labor hours.

TABLE 5-6
CRANE MANUFACTURING COMPANY
TOTAL OVERHEAD COST

Service Departments:	
Department X, Building and Grounds Maintenance	$10,000
Department Y, General Factory Administration	7,500
Producing Departments:	
Department A, Machinery	36,500
Department B, Assembly	44,600

Additional Information:

DEPARTMENT	DIRECT LABOR HOURS	SQUARE FEET	ESTIMATED TOTAL LABOR HOURS
X, Building and Grounds Maintenance	—	700	1,000
Y, General Factory Administration	—	500	700
A, Machinery	1,800	1,000	2,800
B, Assembly	950	3,000	1,200
Total	2,750	5,200	5,700

The allocation of service department costs to producing departments under the direct method is computed in Table 5-7 (pages 136–137).

Step Method

The step method is more accurate than the direct method because it takes into consideration the services provided to other service departments. The allocation of service department costs is performed by a series of steps as follows:

1 The costs of the service department that provides services to the *greatest* number of other service departments are usually allocated first.
2 The costs of the service department that provides services to the *next greatest* number of service departments are then allocated. Any costs added to this department from step 1 are included. Note that under this method, once a service department's costs have been allocated to other departments, no additional costs can be allocated to it in the future. That is, the department whose costs were allocated in step 1 will not receive any cost allocation from the second department.
3 This sequence is continued, step by step, until all the service department costs have been allocated to producing departments.

Using the facts given above, assume that the costs of the building and grounds maintenance department are allocated first, and then the costs of the general factory administration department are allocated. For the Crane Manufacturing Company, the allocation of service department costs to

TABLE 5-7
ALLOCATION OF COSTS
DIRECT METHOD

	SERVICE DEPARTMENTS		PRODUCING DEPARTMENTS	
	DEPARTMENT X BUILDING AND GROUNDS MAINTENANCE	DEPARTMENT Y GENERAL FACTORY ADMINISTRATION	DEPARTMENT A MACHINERY	DEPARTMENT B ASSEMBLY
Total cost	$ 10,000	$ 7,500	$36,500	$44,600
Allocated to producing Departments A and B	(10,000)		2,500 (1)	7,500 (2)
		(7,500)	5,250 (3)	2,250 (4)
Balance after allocation	$ 0	$ 0	$44,250	$54,350
Factory overhead rates			$ 24.58 (5)	$ 57.21 (6)

Computations:

Allocation of Department X—Building and Grounds Maintenance:

$$\frac{\text{Total cost}}{\text{Square feet of Departments A and B}} = \frac{\$10,000}{4,000} = \$2.50 \text{ per square foot}$$

	SQUARE FOOT		RATE PER SQUARE FOOT
(1) To Department A—Machinery = $ 2,500	(1,000	×	$2.50)
(2) To Department B—Assembly = 7,500	(3,000	×	2.50)
Total	$10,000		

Allocation of Department Y—General Factory Administration:

$$\frac{\text{Total cost}}{\text{Total labor hours of Departments A and B}} = \frac{\$7,500}{4,000} = \$1.875 \text{ per total labor hour}$$

		TOTAL LABOR HOURS	×	RATE PER TOTAL LABOR HOUR
(3) To Department A—Machinery	= $5,250	(2,800	×	$1.875)
(4) To Department B—Assembly	= 2,250	(1,200	×	1.875)
Total	$7,500			

Factory overhead rate (based on total labor hours) for producing departments:

		TOTAL COST AFTER ALLOCATION	÷	DIRECT LABOR HOURS
(5) For Department A—Machinery	= $24.58	($44,250	÷	1,800)
(6) For Department B—Assembly	= 57.21	($54,350	÷	950)

producing departments under the step method is computed in Table 5-8 (pages 140–141). Note that the difference between the direct method and the step method is the allocation of the cost of one service department (Department X) to the other (Department Y), which is made only under the step method.

Algebraic Method

This is the most accurate method of the three because it considers any reciprocal services provided among the service departments. For example, the building and grounds maintenance department may service the personnel department, and the personnel department may provide services to the building and grounds maintenance department.

Under the direct method, *no* service department costs are allocated to other service departments. In the step method, service department costs *are* allocated to other service departments. However, reciprocal allocation is not possible because each service department account is closed once its costs have been allocated and no further costs can be allocated to it. Thus, the direct and step methods ignore the allocation of reciprocal services. With the algebraic method, the use of "simultaneous equations" allows for reciprocal allocation because every department serviced will be allocated costs from the department providing the service. When reciprocal services are not extensive, it is possible to arrive at an acceptable approximation by using the step method. In our example, there are two service and two producing departments; thus, two simultaneous equations are required. When the number of departments is large, more equations are required, in which case, the use of a computer facilitates the computations.

Continuing the example of the Crane Manufacturing Company (data from Table 5-6), assume the following additional facts:

	SERVICES PROVIDED BY	
	DEPARTMENT X	DEPARTMENT Y
Service Departments:		
Department X, Building and Grounds Maintenance	—	20%*
Department Y, General Factory Administration	10%	—
Producing Departments:		
Department A, Machinery	40	60
Department B, Assembly	50	20
Total	100%	100%

*The percentages of services provided by one department for another, as used in the equations, are based on past experience and current projections made by management.

The allocation of service department costs to producing departments according to the algebraic method is computed as follows.

The cost to be allocated to Department X (Building and Grounds Maintenance) is equal to $10,000 plus 20% of the cost of Department Y (General Factory Administration). Stated algebraically, this appears as follows:

$$X = \$10,000 + .20Y$$

The cost to be allocated to Department Y is equal to $7,500 plus 10% of the cost of Department X. Stated algebraically, this appears as follows:

$$Y = \$7,500 + .10X$$

The next step is to solve the equations simultaneously for either X or Y. In our example, we will solve for Y first (when there are more than two unknowns in the equation, the equation with the greatest number of unknowns must be solved first; in our example, both have only two unknowns so either one may be solved first). The Department X equation is substituted for the X in the Department Y equation as follows:

$$Y = \$7,500 + .10 (\$10,000 + .20Y)$$

Now only one unknown exists in the equation for Department Y, and it may be solved as follows:

$$
\begin{aligned}
Y &= \$7,500 + \$1,000 + .02Y \quad \text{(cleared parentheses)} \\
.98Y &= \$8,500 \quad \text{(bring unknowns to one side of equation)} \\
Y &= \underline{\$8,673} \quad \text{(divide each side by .98)}
\end{aligned}
$$

Now that we have the cost for Department Y, it may be substituted for Y in the Department X equation, as follows:

$$
\begin{aligned}
X &= \$10,000 + .20Y \\
X &= \$10,000 + .20 (\$8,673) \quad \text{(substitution)} \\
X &= \$10,000 + \$1,735 \\
X &= \underline{\$11,735}
\end{aligned}
$$

The allocation of factory overhead continues in Table 5-9 (pages 142–143).

CHAPTER REVIEW

Factory overhead costs may be classified into the following three categories: variable, fixed, or semivariable. The classification of factory overhead cost is based on its behavior relative to production; that is, does it vary according to units produced, remain fixed for wide ranges of production, or remain fixed for very short ranges of production? The range within which fixed costs remain constant is called the relevant range. The wider the relevant range for a cost, the more likely it will be classified as fixed.

Budgeting or estimating factory overhead costs may be based on past experience, industry trends, or economic forecasts. The predetermined over-

TABLE 5-8
ALLOCATION OF COSTS
STEP METHOD

	SERVICE DEPARTMENTS		PRODUCING DEPARTMENTS	
	DEPARTMENT X BUILDING AND GROUNDS MAINTENANCE	*DEPARTMENT Y* GENERAL FACTORY ADMINISTRATION	*DEPARTMENT A* MACHINERY	*DEPARTMENT B* ASSEMBLY
Total cost	$ 10,000	$ 7,500	$36,500	$44,600
Allocated to service Department Y and producing				
Departments A and B	(10,000)	1,111 (1)	2,222 (2)	6,667 (3)
Subtotal		$ 8,611	$38,722	$51,267
Allocated to producing				
Departments A and B		(8,611)	6,028 (4)	2,583 (5)
Balance after allocation	$ 0	$ 0	$44,750	$53,850
Factory overhead rates			24.86 (6)	56.68 (7)

Computations:

Allocation of Department X, Building and Grounds Maintenance:

$$\frac{\text{Total cost}}{\text{Square feet in Departments Y, A, and B}} = \frac{\$10,000}{4,500} = \$2.2222 \text{ per square foot}$$

		SQUARE FEET	×	RATE PER SQUARE FOOT
(1) To Department Y—General Factory Administration	= $ 1,111	(500	×	$2.2222)
(2) To Department A—Machinery	= 2,222	(1,000	×	2.2222)
(3) To Department B—Assembly	= 6,667	(3,000	×	2.2222)
Total	$10,000			

Allocation of Department Y, General Factory Administration:

$$\text{Total cost} = \frac{\$8,611}{4,000} = \$2.1527 \text{ per total labor hour}$$

Total labor hours of Departments A and B

		TOTAL LABOR HOURS	×	RATE PER TOTAL LABOR HOUR
(4) To Department A—Machinery	= $6,028	(2,800	×	$2.1527)
(5) To Department B—Assembly	= 2,583	(1,200	×	2.1527)
Total	$8,611			

Factory overhead rate (based on direct labor hours) for producing departments:

		TOTAL COST AFTER ALLOCATION	÷	DIRECT LABOR HOURS
(6) For Department A—Machinery	= $24.86	($44,750	÷	1,800)
(7) For Department B—Assembly	= 56.68	($53,850	÷	950)

TABLE 5-9
ALLOCATION OF COSTS
ALGEBRAIC METHOD

	SERVICE DEPARTMENTS		PRODUCING DEPARTMENTS	
	DEPARTMENT X BUILDING AND GROUNDS MAINTENANCE	DEPARTMENT Y GENERAL FACTORY ADMINISTRATION	DEPARTMENT A MACHINERY	DEPARTMENT B ASSEMBLY
Total cost	$ 10,000	$ 7,500	$36,500	$44,600
Allocated to service Department Y and producing Departments A and B	(11,735)	1,173 (1)	4,694 (2)	5,868 (3)
Allocated to service Department X and producing Departments A and B	1,735 (4)	(8,673)	5,203 (5)	1,735 (6)
Balance after allocation	$ 0	$ 0	$46,397	$52,203
Factory overhead rates			$ 25.78 (7)	$ 54.95 (8)

Computations:

Allocation of Department X, Building and Grounds Maintenance:

		% OF SERVICE RECEIVED × TOTAL COST
(1) To Department Y—General Factory Administration	= $ 1,173	(10 × $11,735)
(2) To Department A—Machinery	= 4,694	(40 × 11,735)
(3) To Department B—Assembly	= 5,868	(50 × 11,735)
Total	$11,735	

Allocation of Department Y, General Factory Administration:

			% OF SERVICE RECEIVED	× TOTAL COST
(4)	To Department X—Building and Grounds Maintenance	= $ 1,735	(20	× $8,673)
(5)	To Department A—Machinery	= 5,203	(60	× 8,673)
(6)	To Department B—Assembly	= 1,735	(20	× 8,673)
	Total	$ 8,673		

Factory overhead rates (based on direct labor hours) for producing departments:

		TOTAL COST	÷	DIRECT LABOR HOURS
(7)	For Department A—Machinery	$25.78	($46,397 ÷	1,800)
(8)	For Department B—Assembly	54.95	(52,203 ÷	950)

head rate is commonly computed by using one or more of the four following levels of production: theoretical capacity, practical capacity, normal capacity, and expected actual capacity.

Theoretical capacity is the maximum production capable under ideal conditions. Practical capacity is theoretical capacity less allowances for external constraints. Normal capacity is based on a constant, average level of production encompassing highs and lows actually experienced. Expected actual capacity is the output anticipated for the next period. Only normal and expected actual capacity take into account the relationship between demand and production; therefore, they are most relevant for computing factory overhead rates. Normal capacity results in constant, predetermined unit costs for different periods, whereas expected actual capacity may result in unit costs which vary from period to period.

Factory overhead rates are computed as a percent or dollar amount of some form of production. Any base may be used as long as it relates to factory overhead cost behavior and is relatively simple to use. Factory overhead is applied to production at a predetermined rate as the goods are produced.

Expenses incurred from operating a service department are allocated by the direct method, step method, or algebraic method to the appropriate producing departments as part of factory overhead costs. The direct method involves allocation of service department cost directly to producing departments, and ignores any services provided by one service department to another. Costs are allocated under this method by a base relevant to the services provided. The step method allocates service department costs to other service departments, as well as to producing departments. However, this method ignores any reciprocal services between service departments because once a service department's costs have been allocated, no other costs may be allocated to it. The algebraic method takes into account reciprocal services and involves simultaneous equations. It is more accurate than the direct or step methods, but can be somewhat complex and is most often used in computerized systems. Each method results in a different predetermined overhead rate.

GLOSSARY

Applied Factory Overhead—factory overhead costs that are applied (or matched) to production as goods are produced, through the use of a predetermined rate.

Expected Actual or Short-Run Capacity—anticipated output for the next period.

Factory Overhead Costs—includes all manufacturing costs other than direct materials and direct labor (Selling, general, and administrative expenses are period costs and not included in factory overhead costs.)

Factory Overhead Rate—a rate is a quantitative measure of a part to the whole and is used to allocate estimated factory overhead to production. The formula for computing the factory overhead rate is the same, regardless of the base chosen, as follows:

Estimated factory overhead
Estimated base activity
= factory overhead rate

Fixed Factory Overhead Costs—the total factory overhead cost which remains constant within a relevant range of output, regardless of the varying levels of production within that range. Fixed overhead costs per unit will vary at different levels of production.

Normal or Long-Run Capacity—the constant, average level of utilization of plant and workers over a length of time sufficient to even out the high and low levels of production.

Practical or Realistic Capacity—the theoretical output, less practical contingencies, such as anticipated breakdowns, strikes, and delays.

Relevant Range—the various levels of production in which certain factory overhead costs remain constant.

Semivariable Factory Overhead Costs—costs which possess characteristics of both fixed and variable overhead costs.

Theoretical or Ideal Capacity—the maximum output which a department or factory is capable, under perfect conditions.

Variable Factory Overhead Costs—the overhead costs, which vary in direct proportion to the production of units but remain constant per unit. The greater the number of units produced, the higher the total variable costs.

SUMMARY PROBLEMS

PROBLEM 1

The Olca Ashtray Company has provided the following information about factory overhead costs and production levels:

Normal capacity	350,000 units
Expected actual capacity	310,000 units
Fixed expenses	$610,000
Variable expenses	$1.76 per unit

REQUIRED:

Compute the factory overhead rate for both normal and expected actual capacity.

PROBLEM 2

Assume the following information for the G. Long Company (all estimated figures):

Factory overhead	$ 425,000
Units of production	500,000
Direct materials cost	$1,000,000
Direct labor costs	$1,500,000
Direct labor hours	250,000
Machine hours	110,000

REQUIRED:

Compute the factory overhead rate for the G. Long Company under the following bases:

a   Units of production
b   Direct materials cost
c   Direct labor cost

d   Direct labor hours
e   Machine hours

PROBLEM 3

Indrex Corporation applies factory overhead based upon the following rates:

DEPARTMENT	PER DIRECT LABOR HOUR	ACTUAL DIRECT LABOR HOURS
Dyeing	$3.10	7,600
Weaving	6.04	11,000
Blocking	.85	2,200

Actual overhead costs for the period were $91,900.

REQUIRED:

Prepare journal entries for applying factory overhead, recording actual factory overhead, and closing out applied factory overhead costs, using an applied factory overhead account. Assume that the corporation uses under- or overapplied factory overhead accounts when closing out the applied factory overhead costs. Use T accounts if desired.

PROBLEM 4

The Capricorn Corporation has the following information relating to applied and actual factory overhead:

Factory overhead control	$30,500
Applied factory overhead	36,750
Cost of goods sold	32,000
Ending work-in-process inventory	3,500
Ending finished goods inventory	4,200

REQUIRED:

a   What should the balance in the factory overhead control account be at the end of the period? Is this a debit or a credit balance?
b   Allocate the under- or overapplied factory overhead to those accounts distorted by using the incorrect rate.
c   Prepare the entry to record the allocation.

PROBLEM 5

YLD Incorporated has five service departments and two producing departments. The total overhead costs for the period for each department were as follows:

Service Departments

Buildings and grounds	$20,000
Personnel	2,000
General factory administration	52,180
Cafeteria—operating loss	3,280
Storeroom	5,340

Producing Departments

Machinery	$69,400
Assembly	97,800

The following schedule was prepared for the accounting department to aid in allocating service department costs.

DEPARTMENT	DIRECT LABOR HOURS	NUMBER OF EMPLOYEES	SQUARE FEET	TOTAL LABOR HOURS	NUMBER OF REQUISITIONS
Buildings and Grounds					
Personnel			4,000		
General Factory Administration		70	14,000		
Cafeteria		20	8,000	2,000	
Storeroom		10	14,000	2,000	
Machinery	10,000	100	60,000	16,000	4,000
Assembly	30,000	200	100,000	34,000	2,000
	40,000	400	200,000	54,000	6,000

Management decided that the appropriate bases used by each service department would be the following:

Buildings and Grounds—square feet
Personnel Department—employees
General Factory Administration—total labor hours
Cafeteria—employees
Storeroom—requisitions

Direct labor hours are used as the basis for computing the producing departments' factory overhead rates.

REQUIRED:

Allocate costs to the producing departments by using the following methods. Also determine the factory overhead rates for the producing department in both answers.

a The direct method
b The step method, assuming the allocation of service departments in the following order:
Buildings and Grounds
Personnel
General Factory Administration
Cafeteria
Storeroom

PROBLEM 6

The Dotto Company has two service and two producing departments. It uses the algebraic method to allocate service department costs. The following information is available:

| | | SERVICES PROVIDED BY | |
DEPARTMENT	CLOSING BALANCE	DEPARTMENT A	DEPARTMENT B
Service A	$10,000	—	20%
Service B	20,000	35%	—
Production 1	14,000	15	45
Production 2	6,000	50	35
	$50,000	100%	100%

Direct Labor Hours:

Production 1	10,000
Production 2	5,000

REQUIRED:

Based on the preceding information, allocate the service departments costs, using the algebraic method.

SOLUTIONS TO SUMMARY PROBLEMS

PROBLEM 1

	EXPECTED ACTUAL CAPACITY	NORMAL CAPACITY
Fixed expenses	$ 610,000	$ 610,000
Variable expenses:		
310,000 units × $1.76	545,600	—
350,000 units × $1.76	—	616,000
Total factory overhead costs.................	$1,155,600	$1,226,000
Base for units of production	310,000	350,000
Factory overhead rate	$ 3.728 (1)	$ 3.503 (2)

Computations:

(1) $\dfrac{\$1,155,600}{310,000 \text{ units}} = \$3.728$

(2) $\dfrac{\$1,226,000}{350,000 \text{ units}} = \$3.503$

PROBLEM 2

a Units of Production:

$$\frac{\$425,000}{500,000 \text{ units}} = \underline{\$.85} \text{ per unit}$$

b Direct Materials Cost:

$$\frac{\$425,000}{\$1,000,000} \times 100 = \underline{42.5\%} \text{ of material cost}$$

c Direct Labor Cost:

$$\frac{\$425,000}{\$1,500,000} \times 100 = \underline{28\frac{1}{3}\%} \text{ of direct labor cost}$$

d Direct Labor Hours:

$$\frac{\$425,000}{250,000 \text{ direct labor hours}} = \underline{\$1.70} \text{ per direct labor hour}$$

e Machine Hours:

$$\frac{\$425,000}{110,000 \text{ machine hours}} = \underline{\$3.864} \text{ per machine hour}$$

PROBLEM 3

Applying Factory Overhead Costs:

(1)	Work-in-process	91,870	
	Applied factory overhead		91,870

Computations:

DEPARTMENT	RATE	× HOURS	= TOTAL
Dyeing	$3.10	× 7,600	= $23,560
Weaving	6.04	× 11,000	= 66,440
Blocking	.85	× 2,200	= 1,870
Total applied			$91,870

Recording actual factory overhead costs:

(2)	Factory overhead control	91,900	
	Various payables		91,900

Closing applied factory overhead to factory overhead control:

(3)	Applied factory overhead	91,870	
	Underapplied factory overhead	30	
	Factory overhead control		91,900

Using T Accounts:

Applied Factory Overhead

Entry 3	91,870	Entry 1	91,870
	0		0

Factory Overhead Control

Entry 2	91,900	Entry 3	91,900
	0		0

Work-in-Process

Entry 1	91,870

Underapplied Factory Overhead

Entry 3	30

PROBLEM 4

a The factory overhead control account has a credit balance of $6,250 ($30,500 − $36,750).

b The overapplied balance is allocated as follows:

Balances before Allocation

Cost of goods sold	$32,000
Ending work-in-process inventory	3,500
Ending finished goods inventory	4,200
	$39,700

To cost of goods sold $\dfrac{\$32,000}{\$39,700} \times \$6,250 = \$5,038$

To ending work-in-process inventory $\dfrac{\$\,3,500}{\$39,700} \times \$6,250 = 551$

To ending finished goods inventory $\dfrac{\$\,4,200}{\$39,700} \times \$6,250 = 661$

Total allocated $6,250

c

Factory overhead control 6,250	
Cost of goods sold	5,038
Work-in-process inventory	551
Finished goods inventory	661

PROBLEM 5

a The Direct Method:

	SERVICE DEPARTMENTS					PRODUCING DEPARTMENTS	
	BUILDINGS AND GROUNDS	PERSONNEL	GENERAL FACTORY ADMINISTRATION	CAFETERIA	STOREROOM	MACHINERY	ASSEMBLY
Total cost	$20,000	$2,000	$52,180	$3,280	$5,340	$69,400	$97,800
Allocated to producing departments	(20,000)					7,500 (1)	12,500 (2)
		(2,000)				667 (3)	1,333 (4)
			(52,180)			16,698 (5)	35,482 (6)
				(3,280)		1,093 (7)	2,187 (8)
					(5,340)	3,560 (9)	1,780 (10)
Balance after allocation	$ 0	$ 0	$ 0	$ 0	$ 0	$98,918	$151,082
Factory overhead rates						$9.8918 (11)	$ 5.0316 (12)

See next page for computations.

Computations:

Allocation of Building and Grounds Department:

$$\frac{\$20,000}{160,000 \text{ (square feet)}} = \underline{\$.125} \text{ per square foot}$$

				SQUARE FEET ×	RATE PER SQUARE FOOT
(1)	To machinery department	=	$ 7,500	(60,000	× $.125)
(2)	To assembly department	=	12,500	(100,000	× .125)
	Total		$20,000		

Allocation of Personnel Department:

$$\frac{\$2,000}{300 \text{ (employees)}} = \underline{\$6.6667} \text{ per employee}$$

				EMPLOYEES ×	RATE PER EMPLOYEE
(3)	To machinery department	=	$ 667	(100	× $6.6667)
(4)	To assembly department	=	1,333	(200	× 6.6667)
	Total		$2,000		

Allocation of General Factory Department:

$$\frac{\$52,180}{50,000 \text{ (labor hours)}} = \underline{\$1.0436} \text{ per labor hour}$$

				LABOR HOURS ×	RATE PER LABOR HOUR
(5)	To machinery department	=	$16,698	(16,000	× $1.0436)
(6)	To assembly department	=	35,482	(34,000	× 1.0436)
	Total		$52,180		

Allocation of Cafeteria Department:

$$\frac{\$3,280}{300 \text{ (employees)}} = \underline{\$10.9333} \text{ per employee}$$

				EMPLOYEES ×	RATE PER EMPLOYEE
(7)	To machinery department	=	$1,093	(100	× $10.9333)
(8)	To assembly department	=	2,187	(200	× 10.9333)
	Total		$3,280		

Allocation of Storeroom Department:

$$\frac{\$5,340}{6,000 \text{ (requisitions)}} = \underline{\$.89} \text{ per requisition}$$

		REQUISITIONS ×	RATE PER REQUISITION
(9)	To machinery department = $3,560	(4,000	× $.89)
(10)	To assembly department = 1,780	(2,000	× .89)
	Total $5,340		

Factory overhead rate (based on direct labor hours) for producing departments:

		TOTAL ALLOCATED COST ÷	DIRECT LABOR HOURS
(11)	For machinery department = $9.8918	($98,918	÷ 10,000)
(12)	For assembly department = 5.0361	($151,082	÷ 30,000)

b The Step Method:

	SERVICE DEPARTMENTS					PRODUCING DEPARTMENTS	
	BUILDINGS AND GROUNDS	PERSONNEL	GENERAL FACTORY ADMINISTRATION	CAFETERIA	STOREROOM	MACHINERY	ASSEMBLY
Total cost	$ 20,000	$ 2,000	$ 52,180	$ 3,280	$ 5,340	$ 69,400	$ 97,800
Allocated to service departments and producing departments	(20,000)	400 (1)	1,400 (2)	800 (3)	1,400 (4)	6,000 (5)	10,000 (6)
		$ 2,400					
		(2,400)	420 (7)	120 (8)	60 (9)	600 (10)	1,200 (11)
			$ 54,000				
			(54,000)	2,000 (12)	2,000 (13)	16,000 (14)	34,000 (15)
				$ 6,200			
				(6,200)	200 (16)	2,000 (17)	4,000 (18)
					$ 9,000		
					(9,000)	6,000 (19)	3,000 (20)
Balance after allocation	$ 0	$ 0	$ 0	$ 0	$ 0	$ 100,000	$ 150,000
Factory overhead rates						$ 10.00 (21)	$ 5.00 (22)

Computations:

Allocation of Buildings and Grounds Departments:

$$\frac{\$20,000}{200,000 \ (square \ feet)} = \underline{\$.10} \ per \ square \ foot$$

				SQUARE FEET	×	RATE PER SQUARE FOOT
(1)	To personnel	=	$ 400	(4,000	×	.10)
(2)	To general factory administration	=	1,400	(14,000	×	.10)
(3)	To cafeteria	=	800	(8,000	×	.10)
(4)	To storeroom	=	1,400	(14,000	×	.10)
(5)	To machinery	=	6,000	(60,000	×	.10)
(6)	To assembly	=	10,000	(100,000	×	.10)
	Total		$20,000			

Allocation of Personnel Department:

$$\frac{\$2,400}{400 \ (Employees)} = \underline{\$6.00} \ per \ employee$$

				EMPLOYEES	×	RATE PER EMPLOYEE
(7)	To general factory administration	=	$ 420	(70	×	$6)
(8)	To cafeteria	=	120	(20	×	6)
(9)	To storeroom	=	60	(10	×	6)
(10)	To machinery	=	600	(100	×	6)
(11)	To assembly	=	1,200	(200	×	6)
	Total		$2,400			

Allocation of General Factory Administration:

$$\frac{\$54,000}{54,000 \ (labor \ hours)} = \underline{\$1.00} \ per \ labor \ hour$$

				LABOR HOURS	×	RATE PER HOUR
(12)	To cafeteria	=	$ 2,000	(2,000	×	$1)
(13)	To storeroom	=	2,000	(2,000	×	1)
(14)	To machinery	=	16,000	(16,000	×	1)
(15)	To assembly	=	34,000	(34,000	×	1)
	Total		$54,000			

Allocation of Cafeteria:

$$\frac{\$6,200}{310 \ (employees)} = \underline{\$20.00} \ per \ employee$$

			EMPLOYEES ×	RATE PER EMPLOYEE
(16)	To storeroom =	$ 200	(10	× $20)
(17)	To machinery =	2,000	(100	× 20)
(18)	To assembly =	4,000	(200	× 20)
	Total	$6,200		

Allocation of Storeroom:

$$\frac{\$9,000}{6,000 \text{ (requisitions)}} = \underline{\$1.50} \text{ per requisition}$$

			REQUISITIONS ×	RATE PER REQUISITION
(19)	To machinery =	$6,000	(4,000	× $1.50)
(20)	To assembly =	3,000	(2,000	× 1.50)
	Total	$9,000		

Factory overhead rates (based on direct labor hours) for producing departments:

			TOTAL ALLOCATED COST	÷	DIRECT LABOR HOURS
(21)	For machinery department =	$10.00	($100,000	÷	10,000)
(22)	For assembly department =	5.00	(150,000	÷	30,000)

PROBLEM 6

Let: $A = \$10,000 + .20\ B$
$B = \$20,000 + .35\ A$

Substitute:

$A = \$10,000 + .20\ (\$20,000 + .35\ A)$
$A = \$10,000 + \$4,000 + .07\ A$
$.93\ A = \$14,000$
$A = \underline{\$15,053.76}$

Substitute: $B = \$20,000 + .35\ (\$15,053.76)$
$B = \$20,000 + \$5,268.82$
$B = \$25,268.82$

| | SERVICE DEPARTMENTS | | PRODUCING DEPARTMENTS | |
	DEPARTMENT A	DEPARTMENT B	PRODUCTION 1	PRODUCTION 2
Total cost	$ 10,000.00	$ 20,000.00	$ 14,000.00	$ 6,000.00
Allocated to service department B and producing departments 1 and 2	(15,053.76)	5,268.82 (1)	2,258.06 (2)	7,526.88 (3)
Allocated to service department A and producing departments 1 and 2	5,053.76 (4)	(25,268.82)	11,370.97 (5)	8,844.09 (6)
Balance after allocation	$ 0	$ 0	$ 27,629.03	$ 22,370.97
Factory overhead rates			$2.7629 (7)	$4.4742 (8)

See next page for computations.

Computations:

Allocation of Department A:

			% OF SERVICE RECEIVED	×	TOTAL COST
(1)	To Department B =	$ 5,268.82	(.35	×	$15,053.76)
(2)	To Production 1 =	2,258.06	(.15	×	15,053.76)
(3)	To Production 2 =	7,526.88	(.50	×	15,053.76)
	Total	$15,053.76			

Allocation of Department B:

			% OF SERVICE RECEIVED	×	TOTAL COST
(4)	To Department A =	$ 5,053.76	(.20	×	$25,268.82)
(5)	To Production 1 =	11,370.97	(.45	×	25,268.82)
(6)	To Production 2 =	8,844.09	(.35	×	25,268.82)
	Total	$25,268.82			

Factory overhead rate (based on direct labor hours) for producing departments:

			TOTAL COST	÷	DIRECT LABOR HOURS
(7)	For Production 1 =	$2.7629	($27,629.03	÷	10,000)
(8)	For Production 2 =	4.4742	($22,370.97	÷	5,000)

QUESTIONS

1 Explain the importance of classifying a factory overhead cost as variable, fixed, or semivariable.

2 What two key factors determine the factory overhead rate for a period? Why are these factors important?

3 What characteristics should the denominator used to compute a factory overhead rate possess?

4 What are the five bases commonly used to compute the factory overhead rate, and when is each one appropriate to use?

5 How is the estimated factory overhead cost applied to production?

6 How does the difference between applied and actual factory overhead come about? If the difference is significant, how is it treated?

7 State whether the following are true or false:

   a Selling, general, and administration expenses are manufacturing costs.

   b The greater the number of units produced, the higher the total fixed cost.

   c Variable costs per unit will vary as output changes because these costs are spread over a varying number of units.

    d Semivariable costs vary with production, but not in direct proportion to changes in the level of production.

    e Both theoretical and practical capacity are based solely on the physical capacity of a department or factory.

    f Expected actual capacity is generally used only when normal production activity is easy to determine.

    g The direct labor cost method and the direct labor hours method would be inappropriate if factory overhead were comprised of costs unrelated to the labor activity.

    h The use of subsidiary ledgers permits a greater degree of control over factory overhead costs.

    i The direct method is more accurate than the step method because it takes into consideration the services provided to other service departments.

    j The direct and step methods both ignore the allocation of reciprocal services.

8 What are some examples of factory overhead costs?

9 For each of the following statements, select the item which gives the *most* adequate answer.

    a If production increases to a point at which current facilities are inadequate and additional facilities must be rented, (1) total variable costs will increase; (2) total fixed costs will decrease; (3) total fixed costs will increase; (4) semivariable costs will decrease.

    b Factory overhead should be allocated on the basis of (1) direct materials costs; (2) units of production; (3) direct labor cost; (4) an activity which relates to cost incurrence.

10 Why is the allocation method used in accounting for the difference between applied and actual factory overhead better than charging or crediting the difference to cost of goods sold?

11 Differentiate between a producing department and a service department.

12 Describe how costs are allocated under the direct method, the step method, and the algebraic method.

EXERCISES

EXERCISE 1

Fixed, Variable, and Semivariable Overhead

Donahue and Daughters, Inc., produced 225,000 bottles of perfume during the year. The production costs for the bottles of perfume were the following:

Direct materials	$940,000
Direct labor	550,500
Indirect materials	348,750

Factory rent	$ 40,000
Depreciation	33,750
Indirect labor	213,750
Factory supervisors	60,000

Each worker can produce 2,500 bottles. Each supervisor can handle up to 30 workers; the supervisors are paid equal salaries. Depreciation is determined using the units of production method.

REQUIRED:

Determine the total overhead for Donahue and Daughters, Inc., if the company had produced 375,000 bottles during the year.

EXERCISE 2

Capacities

The Coastin' On Air Co. estimated its levels of production as follows:

Maximum capacity	650,750 units
Long-run capacity	450,500 units
Short-run capacity	370,000 units

Because of actual conditions, theoretical capacity would be reduced by 85,000 units. Total fixed expenses were expected to be $260,000; variable expenses were expected to be $.85 per unit.

REQUIRED:

a   Determine the estimated factory overhead costs, using each of the following volumes of production:
  1 Ideal capacity
  2 Realistic capacity
  3 Normal capacity
  4 Expected actual capacity
b   What would the overhead rates be for the volumes of production in (a)?

EXERCISE 3

Factory Overhead Rates

The Sullivan Manufacturing Company makes hammers that it sells to hardware stores in Karen County, North Carolina. For year 5, the overhead expenses were expected to be:

Fixed	$100,250
Variable	125,750
Semivariable	17,000

For year 5, the company expected production to be 175,500 hammers; machine hours, 180,000; and direct labor hours, 36,400. The estimated direct materials cost was predicted to be $265,000, and the estimated direct labor cost, $172,460.

The actual data for January was as follows:

12,000 hammers
25,000 machine hours
5,000 direct labor hours
$44,020 direct materials cost
$18,000 direct labor cost

REQUIRED:

Compute the rates used to apply the factory overhead, and determine the applied overhead during January for each of the following bases:

a   Units of production   d   Direct labor cost
b   Direct materials cost   e   Machine hours
c   Direct labor hours

EXERCISE 4

Journal Entries

The Winslow Corporation sells stacks of poker chips to several casinos in the Los Angeles area. The corporation collected the following information pertaining to its factory overhead:

Actual factory overhead for 19X8
$25,000
Expected factory overhead for 19X8
Variable $.72/stack
Fixed $1,400
Semivariable   0–15,000 stacks $ 950
                   15,000–30,000   1,300
                   30,000–45,000   1,650
                   45,000–up   2,000
Expected actual capacity for 19X8
30,500 stacks
Units of production for July 19X8
3,250 stacks
Actual factory overhead for July 19X8
10.5% of actual factory overhead for 19X8

Assume the following facts:
Winslow uses only the factory overhead control account.
Estimated actual capacity is used to determine estimated factory overhead.
Units of production is used to determine the applied factory overhead.

REQUIRED:

Prepare journal entries for July 19X8 to record the following:

a   The applied factory overhead
b   The actual factory overhead

c The closing of the Factory Overhead Control account to Cost of Goods Sold.

EXERCISE 5

Journal Entries

Polkadot, Inc., manufactures swimsuits for various shops in Forney, Tex. The estimated overhead for the year was $456,120; the actual overhead was $470,800. Machine hours were used in determining the applied overhead. There were 84,500 actual machine hours and 81,450 estimated machine hours during the year. Polkadot used an Applied Factory Overhead account and an Over- and Underapplied Factory Overhead account.

REQUIRED:

a Prepare journal entries to record the following:
1 The applied factory overhead
2 The actual factory overhead
3 The closing of the Applied Factory Overhead account
b Assume the following facts:

Cost of goods sold $85,725
Finished goods, ending inventory 57,150
Work-in-process, ending inventory 47,625

Allocate the over- or underapplied factory overhead to these three accounts.

EXERCISE 6

Multiple Choice

a Depreciation based on the number of units produced would be classified as what type of cost?
1 Out-of-pocket
2 Marginal
3 Variable
4 Fixed
b The variable factory overhead rate under the normal, practical, and expected activity levels would be the same
1 except for normal volume.
2 except for practical capacity.
3 except for expected activity.
4 for all three activity levels.
c Cox Company found that the differences in product costs, resulting from the

application of predetermined overhead rates rather than actual overhead rates, were immaterial—even though actual production was substantially less than planned production. The most likely explanation is that

1 Overhead was composed chiefly of variable costs.
2 Several products were produced simultaneously.
3 Fixed factory overhead was a significant cost.
4 Costs of overhead items were substantially higher than anticipated.

d If a predetermined overhead rate is not employed and the volume of production is increased over the level planned, the cost per unit would be expected to

1 decrease for fixed costs and remain unchanged for variable costs.
2 remain unchanged for fixed costs and increase for variable costs.
3 decrease for fixed costs and increase for variable costs.
4 increase for fixed costs and increase for variable costs.

e The Carlo Company budgeted overhead at $255,000 for the period for Department A, based on a budgeted volume of 100,000 direct labor hours. At the end of the period, the Factory Overhead Control account for Department A had a balance of $270,000; actual direct labor hours were 105,000. What was the over- or underapplied overhead for the period?

1 $2,250, overapplied
2 $2,250, underapplied
3 $15,000, overapplied
4 $15,000, underapplied

$$\frac{255\,000}{100\,000} = 2.55 \times 105{,}000 = 267\,750$$

f Factory overhead rates best reflect anticipated fluctuations in sales over several years when the rates are computed using figures based on

1 maximum capacity.
2 normal capacity.
3 practical capacity.
4 expected actual capacity.

g Preferably, underapplied overhead resulting from unanticipated price increases should be written off by

1 decreasing cost of goods sold.
2 increasing cost of goods sold.
3 decreasing cost of goods sold, work-in-process inventory, and finished goods inventory.
4 increasing cost of goods sold, work-in-process inventory, and finished goods inventory. if large amount

EXERCISE 7

Service Department Costs—Direct Method

Nana, Inc., has two service departments and three producing departments. The following information was collected by Nana's accountants.

	SERVICE DEPARTMENTS		PRODUCING DEPARTMENTS		
	ONE	TWO	A	B	C
Total indirect labor costs	$10,400	$9,600	$40,000	$24,820	$38,560
Repairs—factory	4,200	6,440	25,000	36,460	10,000
Depreciation—factory equipment	1,000	2,500	6,050	4,000	7,320
Electricity—factory	2,300	1,060	4,400	6,660	2,000
Fuel—factory	3,000	2,100	7,000	2,740	6,080
Supplies—factory	900	400	950	650	700
Miscellaneous factory overhead	100	200	250	450	1,000

Additional Information:

DEPARTMENT	NUMBER OF EMPLOYEES	TOTAL LABOR HOURS
One	40	1,250
Two	65	3,000
A	275	10,500
B	130	4,750
C	205	11,250

The costs of operating Departments One and Two are allocated to the producing departments based upon total labor hours and number of employees, respectively. The producing departments' factory overhead rates would be based upon direct labor hours: 9,000 in Department A; 3,500 in Department B; and 10,000 in Department C.

REQUIRED:

Allocate the costs of the service departments to the producing departments, using the direct method. Include the factory overhead rates for the producing departments.

EXERCISE 8

Service Department Costs—Step Method

The Franfred Company allocated service department costs using the step method. The overhead costs for the period for the service and producing departments were as follows:

SERVICE DEPARTMENTS		PRODUCING DEPARTMENTS	
W	$1,550	37	$10,750
X	3,000	54	25,300
Y	4,400		
Z	900		

Assume the following facts:

	PERCENT OF SERVICES PROVIDED BY DEPARTMENTS			
DEPARTMENTS	W	X	Y	Z
W	10%	2.5%	10%	15%
X	—	14%	17%	—
Y	15%	17.5%	—	—
Z	5%	16%	13%	20%
37	45%	20%	30%	10%
54	25%	30%	30%	55%

The service departments should be allocated in the following order: Y, X, W, Z. Each service department allocates its costs by using "percentage of services provided." The direct labor hours during the period were 3,400 for Department 37 and 2,600 for Department 54. Direct labor hours are used in determining the overhead rates for the producing departments.

REQUIRED:

Using the step method, allocate the service departments' overhead costs to the producing departments. Include the factory overhead rates for the producing departments.

EXERCISE 9

Service Department Costs—Direct Method

	PRODUCING DEPARTMENTS		SERVICE DEPARTMENTS		
	ONE	TWO	A	B	C
Overhead costs	$1,000,000	$ 975,000	$ 300,000	$ 400,125	$ 150,875
Allocation of Department C	45,225	72,360	18,090	15,200	(150,875)
Allocation of Department B	166,130	166,130	83,065	(415,325)	
Allocation of Department A	240,693	160,462	(401,155)		
Balance after allocation	$1,452,048	$1,373,952	0	0	0
Rates (based on direct labor hours)	$ 48.4016	$ 68.6976			

The above schedule was used by Junes, Inc., in order to change their method of allocation from the step method to the direct method.

REQUIRED:

Using the direct method, allocate the costs of the service departments. Use the data supplied to determine the allocation, and include the new factory overhead rates for the producing departments.

EXERCISE 10

Service Department Costs—Algebraic Method

DATA	PRODUCING DEPARTMENTS			SERVICE DEPARTMENTS	
	ASSEMBLY	PACKAGING	MIXING	MATERIALS HANDLING	INSPEC-TION
Direct labor hours	2,750	3,400	2,050	—	—
Kilowatthours	1,000	750	1,250	300	600
Floor area (square feet)	4,000	2,500	3,800	1,200	900
Manufacturing costs before allocation of service costs	$25,000	$19,500	$20,300	$1,750	$2,150
Direct labor costs	5,500	4,500	3,000	—	—
Direct materials costs	7,750	6,750	7,000	—	—

The allocation of the materials handling department's costs is based on floor area; the inspection department's costs are allocated based on kilowatthours. The producing department's factory overhead rates are based on direct labor hours.

REQUIRED:

Using the algebraic method, allocate the service department's costs to the producing departments. Include the factory overhead rates for the producing departments.

PROBLEMS

PROBLEM 1

Overhead Rates—Normal and Maximum Capacities

Prunka's Pranks, Inc., manufactures toys and sells them to Games-R-Fun retail stores throughout the United States. In 19X9, Prunka estimated that the maximum capacity for Ready-Set-Go, a new and challenging game, would be 170,000 units. The normal capacity for this game in 19X9 was 135,000 units. The actual output was 142,575 units. The estimated overhead for Ready-Set-Go during the year was

Variable overhead	$.54/unit
Fixed overhead	$36,500
Semivariable overhead	
0– 80,000 units	$10,000
80,000–160,000 units	20,000
160,000–240,000 units	30,000
240,000 up	40,000

Prunka's analysts used the following data in order to establish a base for applying the overhead during 19X9.

Estimated machine hours	61,500
Estimated direct labor hours........	96,720
Estimated materials cost	$125,500
Estimated direct labor cost	$213,000

The actual data for 19X9 was the following:

Machine hours	62,000
Direct labor hours	96,720
Materials cost	$120,000
Direct labor cost	$220,000

REQUIRED:

a Using 19X9 normal capacity, compute the overhead estimated for Ready-Set-Go. Determine the rate used during the year to apply overhead and compute the overhead applied, using each of the following bases:
1 Units of production
2 Machine hours
3 Direct labor hours
4 Direct materials cost
5 Direct labor cost
b Compute the same items as required in (a), using maximum capacity instead of normal capacity.

PROBLEM 2

Journal Entries—Factory Overhead

Assume the following information for the M.L.&O. Corporation, Year 2:

Estimated overhead: Fixed	$76,000
Variable	$ 6/unit
Expected actual capacity	30,000 units
Estimated direct labor hours	25,000
Estimated machine hours	20,000

The following data was supplied for the month of March, Year 2:

Actual direct labor hours 2,400
Actual machine hours 2,200
Actual overhead $25,000

M.L.&O. uses short-run capacity to estimate its overhead. The company uses an Applied Factory Overhead account and an Over- or Underapplied Factory Overhead account. At the end of the month, the Over- or Underapplied Factory Overhead account is closed to Cost of Goods Sold.

REQUIRED:

Using the data given, prepare two sets of journal entries—one using direct labor hours and the other using machine hours—to apply the factory overhead to the units produced. Do the following:

a   Record the applied overhead.
b   Record the actual overhead.
c   Close the Applied Factory Overhead account and the Factory Overhead Control account.
d   Close the Over- or Underapplied Factory Overhead account.

PROBLEM 3

Journal Entries—Factory Overhead

Data:

	DEPARTMENT 1	DEPARTMENT 2	DEPARTMENT 3
Actual direct labor hours	420	550	375
Overhead rate per direct labor hour	$ 3.95	$ 2.10	$ 4.00
Actual overhead costs:			
Rent on factory	$ 400	$ 250	$ 360
Factory supplies	233	141	220
Indirect labor	407	324	175
Fuel, factory	385	400	620
Small tools	120	80	75
Cost of goods sold	$9,000	$8,750	$7,050
Ending work-in-process inventory	2,300	1,760	940
Ending finished goods inventory	5,400	2,800	1,500

REQUIRED:

Using the data given, prepare two sets of journal entries, one with and one without an Applied Factory Overhead account. Do the following:

a   Record the applied overhead.
b   Record the actual overhead.
c   Close the applied overhead to the control account.

d Allocate the over- or underapplied overhead among work-in-process inventory, ending finished goods inventory, and cost of goods sold.

PROBLEM 4
Overhead Rates, Applied and Underapplied

Data for 19X8:

	DEPARTMENTS		
	A	B	C
Estimated factory overhead	$56,000	$45,400	$60,100
Estimated direct labor cost	$60,500	$45,000	$71,200
Estimated direct labor hours	20,100	14,200	15,000
Estimated machine hours	22,000	14,000	17,700

Department A uses machine hours as the base to apply overhead, Department B uses direct labor costs, and Department C uses direct labor hours.

REQUIRED:

a Compute the predetermined overhead rates for each of the departments.
b Determine the factory overhead applied during October 19X8, based on the following actual data for that month:

	DEPARTMENTS		
	A	B	C
Direct labor costs	$6,200	$4,000	$7,300
Direct labor hours	1,250	1,000	1,410
Machine hours	2,000	1,100	1,150

c What would be the over- or underapplied factory overhead if the 19X8 actual overhead for Departments A, B, and C were $57,500, $45,400, and $60,000, respectively? Assume estimated overhead is equivalent to the applied overhead in 19X8.
d Using an Applied Factory Overhead account, record the actual and applied factory overhead in 19X8 for Department B. Close the applied account.

PROBLEM 5
Journal Entries—Factory Overhead

The B. W. Markowitz Corporation has collected the following information in order to estimate the total factory overhead costs for 19X9:

Normal capacity	100,000 lb
Total fixed factory overhead	$236,000
Total variable factory overhead	$1.25/lb
Total semivariable factory overhead:	
Fixed	$24,000
Variable	$.25/lb

The corporation estimated that 30% of the estimated total factory overhead costs would be incurred by Department A. Department A uses materials cost as a base to compute the overhead rate. For 19X9, the estimated and the actual materials cost for Department A were $307,500 and $300,000, respectively. Department A records both actual and applied factory overhead using only the Factory Overhead Control account. This department charges or credits the under- or overapplied factory overhead to cost of goods sold. During 19X9, the actual factory overhead was $126,000 for Department A.

REQUIRED:

Prepare all necessary journal entries to record the 19X9 actual and applied factory overhead in Department A. Include the journal entries for disposing of the under- or overapplied factory overhead by charging it to cost of goods sold.

PROBLEM 6

Overhead Distribution—Service Departments

The Maynard Company has three service departments and two producing departments. They are presently evaluating several methods of allocating the service departments' overhead costs to producing departments. Accordingly, the following information has been prepared for the month of August, year 1:

	SERVICE DEPARTMENTS			PRODUCING DEPARTMENTS	
	FACTORY ADMIN- ISTRATION	FACTORY MAINTE- NANCE	BUILDING AND GROUNDS	MACHINING	ASSEMBLY
Overhead costs	$48,200	$60,000	$53,000	$1,520,000	$1,760,000
Square footage	1,625	2,000	3,750	75,000	68,000
Total labor hours	28,000	24,000	39,000	481,300	326,250

The costs of the factory administration and building and grounds departments are allocated on the basis of total labor hours and square footage, respectively. However, the costs of the factory maintenance department are allocated on the basis of percent of services rendered, which is 33% to Buildings and Grounds, 35% to Assembly, and 32% to Machining.

REQUIRED:

a Assume Factory Maintenance is allocated first, then Factory Administration, and finally Buildings and Grounds. Allocate the overhead costs of the service departments to the producing departments by using the following: **(1)** direct method, **(2)** step method.

b Determine the factory overhead rates for the producing departments. The bases used are machine hours, with 400,000 for Machining and 300,000 for Assembly.

PROBLEM 7

Direct, Step, and Algebraic Methods

The Snowman Ice Company has two service departments and two production departments.

Service Departments' Overhead Costs:
                Department 1, Repair $14,000
                Department 2, Cafeteria 11,000

Producing Departments' Overhead Costs:
                Department 10, Machinery 52,500
                Department 11, Assembly 48,000

Additional Information:

DEPARTMENT	SQUARE FEET	ESTIMATED TOTAL LABOR HOURS
1, Repair	1,500	3,500
2, Cafeteria	1,800	1,200
10, Machinery	2,000	2,300
11, Assembly	3,000	1,700
Total	8,300	8,700

The costs of the repair department are allocated based on square feet. The costs of the cafeteria department are allocated based on estimated total labor hours. The producing departments use estimated direct labor hours: 1,500 in Department 10 and 1,250 in Department 11.

REQUIRED:

Allocate the costs of the service departments to the producing departments by using the following:
    a Direct method
    b Step method (allocate the costs of the Repair Shop first)
    c Algebraic method
Include the factory overhead rates for the two producing departments in all three solutions.

PROBLEM 8

Direct, Step, and Algebraic Methods

The Ippolito Ink Company prepared the following list in order to determine the overhead in each department for the Year 19X0:

	PRODUCTION DEPARTMENTS		SERVICE DEPARTMENTS		
	H	G	U	V	W
Rent	$ 25,000	$ 77,000	$ 1,500	$ 1,450	$ 700
Repairs	10,000	12,050	2,300	3,000	750
Fuel	35,000	42,000	950	700	600
Indirect labor	15,750	17,000	14,500	10,000	9,750
Indirect materials	6,100	5,650	12,700	9,450	6,000
Heat and light	20,250	15,120	900	600	750
Depreciation	9,400	7,130	300	150	175
Miscellaneous	6,000	5,050	70	60	50
Total	$127,500	$181,000	$33,220	$25,410	$18,775

Additional Data Needed for Allocation of Overhead:

Department U services Departments G, V, and W in the ratio of 2:1:1, respectively.

Department V services Departments H, G, U, and W in the ratio of 4:3:2:1, respectively.

Department W services Departments H and G in the ratio of 3:1, respectively.

REQUIRED:

Assume Department U is allocated first, V is second, and W is last.

a Allocate the overhead costs of the service departments to the producing departments by using the following methods: (1) direct, (2) step, (3) algebraic.

b Determine the factory overhead rates for the producing departments using the following bases: Department H, 100,000 direct labor hours; Department G, 195,000 direct labor hours.

PART TWO

COST ACCOUNTING SYSTEMS

CHAPTER SIX
COST ACCUMULATION SYSTEMS

Most nonaccountants are not aware of the volume of paperwork that is processed in a manufacturing company. Small and medium-sized manufacturing companies may handle thousands of requisitions, purchase orders, receiving reports, vendors' invoices, vouchers, checks, stock issues, and similar business documents each month. A large manufacturing company may handle tens of thousands of such documents a month. Thus, it is obvious that clearly defined cost accumulation systems are required to handle and control this volume of paperwork.

The accumulation and classification of routine cost data is a very important and time-consuming task. Cost accumulation is the organized collection of cost data via a set of procedures, or system. Cost classification is the grouping of all manufacturing costs into various categories in order to meet the needs of management (see Chapter 2 for a detailed discussion of cost classifications). This chapter covers periodic cost accumulation systems and introduces perpetual cost accumulation systems.

COMMON OBJECTIVE OF
COST ACCUMULATION: UNIT COST

A figure indicating the *total cost* of production provides little useful information about a company's operations, since the volume of production (and therefore cost) varies from period to period. Thus, some common denominator, such as *unit costs*, must be available in order to compare various volumes and costs. Unit cost figures can be readily computed by dividing the total cost of goods manufactured by the number of units produced. Unit costs are stated in the same terms of measurement used for units of output, such as cost per *ton*, per *gallon*, per *foot*, per *assembly*, and so on.

Unit costs also facilitate the valuation of cost of goods sold and closing inventory. For example, assume that 5,000 units are produced at a total cost of $8,000, or $1.60 per unit ($8,000 ÷ 5,000). If 3,500 units are sold, the closing inventory consists of 1,500 units. The computation for cost of goods sold and closing inventory is as follows:

DESCRIPTION	UNITS	COST
Total production	5,000	$8,000
Cost of goods sold		
(3,500 units at $1.60)*	3,500	$5,600
Closing inventory		
(1,500 units at $1.60)*	1,500	2,400
Total	5,000	$8,000

* $8,000 ÷ 5,000 units = $1.60 per unit

COST ACCUMULATION— PERIODIC VERSUS PERPETUAL

Proper cost accumulation provides management with a basis for predicting the economic consequences of its decisions. Some of these decisions include the following:

1 Which products should we manufacture?
2 Should we expand the department?
3 Should we reduce the department?
4 Should we expand our product lines?

Cost data is accumulated under either periodic cost accumulation or perpetual cost accumulation systems.

Periodic cost accumulation systems provide only limited cost information during a period and require quarterly or year-end adjustments to arrive at the cost of goods manufactured. In most cases, the additional ledger accounts needed are simply added to a financial accounting system. Periodic physical inventories are taken to adjust inventory accounts to arrive at the cost of goods manufactured. A periodic cost accumulation system is *not* considered a complete cost accumulation system since the costs of work-in-process and finished goods can only be determined after physical inventories are taken. Because of this limitation, periodic cost accumulation systems are generally used by small manufacturing companies.

A perpetual cost accumulation system is a manner of accumulating cost data, through a work-in-process account, that provides continuous information about work-in-process, finished goods, and cost of goods manufactured. Such cost systems are usually very extensive and are used by most medium and large manufacturing companies.

COST ACCUMULATION—
ACTUAL VERSUS STANDARD

All cost accumulation systems accumulate *actual* cost data; some also record *standard* costs. Standard costing involves the determination of standards and estimates of output prior to the start of production. Differences between actual and standard costs are shown in variance accounts, which are used by management as an aid in planning and control decisions. A variance is the difference arising when actual results do not equal standards, due to either external or internal forces.

Periodic cost accumulation systems generally use only actual costs, whereas a perpetual cost accumulation system may accumulate both actual and standard costs. For purposes of illustration, this chapter will accumulate only actual cost data (with the exception of factory overhead in which a predetermined factory overhead rate may also be used). A detailed discussion of standard costing will be presented in Chapters 11 and 12.

PERIODIC COST ACCUMULATION SYSTEMS

The first step in comprehending a periodic cost accumulation system is to understand the flow of costs as goods pass through the various stages of production. The flow of costs in a manufacturing company, under a periodic cost accumulation system, is shown in Figure 6-1.

FIGURE 6-1   **Flow of Costs, Periodic Cost Accumulation System**

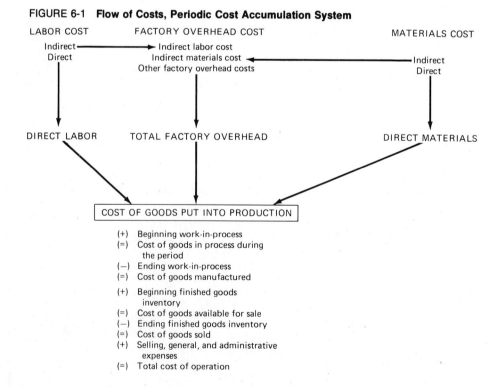

The cost of goods put into production (direct materials + direct labor + factory overhead) plus the cost of work-in-process inventory at the beginning of the period equals the cost of goods in process during the period. In order to determine the cost of goods manufactured, the cost of ending work-in-process inventory is subtracted from the cost of goods in process during the period. The cost of goods manufactured, plus beginning finished goods inventory, equals the cost of goods available for sale. When the ending finished goods inventory is deducted from this figure, the cost of goods sold results. The total cost of operations can now be computed by adding selling, general, and administrative expenses to the cost of goods sold. For example, assume the following information for a period:

Materials Cost:		
Direct	$60,000	
Indirect	20,000	$80,000
Labor Cost:		
Direct	$18,000	
Indirect	17,000	35,000
Other Factory Overhead:		
Power and heat		30,000
Selling, general, and administrative expenses		10,000
Inventories: *		
Beginning		
Work-in-process		2,000
Finished goods		15,000
Ending		
Work-in-process		8,000
Finished goods		20,000

* Assume no beginning or ending materials inventory.

Figure 6-2 (page 180) presents the computation of costs based on the preceding information.

Ledger Accounts Used in the Periodic Cost Accumulation System

The ledger accounts used in conjunction with periodic cost accumulation systems assemble the flow of costs from the beginning of production (materials purchased and issued), through factory operations (labor and overhead added), to the end of the manufacturing process (cost of goods manufactured). Although most accounts relating to sales, administrative expenses, assets, liabilities, and owners' equity are handled similarly in merchandising and manufacturing businesses, there are many additional accounts used in a manufacturing operation.

The following additional manufacturing accounts are used with periodic cost accumulation systems:

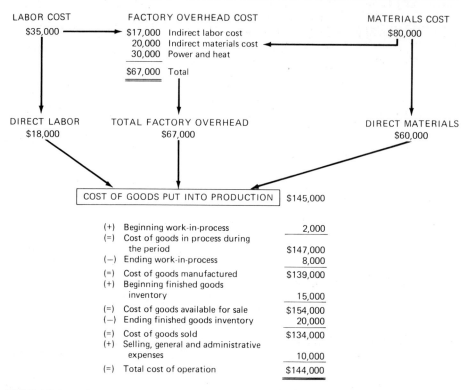

FIGURE 6-2   **Computation of Costs in a Periodic Cost Accumulation System**

Materials Inventory. Either the beginning or ending portion of unused raw materials on hand. When using a periodic cost accumulation system, materials inventory is usually determined by taking a physical count of raw materials on hand. When materials are purchased, the cost is charged to the Purchase of Raw Materials account. At the end of the period, the cost of materials in the beginning Materials Inventory account is added to the cost of purchases during the period to arrive at the cost of materials available for use. The cost of materials on hand at the end of the period is deducted from the cost of materials available for use to arrive at the cost of materials used during the period. The cost of materials on hand at the end of a period is a current asset; it appears on both the balance sheet and the statement of cost of goods manufactured.

Work-in-Process Inventory. The cost of partially completed goods on hand at either the beginning or end of a period. Work-in-process inventory is a current asset and appears on both the balance sheet and statement of cost of goods manufactured.

Finished Goods Inventory. Either the beginning or ending portion of goods that have been completed and are still on hand for sale to customers. Finished goods inventory is a current asset and appears on both the balance sheet and the income statement.

Factory Overhead Accounts. Additional accounts added to the general ledger balances to record various manufacturing costs, other than direct materials and direct labor. In a periodic cost accumulation system, overhead costs are usually added to production as they are incurred. Factory overhead accounts appear on the statement of cost of goods manufactured.

Manufacturing Account. Used to close the manufacturing accounts. It is employed at the end of each period to compute the cost of goods manufactured (the cost of units that have completed the manufacturing cycle and are transferred to finished goods). The Manufacturing account is closed by having its balance transferred to the Income Summary account. The Manufacturing account does not appear on any external financial statement

Journal Entries under a Periodic Cost Accumulation System

The three elements of cost (materials, labor, and factory overhead) must be accumulated under a periodic cost accumulation system in order to arrive at the product cost. Quarterly and annual adjustments are necessary under a periodic cost accumulation system to compute the cost of goods manufactured. The term "periodic" is used because the methods are similar to the record-keeping for a merchandising company that accounts for products by means of a periodic inventory system. In both merchandising and manufacturing companies keeping inventory records under a periodic system, ending inventories must be computed before determining the cost of goods sold, and the cost of goods manufactured—for the manufacturing company. In a perpetual cost accumulation system, a continuous record of the cost of goods manufactured is available because perpetual inventory records are maintained. The journal entries under a perpetual cost accumulation system will be presented later.

The following example shows how costs are recorded under a periodic cost accumulation system. (Assume periodic inventories are used throughout this example; however, it should be noted that in practice some companies may wish to use perpetual inventory recordkeeping procedures to account for certain items, such as raw materials and/or supplies.)

Purchases of Materials. Materials are purchased at a cost of $80,000.

> *Entry 1:*
> Purchases of raw materials 80,000
>   Cash 80,000

When periodic inventories are maintained, the cost of purchases is charged to a separate purchase account.

Issuance of Materials. Direct materials of $60,000 and indirect materials of $20,000 are placed into production.

> No entry

When periodic inventories are maintained, no entry is made to record the issuance of materials. A closing entry is made at the end of the period to record the new ending inventory and eliminate the beginning inventory of materials.

Labor Cost. The total payroll cost is $35,000 (ignore payroll taxes for this example).

> *Entry 2a:*
> Payroll 35,000
>   Accrued payroll payable 35,000

The payroll costs are allocated as follows: $18,000 to direct labor and $17,000 to indirect labor.

> *Entry 2b:*
> Direct labor 18,000
> Indirect labor—factory overhead 17,000
>   Payroll 35,000

The payroll is paid.

> *Entry 2c:*
> Accrued payroll payable 35,000
>   Cash 35,000

Actual Factory Overhead. Power and heat costs for the factory are $30,000.

> *Entry 3:*
> Power and heat—factory overhead 30,000
>   Accounts payable 30,000

Under a periodic cost accumulation system, overhead costs are usually charged to individual accounts rather than factory overhead control.

Applied Factory Overhead

> No entry

Under a periodic cost accumulation system, only the actual factory overhead is recorded because no attempt is made to match overhead costs to units produced until the end of the period.

Goods Transferred to Finished Goods. The cost of goods manufactured for the period was $139,000.

> No entry

When periodic inventories are maintained, no entry is made to record the completion of goods in process. A closing entry is made at the end of the period to the Manufacturing account to accumulate the cost of goods manufactured, record the new ending inventory of finished goods, and eliminate the beginning inventory.

Sale of Goods. Goods costing $134,000 were sold for $150,000 cash.

Entry 4:

Cash	150,000	
Sales		150,000

Under a periodic cost accumulation system, no entry is made at the time of sale to adjust finished goods inventory and record the cost of goods sold. The cost of goods sold is recorded and ending inventories are adjusted with closing entries.

The Worksheet under a Periodic Cost Accumulation System

The worksheet for a manufacturing business using a periodic cost accumulation system is similar to the worksheet for a merchandising business. The difference is the addition of a pair of columns entitled "Manufacturing," which contains the data used in the statement of cost of goods manufactured. The worksheet for a manufacturing company is shown in Table 6-2 (page 184), based on the adjusted trial balance in Table 6-1.

The preceding trial balance is an extension of our previous example, with the addition of nonmanufacturing accounts.

The manufacturing columns are the distinctive aspect of this worksheet. The debit column of the manufacturing statement contains the beginning inventories of work-in-process and raw materials. These items become part of the cost of goods manufactured. The entire debit column contains all

TABLE 6-1
THE MANUFACTURING COMPANY
ADJUSTED TRIAL BALANCE
DECEMBER 31, 19X1

	DEBITS	CREDITS
Cash	20,000	
Accounts receivable	5,000	
Inventories—beginning		
Finished goods	15,000	
Work-in-process	2,000	
Land	10,000	
Accounts payable		15,000
Accrued payroll payable		1,000
Capital stock, $1 par		25,000
Retained earnings, beginning		16,000
Sales		150,000
Purchases of raw materials	80,000	
Direct labor	18,000	
Indirect labor—factory overhead	17,000	
Heat and power—factory overhead	30,000	
Selling, general and administrative expenses	10,000	
	207,000	207,000
Ending inventories are as follows:		
Finished goods	$20,000	
Work-in-process	8,000	

TABLE 6-2
THE MANUFACTURING COMPANY
WORKSHEET (CONDENSED)
FOR THE YEAR ENDED DECEMBER 31, 19X1

	TRIAL BALANCE		MANUFACTURING		INCOME STATEMENT		RETAINED EARNINGS		BALANCE SHEET	
	DR.	CR.	DR.	CR.	DR.	CR.	DR.	CR.	DR.	CR.
Cash	20,000								20,000	
Accounts receivable	5,000								5,000	
Inventories, beginning:										
Finished goods	15,000				15,000					
Work-in-process	2,000		2,000							
Land	10,000								10,000	
Accounts payable		15,000								15,000
Accrued payroll payable		1,000								1,000
Capital stock, $1 par		25,000								25,000
Retained earnings, beginning		16,000						16,000		
Sales		150,000				150,000				
Purchases of raw materials	80,000		80,000							
Direct labor	18,000		18,000							
Indirect labor—factory overhead	17,000		17,000							
Heat and power factory overhead	30,000		30,000							
Selling, general, and administrative expenses	10,000				10,000					
	207,000	207,000								
Inventories, ending:										
Finished goods						20,000			20,000	
Work-in-process				8,000					8,000	
			147,000	8,000						
Cost of goods manufactured				139,000	139,000					
			147,000	147,000	164,000	170,000				
Net income					6,000		0	6,000		
					170,000	170,000	22,000	22,000		
Retained earnings—ending							22,000			22,000
							22,000	22,000	63,000	63,000

manufacturing costs for the period. The ending inventories of work-in-process and raw materials are credited to the manufacturing column. These items are assets and are shown as such by deducting (crediting) them from cost of goods manufactured and adding (debiting) them to the balance sheet columns as ending inventories.

Note also, that beginning and ending inventory balances for finished goods do not appear in the manufacturing columns. Rather, they appear on the income statement, since changes in finished goods inventory do not affect the cost of goods manufactured. The ending finished goods inventory is also on the balance sheet because it is a current asset.

Closing Entries

The closing entries of a manufacturing business can be taken directly from the worksheet. The first step is to open an account called "Manufacturing" by debiting it for the total amount in the debit column in the Manufacturing section, and eliminating the individual accounts with credits as follows:

Entry 1:

Manufacturing	147,000	
Work-in-process inventory (beginning)		2,000
Purchases of raw materials		80,000
Direct labor		18,000
Indirect labor		17,000
Power and heat		30,000

The next entry is a credit to the Manufacturing account for all items in the credit column *other* than Cost of Goods Manufactured:

Entry 2:

Work-in-process inventory (ending)	8,000	
Manufacturing		8,000

	Manufacturing		
Entry 1	147,000	8,000	*Entry 2*
Cost of goods manufactured	139,000		

The $139,000 debit balance in the Manufacturing account is the Cost of Goods Manufactured for the period. This balance is transferred to an Income Summary account, thereby closing the Manufacturing account. All other expenses, finished goods inventories, and sales are closed to Income Summary. The entry presented below closes Finished Goods Inventory (beginning), the Manufacturing account balance, and Selling, General, and Administrative Expenses to the Income Summary account:

Entry 3:

Income Summary	164,000	
Finished goods inventory (beginning)		15,000
Manufacturing		139,000
Selling, general, and administrative expenses		10,000

The following entry closes the Sales account to Income Summary and records Finished Goods Inventory (ending):

Entry 4:

Sales	150,000	
Finished goods inventory (ending)	20,000	
Income summary		170,000

Income Summary		
Entry 3 164,000	170,000	*Entry 4*
	6,000	Net income

The $6,000 credit balance in the Income Summary account is the Net Income for the period. This balance is transferred to the Retained Earnings account, thereby closing the Income Summary as follows:

Entry 5:

Income summary	6,000	
Retained earnings		6,000

Retained Earnings	
16,000	Beginning balance
6,000	*Entry 5*
22,000	Total

The $22,000 credit balance in Retained Earnings is the ending balance of the account for the period.

This completes the cycle of journal entries under a periodic cost accumulation system.

Financial Statements

The financial statements (excluding the statement of changes in financial position) for The Manufacturing Company would appear as in Tables 6-3 through 6-6 (pages 187–188).

INTRODUCTION TO
THE PERPETUAL COST ACCUMULATION SYSTEM

Cost accumulation systems are designed to provide relevant information to management on a timely basis to aid in planning and control decisions. The major objectives in such systems are the accumulation of costs and the computation of unit cost.

The two types of perpetual cost accumulation systems, classified according to attributes, are briefly described below.

Job Order Cost. Costs under this system are accumulated by jobs. This method is suitable when each job or order is unique, such as in the construction of aircraft.

TABLE 6-3
THE MANUFACTURING COMPANY
STATEMENT OF COST OF GOODS MANUFACTURED
FOR THE YEAR ENDED DECEMBER 31, 19X1

Raw materials:		
Inventory, January 1	$ 0	
Purchases of raw materials	80,000	
Total materials available	$80,000	
Inventory, December 31	0	
Materials used		$ 80,000
Direct labor		18,000
Factory overhead:		
Indirect labor	$17,000	
Power and heat	30,000	47,000
Manufacturing costs		$145,000
Plus: Work-in-process, January 1		2,000
Cost of goods in process during the year		$147,000
Less: Work-in-process, December 31		8,000
Cost of goods manufactured		$139,000

Process Cost. Costs under this system are accumulated by departments or cost centers, which are determined according to the process performed. This method is suitable when like products are produced in applicable volume, as in flour mills and steel mills.

The perpetual cost accumulation system must be closely tailored to the organizational structure of the company, the manufacturing process, and the type of information desired by executives. In this section, we will present a general overview of the procedures involved in a perpetual cost accumulation system, with detailed coverage given in later chapters.

TABLE 6-4
THE MANUFACTURING COMPANY
INCOME STATEMENT
FOR THE YEAR ENDED DECEMBER 31, 19X1

Sales		$150,000
Cost of goods sold:		
Finished goods inventory, beginning	$ 15,000	
Plus: Cost of goods manufactured	139,000	
Goods available for sale	$154,000	
Less: Finished goods inventory, ending	20,000	
Cost of goods sold		134,000
Gross profit		$ 16,000
Less: Selling, general, and administrative expenses		10,000
Net income		$ 6,000

TABLE 6-5
THE MANUFACTURING COMPANY
STATEMENT OF RETAINED EARNINGS
FOR THE YEAR ENDED DECEMBER 31, 19X1

Retained earnings—beginning	$16,000
Plus: Net income	6,000
Retained earnings—ending	$22,000

Flow of Cost in a Perpetual Cost Accumulation System

In a perpetual cost accumulation system, the cost of direct materials, direct labor, and factory overhead must first flow through work-in-process in order to reach finished goods. The total costs transferred from work-in-process to finished goods during the period are equal to the cost of goods manufactured. The ending work-in-process is the balance unfinished at the end of the period. As goods are sold, the cost of the goods sold is transferred from the Finished Goods account to the Cost of Goods Sold account. The ending finished goods inventory is the balance on hand at the end of the period. The total cost of operation is equal to the cost of goods sold plus selling, general, and administrative expenses.

Note that in a perpetual cost accumulation system, information is *continuously* available concerning work-in-process, finished goods, cost of goods manufactured, and the cost of goods sold, instead of only at the end of the period as with a periodic cost accumulation system.

The flow of costs through a perpetual cost accumulation system is presented in Figure 6-3 (based on the same cost information provided in Figure 6-2).

TABLE 6-6
THE MANUFACTURING COMPANY
BALANCE SHEET
DECEMBER 31, 19X1

Assets		
Current:		
Cash	$20,000	
Accounts receivable	5,000	
Finished goods inventory....................................	20,000	
Work-in-process inventory	8,000	$53,000
Noncurrent:		
Land		10,000
Total assets		$63,000
Liabilities and Stockholders' Equity		
Current Liabilities:		
Accounts payable	$15,000	
Accrued payroll payable.....................................	1,000	$16,000
Stockholders' Equity:		
Capital stock, $1 par, 25,000 shares authorized and issued	$25,000	
Retained earnings—ending	22,000	47,000
Total liabilities and stockholders' equity		$63,000

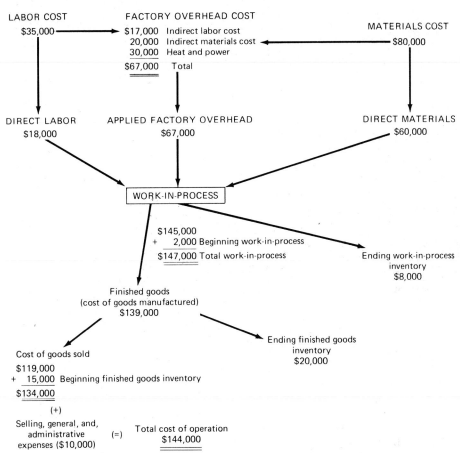

FIGURE 6-3   **Flow of Costs, Perpetual Cost Accumulation System**

Ledger Accounts in a Perpetual Cost Accumulation System

The titles of the ledger accounts under a perpetual cost accumulation system are quite similar to those used for periodic cost accumulation procedures. The major difference is in the way the inventory and work-in-process accounts are maintained. Under a periodic cost accumulation system, these accounts are used only to record beginning and ending inventories. In a perpetual cost accumulation system, the accounts are constantly adjusted as goods are produced and sold.

The following additional accounts are used in a perpetual cost accumulation system:

Materials Inventory.   The unused portion of raw materials on hand at any one time during the period. In a perpetual cost accumulation system, the balance in this account is constantly adjusted when materials are purchased (debited) and put into production (credited).

Work-in-Process. In a perpetual cost accumulation system, the cost of direct materials, direct labor, and factory overhead must first flow through work-in-process in order to reach finished goods. The balance in this account is continually adjusted as direct materials are put into production, direct labor costs are incurred, or factory overhead is applied (all debited), and when completed goods are transferred to finished goods (credited).

Finished Goods. The unsold portion of goods completed and on hand at any one time during the period. In a perpetual cost accumulation system, the balance in this account is continually adjusted when goods in process are completed (debited) and when completed goods are sold (credited).

Factory Overhead Accounts. The factory overhead accounts are added to the other general ledger accounts to record manufacturing costs other than direct materials and direct labor. In a perpetual cost accumulation system, factory overhead may be charged directly to work-in-process when incurred or charged to factory overhead control accounts and then applied to work-in-process by the use of a predetermined factory overhead rate. In either case, the cost of factory overhead must first flow through work-in-process before it finds its way to the Finished Goods account.

Note that the Manufacturing account is not necessary under a perpetual cost accumulation system. The manufacturing accounts are continually adjusted throughout the period rather than only once at the end of the period as with a periodic cost accumulation system.

Journal Entries in a Perpetual Cost Accumulation System

In a perpetual cost accumulation system, journal entries are used *throughout* the period to record the flow of goods and costs through the production process to the eventual sale to customers. The journal entries presented here are based on the same facts given in the example explaining a periodic cost accumulation system. Costs will be accumulated for the entire period instead of by jobs (job order costing) or departments (process costing). The next three chapters will present a detailed discussion of procedures used in job order and process cost systems.

The following example shows how costs are accounted for under a perpetual cost accumulation system. This presentation is intended to provide the reader with a general overview of the journal entries necessary in a perpetual cost accumulation system, and is not intended to cover all transactions that may occur.

Purchase of Materials. Materials are purchased at a cost of $80,000.

Entry 1:

Materials inventory	80,000	
Cash		80,000

When perpetual inventories are kept, the cost of purchases is charged directly to a Materials Inventory account.

Issuance of Materials.   Direct materials of $60,000 and indirect materials of $20,000 are placed into production.

> *Entry 2:*
> | | | |
> |---|---|---|
> | Work-in-process..................... | 60,000 | |
> | Factory overhead control .... | 20,000 | |
> | Materials inventory .... | | 80,000 |

When direct materials are put into production, a journal entry must be made to record the addition of materials to work-in-process. The requisition of indirect materials is generally charged to a Factory Overhead Control account to be applied to work-in-process at a later date.

Labor Cost.   Total payroll cost is $35,000 (ignore payroll taxes for this example).

> *Entry 3a:*
> | | | |
> |---|---|---|
> | Payroll............................ | 35,000 | |
> | Accrued payroll payable .... | | 35,000 |

The payroll costs are allocated as follows: $18,000 to direct labor and $17,000 to indirect labor.

> *Entry 3b:*
> | | | |
> |---|---|---|
> | Work-in-process..................... | 18,000 | |
> | Factory overhead control .... | 17,000 | |
> | Payroll........................... | | 35,000 |

Direct labor costs incurred are charged to work-in-process while indirect labor is charged to the Factory Overhead Control account to be applied to work-in-process at a later date. The payroll is paid.

> *Entry 3c:*
> | | | |
> |---|---|---|
> | Accrued payroll payable .... | 35,000 | |
> | Cash .... | | 35,000 |

Actual Factory Overhead.   Power and heat costs for the factory are $30,000.

> *Entry 4:*
> | | | |
> |---|---|---|
> | Factory overhead control .... | 30,000 | |
> | Accounts payable .... | | 30,000 |

In a perpetual cost accumulation system, the actual factory overhead costs are charged to a Factory Overhead Control account. The final distribution of factory overhead to work-in-process is applied based on a predetermined rate. The balance in the Factory Overhead Control account after this entry is $67,000, computed as follows:

Factory Overhead Control

Entry 2	Indirect materials	20,000	
Entry 3b	Indirect labor	17,000	
Entry 4	Power and heat	30,000	
	Total	67,000	

Applied Factory Overhead. Assume that the amount ($67,000) in the Factory Overhead Control account was applied to work-in-process. (In practice this rarely happens; a discussion on how to account for any difference between the amount applied and the actual balance in the Factory Overhead Control account was presented in Chapter 5.) The entry to apply the $67,000 of factory overhead to work-in-process follows (assume that a Factory Overhead Applied account is not used).

Entry 5:
Work-in-process 67,000
    Factory overhead control   67,000

Goods Transferred to Finished Goods. The cost of goods manufactured for the period was $139,000.

Entry 6:
Finished goods 139,000
    Work-in-process   139,000

In a perpetual cost accounting system, the cost of goods completed is transferred from the Work-in-Process account to the Finished Goods account.

Sale of Goods. Goods costing $134,000 were sold for $150,000 cash.

Entry 7:
Cash 150,000
Cost of goods sold 134,000
    Finished goods   134,000
    Sales   150,000

In a perpetual cost accumulation system, the cost of goods sold is transferred from the Finished Goods account to the Cost of Goods Sold account. The revenue is recorded by a debit to cash (or accounts receivable) and a credit to sales.

The Worksheet for a Perpetual Cost Accumulation System

A worksheet to compute the cost of goods manufactured is rarely used under a perpetual cost accumulation system because financial statements can be prepared directly from the trial balance. (Remember, the accounts have been continuously adjusted and therefore reflect ending balances.)

Closing Entries

Closing entries are only necessary for revenue and expense accounts relating to the income statement; the accounts relating to the manufacture of the products have already been closed, or the remaining balances represent ending inventories. Therefore, the Manufacturing account is not needed.

The only closing entries necessary are those to close the income statement accounts to income summary. The first entry would be to close the cost of goods sold and selling, general, and administrative expenses to income summary as follows:

Entry 1:

Income summary	144,000	
Cost of goods sold.....................................		134,000
Selling, general, and administrative expenses		10,000

The next entry would be to close sales to income summary as follows:

Entry 2:

Sales...	150,000	
Income summary		150,000

	Income Summary		
Entry 1	144,000	150,000	*Entry 2*
		6,000	Net income

The $6,000 credit balance in the Income Summary account is the net income for the period. This balance is transferred to the Retained Earnings account, thereby closing the Income Summary account as follows:

Entry 3:

Income summary	6,000	
Retained earnings		6,000

This completes the cycle of journal entries under a perpetual cost accumulation system.

Financial Statements

The financial statements under a perpetual cost accumulation system are very similar, and in most cases, identical (as in our example), to those for a periodic cost accumulation system and will therefore not be repeated.

COMPARISON OF PERIODIC AND PERPETUAL COST ACCUMULATION SYSTEMS

You will note from the previous two examples that the end results (the cost of goods manufactured, cost of goods sold, and net income) were the same under both cost accumulation systems. Results of the two systems may vary slightly when more complex situations and systems are used. However, on the whole, any resulting differences between periodic and perpetual cost accumulation systems should be insignificant. The major difference is in the information available to management. The systems presented in this chapter were either purely periodic or purely perpetual, but note that any hybrid set of procedures or systems could be developed from parts of both systems, depending on the needs of management and the imagination of the developers.

Table 6-7 (pages 196—197) is a summary of the journal entries under periodic and perpetual methods.

THE FACTORY LEDGER

It is often practical for a manufacturing firm to incorporate a factory ledger in its accounting system. The factory ledger is generally used when manufacturing operations are separated from the main office or when the nature of operations requires many additional accounts. The *factory ledger* contains the data related *only* to manufacturing operations (the information needed to compute cost of goods manufactured). Typically, the accounts in the factory ledger under a perpetual cost accumulation system include Materials, Work-in-Process, Payroll (factory only), Factory Overhead Control, and Finished Goods. A control account or reciprocal account, called General Ledger, is also included on the factory books.

Most firms maintain cash, other factory assets, liabilities, and general revenue and expense accounts on the general office records; thus the *general ledger* includes such accounts as Sales, Cost of Goods Sold, Factory Equipment, Accumulated Depreciation (factory depreciation *expense* for the current period is kept in the factory ledger), and Liabilities. It also includes the control account or reciprocal account, Factory Ledger.

The control accounts, Factory Ledger and General Ledger, are reciprocal in nature; a debit to one requires a corresponding credit to the other. They are used whenever a transaction affects both ledgers. The debit balance in the Factory Ledger account should always equal the credit balance in the General Ledger account. The balances in these two accounts offset each other and are eliminated for statement purposes.

Each ledger is self-balancing and together they make up *one* set of books. For example, in our previous illustration of a perpetual cost accumulation system, only one ledger was used—the general ledger—with the following accounts:

> *General Ledger*
>
> Cash
> Accounts receivable
> Finished goods
> Work-in-process
> Land

> Accounts payable
> Capital stock
> Retained earnings
> Sales
> Cost of goods sold
> Factory overhead control
> Payroll
> Materials
> Selling, general, and administrative expenses

If a factory ledger was also used to record the transactions, the accounts would be allocated between the two ledgers as in Table 6-8 (page 198).

The series of entries in Table 6-9 (page 199) is from our previous example of a perpetual cost accumulation system, now recorded using a general ledger and a factory ledger.

The factory ledger may be used in either a periodic cost accumulation system or a perpetual cost accumulation system. However, when the latter system is in use, a large number of factory accounts and transactions usually exist. The factory ledger is likely to be beneficial in such a situation, and hence is more apt to be used under the perpetual cost accumulation system.

CHAPTER REVIEW

Cost accumulation is the organized collection and classification of cost data by means of accounting procedures, or systems. Cost classification is the grouping of all manufacturing costs into various categories in order to meet the needs of management.

Unit cost values facilitate the computation of figures for closing inventory and cost of goods sold.

Unit cost = total cost of goods manufactured ÷ number of units produced

Cost data is commonly accumulated under either a periodic cost accumulation system or a perpetual cost accumulation system.

A periodic cost accumulation system provides only limited cost information during a period and require quarterly or year-end adjustments to arrive at the cost of goods manufactured. In most cases, additional cost accumulation ledger accounts are simply added to a financial accounting system. Periodic physical inventories are taken to adjust inventory accounts to arrive at the cost of goods manufactured. A periodic cost accumulation system is *not* considered a complete cost accounting system since the costs of work-in-process and finished goods can only be determined after physical inventories have been taken. Because of these limitations, periodic cost accumulation systems are usually found only in small manufacturing companies.

TABLE 6-7
PERIODIC AND PERPETUAL SYSTEMS

TRANSACTION	PERIODIC COST ACCUMULATION SYSTEM		PERPETUAL COST ACCUMULATION SYSTEM	
During the period:				
1 Purchase of materials	Purchases of raw materials	80,000	Materials inventory	80,000
	Cash	80,000	Cash	80,000
2 Issuance of materials	No entry		Work-in-process	60,000
			Factory overhead control	20,000
			Materials inventory	80,000
3 Labor cost	a. Payroll	35,000	a. Payroll	35,000
	Accrued payroll payable	35,000	Accrued payroll payable	35,000
	b. Direct labor	18,000	b. Work-in-process	18,000
	Indirect labor—factory overhead	17,000	Factory overhead control	17,000
	Payroll	35,000	Payroll	35,000
	c. Accrued payroll payable	35,000	c. Accrued payroll payable	35,000
	Cash	35,000	Cash	35,000
4 Actual factory overhead	Power and heat—factory overhead	30,000	Factory overhead control	30,000
	Accounts payable	30,000	Accounts payable	30,000
5 Applied factory overhead	No entry		Work-in-process	67,000
			Factory overhead control	67,000
6 Goods transferred to finished goods	No entry		Finished goods	139,000
			Work-in-process	139,000

7 Sale of goods

Account	Dr	Cr		Account	Dr	Cr
Cash	150,000			Cash	150,000	
Sales		150,000		Cost of goods sold	134,000	
				Finished goods		134,000
				Sales		150,000

Closing entries:

a.

Account	Dr	Cr		Account
Manufacturing	147,000			No entry
Work-in-process (beginning)		2,000		
Purchases of raw materials		80,000		
Direct labor		18,000		
Indirect labor		17,000		
Power and heat		30,000		

b.

Account	Dr	Cr		Account
Work-in-process Inventory (ending)	8,000			No entry
Manufacturing		8,000		

c.

Account	Dr	Cr		Account	Dr	Cr
Income summary	164,000			Income summary	144,000	
Finished goods inventory (beginning)		15,000		Cost of goods sold		134,000
Manufacturing		139,000		Selling, general, and administrative expenses		10,000
Selling, general, and administrative expenses		10,000				

d.

Account	Dr	Cr		Account	Dr	Cr
Sales	150,000			Sales	150,000	
Finished goods Inventory (ending)	20,000			Income summary		150,000
Income summary		170,000				

e.

Account	Dr	Cr		Account	Dr	Cr
Income summary	6,000			Income summary	6,000	
Retained earnings		6,000		Retained earnings		6,000

TABLE 6-8
ALLOCATION OF ACCOUNTS TO GENERAL LEDGER AND FACTORY LEDGER

ACCOUNT	GENERAL LEDGER	FACTORY LEDGER
Cash	Cash	
Accounts receivable	Accounts receivable	
Finished goods		Finished goods
Work-in-process		Work-in-process
Land	Land	
Accounts payable	Accounts payable	
Capital stock	Capital stock	
Retained earnings	Retained earnings	
Sales	Sales	
Cost of goods sold	Cost of goods sold	
Factory overhead control		Factory overhead control
Payroll		Payroll
Materials		Materials
Selling, general, and administrative expenses	Selling, general, and administrative expenses	
New accounts	Factory ledger	General ledger

A perpetual cost accumulation system is a method of accumulating cost data that provides continuous information about work-in-process, finished goods, and cost of goods manufactured. Such cost systems are usually very extensive and are used by most medium and large manufacturing companies.

The factory ledger of a manufacturing firm contains only data related to the manufacturing operations. The factory ledger is tied into the general ledger through control accounts—the Factory Ledger account in the general ledger and the General Ledger account in the factory ledger. These control accounts are reciprocal in nature and therefore are eliminated for purposes of financial statements.

GLOSSARY

Cost Accumulation—the organized collection and classification of cost data.

Cost Classification—the grouping of all manufacturing costs into various categories in order to meet the needs of management.

Cost of Goods Manufactured—the total cost (materials, labor, and factory overhead) involved in manufacturing a product.

Factory Ledger—a ledger containing accounts that relate to a manufacturing operation.

Factory Ledger Control—a control account in the general ledger that functions as a reciprocal account to the General Ledger account.

General Ledger—a ledger containing accounts that relate to the general operations of a business.

General Ledger Control—a control

TABLE 6-9

JOURNAL ENTRIES IN GENERAL LEDGER AND FACTORY LEDGER

TRANSACTION	GENERAL LEDGER		FACTORY LEDGER	
1 Purchases of materials	Factory ledger	80,000	Materials inventory	80,000
	Cash	80,000	General ledger	80,000
2 Issuance of materials	No entry		Work-in-process	60,000
			Factory overhead control	20,000
			Materials inventory	80,000
3 Labor cost	Factory ledger	35,000	Payroll	35,000
	Accrued payroll payable	35,000	General ledger	35,000
	No entry		Work-in-process	18,000
			Factory overhead control	17,000
			Payroll	35,000
	Accrued payroll payable	35,000	No entry	
	Cash	35,000		
4 Actual factory overhead	Factory ledger	30,000	Factory overhead control	30,000
	Accounts payable	30,000	General ledger	30,000
5 Applied factory overhead	No entry		Work-in-process	67,000
			Factory overhead control	67,000
6 Goods transferred to finished goods	No entry		Finished goods	139,000
			Work-in-process	139,000
7 Sales of goods	Cash	150,000	General ledger	134,000
	Cost of goods sold	134,000	Finished goods	134,000
	Sales	150,000		
	Factory ledger	134,000		

account in the factory ledger that functions as a reciprocal account to the Factory Ledger account.

Periodic Cost Accumulation System—a method of accumulating cost data which provides only limited cost information during a period and requires quarterly or year-end adjustments to arrive at the cost of goods manufactured.

Perpetual Cost Accumulation Sys- tem—a system of accumulating cost data through a work-in-process account that provides continuous information about work-in-process, finished goods, and the costs of goods manufactured.

Unit Cost—total cost of goods manufactured divided by the units produced. This figure can be stated in terms of cost per ton, gallon, foot, or any other measurement base.

SUMMARY PROBLEMS

PROBLEM 1

The adjusted trial balance of Anzalone Corporation on June 30 (the end of the company's fiscal year), Year 8, is as follows:

ANZALONE CORPORATION
ADJUSTED TRIAL BALANCE
JUNE 30, YEAR 8

Cash	85,730	
Accounts receivable	101,210	
Allowance for doubtful accounts		8,170
Raw materials inventory, July 1, Year 7	25,950	
Work-in-process inventory, July 1, Year 7	23,290	
Finished goods inventory, July 1, Year 7	18,750	
Equipment—factory	537,860	
Accumulated depreciation—factory equipment		53,790
Office equipment	229,050	
Accumulated depreciation—office equipment		89,750
Accounts payable		59,000
Income taxes payable		92,720
Capital stock, $10 par		250,000
Paid-in capital in excess of par		75,000
Retained earnings, July 1, Year 7		101,250
Dividends	38,000	
Sales (net)		2,125,930
Purchases (net)	489,000	
Direct labor	617,000	
Factory overhead (control)	302,730	
Selling expenses (control)	174,320	
Administrative expenses (control)	120,000	
Income taxes	92,720	
	2,855,610	2,855,610

Inventories at June 30, Year 8, are as follows:

Raw materials inventory $28,010
Work-in-process inventory 25,870
Finished goods inventory 15,220

REQUIRED:

Prepare the following:

a Worksheet (include a pair of columns each for adjusted trial balance, manufacturing, income statement, retained earnings, and balance sheet), assuming a periodic cost accumulation system.

b Closing entries for the period.

PROBLEM 2

E-Lee's Plastic Company uses a perpetual cost accumulation system and maintains a general ledger and a factory ledger. The following transactions occurred during January and February:

1/1 Purchased $10,000 of materials to be used in the factory and $2,500 of supplies for use in the home office.

1/8 Placed $7,500 of direct materials into process.

1/15 Factory and office payroll (prepared and paid) for the first two weeks of January:

Factory payroll:
  Direct labor $2,500
  Indirect labor 1,500 $4,000
Office payroll   1,000
FICA taxes   250
Federal withholding   700

1/16 Recorded employer's share of payroll taxes:

FICA taxes $250
State unemployment......................... 25
Federal unemployment 100

1/19 Paid rent of $600 for factory.

1/31 Recorded depreciation on factory equipment of $175.

1/31 Applied factory overhead—40% of direct labor cost.

2/2 Recorded finished goods of $5,000.

2/4 Sold finished goods costing $3,500 for $5,500.

REQUIRED:

Record the preceding transactions in the appropriate ledgers.

SOLUTIONS TO SUMMARY PROBLEMS

PROBLEM 1

a Worksheet

ANZALONE CORPORATION
WORKSHEET
JUNE 30, YEAR 8

	TRIAL BALANCE		MANUFACTURING	
	DR.	CR.	DR.	CR.
Cash	85,730			
Accounts receivable	101,210			
Allowance for doubtful accounts		8,170		
Raw materials inventory —July 1, Year 7	25,950		25,950	
Work-in-process inventory —July 1, Year 7	23,290		23,290	
Finished goods inventory —July 1, Year 7	18,750			
Equipment—factory	537,860			
Accumulated depreciation— factory equipment		53,790		
Office equipment	229,050			
Accumulated depreciation— office equipment		89,750		
Accounts payable		59,000		
Income taxes payable		92,720		
Capital stock, $10 par		250,000		
Paid-in capital in excess of par		75,000		
Retained earnings—July 1, Year 7		101,250		
Dividends	38,000			
Sales (net)		2,125,930		
Purchases (net)	489,000		489,000	
Direct labor	617,000		617,000	
Factory overhead (control)	302,730		302,730	
Selling expenses (control)	174,320			
Administrative expenses (control)	120,000			
Income taxes	92,720			
	2,855,610	2,855,610		
Raw materials inventory, June 30, Year 8				28,010
Work-in-process inventory, June 30, Year 8				25,870
Finished goods inventory, June 30, Year 8				
Cost of goods manufactured				1,404,090
Net income			1,457,970	1,457,970
Retained earnings—ending				

INCOME STATEMENT		RETAINED EARNINGS		BALANCE SHEET	
DR.	CR.	DR.	CR.	DR.	CR.
				85,730	
				101,210	
					8,170
18,750					
				537,860	
					53,790
				229,050	
					89,750
					59,000
					92,720
					250,000
					75,000
			101,250		
		38,000			
	2,125,930				
174,320					
120,000					
92,720					
				28,010	
				25,870	
	15,220			15,220	
1,404,090					
331,270			331,270		
2,141,150	2,141,150				
		394,520			394,520
		432,520	432,520	1,022,950	1,022,950

b Closing Entries:

1 Manufacturing 1,457,970

Raw materials inventory (beginning) 25,950
Work-in-process inventory (beginning) 23,290
Purchases (net)................................. 489,000
Direct labor 617,000
Factory overhead 302,730

2 Raw materials inventory (ending) 28,010
Work-in-process inventory (ending) 25,870
Manufacturing 53,880

3 Income summary 1,809,880

Finished goods inventory (beginning) 18,750
Manufacturing 1,404,090
Selling expenses 174,320
Administrative expenses 120,000
Income taxes 92,720

4 Sales 2,125,930
Finished goods inventory (ending) 15,220
Income summary 2,141,150

5 Income summary 331,270
Retained earnings 331,270

6 Retained earnings 38,000
Dividends 38,000

PROBLEM 2

		GENERAL LEDGER		FACTORY LEDGER	
Jan. 1	Factory ledger	10,000			
	Office supplies	2,500			
	Accounts payable		12,500		
	Materials			10,000	
	General ledger				10,000
Jan. 8	Work-in-process			7,500	
	Materials				7,500
Jan. 15	Factory ledger	4,000			
	Payroll	1,000			
	FICA taxes payable		250		
	Federal withholding				
	taxes payable		700		
	Accrued payroll		4,050		
	Accrued payroll	4,050			
	Cash		4,050		
	Payroll			4,000	
	General ledger				4,000

		GENERAL LEDGER		FACTORY LEDGER	
	Administrative expense control	1,000			
	Payroll		1,000		
	Work-in-process			2,500	
	Factory overhead control			1,500	
	Payroll				4,000
Jan. 16	Factory ledger				
	(375 × 4/5)	300			
	Administrative expense control				
	(375 × 1/5)	75			
	FICA taxes payable		250		
	State unemployment taxes				
	payable		25		
	Federal unemployment taxes				
	payable		100		
	Factory overhead control			300	
	General ledger				300
Jan. 19	Factory ledger	600			
	Cash		600		
	Factory overhead control			600	
	General ledger				600
Jan. 31	Factory ledger	175			
	Accumulated depreciation		175		
	Factory overhead control			175	
	General ledger				175
Jan. 31	Work-in-process				
	(2,500 × 40%)			1,000	
	Applied factory overhead				1,000
Feb. 2	Finished goods			5,000	
	Work-in-process				5,000
Feb. 4	Accounts receivable	5,500			
	Sales		5,500		
	Cost of goods sold	3,500			
	Factory ledger		3,500		
	General ledger			3,500	
	Finished goods				3,500

QUESTIONS

1 Define the term *cost classification*.
2 Differentiate between periodic cost accumulation systems and perpetual cost accumulation systems.
3 What type of companies use a periodic cost accumulation system and what type use a perpetual cost accumulation system?
4 What type of assets are the following and where do they appear on the financial statements under a periodic cost accumulation system?
  a Materials inventory
  b Work-in-process inventory
  c Finished goods inventory

5 What are the major objectives of a cost accumulation system?

6 How is the information obtained in a perpetual cost accumulation system different from that obtained in a periodic cost accumulation system?

7 Explain how the Inventory and Work-in-Process accounts are maintained under both a periodic cost accumulation system and the perpetual cost accumulation system.

8 In which cost accumulation system is the Manufacturing account used? Why isn't it used in the other one?

9 State whether the following are true or false.

  a There are four elements of cost—materials, labor, factory overhead, and indirect expenses.

  b In a periodic cost accumulation system, journal entries are used throughout the period to record the flow of goods and costs through the production process to the eventual sale to customers.

  c The entry to record the cost of goods manufactured for the period under a perpetual cost accumulation system is

      Finished goods   xxx

        Work-in-process   xxx

  d A worksheet is always used in a perpetual cost accumulation system.

  e The Manufacturing account is not needed in a perpetual cost accumulation system.

  f The financial statements under a periodic cost accumulation system is generally the same as those under the perpetual cost accumulation system.

10 When is a factory ledger used by a manufacturing firm?

11 a What kind of data is contained in the factory ledger?

  b What type of accounts are included in the factory ledger under a perpetual cost accumulation system?

EXERCISES

EXERCISE 1

Cost of Goods Sold and Closing Finished Goods Inventory

The T. P. Company produced 8,000 tents at a cost of $10,000; 5,250 tents have been sold and the remainder are in inventory.

REQUIRED:

Compute the cost of goods sold and closing finished goods inventory.

EXERCISE 2

Determination of Work-in-Process Inventory

At the end of its fiscal year, December 31, Year 2, the following information appeared on the financial statements of the ABC Company:

Cost of goods manufactured	$405,000
Cost of raw materials used	160,000
Factory overhead, 80% of direct labor	92,000
Work-in-process inventory, ending	48,000

REQUIRED:

Using good form, determine the work-in-process inventory on January 1.

EXERCISE 3

Cost of Operation—Periodic Cost Accumulation System

XYZ Corporation had the following information available for a period and follows a periodic cost accumulation system:

Inventories:
Beginning

Work-in-process	$ 5,000
Finished goods	18,000

Ending

Work-in-process	6,000
Finished goods	25,000

Materials Costs

Direct	75,000
Indirect	30,000

Labor Costs

Direct	22,000
Indirect	20,000

Other Factory Overhead

Electricity..	45,000
Selling, general, and administration expenses	16,000

REQUIRED:

Compute the total cost of operation assuming no beginning or ending materials inventory.

EXERCISE 4

Entries under a Periodic Cost Accumulation System

The Chimienti Company purchased for cash materials costing $125,000. Direct materials of $90,000 and indirect materials of $35,000 were placed into production. The total payroll cost was $50,000, of which $30,000 was allocated to direct labor and $20,000 to indirect labor. The company paid the payroll on May 5. Maintenance and repairs for the factory were $33,000 paid on account. The cost of goods manufactured by the company totaled $122,000. The company sold goods costing $116,000 for $125,000 cash.

REQUIRED:

Prepare the necessary entries for the Chimienti Company, assuming it uses a periodic cost accumulation system and that this is one month and not year end.

EXERCISE 5

Cost of Goods Manufactured and Sold Statement

In September 19X7, the B. B. Gun Company put into process $60,000 of raw materials. Department A used 15,000 direct labor hours at a cost of $40,000, and Department B used 10,500 direct labor hours at a cost of $3 per hour. Factory overhead is applied in Departments A and B at a rate of $3.75 and $4.50 per direct labor hour, respectively. Inventories on September 1 were the following: materials, $20,000; work-in-process, $28,200; finished goods, $15,100. On September 30, the inventories were the following: materials, $18,725; work-in-process, $24,500; finished goods, $16,500. The company produced 30,000 units during the month.

REQUIRED:

Prepare a combined statement of cost of goods manufactured and sold.

EXERCISE 6

Closing Entries

The manufacturing account of the Safe-T-Lock Manufacturing Company was made up of the following accounts:

Factory overhead (actual)	$45,000
Indirect labor	25,000
Direct labor	40,000
Indirect materials	10,000
Direct materials	45,000
Raw materials Inventory—beginning . . .	10,250
Raw materials inventory—ending	20,000
Purchases of raw materials	64,750

REQUIRED:

a Prepare the entry that is needed to close the individual accounts.
b What is the balance remaining in the Manufacturing account and what does this balance represent?
c How is the Manufacturing account closed?

EXERCISE 7

Statement of Cost of Goods Manufactured

The Avocado Company had the following information available on May 31, 19X8: raw materials put into process, $47,000; direct labor paid at a rate of $4.35 an hour in Department S, $3.75 in Department T, and $5.00 in Department P. Department S worked 9,725 hours, Department T worked 11,000 hours, and Department P worked 15,475 hours. Factory overhead was $60,000 for all three departments combined.

	INVENTORIES	
	MAY 1	MAY 31
Raw materials	$14,000	$12,750
Work-in-process	16,250	18,500
Finished goods	22,000	20,000

REQUIRED:

a Prepare a statement of cost of goods manufactured.
b What is the amount of the cost of goods sold?

EXERCISE 8

Entries under Perpetual Cost Accumulation System

The Star Company purchased materials for cash at a cost of $12,795. Direct materials of $9,250 and indirect materials of $3,545 were placed into production of the company's most popular product—78XT. The total payroll cost was $37,000, of which $25,000 was allocated to direct labor and $12,000 to indirect labor. The payroll was paid on March 3. The insurance and depreciation expenses for the manufacturing operations amounted to $16,000. Assume the exact amount in Factory Overhead Control was applied to Work-in-Process. The cost of the goods manufactured for the period was $64,000. Sales of 78XT amounted to $65,000 in cash, and the cost was $60,000.

REQUIRED:

Prepare the entries the Star Company should make, assuming a perpetual cost accumulation system is used.

EXERCISE 9

General Ledger and Factory Ledger

REQUIRED:

Based on the information in Exercise 8, prepare the necessary entries if both a general ledger and a factory ledger are used.

PROBLEMS

PROBLEM 1

Determination of the Total Cost of Operation—Periodic Cost Accumulation System

On December 31, Year 1, the following information was available for the Tweedle Company: Materials used during the year amounted to $94,000, of which $30,000 was for indirect materials. Labor cost for the company included $22,000 for direct labor and $18,000 for indirect labor. The combined cost of heat and electricity was $34,000. Selling, general, and administrative expenses were $16,000. Inventories were as follows: beginning work-in-process, $9,500; ending work-in-process, $12,000; beginning finished goods, $18,000; ending finished goods, $22,000.

REQUIRED:

Using good form, determine the total cost of operation for the Tweedle Company, assuming a periodic cost accumulation system is followed.

PROBLEM 2

Entries for Periodic Cost Accumulation Procedures

Assume the following information for Joan and Mary's Manufacturing Corporation:

May 1   Purchased materials for cash at a cost of $57,000.

May 5   Direct materials of $45,000 and indirect materials of $12,000 were placed into production.

May 12   Payroll was as follows: direct labor, $26,000; indirect labor, $20,000.

May 14   The payroll is paid.

May 20   Heat and power for the factory cost $33,000.

May 30   The cost of goods manufactured was $97,250.

June 6   Sold finished goods costing $85,000 for $92,000 cash.

REQUIRED:

Prepare the necessary entries, assuming a periodic cost accumulation system was followed.

PROBLEM 3

Entries for a Perpetual Cost Accumulation System

The following information was available for the Beaken Company:

July 1   Purchased raw materials for cash, $41,000.

July 3   Materials placed into production, $32,000 ($15,000 were indirect materials).

July 15   Payroll for the first 2 weeks of July: direct labor $18,000; indirect labor $14,000.

July 17   Paid payroll.

July 20   Factory overhead cost, $22,000.

July 24   Factory overhead is applied at a rate of 30% of direct labor.

July 30   Cost of goods manufactured, $81,150.

August 10 Finished goods costing $72,000 sold for $78,000.

REQUIRED:

Prepare the necessary entries, assuming a perpetual cost accumulation system is followed.

PROBLEM 4

Worksheet and Closing Entries—A Periodic Cost Accumulation System

The adjusted trial balance for the Satellite Corporation as of April 10, 19X2, the close of its fiscal year, is as follows:

SATELLITE CORPORATION
ADJUSTED TRIAL BALANCE
APRIL 10, 19X2

	DEBITS	CREDITS
Cash	98,750	
Accounts receivable	125,875	
Allowance for doubtful accounts...........................		9,250
Raw materials inventory, April 11, 19X1	36,700	
Work-in-process inventory, April 11, 19X1	32,000	
Finished goods inventory, April 11, 19X1	25,950	
Land	52,000	
Building ....'...............	45,000	
Accumulated depreciation—building		4,500
Office equipment	39,480	
Accumulated depreciation—office equipment.................		4,000
Accounts payable		65,275
Income taxes payable		100,000
Capital stock $20 par		550,000
Paid in capital in excess of par		100,250
Retained earnings, April 11, 19X1		176,760
Dividends	27,000	
Sales..		1,942,520
Purchases	525,270	
Direct labor	750,985	
Indirect labor—factory overhead	525,225	
Electricity—factory overhead	250,000	
Selling expenses..	185,000	
Administrative expenses...................................	133,320	
Income taxes	100,000	
	2,952,555	2,952,555

Inventories at April 10, 19X2, are as follows:

Raw materials inventory	$32,950
Work-in-process inventory	35,270
Finished goods inventory	22,516

REQUIRED:

a Prepare a worksheet (include a pair of columns each for adjusted trial balance, manufacturing, income statement, retained earnings, and balance sheet), assuming a periodic cost accumulation system is used.

b Prepare the closing entries for the period.

PROBLEM 5

Worksheet—A Periodic Cost Accumulation System

On June 30, the end of its fiscal year, Year 5, the adjusted trial balance for the Smalley Corporation appeared as follows:

SMALLEY CORPORATION
ADJUSTED TRIAL BALANCE
JUNE 30, YEAR 5

	DEBITS	CREDITS
Cash	76,520	
Accounts receivable	96,150	
Allowance for doubtful accounts...........................		6,120
Raw materials inventory, July 1, Year 4	18,520	
Work-in-process inventory, July 1, Year 4	16,290	
Finished goods inventory, July 1, Year 4	14,435	
Office equipment	133,165	
Accumulated depreciation—office equipment..............		63,270
Building...	47,560	
Accumulated depreciation—building		38,045
Land	233,040	
Accounts payable		93,705
Income taxes payable		86,280
Capital stock $15 par		190,840
Paid-in-capital in excess of par		63,105
Retained earnings, July 1, Year 4		92,025
Dividends	22,000	
Sales..		1,676,515
Purchases	327,050	
Direct labor	509,000	
Indirect labor	304,680	
Factory overhead control................................	204,670	
Selling expenses.......................................	132,020	
Administrative expenses.................................	92,015	
Income taxes	82,790	
	2,309,905	2,309,905

Inventories on June 30, Year 5 are the following:

Raw materials	$19,000
Work-in-process	16,000
Finished goods	10,000

REQUIRED:

Prepare a worksheet (include a pair of columns each for adjusted trial balance, manufacturing, income statement, retained earnings, and balance sheet), assuming a periodic cost accumulation system was used.

PROBLEM 6

Statement of Cost of Goods Manufactured and Income Statement

The following information is available for the Silverman Company on December 31, Year 3:

RAW MATERIALS		LABOR COSTS	
Inventory, January 1	$ 9,000	Direct	$19,000
Inventory, December 31	$12,000	Indirect	$17,000
	Heat and electricity for the factory $25,000		

Additional information for the company is as follows:

Materials purchased during the year	$ 40,000
Cost of goods in process during the year	103,000
Work-in-process, December 31	7,000
Sales	125,000
Finished goods inventory, January 1	25,000
Cost of goods sold	105,000
Selling, general, administrative expenses	11,000

REQUIRED:

Prepare a statement of cost of goods manufactured and an income statement.

PROBLEM 7

General Ledger and Factory Ledger—Periodic Cost Accumulation System

The Muppet Corporation uses a periodic cost accumulation system and maintains a factory ledger and a general ledger. The following transactions occurred during November and December:

11/1   The company purchased $26,000 of materials to be used in the factory and $6,000 of supplies and tools for use in the home office. These were all purchased on account.

11/7   Direct materials of $20,000 were placed into production.

11/16   The factory and office payrolls (prepared and paid) for the first 2 weeks of November were as follows:

Factory payroll	
Direct labor	$10,000
Indirect labor	8,500
Office payroll	5,000

The home office prepared the payroll and the checks, and also deducted $3,690 for federal withholding taxes (ignore other payroll taxes).

11/20   Paid insurance of $1,200 for factory.

11/23   Materials costing $500 were defective and returned to supplier.

12/5   Paid supplier for materials and supplies and tools purchased on account on 11/1.

12/10   Finished goods completed totaled $28,500.

12/16   Finished goods costing $19,750 were sold on credit for $24,500.

REQUIRED:

Prepare journal entries on the books of the general ledger and the factory ledger to record the preceding transactions.

PROBLEM 8

General Ledger and Factory Ledger—Perpetual Cost Accumulation System

The following transactions occurred during June and July for the Greenport Company. The company uses a perpetual cost accumulation system and records all transactions in a factory ledger and general ledger.

6/1   Purchased $34,000 of raw materials on account to be used in the factory.

6/4   Office supplies costing $8,000 were purchased on account for use in the home office.

6/8   Placed $13,000 of direct materials into production.

6/11   Payrolls for the factory and the home office were as follows:

Home office payroll	$ 6,200
Factory payroll:	
Direct labor	12,000
Indirect labor	8,100

Payroll taxes deducted and employer payroll expenses were as follows:

FICA	5.7%
Federal withholding tax	10%
State unemployment tax	3.2%
Federal unemployment tax	.5%

Payroll is prepared and paid on the same day.

6/22   Paid rent for factory, $4,000.

6/25   Factory overhead applied at a rate of 95% of direct labor dollars.

7/6   Paid supplier for raw materials and office supplies bought on account.

7/10   Finished goods, $34,300.

7/13   Finished goods costing $18,175 were sold on account for $23,450.

REQUIRED:

Record the transactions for the Greenport Company in the factory ledger and general ledger.

CHAPTER SEVEN
JOB ORDER COST SYSTEM

A general introduction to cost accumulation systems was presented in the previous chapter. It was stated that factory costs are usually accounted for either by jobs (job order cost system) or by departments (process cost system). This chapter will focus on a job order cost system, and the next two chapters will present the procedures used in a process cost system.

JOB ORDER COSTING

A job order cost system is most suitable where the products manufactured differ in materials and labor requirements. Each product is made according to customer's specifications and the price quoted is closely tied to estimated cost. The cost incurred in manufacturing a particular job must therefore be matched to the goods produced. Examples of types of companies which might use job order costing are printing, shipbuilding, aircraft, construction, and engineering firms.

Under a job order cost system, the three basic elements of cost—direct materials, direct labor, and factory overhead—are accumulated according to assigned job numbers. The unit cost for each job is obtained by dividing the total units for the job into the total cost. Selling and administrative expenses based on a percentage of manufacturing cost are listed on the cost sheet to arrive at total cost. A cost sheet is used to summarize the applicable job costs.

In order for a job order cost system to function properly, it must be possible to identify each job physically and segregate its related costs. Direct material requisitions and direct labor costs carry the particular job number, and factory overhead is usually applied to individual jobs based on a predetermined overhead rate. The profit or loss can be determined for each job and the unit cost computed for purposes of inventory costing. Schedules are prepared to accumulate the information for the required journal entries.

Following is an illustration of the flow of costs through a job order cost system together with the required journal entries and necessary source documents.

JOB ORDER COST SYSTEM—ILLUSTRATED

Fork Company is a small furniture manufacturing company specializing in custom-made office furniture. All orders are made to specifications indicated by customers, and costs are accumulated according to job. On June 17, 19X9, Maple Company placed an order with Fork Company for a large custom-made conference table with matching wood chairs and wall units at a price of $12,000. Maple Company wants shipment on or before July 10, 19X9.

The Maple Company order was designated Job 85. We will follow this job through the manufacturing process and the accumulation of production costs. The following information relates to Job 85:

1 *Purchase of materials*—On July 3, 19X9, the purchasing department received $11,000 of materials, as indicated below. (Not all the materials will be used for Job 85.)

20 sheets mahogany wood	73A61	at $500/sheet	$10,000
100 gallons stain	27530	at $5/gallon	500
15 cases glue	67G21	at $20/case	300
5 cases nails	13N13	at $40/case	200
		Total	$11,000

2 *Issuance of materials*—On July 3, 19X9, the production department requisitioned the following materials and began work on Job 85:

Direct material for Job 85:				
Mahogany	5 sheets	at $500 each		$2,500
Indirect materials (not all the indirect materials				
will be used for Job 85):				
Stain	10 gallons	at $ 5	$ 50	
Glue	1 case	at $ 20	20	
Nails	1 case	at $ 40	40	110
	Total materials cost			$2,610

3 *Labor cost*—The production department incurred the following payroll costs for the week ended July 7, 19X9 (July 3, 19X9–July 7, 19X9):

Direct labor for Job 73	$ 300
Direct labor for Job 85	3,500
Indirect labor	1,000
Total labor cost	$4,800

4 *Actual factory overhead*—The production department incurred other factory overhead costs (in addition to indirect materials and indirect labor) amounting to $2,000 for the week ended July 7, 19X9. Actual factory overhead is not charged directly to jobs; instead, an applied factory overhead rate is used.

5 *Applied factory overhead*—Factory overhead was applied at a rate of 75% of direct labor cost for Job 85.

6 *Completion of job*—Job 85 was completed on July 7, 19X9 and transferred to the finished goods storeroom.

7 *Sale of job*—Job 85 was picked up by Maple Company on July 10, 19X9. Payment is to be made in 20 days.

The following journal entries and reports are for the week ended July 7, 19X9 when production of Job 85 was started and completed:

Purchase of Materials

Raw materials and supplies used in production are ordered by the purchasing department. These materials are kept in a materials storeroom under the control of a clerk and are issued only when a properly approved requisition is presented. Entry 1 records the purchase of materials (assuming a perpetual inventory system is used):

> *Entry 1:*
> Materials inventory 11,000
> Accounts payable (or cash)   11,000

Issuance of Materials

The next step in the manufacturing process is to obtain the needed raw materials from the materials storeroom. There is one source document for the issuance of materials in a job order cost system—a materials requisition.

Any issuance of materials by the materials clerk must be substantiated by a materials requisition approved by the production manager or the department supervisor. Each requisition form shows the job order number, the department number, and the quantities and description of materials requested. The materials clerk enters the unit cost and total cost on the requisition form.

On a regular basis, perhaps weekly, materials requisitions are sorted by job number and the totals recorded on a cost summary sheet. Figure 7-1 (page 218) is an example of a materials requisition form (the data relates to Job 85).

When direct materials are put into production, a journal entry is made to record the addition of materials to work-in-process.

When indirect materials are requisitioned, they are generally charged to a departmental Factory Overhead Control account. Indirect materials costs are included in the applied factory overhead rate, as it is often impractical to trace these materials to each job. Entry 2 records the requisition of direct and indirect materials for Job 85:

```
+-------------------------------------------------------------------+
|                 MATERIALS REQUISITION FORM                        |
|                                                                   |
|  DATE REQUESTED: ___7/3/x9___   DATE ISSUED: ___7/3/x9___          |
|                                                                   |
|  DEPARTMENT REQUESTING: Production   APPROVED BY: ___JR___         |
|                                                                   |
|  REQUISITION #: ___430___           ISSUED TO: ___uS___           |
+-------------------------------------------------------------------+
```

QUANTITY	DESCRIPTION	JOB NUMBER	UNIT COST	TOTAL COST
5 sheets	Mahogany #73A61	85	$500/sheet	$2,500
10 gal	Stain #27530	—	5/gal	50
1 case	Glue #67G21	—	20/case	20
1 case	Nails #13N13	—	40/case	40
RETURNED:			SUBTOTAL	$2,610
				(—0—)
			TOTAL	$2,610

FIGURE 7-1 **Materials Requisition Form**

Entry 2:

```
Work-in-process—Job 85 ...................................  2,500
Factory overhead control—production department ............   110
    Materials inventory ......................................        2,610
```

Each account is supported by a subsidiary ledger.

Labor Cost

There are two source documents for labor in a job order cost system—a time card and a labor job ticket. Time cards are inserted in a time clock by employees each day when they arrive, go to and return from lunch, take breaks, and leave work for the day. This procedure mechanically provides a record of total hours worked each day by each employee and thus provides a reliable source for the computation and recording of payroll. Labor job tickets are prepared daily by each employee indicating the job worked on, and the number of hours worked. The wage rate of the employee is inserted by the payroll department. The sum of the labor cost and hours incurred on various jobs (labor tickets) should be equal to the total labor cost and total labor hours for the period (time cards).

The following information is available concerning Job 85 for the week ended July 7, 19X9:

1 Ten employees worked 40 hours each, entirely on Job 85. Their pay rate was $8 per hour. (10 × 40 hours × $8 per hour = $3,200 direct labor for Job 85)

2 Two employees (X and Y) worked 40 hours each; 20 hours each on Job

85 and 20 hours each on Job 73; their pay rate is \$7.50 per hour. (2 ×
20 × \$7.50 = \$300 direct labor for Job 85 and \$300 for Job 73)

3 The salaries for supervisors and maintenance personnel in the production
department amounted to \$1,000.

Figures 7-2 and 7-3 are the time card and labor job ticket for Y on July 3, 19X9
(only one job ticket is presented, as Y worked the same hours on Job 85 each
day). Time accumulated for employees working directly on production (direct
labor) is charged to each job. Time accumulated for workers who cannot be
identified directly with a particular job is indirect labor and charged to factory
overhead.

FIGURE 7-2 **Labor Job Ticket—Prepared for Each Day**
FIGURE 7-3 **Time Card**

LABOR JOB TICKET

JOB NO.: 85   DEPT: Production

DATE: 7/3   EMPLOYEE: Y

START: 1:00 PM   RATE: \$7.50

STOP: 5:00 PM

TOTAL: 4 hours   TOTAL: \$30.00

EMPLOYEE NAME: Y

EMPLOYEE NUMBER: 70071

WEEK OF: 7/3

	7/3	7/4	7/5	7/6	7/7	
SUN	MON	TUES	WED	THURS	FRI	SAT
	8:00 AM	8:00 AM	8:00 AM	8:00 AM	8:00 AM	
	12:00 PM	12:00 PM	12:00 PM	12:00 PM	12:00 PM	
	1:00 PM	1:00 PM	1:00 PM	1:00 PM	1:00 PM	
	5:00 PM	5:00 PM	5:00 PM	5:00 PM	5:00 PM	
	8	8	8	8	8	

REGULAR: 40

OVERTIME: —

TOTAL: 40

At periodic intervals, time cards are summarized to record the payroll and labor job tickets are summarized to be charged to work-in-process or factory overhead. Time card and job ticket hours should be reconciled.

The entry to record the payroll from the time cards is as follows:

Entry 3a:
Payroll	4,800	
Accrued Payroll*		4,800

Computed as follows:

10 employees (400 hours × $8)	$3,200
2 employees (80 hours × $7.50)	600
Supervisors and maintenance	1,000
Total payroll	$4,800

Entry 3b is made to distribute the labor cost (based on labor job tickets) as follows:

Entry 3b:
Work-in-process—Job 73	300	
Work-in-process—Job 85 ($3,200 + $300)	3,500	
Factory overhead control	1,000	
Payroll		4,800

Factory Overhead

The third element to be included in determining the total cost in a job order cost system is factory overhead. There is one source document for the computation of factory overhead costs in a job order cost system—a departmental factory overhead cost sheet. Each department maintains a departmental factory overhead cost sheet, which is a subsidiary ledger of the Factory Overhead Control account. Reconciliation of the control and subsidiary ledgers should be performed at regular intervals.

A departmental factory overhead cost sheet is illustrated in Table 7-1 for the week ended July 7, 19X9. Factory overhead incurred by the production department for the week ended July 7, 19X9 totaled $3,110. This total comprises

Indirect materials........................	$ 110
Indirect labor	1,000
Miscellaneous invoices	1,000
Utilities	490
Depreciation—machinery	220
Depreciation—factory	290
Total	$3,110

*Payroll withholdings are ignored in this example.

TABLE 7-1
DEPARTMENTAL FACTORY OVERHEAD COST SHEET
PRODUCTION DEPARTMENT

DATE	SOURCE	INDIRECT MATERIALS	INDIRECT LABOR		OTHER			MISCELLANEOUS	TOTAL OVERHEAD
			REGULAR	OVER-TIME	DEPRECIATION MACHINERY	DEPRECIATION FACTORY	UTILITIES		
7/3	Materials requisitions	$110							$ 110
7/3–7/7	Job tickets		$1,000						1,000
7/7	Miscellaneous invoices							$1,000	1,000
7/15	Utilities						$490		490
7/30	Adjusting entries				$220	$290			510
	Total	$110	$1,000		$220	$290	$490	$1,000	$3,110

Entry 4 is made to record the overhead expenses (except indirect materials, which were recorded in Entry 2, and indirect labor, which was recorded in Entry 3):

Entry 4:

Factory overhead control—production department	2,000	
Accumulated depreciation—machinery		220
Accumulated depreciation—factory		290
Accounts payable (utilities and miscellaneous)		1,490

Entry 4 recorded the balance of the expenses incurred by the department. In our example, factory overhead costs are accumulated by department. It should be noted, however, that factory overhead costs may be recorded for the factory in total, and then distributed to the departments for ultimate distribution to jobs.

The distribution of factory overhead is based on a predetermined rate. Factory overhead applied rates are expressed in terms of direct labor hours, direct labor dollars, direct materials dollars, machine hours, or some other reasonable basis. When factory overhead is accumulated on a factory-wide level for distribution to several departments, *each department* will generally have a *different* rate.   Department A's rate may be $2.30 per direct labor hour while Department B's rate may be $2.70 per direct labor hour. In addition, each department may use separate bases to determine the rate of application. For example, overhead in Department A may be based on direct labor hours and in Department B on the basis of machine hours. Application rates vary because of the differences in activity and function of departments.

In our example, the production department applies factory overhead at a rate of 75% of direct labor dollars. Total direct labor dollars for Job 85 amounted to $3,500. Factory overhead applied would therefore be $2,625 (75% of $3,500). Assume any under- or overapplied factory overhead is not adjusted until the end of the period.

Entry 5 is made to record the application of factory overhead to Job 85:

Entry 5:

Work-in-process—Job 85	2,625	
Factory overhead control		2,625

Job Order Cost Sheet

A job order cost sheet summarizes the amount of direct materials, direct labor, and factory overhead for each job processed. Materials and labor cost information is obtained from materials requisitions and labor summaries, and is posted to the job order cost sheet daily or weekly. Factory overhead is usually applied at the end of the job, as are selling and administrative expenses.

Job order cost sheets are designed to provide information needed by management and therefore will vary according to management's desires or needs. For example, some forms include selling and administrative expenses and selling price so that estimated profit can be readily determined for each job. Other forms provide only basic factory cost data—materials, labor, and factory overhead. Forms will also vary depending upon whether a firm is departmentalized or maintains no departments.

Figure 7-4 is an example of a job order cost sheet for Job 85 of the Fork Company, which has only one production department.

Entry 6 is made to transfer finished goods out of Work-in-Process to Finished Goods for Job 85 (direct materials $2,500 + direct labor $3,500 + factory overhead $2,625):

> Entry 6:
> Finished goods 8,625
> Work-in-process 8,625

Entry 7 is made to record the delivery of Job 85 to Maple Company:

FIGURE 7-4 **Job Order Cost Sheet**

JOB ORDER COST SHEET

CUSTOMER: _Maple Company_   JOB NO. _85_

PRODUCT: _Conference table, chairs, wall units_   Date Ordered: _6/17/X9_

QUANTITY: _1 SET_   Date Started: _7/3/X9_

SPECIFICATIONS: _Mahogany_   Date Wanted: _7/10/X9_

SET SIZE: _#14_   Date Completed: _7/7/X9_

DIRECT MATERIALS			DIRECT LABOR		FACTORY OVERHEAD (APPLIED)	
Date	Requisition number	Amount	Date	Amount	Date	Amount
7/3	430	$2,500	7/3	$ 700	7/7	$2,625
			7/4	700		
			7/5	700		
			7/6	700		
			7/7	700		
TOTAL		$2,500	TOTAL	$3,500	TOTAL	$2,625

Selling price		$12,000	
Factory costs:			
Direct materials	$2,500		
Direct labor	3,500		
Factory overhead	2,625	8,625	
Gross profit		$ 3,375	
Selling and administrative			
expenses — 5% of selling price		600	
Estimated profit		$ 2,775	

Entry 7:

Accounts receivable—Maple Company	12,000	
Cost of goods sold	8,625	
Finished goods		8,625
Sales		12,000

Figure 7-5 presents a flow of costs for Job 85: The numbers in parentheses relate to the journal entries that were made to record the costs and revenue from the job. Figure 7-6 presents a general flow of costs in a job order cost system where more than one job is involved.

FIGURE 7-5   **Flow of Costs, Job 85**

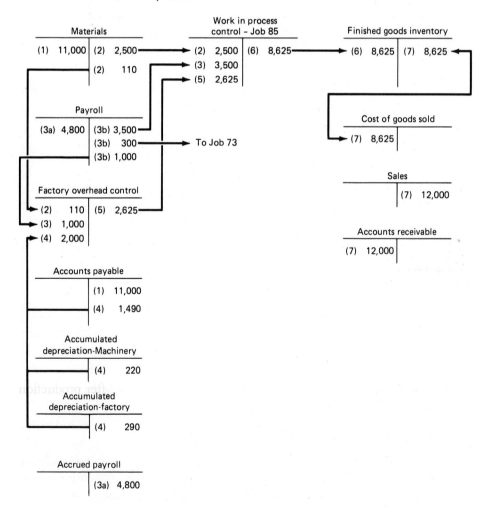

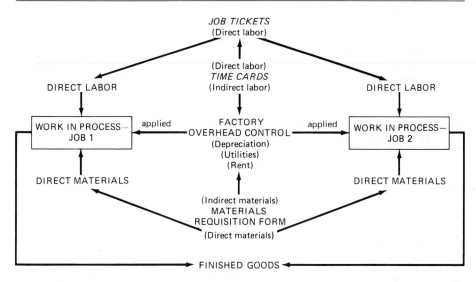

FIGURE 7-6   **Flow of Costs for More than One Job**

SPOILED GOODS, DEFECTIVE GOODS, SCRAP MATERIAL, AND WASTE MATERIAL IN A JOB ORDER COST SYSTEM

The terms spoiled or defective goods, scrap material, and waste material are not synonymous; and they should not be used interchangeably. For our discussion, the following definitions will apply:

Spoiled Goods.   Goods that do not meet production standards and are either sold for their salvage value or discarded. When spoiled goods are discovered, they are taken out of production and no further work is performed on them.

Defective Goods.   Goods that do not meet production standards and must be processed further in order to be salable as good units or as irregulars.

Scrap Material.   Raw materials that are left over from the production process that cannot be put back into production for the same purpose but may be usable for a different purpose or production process, or may be sold to outsiders for a nominal amount. Scrap material such as shavings, filings, and sawdust is similar to a by-product that results from the production of a main product and has a small sales value in comparison with the main product.

Waste Materials.   The part of raw materials that is left over after production and has no further use or resale value.

Accounting for Spoiled Goods (Units)

A system of accounting for spoilage should be developed for all cost accounting systems. This system should provide management with the information necessary to determine the nature and cause of spoiled goods.

Spoilage is an important consideration in any planning and control decision. Management must determine the most efficient production process that will keep spoilage to a minimum.

Spoilage that results from an *efficient* production process is called *normal spoilage*. Normal spoilage costs are considered to be an unavoidable cost of producing good units. Normal spoilage costs have commonly been accounted for by either of the following methods:

1. An estimate of the cost of net spoilage (normal spoilage cost less any estimated salvage value) is made and included in the computation of the factory overhead rate to be applied to jobs. When spoiled units develop, the *total cost* of the spoiled unit is removed from work-in-process because it has already been accounted for in work-in-process as part of applied factory overhead.

2. Spoilage is *ignored* in the computation of the factory overhead rate to be applied to jobs. When spoiled units develop, only the *net salvage value* is removed from work-in-process, leaving in the unsalvageable costs. in WIP

Both methods will result in the same unit cost of goods produced if the *estimates* of the cost of the net spoiled goods that is used in Method 1 equals the *actual* net spoilage cost. Method 2 will be followed by the authors because it is simpler and more accurate (estimates rarely equal actual results). The entry to record spoiled units when spoilage has not been included in the factory overhead rate (Method 2) takes only the salvage value of the spoiled goods out of work-in-process as follows:

Spoiled goods inventory (salvage value of spoiled goods)   X
    Work-in-process—Job A   X

The *unit cost* of the remaining good units will increase because the unsalvageable *cost* of the spoiled units remains in work-in-process while the *units* are removed. For example, a company puts 156 units into production for Job 25. The total cost of production is $2,496. The Work-in-Process account for Job 25 will have a debit balance of $2,496:

Work-in-Process—Job 25

2,496 |

A separate work-in-process account for each job will be used in our examples; in practice, this may not be feasible or practical.

If there are no spoiled units, the unit cost on Job 25 will be $16.00 ($2,496 ÷ 156). However, if we assume that only 150 *good* units are produced and six are spoiled, with a salvage value of $3 each, the adjusting journal entry will be as follows:

Spoiled goods inventory (6 units × $3.00)   18
    Work-in-process—Job 25   18

The Work-in-Process account appears as follows:

Work-in-Process—Job 25

	2,496	18
Balance	2,478	

The unit cost for Job 25 has now increased to $16.52 ($2,478 ÷ 150) because the remaining good units have absorbed the cost of the spoiled units.

In addition to normal spoilage costs, there are *abnormal spoilage costs*. Abnormal spoilage is any excess over what is considered usual for a particular production process. Abnormal spoilage is considered to be controllable by line or production personnel and is usually the result of inefficient operations. While normal spoilage is acceptable and expected in most production activities and is usually considered a part of production costs, abnormal spoilage is not anticipated and thus is usually not considered a part of the cost of production. Instead, the *total cost* of the abnormal spoiled goods should be removed from the work-in-process job accounts, and any salvage value is recorded in a Spoiled Goods Inventory account, with the difference between the total cost of abnormal spoilage and the salvage value being charged to an Abnormal Spoilage account. This account would appear on the income statement as a period cost. The entry to remove abnormal spoilage from work-in-process appears as follows:

Spoiled goods inventory (salvage value of spoiled goods) X
Abnormal spoilage (total cost of spoiled goods less salvage value) X
   Work-in-process—Job A X

The unit cost of the good units is not affected by the technique. For example, assume 5,000 units are put into production for Job 106 at a cost of $20,000. The Work-in-Process account for Job 106 would have a debit balance of $20,000:

Work-in-Process—Job 106

20,000	

The unit cost on Job 106 would be $4.00 ($20,000 ÷ 5,000). If 20 units are found to be spoiled, with a salvage value of $.50 each, and no spoilage was anticipated for Job 106, the 20 units are deemed to be abnormal spoilage. The total cost of these units must be removed from the Work-in-Process account as follows:

Spoiled goods inventory (20 × $.50) 10
Abnormal spoilage [(20 × $4.00) − $10] 70
   Work-in-process—Job 106 80

The Work-in-Process account for Job 106 would now appear as follows:

Work-in-Process—Job 106

	20,000	80
Balance	19,920	

The unit cost for Job 106 is still $4.00 [$19,920 ÷ 4,980 (5,000 good units − 20 spoiled units)].

The following is an example of a situation involving both normal and abnormal spoilage: Assume 10,000 units are put into production for Job 9 and the total cost of production was $300,000. Normal spoilage for the job is estimated to be 50 units; the factory overhead rate does not include a provision for spoiled units. At the completion of production only 9,910 units were good (90 units were spoiled, with a salvage value of $5 each). Therefore, normal spoilage was 50 units and abnormal spoilage was 40 (90 − 50) units. The following entries would be made:

Normal spoilage (50 units) to remove net salvage value:

Spoiled goods inventory (50 × $5)	250	
Work-in-process—Job 9		250

Abnormal spoilage (40 units) to remove total cost of spoiled units:

Spoiled goods inventory (40 × $5)	200	
Abnormal spoilage (40 × $30 = $1,200 − $200)	1,000	
Work-in-process—Job 9		1,200

The unit cost before the adjustments for spoilage was $30.00 ($300,000 ÷ 10,000 units).

After the above entries are posted, the Work-in-Process account would have a balance of $298,550 shown as follows:

Work-in-Process—Job 9

Costs put into production	300,000	250	Normal spoilage
		1,200	Abnormal spoilage
	300,000	1,450	
Balance	298,550		

The new unit cost for Job 9 is computed as follows:

$$\frac{\$298,550}{9,910} = \$30.126 \text{ per unit}$$

Note: The authors computed the unit cost for abnormal spoilage using $30, which is the unit cost before the adjustment for normal spoilage. Manufacturing firms can either compute the unit cost for abnormal spoilage before or after the adjustment for normal spoilage because the difference between the two methods is usually insignificant. For example, if the unit cost for abnormal spoilage is computed after the adjustment for normal spoilage, the unit cost used to remove abnormal spoilage from work-in-process would have been

$30.13 ($300,000 − $250)/9,950. Thus, abnormal spoilage would equal $1,005 (40 × $30.13 = $1,205 − $200). The method chosen by a company should be consistently applied.

Accounting for Defective Goods (Units)

The difference between spoiled goods and defective goods is that defective goods are reworked to put them into condition to be sold with good units or to be sold as irregulars, while spoiled goods are sold without additional work being performed on them. As with spoiled goods, defective goods are classified as either normal or abnormal.

Normal. The number of defective units and the degree of defects in any particular production process that can be expected under efficient operations. The estimated cost of reworking defective goods may be included in the predetermined factory overhead rate or excluded from it and instead added to work-in-process when it occurs. Since it is simpler and more accurate to add the rework cost of defective goods to work-in-process when defective goods result, the authors will follow the procedure which charges rework costs to work-in-process when it occurs. For example, assume Job 22; 500 units were put into production at a total cost of $80,000 resulting in 20 defective units (which is determined to be a normal number of defective units for this process).

The cost of reworking the defective units is as follows:

Direct materials	$1,000
Direct labor	400
Factory overhead applied (50% of direct labor dollars)	200

The following adjusting entry is required:

Work-in-process—Job 22	1,600	
Materials		1,000
Payroll		400
Factory overhead control		200

If the defective units were not reworked, there would be a loss of $160.00 per unit ($80,000 ÷ 500 units). The rework cost was only $80.00 a unit ($1,600 ÷ 20 units), a reduction of the loss. The new cost per unit is $163.20, computed as follows:

$$\frac{\$80,000 + \$1,600}{500} = \$163.20$$

Abnormal. The number of defective units that exceed what is considered to be normal for an efficient operation. The total cost of reworking abnormal defective units should be charged to an abnormal defective units account instead of to work-in-process because it is the result of inefficient operations and should not become part of the product cost. The cost of reworking abnormal defective goods should be shown on the income statement as a period cost. In our previous example (Job 22), if no defective goods are anticipated, the 20 defective goods would be considered abnormal and the following entry would be made:

Abnormal defective unit loss	1,600	
Materials		1,000
Payroll		400
Factory overhead control		200

The unit cost of Job 22 would still be $160.00 because no addition was made to the work-in-process account.

The following is an example of a situation involving both normal and abnormal defective units: Assume 40,000 units are placed into production for Job 32 and the total cost of production is $200,000. Normal defective units for this job are estimated to be 400; actual defective units were 1,000. The total cost to rework the defective units was as follows:

Direct materials	$ 500
Direct labor	1,000
Factory overhead applied (50% of direct labor dollars)	500
Total	$2,000

Unit cost of reworking is computed as follows:

$$\frac{\text{Total rework costs}}{\text{Total units reworked}} \quad \frac{\$2,000}{1,000} = \$2.00 \text{ rework costs per defective unit}$$

Direct materials	$ 500 ÷ 1,000 = $ .50/unit
Direct labor	1,000 ÷ 1,000 = 1.00/unit
Factory overhead	500 ÷ 1,000 = .50/unit
	$2.00/unit

The following journal entries would be made:

Normal defective goods (400 units):

Work-in-Process—Job 32 (400 × $2)	800	
Materials (400 × $.50)		200
Payroll (400 × $1.00)		400
Factory Overhead Control (400 × $.50)		200

Abnormal defective goods (600 units):

Abnormal Defective Unit Loss (600 × $2.00)	1,200	
Materials (600 × $.50)		300
Payroll (600 × $1.00)		600
Factory Overhead Control (600 × $.50)		300

The unit cost before the adjustment for defective units was $5 ($200,000 ÷

40,000). After the above entries are posted, the Work-in-Process account would have a balance of $200,800 shown as follows:

Work-in-Process Job 32	
	200,000
Normal rework costs	800
Balance	200,800

The new unit cost of Job 32 is computed as follows:

$$\frac{\$200,800}{40,000} = \$5.02$$

Accounting for Scrap Material

A cost accounting system should provide a system of control and costing for scrap as it does for spoilage and defective units. When the amount of scrap produced exceeds the norm, it could be an indication of some type of inefficiency. A predetermined rate for scrap should be prepared as a guide for comparison with the actual scrap that results. If large variances occur, management should find the reason and correct the problem.

Scrap materials have commonly been accounted for in either of the following two ways:

1 The resale value of scrap may be considered when the predetermined factory overhead rate is prepared if it represents a significant dollar amount. If this is the case, the entry to record the sale of scrap would reduce factory overhead control. For example, scrap from Job 402 was sold for $100 and had been considered in computing the factory overhead rate. The following entry is made to record the sale:

Cash	100	
Factory overhead control		100

2 If the value of scrap was not considered in the computation of the factory overhead rate, the proceeds from its sale would be credited to the specific job's work-in-process account. If this were the case, the scrap from our previous example (Job 402) would be recorded as follows:

Cash	100	
Work-in-process—Job 402		100

No entry is made on the books when scrap is returned to the materials inventory—only a memorandum is made as to the type and quantity returned. Only when the dollar amount of scrap is material and there is a significant time lag before it can be sold is an inventory value assigned to the scrap.

Accounting for Waste Material

No separate recognition is given to waste materials because they are (1) unavoidable in the production process, (2) relatively insignificant with respect to total cost, and (3) not usable or salable. Waste exceeding a normal level indicates inefficiencies somewhere in the production process and signals management to take corrective action.

The cost incurred in disposing of waste material is generally charged to Factory Overhead Control.

CHAPTER REVIEW

Job order costing is a method of cost accumulation and distribution used by companies which manufacture products according to customer specifications. In a job order cost system, materials and labor are accumulated by jobs. Factory overhead is accumulated by department and then allocated to jobs. In essence, all factory costs are matched to the products produced.

Direct and indirect materials are obtained from the materials storeroom with an approved materials requisition. Direct materials are charged to specific jobs by a debit to work-in-process. Indirect materials are charged to factory overhead control by department and are allocated to individual jobs upon completion, through a factory overhead applied rate.

Labor cost (payroll) is *accumulated* from time cards which mechanically record total hours worked by employees on a daily basis. Labor cost is *distributed* (charged) to the individual jobs in process based on labor job tickets which indicate the number of direct hours worked on each job or indirect hours worked in each department, by each employee, on a daily basis. Total labor hours and cost from job tickets should equal total labor hours and cost from time cards.

Direct labor hours/dollars are distributed to jobs by a debit to the appropriate work-in-process account. Indirect labor hours/dollars are distributed to the appropriate departments by a debit to factory overhead control and later distributed to individual jobs at the factory overhead applied rate.

Factory overhead incurred is accumulated by the appropriate departmental factory overhead cost sheet and applied to the particular jobs.

Two general types of spoilage result from the production process—normal and abnormal. The cost of normal spoilage is absorbed by good units. Unit cost increases as a result of normal spoilage because total cost is distributed over fewer units (only the good units are in the computation of unit cost). The cost of abnormal spoilage is removed from work-in-process and isolated in a loss account, Abnormal Spoilage. Therefore, the unit cost is not increased as a result of inefficient operations that cause abnormal spoilage.

Defective goods (goods that are reworked) are also classified as normal and abnormal.

The cost of reworking normal defective units is added to work-in-process, thereby increasing unit cost. The cost of reworking abnormal defective units is isolated in an Abnormal Defective Units Loss account, and is not added to work-in-process; unit cost would thus not be affected.

The sales value of scrap materials may be considered in the predetermined factory overhead rate or accounted for as a credit (reduction) to work-in-process.

No separate accounting recognition is given to waste materials.

GLOSSARY

Abnormal Defective Goods—the number of defective units that exceed what is considered to be normal for an efficient operation.

Abnormal Spoilage—any spoilage in excess of what is considered normal for a particular production process. Abnormal spoilage is considered to be controllable by line or production personnel and is usually the result of inefficient operations.

Defective Goods—goods that do not meet production standards and must be reworked in order to be salable along with good units or as irregulars.

Departmental Factory Overhead Cost Sheet—a summary of factory overhead expenses incurred; it functions as a subsidiary ledger of the Factory Overhead Control account.

Job Order Costing—method of cost accumulation and distribution by jobs manufactured.

Job Order Cost Sheet—a summary of costs (direct materials, direct labor, and factory overhead) charged to a job.

Labor Job Ticket—a summary of hours worked on a job by an employee. The labor job ticket is prepared daily and is the source for labor cost distribution to jobs.

Materials Requisition—a form submitted to the materials storeroom by production departments to obtain direct and indirect materials.

Normal Defective Goods—the number of defective units and the degree of defects in any particular production process that can be expected under *efficient* operations.

Normal Spoilage—spoilage that would be expected in an *efficient* production process.

Scrap Material—raw materials left over from the production process that cannot be put back into production for the same purpose as before but that may be usable for a different purpose or production process or may be sold to outsiders for a nominal amount.

Spoiled Goods—goods that do not meet production standards and are either sold for their salvage value or discarded.

Time Card—a card used to mechanically record time in and time out for employees by insertion in a time clock. It is the source for the recording and payment of payroll.

Waste Material—raw material that is left over after production and has no further use or resale value.

SUMMARY PROBLEMS

PROBLEM 1

The R & S Metal Company received two orders from customers on January 17, 19X9 as follows:

ASSIGNED
JOB NO.

101   Smith's Auto Parts placed an order for 10,000 aluminum rods, ¾ inch diameter, 12 inches long. The price agreed upon for the job is $7,000. Smith's Auto Parts requested a completion date of January 21, 19X9

102   The Fortune Lamp Company placed an order for 3,000 aluminum switch plates of standard size. The price for this job is $3,000 and requested completion date is January 25, 19X9.

Both jobs will be shaped in the forming department and cleaned in the finishing department. The R & S Metal Company uses a job order cost system. The following transactions relate to Jobs 101 and 102:

1 On January 7, 19X9, the purchasing department bought:
   50,000 lb of aluminum for $37,500; unit cost is $.75 per lb
   500 gallons of cleaning fluid for $2,500; unit cost $5/gal
2 The following materials were requisitioned:

	DATE	QUANTITY	DESCRIPTION	AMOUNT
Forming Department				
Job 101	1/17	2,500 lb	Aluminum	$1,875
Job 102	1/17	300 lb	Aluminum	225
Total				$2,100
Finishing Department				
	1/24	10 gal	Cleaning fluid	$ 50
Total				$ 50

3 Labor costs incurred according to labor job tickets and payroll summary were as follows:

	FORMING	FINISHING	TOTAL
Week of 1/17/X9:			
Direct labor—Job 101	$1,550	$350	$1,900
Direct labor—Job 102	750	100	850
Indirect labor—forming department	550	—	550
Week of 1/24/X9:			
Direct labor—Job 102	—	200	200
Indirect labor—finishing department	—	75	75
Total	$2,850	$725	$3,575

4 Additional factory overhead incurred by the forming department:

Insurance expense ...	$1,200
Depreciation	150
Payroll taxes	200
Total	$1,550

5 Factory overhead is applied to each job upon completion as follows:

Forming department —100% direct labor dollars
Finishing department— 50% direct labor dollars

6 Job 101 was completed on January 21 and Job 102 was completed on January 25. Both jobs were transferred to the finished goods storeroom upon completion.

7 Both jobs were picked up on January 25 by the customers, who paid cash.

REQUIRED:

a Prepare journal entries for the above transactions.
b Prepare a job order cost sheet for Job 101.

PROBLEM 2

The S. Loppy Manufacturing Company produces items made to order and uses a job order cost system to record and distribute costs. The following information relates to Job 86 for 30,000 units:

Cost of normal spoilage (500 units) (assume spoilage was ignored in the computation of the overhead rate)	$20,000
Cost of abnormal spoilage (100 units)	$ 4,000
Salvage value of spoiled goods	$ 10 (per unit)
Cost of reworking defective units (required only labor and assume rework costs were ignored in the computation of the overhead rate)	$ 5 (per unit)
Normal defective units	140
Abnormal defective units	20
Cash received from sale of scrap materials (assume scrap was ignored in the computation of the overhead rate) ...	$ 300
Cost of disposing of waste materials	$ 40

REQUIRED:

Write the journal entries necessary to record the above information.

SOLUTIONS TO SUMMARY PROBLEMS

PROBLEM 1

a Journal Entries

1 | Materials inventory .... | 40,000 | |
| Accounts payable .... | | 40,000 |

2a Work-in-process—materials, Job 101 1,875

    Work-in-process—materials, Job 102 225

      Materials inventory 2,100

b Factory overhead control—finishing 50

    Materials inventory 50

3a *Week of January 17, 19X9:*

    Work-in-process—labor, Job 101 1,900

    Work-in-process—labor, Job 102 850

    Factory overhead control—forming 550

      Payroll 3,300

b *Week of January 24, 19X9:*

    Work-in-process—labor, Job 102 200

    Factory overhead control—finishing 75

      Payroll 275

4 Factory overhead control—forming 1,550

    Accounts payable (insurance) 1,200

    Accumulated depreciation 150

    Payroll taxes payable 200

5 Work-in-process—Job 101 (factory overhead) 1,725

    Work-in-process—Job 102 (factory overhead) 900

      Factory overhead control—forming 2,300

      Factory overhead control—finishing 325

DEPARTMENT	JOB 101		JOB 102		TOTAL
Forming	100% × ($1,550)	$1,550	100% × ($750)	$750	$2,300
Finishing	50% × ($ 350)	175	50% × ($100 + $200)	150	325
	Total	$1,725	Total	$900	

6a *January 21, 19X9—Job 101*

    Finished goods inventory 5,500

      Work-in-process—Job 101 5,500

    Computations:

      Direct materials $1,875

      Direct labor 1,900

      Factory overhead 1,725

        Total $5,500

b *January 25, 19X9—Job 102*

    Finished goods inventory 2,175

      Work-in-process—Job 102 2,175

    Computations:

      Direct materials .... $ 225

      Direct labor 1,050

      Factory overhead 900

        Total $2,175

7	Cost of goods sold ($5,500 + $2,175)	7,675	
	Finished goods inventory		7,675
	Cash	10,000	
	Sales		10,000

b

JOB ORDER COST SHEET

JOB ORDER NO. _101_

CUSTOMER: _Smith's Auto Parts_   Date Ordered: _1/17/x9_

PRODUCT: _Aluminum Rods_   Date Started: _1/17/x9_

QUANTITY: _10,000_   Date Requested: _1/21/x9_

SPECIFICATION: _12 inches 3/4 inch diameter_ Date Completed: _1/21/x9_

FORMING DEPARTMENT

DIRECT MATERIALS				DIRECT LABOR		FACTORY OVERHEAD: 100% DL $	
Date	Description	Quantity	Amount	Week of	Amount	Date	Amount
1/17	Aluminum	2,500 lb	$1,875	1/17	$1,550	1/21	$1,550
Subtotal			$1,875		$1,550		$1,550

FINISHING DEPARTMENT

DIRECT MATERIALS				DIRECT LABOR		FACTORY OVERHEAD: 50% DL $	
Date	Description	Quantity	Amount	Week of	Amount	Date	Amount
				1/17	$ 350	1/21	$ 175
Subtotal			—0—		$ 350		$ 175
Total—Forming and Finishing			$1,875		$1,900		$1,725

Selling Price:		$7,000
Cost:		
Direct Materials	$1,875	
Direct Labor	1,900	
Factory Overhead	1,725	5,500
Gross Profit		$1,500

PROBLEM 2

1	Spoiled goods inventory	5,000	
	Work-in-process—Job 86		5,000
	To remove the salvage value of normal spoilage from work-in-process (500 units × $10)		

2 Spoiled goods inventory (100 × $10) 1,000
    Abnormal spoilage 3,000
       Work-in-process—Job 86 4,000
    To remove the total cost of abnormal spoilage from work-
in-process

3 Work-in-process—Job 86 700
      Payroll 700
    To add the rework costs of normal defective goods to
work-in-process (140 × $5)

4 Abnormal defective unit loss 100
      Payroll 100
    To record the rework costs of abnormal defective goods
(20 × $5)

5 Cash 300
      Work-in-process—Job 86 300
    To record the sale of scrap and remove its cost from work-
in-process

6 Factory overhead control 40
      Cash 40
    To charge cost of removing waste to factory overhead
control

QUESTIONS

1 When is a job order cost system most suitable?
2 What is needed for a job order cost system to function properly?
3 What information is included on a materials requisition form?
4 Differentiate between direct labor and indirect labor.
5 Each department maintains a departmental factory overhead cost sheet. Describe this cost sheet.
6 Where is the information needed for materials, labor cost, and factory overhead obtained from?
7 Describe the two ways normal spoilage costs have been accounted for.
8 What is the difference between spoiled goods and defective goods?
9 Describe the two ways scrap materials have been accounted for.
10 State whether the following are true or false:
   a A job order cost system is most suitable when the products manufactured differ in material and labor requirements.
   b It is not necessary to be able to identify each job physically and segregate its related costs in a job order cost system.
   c Raw materials and supplies used in production are purchased by each department individually.

d   The first step in the manufacturing process is to obtain the raw materials that will be used in production from the storeroom.

e   The sum of the labor cost and hours incurred on different jobs should be equal to the total labor cost and total labor hours for the period.

f   Factory overhead applied rates can be expressed only on one basis— direct labor hours.

g   When factory overhead is accumulated on a factory-wide level for distribution to several departments, each department will have the same rate.

h   Job order cost sheets vary by firm.

i   Normal spoilage costs are considered to be an avoidable cost of producing good units.

j   Abnormal spoilage is considered to be controllable by line or production personnel and is usually the result of inefficient operations.

k   Abnormal spoilage is considered a part of the cost of production.

l   No entry is made on the books when scrap is returned to the materials inventory—only a memorandum is made as to the type and quantity returned.

11   What are the source documents for the issuance of materials, for labor cost, and for factory overhead?

EXERCISES

EXERCISE 1

Entries for Purchase and Issuance of Materials

The purchasing department of Rainbow Paint Company ordered and received $6,600 of materials on September 24, 19XX as indicated below:

> 100 gallons of paint A9786 at $50 per gallon
> 50 gallons of varnish B1234 at $30 per gallon
> 20 cases of brushes C1331 at $5 per case

On September 25, 19XX the production department requisitioned the following materials for Job 16:

> *Direct materials:* 20 gallons of paint
> *Indirect materials:* 8 gallons of varnish and 2 cases of brushes

On September 29, 19XX the production department requisitioned the rest of the materials, and divided them between Jobs 17 and 18.

REQUIRED:

Entries for the purchase of materials, and the issuance to each job, assuming a perpetual inventory system.

EXERCISE 2

Entries for Labor Cost

SJG Company has just completed Jobs 22 and 23. The following information is available for the week ended June 6, 19XX:

1 Fifteen employees worked 35 hours each, entirely on Job 22. Their pay rate was $7.50 per hour.
2 Nine employees worked 35 hours each, entirely on Job 23, at a pay rate of $8.25 per hour.
3 Three employees worked 35 hours each, half on Job 22 and half on Job 23. Their pay rate was $6.25 per hour.
4 The salaries for supervisors and maintenance personnel amounted to $785 for each job.

REQUIRED:

Entries to record the payroll and to distribute the labor cost to Jobs 22 and 23.

EXERCISE 3

Entries for Factory Overhead:

Factory overhead incurred by the production department of Duffy's Dinette Manufacturing Company for the week ended January 8, 19XX was as follows:

Depreciation—factory	$ 425
Depreciation—machinery	375
Utilities	500
Miscellaneous	1,200
Total	$2,500

The production department applies factory overhead at a rate of 125% of direct labor dollars. Total direct labor dollars amounted to $2,700.

REQUIRED:

Entries to record the expenses and the application of factory overhead.

EXERCISE 4

Applied Overhead

Narrows Company applies overhead on a direct labor hour basis in Department F, on a materials dollar basis in Department M, and on a machine hours basis in Department S. The Narrows Company made the following estimates for the fiscal year beginning May 1, 19XX:

	DEPARTMENT F	DEPARTMENT M	DEPARTMENT S
Direct labor hours	8,500	10,500	5,000
Direct labor dollars	$7,250	$9,200	$4,500
Material dollars	$6,000	$9,500	$3,250
Machine hours	3,500	6,295	900
Factory overhead cost	$16,000	$22,000	$10,000

The cost sheet for Job 525 shows the following information for the month of September:

	DEPARTMENT F	DEPARTMENT M	DEPARTMENT S
Direct labor hours	5 per unit	7 per unit	3 per unit
Direct labor dollars	$7.50 per unit	$11.00 per unit	$4.50 per unit
Material dollars	$4.75 per unit	$6.25 per unit	$2.00 per unit
Machine hours	3 per unit	2 per unit	.5 per unit

REQUIRED:

a What predetermined overhead rate would be used in Departments F, M, and S?

b How much overhead will be applied to each product in Job 525?

c Job 525 consists of 75 units of product. What is the total cost of this job?

EXERCISE 5

Job Order Cost Sheet

The following is the job order cost sheet for the Street Manufacturing Company:

JOB ORDER COST SHEET

CUSTOMER: Dinnerware Company   JOB NO.: 26

PRODUCT: Forks, spoons, knives   DATE ORDERED: 5/1/X

QUANTITY: 1 SET   DATE STARTED: 5/11/X

SPECIFICATIONS: Sterling Silver   DATE WANTED: 5/25/X

SET SIZE: #12   DATE COMPLETED: 5/15/X

DIRECT MATERIALS			DIRECT LABOR		FACTORY OVERHEAD (APPLIED)	
Date	Requisition Number	Amount	Date	Amount	Date	Amount
5/10	123	$1,250	5/11	$ 525	5/15	$1,575
			5/12	$ 525		
			5/13	$ 525		
			5/14	$ 525		
Total		$1,250	Total	$2,100	Total	$1,575

The selling price was $5,500.

REQUIRED:

Entries to transfer goods from work-in-process to finished goods for Job 26 and to record the delivery of Job 26 to Dinnerware Company.

EXERCISE 6

Spoiled Goods

Wellgoes Company put 1,331 units into production for Job 3. The total cost of production is $34,606. Only 1,300 good units are produced and the rest are spoiled, with a salvage value of $6 each. Spoilage of 20 units was anticipated.

REQUIRED:

a Entries to record the normal and abnormal spoilage.
b What is the unit cost before the adjustments for spoilage?
c What is the balance in the Work-in-Process account for Job 3?
d What is the new unit cost after the adjustments for spoilage?

EXERCISE 7

Defective Units

Cosmo Corporation placed 16,500 units into production for Job 16. The total cost of production is $412,500. Normal defective units for this job are estimated to be 100 units. The actual defective units were 250. The total cost to rework the defective units is as follows:

Direct materials	$300
Direct labor	450
Applied factory overhead (30% of direct labor)	135
Total	$885

REQUIRED:

a Compute rework cost per defective unit and split this cost into direct material, direct labor, and factory overhead cost per unit.
b Prepare the journal entries to record the normal defective units and the abnormal defective units.
c What is the balance in the Work-in-Process account?
d What is the unit cost before the adjustments for defective units, and after the adjustments for defective units?

EXERCISE 8

Job Order Cost Sheet

Handy Manufacturing has accumulated the following information for Job 453:

a $3,700 of direct materials were requisitioned on No. 76.

b Eleven hours of direct labor were needed each day for 5 days. Labor rate is $9.00 per hour. Any hours over 40 are considered overtime and are charged at 1½ times the normal labor rate.

c Factory overhead is applied at 80% of direct labor cost.

This job will produce 25 size 4 crankshafts for Al's Auto Supply Store. The goods were ordered on April 27, and work was begun on that day. The job was completed on May 3 and was to be delivered on May 9. The crankshafts were sold for $100 apiece.

REQUIRED:

Based on the above information, and assuming that selling and administrative expenses equal 3% of total sales, prepare a job order cost sheet for Job 453.

EXERCISE 9

Defective Units and Scrap Materials

Register, Inc., had both defective units and scrap materials from Job 186. There were 70 defective units, 20 of which were abnormal. The scrap materials were sold for $125 and were not considered in the computation of the factory overhead rate.

REQUIRED:

a Prepare journal entries for the normal and abnormal defective units, assuming the following rework costs:

Materials	$105
Labor	70
Overhead	35
Total	$210

b Prepare journal entries for the sale of the scrap materials. Assume scrap is still in work-in-process.

PROBLEMS

PROBLEM 1

T Accounts

Cloudy Glass Manufacturing Company purchased materials on account for $22,000. Job 30 required direct materials of $15,000 and indirect materials of $3,000. It incurred a direct labor cost of $12,000 and an indirect labor cost of $5,000.

Depreciation for the factory was $1,600, rent payable was $2,400, and depreciation on the machinery was $1,500. Factory overhead is applied at a rate of 90% of direct labor. Goods costing $17,500 were transferred out of work-in-process. These goods were sold for $20,000.

REQUIRED:

Record the above information in T accounts. Assume in your solution a perpetual inventory system and no beginning inventories.

PROBLEM 2

Journal Entries under Job Order Cost System

The Table and Chair Manufacturing Company received two orders from customers on February 16, 19XX, as follows:

ASSIGNED
JOB NO.

66   Oak Company placed an order for 50 tables. The price agreed upon for the job is $25,000. February 28, 19XX is the requested date of completion.

67   The Kitchen Company placed an order for 24 chairs. The price agreed upon for the job is $4,200. February 20, 19XX is the requested date of completion.

Both jobs will be formed in the Setting Department and cleaned and checked in the Finishing Department. The Table and Chair Manufacturing Company uses a Job Order Cost System. The following information relates to Jobs #66 and #67:

1 On February 16, 19XX the Purchasing Department bought:
  100 sheets of oakwood for $14,000; unit cost of $140 } Direct materials
  20 cases of glue for $500; unit cost of $25 ⎱
  10 cases of nails for $300; unit cost of $30   } Indirect
  50 gallons of varnish for $200; unit cost of $4 ⎰ materials

2 The following materials were requisitioned:

	DATE	QUANTITY	DESCRIPTION	AMOUNT
Setting Department				
Job 66	2/16	75 sheets	Oakwood	$10,500
Job 67	2/16	7 sheets	Oakwood	980
				$11,480
Finishing Department				
	2/18	10 gallons	Varnish	$ 40
				$ 40

3 Labor costs according to labor time cards and payroll summary were as follows:

	SETTING	FINISHING	TOTAL
Week of 2/16:			
Direct labor—Job 66	$2,750	$425	$3,175
Direct labor—Job 67	1,200	120	1,320
Indirect labor	700	—	700
Week of 2/23:			
Direct labor—Job 67	—	150	150
Indirect labor	—	100	100
	$4,650	$795	$5,445

4 Additional factory overhead incurred by the setting department:

Rent expense	$1,500
Depreciation—machinery	360
Depreciation—factory	490
Utilities	225
Payroll taxes	300
Total.........................	$2,875

5 Factory overhead is applied to each job upon completion as follows:
   Setting department—120% of direct labor dollars
   Finishing department—75% of direct labor dollars

6 Job 66 was completed on February 27, 19XX and Job 67 was completed on February 20, 19XX. Both jobs were transferred to the finished goods storeroom upon completion.

7 Job 66 was picked up on February 28, 19XX and Job 67 was picked up on February 20, 19XX. The customer for Job 66 paid cash, and the customer for Job 67 charged his account.

REQUIRED:

a Prepare the journal entries for the above transactions.
b Prepare a job order cost sheet for Job 67.

PROBLEM 3
Spoiled and Defective Units

The Dapper Dan Company makes jackets and uses a job order cost system to record and distribute costs. The following information relates to Job 22, which is the production of 1,000 jackets. Normal spoilage is estimated to be 25 jackets. Abnormal spoilage consisted of 4 jackets. The factory overhead rate does not include a provision for spoiled units. Normal defective units for this job are estimated to be 11 jackets. Actual defective units were 16. At completion of production only 955 jackets were good. The salvage value of the spoiled goods is $3 per jacket. The total cost to rework the defective units was as follows:

Direct materials	$ 50
Direct labor	40
Applied factory overhead	10
Total	$100

Cash received from the sale of scrap materials was $150. A special inventory account for scrap is not maintained. The cost of disposing of waste materials was $25. The total cost of production was $15,000.

REQUIRED:

Entries to record the above information.

PROBLEM 4

Journal Entries under Job Order Cost System

The Hungry Frozen Food Company maintains a job order cost system. For the month of June it had the following information: Work-in-process on June 1 was $12,500; raw materials purchased amounted to $15,000; materials requisitioned were $11,000, of which $3,000 was indirect. Payroll for the month was $36,000, $12,000 of which was indirect. The actual factory overhead was $42,000. Factory overhead is applied at 85% of direct labor. Jobs with a total cost of $52,000 were completed during June. Jobs costing $76,000 were sold at a markup of 30% of cost. Assume a perpetual inventory system.

REQUIRED:

a Prepare the entries for the above transactions.
b Compute the amount in the work-in-process inventory on June 30.

PROBLEM 5

Journal Entries and Job Order Cost Sheet

Ajax Assembling Company is manufacturing 500 radios for Sonar Sound Supply via Job 821. The radios were ordered on April 11, 19XX, and work was commenced 3 days later. They were completed and delivered on April 18, 19XX. There were no specifications for the job, and the radios were to be standard size.

Ajax accumulated the following costs in connection with Job 821:

Materials requisitioned on No. 492:
500 transistors at $.50 each
2,500 circuits at $.25 each
200 dials at $.40 each
2,000 wires at $.05 each

For the purposes of this job, the dials and wires are considered to be indirect materials.

For the duration of Job 821, 3 permanent employees worked a total of 180 hours at a rate of $9.25 per hour. Any hours in excess of 40 per worker is overtime and is to be paid at 1½ times the normal hourly rate.

In addition, 5 employees worked 20 hours each on Job 821, at an hourly rate of $5.85.

Salaries for supervisors and repair personnel amounted to $550 for the job.

Factory overhead is applied on a basis of $1.25 per direct labor hour.

The radios were sold for $15 each, and selling and administrative expenses were 2% of total sales. The company uses a perpetual cost accumulation system.

REQUIRED:

a Journalize the above transactions.

b Prepare a job order cost sheet for Job 821.

c Prepare journal entries to transfer the goods from work-in-process to finished goods, and to record the sale and delivery of the merchandise.

PROBLEM 6

Journalizing, Posting, and Preparation of Trial Balance

Shamrock, Inc., entered into the following transactions during May of 19XX:

1 Purchased materials on account for $56,000. Assume no beginning inventories.

2 Job 67 requisitioned direct materials of $32,000 and supplies of $6,000.

3 Job 67 incurred labor costs of $4,400 for direct labor and $1,200 for supervision.

4 Rent of $2,000 was accrued but not paid. Depreciation was $800 on the building and $1,750 on the equipment.

5 Factory overhead was applied at a rate of 75% of direct labor dollars.

6 Goods costing $30,000 were transferred to finished goods and then sold on account for $40,000. The company uses a perpetual cost accumulation system.

REQUIRED:

a Journalize the above transactions, and post them to T accounts.

b Prepare a trial balance for May 19XX.

PROBLEM 7

Job Order Cost Sheet

Steinwin Corporation produces high-quality pianos. Work is completed in one department, production. The following transactions occurred relative to Job 491:

1 Purchased for cash and requisitioned Job No. 26 on June 14, 19XX:

          50 lb of oak at $12.00 per pound

          600 lb of ivory at $6.50 per pound

          100 ft of string at $2.60 per foot

2 Accounted for the following labor costs on June 18, 19XX: 100 hours of direct labor, 60% of which was paid $7.75 per hour. The remaining hours were paid at $6.35 per hour. Supervision costs amounted to $895.

3 Utility costs for the job were $605

   Depreciation on machinery was $715

   Miscellaneous expenses totaled $545

4 Factory overhead is applied on the basis of 110% of direct labor cost.

5 On June 21, 19XX, as a result of a breakdown in the production department,

three pianos were considered to be defective. Normal rework costs amounted to $640 for direct materials and $1,175 for direct labor. In addition, 10% of the ivory was wasted. It cost $230 in cash to remove the materials from the factory.

6 At the completion of the job, the units were transferred to finished goods. The following week, they were sold for $12,000. Fifty percent of the sales price was paid in cash, the rest by a 30-day note.

REQUIRED:

a Journal entries reflecting the above transactions. The company uses a perpetual cost accumulation system.

b A job order cost sheet for Job 491, assuming that selling and administrative expenses equal 5% of sales. The 10 pianos were sold to the Sharp School of Music, which ordered the pianos on June 14, 19XX, the day that work was begun. Work was completed on June 21, 19XX, and the goods were to be delivered on that day.

PROBLEM 8

Cost of Goods Manufactured Statement

The Helper Corporation manufactures one product and accounts for costs by a job order cost system. You have obtained the following information for the year ended December 31, 19X3, from the corporation's books and records:

1 Total manufacturing cost added during 19X3 (sometimes called cost to manufacture) was $1,000,000 based on actual direct material, actual direct labor, and applied factory overhead on actual direct labor dollars.

2 Cost of goods manufactured was $970,000 also based on actual direct material, actual direct labor, and applied factory overhead.

3 Factory overhead was applied to work-in-process at 75% of direct labor dollars. Applied factory overhead for the year was 27% of the total manufacturing cost.

4 Beginning work-in-process inventory, January 1, was 80% of ending work-in-process inventory, December 31.

REQUIRED:

Prepare a formal statement of cost of goods manufactured for the year ended December 31, 19X3, for Helper Corporation. Use actual direct material used, actual direct labor, and applied factory overhead. Show supporting computations in good form.

(AICPA Adapted)

CHAPTER EIGHT

THE NATURE AND CHARACTERISTICS OF A PROCESS COST SYSTEM— THE BASICS

The design of a cost accumulation system must be compatible with the nature and type of operations performed in a manufacturing company. When the products are manufactured through mass production or continuous process, a process cost system is usually appropriate. Examples of industries using process cost systems are paper, steel, chemical, and textile.

This chapter will introduce process costing and present the basic procedures used in a process cost system.

PROCESS COSTING

Process costing is a system of accumulating costs of production by department or cost center. A department is a major functional division in a factory where related manufacturing processes are performed. When two or more processes are performed within a department, it may be desirable to further divide the departmental unit into cost centers. Each process would be designated a cost center and costs would be accumulated by cost centers instead of departments. For example, the "assembly" department of an electronics manufacturing company may be divided into the following cost centers: materials setup, wiring, and soldering. Departments, or cost centers, are responsible for costs incurred within their area and their supervisors must account to management for the costs incurred by periodically preparing a cost of production report. This report is a detailed record of the unit and cost activities in each department, or cost center, during a period.

OBJECTIVES OF
PROCESS COSTING

A process cost system determines how manufacturing costs incurred during each period will be allocated. The allocation of costs within a department is only an intermediate step, and the ultimate goal is to compute total unit cost for income determination. During a period, some units will be started but will not be completed by the end of that period. Consequently, each department must determine how much of the total costs incurred by the department is attributed to units still in process and how much to the completed units. For example, assume that during January, 2,000 units were put into process in Department A. During the month, costs incurred were as follows: materials—$2,000, labor—$1,000, and factory overhead—$500. At the end of the month, 1,000 units were completed and transferred to Department B.

The objective of a process cost system is to determine how much of the $2,000 materials, $1,000 labor, and $500 factory overhead costs applies to the 1,000 units completed and transferred, and how much applies to the 1,000 units still in process. A cost of production report is prepared for each department to illustrate this allocation. A detailed discussion of this report will be presented later in this chapter.

CHARACTERISTICS OF
A PROCESS COST SYSTEM

Process costing deals with the flow of units through several operations or departments acquiring additional costs as they progress. Unit costs for each department are based on the relationship between costs incurred over a period of time and units completed over the identical period.

A process cost system has the following characteristics:

1 Costs are accumulated and recorded by department or cost center.
2 Each department has its own general ledger work-in-process account. This account is charged with the processing costs incurred by the department.
3 Equivalent units are used to restate work-in-process in terms of completed units at the end of a period.
4 Unit costs are determined by department for each period.
5 Completed units and their corresponding costs are transferred to the next department or to finished goods. By the time units leave the last processing department, total costs for the period have been accumulated and can be used to determine finished goods unit cost.

6   Total cost and unit costs for each department are periodically aggregated, analyzed, and calculated through the use of departmental cost of production reports.

PRODUCTION BY DEPARTMENT

In a process cost system, major emphasis is placed on departments, or cost centers. Different processes or functions, such as mixing in Department A or refining in Department B, are performed in each department, or cost center. A product generally flows through two or more such departments, or cost centers, before it reaches the finished goods storeroom.

Materials, labor, and factory overhead costs for each department are charged to separate work-in-process accounts. When units are completed in one department, they are transferred to the next processing department accompanied by their corresponding costs. The completed unit of one department becomes the raw material of the next until the units reach finished goods. The cost per unit generally increases as goods flow through each department. The departmental handling of production costs is illustrated in the following example:

The Moonglow Company manufactures Product Z, which requires processing in Departments A and B. During February 19X1, 4,500 units were placed in production and completed during the month. The costs were as follows: materials—$9,000, labor—$7,875, and factory overhead—$5,625. The computations are as follows:

WORK-IN-PROCESS—DEPARTMENT A

	TOTAL COST	UNIT COST	COMPUTATIONS OF UNIT COST
Materials placed in production	$ 9,000	$2.00	($9,000 ÷ 4,500)
Labor	7,875	1.75	($7,875 ÷ 4,500)
Factory overhead	5,625	1.25	($5,625 ÷ 4,500)
Total	$22,500	$5.00	

The unit cost is determined by dividing total cost by the number of completed units. Since the 4,500 units started were completed, they are transferred to Department B. In this example, there were no units still in process at the beginning or end of the period; additional evaluations and computations would have been necessary to allocate costs to those units in process and those transferred to the next department.

At the end of the period, a cost of production report is prepared for each department. The report (which is explained later in this chapter) is used in the calculation of total and unit costs.

SYSTEM FLOW

Units and costs flow through a process cost system together. The following equation summarizes the *physical* flow of units in a department.

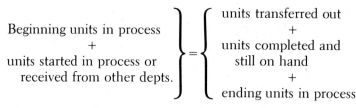

$$
\left.\begin{array}{c}
\text{Beginning units in process} \\
+ \\
\text{units started in process or} \\
\text{received from other depts.}
\end{array}\right\} = \left\{\begin{array}{c}
\text{units transferred out} \\
+ \\
\text{units completed and} \\
\text{still on hand} \\
+ \\
\text{ending units in process}
\end{array}\right.
$$

This equation illustrates how units received, or started, must be accounted for in a department. A department need not have all components of the equation. If all completed units are transferred out, there will be no "units still on hand." If all but one of the components are known, the missing component can be computed. The following example illustrates the flow of units within a department.

The Vinjoan Company had in Department A 2,000 units in process at the beginning of the month, placed 6,000 units into process during the month, and had 3,000 units in process at the end of the month. *All* completed units were transferred to Department B. By placing all known figures in the equation, the unknown component (units transferred out) can be found.

$$
\left.\begin{array}{lr}
\text{Beginning units in process} & 2,000 \\
+ & \\
\text{units started in process} & 6,000 \\
\end{array}\right\} = \left\{\begin{array}{ll}
? & \text{units transferred out} \\
+ & \\
3,000 & \text{ending units in process}
\end{array}\right.
$$

$$
\begin{array}{rcl}
8,000 & = & 3,000 + ? \\
8,000 - 3,000 & = & ? \\
5,000 & = & ? \quad \text{units transferred to} \\
& & \text{Department B}
\end{array}
$$

The input and output of costs is reflected in the departmental work-in-process account. Work-in-process is debited for production costs (materials, labor, factory overhead) and transferred-in costs. When completed units are transferred out, work-in-process is credited for the costs associated with these completed units.

A product may flow through a factory in different ways on route to completion. The most common product flows are sequential, parallel, and selective. The same process cost system can be used for all product flows.

In a *sequential* product flow, the initial raw materials are placed into process in the first department and flow through every department in the factory; additional materials may or may not be added in the other departments. All items produced go through the same processes in the same sequence.

A graphic presentation of *sequential* product flow is presented in Figure 8-1.

In a *parallel* product flow, the initial raw material is added during different processes, beginning in different departments, and then joining in a final process or processes. A graphic presentation of *parallel* product flow appears in Figure 8-2.

In the *selective* product flow, several products are produced from the initial raw materials. The finished product is determined by the processes which it

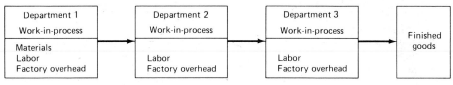

FIGURE 8-1 **Sequential Product Flow**

undergoes. Each process will yield a different finished product. A graphic presentation of selected product flow appears in Figure 8-3 (page 254).

PROCEDURES—MATERIALS, LABOR, AND FACTORY OVERHEAD

The use of a process cost system does not alter the manner of *accumulating* materials, labor, and factory overhead costs. The normal procedures of cost accounting are used to accumulate the three cost elements. Process costing is concerned, however, with the *allocation* of these costs to the appropriate departmental work-in-process accounts.

Materials

The journal entry to record the use of $10,000 of materials by Department A during the period is as follows:

Work-in-process—Department A 10,000
    Materials   10,000

Most often materials are added only in the first processing department, but occasionally, materials are added in other departments. The journal entry would be the same for adding materials in the later processing departments.

FIGURE 8-2 **Parallel Product Flow**

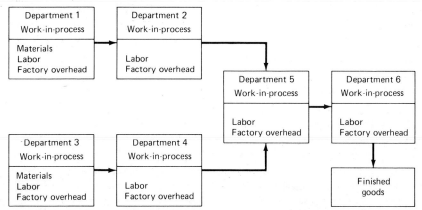

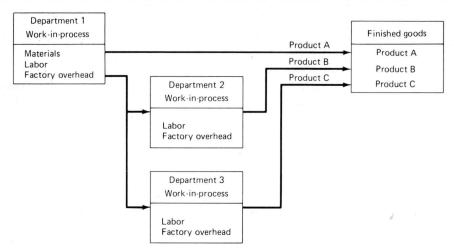

FIGURE 8-3 **Selected Product Flow**

The cost of materials to be charged can be obtained by various methods: (1) Individual materials requisitions can be issued to the department; thus, the total of all materials requisitions will be the total materials cost. (2) The cost of materials used can be determined by adding purchases to beginning inventory, and subtracting the ending inventory. The difference is materials consumed. (3) When there is continuous use of identical materials, the usage each day or week can be obtained from consumption reports. (4) In some industries, such as pharmaceuticals and engineering concerns, specifications or formulas can be used to determine type and quantity of materials used. It should be noted, however, that the method of computing materials cost does not affect the journal entry to record the cost of materials in the work-in-process account.

The accumulation of materials costs is much simpler in a process cost system than a job order cost system. Process costing generally requires fewer journal entries. The number of departments using materials is usually less than the number of jobs requiring materials in a job order cost system. One journal entry at the end of the month for each department is often all that is necessary under process costing.

Labor

The entry to distribute manufacturing labor costs of Department A—$5,000, Department B—$6,200, and Department C—$4,800, is as follows:

Work-in-process—Department A	5,000	
Work-in-process—Department B	6,200	
Work-in-process—Department C	4,800	
Payroll		16,000

The amounts to be charged to each department are determined by the *gross* earnings of the employees assigned to each department. If John Jones works in Department B, his gross salary is charged to Department B. Under a job order cost system, Jones' salary would have to be distributed among all the jobs he worked on. Process costing reduces the amount of paper work needed to assign labor costs. As with materials costs, there is no need to distinguish between direct and indirect cost components.

Factory Overhead

In a process cost system, factory overhead costs may be applied using either of the following two methods. The first method, which is also common in job order costing, applies factory overhead to work-in-process at a *predetermined rate*. This rate is expressed in terms of some form of production activity (for example, 150% of labor costs). The actual factory overhead expenses are accumulated in a Factory Overhead Control account. A subsidiary ledger is maintained to record in greater detail the actual factory overhead costs incurred by each department. When the amount to be applied has been computed, and assuming a rate of 150% of the previous example's labor cost; the following entry is made:

Work-in-process—Department A	7,500	
Work-in-process—Department B	9,300	
Work-in-process—Department C	7,200	
Factory Overhead Control		24,000

A predetermined factory overhead rate is appropriate when production volume or factory overhead expenses fluctuate substantially from month to month. The use of predetermined rates thereby eliminates distortions in monthly unit costs caused by such fluctuations.

The second method applies *actual* factory expenses incurred to work-in-process. This method is appropriate when production volume and factory overhead costs remain relatively constant from month to month. In a process cost system where there is continuous production, either method may be used.

The total factory overhead costs for the month include direct costs applied by either of the two methods and service department costs allocated to producing departments or cost centers.

THE COST OF PRODUCTION REPORT

The cost of production report is an analysis of the activity in the department or cost center for the period. All costs chargeable to a department or cost center are presented according to cost elements.

In addition to total and unit costs, each cost element may be listed separately, either on the report or on a supporting schedule. The amount of detail depends on the needs and desires of management. The cost of production report is often the source for summary journal entries for the period.

The cost of production report generally contains the following three schedules:

1 Quantities (unit input and output)
2 Costs to account for (cost input)
3 Costs accounted for (cost output)

These schedules and computations are illustrated in the cost of production reports of the King Company, which manufactures a product in two departments. The following data relates to King Company production for January 19XX:

	DEPARTMENT A	DEPARTMENT B
Units:		
Started in process	60,000	
Received from Department A		46,000
Transferred to Department B	46,000	
Transferred to finished goods		40,000
Ending units in process:		
Department A—all materials, ²/₅ labor and factory overhead complete	14,000	
Department B—all materials, ¹/₃ labor and factory overhead complete		6,000
Costs:		
Materials	$31,200	0
Labor	36,120	$35,700
Overhead	34,572	31,920

Quantities

This section accounts for the *physical flow of units* into and out of departments. The quantity schedules of the King Company are shown below.

DEPARTMENT A

Units started in process		60,000
Units transferred to next department	46,000	
Ending units in process	14,000	60,000

DEPARTMENT B

Units received from preceding department		46,000
Units transferred to finished goods....................	40,000	
Ending units in process	6,000	46,000

From the quantities schedule, it can be seen that the King Company placed 60,000 units into process in Department A during the month. The quantity schedule for Department A accounts for the distribution of these units by showing the quantity completed and transferred, and the quantity still in process. Of the 46,000 units received by Department B, 40,000 units were completed and transferred to finished goods, while 6,000 units are still in process. It should be noted that units must be expressed in the same denomination as the finished product. For example, if raw materials are added in quarts and the finished product is in gallons, the quantity schedule should state units in terms of gallons.

Equivalent Production (Units). The concept of equivalent production is basic to process costing. In most cases, all units are not completed during the period. Thus, there are units which are still in process at varying stages of completion. All units must be expressed in terms of completed units to determine unit costs. Equivalent production is the restatement of incomplete units in terms of completed units.

Because the degree of completion for materials and conversion costs (labor and factory overhead) are rarely the same, two separate equivalent production computations are needed. Materials are generally added at one specific point in production, such as at the beginning or at the end of the process. If materials are added at the beginning, all work-in-process units will have complete materials costs (100% of materials cost). Labor and factory overhead costs are usually assumed to be applied evenly throughout the process. For example, equivalent units for Departments A and B of King Company are computed as follows:

	DEPARTMENT A	DEPARTMENT B
Materials:		
Units completed and transferred to:		
Department B	46,000	
Finished goods		40,000
Ending units in process:		
14,000 × 100%	14,000	
6,000 × 100%		6,000
Equivalent units for materials	60,000	46,000
Conversion costs:		
Units completed and transferred to:		
Department B	46,000	
Finished goods		40,000
Ending units in process:		
14,000 × $^2/_5$ complete	5,600	
6,000 × $^1/_3$ complete		2,000
Equivalent units for conversion costs	51,600	42,000

The total equivalent units of production for each cost element is found by adding the number of completed units to the work-in-process equivalent units. The units in process are restated as equivalent units by multiplying units in process by the percentage of completion. The equivalent units of production are then used in the computation of unit cost.

Costs to Account For

This section of the cost of production report shows which costs were accumulated by the department. These costs may be transferred in during the period, and/or added by the department during the period. Unit costs, broken down by elements, are also presented in this section. Unit cost computations for the first processing department are as follows:

(1) Materials unit cost $= \dfrac{\text{materials cost added during the period}}{\text{equivalent units for materials}}$

(2) Labor unit cost $= \dfrac{\text{labor cost added during the period}}{\text{equivalent units for labor}}$

(3) Overhead unit cost $= \dfrac{\text{overhead cost added during the period}}{\text{equivalent units for overhead}}$

(4) Total unit cost $= (1) + (2) + (3)$

Unit cost calculations for subsequent departments are computed as follows:

Cost from Preceding Department:

(1) Transferred-in unit cost $= \dfrac{\text{transferred-in cost for units transferred in during the period}}{\text{total units in the department}}$

Cost from This Department:

(2) Materials unit cost $= \dfrac{\text{materials cost added during the period}}{\text{equivalent units for materials}}$

(3) Labor unit cost $= \dfrac{\text{labor cost added during the period}}{\text{equivalent units for labor}}$

(4) Overhead unit cost $= \dfrac{\text{overhead cost added during the period}}{\text{equivalent units for overhead}}$

(5) Total unit cost $= (1) + (2) + (3) + (4)$

The "Costs to Account For" schedule of the King Company's cost of production report is presented on page 259:

COSTS TO ACCOUNT FOR

DEPARTMENT A

	TOTAL COST	UNIT COST
Costs added by department:		
Materials	$ 31,200	$ .52 (A)
Labor	36,120	.70 (B)
Overhead	34,572	.67 (C)
Total cost to account for	$101,892	$1.89

DEPARTMENT B

	TOTAL COST	UNIT COST
Cost from preceding department:		
Transferred in	$ 86,940 (D)	$1.89 (E)
Costs added by department:		
Labor	$ 35,700	$ .85 (F)
Overhead	31,920	.76 (G)
Total costs added	$ 67,620	$1.61
Total costs to account for	$154,560	$3.50

Computations of unit cost:
(A) $31,200 ÷ 60,000 = $.52
(B) $36,120 ÷ 51,600* = $.70
(C) $34,572 ÷ 51,600 = $.67
(D) 46,000 × $1.89 = $86,940
(E) $86,940 ÷ 46,000 = $1.89
(F) $35,700 ÷ 42,000† = $.85
(G) $31,920 ÷ 42,000 = $.76

* 46,000 + 5,600 (14,000 × $2/5$)
† 40,000 + 2,000 (6,000 × $1/3$)

Department A, which is the first processing department, must only account for costs it added. Department B must account for the costs it added plus those transferred in from Department A. The transferred-in costs of Department B must be equal to the transferred-out costs of Department A.

During the month, it cost $1.89 to produce a completed unit in Department A and $3.50 in Department B. In Department A, it took $31,200 in material costs to complete 60,000 units, $36,120 in labor costs to complete 51,600 equivalent units, and $34,572 of factory overhead to complete 51,600 equivalent units. In Department B, it required $35,700 of labor costs and $31,920 of factory overhead costs to complete 42,000 equivalent units [40,000 units transferred to finished goods + 2,000 (6,000 × $1/3$ still in process)].

Costs Accounted For

This section of the cost of production report illustrates the distribution of accumulated costs to units still in process, units completed and still on hand, and/or units transferred to another department or to finished goods. The total

Costs to Account For section must equal the total Costs Accounted For section.

The costs of the King Company for the month are accounted for in the cost of production report as follows:

COSTS ACCOUNTED FOR		
DEPARTMENT A		
Transferred to next department		
(46,000 × $1.89)		$ 86,940
Work-in-process—ending:		
Materials (14,000 × $.52)	$7,280	
Labor (14,000 × 2/5 × $.70)	3,920	
Overhead (14,000 × 2/5 × $.67)	3,752	14,952
Total costs accounted for		$101,892

DEPARTMENT B		
Transferred to finished goods		
(40,000 × $3.50)		$140,000
Work-in-process—ending:		
Costs from preceding department		
(6,000 × $1.89)	$11,340	
Labor (6,000 × 1/3 × $.85)	1,700	
Overhead (6,000 × 1/3 × $.76)	1,520	14,560
Total costs accounted for		$154,560

The transferred-out cost figure is equal to the number of completed units multiplied by the completed unit cost. Additional computations are required to determine ending work-in-process. In Department A, the units still in process have received all their materials but only 2/5 of their conversion costs. The labor and factory overhead *unit costs* are expressed in terms of cost per completed units. The 14,000 units still in process must therefore be expressed in completed units or equivalent production. This is derived by multiplying the units in process by the degree of completion (14,000 × 2/5 completed = 5,600). The equivalent production is then multiplied by the unit cost for each cost element.

In computing the work-in-process costs for Department B, it is necessary to include the costs from the preceding department. To calculate the cost from the preceding department for ending work-in-process, the number of units in process are multiplied by the transferred-in unit cost. The same computations as applied in Department A are used to determine labor and factory overhead costs. The work-in-process units are multiplied by the percentage of completion [to arrive at equivalent production of 2,000 (6,000 × 1/3)] and then multiplied by the unit cost for each cost element.

The cost of production report for each department may be combined or presented separately. Illustrated in Table 8-1 is the combined cost of production report for the King Company with journal entries for Department A and B for the month, and a diagram of the flow of costs using T accounts.

TABLE 8-1
KING COMPANY
COST OF PRODUCTION REPORT
MONTH OF JANUARY 19XX

	DEPARTMENT A		DEPARTMENT B	
Quantities:				
Units started in process	60,000			
Units received from preceding department				46,000
Units transferred to next department	46,000			
Units transferred to finished goods			40,000	
Ending units in process	14,000	60,000	6,000	46,000
	TOTAL COST	UNIT COST	TOTAL COST	UNIT COST
Costs to Account For:				
Costs from preceding department:				
Transferred in during the month			$ 86,940	$ 1.89 (D)
Costs added by department:				
Materials	$ 31,200	$ .52 (A)		
Labor	36,120	.70 (B)	$ 35,700	$ .85 (E)
Overhead	34,572	.67 (C)	31,920	.76 (F)
Total cost added	$101,892	$ 1.89	$ 67,620	$ 1.61
Total cost to account for	$101,892	$ 1.89	$154,560	$ 3.50
Costs Accounted For:				
Transferred to next department		$ 86,940 (G)		
Transferred to finished goods				$140,000 (K)
Work-in-process—ending:				
Costs from preceding department			$ 11,340 (L)	
Materials	$ 7,280 (H)			
Labor	3,920 (I)		1,700 (M)	
Overhead	3,752 (J)	14,952	1,520 (N)	14,560
Total costs accounted for		$101,892		$154,560

Computations of unit cost:

(A) $31,200 ÷ 60,000 = $.52
(B) $36,120 ÷ 51,600 = $.70
(C) $34,572 ÷ 51,600 = $.67
(D) $86,940 ÷ 46,000 = $1.89
(E) $35,700 ÷ 42,000 = $.85
(F) $31,920 ÷ 42,000 = $.76
(G) 46,000 × $1.89 = $86,940

(H) 14,000 × $.52 = $7,280
(I) 14,000 × $^2/_5$ × $.70 = $3,920
(J) 14,000 × $^2/_5$ × $.67 = $3,752
(K) 40,000 × $3.50 = $140,000
(L) 6,000 × $1.89 = $11,340
(M) 6,000 × $^1/_3$ × $.85 = $1,700
(N) 6,000 × $^1/_3$ × $.76 = $1,520

TABLE 8-1 (Continued)
JOURNAL ENTRIES FOR KING COMPANY

Department A:

1. Work-in-process—Department A   101,892
        Materials   31,200
        Payroll   36,120
        Overhead   34,572
    Costs added by Department A

2. Work-in-process—Department B   86,940
        Work-in-process—Department A   86,940
    To transfer costs of completed goods to Department B

Department B:

3. Work-in-process—Department B   67,620
        Payroll   35,700
        Overhead   31,920
    Costs added by Department B

4. Finished goods   140,000
        Work-in-process—Department B   140,000
    To transfer costs of completed goods to finished goods
        inventory

FLOW OF COSTS

DEPARTMENT A WORK-IN-PROCESS		DEPARTMENT B WORK-IN-PROCESS	
Costs added by dept. (*entry 1*) $101,892		Costs added by dept. (*entry 3*) $67,620	
	$86,940	Trans. to Dept. B (*entry 2*) → 86,940	$140,000 Trans. to finished Goods (*entry 4*)
Ending balance (same as on Costs Accounted For Schedule) $ 14,952		Ending balance (same as on Costs Accounted For schedule) $14,560	

MATERIALS ADDED AFTER THE FIRST DEPARTMENT

Many manufacturing operations require raw materials only in the initial processing department; subsequent departments generally add labor and factory overhead (conversion costs), but no additional materials. Some manufacturing operations, however, call for the addition of materials in subsequent departments. Materials added after the first department may have the following effects on units and costs:

1   No increase in units but cost increases (for example, adding tires to the production of an automobile).

2 Increase in units with no increase in cost (for example, adding water when producing latex paint if a company is not charged for the water they use).

3 Increase in units and in cost (for example, adding sugar when producing a beverage drink).

In situation 1, the subsequent department is usually adding an additional component that becomes part of the unit. The *number* of units remains unchanged; total and unit *costs increase*. A variation of a previous example will be used to illustrate this situation. Refer to the King Company example and assume the following information for Department B:

Units:

Received from Department A	46,000
Units transferred to finished goods	40,000
Ending units in process (all materials, $1/3$ labor and	
factory overhead complete)	6,000

Costs:

Transferred in from Department A	$86,940
Materials added this period (beginning of the process)	20,700
Labor added this period	35,700
Overhead added this period	31,920

Note that the information above is identical to the previous data assumed for Department B of the King Company except that it is now assumed that materials costing $20,700 were added with no additional increase in units. An analysis of the effects on the cost of production report follows.

Quantity Schedule

The quantity schedule for Department B does not change in this situation because the number of units in the department did not increase. The quantity schedule for Department B would appear as follows:

Units received from preceding department		46,000
Units transferred to finished goods	40,000	
Ending units in process	6,000	46,000

Costs to Account For Schedule

Department B is charged for the additional materials used. Therefore, total costs for Department B increase by $20,700 (from $154,560 to $175,260) and the unit cost increases by $.45 (from $3.50 to $3.95). Equivalent units of production for materials must also be calculated. Since materials are added at the beginning of the process, the total cost and unit cost increases as additional materials costs were added but no additional units were added. Materials cost is the only item different in this schedule as compared with the schedule in the previous example. The cost to account for schedule for Department B would appear as follows:

	TOTAL COST	UNIT COST
Costs from preceding department:		
Transferred in during the month	$ 86,940	$1.89 (A)
Costs added by department:		
Materials	$ 20,700	$ .45 (B)
Labor	35,700	.85 (C)
Overhead	31,920	.76 (D)
Total costs added	$ 88,320	$2.06
Total costs to account for	$175,260	$3.95

Computations of unit cost:
(A) $86,940 ÷ 46,000 = $1.89
(B) $20,700 ÷ 46,000 = $.45
(C) $35,700 ÷ 42,000 = $.85
(D) $31,920 ÷ 42,000 = $.76

Costs Accounted For Schedule

The procedures used to prepare this schedule do not change; costs are still accounted for in the manner previously discussed. The addition of materials increased only the amount of costs to be accounted for. The costs accounted for schedule for Department B would appear as follows:

Transferred to finished goods ($3.95 × 40,000)		$158,000
Work-in-process—ending:		
Transferred-in costs (6,000 × $1.89)....................	$11,340	
Materials (6,000 × 100% × $.45)	2,700	
Labor (6,000 × 1/3 × $.85)	1,700	
Overhead (6,000 × 1/3 × $.76)........................	1,520	17,260
Total costs accounted for		$175,260

A comparison of the cost of production report for Department B with no materials added (previous example) to that with materials added for the King Company (current example) is shown in Table 8-2. This comparison illustrates that the addition of materials affects both total cost and unit cost while the number of units remains the same.

In manufacturing processes that use weight or volume to measure units of production, the addition of materials in subsequent departments will have the effect of increasing the number of units and possibly total costs. Assume a product is measured in gallons (volume); Department A places 6,000 gallons into process and during the month transfers all 6,000 gallons to Department B. If Department B adds 2,000 gallons of another ingredient, the department is now responsible for 8,000 gallons (units). Depending on whether the added

TABLE 8-2
KING COMPANY
COMPARATIVE COST OF PRODUCTION REPORT
DEPARTMENT B
MONTH OF JANUARY, 19XX

	COST OF PRODUCTION REPORT (NO MATERIALS ADDED)		COST OF PRODUCTION REPORT (MATERIALS ADDED)	
Quantities:				
Units received from preceding department		46,000		46,000
Units transferred to finished goods	40,000		40,000	
Ending units in process	6,000	46,000	6,000	46,000
	TOTAL COST	UNIT COST	TOTAL COST	UNIT COST
Costs to Account For:				
Costs from preceding department:				
Transferred in during month	$ 86,940	$ 1.89 (A)	$ 86,940	$ 1.89 (A)
Costs added by department:				
Materials			$ 20,700	$ .45 (B)
Labor	$ 35,700	$ .85 (C)	35,700	.85 (C)
Overhead	31,920	.76 (D)	31,920	.76 (D)
Total cost added	$ 67,620	$ 1.61	$ 88,320	$ 2.06
Total cost to account for	$154,560	$ 3.50	$175,260	$ 3.95
Costs Accounted For:				
Transferred to finished goods		$140,000 (E)		$158,000 (I)
Work-in-process—ending:				
Costs from preceding department	$ 11,340 (F)		$ 11,340 (F)	
Materials			2,700 (J)	
Labor	1,700 (G)		1,700 (G)	
Overhead	1,520 (H)	14,560	1,520 (H)	17,260
Total costs accounted for		$154,560		$175,260

Computations of unit costs:
(A) $86,940 ÷ 46,000 = $1.89
(B) $20,700 ÷ 46,000 = $.45
(C) $35,700 ÷ 42,000 = $.85
(D) $31,920 ÷ 42,000 = $.76
(E) 40,000 × $3.50 = $140,000

(F) 6,000 × $1.89 = $11,340
(G) 6,000 × 1/3 × $.85 = $1,700
(H) 6,000 × 1/3 × $.76 = $1,520
(I) 40,000 × $3.95 = $158,000
(J) 6,000 × 100% × $.45 = $2,700

ingredient has a cost, the total cost and unit cost might also be increased. The following information will be used to illustrate a cost of production report where the addition of materials increases the number of units after the first department. Assume that the Juicy Apple Drink Company has the following two departments:

> Department 1—removes juice from apples.
> Department 2—adds sugar and water and packages the juice into plastic quart containers.

The following unit and cost data pertains to Departments 1 and 2:

	DEPARTMENT	
	1	2
Units (quarts):		
Started in process during the period	50,000	
Units transferred to Department 2	40,000	
Units added to production		10,000
Transferred to finished goods		45,000
Ending units in process:		
All materials, 20% complete as to		
conversion costs	10,000	
All materials, 70% complete as to		
conversion costs		5,000
Costs:		
Materials	$150,000	$60,000
Labor	84,000	48,500
Overhead	42,000	24,250

Table 8-3 shows the cost of production report for Department 1. The effect on the cost of production report when materials are added after the first department is presented in the following paragraphs.

Quantity Schedule

The basic physical flow equation introduced earlier must now be modified when additional materials cause units to increase after the first department. An additional line called "units added to production" must now be included in the quantity schedule. For subsequent departments, the modified equation would appear as follows:

$$\left.\begin{array}{c}\text{Beginning units in process}\\ +\\ \text{units started in process or received from other departments}\\ +\\ \text{units added to production}\end{array}\right\} = \left\{\begin{array}{c}\text{units transferred out}\\ +\\ \text{units completed and still on hand}\\ +\\ \text{ending units in process}\end{array}\right.$$

TABLE 8-3
JUICY APPLE DRINK COMPANY
COST OF PRODUCTION REPORT
DEPARTMENT 1

Quantities:

Units started in process		50,000
Units transferred to next department	40,000	
Ending units in process	10,000	50,000

	TOTAL COST	UNIT COST
Costs to Account For:		
Costs added by department:		
Materials	$150,000	$ 3.00 (A)
Labor	84,000	2.00 (B)
Overhead	42,000	1.00 (C)
Total costs to account for	$276,000	$ 6.00

Costs Accounted For:		
Transferred to next department:		
(40,000 × $6.00)		$240,000
Work-in-process—ending:		
Materials (10,000 × $3.00)	$30,000	
Labor (10,000 × $2.00 × 20%)	4,000	
Overhead (10,000 × $1.00 × 20%)	2,000	36,000
Total costs accounted for		$276,000

EQUIVALENT PRODUCTION	MATERIALS	CONVERSION COSTS
Units completed and transferred to Department 2	40,000	40,000
+ Ending units in process	10,000	2,000 (10,000 × 20%)
Equivalent production	50,000	42,000

Computations of unit cost:
(A) $150,000 ÷ 50,000 = $3.00
(B) $84,000 ÷ 42,000 = $2.00
(C) $42,000 ÷ 42,000 = $1.00

The quantity schedule for Department 2 would appear as follows:

Quantities:

Units transferred in	40,000	
Units added to production	10,000	50,000
Units transferred to finished goods	45,000	
Ending units in process	5,000	50,000

Department 2 has an additional line, "units added to production," in its quantity schedule which is an input component. Department 2 must now account for 50,000 units, rather than the 40,000 units transferred in. The technique of computing equivalent production remains the same because it is based on output expressed as completed units. The addition of units to production affects only units of input.

Costs to Account For Schedule

Units added in subsequent departments affect the costs to account for schedule as to transferred-in costs. Transferred-in costs from the previous department are now being spread over more units. All units in subsequent departments are considered to be complete as to the previous department's costs. Therefore, the $240,000 of cost from Department 1 must be allocated to the 50,000 units now in Department 2. Whenever a subsequent department increases the units in process by the addition of materials, the transferred-in unit cost will be *decreased* because a fixed amount of cost is being spread over a larger number of units. The unit cost transferred in from Department 1 is $6.00; however, the addition of 10,000 units in Department 2 decreases the unit cost to $4.80 ($240,000 ÷ 50,000).

There is no change in the procedure for handling costs added by the department. In this example, the materials added also increased the department's costs. However, this is not always true. If the materials added have no significant cost (such as water), the department would not be charged an additional cost, and the unit cost would decrease (total cost would be spread over more units).

The costs to account for schedule for Department 2 would appear as follows:

	UNITS	TOTAL COST	UNIT COST
Costs to Account For:			
Costs from preceding department	40,000	$240,000	$6.00
Units added to production	10,000		
Adjusted units and unit cost	50,000		$4.80 (A)
Costs added by department:			
Materials		$ 60,000	$1.20 (B)
Labor		48,500	1.00 (C)
Overhead		24,250	.50 (D)
Total costs added		$132,750	$2.70
Total costs to account for		$372,750	$7.50

Computations of unit cost:
(A) $240,000 ÷ 50,000* = $4.80
(B) $60,000 ÷ 50,000 = $1.20
(C) $48,500 ÷ 48,500† = $1.00
(D) $24,250 ÷ 48,500 = $.50

* 45,000 + 5,000
† 45,000 + 3,500 (5,000 × 70%)

Costs Accounted For Schedule

Costs are accounted for in the same manner discussed in previous examples.

Illustrated in Table 8-4 are the cost of production reports for Departments 1 and 2 of the Juicy Apple Drink Company and the appropriate journal entries.

TABLE 8-4
JUICY APPLE DRINK COMPANY
COST OF PRODUCTION REPORT
DEPARTMENT 2

Quantities			
Units transferred in		40,000	
Units added to production		10,000	50,000
Units transferred to finished goods		45,000	
Ending units in process		5,000	50,000

	UNITS	TOTAL COST	UNIT COST
Costs to Account For:			
Cost from preceding department	40,000	$240,000	$ 6.00
Units added to production	10,000		
Adjusted units and unit cost	50,000		$ 4.80 (A)
Costs added by department:			
Materials		$ 60,000	1.20 (B)
Labor		48,500	1.00 (C)
Overhead		24,250	.50 (D)
Total costs added		$132,750	$ 2.70
Total costs to account for		$372,750	$ 7.50
Costs Accounted For:			
Transferred to finished goods (45,000 × $7.50)		$337,500	
Work-in-process—ending:			
Costs from preceding			
department (5,000 × $4.80)	$24,000		
Materials (5,000 × $1.20)	6,000		
Labor (5,000 × $1.00 × 70%)	3,500		
Overhead (5,000 × $.50 × 70%)	1,750	35,250	
Total costs accounted for		$372,750	

EQUIVALENT PRODUCTION	MATERIALS	CONVERSION COSTS
Units completed and transferred to finished goods	45,000	45,000
+ Ending units in process	5,000	3,500 (5,000 × 70%)
Equivalent production	50,000	48,500

Computations of unit cost:
(A) $240,000 ÷ 50,000 = $4.80
(B) $60,000 ÷ 50,000 = $1.20
(C) $48,500 ÷ 48,500 = $1.00
(D) $24,250 ÷ 48,500 = $.50

JOURNAL ENTRIES FOR JUICY APPLE DRINK COMPANY

Work-in-process—Department 1 ($150,000 + $84,000 + $42,000)	276,000	
Work-in-process—Department 2 ($60,000 + $48,500 + $24,250)	132,750	
Materials ($150,000 Department 1 + $60,000 Department 2)		210,000
Payroll ($84,000 Department 1 + $48,500 Department 2)		132,500
Overhead ($42,000 Department 1 + $24,250 Department 2)		66,250
Costs added by Departments 1 and 2		

TABLE 8-4 (Continued)

Work-in-process—Department 2	240,000	
Work-in-process—Department 1		240,000
Units transferred to Department 2 ($6.00 × 40,000)		
Finished goods	337,500	
Work-in-process—Department 2		337,500
Units transferred to finished goods ($7.50 × 45,000)		

SPOILED UNITS

Subsequent departments which add units may also experience units spoiled during processing. Spoiled units may be handled in either of the following two ways. In one case, the units spoiled may be offset against the units added to production. Under this method, no mention of spoiled units is made if the number of units added exceed the number of units spoiled. In another method, the gross amount of units added and spoiled is shown. The treatment of spoiled units is illustrated in the next chapter.

CHAPTER REVIEW

Process costing is the system of accumulating product costs according to department, cost center, or process. This system is used when finished goods are part of a continuous process and therefore have no individual identity.

In a process cost system, units and costs flow through departments where they undergo different processes. The product flow may be sequential, parallel, or selective. All units started by a department or received from another department must be accounted for. The units can be completed and transferred, completed and still on hand, or still in process. As the units pass through each department, they acquire additional costs. One objective of process costing is the allocation of accumulated costs to the units completed and the units still in process.

Materials, labor, and factory overhead costs for the period are charged to departmental work-in-process accounts. Process costing is usually less detailed and involves fewer journal entries than a job order cost system.

Equivalent production is a major concept in process costing. All units in production are rarely completed during the period. Some units are usually still in process and at varying stages of completion. For purposes of determining unit costs, all units must be expressed in terms of completed units. The degree of completion for each cost element (materials, labor, factory overhead) must be determined. The units still in process are multiplied by the degree of completion to arrive at the equivalent completed units. The restated work-in-process units plus units completed equals the units of equivalent production.

Total costs are divided by equivalent production to determine the unit costs for the period.

In a process cost system, the cost of production report is the main reporting schedule. All costs chargeable to a department, or cost center, are presented there. The three sections of the cost of production report are (1) *quantities*—this schedule accounts for the physical flow of units in and out of a department; (2) *costs to account for*—this schedule accounts for costs added or received during a period (costs are presented in total and as unit costs); (3) *costs accounted for*—this schedule accounts for the distribution of the accumulated costs to units still in process, units completed and still on hand, and units completed and transferred to another department or finished goods.

The cost of production report for each department may be presented separately or jointly. This report is often a source for summary journal entries at the end of each period.

When materials are added after the first department, the following may result: no increase in units but cost increases; increase in units with no increase in cost; or increase in units and cost. When materials are added and only costs increase, the costs to account for schedule is adjusted to include the *cost* of the materials added. When materials added increase units *and* costs, the quantity schedule and the costs to account for schedule must be adjusted to account for the change.

GLOSSARY

Cost of Production Report—a detailed record of the unit and cost activities in each department during a period. It is divided into three sections: (1) quantities, (2) costs to account for, and (3) costs accounted for.

Equivalent Production—the sum of units still in process restated in terms of completed units plus total units actually completed.

Parallel Product Flow—a manufacturing system in which initial raw materials flow through different processes until combined in a final process or processes.

Process Costing—the system of ac-

cumulating product costs according to department, cost center, or process, used when a product is manufactured through mass production or a continuous process.

Selective Product Flow—a manufacturing system in which several finished products are produced from the initial raw material. The finished product is determined by which process it undergoes.

Sequential Product Flow—a manufacturing system in which units flow through all departments of the factory in the same order (or in sequence).

SUMMARY PROBLEMS

PROBLEM 1

The NBG Company manufactures a product using two processing departments. Materials are added in the beginning of Department A. Labor and factory overhead costs are applied evenly throughout the process.

During January, Department A was charged the following costs: materials, $52,650; labor, $42,000; and factory overhead, $39,600.

January's quantity schedule for Department A appears below:

Units started in process		65,000
Units completed and transferred to Department B	50,000	
Ending units in process	15,000	65,000

All materials, ⅔ labor, and factory overhead complete

REQUIRED:

a Calculate the equivalent units of production for materials and conversion costs.

b Calculate the unit cost of each cost element.

c Calculate the total unit cost for a completed unit in Department A.

PROBLEM 2

The TMG Company uses two processing departments (Departments A and B) to manufacture its finished product. The cost department obtained the following information for the month of July:

	DEPARTMENT A	DEPARTMENT B
Beginning units in process	0	0
Units started in process	35,000	
Units received from other department		30,000
Ending units in process	5,000	6,000
Costs added by department:		
Materials	$31,500	$ 0
Labor	24,180	15,680
Overhead	20,460	13,440
Degree of completion of ending work-in-process:		
Materials	100%	—
Conversion costs	⅕	⅔

REQUIRED:

a Prepare a quantity schedule for both departments.

  b   Calculate the completed unit costs for Department A.

  c   Prepare a cost of production report for Department B.

PROBLEM 3

Two processing departments are used by Grieser Chemical Company to produce its product. The two departments had the following activities and costs during the month of January:

	DEPARTMENT 1	DEPARTMENT 2
Units:		
Started in process during the period	80,000	
Units received from department 1		76,000
Units added to production		4,000
Transferred to finished goods		78,000
Ending units in process:		
All materials, 30% complete		
as to conversion costs	4,000	
All materials, 60% complete		
as to conversion costs		2,000
Costs:		
Materials	$200,000	$160,000
Labor	289,500	237,600
Overhead	96,500	198,000

REQUIRED:

  Prepare a cost of production report for the month of January for Departments 1 and 2.

SOLUTIONS TO SUMMARY PROBLEMS

PROBLEM 1

a   Equivalent production = completed units + (units still in process × % of completion)

Materials:

$$50,000 + (15,000 \times 100\%)$$
$$50,000 + 15,000 = 65,000 \text{ equivalent units}$$

Labor and Overhead:

$$50,000 + (15,000 \times \tfrac{2}{3})$$
$$50,000 + 10,000 = 60,000 \text{ equivalent units}$$

b

$$\text{Unit cost} = \frac{\text{cost}}{\text{equivalent production}}$$

$$\text{Materials} = \frac{\$52,650}{65,000} = \$.81$$

$$\text{Labor} = \frac{\$42,000}{60,000} = \$.70$$

$$\text{Overhead} = \frac{\$39,600}{60,000} = \$.66$$

c Total unit cost:

Materials	=	$.81
+ labor	=	.70
+ overhead	=	.66
Total		$2.17

PROBLEM 2

	DEPARTMENT A		DEPARTMENT B	
a Quantities:				
Units started in process	35,000			
Units received from preceding department				30,000
Units completed and transferred	30,000 (A)		24,000 (B)	
Ending units in process	5,000	35,000	6,000	30,000

(A) Same as units received in Dept. B
(B) Units received in Dept. B = 30,000 less 6,000 units in ending work-in-process

b

$$\text{Materials} \quad \frac{\$31,500}{35,000^*} = \$ .90$$

$$\text{Labor} \quad \frac{\$24,180}{31,000^*} = \$ .78$$

$$\text{Overhead} \quad \frac{\$20,460}{31,000^*} = \$ .66$$

Total unit cost	$2.34
(Department A)	

* Equivalent Production—Department A

EQUIVALENT PRODUCTION—DEPT. A	MATERIALS	CONVERSION COSTS
Units completed and transferred to Department B	30,000	30,000
Ending units in process	5,000	1,000 (5,000 × 1/5)
Equivalent production	35,000	31,000

c

THE TMG COMPANY
COST OF PRODUCTION REPORT
DEPARTMENT B
MONTH OF JULY

Quantities:

Units received from preceding department		30,000
Units transferred to finished goods	24,000	
Ending units in process	6,000	30,000

Costs to Account For	TOTAL COST	UNIT COST
Costs from preceding department:		
Transferred in during the month (30,000) (A)$70,200 (A)		$2.34 (B)
Costs added by department:		
Labor	$15,680	$ .56 (C)
Overhead	13,440	.48 (D)
Total cost added	$29,120	$1.04
Total cost to account for	$99,320	$3.38

Costs Accounted For:		
Transferred to finished goods		
(24,000 × $3.38)		$81,120
Work-in-process—ending:		
Costs from preceding department		
($2.34 × 6,000)	$14,040	
Labor (6,000 × ⅔ × $.56)	2,240	
Overhead (6,000 × ⅔ × $.48)	1,920	18,200
Total costs accounted for		$99,320

EQUIVALENT PRODUCTION	CONVERSION COSTS
Units transferred to finished goods	24,000
Ending units in process	4,000 (6,000 × ⅔)
Equivalent production	28,000

Computations of unit cost:
(A) $30,000 × $2.34 = $70,200
(B) $70,200 ÷ 30,000 = $2.34
(C) $15,680 ÷ 28,000 = $.56
(D) $13,440 ÷ 28,000 = $.48

PROBLEM 3

GRIESER CHEMICAL COMPANY
COST OF PRODUCTION REPORT
DEPARTMENT 1
MONTH OF JANUARY

Quantities:

Units started in process		80,000
Units transferred to next department	76,000	
Ending units in process	4,000	80,000

	TOTAL COST	UNIT COST
Costs to Account For:		
Costs added by department:		
Materials	$200,000	$ 2.50 (A)
Labor	289,500	3.75 (B)
Overhead	96,500	1.25 (C)
Total cost to account for	$586,000	$ 7.50
Costs Accounted For:		
Transferred to next department		
(76,000 × $7.50)	$570,000	
Work-in-process—ending		
Materials (4,000 × $2.50)	$10,000	
Labor (4,000 × $3.75 × 30%)	4,500	
Overhead (4,000 × $1.25 × 30%)	1,500	16,000
Total costs accounted for		$586,000

EQUIVALENT PRODUCTION	MATERIALS	CONVERSION COSTS
Units transferred to next department	76,000	76,000
+ Ending units in process	4,000	1,200 (4,000 × 30%)
Equivalent production	80,000	77,200

Computations of Unit Cost:
(A) $200,000 ÷ 80,000 = $2.50
(B) $289,500 ÷ 77,200 = $3.75
(C) $96,500 ÷ 77,200 = $1.25

GRIESER CHEMICAL COMPANY
COST OF PRODUCTION REPORT
DEPARTMENT 2
MONTH OF JANUARY

Quantities:		
Units transferred in	76,000	
Units added to production	4,000	80,000
Units transferred to finished goods	78,000	
Ending units in process	2,000	80,000

	UNITS	TOTAL COST	UNIT COST
Costs to Account For:			
Cost from preceding department	76,000	$ 570,000	$ 7.500
Units added to production	4,000		
Adjusted units and unit cost	80,000		$ 7.125 (A)
Costs added by department:			
Materials		$ 160,000	$ 2.000 (B)
Labor		237,600	3.000 (C)
Overhead		198,000	2.500 (D)
Total costs added		$ 595,600	$ 7.500
Total costs to account for		$1,165,600	14.625

		TOTAL COST	UNIT COST
Costs Accounted For:			
Transferred to finished goods			
(78,000 × $14.625)		$1,140,750	
Work-in-process—ending			
Costs from preceding depart-			
ment (2,000 × $7.125)	$14,250		
Materials (2,000 × $2.00)	4,000		
Labor (2,000 × $3.00 × 60%)	3,600		
Overhead			
(2,000 × $2.50 × 60%)	3,000	24,850	
Total costs accounted for		$1,165,600	

EQUIVALENT PRODUCTION	MATERIALS	CONVERSION COSTS	
Units transferred to			
finished goods	78,000	78,000	
+ Ending units in process	2,000	1,200	(2,000 × 60%)
Equivalent production	80,000	79,200	

Computations of unit cost:
(A) $570,000 ÷ 80,000 = $7.125
(B) $160,000 ÷ 80,000 = $2.000
(C) $237,600 ÷ 79,200 = $3.000
(D) $198,000 ÷ 79,200 = $2.500

QUESTIONS

1   What types of manufacturing processes are usually associated with process costing?
2   In job order costing, costs are accumulated by jobs. How are costs accumulated under a process cost system?
3   What is the main objective of a process cost system?
4   What are the three common ways a product flows through production?
5   Explain how the recording of labor costs under process costing differs from job order costing.
6   Briefly explain the two methods that may be used to apply factory overhead to work-in-process. Under what conditions is each method appropriately used?
7   Name the three sections that make up the cost of production report. What information is included in each section?
8   Define equivalent production. Why is it necessary?
9   Why is it usually necessary to have two separate equivalent production computations?
10 What effects may adding materials in a subsequent department have on units and costs?

11   Name three methods used to determine the amount of materials costs to be charged to work-in-process. Will the method chosen affect the journal entry?

12   If the addition of materials by a subsequent department increases the units, what effect will this have on the transferred-in unit cost?

13   What effect will overstating the percentage of completion of ending units in process have on the period's unit cost?

14   What should be taken into consideration in deciding whether to use a process cost system?

EXERCISES

EXERCISE 1

Quantity Flow

The ABC Manufacturing Corp. has five processing departments. An examination of its cost of production report reveals the following incomplete information:

	DEPARTMENTS				
QUANTITIES:	1	2	3	4	5
Units started in process	10,000	—	—	—	—
Units received from preceding department	—	B 4,000	3,000	E 2,400	G 2,100
Units transferred to next department	A 4,000	3,000	D 2,400	F 2,100	— 1,600
Units transferred to finished goods	—	—	—	—	H
Ending units in process	6,000	C 1,000	600	300	500

REQUIRED:

Complete the quantity schedule by replacing the letters with the correct unit amount. Assume that the process is segmental (that is, the output of Department 1 is the input of Department 2) and that no beginning work-in-process inventory exists.

EXERCISE 2

Equivalent Production

The Happy Tot Co. manufactures a wide variety of plastic toys. All materials are added at the beginning of Department A. Departments A, B, and C add labor and factory overhead evenly throughout the process. January's quantity schedules appear on page 279.

	DEPARTMENT A	DEPARTMENT B	DEPARTMENT C
Units started in process	25,000		
Units received from preceding department	—	15,000	12,000
Units transferred to next department	15,000	12,000	
Units transferred to finished goods			9,000
Ending units in process	10,000 (75% complete)	3,000 (50% complete)	3,000 (30% complete)
	25,000	15,000	12,000

REQUIRED:

Determine the equivalent units of production for both materials and conversion costs for each department. No beginning work-in-process inventory exists.

EXERCISE 3

Journal Entries

Department 1002 of a manufacturing company had the following transactions for the month of May:

1 Requisitioned $24,300 of raw materials from the storeroom.
2 Distributed monthly payroll costs. Four of the ten factory workers had worked 160 hours each in Department 1002. All factory workers are paid $2.75 an hour.
3 Factory overhead is applied at a predetermined rate based on direct labor cost. Total estimated factory overhead was $110,880 and total estimated labor cost was $52,800.
4 Ending work-in-process was $9,254. Units transferred went to Department 1022. No beginning work-in-process inventory exists.

REQUIRED:

Give the appropriate journal entries for the above transactions under a process cost system.

EXERCISE 4

Costs to Account For Schedule

Below is the quantity schedule for Department 2 of a manufacturing firm.

Units received from Department 1		37,000
Units transferred to finished goods	28,000	
Ending units in process		
(all materials; 35% complete as		
to conversion costs)	9,000	37,000

Additional Information:

Costs transferred in	=	$24,050
Costs added this period:		
Labor	=	$ 7,476
Factory overhead	=	11,214
		$18,690

REQUIRED:

Prepare a costs to account for schedule.

EXERCISE 5

Materials Added in Subsequent Department—Unit Cost Computations

Below is data pertaining to Department B:

Units transferred in	55,000
Units added to production	5,000
Units transferred out	48,000
Ending units in process (all materials; 70% as to conversion costs)	12,000
Costs transferred in	$24,750
Costs added by department:	
Materials	7,200
Labor	21,432
Factory overhead	32,148

REQUIRED:

Determine the following unit costs:

a Transferred-in unit cost   d Factory overhead
b Materials   e Total unit cost
c Labor

EXERCISE 6

Subsequent Department—Increased Material Costs

The M. K. Wheelie Corp. manufactures toy cars. In Department 1, the body of the toy car is formed out of plastic. In Department 2 four rubber wheels are placed on each car at the end of the process. Below is the activity of Department 2 for March:

Units transferred in	15,000
Cost transferred in	$13,500
Costs incurred by department:	
Materials	$.02 for each rubber wheel
Labor	$8,120
Factory overhead	$6,090
Ending units in process	3,000 (⅔ complete)

Conversion costs are added evenly throughout the process.

REQUIRED:

a What materials costs were incurred during March?
b What was the total cost of a completed unit transferred out of Department 2?

EXERCISE 7

Equivalent Production

KYZ Corp. produces a finished product requiring materials to be added at uneven intervals of production. Materials are added only in Department A. The schedule of when materials are added in Department A is as follows:

STAGE OF PRODUCTION, PERCENTAGE COMPLETE	PERCENTAGE OF MATERIALS ADDED
10	20
40	30
75	30
90	20
	100

Conversion costs are added *evenly* throughout the process. Following is the August data for Department A:

No beginning units in process

50,000 units started in process

10,000 ending units in process (25% were 35% complete, 30% were 55% complete, 25% were 80% complete, and 20% were 95% complete)

REQUIRED:

Calculate the equivalent units of production for Department A for both materials and conversion costs for the month of August.

EXERCISE 8

Materials Added in Subsequent Department

Below is data concerning Department B of a manufacturing corporation that uses a process cost system:

Units received from Department A	500,000
Units added in production	100,000
Units transferred to finished goods	530,000
Ending units in process	10% are 30% complete, 40% are 60% complete, 15% are 75% complete, 35% are 85% complete

Costs transferred in	$300,000
Costs added by department:	
Materials	$560,272
Labor	363,888
Overhead	242,592

Both materials and conversion costs are added evenly throughout the process. No beginning work-in-process inventory exists.

REQUIRED:

a Calculate the equivalent units of production for materials and conversion costs.

b Calculate the cost of ending work-in-process.

EXERCISE 9

Subsequent Departments Adding More Units

The Gulpy Beverage Corp. produces a cola beverage. Three liquid raw materials (syrup, water, and phosphoric acid) are used in production. Syrup enters production at the beginning of Department 1. In Department 2, water is added at the beginning of the process and phosphoric acid is added at the end.

For every gallon (unit) of syrup that is transferred into Department 2, two gallons of water and one gallon of phosphoric acid are required to produce the finished beverage. No gallons are lost through evaporation.

During May, 100,000 gallons were transferred into Department 2 at a cost of $.45 per gallon. Finished goods was debited for $240,000 during May. Of units transferred in during the period, 75% were completed.

REQUIRED:

a How many gallons of water and phosphoric acid were added to production?

b Calculate the revised unit cost for units transferred in to Department 2 during May.

c Calculate the units of equivalent production for materials, if Department 2's ending work-in-process was 45% complete.

PROBLEMS

PROBLEM 1

Cost of Production Report—Two Departments

The Acme Plastic Co. has two processing departments. All materials are added in Department 1 at the beginning of the process. Conversion costs are incurred evenly throughout the process. Data for January 19XX is on page 284.

	DEPARTMENT 1	DEPARTMENT 2
Units started in process	75,000	
Units transferred to next department	60,000	
Units transferred to finished goods		55,000
Ending units in process	15,000	5,000
	(60% complete)	(80% complete)
Costs added by department:		
Materials	$300,000	
Labor	172,500	$162,250
Overhead	86,250	81,125

No beginning work-in-process inventory exists.

REQUIRED:

Prepare a cost of production report for both departments.

PROBLEM 2

Materials Added in Subsequent Department

Department 112A adds additional materials at the end of processing. It is the second department in a four-processing-department operation. The materials added do not increase the number of units. Data for Department 112A for the month of July 19XX follows:

Units transferred in	13,000
Costs transferred in	$16,120
Ending units in process (45% complete)	2,000
Costs added during period:	
Materials	$2,860
Labor	6,664
Overhead	3,332

No beginning work-in-process inventory exists.

REQUIRED:

Prepare a cost of production report for Department 112A.

PROBLEM 3

Cost of Production Report—Three Departments

The Simon Soap Corporation requires three processing departments to produce its soap. All raw materials are entered at the beginning of Department 1. Departments 1 through 3 add conversion costs evenly throughout the process.

The cost accountant obtained the following information for December 19XX:

	DEPARTMENTS		
	1	2	3
Units started in process	150,000		
Units transferred to the next department	125,000	115,000	
Units transferred to finished goods			112,000
Ending units in process—% of completion	40%	10%	90%
Costs added by department:			
Materials	$21,000		
Labor	8,100	$11,600	$ 8,029
Overhead	16,200	23,200	16,058

REQUIRED:

Prepare a cost of production report for each department.

PROBLEM 4

Cost of Production Report—Two Departments

The October data for a manufacturing firm is shown below:

	DEPARTMENT 1	DEPARTMENT 2
Units started in process	25,000	
Units received from previous department		15,000
Units transferred to finished goods		7,000
Units completed but not transferred		1,000
Ending units in process	10,000	7,000
	(80% materials	(75% conversion
	65% conversion	costs)
	costs)	
Costs added by department:		
Materials	$12,650	—
Labor	13,545	$9,805
Overhead	5,160	6,625

REQUIRED:

a   Prepare a cost of production report for Departments 1 and 2.
b   If finished goods had a beginning balance of $25,000 and an ending balance of $13,300, what amount was charged to cost of goods sold?

PROBLEM 5

Equivalent Production (Several Raw Materials Added at Different Points of Production)

The Able Medicine Co. manufactures an all-purpose capsule. Four raw materials are put into production in Department A. Department B places the units received from Department A into quick-dissolving capsules. Raw materials are placed into production as follows:

Raw material 101 (aspirin) — beginning of process
Raw material 102 (caffeine) — when units are 40% complete
Raw material 103 (decongestant) — when units are 60% complete
Raw material 104 (muscle relaxer) — when units are 95% complete

July Data, Department 1:

Units started in process	300,000
Units transferred out	250,000
Ending units in process (30% are 45% complete, 35% are 50% complete, 15% are 65% complete, 20% are 98% complete)	50,000

Costs incurred:
Materials:

101	=	$ 6,000.00
102	=	3,000.00
103	=	9,362.50
104	=	13,000.00

Conversion costs:

Labor	=	$81,250.75
Overhead	=	36,422.75

REQUIRED:

a Calculate the units of equivalent production for raw materials and conversion costs.

b Calculate the cost of ending work-in-process.

PROBLEM 6

Materials Added in Subsequent Department—Increase in Units

The Aroma Perfume Co. has two processing departments. Raw materials are added at the beginning of the process in both departments. Below is the cost of production report for February for Department 1.

THE AROMA PERFUME CO.
DEPARTMENT 1
COST OF PRODUCTION REPORT
MONTH OF FEBRUARY

Quantities:		
Units started in process		8,000
Units transferred to next department	6,000	
Ending units in process	2,000	8,000

	TOTAL COST	UNIT COST
Costs to Account For:		
Costs added by the department		
Materials	$ 8,400	$ 1.05 (A)
Labor	4,950	.75 (B)
Overhead	3,960	.60 (C)
Total costs to account for	$17,310	$ 2.40
Costs Accounted For:		
Transferred to next department (6,000 × $2.40)		$14,400
Work-in-process—ending		
Materials (2,000 × $1.05)	$ 2,100	
Labor (2,000 × .30 × $.75)	450	
Overhead (2,000 × .30 × $.60)	360	2,910
Total costs accounted for		$17,310

Data for Department 2 for February:

Units added to production 3,000
Units transferred to finished goods 8,100
Costs added by the department:
Materials $6,660
Labor 5,046
Overhead 3,654
Ending units in process are ⅔ complete as to conversion costs.

No beginning work-in-process inventory exists.

REQUIRED:

a Prepare a cost of production report for Department 2.
b Give the journal entries to record February's activity in both departments.

PROBLEM 7

Materials Added in Subsequent Department—Spoiled Units

The Clean Cold Cream Co. has two processing departments. Raw materials are added at the end of Department 1 processing and at the beginning of Department 2 processing. Materials added in Department 2 increase the number of units. It is company policy to offset spoiled units against those added to production. Below is information concerning production for April 19XX:

	DEPARTMENT 1	DEPARTMENT 2
Units started in process	54,000	
Units transferred to the next department	38,000	
Units transferred to finished goods		38,900
Units added to production		2,400
Spoiled units		500
Ending units in process	16,000	1,000
	(⅜ complete)	(⅕ complete)

	DEPARTMENT 1	DEPARTMENT 2
Costs incurred:		
Materials	$21,660	$18,354
Labor	12,760	22,287
Overhead	8,360	14,076

No beginning work-in-process inventory exists.

REQUIRED:

Prepare cost of production reports for both departments.

PROBLEM 8

Materials Added in Subsequent Department (Increase in Units)

The Soupy Soup Company produces two kinds of soups—plain chicken and cream of chicken. Both kinds of soups enter production in Department 1, where chicken broth is added at the beginning of the process. Completed units (one unit = one gallon) are then transferred to either Department 2B or Department 3B. Department 2B adds only water and produces plain chicken soup. The water is added at the end of the process. Department 3B adds cream and produces cream of chicken soup. The cream is added at the beginning of the process. From Departments 2B and 3B, the soups are transferred to the canning department.

The cost accountant obtained the following information concerning March 19XX production:

	DEPARTMENT 1	DEPARTMENT 2B	DEPARTMENT 3B
Units started in process	85,000		
Units transferred to Department 2B	55,000		
Units transferred to Department 3B	20,000		
Ending units in process	10,000	20,000	7,000
	(65% complete)	(50% complete)	(20% complete)
Costs added by department:			
Materials	$76,500	—	$17,400
Labor	36,675	$46,000	10,492
Overhead	17,930	28,750	7,320

For every gallon that is transferred into Department 2B, 2 gallons of water are added at the end of the processing. For every gallon that is transferred into Department 3B, ½ gallon of cream is added. No beginning work-in-process inventory exists.

REQUIRED:

Prepare cost of production reports for all three departments.

PROBLEM 9

Determining Finished Unit Cost

The Runfast Sneaker Co. has just started business. It has been determined that three processing departments will be required. Department A will make the canvas upper section of the sneaker. Department B will attach the rubber sole to the upper portion. Department C will place the finishing touches on the sneakers. No additional materials are added in Department C.

Raw materials are added at the beginning of each process in Departments A and B.

Below is the information for the first month of operations:

	DEPARTMENT A	DEPARTMENT B	DEPARTMENT C
Units started in process	89,000		
Units received from previous department		70,000	64,000
Units transferred to finished goods			60,000
Ending units in process—% of completion:	70%	25%	60%

Costs:

Department A:
    Materials ....$5 per unit
    Labor $50,813
    Overhead ....150% of labor cost

Department B:
    Materials ....$2 per unit
    Labor $35,370
    Overhead ....150% of labor cost

Department C:
    Labor $48,672
    Overhead ....150% of labor cost

REQUIRED:

If management wishes to have a gross profit of 20% of sales, what should be the price of the sneakers completed during the first month of operation?

CHAPTER NINE
PROCESS COST SYSTEM– EXPANDED

The basic procedures to account for goods under a process cost system were presented in the previous chapter. Techniques for handling the following situations under a process cost system will be presented in this chapter.

1 Beginning work-in-process inventories
2 Spoiled goods, defective goods, scrap, and waste material

BEGINNING WORK-IN-PROCESS INVENTORIES

The examples given in the previous chapter did not have a beginning work-in-process inventory. This situation would probably exist only in the first month of a new business or in a new production process because production is usually continuous and some units will therefore still be in process at the end of a period. The ending work-in-process inventory of the last period becomes this period's beginning work-in-process.

The existence of beginning work-in-process inventories creates a problem in process costing because the following questions must be considered:

1 Should a distinction be made between completed units from beginning work-in-process and completed units from the present period?
2 Should all the units completed during the present period be included at 100% in equivalent production regardless of the stage of completion of beginning work-in-process?
3 Should the costs of beginning work-in-process be added to costs which have been added to production during the present period to arrive at "costs added during the period"?

The answers to these questions will depend on the method chosen to account for beginning work-in-process. Beginning work-in-process is commonly accounted for by either of the following two methods:

1   Weighted average costing
2   First-In, First-Out (fifo) costing

Under *weighted average costing*, the costs of beginning work-in-process are added to the period's current costs, and this total is divided by equivalent production to arrive at weighted average unit costs. Costs associated with the units still in process lose their identity because of the merger. The beginning inventory cost is therefore treated as if it were a current period cost. No distinction is made between completed units from beginning work-in-process and completed units from new production. There is only *one* final unit cost for all completed units—a weighted average unit cost.

Under *fifo costing*, the units in the beginning inventory are reported separately from units of the present period. Work-in-process units are assumed to be completed before the units started during this period are completed. Costs associated with the beginning units in process are separated from costs of units started and completed during the period. Because of this separation, there are two final unit cost figures for completed units.

The three schedules in the cost of production report and the equivalent production calculation will be individually analyzed in explaining the procedures associated with beginning work-in-process.

The information in Table 9-1 will be used in the discussion.

TABLE 9-1
NELLIE CORPORATION

	DEPARTMENT 1	DEPARTMENT 2
Units:		
Beginning units in process:		
All materials; 40% complete as to conversion costs	4,000	
All materials; 20% complete as to conversion costs		6,000
Started in process during the period	40,000	
Units transferred to Department 2	35,000	
Units added to production		5,000
Transferred to finished goods		44,000
Ending units in process:		
All materials; 60% complete as to conversion costs	9,000	
All materials; 30% complete as to conversion costs		2,000
Costs:		
Beginning work-in-process from preceding department	0	$ 40,000
Beginning work-in-process from this department:		
Materials	$ 14,000	12,000
Labor	6,560	10,280
Overhead	11,000	4,600
Total	$ 31,560	$ 66,880
Added during the period:		
Materials	$140,000	$ 80,000
Labor	50,000	70,000
Overhead	90,000	40,000
Total	$280,000	$190,000

Quantity Schedule

The physical flow equation as presented in Chapter 8, is repeated below for further discussion of beginning work-in-process. The physical flow equation is as follows:

$$
\left.\begin{array}{c}
\text{Beginning units in process} \\
+ \\
\text{units started in process or} \\
\text{received from other departments} \\
+ \\
\text{units added to production}
\end{array}\right\} = \left\{\begin{array}{c}
\text{units transferred out} \\
+ \\
\text{units completed and} \\
\text{still on hand} \\
+ \\
\text{ending units in process}
\end{array}\right.
$$

The new input component appears as an additional line in the quantity schedule called "beginning units in process." Illustrated below are the quantity schedules of the Nellie Corporation for the period.

	DEPARTMENT 1		DEPARTMENT 2	
Quantities:				
Beginning units in process	4,000		6,000	
Units started in process	40,000	44,000		
Units received from preceding department			35,000	
Units added to production			5,000	46,000
Units completed and transferred	35,000		44,000	
Ending units in process	9,000	44,000	2,000	46,000

The 46,000 units in Department 2 came from three sources: 6,000 units not completed in the previous period (beginning work-in-process inventory), 35,000 units received from Department 1 during the period, and 5,000 units added by the department during the period. The quantity schedule is the same under weighted average and fifo costing.

Equivalent Production. In previous examples, all units completed at the end of a period had been started in production or received from another department during that same period. Therefore, all completed units received 100% of their departmental cost during the current period. In the calculation of equivalent production, all units are restated as whole units.

If, however, the department had units in process at the beginning of the period (beginning work-in-process inventory), those units were partially completed in the previous period, and therefore receive only a portion of their cost in the current period.

Under weighted average costing, units in process at the beginning of the period are treated as though they had been started and completed during the current period. All units completed during the period are included in equivalent production at 100%, regardless of the stage of completion of beginning work-in-process.

Under fifo, beginning work-in-process is included in equivalent production only to the extent that the units were completed during the current period.

Fifo assumes that units in beginning work-in-process are completed first, and the *actual* flow of units is therefore considered for purposes of computing unit cost.

It should be noted, however, that in most cases the difference in unit costs calculated under the two methods is immaterial. The method selected is usually based on ease of application to the cost system. Below are the computations for equivalent production for Nellie Corporation, Departments 1 and 2, under weighted average and fifo costing:

	WEIGHTED AVERAGE		FIFO	
	MATERIALS	CONVERSION COSTS	MATERIALS	CONVER- SION COSTS
Department 1				
Units completed and trans- ferred	35,000	35,000	35,000	35,000
− Beginning units in process			4,000	4,000
= Units started and completed			31,000	31,000
+ Amount needed to complete beginning work-in-process (units X % to complete)				2,400 (A)
+ Ending units in process, amount completed (units X % completed)	9,000 (B)	5,400 (C)	9,000 (B)	5,400 (C)
Equivalent production	44,000	40,400	40,000	38,800
Department 2				
Units completed and trans- ferred	44,000	44,000	44,000	44,000
− Beginning units in process			6,000	6,000
= Units started and completed			38,000	38,000
+ Amount needed to complete beginning work-in-process (units X % to complete)				4,800 (D)
+ Ending units in process, amount completed (units X % completed)	2,000 (E)	600 (F)	2,000 (E)	600 (F)
Equivalent production	46,000	44,600	40,000	43,400

(A) 4,000 × 60% = 2,400
(B) 9,000 × 100% = 9,000
(C) 9,000 × 60% = 5,400
(D) 6,000 × 80% = 4,800
(E) 2,000 × 100% = 2,000
(F) 2,000 × 30% = 600

Costs to Account For Schedule

To illustrate weighted average costing and fifo costing, the costs to account for schedule for the Nellie Corporation will be presented for each method.

Weighted Average Costing—First Department. In the first processing department, the costs to be considered are the costs of beginning work-in-process and costs added by the department. Under weighted average costing, the cost of beginning work-in-process is separated into the three elements of cost (materials, labor, and overhead) in the costs to account for schedule. These elements are added to their related cost elements, which have been added to production *during* the period to arrive at a total cost of materials, total cost of labor, and total cost of overhead. Each total is divided by its related equivalent production to obtain a weighted average unit cost by element. The unit cost computation for costs added during the period and for beginning work-in-process cost by element is not presented in the body of the schedule; rather, it is presented in a computation at the foot of the cost of production report.

Unit cost computations by element for the first department under weighted average costing are as follows:

(1)   Materials unit cost $= \dfrac{\text{materials cost in beginning work-in-process} + \text{materials cost added during period}}{\text{equivalent units for materials}}$

(2)   Labor unit cost $= \dfrac{\text{labor cost in beginning work-in-process} + \text{labor cost added during period}}{\text{equivalent units for labor}}$

(3)   Overhead unit cost $= \dfrac{\text{overhead cost in beginning work-in-process} + \text{overhead cost added during period}}{\text{equivalent units for overhead}}$

(4)   Total unit cost $= (1) + (2) + (3)$

Illustrated below is the costs to account for schedule for Department 1 under weighted average costing.

COSTS TO ACCOUNT FOR

	TOTAL COST	UNIT COST
Costs added by department:		
Work-in-process—beginning:		
Materials	$ 14,000	
Labor	6,560	
Overhead	11,000	
Costs added during the period:		
Materials	$140,000	$3.50 (A)
Labor	50,000	1.40 (B)
Overhead	90,000	2.50 (C)
Total costs to account for	$311,560	$7.40

Computations of unit cost:
(A) ($140,000 + $14,000) ÷ 44,000 = $3.50
(B) ($50,000 + $6,560) ÷ 40,400 = $1.40
(C) ($90,000 + $11,000) ÷ 40,400 = $2.50

Weighted Average Costing—After First Department. The same principle for calculating unit costs for beginning work-in-process costs and costs added by the first department is used for subsequent departments. There is, however, an additional "costs to account for" in subsequent departments—the cost of units transferred in from previous departments. For purposes of unit costing, the cost of units from the preceding department is considered an additional cost element and is presented separately. The costs to account for schedule will now have two sections: (1) costs from preceding department and (2) costs added by department. Within the first section, beginning work-in-process (the remaining portion of the last period's transferred-in costs) and transferred-in costs during the current period are added to arrive at a total cost from the preceding department. This total is divided by the total number of units (beginning work-in-process + transferred-in + added during the period) in the department to arrive at a weighted average unit cost for transferred-in costs.

The second section, costs added by department, follows the same procedures as the first department. We now have five weighted average unit cost computations, as follows:

Costs from Preceding Department:

$$(1) \quad \text{Transferred-in unit cost} = \frac{\text{beginning work-in-process} + \genfrac{}{}{0pt}{}{\text{transferred-in costs}}{\text{during the period}}}{\text{total units in department}}$$

Costs Added by Department:

$$(2) \quad \text{Materials unit cost} = \frac{\genfrac{}{}{0pt}{}{\text{materials cost in}}{\text{beginning work-in-process}} + \genfrac{}{}{0pt}{}{\text{materials cost}}{\text{added during period}}}{\text{equivalent units for materials}}$$

$$(3) \quad \text{Labor unit cost} = \frac{\genfrac{}{}{0pt}{}{\text{labor cost in}}{\text{beginning work-in-process}} + \genfrac{}{}{0pt}{}{\text{labor cost}}{\text{added during period}}}{\text{equivalent units for labor}}$$

$$(4) \quad \text{Overhead unit cost} = \frac{\genfrac{}{}{0pt}{}{\text{overhead costs in}}{\text{beginning work-in-process}} + \genfrac{}{}{0pt}{}{\text{overhead cost}}{\text{added during period}}}{\text{equivalent units for overhead}}$$

$$(5) \quad \text{Total unit cost} = (1) + (2) + (3) + (4)$$

The costs to account for schedule for Department 2 under weighted average costing is shown at the top of page 296.

COSTS TO ACCOUNT FOR

	UNITS	TOTAL COST	UNIT COST
Costs from preceding department:			
Work-in-process—beginning	6,000	$ 40,000	
Transferred in during the period	35,000	259,000 (A)	
Units added to production	5,000		
Adjusted units and unit cost	46,000	$299,000	$ 6.50 (B)
Cost added by department:			
Work-in-process—beginning:			
Materials		12,000	
Labor		10,280	
Overhead		4,600	
Cost added during the period:			
Materials		80,000	2.00 (C)
Labor		70,000	1.80 (D)
Overhead		40,000	1.00 (E)
Total costs to account for		$515,880	$11.30

Computations of unit cost:
(A) 35,000 units × $7.40 total unit cost from Dept. 1 = $259,000
(B) $299,000 ÷ 46,000 = $6.50
(C) ($80,000 + $12,000) ÷ 46,000 = $2.00
(D) ($70,000 + $10,280) ÷ 44,600 = $1.80
(E) ($40,000 + $4,600) ÷ 44,600 = $1.00

First-In, First-Out Costing—First Department. The fifo method of costing assumes the beginning work-in-process inventory will be completed before all other units. This technique attempts to match *cost* flow to the actual *unit* flow by keeping the beginning work-in-process costs separate from the costs of units started and completed during the period. Therefore, under this method, beginning work-in-process costs are isolated and do not enter into the computation of unit costs for "costs added during the period."

Unit costs are determined by dividing equivalent production into the costs added this period. Fifo equivalent production includes only production performed during the period.

The following are formulas for unit cost calculations necessary for the first department under fifo costing:

(1) Materials $= \dfrac{\text{materials cost added during the period}}{\text{equivalent units for materials}}$

(2) Labor $= \dfrac{\text{labor cost added during the period}}{\text{equivalent units for labor}}$

(3) Overhead $= \dfrac{\text{overhead cost added during the period}}{\text{equivalent units for overhead}}$

(4) Total unit cost = (1) + (2) + (3)

The schedule of costs to account for of the Nellie Corporation under fifo costing for Department 1 is shown below

COSTS TO ACCOUNT FOR

	TOTAL COST	UNIT COST
Work-in-process—beginning	$ 31,560	
Costs added during the period:		
Materials	$140,000	$3.50000 (A)
Labor	50,000	1.28866 (B)
Overhead	90,000	2.31959 (C)
Total costs added	$280,000	$7.10825
Total costs to account for	$311,560	

Computations of unit cost:
(A) $140,000 ÷ 40,000 = $3.50000
(B) $50,000 ÷ 38,800 = $1.28866
(C) $90,000 ÷ 38,800 = $2.31959

First-In, First-Out Costing—After First Department. As with fifo costing in the first department, the cost of beginning work-in-process in subsequent departments is accounted for in *total only* and is isolated from all other costs. This beginning work-in-process includes an additional cost to account for—the remaining portion of last period's transferred-in costs (plus the costs added last period by this department).

The transferred-in costs for units received from the preceding department during the current period are presented in total, and a separate unit cost is calculated. The transferred-in unit cost is determined by dividing current transferred-in costs by the number of units transferred in (plus any additional units added to production).

Unit costs for "costs added during the period" are calculated in the same manner presented for the first department. These unit costs are added to the transferred-in unit cost to obtain one unit cost, excluding beginning inventory.

The costs to account for schedule for subsequent departments under fifo costing is therefore divided into three sections:

1 Work-in-process—beginning
2 Transferred in during the period
3 Costs added during the period

Unit cost computations are made as follows:

Cost from Preceding Department:

$$(1) \quad \text{Transferred-in unit cost} = \frac{\text{total cost transferred in during the period}}{\text{units transferred in} + \text{units added}}$$

Costs Added during the Period:

$$(2) \quad \text{Materials unit cost} = \frac{\text{total materials cost added during the period}}{\text{equivalent units for materials}}$$

(3)   Labor unit cost $= \dfrac{\text{total labor cost added during the period}}{\text{equivalent units for labor}}$

(4)   Overhead unit cost $= \dfrac{\text{total overhead cost added during the period}}{\text{equivalent units for overhead}}$

(5)   Total unit cost $= (1) + (2) + (3) + (4)$

Illustrated below is the costs to account for schedule for Department 2 under fifo costing:

COSTS TO ACCOUNT FOR

	UNITS	TOTAL COST	UNIT COST
Work-in-process—beginning	6,000	$ 66,880	
Transferred in during the period	35,000	$260,576*	
Units added to production	5,000		
Adjusted units and unit cost	40,000		$ 6.51440 (A)
Costs added during the period:			
Materials		$ 80,000	2.00000 (B)
Labor		70,000	1.61290 (C)
Overhead		40,000	.92166 (D)
Total cost added		$190,000	$ 11.04896
Total costs to account for		$517,456	

Computations of unit cost:
(A) $\$260,576 \div 40,000 = \$6.51440$
(B) $\$80,000 \div 40,000 = \$2.00000$
(C) $\$70,000 \div 43,400 = \$1.61290$
(D) $\$40,000 \div 43,400 = \$.92166$

* This figure represents the total cost of goods transferred in from the preceding department and will be explained later in the "costs accounted for schedule" for Department 1.

It should be noted, however, that fifo costing as used in a process cost system is not a pure fifo cost flow. Costs transferred to subsequent departments (called "transferred-in costs" by the next department) are "averaged" among all the units in the department at that time. In other words, they lose their identity in subsequent departments and become an average cost.

Illustrated below is a summary of the section headings in the costs to account for schedule under weighted average and fifo:

DEPARTMENT	WEIGHTED AVERAGE	FIFO
First	I Costs added by dept.	I Work-in-process—beginning
	1 Work-in-process—beginning	II Costs added during the period
	2 Costs added during the period	

DEPARTMENT	WEIGHTED AVERAGE	FIFO
After first	I Costs from preceding dept.	I Work-in-process—beginning
	1 Work-in-process—beginning	II Transferred in during the period
	2 Transferred in during the period	1 Units added to production (if any)
	3 Units added to production (if any)	
	II Costs added by dept.	III Costs added during the period
	1 Work-in-process—beginning	
	2 Costs added during the period	

Costs Accounted For Schedule

The procedures used in preparing a costs accounted for schedule depends upon whether weighted average costing or fifo costing is used in accounting for beginning work-in-process. If weighted average costing is used, there is no change in the procedures shown in previous problems.

When fifo is used, it is assumed that the units in process at the beginning are the first to be completed and first to be transferred out. Costs associated with the beginning work-in-process are kept separate from the other costs. Beginning work-in-process units that were completed have one completed unit cost and units started and completed during the period will usually have another completed unit cost.

Costs are accounted for under two captions: (1) transferred to finished goods or the next department or (2) still in process at the end of the period.

The first caption of the costs accounted for schedule appears as follows:

Total costs transferred to finished goods or the next department:

From beginning work-in-process

1 Inventory cost (at beginning of the period)

2 Materials $= \dfrac{\text{beginning units}}{\text{in process}} \times \dfrac{\text{percent to}}{\text{complete}} \times \dfrac{\text{materials}}{\text{unit cost}}$

3 Labor $= \dfrac{\text{beginning units}}{\text{in process}} \times \dfrac{\text{percent to}}{\text{complete}} \times \dfrac{\text{labor}}{\text{unit cost}}$

4 Overhead $= \dfrac{\text{beginning units}}{\text{in process}} \times \dfrac{\text{percent to}}{\text{complete}} \times \dfrac{\text{overhead}}{\text{unit cost}}$

From current production

Units started and completed during the period $\times$ Total unit cost for materials, labor and overhead added during this period (found on the costs to account for schedule)

Units started and completed during the period can be obtained by subtracting the beginning work-in-process units from the total completed units (this figure can also be found on the equivalent production schedule).

The second caption of the costs accounted for schedule appears as follows:

Work-in-process—ending

1   $\dfrac{\text{Cost from preceding}}{\text{department (if any)}} = \dfrac{\text{ending units}}{\text{in process}} \times \dfrac{\text{transferred-in}}{\text{unit cost}}$

2   Materials $= \dfrac{\text{ending units}}{\text{in process}} \times \dfrac{\text{percent}}{\text{completed}} \times \dfrac{\text{materials}}{\text{unit cost}}$

3   Labor $= \dfrac{\text{ending units}}{\text{in process}} \times \dfrac{\text{percent}}{\text{completed}} \times \dfrac{\text{labor}}{\text{unit cost}}$

4   Overhead $= \dfrac{\text{ending units}}{\text{in process}} \times \dfrac{\text{percent}}{\text{completed}} \times \dfrac{\text{overhead}}{\text{unit cost}}$

A comparison of weighted average costing and fifo costing is presented in Table 9-2.

Table 9-3 shows the Nellie Corporation costs accounted for schedules for both departments under the fifo costing method.

TABLE 9-2
COMPARISON BETWEEN WEIGHTED AVERAGE COSTING AND FIFO COSTING

	WEIGHTED AVERAGE	FIFO
Overview	No distinction is made between completed units from beginning work-in-process and completed units from the present period	Units in the beginning work-in-process inventory are reported separately from units of the present period
Cost of production report:		
Quantities	Same procedure for both methods	
Equivalent production	All units completed during the period are included at 100%, regardless of the stage of completion of beginning work-in-process	Beginning work-in-process is included only to the extent that the units were completed during the present period
Costs to account for	Cost of beginning work-in-process is added to costs which have been added to production during the present period to arrive at "costs added during the period"	Beginning work-in-process costs are isolated and do not enter into the computation of unit costs for "costs added during the period"

	WEIGHTED AVERAGE	FIFO
Costs accounted for	Transferred-out costs are determined by multiplying completed units by the completed unit cost (there is only one completed unit cost)	Transferred-out costs are assumed to come first from beginning work-in-process and then from current production (there are two completed unit costs—beginning work-in-process and current production)
Comment	Weighted average costing results in less product cost information than provided by fifo (because of one set of unit costs rather than two)	

TABLE 9-3
NELLIE CORPORATION
COSTS ACCOUNTED FOR
FIFO

		DEPARTMENT 1
Transferred to next department:		
From beginning inventory:		
Inventory cost	$31,560	
Labor (4,000 × $1.28866 × 60%)	3,093	
Overhead (4,000 × $2.31959 × 60%)	5,567	$ 40,220
From current production:		
Units started and completed (31,000 × $7.10825)		220,356
Total transferred		$260,576
Work-in-process—ending:		
Materials (9,000 × $3.50)	$31,500	
Labor (9,000 × $1.28866 × 60%)	6,959	
Overhead (9,000 × $2.31959 × 60%)	12,526	50,985
Total		$311,561
Less rounding difference		1
Total costs accounted for		$311,560

		DEPARTMENT 2
Transferred to finished goods:		
From beginning inventory:		
Inventory cost	$66,880	
Labor (6,000 × $1.61290 × 80%)	7,742	
Overhead (6,000 × $.92166 × 80%)	4,424	$ 79,046
From current production:		
Units started and completed (38,000 × $11.04896)		.419,860
Total transferred		$498,906
Work-in-process—ending:		
Cost from preceding department (2,000 × $6.51440)	$13,029	
Materials (2,000 × $2.00)	4,000	
Labor (2,000 × $1.6129 × 30%)	968	
Overhead (2,000 × $.92166 × 30%)	553	18,550
Total costs accounted for		$517,456

Illustrated below is a summary of the section headings in the Costs Accounted for schedule under weighted average and fifo:

DEPARTMENT	WEIGHTED AVERAGE	FIFO
First	I Transferred to next dept.	I Transferred to next dept.
	II Work-in-process—ending	1 From beginning inventory
		2 From current production
		II Work-in-process—ending
After first	I Transferred to finished goods	I Transferred to finished goods
	(or next dept.)	(or next dept.)
	II Work-in-process—ending	1 From beginning inventory
		2 From current production
		II Work-in-process—ending

Tables 9-4 through 9-8 are the completed cost of production reports for Nellie Corporation under both weighted average and fifo and a chart comparing weighted average and fifo costs with each other.

TABLE 9-4
NELLIE CORPORATION
COST OF PRODUCTION REPORT
WEIGHTED AVERAGE
DEPARTMENT 1

Quantities:		
Beginning units in process	4,000	
Units started in process	40,000	44,000
Units transferred to next department	35,000	
Ending units in process	9,000	44,000

	TOTAL COST	UNIT COST
Costs to Account For:		
Costs added by department:		
Work-in-process—beginning:		
Materials	$ 14,000	
Labor	6,560	
Overhead	11,000	
Costs added during the period:		
Materials	140,000	$ 3.50 (A)
Labor	50,000	1.40 (B)
Overhead	90,000	2.50 (C)
Total costs to account for	$311,560	$ 7.40

Costs Accounted For:		
Transferred to next department (35,000 × $7.40)	$259,000	
Work-in-process—ending:		
Materials (9,000 × $3.50)	$31,500	
Labor (9,000 × $1.40 × 60%)	7,560	
Overhead (9,000 × $2.50 × 60%)	13,500	52,560
Total costs accounted for		$311,560

EQUIVALENT PRODUCTION	MATERIALS	CONVERSION COSTS
Units completed and transferred to		
Department 2	35,000	35,000
Ending units in process	9,000	5,400 (9,000 × 60%)
Total	44,000	40,400

Computations of unit cost:
(A) ($140,000 + $14,000) ÷ 44,000 = $3.50
(B) ($50,000 + $6,560) ÷ 40,400 = $1.40
(C) ($90,000 + $11,000) ÷ 40,400 = $2.50

TABLE 9-5
NELLIE CORPORATION
COST OF PRODUCTION REPORT
WEIGHTED AVERAGE
DEPARTMENT 2

Quantities:		
Beginning units in process	6,000	
Units received from preceding department	35,000	
Units added to production	5,000	46,000
Units transferred to finished goods	44,000	
Ending units in process	2,000	46,000

	UNITS	TOTAL COST	UNIT COST
Costs to Account For:			
Cost from preceding department:			
Work-in-process—beginning	6,000	$ 40,000	
Transferred in during the period	35,000	259,000 (A)	
Units added to production	5,000		
Adjusted units and unit cost	46,000	$299,000	$ 6.50 (B)
Costs added by department:			
Work-in-process—beginning:			
Materials		12,000	
Labor		10,280	
Overhead		4,600	
Costs added during the period:			
Materials		80,000	2.00 (C)
Labor		70,000	1.80 (D)
Overhead		40,000	1.00 (E)
Total costs to account for		$515,880	$11.30
Costs Accounted For:			
Transferred to finished goods			
(44,000 × $11.30)		$497,200	
Work-in-process—ending:			
Costs from preceding department:			
(2,000 × $6.50)	$13,000		
Materials (2,000 × $2.00)	4,000		
Labor (2,000 × 1.80 × 30%)	1,080		
Overhead (2,000 × $1.00 × 30%)	600	18,680	
Total costs accounted for		$515,880	

TABLE 9-5 (Continued)

EQUIVALENT PRODUCTION	MATERIALS	CONVERSION COSTS
Transferred to finished goods	44,000	44,000
Ending units in process	2,000	600 (2,000 × 30%)
Total	46,000	44,600

Computations of unit cost:
(A) $35,000 units × $7.40 total unit cost from Dept. 1 = $259,000
(B) $299,000 ÷ 46,000 = $6.50
(C) ($80,000 + $12,000) ÷ 46,000 = $2.00
(D) ($70,000 + $10,280) ÷ 44,600 = $1.80
(E) ($40,000 + $4,600) ÷ 44,600 = $1.00

JOURNAL ENTRIES

Work-in-process—Department 1 ($140,000 + $50,000 + $90,000)	280,000	
Work-in-process—Department 2 ($80,000 + $70,000 + $40,000)	190,000	
Materials ($140,000 Department 1 + $80,000 Department 2)		220,000
Payroll ($50,000 Department 1 + $70,000 Department 2)		120,000
Overhead ($90,000 Department 1 + $40,000 Department 2)		130,000
Costs added by Departments 1 and 2		
Work-in-process—Department 2	259,000	
Work-in-process—Department 1		259,000
Units transferred to Department 2 (35,000 × $7.40)		
Finished goods	497,200	
Work-in-process—Department 2		497,200
Units transferred to finished goods (44,000 × $11.30)		

TABLE 9-6
NELLIE CORPORATION
COST OF PRODUCTION REPORT
FIFO, DEPARTMENT 1

Quantities:		
Beginning units in process	4,000	
Units started in process	40,000	44,000
Units transferred to next department	35,000	
Ending units in process	9,000	44,000

	TOTAL COST	UNIT COST
Costs to Account For:		
Work-in-process—beginning	$ 31,560	
Costs added during the period:		
Materials	$140,000	$3.50000 (A)
Labor	50,000	1.28866 (B)
Overhead	90,000	2.31959 (C)
Total costs added	$280,000	$7.10825
Total costs to account for	$311,560	

Costs Accounted For:
  Transferred to next department:
    From beginning inventory:

Inventory cost	$31,560	
Labor (4,000 × $1.28866 × 60%)	3,093	
Overhead (4,000 × $2.31959 × 60%)	5,567	$ 40,220

  From current production:
    Units started and completed

(31,000 × $7.10825)		220,356
Total transferred		$260,576

  Work-in-process—ending:

Materials (9,000 × $3.50)	$31,500	
Labor (9,000 × $1.28866 × 60%)	6,959	
Overhead (9,000 × $2.31959 × 60%)	12,526	50,985
Total		$311,561
Less rounding difference		1
Total costs accounted for		$311,560

EQUIVALENT PRODUCTION	MATERIALS	CONVERSION COSTS
Units completed and transferred	35,000	35,000
− Beginning units in process	4,000	4,000
= Units started and completed	31,000	31,000
+ Amount needed to complete beginning		
work-in-process	0	2,400 (4,000 × 60%)
+ Ending units in process	9,000	5,400 (9,000 × 60%)
Total	40,000	38,800

Computations of unit cost:
(A) $140,000 ÷ 40,000 = $3.50000
(B) $50,000 ÷ 38,800 = $1.28866
(C) $90,000 ÷ 38,800 = $2.31959

TABLE 9-7
NELLIE CORPORATION
COST OF PRODUCTION REPORT
FIFO
DEPARTMENT 2

Quantities:		
Beginning units in process	6,000	
Received from preceding department	35,000	
Units added to production	5,000	46,000
Units transferred to finished goods	44,000	
Ending units in process	2,000	46,000

TABLE 9-7 (Continued)

	UNITS	TOTAL COST	UNIT COST
Costs to Account For:			
Work-in-process—beginning	6,000	$ 66,880	
Transferred in during the period	35,000	$260,576	
Units added to production	5,000		
Adjusted units and unit cost	40,000		$ 6.51440 (A)
Costs added during the period:			
Materials		$ 80,000	2.00000 (B)
Labor		70,000	1.61290 (C)
Overhead		40,000	.92166 (D)
Total cost added		$190,000	$11.04896
Total costs to account for		$517,456	
Costs Accounted For:			
Transferred to finished goods:			
From beginning inventory:			
Inventory cost	$66,880		
Labor (6,000 × $1.61290 × 80%)	7,742		
Overhead (6,000 × $.92166 ×			
80%)	4,424	$ 79,046	
From current production:			
Units started and completed (38,000 × $11.04896)	419,860		
Total transferred		$498,906	
Work-in-process—ending:			
Costs from preceding department			
(2,000 × $6.51440)	$13,029		
Materials (2,000 × $2.00)	4,000		
Labor (2,000 × $1.6129 × 30%)	968		
Overhead (2,000 × $.92166 × 30%)	553	18,550	
Total costs accounted for		$517,456	

EQUIVALENT PRODUCTION		MATERIALS	CONVERSION COSTS
	Units completed and transferred	44,000	44,000
−	Beginning units in process	6,000	6,000
=	Units started and completed	38,000	38,000
+	Amount needed to complete beginning		
	work-in-process	0	4,800 (6,000 × 80%)
+	Ending units in process	2,000	600 (2,000 × 30%)
	Total	40,000	43,400

Computations of unit cost:
(A) $260,576 ÷ 40,000 = $6.51440
(B) $80,000 ÷ 40,000 = $2.00000
(C) $70,000 ÷ 43,400 = $1.61290
(D) $40,000 ÷ 43,400 = $.92166

JOURNAL ENTRIES

Work-in-process—Department 1 ($140,000 + $50,000 + $90,000)	280,000	
Work-in-process—Department 2 ($80,000 + $70,000 + $40,000)	190,000	
Materials ($140,000 Department 1 + $80,000 Department 2)		220,000
Payroll ($50,000 Department 1 + $70,000 Department 2)		120,000
Overhead ($90,000 Department 1 + $40,000 Department 2)		130,000
Costs added by Departments 1 and 2		

Work-in-process—Department 2	260,576	
Work-in-process—Department 1		260,576
Units transferred to Department 2 ($40,220 + $220,356)		

Finished goods	498,906	
Work-in-process—Department 2		498,906
Units transferred to finished goods ($79,046 + $419,860)		

TABLE 9-8
NELLIE CORPORATION
COMPUTATION OF UNIT COST
WEIGHTED AVERAGE AND FIFO
DEPARTMENTS 1 AND 2

	TOTAL COST TRANSFERRED OUT	UNITS COMPLETED AND TRANSFERRED	UNIT COST
Weighted average:			
Department 1	$259,000	35,000	$ 7.40
Department 2	497,200	44,000	11.30
Fifo:			
Department 1	260,576	35,000	7.44503 (A)
Department 2	498,906	44,000	11.33877 (B)

Computations of unit cost:
(A) $260,576 ÷ 35,000 = $7.44503
(B) $498,906 ÷ 44,000 = $11.33877

SPOILED GOODS, DEFECTIVE GOODS, SCRAP, AND WASTE MATERIAL

Spoiled goods, defective goods, scrap, and waste material must also be accounted for under a process cost system. It is important that the distinctions between these four terms be understood because different accounting procedures are used for each. To help ensure understanding of the subsequent discussion, the terms are redefined below:

Spoiled Goods. Goods that do not meet production standards and are either sold for their salvage value or discarded. When spoiled goods are discovered, they are taken out of production and no further work is performed on them.

Defective Goods. Goods that do not meet production standards and must be processed further in order to be salable along with good units, or sold as irregulars.

Scrap Material. Raw materials that are left over from the production process that cannot be put back into production for the same purpose but may be usable for a different purpose or production process, or sold to outsiders for a nominal amount. Scrap material is similar to a by-product—a product that results from the production of a main product and has a small sales value in comparison with the main product. The distinction between scrap material and a by-product usually rests on the relative sales value of the item in relation to the main product—the smaller the sales value, the more likely it is to be classified as scrap material. A discussion of by-products will be given in the next chapter.

Waste Material.   That part of the raw materials that is left over after production and has no further use or resale value.

Accounting for Spoiled Goods (Units)

Spoiled units in a process cost system may be handled using either of two methods. Under the first method, spoiled units are considered as never having been put into production. By completely ignoring the spoiled units, the cost per unit is increased. Costs for the period are divided by a smaller number of equivalent units, thereby increasing the cost per unit. Cost allocation to goods completed and goods still in process is computed using the higher unit cost. Thus normal spoilage costs are automatically spread over all the good units.

This method is not recommended because it becomes inaccurate if there are work-in-process inventories or if materials, conversion, and spoilage costs are not incurred evenly throughout the production process. In addition, units that are still in process will be charged with spoilage costs even in situations where they have not been inspected.

Under the second method, a separate cost is calculated for the spoiled units. Management then has a choice as to the allocation of the costs. In the first method, spoiled costs are automatically allocated to work-in-process and completed goods. Under the second method, spoiled unit costs can be allocated to both work-in-process and completed units, to completed units alone, or to neither work-in-process nor completed units (abnormal spoilage). When there is both normal and abnormal spoilage, this method makes it possible to independently allocate normal and abnormal spoilage. This is preferable because abnormal spoilage is considered a period cost and should not be accounted for as a product cost (included in the cost of finished goods).

The actual cost of both normal and abnormal spoilage can be computed and reported under the second method. Because of its explicit recognition of such costs, the second method is preferred and will therefore be followed here.

The information in Table 9-9 will be used in the discussion of spoiled units.

Additional Information.   Materials are applied at the beginning of each department; conversion costs are applied evenly throughout the process.

Department 1.   Units are inspected at the *end* of the process. Work-in-process at the end was 40% complete; therefore, the units in work-in-process had not reached the inspection stage.

Department 2.   Units were inspected and spoiled units were discovered 40% of the way through the process. Work-in-process at the end was 60% complete; therefore, the units in work-in-process were inspected, and the cost of normal

TABLE 9-9
EXAMPLE OF NORMAL AND ABNORMAL SPOILED UNITS
UNDER WEIGHTED AVERAGE AND FIFO

	DEPARTMENT 1	DEPARTMENT 2
Units:		
Beginning units in process:		
All materials; 75% complete as to conversion costs	3,000	
All materials; 25% complete as to conversion costs		7,000
Units started in process	21,000	
Units received from preceding department		18,000
Units transferred to finished goods		19,000
Ending units in process:		
All materials; 40% complete as to conversion costs	2,000	
All materials; 60% complete as to conversion costs		4,000
Spoiled units:		
Normal	3,000	1,000
Abnormal	1,000	1,000
Costs:		
Work-in-process—beginning:		
From preceding department	0	$ 21,300
Materials	$ 9,000	25,000
Labor	14,000	66,760
Overhead	2,360	6,800
Total	$ 25,360	$119,860
Added during the period:		
Materials	$ 75,000	$ 50,000
Labor	100,000	200,000
Overhead	25,000	40,000
Total	$200,000	$290,000

spoilage should be allocated between finished goods and ending work-in-process. Materials added did not increase the number of units.

First Method—Spoiled Units Ignored for Computation of Equivalent Production. The solution under the first method of accounting for spoiled units (where spoiled units are ignored for computation of equivalent production) is presented in Table 9-10 (page 310) for Department 1 under weighted average costing to illustrate the shortcomings of this method.

Note the following shortcomings in this solution:

1 The cost of spoiled units was not identified.
2 The total cost of spoiled units was automatically spread over all the good units.
3 No distinction was made between normal spoilage and abnormal spoilage.

TABLE 9-10
COST OF PRODUCTION REPORT
WEIGHTED AVERAGE
DEPARTMENT 1

Quantities:		
Beginning units in process	3,000	
Units started in process	21,000	24,000
Units transferred to next department	18,000	
Ending units in process	2,000	
Spoiled units	4,000	24,000

	TOTAL COST	UNIT COST
Costs to Account For:		
Costs added by department:		
Work-in-process—beginning:		
Materials	$ 9,000	
Labor	14,000	
Overhead	2,360	
Costs added during the period:		
Materials	75,000	$ 4.2000 (A)
Labor	100,000	6.0638 (B)
Overhead	25,000	1.4553 (C)
Total costs to account for	$225,360	$11.7191
Costs Accounted For:		
Transferred to next department completed (18,000 × $11.7191)		$210,944
Work-in-process—ending:		
Materials (2,000 × $4.20)	$ 8,400	
Labor (2,000 × $6.0638 × 40%)	4,851	
Overhead (2,000 × $1.4553 × 40%)	1,164	14,415
Add rounding difference		1
Total costs accounted for		$225,360

EQUIVALENT PRODUCTION	MATERIALS	CONVERSION COSTS
Units completed and transferred	18,000	18,000
+ Ending units in process, amount completed (units × percent completed)	2,000	800 (2,000 × 40%)
Equivalent production	20,000	18,800

Computations of unit cost:
(A) ($75,000 + $9,000) ÷ 20,000 = $4.2000
(B) ($100,000 + $14,000) ÷ 18,800 = $6.0638
(C) ($25,000 + $2,360) ÷ 18,800 = $1.4553

4 Ending work-in-process will always be charged with spoilage costs under this method. This is not appropriate when ending work-in-process has not reached the inspection point.

Second Method—Spoiled Units Included in the Computation of Equivalent Production. As was stated earlier, the second method of accounting for spoiled units (where spoiled units are included in the computation of equivalent production) is the preferred method, and a detailed solution will therefore be presented.

Quantity Schedule. When spoiled units are found, they should be immediately taken out of the production process. Accounting for the removal of these units requires an additional output component to the physical unit flow equation. The addition of a line for spoiled units produces the following equation:

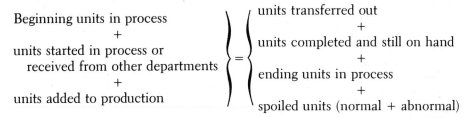

Spoiled units must therefore appear on the quantity schedule on the output side. A breakdown between abnormal and normal is not necessary because *units* alone are being accounted for. The units are still leaving production whether they are normal or abnormal. Below is the quantity schedule for Department 2:

Quantities:		
Beginning units in process	7,000	
Units received from preceding department	18,000	25,000
Units transferred to finished goods	19,000	
Ending units in process	4,000	
Spoiled units	2,000	25,000

Equivalent Production. Spoiled goods have absorbed costs up to the point of inspection. The degree of completion of spoiled goods therefore depends upon where inspection takes place and how costs are added to production.

In this example, Department 1 had 4,000 spoiled units. Because inspection was at the end of the process, the spoiled units were 100% complete for both materials and conversion costs. Spoiled goods were completed before removal from production; so all 4,000 units should be included in equivalent production.

In Department 2, the 2,000 spoiled units were discovered 40% of the way through the process. Because the materials were added at the beginning and conversion costs were added evenly, the spoiled units at the time of inspection had all their materials but only 40% of their conversion costs. Equivalent production for spoiled units is 2,000 (2,000 × 100%) for materials and 800 (2,000 × 40%) for conversion costs. It would be incorrect to add the entire 2,000 spoiled units to equivalent production for conversion costs because the units had received only 40% of their conversion costs.

The calculation of equivalent production for Departments 1 and 2, under weighted average and fifo costing is presented on page 312.

	WEIGHTED AVERAGE		FIFO	
	MATERIALS	CONVERSION COSTS	MATERIALS	CONVERSION COSTS
Department 1:				
Units completed and transferred	18,000	18,000	18,000	18,000
− Beginning units in process			3,000	3,000
= Units started and completed			15,000	15,000
+ Amount needed to complete beginning work-in-process (units X % to complete)				750 (A)
+ Ending units in process, amount completed (units × % completed)	2,000 (B)	800 (C)	2,000 (B)	800 (C)
+ Total spoiled units (units × % completed), which depends upon where inspection takes place and how costs are added to production	4,000 (D)	4,000 (D)	4,000 (D)	4,000 (D)
Equivalent production	24,000	22,800	21,000	20,550
Department 2:				
Units completed and transferred	19,000	19,000	19,000	19,000
− Beginning units in process			7,000	7,000
= Units started and completed			12,000	12,000
+ Amount needed to complete beginning work-in-process (units × % to complete)				5,250 (E)
+ Ending units in process, amount completed (units × % completed)	4,000 (F)	2,400 (G)	4,000 (F)	2,400 (G)
+ Total spoiled units (units × % complete), which depends upon where inspection takes place and how costs are added to production	2,000 (H)	800 (I)	2,000 (H)	800 (I)
Equivalent production	25,000	22,200	18,000	20,450

(A) 3,000 × 25% = 750
(B) 2,000 × 100% = 2,000
(C) 2,000 × 40% = 800
(D) 4,000 × 100% = 4,000
(E) 7,000 × 75% = 5,250

(F) 4,000 × 100% = 4,000
(G) 4,000 × 60% = 2,400
(H) 2,000 × 100% = 2,000
(I)   2,000 × 40% = 800

Schedule of Costs to Account For. The schedule of costs to account for is not affected by spoiled units under either weighted average costing or fifo costing. For illustrative purposes, the example problem has been solved using both methods.

Schedule of Costs Accounted For. One of the primary advantages of this method is the ability to allocate spoilage costs on the costs accounted for schedule between normal and abnormal spoilage. All necessary information is readily available. The cost allocation is based on the definition of abnormal and normal spoilage. Abnormal spoilage is the spoilage that exceeds what is considered normal for a particular production process. Such spoilage is considered controllable and a result of inefficient operations. Abnormal spoilage should not, therefore, be included in the cost of producing good units. Spoilage costs that are abnormal are a period cost and should be removed from the work-in-process account and listed separately. Abnormal spoilage has no effect on the unit costs because both units and costs are removed from production.

Normal spoilage is the unavoidable cost of producing good units. Spoilage that is a result of efficient production is therefore considered normal. Costs associated with normal spoilage should be included in the cost of producing good units.

In accounting for costs, abnormal and normal spoilage must be listed separately. Normal spoilage must also be properly allocated to completed units and to units still in process if work-in-process was inspected along with completed goods. Before allocation takes place, total spoilage costs must be calculated. Spoilage costs are determined in the first department by use of the following equation: Equivalent units spoiled × total unit cost (materials and/ or conversion costs). If costs are added at the beginning of production, the spoiled units are translated into equivalent production at 100%. If costs are added evenly through the process and inspection occurs before the end of the process, then equivalent spoiled units are found by multiplying all spoiled units by the point in production where inspection took place.

In subsequent departments, the transferred-in costs associated with the units must also be added to the spoilage cost total. The additional calculation would be: Spoiled units × transferred-in unit cost. All spoiled units in subsequent departments will be complete as far as the previous department's costs. Spoilage costs for Department 2 (under fifo) are computed as follows [see cost of production report (Table 9-14, page 319) for computations of unit cost]:

Spoilage (2,000 units):

From preceding department: (2,000 × $11.31644)	$22,633
Materials (2,000 × $2.77778)	5,556
Labor (2,000 × $9.77995 × 40%)	7,824
Overhead (2,000 × $1.95599 × 40%)	1,565
Total spoilage costs	$37,578

Once total spoilage costs are determined, they can be separated into abnormal and normal. The cost associated with each type of spoilage is calculated by multiplying the total spoilage cost by the ratio of the units in each type of spoilage to the total number of spoiled units as follows:

$$\text{Normal spoilage cost} \quad = \text{total spoilage cost} \times \frac{\text{normal spoiled units}}{\text{total spoiled units}}$$

$$\text{Abnormal spoilage cost} = \text{total spoilage cost} \times \frac{\text{abnormal spoiled units}}{\text{total spoiled units}}$$

The spoilage cost can also be found by dividing the total spoiled units into the total spoilage cost to get a *spoilage unit cost* and then multiplying the spoilage unit cost by either the abnormal or normal units to arrive at abnormal or normal spoilage costs, respectively. The equation would appear as follows:

Spoilage unit cost = total spoilage cost ÷ total spoiled units
Normal spoilage cost = spoilage unit cost × normal spoiled units
Abnormal spoilage cost = spoilage unit cost × abnormal spoiled units

For example, in Department 1 (under fifo), total spoilage is $38,616 [4,000 spoiled units × $9.65416 total unit cost; see Table 9-13 (page 318)]. Normal spoilage was 3,000 units at $28,962, computed as follows:

$$\$38,616 \times \frac{3,000}{4,000} = \underline{\$28,962}$$

or

$$\$38,616 \div 4,000 = \$9.654 \times 3,000 = \underline{\$28,962}$$

Abnormal spoilage was 1,000 units at $9,654 computed as follows:

$$\$38,616 \times \frac{1,000}{4,000} = \underline{\$9,654}$$

or

$$\$38,616 \div 4,000 = \$9.654 \times 1,000 = \underline{\$\ 9,654}$$

Normal spoilage costs may have to be allocated between work-in-process units and/or completed units. Under fifo costing, an attempt should be made to identify any spoiled units from beginning work-in-process. If spoilage can be traced to beginning work-in-process then normal spoilage should be allocated between beginning work-in-process and units started and completed. (To simplify matters, it will be assumed in all our illustrations and homework problems that spoilage occurred only in units started and completed and/or ending work-in-process.) When ending work-in-process has reached or is past the inspection stage, normal spoilage cost should also be allocated to ending work-in-process. The allocation of normal spoilage to all three areas would be computed as follows:

$$\begin{matrix} \text{To beginning} \\ \text{work-in-process} \end{matrix} = \begin{matrix} \text{normal spoil-} \\ \text{age costs} \end{matrix} \times \frac{\text{total units in beginning work-in-process}}{\text{total units*}}$$

* Total units = beginning work-in-process units + started and completed units + ending work-in-process units.

$$\frac{\text{To units started}}{\text{and completed}} = \frac{\text{normal spoil-}}{\text{age costs}} \times \frac{\text{total units started and completed}}{\text{total units*}}$$

$$\frac{\text{To ending}}{\text{work-in-process}} = \frac{\text{normal spoil-}}{\text{age costs}} \times \frac{\text{total units in ending work-in-process}}{\text{total units*}}$$

The costs accounted for schedule is not any different from previous examples except for the accounting for spoiled units.

In Department 1, inspection occurred at the end of the process; thus no spoilage was allocated to work-in-process (only 40% complete and therefore never reached inspection). Inspection occurs 40% of the way through the process in Department 2. Since the work-in-process units were 60% complete, they had gone through inspection and the normal spoilage has to be allocated to both work-in-process and finished goods.

Completed cost of production reports and journal entries under both weighted average and fifo costing are shown in Tables 9-11 through 9-14.

TABLE 9-11
COST OF PRODUCTION REPORT
WEIGHTED AVERAGE
DEPARTMENT 1

Quantities:		
Beginning units in process	3,000	
Units started in process	21,000	24,000
Units transferred to next department	18,000	
Ending units in process	2,000	
Spoiled units	4,000	24,000
	TOTAL COST	**UNIT COST**
Costs to Account For:		
Costs added by department:		
Work-in-process—beginning:		
Materials	$ 9,000	
Labor	14,000	
Overhead	2,360	
Costs added during the period:		
Materials	75,000	$ 3.50 (A)
Labor	100,000	5.00 (B)
Overhead	25,000	1.20 (C)
Total costs to account for	$225,360	$ 9.70
Costs Accounted For:		
Transferred to next department:		
Completed (18,000 × $9.70)	$174,600	
Normal spoilage (3,000 × $9.70)	29,100	$203,700
Work-in-process—ending:		
Materials (2,000 × $3.50)	$ 7,000	
Labor (2,000 × $5.00 × 40%)	4,000	
Overhead (2,000 × $1.20 × 40%)	960	11,960
Abnormal spoilage (1,000 × $9.70)		9,700
Total costs accounted for		$225,360

TABLE 9-11 (continued)

EQUIVALENT PRODUCTION	MATERIALS	CONVERSION COST	
Units completed and transferred to Department 2	18,000	18,000	
+ Ending units in process	2,000	800	(2,000 × 40%)
+ Spoiled units	4,000	4,000	(100% because in-
Total	24,000	22,800	spected at the end of process)

Computations of unit cost:
(A) ($75,000 + $9,000) ÷ 24,000 = $3.50
(B) ($100,000 + $14,000) ÷ 22,800 = $5.00
(C) ($25,000 + $2,360) ÷ 22,800 = $1.20

JOURNAL ENTRIES

Work-in-process—Department 1	200,000	
Materials		75,000
Payroll		100,000
Overhead (various credits)		25,000
To record costs added during the period		
Work-in-process—Department 2	203,700	
Work-in-process—Department 1		203,700

To record cost of goods transferred to Department 2
Note: Unit cost is $11.3167 ($203,700 ÷ 18,000 units) due to addition of normal spoilage cost. Normal spoilage was completely allocated to completed goods since work-in-process did not reach the inspection stage.

Abnormal spoilage	9,700	
Work-in-process—Department 1		9,700

To remove the cost of abnormal spoilage from work-in-process
(abnormal spoilage is a period cost account)

TABLE 9-12
COST OF PRODUCTION REPORT
WEIGHTED AVERAGE
DEPARTMENT 2

Quantities:		
Beginning units in process	7,000	
Received from preceding department	18,000	25,000
Units transferred to finished goods	19,000	
Ending units in process	4,000	
Spoiled units	2,000	25,000

	UNITS	TOTAL COST	UNIT COST
Costs to Account For:			
Costs from preceding department:			
Work-in-process—beginning	7,000	$ 21,300	
Transferred in during the period	18,000	203,700	
Total	25,000	$225,000	$ 9.00000 (A)
Costs added by department:			
Work-in-process—beginning:			
Materials		25,000	
Labor		66,760	
Overhead		6,800	
Costs added during the period:			
Materials		50,000	3.00000 (B)
Labor		200,000	12.01622 (C)
Overhead		40,000	2.10811 (D)
Total costs to account for		$613,560	$26.12433
Costs Accounted For:			
Transferred to finished goods:			
Completed (19,000 × $26.12433)	$496,362		
Normal spoilage	14,580 (E)	$510,942	
Work-in-process—ending:			
Costs from preceding department			
(4,000 × $9.00)	$ 36,000		
Materials (4,000 × $3.00)	12,000		
Labor (4,000 × $12.01622 × 60%)	28,839		
Overhead (4,000 × $2.10811 × 60%)	5,059		
Normal spoilage to work in process	3,070 (E)	84,968	
Abnormal spoilage		17,649 (E)	
Add rounding difference		1	
Total costs accounted for		$613,560	

EQUIVALENT PRODUCTION	MATERIALS	CONVERSION COSTS	
Units completed and transferred to finished goods	19,000	19,000	
+ Ending units in process	4,000	2,400	(4,000 × 60%)
+ Spoiled units	2,000	800	(2,000 × 40%—
Total	25,000	22,200	point of inspection)

Computations of unit cost:
(A) $225,000 ÷ 25,000 = $9.00000
(B) ($50,000 + $25,000) ÷ 25,000 = $3.00000
(C) ($200,000 + $66,760) ÷ 22,200 = $12.01622
(D) ($40,000 + $6,800) ÷ 22,200 = $2.10811
(E) *Spoilage (2,000 units)*

From preceding department (2,000 × $9.00)	$18,000	
Added during the period:		
Materials (2,000 × $3.00)	6,000	
Labor (2,000 × $12.01622 × 40%)	9,613	
Overhead (2,000 × $2.10811 × 40%)	1,686	
Total spoilage	$35,299	

TABLE 9-12 (Continued)

To Abnormal:	
[(1,000 ÷ 2,000) × $35,299]	$17,649*
To Normal:	
[(1,000 ÷ 2,000) × $35,299]	$17,650*
Further allocated Normal to:	
Finished goods:	
(19,000 ÷ 23,000 × $17,650)	$14,580
Work-in-process:	
(4,000 ÷ 23,000 × $17,650)	$ 3,070

JOURNAL ENTRIES

Work-in-process—Department 2	290,000	
Materials		50,000
Payroll		200,000
Overhead (various credits)		40,000
To record costs added during the period		
Finished goods	510,942	
Work-in-process—Department 2		510,942
To record cost of finished goods		

Note: Unit cost is $26.89 ($510,942 ÷ 19,000); the increase is due to the addition of normal spoilage cost

Abnormal spoilage	17,649	
Work-in-process—Department 2		17,649

To remove the cost of abnormal spoilage from work-in-process. Abnormal spoilage account reflects this cost as a period cost.

* Dollar difference due to rounding

TABLE 9-13
COST OF PRODUCTION REPORT
FIFO
DEPARTMENT 1

Quantities:		
Beginning units in process	3,000	
Units started in process	21,000	24,000
Units transferred to next department	18,000	
Ending units in process	2,000	
Spoiled units	4,000	24,000

	TOTAL COST	UNIT COST
Costs to Account For:		
Work-in-process—beginning	$ 25,360	
Costs added during the period:		
Materials	$ 75,000	$3.57143 (A)
Labor	100,000	4.86618 (B)
Overhead	25,000	1.21655 (C)
Total costs added	$200,000	$9.65416
Total costs to account for	$225,360	

Costs Accounted For:
  Transferred to next department:
    From beginning inventory:

Inventory cost	$25,360	
Labor (3,000 × $4.86618 × 25%)	3,650	
Overhead (3,000 × $1.21655 × 25%)	912	$ 29,922

    From current production:

Units started and completed		
(15,000 × $9.65416)		144,812
Normal spoilage (3,000 × $9.65416)		28,962
Total transferred		$203,696
Work-in-process—ending:		
Materials (2,000 × $3.57143)	$ 7,143	
Labor (2,000 × $4.86618 × 40%)	3,893	
Overhead (2,000 × $1.21655 × 40%)	973	12,009
Abnormal spoilage (1,000 × $9.65416)		9,654
Add rounding difference		1
Total costs accounted for		$225,360

EQUIVALENT PRODUCTION	MATERIALS	CONVERSION COSTS	
Units completed and transferred	18,000	18,000	
− Beginning units in process	3,000	3,000	
= Units started and completed	15,000	15,000	
+ Amount needed to complete beginning			
work-in-process	0	750	(3,000 × 25%)
+ Ending units in process	2,000	800	(2,000 × 40%)
+ Spoiled units	4,000	4,000	
Equivalent production	21,000	20,550	

Computation of unit cost:
(A) $75,000 ÷ 21,000 = $3.57143
(B) $100,000 ÷ 20,550 = $4.86618
(C) $25,000 ÷ 20,550 = $1.21655

JOURNAL ENTRIES

Work-in-process—Department 1	200,000	
Materials		75,000
Payroll		100,000
Overhead (various credits)		25,000
To record costs added during the period		
Work-in-process—Department 2	203,696	
Work-in-process—Department 1		203,696
To record cost of goods transferred to Department 2.		
Note: Unit cost is $11.3164 ($203,696 ÷ 18,000)		
Abnormal spoilage	9,654	
Work-in-process—Department 1		9,654
To remove the cost of abnormal spoilage from work-in-process		

TABLE 9-14
COST OF PRODUCTION REPORT
FIFO
DEPARTMENT 2

Quantities:

Beginning units in process	7,000	
Received from preceding department	18,000	25,000
Units transferred to finished goods	19,000	
Ending units in process	4,000	
Spoiled units	2,000	25,000

	UNITS	TOTAL COST	UNIT COST
Costs to Account For:			
Work-in-process—beginning	7,000	$119,860	
Transferred in during the period	18,000	$203,696	$11.31644 (A)
Costs added during the period:			
Materials		$ 50,000	2.77778 (B)
Labor		200,000	9.77995 (C)
Overhead		40,000	1.95599 (D)
Total costs added		$290,000	$25.83016
Total costs to account for		$613,556	

Costs Accounted For:

Transferred to finished goods:

From beginning inventory:

Inventory cost	$119,860	
Labor (7,000 × $9.77995 × 75%)	51,345	
Overhead (7,000 × $1.95599 × 75%)	10,269	$181,474

From current production:

Units started and completed (12,000 × $25.83016)		309,962
Normal spoilage		15,521 (E)
Total transferred		$506,957

Work-in-process—ending:

Costs from preceding department (4,000 × $11.31644)	$ 45,266	
Materials (4,000 × $2.77778)	11,111	
Labor (4,000 × $9.77995 × 60%)	23,472	
Overhead (4,000 × $1.95599 × 60%)	4,694	
Normal spoilage	3,268 (E)	87,811
Abnormal spoilage		18,789 (E)
Total		$613,557
Less rounding difference		1
Total costs accounted for		$613,556

EQUIVALENT PRODUCTION	MATERIALS	CONVERSION COSTS	
Units completed and transferred	19,000	19,000	
− Beginning units in process	7,000	7,000	
= Units started and finished	12,000	12,000	
+ Amount needed to complete beginning			
work-in-process	0	5,250	(7,000 × 75%)
+ Ending units in process	4,000	2,400	(4,000 × 60%)
+ Spoiled units	2,000	800	(2,000 × 40%
Total	18,000	20,450	point of in-spection)

Computations of unit cost:
(A) $203,696 ÷ 18,000 = $11.31644
(B) $50,000 ÷ 18,000 = $2.77778
(C) $200,000 ÷ 20,450 = $9.77995
(D) $40,000 ÷ 20,450 = $1.95599
(E) Spoilage (2,000 units):

From preceding department (2,000 × $11.31644)	$22,633
Added during the period:	
Materials (2,000 × $2.77778)	5,556
Labor (2,000 × $9.77995 × 40%)	7,824
Overhead (2,000 × $1.95599 × 40%)	1,565
Total spoilage	$37,578
To Abnormal:	
[(1,000 ÷ 2,000) × $37,578]	$18,789
To Normal:	
[(1,000 ÷ 2,000) × $37,578]	$18,789
Further Allocated Normal to:	
Finished goods:	
[(19,000 ÷ 23,000) × $18,789]	$15,521
Work-in-process:	
[(4,000 ÷ 23,000) × $18,789]	$ 3,268

JOURNAL ENTRIES

Work-in-process—Department 2	290,000	
Materials		50,000
Payroll		200,000
Overhead (various credits)		40,000
To record costs added during the period		
Finished goods	506,957	
Work-in-process—Department 2		506,957
To record costs of finished goods		
Unit cost is $26.68 ($506,957 ÷ 19,000)		
Abnormal spoilage	18,789	
Work-in-process—Department 2		18,789
To remove the cost of abnormal spoilage from work-in-process		

DEFECTIVE GOODS

Defective goods, as explained earlier, also do not meet production standards but are not removed from production as are spoiled units. The defective units are, instead, reworked in order to pass inspection or at least be salable as irregulars.

The main concept in defective units is that additional work is performed on them. Since units are not removed from production, the quantity schedule and the unit physical flow equation are not affected by defective units. The costs to account for schedule is the only section of the cost of production report that may be affected. In order to repair the units, additional materials, labor, or factory overhead may be necessary (rework may require all three elements, or only conversion costs).

Defective units may be normal and/or abnormal. The recording of cost expenditures depends on the units' classification. Costs associated with the reworking of normal defective units are charged to the production department where they occurred. The journal entry for normal defective units is as follows:

Work-in-process—Department B	X	
Materials		X
Payroll		X
Overhead		X

"Costs added by the department" for the period are increased because of the additional work required. Unit cost will therefore be increased by the cost to rework defective units.

Abnormal defective units are the number of defective units which exceed what is expected under efficient operations. Such costs are considered a result of inefficiency and as such should not be included in the products' cost. They would therefore not appear on the cost of production report. Abnormal costs are journalized as follows:

Abnormal defective unit loss	X	
Materials		X
Payroll		X
Overhead		X

An example of defective units is shown in the Summary Problem.

SCRAP MATERIAL

Scrap material is a raw material that is left over from the production process which cannot be used again in production but may have a nominal value if sold.

Scrap material may be handled in two ways:

1 If the value of the scrap was considered when preparing the factory overhead rate, the sale of the scrap would reduce the Factory Overhead Control account. For example, Department B took scrap into consid-

eration when preparing its factory overhead rate. During the month, 500 pounds of scrap were sold at $.30 a pound. The entry would be

```
Cash (500 × $.30) . . . . . . . . . . . . . . . . . . . . . . . .   150
        Factory overhead control . . . . . . . . . . . . . . .          150
```

2   If such consideration was not made in preparing the factory overhead rate, the proceeds would be credited to the departmental work-in-process account. Using the same information as in the previous example, except that scrap was not considered in the factory overhead rate, the journal entry would be

```
Cash (500 × $.30) . . . . . . . . . . . . . . . . . . . . . . . .   150
        Work-in-process—Department B . . . . . . . . .          150
```

The credit to work-in-process will reduce the materials costs on the costs to account for schedule of the cost of production report. No entry is made on the books when scrap is returned to the materials inventory— only a memorandum is made as to the type and quantity returned. An inventory value is assigned if the dollar amount is material and there is a time lag before it can be sold.

WASTE MATERIAL

No separate recognition is given to waste material because waste is usually unavoidable, is insignificant when compared with total cost, or has no value. Waste exceeding the norm should be investigated by management because it indicates inefficiencies somewhere in the production process. Costs incurred in disposing of waste materials are generally charged to factory overhead control.

CHAPTER REVIEW

Techniques used in a process cost system for handling beginning work-in-process inventories, spoiled goods, defective goods, scrap, and waste material were presented.

Beginning work-in-process inventories may be handled under either weighted average or first-in, first-out (fifo) costing techniques. Under weighted average costing, the costs from the beginning work-in-process are added to the current costs for the period and the total is divided by equivalent production to arrive at weighted average unit costs. Costs associated with the units still in process lose their identity because of the merger. The beginning inventory is treated as if it were a current period cost. There is no distinction between completed units and beginning work-in-process. There is only one completed unit cost for all units completed.

Under fifo costing, the units in the beginning inventory are reported separately from units of the present period. The assumption is that the work-in-process units are completed before units started this period are completed. Costs associated with the beginning units in process are separated from costs of units started and completed during the period. Because of the separation, there are two completed unit cost figures.

Two methods were discussed for computing spoiled unit cost in a process cost system. In the first method, spoiled unit costs are automatically absorbed into work-in-process and completed goods. Under the second method, spoiled unit costs can be allocated to *both* work-in-process and completed units, to completed units *only*, or to *neither* work-in-process nor completed units (abnormal spoilage). The second method was preferred and shown in detail because this method makes it possible to allocate normal and abnormal spoilage independently.

Defective units may be considered by management to be either normal and/or abnormal. The costs incurred in reworking the portion considered to be normal are charged to the production department where rework costs were incurred. The costs of reworking the number of units considered to be abnormal are charged as a period cost.

Value received for scrap material should be credited to factory overhead control if the value of scrap was considered in determining the overhead rate. If consideration was not made in determining the factory overhead rate, the department that produced the scrap should be credited.

No separate recognition is given to waste material because it is usually unavoidable, insignificant, and has no value.

GLOSSARY

Defective Goods—goods that do not meet production standards and must be processed further in order to be salable along with good units, or sold as irregulars.

First-In, First-Out (Fifo) Costing—a costing method by which units in the beginning inventory are reported separately from units of the present period. The assumption is that the work-in-process units are completed before units started this period are completed. Costs associated with the beginning units in process are separated from costs of units started and completed during the period. Because of the separation, there are two completed unit cost figures.

Scrap Material—raw materials that are left over from the production process that cannot be put back into production for the same purpose but may be usable for a different purpose or production process, or sold to outsiders for a nominal amount.

Spoiled Goods—goods that do not meet production standards and are either sold for their salvage value or discarded.

Waste Material—that part of the raw materials that is left over after production, and has no further use or resale value.

Weighted Average Costing—a costing method by which costs from the beginning work-in-process are added to the period's current costs and the total is divided by equivalent production to arrive at unit costs. Costs associated with the units still in process lose their identity because of the merger. The beginning inventory is treated as if it were current period costs. There is no distinction between completed units and beginning work-in-process. There is only one completed unit cost for all completed units.

SUMMARY PROBLEM

The following information relates to Grimsley Company:

	GRIMSLEY COMPANY DEPARTMENTS	
	1	2
Units:		
Beginning units in process:		
All materials; 30% complete as to conversion costs	10,000	
All materials; 60% complete as to conversion costs		5,000
Started in process during the period:	40,000	
Units received from Department 1		37,000
Units added to production		4,000
Transferred to finished goods		34,000
Ending units in process:		
All materials; 65% complete as to conversion costs	6,000	
All materials; 40% complete as to conversion costs		8,000
Spoiled units:		
Normal	5,000	3,000
Abnormal	2,000	1,000
Total spoilage	7,000	4,000
Costs:		
Beginning work-in-process:		
From preceding department	0	$ 40,000
Materials	$ 15,000	30,000
Labor	18,000	25,000
Overhead	7,000	12,000
Total	$ 40,000	$107,000
Added during the period:		
Materials	$ 80,000	$ 50,000
Labor	110,000	70,000
Overhead	50,000	40,000
Total	$240,000	$160,000
Rework costs for:		
Normal defective units		
Labor	$ 4,000	
Overhead	2,500	
Abnormal defective units		
Labor		$ 7,000
Overhead		4,000
Total	$ 6,500	$ 11,000

Additional Information: All materials are applied at the beginning of each department; conversion costs are applied evenly throughout the process.

Department 1: Spoiled units are inspected 60% of the way through the process.

Department 2: Spoiled units are inspected at the end of the process.

REQUIRED:

a Prepare a cost of production report and journal entries for both departments under the
1 Weighted average method
2 Fifo method

b Compute the unit cost of completed goods transferred out of each department under the weighted average and fifo methods.

SOLUTION TO SUMMARY PROBLEM

a.1

GRIMSLEY COMPANY
COST OF PRODUCTION REPORT
WEIGHTED AVERAGE
DEPARTMENT 1

Quantities:		
Beginning units in process	10,000	
Units started in process	40,000	50,000
Units transferred to next department	37,000	
Ending units in process	6,000	
Spoiled units	7,000	50,000

	TOTAL COST	UNIT COST
Costs to Account For:		
Costs added by department:		
Work-in-process—beginning:		
Materials	$ 15,000	
Labor	18,000	
Overhead	7,000	
Costs added during the period:		
Materials	80,000	$ 1.90000 (A)
Labor ($110,000 + $4,000 rework costs)	114,000	2.92683 (B)
Overhead ($50,000 + $2,500 rework costs)	52,500	1.31929 (C)
Total costs to account for	$286,500	$ 6.14612
Costs Accounted For:		
Transferred to Department 2		
(37,000 × $6.14612)	$227,406	
Normal spoilage	19,136 (D)	$246,542
Work-in-process—ending:		
Materials ($6,000 × $1.9)	$ 11,400	
Labor (6,000 × $2.92683 × 65%)	11,415	
Overhead (6,000 × $1.31929 × 65%)	5,145	
Normal spoilage to work in process	3,103 (D)	31,063
Abnormal spoilage		8,895 (D)
Total costs accounted for		$286,500

EQUIVALENT PRODUCTION	MATERIALS	CONVERSION COSTS	
Units completed and transferred to Department 2	37,000	37,000	
+ Ending units in process	6,000	3,900	(6,000 × 65%)
+ Spoiled units	7,000	4,200	(7,000 × 60%)
Total	50,000	45,100	

Computations of unit cost:
(A) ($80,000 + $15,000) ÷ 50,000 = $1.90000
(B) ($114,000 + $18,000) ÷ 45,100 = $2.92683
(C) ($52,500 + $7,000) ÷ 45,100 = $1.31929

(D) *Spoilage:* (7,000 units)

Materials (7,000 × $1.9)	$13,300
Labor (7,000 × $2.92683 × 60%)	12,293
Overhead (7,000 × $1.31929 × 60%)	5,541
Total spoilage	$31,134

To Abnormal:

(2,000/7,000 × $31,134)	$8,895

To Normal:

(5,000/7,000 × $31,134)	$22,239

Further Allocate Normal to:
Goods transferred to Department 2

(37,000/43,000 × $22,239)	$19,136

Work-in-process—ending

(6,000/43,000 × $22,239)	$ 3,103

JOURNAL ENTRIES

1	Work-in-process—Department 1	246,500	
	Materials		80,000
	Payroll ($110,000 + $4,000)		114,000
	Overhead (various credits) ($50,000 + $2,500)		52,500
2	Work-in-process—Department 2	246,542	
	Work-in-process—Department 1		246,542
3	Abnormal spoilage	8,895	
	Work-in-process—Department 1		8,895

GRIMSLEY COMPANY
COST OF PRODUCTION REPORT
WEIGHTED AVERAGE
DEPARTMENT 2

Quantities:		
Beginning units in process	5,000	
Received from preceding department	37,000	
Units added to production	4,000	46,000
Units transferred to finished goods	34,000	
Ending units in process	8,000	
Spoiled units	4,000	46,000

	UNITS	TOTAL COST	UNIT COST
Costs to Account For:			
Costs from preceding department:			
Work-in-process—beginning	5,000	$ 40,000	
Transferred in during the period	37,000	246,542	
Units added to production	4,000		
Adjusted units and unit cost	46,000	$286,542	$ 6.22917 (A)
Costs added by department:			
Work-in-process—beginning:			
Materials		30,000	
Labor		25,000	
Overhead		12,000	
Costs added during the period:			
Materials		50,000	1.73913 (B)
Labor		70,000	2.30583 (C)
Overhead		40,000	1.26214 (D)
Total costs to account for		$513,542	$11.53627
Costs Accounted For:			
Transferred to finished goods:			
Completed (34,000 × $11.53627)	$392,233		
Normal spoilage (3,000 ×			
$11.53627)	34,609	$426,842	
Work-in-process—ending:			
Costs from preceding department			
(8,000 × $6.22917)	$ 49,833		
Materials (8,000 × $1.73913)	13,913		
Labor (8,000 × $2.30583 × 40%)	7,379		
Overhead (8,000 × $1.26214 × 40%)	4,039	75,164	
Abnormal spoilage			
(1,000 × $11.53627)		11,536	
Total costs accounted for		$513,542	

EQUIVALENT PRODUCTION	MATERIALS	CONVERSION COSTS	
Units completed and transferred to finished goods	34,000	34,000	
+ Ending units in process	8,000	3,200	(8,000 × 40%)
+ Spoiled units	4,000	4,000	(4,000 × 100%)
Total	46,000	41,200	

Computations of unit cost:
(A) $286,542 ÷ 46,000 = $6.22917
(B) ($50,000 + $30,000) ÷ 46,000 = $1.73913
(C) ($70,000 + $25,000) ÷ 41,200 = $2.30583
(D) ($40,000 + $12,000) ÷ 41,200 = $1.26214

JOURNAL ENTRIES

1	Work-in-process—Department 2	160,000	
	Materials		50,000
	Payroll		70,000
	Overhead (various credits)		40,000

2	Finished goods	426,842	
	Work-in-process—Department 2		426,842
3	Abnormal spoilage	11,536	
	Work-in-process—Department 2		11,536
4	Abnormal defective unit loss	11,000	
	Payroll		7,000
	Overhead		4,000

a.2

GRIMSLEY COMPANY
COST OF PRODUCTION REPORT
FIFO
DEPARTMENT 1

Quantities:
Beginning units in process	10,000	
Units started in process	40,000	50,000
Units transferred to next department	37,000	
Ending units in process	6,000	
Spoiled units	7,000	50,000

	TOTAL COST	UNIT COST
Costs to Account For:		
Work-in-process—beginning	$ 40,000	
Costs added during the period:		
Materials	$ 80,000	$ 2.00000 (A)
Labor ($110,000 + $4,000 rework costs)	114,000	2.70784 (B)
Overhead ($50,000 + $2,500 rework costs)	52,500	1.24703 (C)
Total costs added	$246,500	$ 5.95487
Total costs to account for	$286,500	

Costs Accounted For:
Transferred to next department:			
From beginning inventory:			
Inventory cost	$40,000		
Labor added (10,000 × $2.70784 × 70%)	18,955		
Overhead added (10,000 × $1.24703 × 70%)	8,729	$ 67,684	
From current production:			
Units started and finished (27,000 × $5.95487)		160,781	
Normal spoilage to goods transferred		18,814 (D)	
Total transferred		$247,279	
Work-in-process—ending:			
Materials (6,000 × $2.00)	$12,000		
Labor (6,000 × $2.70784 × 65%)	10,561		
Overhead (6,000 × $1.24703 × 65%)	4,863		
Normal spoilage to work in process	3,051 (D)	30,475	
Abnormal spoilage		8,746 (D)	
Total costs accounted for		$286,500	

EQUIVALENT PRODUCTION	MATERIALS	CONVERSION COSTS	
Units completed and transferred to Department 2	37,000	37,000	
− Beginning units in process	10,000	10,000	
= Units started and completed	27,000	27,000	
+ Amount needed to complete beginning work-in-process	0	7,000	(10,000 × 70%)
+ Ending units in process	6,000	3,900	(6,000 × 65%)
+ Spoiled units	7,000	4,200	(7,000 × 60%)
Total	40,000	42,100	

Computations of unit cost:

(A) $80,000 ÷ 40,000 = $2.00000

(B) $114,000 ÷ 42,100 = $2.70784

(C) $52,500 ÷ 42,100 = $1.24703

(D) *Spoilage* (7,000 units)

Materials (7,000 × $2.00000)	$14,000
Labor (7,000 × $2.70784 × 60%)	11,373
Overhead (7,000 × $1.24703 × 60%)	5,238
Total spoilage	$30,611

To Abnormal:

(2,000/7,000 × $30,611)	$ 8,746

To Normal:

(5,000/7,000 × $30,611)	$21,865

Further Allocate Normal to:

Goods transferred to Department 2 (37,000/43,000 × $21,865)	$18,814
Work-in-process—ending (6,000/43,000 × $21,865)	$ 3,051

JOURNAL ENTRIES

1	Work-in-process—Department 1	246,500	
	Materials		80,000
	Payroll ($110,000 + $4,000)		114,000
	Overhead ($50,000 + $2,500)		52,500
2	Work-in-process—Department 2	247,279	
	Work-in-process—Department 1		247,279
3	Abnormal spoilage	8,746	
	Work-in-process—Department 1		8,746

GRIMSLEY COMPANY
COST OF PRODUCTION REPORT
FIFO
DEPARTMENT 2

Quantities:			
Beginning units in process		5,000	
Received from preceding department		37,000	
Units added to production		4,000	46,000
Units transferred to finished goods		34,000	
Ending units in process		8,000	
Spoiled units		4,000	46,000

	UNITS	TOTAL COST	UNIT COST
Costs to Account For:			
Work-in-process—beginning	5,000	$107,000	
Transferred in during the period	37,000	$247,279	
Units added to production	4,000		
Adjusted units and unit cost	41,000		$ 6.03120 (A)
Costs added during the period:			
Materials		$ 50,000	1.21951 (B)
Labor		70,000	1.83246 (C)
Overhead		40,000	1.04712 (D)
Total cost added		$160,000	$10.13029
Total costs to account for		$514,279	
Costs Accounted For:			
Transferred to finished goods			
From beginning inventory:			
Inventory cost	$107,000		
Labor added			
(5,000 × $1.83246 × 40%)	3,665		
Overhead added			
(5,000 × $1.04712 × 40%)	2,094	$112,759	
From current production:			
Units started and finished			
(29,000 × $10.13029)		293,778	
Normal spoilage			
(3,000 × $10.13029)		30,391	
Total transferred		$436,928	
Work-in-process—ending:			
Costs from preceding			
department (8,000 × $6.03120)	$ 48,250		
Materials (8,000 × $1.21951)	9,756		
Labor (8,000 × $1.83246 × 40%)	5,864		
Overhead			
(8,000 × $1.04712 × 40%)	3,351	67,221	
Abnormal spoilage			
(1,000 × $10.13029)		10,130	
Total costs accounted for		$514,279	

EQUIVALENT PRODUCTION	MATERIALS	CONVERSION COSTS	
Units completed and transferred to finished goods	34,000	34,000	
− Beginning units in process	5,000	5,000	
= Units started and completed	29,000	29,000	
+ Amount needed to complete beginning work-in-process	0	2,000	(5,000 × 40%)
+ Ending units in process	8,000	3,200	(8,000 × 40%)
+ Spoiled units	4,000	4,000	(4,000 × 100%)
Total	41,000	38,200	

Computations of unit cost:

(A) $247,279 ÷ 41,000 = $6.03120
(B) $50,000 ÷ 41,000 = $1.21951
(C) $70,000 ÷ 38,200 = $1.83246
(D) $40,000 ÷ 38,200 = $1.04712

JOURNAL ENTRIES

1	Work-in-process—Department 2	160,000	
	Materials		50,000
	Payroll		70,000
	Overhead (various credits)		40,000
2	Finished goods	436,928	
	Work-in-process—Department 2		436,928
3	Abnormal spoilage	10,130	
	Work-in-process—Department 2		10,130
4	Abnormal defective unit loss	11,000	
	Payroll		7,000
	Overhead		4,000

b

GRIMSLEY COMPANY
COMPUTATION OF UNIT COST
WEIGHTED AVERAGE—FIFO
DEPARTMENTS 1 AND 2

	TOTAL COST TRANSFERRED OUT	UNITS COMPLETED AND TRANSFERRED	UNIT COST
Weighted Average:			
Department 1	$246,542	37,000	$ 6.66330 (A)
Department 2	426,842	34,000	12.55418 (B)
Fifo:			
Department 1	247,279	37,000	6.68321 (C)
Department 2	436,928	34,000	12.85082 (D)

(A) $246,542 ÷ 37,000 = $6.66330
(B) $426,842 ÷ 34,000 = $12.55418
(C) $247,279 ÷ 37,000 = $6.68321
(D) $436,928 ÷ 34,000 = $12.85082

QUESTIONS

1 What two methods are used to account for beginning work-in-process inventory?
2 How are the beginning work-in-process costs treated under weighted average costing?
3 Why is waste material given no separate recognition?
4 What is the physical flow equation that takes into account both beginning work-in-process and spoiled units?
5 In preparing an equivalent production schedule, how does the treatment of the beginning units in process differ under weighted average costing and fifo costing methods?
6 Explain why there may be two completed unit costs under the fifo costing method.
7 Explain why a cost flow assumption (weighted average or fifo) is necessary when there are beginning work-in-process inventories.
8 Fifo costing is often selected over the weighted average costing method by companies that wish to use the unit costs for efficiency evaluation purposes. Explain the reasoning behind their selection of fifo.
9 What is the difference between spoiled goods and defective goods?
10 Explain the accounting difference in how normal and abnormal spoilage costs are treated under process costing.
11 One method of treating spoiled units is to treat them as if they never existed. Why is this not a good method?
12 Name the principal advantage of having a separate cost calculation for spoiled units.
13 In determining degree of completion for spoiled units, what two items must be known in order to do the calculation?
14 How is the balance sheet of a company affected by an improper classification of spoiled units as normal rather than as abnormal?
15 When should normal spoilage be allocated to both completed units and ending work-in-process?

EXERCISES

EXERCISE 1

Equivalent Production: Weighted Average vs. Fifo

Selected quantity data from a manufacturing firm for a 2-month period is shown on page 334.

	DEPARTMENT A	DEPARTMENT B
May:		
Units started in process	120,000	
Units received from preceding department		86,000
Units transferred to next department	86,000	53,000
Ending units in process	34,000	33,000
	(100% materials, 20% conversion costs)	(100% materials, 80% conversion costs)
June:		
Units started in process	117,000	
Units received from preceding department		132,500
Units transferred to next department	132,500	131,200
Ending units in process	?	?
	(100% materials, 45% conversion costs)	(100% materials 75% conversion costs)

All units were transferred out as they were completed.

REQUIRED:

a How many units were still in process at the end of June in both departments?
b Calculate the units of equivalent production for materials and conversion costs for both departments for June using *both* weighted average and fifo.

EXERCISE 2

Equivalent Production—Spoiled Units (Fifo)

The We-Make-It-You-Bake-It Dough Company manufactures frozen pizzas. There are two processing departments. Inspection for spoiled units takes place as follows:

> *Department 1:* at the end of the process
> *Department 2:* 50% of the way through the process

December's records showed the following data:

	DEPARTMENT 1	DEPARTMENT 2
Units:		
Beginning work-in-process:		
100% materials, 60% conversion costs	19,000	
100% materials, 30% conversion costs		24,000
Units started in process	28,000	
Units received from preceding department		40,000
Units transferred to finished goods		60,000
Ending units in process:		
100% materials, 85% conversion costs	4,500	
100% materials, 62% conversion costs		3,000
Spoiled units:		
Normal	2,000	500
Abnormal	500	500

Additional Information:

Materials are added at the beginning of the process in both departments. Department 2's materials do not increase the number of units in production. Conversion costs are incurred evenly throughout both processes.

REQUIRED:

For both departments, prepare an equivalent production schedule for both materials and conversion costs assuming a fifo costing method is used.

EXERCISE 3

Cost of Production Report—Fifo Costing

The XYZ Corp. uses a process cost system. Since the beginning of the operation, it has used weighted average costing to account for beginning work-in-process. Below is the cost of production report for March for Department 182.

THE XYZ CORP.
COST OF PRODUCTION REPORT—DEPARTMENT 182
FOR THE MONTH OF MARCH

Quantities:		
Beginning units in process		
(70% complete as to conversion costs)	4,300	
Units received from preceding department	21,700	
Units added to production	4,000	30,000
Units transferred to finished goods	23,600	
Ending units in process	6,400	30,000

	UNITS	TOTAL COST	UNIT COST
Costs to Account For:			
Costs from preceding department:			
Work-in-process—beginning	4,300	$ 21,740	
Transferred in during period	21,700	60,760	
Units added to production	4,000		
Adjusted units and unit cost	30,000	$ 82,500	$ 2.75 (A)
Costs added by department:			
Work-in-process—beginning			
Materials		$ 3,140	
Labor		2,150	
Overhead		1,200	
Costs added during the period:			
Materials		24,000	1.15 (B)
Labor		21,970	.90 (C)
Overhead		18,900	.75 (D)
Total costs to account for		$153,860	$ 5.55
Costs Accounted For:			
Transferred to finished goods			
(23,600 × $5.55)			$130,980
Work-in-process—ending			
Costs from preceding department			
(6,400 × $2.75)		$ 17,600	
Materials (6,400 × $1.15 × 0%)		0	
Labor (6,400 × $.90 × 50%)		2,880	
Overhead (6,400 × $.75 × 50%)		2,400	22,880
Total costs accounted for			$153,860

	MATERIAL	CONVERSION COSTS
Computations:		
Equivalent production:		
Transferred to finished goods	23,600	23,600
Ending units in process	0*	3,200†
Total	23,600	26,800

(A) $82,500 ÷ 30,000 = $2.75
(B) ($24,000 + $3,140) ÷ 23,600 = $1.15
(C) ($21,970 + $2,150) ÷ 26,800 = $.90
(D) ($18,900 + $1,200) ÷ 26,800 = $.75

  * Materials added at end of process
  † 6,400 × 50%

Management is contemplating switching to the fifo costing method.

REQUIRED:

Prepare the cost of production report for March for Department 182 assuming that fifo was being used.

EXERCISE 4

Unit Cost Calculations under Weighted Average Costing

The Pointed Pencil Company uses the weighted average costing method in its three processing departments. Materials are used in Departments 1 and 2. Raw materials in Department 2 consist of erasers which are placed immediately on each unit as it is transferred in.

Below is a portion of October's cost of production report for Department 2:

Work-in-process—ending
Costs from preceding department (8,900 × $.23)	$2,047.00
Materials (8,900 × 100% × $.03)	267.00
Labor (8,900 × 60% × $.28)	1,495.20
Overhead (8,900 × 60% × $.10).......................	534.00
	$4,343.20

During November the following activity occurred in Department 2:

Units transferred in	30,100
Costs transferred in	$8,483
Costs incurred:	
Materials	$1,683
Labor	$7,994.80
Overhead	$2,021
Units transferred out	29,000
Ending work-in-process	75% complete

REQUIRED:

Calculate the following unit costs for the month of November:
- **a** Transferred-in unit cost
- **b** Materials unit cost
- **c** Labor unit cost
- **d** Overhead unit cost
- **e** Total unit cost

EXERCISE 5

Cost of Transferred Units—Fifo Costing

Below is July's unit and cost data for a manufacturing firm that uses fifo costing.

	DEPARTMENT 2
Beginning units in process (55% materials, 15% of conversion costs)	135,000
Work-in-process—beginning	$472,500
Units transferred in during the period	420,000
Costs transferred in this period	$588,000

	DEPARTMENT 2
Costs added this period:	
Materials	$812,700
Labor...	$676,260
Overhead	$487,305
Units transferred out to finished goods	430,000
Ending units in process (25% materials,	
70% conversion costs	125,000

REQUIRED:

a Calculate the equivalent units for materials and conversion costs.

b Prepare the costs accounted for section of the cost of production report for Department 2.

EXERCISE 6

Spoiled Units: Allocation of Costs

The N. H. Jones Manufacturing Company produces china figurines. The molding department inspects for spoiled units when units are 65% complete. Materials are added at the beginning of the process, and labor and factory overhead are added evenly throughout the process. May's data for the department is as follows:

Beginning units in process (all materials, ⅓ conversion costs)	3,390
Beginning work-in-process inventory	$6,271.50
Units transferred in during the period	12,150
Costs transferred in during the period	$20,290.50
Units transferred out	11,000
Ending units in process (all materials, 60% conversion costs)	3,040
Spoiled units:	
Normal	800
Abnormal	700
Costs added during the period:	
Materials	$10,449.00
Labor	$3,420.63
Overhead...	$2,407.11

Additional Information:

Fifo costing is used to account for beginning work-in-process.

REQUIRED:

a Determine the total costs of the spoiled units.

b Allocate the total spoiled unit cost to normal and abnormal spoilage.

EXERCISE 7

Fifo Costing: Cost of Production Report—One Department

The Blondie Dye Company manufactures hair rinses and colorings. Raw materials are introduced into production at the 50% stage of completion in Department A. Labor and overhead are incurred evenly throughout the process. Because of the timing of certain chemical processes, units are often at different stages of completion.

Management uses the fifo costing method in an effort to analyze costs.

Beginning units in process in Department A for May were at the following stages of completion:

> 40% of the units were 10% complete
> 15% of the units were 40% complete
> 20% of the units were 55% complete
> 25% of the units were 70% complete

Beginning units in process amounted to 26,000 units. They had a total cost of $37,700.

During May, 68,000 units were started in process. The following costs were incurred: materials—$47,092; labor—$34,658; and overhead—$51,987.

Ending units in process for May amounted to 6,000 units. They were at the following stages of completion:

> 35% of the units were 25% complete
> 50% of the units were 45% complete
> 10% of the units were 75% complete
> 5% of the units were 95% complete

There were no spoiled units during the month.

REQUIRED:

Prepare a cost of production report for Department A for May.

EXERCISE 8

Multiple Choice

a The type of spoilage which should have *no* effect on the recorded cost of inventory is
1 Normal spoilage
2 Standard spoilage
3 Abnormal spoilage
4 Seasonal spoilage (AICPA Adapted)
b A company uses the fifo method of costing in a process cost system. In Department A, materials are added at the beginning of the process and conversion costs are incurred evenly throughout the process. Beginning work-in-process inventory on April 1 in Department A consisted of 50,000 units

estimated to be 30% complete. During April, 150,000 units were started in Department A, and 160,000 units were completed and transferred to Department B. Ending work-in-process inventory on April 30 in Department A was estimated to be 20% complete. The total equivalent production in Department A for April for materials and conversion costs, respectively, was

1 200,000 and 153,000
2 150,000 and 153,000
3 150,000 and 133,000
4 200,000 and 133,000   (AICPA Adapted)

c Material is added at the beginning of a process in a process costing system. The beginning work-in-process inventory for the process this period was 20% complete as to conversion costs. Using the first-in, first-out method of costing, the total equivalent units for material for this process during this period are equal to the

1 Beginning inventory this period for this process
2 Units started this period in this process
3 Units started this period in this process plus the beginning inventory
4 Units started this period in this process plus 80% of the beginning inventory this period   (AICPA Adapted)

d On April 1, 19X7, the Collins Company had 6,000 units of work-in-process in Department B, the second and last stage of their operations. The costs associated with these 6,000 units were $12,000 of costs transferred in from Department A, $2,500 of material costs added in Department B, and $2,000 of conversion costs added in Department B. Materials are added in the beginning of the process in Department B. Conversion was 50% complete on April 1, 19X7. During April, 14,000 units were transferred in from Department A at a cost of $27,000; and material costs of $3,500 and conversion costs of $3,000 were added in Department B. On April 30, 19X7, Department B had 5,000 units in work-in-process, 60% complete as to conversion costs. The costs attached to these 5,000 units were $10,500 of costs transferred in from Department A, $1,800 of material costs added in Department B, and $800 of conversion costs added in Department B.

Using the weighted average method, what were the equivalent units of production for the month of April?

	TRANSFERRED IN FROM DEPARTMENT A	MATERIALS	CONVERSION	
1	15,000	15,000	15,000	
2	19,000	19,000	20,000	
3	20,000	20,000	18,000	
4	25,000	25,000	20,000	(AICPA Adapted)

e Assume the same information that was in item d. Using the weighted average method, what was the cost per equivalent unit for conversion costs?

1   $4,200 ÷ 15,000
2   $5,800 ÷ 18,000
3   $5,800 ÷ 20,000
4   $5,000 ÷ 18,000   (AICPA Adapted)

REQUIRED:

Select the best answer to the above.

EXERCISE 9

Spoilage and Defective Units: One Department Using Weighted Average Costing

The Donough Manufacturing Company uses a process cost system. In the second department, Department X, both spoiled units and defective units occur during operations. Inspection for spoiled units occurs when units are 70% complete. Materials are added at the end of the process. Conversion costs are added evenly throughout the process.

Data pertaining to December's activity in Department X is shown below:

Units:

Beginning units in process—90% complete	17,000
Units received from preceding department	38,000
Units transferred to next department	40,000
Ending units in process	75% complete
Spoiled units:	
Normal	6,000
Abnormal	2,000

Costs:

Beginning work-in-process:	
From preceding department	$ 9,000.00
Materials	2,600.00
Labor...	5,290.00
Overhead	3,500.50
Added during the period:	
Materials	37,000.00
Labor...	30,005.00
Overhead	15,052.00
Rework costs for:	
Normal defective units:	
Labor...	1,317.00
Overhead	1,279.00
Abnormal defective units:	
Labor...	898.00
Overhead	526.00
Costs transferred in during the period from preceding department	48,750.00

Additional Information:

The company uses weighted average costing.

REQUIRED:

Prepare a cost of production report for Department X for December.

PROBLEMS

PROBLEM 1

Cost of Production Report: Two Months—Weighted Average

The Four-Eyes Optical Company manufactures eyeglass frames. In Department 3, the final processing department, the ornamentation is added to the frames at the beginning of the process. Labor and factory overhead are added evenly throughout the process. The department uses weighted average costing.

An examination of the records for Department 3 revealed the following for a 2-month period:

	APRIL	MAY
Units:		
Beginning units in process		
(all materials; 45% of conversion costs)	89,000	
Units received from preceding department	274,000	252,000
Units transferred to finished goods	300,000	295,000
Ending units in process:		
All materials; 25% conversion	63,000	
All materials; 50% conversion		20,000
Costs:		
Beginning work-in-process:		
From preceding department	$1,427,500	
Materials	12,380	
Labor	65,200	
Overhead	19,025	
Costs transferred in during the period	5,560,250	$4,788,000
Costs added during the period:		
Materials	89,260	76,860
Labor	200,030	249,070
Overhead	549,325	529,800

REQUIRED:

Prepare Department 3's cost of production report for April and May.

PROBLEM 2

Cost of Production Report: Weighted Average and Fifo Costing Methods

At the beginning of February, the A. B. Cee Company had $26,400 (materials—$10,200; labor—$8,200; and overhead—$8,000) in Department 1's beginning work-in-process inventory. The inventory consisted of 15,500 units which had all their materials costs and 65% of their labor and overhead costs.

During February, 36,000 units were started in process in Department 1. Costs incurred during the month were: materials—$20,292.00; labor—$27,266.25; over-head—$26,274.75. As units were completed, they were immediately transferred to Department 2. At the end of February, 3,500 units were still in process in Department 1. The units had all their material costs and 45% of their labor and overhead costs.

No spoilage occurred during February.

REQUIRED:

a Prepare a cost of production report for February using the weighted average costing method.

b Prepare a cost of production report for February using the fifo costing method.

(Round to four decimal places.)

PROBLEM 3

Cost of Production Report: Two Departments, Fifo Costing

The Slowburn Candle Company makes decorative candles. The company uses a process cost system which involves two processing departments. At the beginning of Department 1, liquid wax is placed into process. In Department 2, liquid dyes are added to the units transferred in. The dyes are added at the beginning of the process and increase the number of units. The company uses fifo costing to account for beginning work-in-process.

The company's data for June is shown below:

	DEPARTMENT 1	DEPARTMENT 2
Beginning units in process:		
All materials; 50% conversion costs	30,000	
All materials; 70% conversion costs		20,000
Units started in process	160,000	
Units received from previous department		150,000
Units added to production		5,000
Ending units in process:		
All materials; 20% conversion costs	40,000	
All materials; 80% conversion costs		35,000
Beginning work-in-process	$21,300	$19,500
Costs added by department during the period:		
Materials	$17,600	$ 9,300
Labor	54,340	87,780
Overhead	27,170	43,120

REQUIRED:

Prepare a cost of production report for Departments 1 and 2.

PROBLEM 4

Cost of Production Report: Two Departments, Weighted Average Costing

The Alena Manufacturing Company produces one product in two departments, 1002 and 1003. Raw materials are added at the beginning of Department 1002 and at the end of Department 1003. When the materials in Department 1003 are added, the number of final units are increased. Conversion costs are added evenly throughout both departments.

An examination of July's cost of production reports revealed the following unit cost information:

	DEPARTMENT 1002	DEPARTMENT 1003
Costs from preceding department		$.95
Materials	$.75	
Labor	.30	.10
Overhead	.15	.05

At the end of July, Department 1002 had 62,000 units still in process which were 12.5% complete. Department 1003 had 28,000 units still in process which were 25% complete.

During August, the following activity took place:

	DEPARTMENT 1002	DEPARTMENT 1003
Units started in process	139,000	
Units added to production		13,000
Units transferred to next department	175,000	
Units transferred to finished goods		200,000
Ending units in process	80% complete	40% complete
Costs added during the period:		
Materials	$116,310.00	$84,000
Labor	72,079.00	26,132
Overhead	32,123.50	13,066

REQUIRED:

Prepare the cost of production reports for Departments 1002 and 1003 using the weighted average costing method.

PROBLEM 5

Cost of Production Reports: Spoiled Units and Defective Units

The GGK Doll Company manufactures small vinyl dolls. In the molding department, the first department, the doll bodies are formed. Raw materials are added at the beginning of the process. Conversion costs are added evenly throughout the process. Inspection for spoiled units occurs at the 60% stage of completion. Completed units are transferred to the finishing department.

In the finishing department, the final necessities such as hair and clothing are placed on the doll bodies. Any defective units are reworked. Raw materials and conversion costs are added evenly throughout the process.

	MOLDING DEPARTMENT	FINISHING DEPARTMENT
September data		
Beginning units in process	520	780
% of completion	75%	10%
Units started in process	1,780	
Units transferred out of department	1,950	2,430
Ending units in process	150	300
% of completion	40%	70%
Spoiled units:		
Normal	150	
Abnormal	50	
Beginning work-in-process:		
Costs from preceding department		$ 495.30
Materials	$254.80	270.40
Labor	171.60	225.00
Overhead	104.00	250.00
Costs added during the period:		
Materials	$941.20	$1,580.00
Labor	552.60	1,475.00
Overhead	279.40	1,330.00
Rework costs for normal defective units:		
Materials		$ 24.00
Labor		16.00
Overhead		4.00

REQUIRED:

a Prepare a cost of production report for September for both departments using the weighted average costing method.

b Prepare a cost of production report for September for both departments using the fifo costing method.

PROBLEM 6

Cost of Production Report: Two Departments, Fifo, Spoilage

The A. B. Chemical Corp. produces an industrial cleaner. Three processing departments are used in its manufacture. Raw materials are added at the beginning of the first two departments, Department A and Department B. Units are measured in terms of gallons. The raw materials added in Department B increase the gallons transferred in by 5%.

Inspection for spoiled units occurs at the 30% stage of completion in Department A, and at the 70% stage of completion in Department B.

The cost accountant obtained the following information concerning October's activity:

	DEPARTMENT A	DEPARTMENT B
Units:		
Beginning units in process:	170,000 gallons	115,000 gallons
% of completion	15%	45%
Units started in process	430,000 gallons	
Units transferred to next		
department	490,000 gallons	595,000 gallons
Ending units in process	98,000 gallons	31,000 gallons
% of completion	25%	75%
Spoiled units:		
Normal	9,000 gallons	3,000 gallons
Abnormal	3,000 gallons	500 gallons
Costs:		
Beginning work-in-process:		
Costs from preceding department		$ 805,000
Materials	$ 595,000	195,500
Labor	31,875	103,500
Overhead	57,375	155,250
Costs added during the period:		
Materials	$1,612,500	$ 900,375
Labor	738,900	1,137,900
Overhead	1,108,350	1,706,850

REQUIRED:

Using the FIFO costing method, prepare a cost of production report for Department A and Department B for October.

PROBLEM 7

Comparison of Methods to Handle Spoiled Units and Spoilage Costs

The Waylon Manufacturing Company adds a second raw material in Department 2 at the 40% stage of completion. The raw material increases the number of units in process. Conversion costs are added evenly throughout the process. Spoiled units are detected 50% of the way through the process.

The cost accountant has not been allocating spoiled unit costs but has followed the policy of offsetting the spoiled units against those added to production.

Below is January data for Department 2.

	DEPARTMENT 2
Units:	
Beginning units in process (35% complete)	16,000
Units received from Department 1	54,000
Units added to production	6,000
Units transferred to finished goods	59,000
Ending units in process (80% complete)	14,000
Spoiled units:	
Normal	2,050
Abnormal	950
Costs:	
Beginning work-in-process:	
Costs from previous department	$ 30,142
Materials	11,200
Labor	4,480
Overhead	2,240
Costs added during this period:	
Materials	139,180
Labor	53,084
Overhead	26,542
Costs transferred in during the period	634,158

Additional Information:

No spoilage occurred in Department 1 during December and January. Weighted average costing is used.

REQUIRED:

a Prepare a cost of production report for January using the cost accountant's method for spoiled units.

b Prepare a cost of production report using the recommended method (recognition of spoilage costs).

c Because the cost accountant ignores spoiled unit costs, by how much are the inventories (work-in-process and finished goods) overstated?

PROBLEM 8

Cost of Production Report: Spoilage, Fifo Costing

The XYZ Company has three processing departments. Units must go through all three departments before they are transferred to finished goods. Raw materials are added in the first and third departments.

Information Concerning Department C (last processing department):

Materials are added at the 70% stage of completion. For every unit transferred in, $2.05 of raw materials are added.

Raw material addition does not increase the number of units.

Inspection for spoiled units occurs when units are 55% complete. Conversion costs are added evenly throughout the process.

March Activity Data—Department C:

Units:

Beginning units in process	18,900
10% are 40% complete	
60% are 65% complete	
30% are 90% complete	
Units received from preceding department	25,300
Units transferred to finished goods	38,000
Ending units in process	5,800
5% are 30% complete	
25% are 50% complete	
40% are 60% complete	
30% are 80% complete	

Spoiled units:

Normal	300
Abnormal	100

Costs:

Beginning work-in-process	$35,025.00
Transferred-in cost during the period	37,697.00
Labor	17,151.60
Overhead—50% of materials cost	

REQUIRED:

Using the fifo costing method, prepare a cost of production report for Department C for March.

PROBLEM 9

Spoiled Units

The Dexter Production Company manufactures a single product. Its operations are a continuing process carried on in two departments—machining and finishing. In the production process, materials are added to the product in each department without increasing the number of units produced.

For the month of June 19X5, the company records indicated the following production statistics for each department:

	MACHINING DEPARTMENT	FINISHING DEPARTMENT
Units in process, June 1, 19X5	0	0
Units transferred from preceding department	0	60,000
Units started in production	80,000	0
Units completed and transferred out	60,000	50,000
Units in process, June 30, 19X5	20,000	8,000
Units spoiled in production	0	2,000
Percentage of completion of units in process at June 30, 19X5:		
Materials	100%	100%
Labor	50%	70%
Overhead	25%	70%

The units spoiled in production had no scrap value and were 50% complete as to material, labor, and overhead.

Cost records showed the following charges for the month of June:

	MACHINING DEPARTMENT	FINISHING DEPARTMENT
Materials	$240,000	$ 88,500
Labor	140,000	141,500
Overhead	65,000	25,700

REQUIRED:

Prepare a cost of production report for June for both departments. (Assume spoilage was normal.)

(AICPA Adapted)

PROBLEM 10

Equivalent Production: Spoiled Units, Additional Materials

Poole, Inc., produces a chemical compound by a unique chemical process which Poole has divided into two departments, A and B, for accounting purposes. The process functions are as follows:

The formula for the chemical compound requires one pound of chemical X and one pound of chemical Y. In the simplest sense, one pound of chemical X is processed in Department A and transferred for further processing to Department B, where one pound of chemical Y is added when the process is complete. When the processing is complete in Department B, the finished chemical compound is transferred to finished goods. The process is continuous, operating 24 hours a day.

Normal spoilage occurs in Department A. Five percent of chemical X is spoiled in the first few seconds of processing.

No spoilage occurs in Department B.

In Department A, conversion costs are incurred uniformly throughout the process.

In Department B, conversion costs are allocated equally to each equivalent pound of output.

Poole's unit of measure for work-in-process and finished goods inventories is pounds. The following data are available for the month of October.

	DEPARTMENT A	DEPARTMENT B
Work-in-process, October 1	8,000 lb	10,000 lb
Stage of completion of beginning		
inventory (one batch per department)	$3/4$	$3/10$
Started or transferred in	50,000 lb	?
Transferred out	46,500 lb	?
Work-in-process, October 31	?	?
Stage of completion of ending inventory	$1/3$	$1/5$
Total equivalent pounds of material		
added in Department B	—	44,500 lb

(AICPA Adapted)

REQUIRED:

a Complete the above schedule.

b Prepare equivalent production schedules for Department A and Department B for October under fifo.

PROBLEM 11

Spoiled Units under Fifo Costing

In the course of your examination of the financial statements of the Zeus Company for the year ended December 31, you have ascertained the following concerning its manufacturing operations:

Zeus has two production departments (fabricating and finishing) and a service department. In the fabricating department, polyplast is prepared from Miracle Mix and Bypro. In the finishing department, each unit of polyplast is converted into six tetraplexes and three uniplexes. The service department provides services to both production departments.

Fabricating and finishing both use process cost accounting systems. Actual production costs, including overhead, are allocated monthly. Service department expenses are allocated to production departments as follows:

EXPENSE	ALLOCATION BASE
Building maintenance	Space occupied
Timekeeping and personnel	Number of employees
Other	One-half to fabricating, one-half to finishing

Raw materials inventory and work-in-process are priced on a fifo basis. Inspection for spoilage occurs at the end of the process. The following data were taken from the fabricating department's records for December.

Quantities (units of polyplast):

In process, December 1	3,000
Started in process during month	25,000
Total units to be accounted for	28,000
Transferred to finishing department	19,000
In process, December 31	6,000
Spoiled units (normal)	3,000
Total units accounted for	28,000

Cost of work-in-process, December 1:

Materials	$ 13,000
Labor......................................	17,500
Overhead	21,500
	$ 52,000
Direct labor costs, December	$154,000
Departmental overhead, December	$132,000

Polyplast work-in-process at the beginning and end of the month was partially completed as follows:

	MATERIALS	LABOR AND OVERHEAD
December 1	66 2/3%	50%
December 31	100%	75%

The following data were taken from raw materials inventory records for December:

	MIRACLE MIX		BYPRO	
	QUANTITY	AMOUNT	QUANTITY	AMOUNT
Balance, December 1	62,000	$62,000	265,000	$18,550
Purchases:				
December 12	39,500	49,375		
December 20	28,500	34,200		
Fabricating department usage	83,200		50,000	

Service department expenses for December (not included in departmental overhead above) were

Building maintenance	$ 45,000
Timekeeping and personnel	27,500
Other	39,000
	$111,500

Other information for December is presented below:

	SQUARE FEET OF SPACE OCCUPIED	NUMBER OF EMPLOYEES
Fabricating	75,000	180
Finishing	37,500	120
	112,500	300

REQUIRED:

a Prepare a schedule of equivalent production for materials and conversion costs for the fabricating department for December.

b Calculate the dollar amount of raw materials used by the fabricating department for December.

c Calculate the total amount of overhead incurred by the fabricating department during December.

d Prepare the cost of production report for December for the fabricating department.

(AICPA Adapted)

CHAPTER TEN
JOINT PRODUCT AND BY-PRODUCT COSTING

In many industries, one production process will yield several different products. For example, petroleum industries produce gasoline, heating oils, and kerosene from the refining of crude oil; meat-packing industries derive various cuts of meats, skins, and trimmings from an animal carcass. When more than one product results from one production process, the products are called joint products or by-products, depending primarily upon their relative sales value. Joint product and by-product costing involves the allocation of joint costs to the appropriate product. Such allocation is necessary for income and inventory determinations. Costing procedures for joint products and by-products do not constitute separate cost-accumulation systems but rather are part of either a job-order cost system or a process cost system. This chapter will present the techniques involved in accounting for joint products and by-products.

JOINT PRODUCTS

Joint products are individual products, each with significant sales values, which are produced simultaneously as a result of a common process or series of processes. For example, soybean oil and meal are joint products which result from the processing of soybeans. Joint products also occur in the meat-packing industry, and in many natural-resource refining industries. The basic characteristics of joint products are

1 Joint products have a physical relationship that requires simultaneous common processing. Processing of one of the joint products simultaneously results in the processing of the other joint products. When

additional quantities of one product are produced, the quantity of the other joint products will increase proportionately.

2 Manufacturing of joint products always has a split-off point at which separate products emerge, to be sold or processed further. Costs incurred after the split-off point do not generally cause allocation problems because they can be identified for the specific products.

3 None of the joint products are significantly greater in value than other joint products. This is the characteristic that distinguishes joint products from by-products.

JOINT COSTS AND THE SPLIT-OFF POINT

Joint costs are those incurred up to the point in a given production process where individual products can be identified. This point, known as the split-off point, occurs when each separate product, having a significant sales value, can be identified. The split-off point of by-products is the point at which the main product, having a significant value, is identified and associated by-products, having a lesser value, emerge.

DIFFICULTIES ASSOCIATED WITH JOINT COSTS

A major difficulty inherent in joint costs is that they are indivisible; that is, joint costs are not specifically identifiable with any of the products being produced simultaneously. For example, the costs of a refining company to locate, mine, and process the ore are joint costs that must be matched to the iron, zinc, or lead which are later extracted from the ore. Since the joint costs cannot be specifically identified for iron, zinc, or lead, the joint costs must be allocated. Joint costs are sometimes confused with common costs. Common costs are those incurred to produce products simultaneously, but each of the products could have been produced separately. Therefore, common costs are divisible and can be specifically identified for each of the products produced, while joint costs are indivisible.

ACCOUNTING FOR JOINT PRODUCTS

Joint product costs must be allocated to individual products in order to determine the net income and the ending inventory. As discussed previously, specific allocation is not possible. Therefore, an appropriate method must be used to allocate a proportion of the joint costs to individual products. The following methods are commonly used to allocate joint costs:

1 Market or sales value method
2 Quantitative unit method
3 Unit cost method

The information below will illustrate the above methods (see also Figure 10-1).

JOINT PRODUCT	X	Y	Z
Number of units produced	30,000	32,000	20,000
Market value at split-off point:			
Unit	$ 3.00	$ 2.50	$ 3.50
Total	$90,000	$80,000	$70,000
Total joint costs—$132,000			

Market or Sales Value Method

Under this method, joint costs are allocated according to the sales values of the individual products. Advocates of this method argue that a direct relationship exists between cost and selling price. They contend that selling prices of products are determined primarily by the costs involved in producing that product. Therefore, joint product costs should be allocated on the basis of the market value of the individual product. The allocation of joint costs on the basis of market or sales value is the most popular allocation method. The procedures to be used under this method will depend on whether:

1 The market value is known at split-off point.
2 The market value is not known at split-off point.

Market Value Known at Split-Off Point. When the market value is known at the split-off point, the total joint cost is allocated among the joint products by dividing the total market value of each product produced by the total market

FIGURE 10-1 **Diagram of Joint Cost Facts**

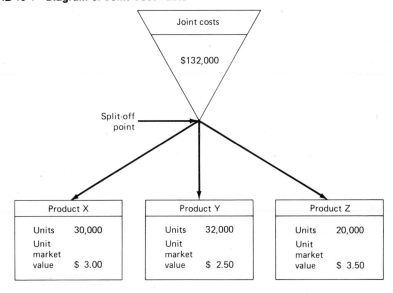

value of all products produced to arrive at a ratio of individual market values to total market values. This ratio is then multiplied by the total joint costs.

Formula:

$$\frac{\text{Joint cost allocation}}{\text{of } each \text{ product}} = \frac{\text{total market value of } each \text{ product}^1}{\text{total market value of } all \text{ products}^2} \times \text{joint costs}$$

[1] Total market value of *each* product = units produced of *each* product × unit market value of *each* product

[2] Total market value of *all* products = sum of all the total market values of each product

Computations:

Joint Cost Allocation of Each Product:

Product X

$$\frac{\$90,000 \ (1)}{\$240,000 \ (4)} \times \$132,000 = \$ \ 49,500$$

Product Y

$$\frac{\$80,000 \ (2)}{\$240,000 \ (4)} \times \$132,000 = \quad 44,000$$

Product Z

$$\frac{\$70,000 \ (3)}{\$240,000 \ (4)} \times \$132,000 = \quad 38,500$$

Total $132,000

Total Market Value of Each and All Products:
Total Market Value of Each Product:

PRODUCT	UNITS PRODUCED OF EACH PRODUCT	×	UNIT MARKET VALUE OF EACH PRODUCT	=	TOTAL MARKET VALUE OF EACH PRODUCT
X	30,000	×	$3.00	=	$90,000 (1)
Y	32,000	×	2.50	=	80,000 (2)
Z	20,000	×	3.50	=	70,000 (3)

Total Market Value of All Products:

$90,000 + $80,000 + $70,000 = $240,000 (4)

Under the market value method, all products are equally profitable because of equal gross profit percentages. A shortcoming of this conclusion is that this method considers only the volume of each product produced and not the volume of each product sold.

Market Value Not Known at Split-Off Point. The market value of a joint product may not be readily determinable at the split-off point, especially if additional processing is required to put the product into salable condition. A slight modification must therefore be made to the formula presented above—a *hypothetical* market value at the split-off point must be calculated. The hypothetical market value is determined by subtracting the cost of additional processing from the market value of the completed product.

The total cost of each product (allocation of joint costs + after split-off processing costs) is computed as follows: the total hypothetical market value of each product is divided by the total hypothetical market value of all products to determine the ratio of individual market value to total market value. This ratio is multiplied by the total joint cost, and the result is added to "after split-off" processing costs of each product.

Assume that the following information is added to the example (see also Figure 10-2). Joint products X, Y, and Z do not have a market value at the split-off point. After further processing, the market values are as follows: Product X—$4.50, Product Y—$4.00, and Product Z—$4.00. Additional processing costs after split-off were as follows: Product X—$5,000, Product Y—$10,000, and Product Z—$2,500.

FIGURE 10-2 Diagram of Joint Cost Facts

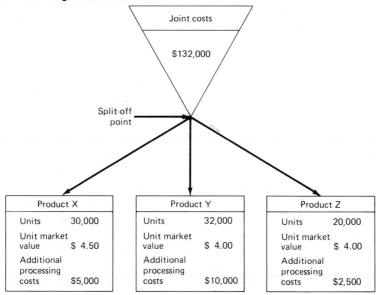

Formula:

Joint cost allocation of *each* product $= \left(\dfrac{\text{total hypothetical market value of } \textit{each} \text{ product}^{\,1}}{\text{total hypothetical market value of } \textit{all} \text{ products}^{\,2}} \times \text{joint costs} \right)$

$\qquad$ + after split-off processing costs of *each* product

[1] Total hypothetical market value of *each* product
$\quad$ = (units produced of *each* product × hypothetical market value of *each* product)
$\qquad\qquad\qquad\qquad$ − after split-off processing costs of *each* product

[2] Total hypothetical market value of *all* products
$\qquad\qquad$ = sum of all the total hypothetical market value of *each* product

Computations:

Joint Cost Allocation of Each Product:

$\qquad$ Product X

$$\left[\frac{\$130{,}000\ (1)}{\$325{,}500\ (4)} \times \$132{,}000 \right] + \$\ 5{,}000 = \$\ 57{,}719$$

$\qquad$ Product Y

$$\left[\frac{\$118{,}000\ (2)}{\$325{,}500\ (4)} \times \$132{,}000 \right] + \$10{,}000 = \quad 57{,}853$$

$\qquad$ Product Z

$$\left[\frac{\$77{,}500\ (3)}{\$325{,}500\ (4)} \times \$132{,}000 \right] + \$\ 2{,}500 = \quad \underline{33{,}928}$$

$\qquad\qquad\qquad\qquad\qquad\qquad\qquad$ Total $\quad \underline{\underline{\$149{,}500}}$

Total Hypothetical Market Value of Each and All Products:
$\qquad$ *Total Hypothetical Market Value of Each Product:*

PRODUCT	UNITS PRODUCED OF EACH PRODUCT	×	MARKET VALUE OF EACH PRODUCT	−	AFTER SPLIT-OFF PROCESSING COSTS OF EACH PRODUCT	=	TOTAL HYPOTHETICAL MARKET VALUE OF EACH PRODUCT
X	(30,000	×	$4.50)	−	$ 5,000	=	$130,000 (1)
Y	(32,000	×	4.00)	−	10,000	=	118,000 (2)
Z	(20,000	×	4.00)	−	2,500	=	77,500 (3)

$\qquad$ *Total Hypothetical Market Value of All Products:*

$\qquad\qquad$ $130,000 + $118,000 + $77,500 = $325,500 (4)

Under the market or sales value method, a change in market value of any of the products will cause a change in costs assigned to those products although no change in production has taken place. This fluctuation of cost allocation ratios as a result of changes in market values is seen as a major criticism of this method.

Quantitative Unit Method

Under this method, the quantity of output is used as a basis for allocating joint costs. The quantity of output is expressed in units which may be tons, quarts, or any other appropriate measurement. The quantity of output of all the joint products must be stated in the same terms. When the measurement basis of output varies from product to product, a common denominator such as quantity per ton must be used. The joint cost allocated to each product under this method is computed by dividing the quantity of output of each product by the total quantity of output of all products produced and multiplying the result by the total joint costs.

The following is an illustration of the allocation of joint costs under this method using the original example (Figure 10-1):

Formula:

$$\frac{\text{Joint cost allocation}}{\text{of \textit{each} product}} = \frac{\text{total units of \textit{each} product}}{\text{total units of \textit{all} products} ^1} \times \text{joint costs}$$

[1] Total units of *all* products = sum of *all* units produced

Computations:

Joint Cost Allocation of Each Product:

    Product X

$$\frac{30,000}{82,000 \ (1)} \times \$132,000 = \$ \ 48,293$$

    Product Y

$$\frac{32,000}{82,000 \ (1)} \times \$132,000 = \quad 51,512$$

    Product Z

$$\frac{20,000}{82,000 \ (1)} \times \$132,000 = \quad 32,195$$

                  Total $132,000

Total Units of All Products:

$$30,000 + 32,000 + 20,000 = \underline{82,000} \ (1)$$

Unit Cost Method

When products are produced in the same unit of measurement, the unit cost method may be appropriate. In order for this method to be used, units produced must be measured in the same terms. Two variations of this method are currently used:

1 Simple average unit cost
2 Weighted average unit cost

Simple Average Unit Cost. Under this method, total joint costs are divided by the total number of units produced to obtain the cost per unit; the cost per unit is multiplied by the number of units of each product produced to determine the portion of joint costs to be allocated to each product.

Allocation of the joint costs under the simple average unit cost method using the original example would be as follows:

Formula:

$$\text{Cost per unit} = \frac{\text{total joint costs}}{\text{total number of units produced}}$$

$$\text{Joint cost allocation} = \text{cost per unit} \times \text{number of units}$$
$$\text{of } \textit{each} \text{ product produced}$$

Computations:

Product X

$$\frac{\$132,000}{82,000} = \$1.60976 \times 30,000 = \$\ 48,293$$

Product Y

$$\frac{\$132,000}{82,000} = \$1.60976 \times 32,000 = \quad 51,512$$

Product Z

$$\frac{\$132,000}{82,000} = \$1.60976 \times 20,000 = \quad 32,195$$

Total $132,000

The basic assumption of this method is that all products produced by a common process should be charged a proportionate share of the total joint costs based on the number of units produced. It is assumed that the products are homogeneous and one product does not require more or less cost than any other product in the group. This method will produce the same results as the quantitative unit method; the difference is in the procedures applied. The quantitative unit method allocates joint costs in total; while the average unit cost method reduces joint costs to a unit cost, which is then multiplied by the quantities produced of each product, to arrive at the portion of joint costs of each product.

Weighted Average Unit Cost. There may be varying complexities affecting the production of joint products such as the difficulty in production, the amount of time involved, or the quality of labor needs or size of the unit. Allocation of joint costs using the simple average method does not always reflect these complexities. Weight factors, based on these complexities, may therefore be used to determine a more appropriate allocation.

The weighted average unit cost method is computed as follows: the number of units of each product is multiplied by its related weight factor to determine the total weighted average units of each product. The total weighted average units of each product are then divided by the total weighted average units of all products to determine the ratio of individual weighted average units to total weighted average units. This ratio is multiplied by the total joint costs to determine the joint cost allocation.

Assume that the joint products in the example are weighted as follows:

$$\text{Product X} = 3.0 \text{ points}$$
$$\text{Product Y} = 2.5 \text{ points}$$
$$\text{Product Z} = 4.0 \text{ points}$$

The cost allocation is as follows:

Formula:

$$\frac{\text{Joint cost}}{\text{allocation}} = \frac{\text{total weighted average units of } each \text{ product}^1}{\text{total weighted average units of } all \text{ products}^2} \times \text{joint costs}$$

[1] Total weighted average units of *each* product = number of units produced × weight factor
[2] Total weighted average units of *all* products = sum of all the total weighted average units of *each* product

Computations:

Joint Cost Allocation:

   Product X

$$\frac{90,000 \ (1)}{250,000 \ (4)} \times \$132,000 = \$ \ 47,520$$

   Product Y

$$\frac{80,000 \ (2)}{250,000 \ (4)} \times \$132,000 = \ \ \ 42,240$$

   Product Z

$$\frac{80,000 \ (3)}{250,000 \ (4)} \times \$132,000 = \ \ \ 42,240$$

$$\text{Total} \quad \underline{\$132,000}$$

Total Weighted Average of Each and All Products:
   Total Weighted Average of Each Product:

PRODUCT	NUMBER OF UNITS PRODUCED	×	WEIGHT FACTOR	=	TOTAL WEIGHTED AVERAGE OF EACH PRODUCT
X	30,000	×	3.0	=	90,000 (1)
Y	32,000	×	2.5	=	80,000 (2)
Z	20,000	×	4.0	=	80,000 (3)

Total Weighted Average of All Products:

$$90,000 + 80,000 + 80,000 = 250,000 \ \ (4)$$

BY-PRODUCTS

By-products are those of limited sales value produced simultaneously with a product of greater sales value, known as the main product. The main product is generally produced in much greater quantity than the by-products. By-products are an incidental result of producing the main product. By-products may result from the cleansing of the main product or the preparing of raw materials before they are used to manufacture the main product, or they may be the leftovers after the main product is processed.

By-products are generally one of the following two types:

1 They may be sold in the same form as originally produced.
2 They may undergo further processing before sale.

Occasionally there is a problem of whether to classify a product as a by-product or as scrap. The basic difference between the two is that by-products have a greater value than scrap. Also, scrap is generally sold immediately, whereas by-products may undergo further processing after the split-off point.

The classification of products as either joint products, by-products, or scrap may change as new uses of the products are discovered or old ones abandoned. Because of technological discoveries, a product may change from a by-product to a joint product. For example, in the petroleum industry, gasoline was originally a by-product of the main product, kerosene. But, after the invention of the automobile, gasoline became the main product and kerosene the by-product. In many cases, uses have been found for by-products formerly considered waste or scrap. For example, sewage plants have found ways to convert their waste into fertilizer. Product markets change relatively frequently; so a product that may have relatively small sales value today may have a high sales value tomorrow. Therefore, management should frequently examine product classifications and reevaluate when necessary.

ACCOUNTING FOR BY-PRODUCTS

By-products, like joint products, are produced from common materials. These costs are not traceable to the main product or to by-products. Since by-products are generally of secondary importance in production, cost allocation methods differ from those used for joint products. The methods of costing by-products fall into two categories.

Category 1

Methods in this category do not allocate specific costs to by-products for costing or inventory purposes. By-products are considered of minor importance, and therefore, no cost of production is assigned to them. Included in this category are the following three methods:

Method 1. Under this method, income from by-products is shown on the income statement under one of the following classifications:
Addition to Revenue:

  a Sales revenue
  b Other income

Deduction from Main Product:

  c A deduction from cost of goods sold of the main product
  d A deduction from total production costs of the main product

For example, assume the following facts:

Total production costs	$31,500 (18,000 units)
Sales from main product	37,500 (15,000 units at 2.50 per unit)
By-product revenue	2,275
Marketing and administrative expenses (main product)	3,250
Ending inventory (3,000 units × $1.75)	5,250

Classification A

Sales Revenue:

Sales:		
Main product (15,000 × $2.50)		$37,500
By-product..		2,275
Total		$39,775
Cost of goods sold:		
Total production costs (18,000 × $1.75)	$31,500	
Less: Ending inventory	5,250	26,250
Gross profit		$13,525
Marketing and administrative expenses		3,250
Net income		$10,275

Classification B

Other Income:

Sales (main product—15,000 × $2.50)		$37,500
Cost of goods sold:		
Total production costs (18,000 × $1.75)	$31,500	
Less: Ending inventory (3,000 × $1.75)	5,250	26,250
Gross profit		$11,250
Marketing and administrative expenses		3,250
Income from operations		$ 8,000
Other income:		
Revenue from sale of by-products		2,275
Net income		$10,275

Classification C

A Deduction from Cost of Goods Sold of the Main Product:

Sales (main product—15,000 × $2.50)		$37,500
Cost of goods sold:		
Total production costs	$31,500	
Less: Ending inventory	5,250	
Total cost of goods sold	$26,250	
Less: Revenue from sale of by-products	2,275	23,975
Gross profit		$13,525
Marketing and administrative expenses		3,250
Net income		$10,275

Classification D

A Deduction from Total Production Costs of the Main Product:

Sales (main product: 15,000 × $2.50)			$37,500
Cost of goods sold:			
Total production costs (18,000 × $1.75)	$31,500		
Less: Revenue from by-product	2,275	$29,225	
Less: Ending inventory (3,000 × $1.6236)*		4,871	24,354
Gross profit			$13,146
Marketing and administrative expenses			3,250
Net income			$ 9,896

*A new unit cost must be recalculated because of the decrease in total production costs by the by-product revenue

$$\frac{\$29,225}{18,000} = \$1.6236$$

In Classifications A, B, and C there is no attempt to distribute the costs assocated with the by-product. The main product's ending inventory is therefore overstated. These classifications are generally used when by-products are of relatively insignificant value. In Classification D, we reduced the total production cost; this reduction is based on sales value rather than on an allocation of costs as in joint cost allocation.

Method 2. The income statement shows by-product income in the same manner as Method 1; however, the amount of by-product income represents revenues from sales of by-products less marketing and administrative expenses and any additional processing costs.

To illustrate Method 2, assume the following additional facts in the previous example:

Marketing and administrative expenses associated with the by-product	$500
Additional processing costs of packaging the by-product	100
Total	$600

If by-products are accounted for as other income, the income statement would appear as follows:

Sales (main product)		$37,500
Cost of goods sold:		
Total production costs......................................	$31,500	
Less: Ending inventory	5,250	26,250
Gross profit		$11,250
Marketing and administrative expenses (main product)		3,250
Income from operations		$ 8,000
Other income:		
Net revenue from sale of by-products ($2,275 – $600)		1,675
Net income		$ 9,675

Method 3. Certain by-products are not sold but are used in manufacturing processes within the plant. The use of the by-product eliminates the need to purchase this material from outside suppliers. Under this situation, the replacement cost method is appropriate. This method credits production costs of the main product at the current market or replacement rate for furnishing such materials. Such a situation is very common in the steel industry. By-product revenue in this method does not appear in the income statement.

For example, assume the following facts:

Total production costs	$31,500 (18,000 units)
Sales from main product	37,500 (15,000 units at $2.50 per unit)
Replacement cost of by-products used	
in production of the main product	2,275
Marketing and administrative expenses............	3,250
Ending inventory (3,000 units × $1.75)	5,250

The income statement would appear as follows:

Sales (main product)			$37,500
Cost of goods sold:			
Total production (18,000 × $1.75)	$31,500		
Less: Replacement cost of by-product used			
in production	2,275	$29,225	
Less: Ending inventory (3,000 × 1.6236)*		4,871	24,354
Gross profit..			$13,146
Marketing and administrative expenses..............			3,250
Net income			$ 9,896

* $\dfrac{\$29,225}{18,000} = \$1.6236$

Note that the facts in the example above are identical to our previous example (Classification D), except that in this example, there was no revenue from the sale of by-products. Instead, these by-products were used in the manufacture of the main product.

Category 2

The methods in this category allocate a portion of joint costs to the by-products. The most commonly used method is the market value (or reversal cost) method (which is similar to Method 1, Classification D). The term reversal cost is commonly used to describe this method because you must work backward from revenue to cost. The estimated cost of the by-product is computed by deducting from its estimated sales value any estimated gross profit and marketing and administrative expenses. Total production costs are then reduced by the estimated cost of the by-product (rather than actual revenues as in Method 1, Classification D). The amount credited to the main product costs is charged to the by-product inventory account. The following data will be used to illustrate the market value (reversal cost) method:

	BY-PRODUCT X	MAIN PRODUCT
Sales (main product)		$150,000
Estimated sales value (by-product)	$12,000	
Process costs before separation		$75,000
Process costs after separation	$2,200	$23,000
Marketing and administrative expenses	$1,500	$12,000
Units produced	9,000	20,000

There are no beginning or ending inventory accounts. The company allows a 20% gross profit for by-product X.

The market value (reversal cost) method is shown below:

	BY-PRODUCT X	MAIN PRODUCT
Process costs before separation		$75,000
Estimated sales value of by-product	$12,000	
Gross profit for by-product (20% × $12,000)	$2,400	
Marketing and administrative expenses	1,500	3,900
Total		$ 8,100
Less: Process costs after separation		2,200
Amount credited to main product		$ 5,900 5,900
Net cost to produce main product at separation		$69,100
Add: Process costs after separation		2,200 23,000
Allocation of total costs		$ 8,100 $92,100
Unit costs:		
By-product ($8,100 ÷ 9,000)		$ .90
Main product ($92,100 ÷ 20,000)		$ 4.605

A basic assumption in this method is that the costs of a by-product are proportional to its market value. The revenue and expense matching lag that was experienced under Method 2 is eliminated under this method. Costs after separation are being matched to the total units produced, not just those sold. Of all the methods discussed, this method is the most similar to those employed in joint product costing.

SPOILED GOODS, DEFECTIVE GOODS, SCRAP, AND WASTE MATERIAL

Costing for joint products and by-products does not constitute a new cost accumulation system; rather, it is a modification to either a job order cost or process cost accumulation system. Therefore, when spoilage, defective goods, scrap, or waste result from the production of joint products and by-products, the accounting treatment of these items will depend on the system employed. For a more detailed discussion, see Chapters 7, 8, and 9.

EFFECTS UPON DECISION MAKING

The allocation techniques discussed in this chapter should not be used by management for decision-making purposes. Decision making generally involves output decisions, further-processing decisions, and pricing decisions. In each of these decisions, joint cost allocation is not necessary information and may prove to be counterproductive. The allocation of joint costs is performed solely for purposes of financial statements. Such allocations should not be influential in the plans made by management.

The very nature of joint products and by-products limits the flexibility of decisions. The physical characteristics of main products require that all the products in the group be produced. When the products manufactured are proportionately fixed, a decision to produce more or less of one product will result in proportionately more or less of the other product or products. Therefore, more useful information is obtained by comparing total input costs with the revenues generated from total output. Individual profit of each product is of little significance in production decisions regarding joint product and by-product production.

When the products can be produced in alternative ratios or "mixes," the decision is based on which mix obtains the most profit. In this situation, income increments are analyzed. Total cost variation under each alternative can be calculated and compared with the resultant total revenues. Although individual product cost cannot be specifically measured, total costs and total revenues can.

Total joint cost allocation has no influence on the decision whether to sell at the split-off point or manufacture a product further. A decision to process further depends on whether the incremental revenue is greater than the incremental cost. Management decisions should therefore be based on the opportunity costs rather than the allocation of historical joint costs.

Joint cost allocations are also not useful in price determinations. All products are expected to be sold; thus individual product pricing is aimed at selling all the joint products in the same proportion to that in which they are manufactured. This circular reasoning occurs because in certain methods, selling price determines allocation. Thus selling prices are used to determine cost and costs then are used to determine selling prices.

CHAPTER REVIEW

Many manufacturing processes produce different products from an initial raw material. Depending on their relative sales value, the products produced are either joint products or by-products. Joint products and by-products by their nature contain an element called joint costs. These are the costs incurred up to the point in a given process where individual products can be identified. The point of production at which separate products are identifiable is known as the split-off point. Joint costs incurred up to the split-off point cannot be identified with specific products.

A major difficulty inherent in joint costs is that they are indivisible; that is, joint costs are not specifically identifiable with any of the products being produced simultaneously.

Joint products are individual products, each of significant sales value, which are produced simultaneously as a result of a common process or series of processes. The manufacture of joint products occurs in the meat-packing industry, in natural-resource refining industries, and in those industries where raw materials must be graded before processing.

Joint product costs are those incurred in the processing of a common raw material. They occur prior to the split-off point. Such costs are indivisible, having been incurred for all products and not for each individually. The finished product cost includes some allocated portion of the joint products costs and any necessary additional processing.

The basic characteristics of joint products are

1 Joint products have an unavoidable physical relationship which requires simultaneous common processing.
2 Manufacturing of joint products has a split-off point at which separate products emerge to be sold or further processed.
3 Joint products have similar sales values.

Because of the importance of each joint product, individual product costs for both income determination and inventory valuation are necessary. Joint product costs should be allocated to each individual product.

The following methods for allocation of joint costs are commonly used:

1 *Market or sales value method*—Joint costs are allocated according to the sales values of the individual products at the split-off point. If the product does not have a market value at the split-off point and must be processed further to be salable, a hypothetical market value at split-off point is used.
2 *Quantitative unit method*—Units of measurement such as units, pounds, and heat content are used as the basis for allocating joint costs. A common unit of measurement must be used.
3 *Unit cost method*—This is a useful method when products are produced in the same unit of measurement and do not vary greatly. A cost per unit

is obtained by dividing the total joint costs by the total units produced. Joint cost allocation is found by multiplying the number of each product produced by cost per unit. A simple average does not always reflect the varying complexities of products sharing joint costs. Products may be assigned weight factors according to the difficulty of production, amount of time involved, labor needs, or size of units. A weighted cost per unit is calculated and used to allocate the joint product costs.

By-products are products of limited sales value produced simultaneously with a product of greater value known as the main product. By-products are an incidental result of producing the main product. By-products may be sold in the same form as originally produced, or they may undergo further processing before sale.

Classifications of products as joint products, by-products, or scrap are not fixed. Depending on market values and technological changes, products can shift from one classification to another.

Because by-products are generally of secondary importance, cost allocation differs from that applied to joint products. Methods for costing by-products fall into two categories.

Category 1. Methods in this category do *not* allocate specific costs to by-products. Three common methods in this category are

Method 1. The income from by-products is shown on the income statement as (a) sales revenue, (b) other income, (c) a deduction from cost of goods sold of main product, or (d) a deduction from total production costs of main product.

Method 2. The income statement shows by-product income in the same manner as Method 1, but the figure used for by-product income represents revenues from sales of by-products less marketing and administrative expenses and any additional processing costs incurred.

Method 3. When certain by-products are not sold but are used in the manufacturing process within the plant, the replacement cost method is generally used. Main product production costs are credited at the going market purchase or replacement price for such materials.

Category 2. Methods in this category allocate a portion of joint costs to the by-products. The market value (reversal cost) method is the most commonly used. Under this method, the total estimated cost of the by-products produced, not by-product revenue, is deducted from the total production cost of the main product. Estimated gross profit, marketing and administrative expenses, and additional processing costs are deducted from the by-product market value before crediting the main product's production costs.

Allocation of joint costs is used primarily for historical cost financial statements. Decisions usually involve output decisions, further processing decisions, and pricing decisions.

GLOSSARY

By-Product—product of limited sales value produced simultaneously with a product of greater value, known as a main product.

Joint Costs—costs incurred up to the point in a given process where individual products can be identified.

Joint Product Costs—common cost factors shared by joint products which are incurred prior to separation into individual joint products.

Joint Products—individual products of significant sales value which are produced simultaneously and are a result of a common process or series of processes.

Main Product—the product of greater value which is produced simultaneously with by-products.

Split-Off Point—the point of production at which separate products, either joint products or by-products, are identifiable.

SUMMARY PROBLEMS

PROBLEM 1

The M & O Company has one production process which yields three different products: P, R, and T. Specific allocation of costs is impossible for these products. At the split-off point the company can sell P at $4.50, R at $2.75, and T at $3.20. The costs incurred for the 75,000 units produced were $225,000 before split-off, and the ratio of units produced for P, R, and T is 2:5:3, respectively.

REQUIRED:

Allocate the total joint costs among the three joint products using:
    a The market value method   **b** The quantitative unit method
Round all answers to the second digit.

PROBLEM 2

The Oilslick Petroleum Company produces three joint products (A, B, and C) and one by-product (X) in its refinery. The split-off point occurs at the end of Department 1. Joint products A and B are not salable at the split-off point and must be further processed. Joint product costs are allocated under the *market or sales value method,* while the by-product is costed using the *reversal cost method.* Below is the cost information for the month ending June 30, 19X8.

Department 1 costs:

Materials	$50,000
Labor	20,000
Factory overhead	10,000
Total	$80,000

Production for the period:

Product A = 20,000 units
Product B = 20,000 units
Product C = 15,000 units
By-product X = 11,250 units

Costs after split-off:

Product A = $3,000
Product B = 2,000
By-product X = 1,000

Selling price of joint products:

Product A = $1.75 per unit (after split-off point)
Product B = 2.50 per unit (after split-off point)
Product C = 3.00 per unit (at split-off point)

Estimated revenue from by-product = $12,000
Estimated gross profit on by-product = 15%
Marketing and administrative expenses of by-product = $1,200

REQUIRED:

a Calculate the value of the by-product that should be credited to the joint products' production costs.

b Allocate the total joint costs among the three joint products.

c Compute total and unit costs for the joint products and the by-product.

PROBLEM 3

The Director Mining Company produces three joint products, X, Y, and Z. Because of the difference in labor needs, the products are weighted as follows: X, 5 points, Y, 8 points, and Z, 6 points. Cost information is as follows:

Department A:	Materials	=	$ 60,000
	Labor	=	40,000
	Factory overhead	=	20,000
	Total costs		$120,000

Units:	Product X	=	14,000
	Product Y	=	10,000
	Product Z	=	15,000
	Total units		39,000

REQUIRED:

a Using the weighted average method, allocate the joint costs of Department A.

b Determine how the joint costs would be allocated if the products were not weighted and the simple average unit cost method was used.

PROBLEM 4

The Huffy Manufacturing Corporation presents you with the following information:

Main product

Sales (20,000 units at $10 each)	$200,000
Marketing expenses	25,000
Ending inventory (5,000 units at $6 each)	30,000

By-product

Sales	$ 5,000
Total production costs	150,000
Administrative expenses	20,000

No specific costs are allocated to by-products because they are considered to be of minor importance.

REQUIRED:

Present the four principal methods of accounting for by-products on the income statement.

SOLUTIONS TO SUMMARY PROBLEMS

PROBLEM 1

Graphic Solution of Summary Problem 1

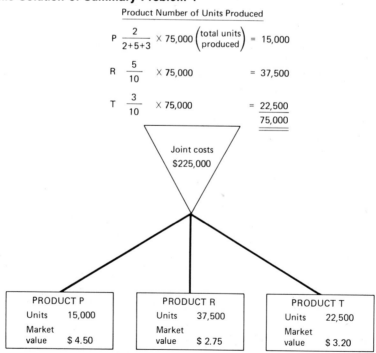

Product Number of Units Produced

$$P \quad \frac{2}{2+5+3} \times 75,000 \left(\frac{\text{total units}}{\text{produced}} \right) = 15,000$$

$$R \quad \frac{5}{10} \times 75,000 = 37,500$$

$$T \quad \frac{3}{10} \times 75,000 = \underline{22,500}$$
$$\phantom{T \quad \frac{3}{10} \times 75,000 = } \overline{\overline{75,000}}$$

Joint costs
$225,000

PRODUCT P		PRODUCT R		PRODUCT T	
Units	15,000	Units	37,500	Units	22,500
Market value	$ 4.50	Market value	$ 2.75	Market value	$ 3.20

a Joint cost allocation of each product $= \dfrac{\text{total market value of each product}}{\text{total market value of all products}} \times$ joint costs

PRODUCT

P $\quad \dfrac{67,500}{242,625} \times \$225,000 = \$\ 62,596.60$

R $\quad \dfrac{103,125}{242,625} \times \$225,000 = \quad 95,633.69$

T $\quad \dfrac{72,000}{242,625} \times \$225,000 = \quad 66,769.71$

$\quad\quad\quad\quad\quad\quad\quad\quad\quad\quad\quad\quad\quad \underline{\underline{\$225,000.00}}$

Total market value of each product = units produced of each product
$\quad\quad\quad\quad\quad\quad\quad\quad\quad\quad\quad\quad\quad \times$ unit market value of each product

Total market value of all products = sum of total market values of each product

PRODUCT	UNITS PRODUCED OF EACH PRODUCT	UNIT MARKET VALUE		TOTAL MARKET VALUE
P	15,000 (A)	× $4.50	=	$ 67,500
R	37,500 (B)	× 2.75	=	103,125
T	22,500 (C)	× 3.20	=	72,000
	Total market value of all products			$242,625

(A) 75,000 × 20%; (B) 75,000 × 50%; (C) 75,000 × 30%

b Total Units Produced:

$$15,000 + 37,500 + 22,500 = \underline{\underline{75,000}}$$

Joint Cost Allocation of Each Product:

Joint cost allocation of each product $= \dfrac{\text{total units of each product}}{\text{total units of all products}} \times$ joint costs

PRODUCT

P $\quad \dfrac{15,000}{75,000} \times \$225,000 = \quad \$\ 45,000$

R $\quad \dfrac{37,500}{75,000} \times \$225,000 = \quad 112,500$

T $\quad \dfrac{22,500}{75,000} \times \$225,000 = \quad 67,500$

$\quad\quad\quad\quad\quad\quad\quad\quad\quad\quad\quad\quad\quad \underline{\underline{\$225,000}}$

PROBLEM 2

a

	BY-PRODUCT		JOINT PRODUCTS
Process costs before separation			$80,000
Estimated sales value of by-product		$12,000	
Gross profit for by-product (15% × $12,000)	$1,800		
Marketing and administrative expenses			
for by-product	1,200	3,000	
Total		$ 9,000	
Less: Process costs after separation		1,000	
Amount credited to joint products		$ 8,000	8,000
Net cost to produce joint products at separation			$72,000

b

Product A:

$$\left(\frac{\$32,000}{\$125,000} \times \$72,000 \right) + \$3,000 = \underline{\$21,432}$$

Product B:

$$\left(\frac{\$48,000}{\$125,000} \times \$72,000 \right) + \$2,000 = \underline{\$29,648}$$

Product C:

$$\frac{\$45,000}{\$125,000} \times \$72,000 \qquad = \underline{\$25,920}$$

Hypothetical Market Value:

PROD-UCT	UNITS PRODUCED PER PRODUCT	MARKET VALUE PER PRODUCT	AFTER SPLIT-OFF PROCESSING COSTS PER PRODUCT	TOTAL
A	(20,000	× $1.75)	− $3,000	$ 32,000
B	(20,000	× 2.50)	− 2,000	48,000
C	(15,000	× 3.00)	0	45,000
			Total	$125,000

c

	PRODUCT A	PRODUCT B	PRODUCT C	BY-PRODUCT X
Cost before separation				$ 8,000
Cost after separation				1,000
Total cost	$21,432	$29,648	$25,920	$ 9,000
Units produced	20,000	20,000	15,000	11,250
Unit cost	$1.0716	$1.4824	$ 1.728	$ .80

PROBLEM 3

a

PRODUCT	UNITS		POINTS		WEIGHTED UNITS		COST PER UNIT*		TOTAL PRODUCTION COSTS
X	14,000	×	5	=	70,000	×	$ .50	=	$ 35,000
Y	10,000	×	8	=	80,000	×	.50	=	40,000
Z	15,000	×	6	=	90,000	×	.50	=	45,000
Total					240,000				$120,000

$$* \quad \frac{\text{Total production cost}}{\text{Total number of weighted units}} = \frac{\$120,000}{240,000} = \$ .50$$

b

$$\frac{\text{Total joint costs}}{\text{Total number of units produced}} = \frac{\$120,000}{39,000} = \$3.0769 \text{ (rounded) per unit}$$

Allocation:

Product X: 14,000 × $3.0769 = $ 43,077
Product Y: 10,000 × 3.0769 = 30,769
Product Z: 15,000 × 3.0769 = 46,154
$120,000

PROBLEM 4

a Sales Revenue:

Sales:		
Main product		$200,000
By-product		5,000
Total		$205,000
Cost of goods sold:		
Total production costs	$150,000	
Less: Ending inventory	30,000	120,000
Gross profit		$ 85,000
Marketing and administrative expenses		45,000
Net income		$ 40,000

b Other Income:

Sales (main product)		$200,000
Cost of goods sold:		
Total production costs	$150,000	
Less: Ending inventory	30,000	120,000
Gross profit		$ 80,000
Marketing and administrative expenses		
($25,000 + $20,000)		45,000
Income from operations		$ 35,000
Other income:		
Revenues from sale of by-products		5,000
Net income		$ 40,000

c A Deduction from Cost of Goods Sold of the Main Product:

Sales (main product)		$200,000
Cost of goods sold:		
Total production costs	$150,000	
Less: Ending inventory	30,000	
Total cost of goods sold	$120,000	
Less: Revenue from sale of by-products	5,000	115,000
Gross profit		$ 85,000
Marketing and administrative expenses		45,000
Net income		$ 40,000

d A Deduction from Total Production Costs of the Main Product:

Sales			$200,000
Cost of goods sold:			
Total production costs	$150,000		
Less: Revenue from by-products	5,000	$145,000	
Less: Ending inventory*		29,000	116,000
Gross profit			$ 84,000
Marketing and administrative expenses ...			45,000
Net income			$ 39,000

$$*\frac{\$145,000}{25,000} = \$5.80 \times 5,000 = \$29,000$$

QUESTIONS

1 Are there any similarities or differences between the natures of joint products and of by-products? Explain. What is the primary factor which determines whether a product is a joint product or a by-product?

2 How does management allocate the joint costs and the common costs to the individual products? Are the joint costs the same as common costs? Explain.

3 Describe the basic characteristics of joint products. What is included in the cost of a finished product that was once a joint product?

4 What are the pros and cons of the market or sales value method?

5 For each of the following, explain the relationship which exists between the two phrases:

a Proportionate share: simple average unit cost

b Hypothetical market value: sales value method

  c Quantity of output: quantitative unit method
  d Weight factor: weighted average unit cost
  e Gross profit percentages: market value method

6 Describe the assumption in the simple average unit cost method of allocating joint costs. Compare this method with the quantitative unit method.

7 How are by-products produced? What categories do they belong to?

8 "Management should frequently examine their product classifications and reevaluate when necessary." Why is this so?

9 The first method of category 1, accounting for by-products, has four separate areas where income from by-products can be shown on the income statement. Discuss these classifications.

10 What are the three methods that are included in category 1, accounting for by-products? Describe their similarities and differences.

11 What is reversal cost and how is it determined? What is the basic assumption in this method?

12 Costing for joint products is useful in decision making and in determining the selling prices. Discuss.

13 Answer true or false to the following statements:
  a By-products are always insignificant and should never have the main product's production cost allocated to them.
  b When joint products are proportionately fixed, the production decision is based on which product obtains the most profit.
  c Joint product and by-product costing is used for income and inventory determinations.
  d The complexities affecting the production of joint products are not reflected in the weighted average unit cost method.
  e Scrap has greater sales value than by-products but never undergoes further processing after split-off.
  f Decision making involves output decisions, further processing decisions, and pricing decisions.
  g The total joint costs influence the decision on whether to sell at split-off point or manufacture the product further.

14 In the reversal cost method, manufacturing costs applicable to the by-product ending inventories should be reported in the
  a Income statement
  b Balance sheet
  c Both a and b
  d None of the above

15 In the reversal cost method, the manufacturing cost of the main product is reduced by
  a The actual revenues received from the by-products
  b The estimated replacement costs of the by-product
  c The estimated market values of the by-products
  d None of the above

EXERCISES

EXERCISE 1

Market or Sales Value Method

Laure Hes, Inc., manufactures four products: Brand W, Brand X, Brand Y, and Brand Z. These products, each with significant sales value, are produced simultaneously. The following information is utilized in order to allocate the joint costs:

1 Brands W, X, and Z are sold at split-off point. Brand Y is processed further and then sold.
2 The market values for all the products total $550,000.
3 The costs of the finished products total $375,000.
4 Additional processing costs total $50,000.
5 Percentage of the total market value of all the products:

Brand W:	35%
Brand X:	15%
Brand Y:	30%
Brand Z:	20%

REQUIRED:

Calculate the joint cost allocation of each product using the market or sales value method.

EXERCISE 2

Sales Value Method

The Mellina Metal Co. locates, mines, and processes iron ore. During one production run, the joint costs totaled $15,000. In order to allocate these costs, management gathered the following additional information:

JOINT PRODUCTS PRODUCED	% OF TOTAL AMOUNT PRODUCED	MARKET VALUE AFTER FURTHER PROCESSING (PER POUND)	ADDITIONAL PROCESSING COSTS (PER POUND)	AMOUNT SOLD IN POUNDS
Iron	35	$1.50	$.65	9,000
Zinc	25	.75	.20	6,000
Lead	40	2.50	.80	10,000

The total amount produced was 30,000 pounds.

REQUIRED:

Using the sales value method, allocate the joint costs to the individual products. Calculate the total cost allocation of each product.

EXERCISE 3

Quantitative Unit and Simple Average Unit Cost Methods:

	GASOLINE	HEATING OILS	KEROSENE
Total market value of gallons sold (dollars)	40,000	28,500	36,540
Market value per gallon (dollars)	1.00	.60	.70
Beginning inventory (gallons)	10,275	20,000	25,000

The above chart was used by the G. E. T. Rich Co. for allocating the $45,000 joint costs incurred in March 19X7.

During this month the company had no ending inventory. No additional processing costs are incurred.

REQUIRED:

a The management of the G. E. T. Rich Co. allocates the joint cost using the quantitative unit method. Show how this is done.

b If management decided to use the simple average unit cost method to allocate the joint cost, what would the joint cost allocation be?

EXERCISE 4

The Unit Cost Method

The Burn T. Meat Corp. sells a variety of cooked meats, skins, and trimmings. Four joint products have varying complexities which affect their production.

PRODUCTS	AMOUNTS PRODUCED	COMPLEXITIES (POINTS)		
		DIFFICULTY IN PRODUCTION	TIME-CONSUMING	SPECIALIZED ATTENTION
1	1,000	3	4	2
2	9,000	0	1	4
3	400	4	4	0
4	5,100	1	3	0

The split-off point for these products occurs in Division 21, and the costs incurred up to this point are

Materials $20,000
Labor 15,000
Overhead 7,000

REQUIRED:

a Calculate the joint cost allocated to each of the joint products by using the simple average unit cost method.

b Using the weighted average unit cost method, determine the joint cost allocation for each product.

EXERCISE 5

Joint Products—Multiple Choice

From a particular joint process, Watkins Company produces three products—X, Y, and Z. Each product may be sold at the point of split-off or processed further. Additional processing requires no special facilities, and production costs of further processing are entirely variable and traceable to the products involved. In 19X3, all three products were processed beyond split-off. Joint production costs for the year were $60,000. Sales values and costs needed to evaluate Watkins' 19X3 production policy follow:

| | | | ADDITIONAL COSTS AND SALES VALUES IF PROCESSED FURTHER | |
| | UNITS | SALES VALUES | | |
PRODUCT	PRODUCED	AT SPLIT-OFF	SALES VALUES	ADDED COSTS
X	6,000	$25,000	$42,000	$9,000
Y	4,000	41,000	45,000	7,000
Z	2,000	24,000	32,000	8,000

Joint costs are allocated to the products in proportion to the relative physical volume of output.

REQUIRED:

Select the right answer for each of the following multiple choices.
  a The joint costs were allocated as follows
  1 X: $16,667, Y: $27,333, Z: $16,000
  2 X: $30,000, Y: $20,000, Z: $10,000
  3 X: $21,177, Y: $22,689, Z: $16,134
  4 X: $20,842, Y: $24,000, Z: $15,158
  b The total cost allocation for each product was
  1 X: $25,667, Y: $34,333, Z: $24,000
  2 X: $29,842, Y: $31,000, Z: $23,158
  3 X: $39,000, Y: $27,000, Z: $18,000
  4 X: $30,000, Y: $20,000, Z: $10,000
  c If the sales value method (known at split-off) was used, the joint cost allocation would be
  1 X: $16,667, Y: $27,333, Z: $16,000
  2 X: $30,000, Y: $20,000, Z: $10,000
  3 X: $21,177, Y: $22,689, Z: $16,134
  4 X: $20,842, Y: $24,000, Z: $15,158
  d If the sales value method (not known at split-off) was used, the total cost allocation would be
  1 X: $25,667, Y: $34,333, Z: $24,000
  2 X: $29,842, Y: $31,000, Z: $23,158
  3 X: $39,000, Y: $27,000, Z: $18,000
  4 X: $30,000, Y: $20,000, Z: $10,000

   e For units of Z, the unit production cost most relevant to a sell-or-process-further decision is

     1 $5

     2 $12

     3 $4

     4 $9

   f To maximize profits, Watkins should subject the following products to additional processing:

     1 X only

     2 X, Y, and Z

     3 Y and Z only

     4 Z only

(AICPA Adapted)

EXERCISE 6

Sell or Process Further—Incremental Revenue

Roberts, Inc., processes soybeans to make soybean oil and meal. The managers must decide whether to sell the soybean meal at split-off or to process it further to make soybean-flavored crackers. The following data was collected and used by the management:

	SOYBEAN OIL	SOYBEAN MEAL
Quantity produced (pounds)	300	550
Selling price at split-off (per pound)	$1.20	$.75
Additional costs (per pound)	—	$.50
Selling price after additional processing (per pound)	—	$1.95

   The total joint cost, $300, was allocated by using the quantitative unit method. There were no beginning or ending inventories.

REQUIRED:

   a Calculate the joint cost allocated to each product.

   b Using opportunity costs, determine whether management should sell the meal or process it further. What is the total incremental cost and incremental revenue?

EXERCISE 7

By-Product and Income Statements

The Sister Steel Co. manufactured 100 lb of Product L and 3,000 lb of Product M during October 19X7. Management did not allocate any joint costs to Product L for costing or inventory purposes and considered this a by-product. The production costs incurred before separation were $15,000. Both products were processed further.

	PRODUCT L	PRODUCT M
Additional costs after separation:		
Labor (dollars)	250	3,600
Fixed overhead (dollars)	60	650
Variable overhead (dollars)	25	1,100
Materials (dollars)	40	2,050
Selling expenses (dollars)	105	1,200
Administrative expenses (dollars)	30	900
Revenue from sales (dollars)	3,000	30,000
Beginning inventory (units)	0	0
Ending inventory (units)	0	500

REQUIRED:

a Management shows income from by-products as a deduction from cost of goods sold of the main product (Category 1, Method 1). Show the income statement for these two products.

b Show the income statement if management decided to use Category 1, Method 2, and show the income from by-products the same as a above.

EXERCISE 8

By-Products and Replacement Costs

The Woody Lumber Manufacturing Corp. uses two by-products, wood pulp and wood shavings, in the manufacturing processes within the plant. Half of the wood pulp is equally used in the manufacture of products A, B, and C, and the other half is used in product D. The wood shavings are used equally between A, B, and D. Since A, B, C, and D are joint products and are the main products of the company, their total production costs consist of joint and separate costs. There were no beginning inventories.

PRODUCTS	TOTAL PRO-DUCTION COSTS	MARKETING AND ADMIN-ISTRATIVE COSTS	REPLACE-MENT COSTS (PER UNIT)	SALES PRICE (PER UNIT)	UNITS PRO-DUCED	ENDING INVEN-TORY (UNITS)
Wood pulp	—	—	$1.05	—	4,000	—
Wood shavings	—	—	1.80	—	2,500	—
A	$12,800	$ 3,000	—	$2.20	12,800	4,300
B	29,450	1,750	—	3.00	19,000	2,000
C	21,175	4,125	—	2.95	16,940	1,340
D	50,000	10,500	—	4.50	25,000	10,100

REQUIRED:

Show a separate income statement for each product, A, B, C, and D. Show one figure for the by-product replacement costs on the income statement. Replacement cost of the by-products allocated is based on the quantity of the by-product used by each department.

EXERCISE 9

By-Products and the Reversal Cost Method

The following income statement is for the Searsites Corp., and the accountant has assumed that the by-product is considered of minor importance:

SEARSITES CORP.
INCOME STATEMENT
YEAR ENDED DECEMBER 31, 19X6

Sales (295,500 tons at $3.10)		$916,050
Cost of goods sold:		
Total production costs	$500,000	
Less: Ending inventory		
(17,000 tons at $1.60)	27,200	472,800
Gross profit on sales		$443,250
Less: Operating expenses		
Marketing expenses	$ 31,000	
Administrative expenses	47,800	78,800
Net operating income		$364,450
Other income:		
Revenue from sale of by-product		25,000
Net income		$389,450

Since management is considering whether or not to inventory the by-products, they assembled the following information:

By-Product Data:

1 Process costs after separation are 2.5% of total production costs.
2 Administrative expenses associated with by-product are 8% of total administrative expenses.
3 Marketing expenses associated with by-product are 5% of total marketing expenses.
4 Gross profit percentage is 15%.

Assume the accountants used Category 1, Method 1, in preparing the above income statement. There are no beginning inventories and no ending by-product inventory.

REQUIRED:

Rewrite the income statement using the reversal cost method (category 2) to allocate a portion of joint costs to the by-products.

PROBLEMS

PROBLEM 1

Joint Products

The Kerwin Chemical Co. produced 720,000 gallons of three joint products during the month of July. Chemical 1, Chemical 2, and Chemical 3 were produced in the ratio of 5:4:3, respectively, and had production costs of $298,000 before split-off.

	CHEMICAL 1	CHEMICAL 2	CHEMICAL 3
Sales value at split-off	$1.33/gal	$ .78/gal	$ .56/gal
Weight factors	4	10	7.5
Additional costs if			
processed further	$150,300	$52,021	$ 6,300
Sales value if			
processed further	$2.45/gal	$ .99 gal	$ .60/gal

REQUIRED:

a Calculate the total cost allocation of each joint product using the following methods:

   1 Market value method; market value known at split-off point

   2 Quantitative unit method

   3 Weighted average unit cost method

b Use total incremental revenue and incremental cost to determine whether you should process the joint products further. Show your calculations for each chemical.

PROBLEM 2

Joint Products

Pigs and Things, Ltd., raises pigs and hogs in order to sell various cuts of meat to the local markets. The following chart is used by management in order to allocate the joint product costs, $4,100, to individual products.

HOG	AMOUNT PRO- DUCED (LB)	AMOUNT SOLD (LB)	ADDITIONAL PRO- DUCTION COSTS (PER LB)	WEIGHT FACTORS	SALES PRICE AT SPLIT-OFF (PER LB)	SALES PRICE AFTER SPLIT-OFF (PER LB)
Bacon	200	170	$1.70	3	$10.70	$15.00
Lard	350	300	.60	1	6.25	7.50
Pork chops	150	150	1.30	4	12.50	17.75
Pigs' feet	100	80	1.00	2	7.30	8.00
Pigs' knuckles	100	100	.30	1	4.15	5.75
Cutlets	250	200	2.00	4	8.70	12.60
Trimmings	50	40	.05	1	1.25	2.00

REQUIRED:

Calculate the total cost allocation to each joint product using the following methods:

  a Market (or sales) value method; market value known at split-off

  b Quantitative unit method

  c Simple average unit cost method

  d Weighted average unit cost method

PROBLEM 3

Joint Products and the Gross Profit Percentage

The Spanish Olives Co. produces four joint products; uno, dos, tres, and cuatro. For the month of September the total processing costs after split-off were $67,600 and the total sales were $304,000.
Ending inventory:

uno	....	10% of production
dos	....	15% of production
tres	....	20% of production
cuatro	....	5% of production

Total sales were split between uno, dos, tres, and cuatro in the ratio 5:4:8:2, respectively.

Total processing costs after split-off were split between uno, dos, tres, and cuatro in the ratio 4:3:5:1, respectively.

167,960 units were produced of uno, dos, tres, and cuatro, and the ratio is 6:3: 7:1, respectively.

Every joint product produced in September was equally profitable. Ignoring the ending inventories, the gross profit percentage was 30%.

There were no beginning inventories.

REQUIRED:

a   Using the sales values, the gross profit percentage, and the further processing costs, determine the processing costs before split-off and the joint cost allocated to each product and determine the total joint cost.

b   Prepare a product line income statement from the facts given in this problem. Include gross profit percentages at the bottom of this five-column income statement.

PROBLEM 4

Joint Products and the Income Statement

Moe, Unlimited, produces five joint products; M-1, N-2, O-3, P-4, and Q-5. The joint production cost in one week is $7,500 and the administrative expenses are $4,000 for one week.
Data for the month of March:

	SALES (UNITS)	SALES PRICE (PER UNIT)	FURTHER PROCESSING COSTS (PER UNIT)	PRODUCTION (UNITS)
M-1	3,000	$3.19	$ .1500	4,500
N-2	10,000	4.50	.1300	15,000
O-3	4,000	6.30	.3125	4,000
P-4	5,000	2.85	.1800	6,300
Q-5	9,600	3.60	.2000	10,000

The manufacturing and administrative expenses are in the ratio of 1:5:3:2:5 for M-1, N-2, O-3, P-4, and Q-5, respectively. There were no beginning inventories.

REQUIRED:

Prepare a product line income statement for the month of March. Have six columns, one column for each product and a total column. (Assume 4 weeks = 1 month and each week the company produces the same amount of joint products.) The simple average unit cost method is used to allocate the joint costs.

PROBLEM 5

Joint Products and By-Products

The Mary Louise Ore Company refines various ores and produces metals used by many countries throughout the world. In Dept. 25 one ore produces two joint products, xium and zeous. Xium is sent to Dept. 36 and zeous is sent to Dept. 37. Further processing of xium creates the by-product, phori. The by-product and main product are sent to Dept. 41, where phori is used in the final processing of xium. After further refining in Dept. 37, zeous is transferred to Dept. 45 and its by-product rasic is sent to Dept. 48. Both main product and by-product are further processed before their sales.

The following information was gathered by the metal analysts:

1

COST DATA	DEPARTMENTS					
	25	36	37	41	45	48
Materials	$250,150	$40,200	$51,300	$20,100	$15,990	$10,000
Labor	100,300	10,150	14,130	9,360	8,800	4,500
Overhead	95,810	8,660	9,370	4,100	2,360	3,750

2

	SALES PRICE
zeous	$3.30/lb
rasic	$ .40/lb
xium	$4.10/lb

3   Rasic is shown on the income statement as a deduction from total production costs of zeous. The amount of by-product income represents revenues from sales of by-products less marketing and administrative expenses and any additional processing costs.
4   The replacement cost of phori is $.52/lb.
5   The amounts produced (no spoilage):

Dept. 25:   500,000 lb
            60% zeous
Dept. 36:   10% phori
Dept. 37:   80% zeous

6 Marketing and administrative expenses, $100,000. The Mary Louise Ore Company allocates 1.5% of the marketing and administrative expenses to every 100,000 lb of rasic.

REQUIRED:

Use the sales value method to allocate the joint costs among the joint products. Assume this company includes the by-product revenue and replacement costs in the hypothetical figures needed to allocate the joint costs.

PROBLEM 6

By-Products and Joint Products

The Crusher Corp. drills oil wells to obtain crude oil and natural gas. Last month the company produced 100,000 gal of crude oil and 15,750 gal of natural gas.

The crude oil sells for $55/gal and the natural gas sells for $12/gal.

After split-off the crude oil and natural gas were processed further at costs of $400,440 and $29,000, respectively.

The costs relating to the four oil wells were $250,000, $400,000, $880,100, and $330,000.

Selling costs were $100,350 for crude oil and $15,000 for natural gas.

Administrative expenses were $11,000 for natural gas and $50,000 for crude oil.

The additional costs incurred before split-off were $550,660.

The ending inventory is 10,000 gal of crude oil; there are no beginning inventories.

REQUIRED:

a Natural gas is a by-product of crude oil. In order to compare Method 1 and Method 2 in category 1, prepare a two-column income statement. By-product revenue is deducted from cost of goods sold.

b Management has decided that natural gas should be treated as a joint cost. Using the sales value method, allocate the joint costs between natural gas and crude oil. Calculate the total cost allocation for each product.

PROBLEM 7

By-Products and Revenues (Category 1, Method 1)

The Lovelife Company utilizes the wastes from its main product by selling these residual products to farmers throughout Southern County. During January, this company sold 100,000 lb of the main products, totaling $650,000, and 25,000 lb of the by-product, totaling $45,000.

January Cost Data:

Materials	$200,700
Labor	50,200
Fixed factory overhead	31,100
Variable factory overhead	30,000
Marketing expenses (total)	180,000
Administrative expenses (total)	70,000

The production costs after split-off are 65% of the total production costs. The by-product's marketing expenses are 3% of its selling price and the by-product's administrative expenses are 5% of the total administrative expenses.

The managers of the Lovelife Company collected a list of ratios that existed between the main product and the by-product. *During January the production costs after split-off were in the ratio:* materials, labor, fixed overhead, and variable overhead at 6:2:1:1, respectively. *The production costs after split-off were further broken down into:*

	MAIN PRODUCT	BY-PRODUCT
Materials	10	2
Labor	10	3
Fixed factory overhead	9	1
Variable factory overhead	7	1

The main product had an ending inventory of 30,000 lb and had no beginning inventory. The by-product had no beginning or ending inventories.

REQUIRED:

Using category 1, method 1, prepare an income statement for each of the following classifications of by-product revenue:

   a Other income
   b Additional sales revenue
   c A deduction from cost of goods sold
   d A deduction from total production costs.
The income statement is for the month of January.

PROBLEM 8

By-Products and Revenues (Category 1, Method 2)

REQUIRED:

Refer to Problem 7 to complete the requirements of this problem. Using category 1, Method 2, prepare an income statement for the month of January for each of the following classifications of by-product revenue:

   a Other income
   b Additional sales revenue
   c A deduction from cost of goods sold
   d A deduction from total production costs

PROBLEM 9

By-Products and Category 1

Williams and Williams, Inc., processes coke for the western region of the United States. During December, Department 1 manufactured 80,000 lb of raw material into 80% coke, 5% minor chemicals, and 15% tar. The minor chemicals are considered scrap and are disposed of immediately. The tar, a by-product, is processed further and is sold to several stores in Kansas. There were no beginning inventories.

DATA	COKE	TAR
Sales (percentage of units produced)	70%	100%
Materials	$50,000	$7,750
Labor	$26,000	$6,000
Factory overhead	$17,500	$3,250
Marketing and administrative expenses	$19,500	$2,500
Sales price/lb	$6.00	$1.75

The joint costs are 35% of the main product's total production costs. Management does not allocate specific costs to by-products for costing or inventory purposes.

REQUIRED:

a Prepare an income statement using category 1, Method 1. The income from by-products is shown as a deduction from total production costs.

b Prepare an income statement using category 1, Method 2. The income from by-products is shown as a deduction from total production costs.

c Prepare an income statement using category 1, Method 3. Assume that the by-products are used in manufacturing processes within the plant. Therefore, there are *no* by-product revenues and *no* by-product costs (production, marketing, and administrative expenses). The replacement cost of the by-products used in production of the main product is $5,000.

PROBLEM 10

By-Products, Reversal Cost, and Replacement Cost

TOTAL PROCESSING COSTS	MATERIALS	LABOR	OVERHEAD
Joint costs	$34,000	$21,160	$10,300
Additional processing costs	56,570	50,170	41,190

The Kathrock Corp. produced 250,500 units of Main Product A and 63,000 units of By-Product B. They sold 200,000 units of Main Product A and 60,000 units of By-Product B. The information pertaining to By-Product B was as follows:

Additional processing costs: 10% of total additional processing costs
Marketing expenses: 8% of total marketing expenses
Administrative expenses: 12% of total administrative expenses
Gross profit percentage: 11% of by-product sales

The total marketing expenses were $26,300 and the total administrative expenses were $24,250. The Kathrock Corp. sold $360,000 of A and $30,500 of B. There were no beginning inventories.

REQUIRED:

a Use the market value (or reversal cost) method to allocate a portion of joint costs to the by-product. Determine the amount of joint cost allocated to the by-product, the total costs for the by-product and the main product, and the unit costs for the by-product and the main product.

b Prepare an income statement using the reversal cost method to allocate a portion of joint costs to the by-product. The by-product's revenues and costs should be classified separately from the main product's.

c Prepare an income statement using category 1, Method 3. Assume that *all* the by-product produced is used in manufacturing processes within the plant. Therefore, there are *no* by-product revenues and *no* additional by-product costs (deduct by-product costs from the total costs). The total replacement cost of By-Product B used in production of the main product is $4,750.

CHAPTER ELEVEN

STANDARD COSTS– MATERIALS AND LABOR

The cost of manufacturing a product may be predetermined before production begins or computed when production is completed. A cost accumulation system (either job order costing or process costing) may therefore apply predetermined costs to units as they are being produced, rather than wait for actual cost data to be accumulated and allocated to completed units.

In previous chapters, costs were accumulated as they were incurred, with one exception: factory overhead was often applied to production, based on a predetermined rate. The use of a predetermined rate to apply factory overhead is a form of standard costing.

This chapter will present a discussion of the concepts and techniques of standard costing for materials and labor. The next chapter will discuss standard costing and variance analysis for factory overhead, and related topics in variance analysis.

ACTUAL VERSUS STANDARD COSTS

The National Association of Accountants (NAA), in their Research Report 7463, Standard Costs and Variance Analysis, defined actual or historical costs as "the cost which is accumulated during the process of production by the usual historical costing methods as opposed to the cost which has been determined in advance of the production process. The term 'actual' is not intended to convey any implication as to the accuracy with which costs are measured." Standard cost represents the "planned" cost of a product and is generally established well before production begins. The establishment of standards thus provides management with goals to attain and bases for comparison with actual results.

Standard costs are those expected to be achieved in a particular production process under normal conditions. Standard costing, on the other hand, is concerned with cost *per unit* and serves basically the same purpose as a budget. Budgets, however, generally provide cost goals in *total* cost figures rather than on a unit cost basis.

Standard costs do not replace actual costs in a cost accumulation system. Instead, standard costs and actual costs complement each other.

USES OF STANDARD COSTS

Cost information may be used for many different purposes. It should be noted that cost information which serves one purpose may not be appropriate for another. Therefore, the purpose for which cost information is to be used should be clearly defined before procedures are developed to accumulate cost data. Standard costs may be used for the following purposes:

1 Cost control
2 Inventory costing
3 Budgetary planning
4 Product pricing
5 Record keeping

Cost Control

The objective of cost control is to aid management in the production of a unit of usable product or service, at the lowest possible cost, in accordance with predetermined quality standards. Standards enable management to make periodic comparisons of actual costs with standard costs in order to measure performance and correct inefficiencies.

Inventory Costing

Two views are held by accountants concerning inventory costing. One group maintains that inventory should be stated in standard cost terms and that cost caused by inefficiency and idle production facilities should be charged as period costs. The other group maintains that all costs incurred in the production of a unit should be included in *inventory cost*. The Committee on Accounting Procedures, in Accounting Research Bulletin 43, has taken the following position:

> Standard costs are acceptable if adjusted at reasonable intervals to reflect current conditions, so that at the balance-sheet date standard costs reasonably approximate costs computed under one of the recognized bases. In such cases, descriptive language should be used which will express this relationship, as, for in-

> stance, "approximate costs determined on a first-in, first-out basis," or, if it is desired to mention standard cost, "at standard costs, approximating actual costs."

Therefore, for purposes of preparing financial statements, inventories costed at standard must be adjusted to approximate actual costs.

Budgetary Planning

Standard costs and budgets are similar, because they both represent planned costs for a specific period. Standard costs are very useful when developing a budget, since they form the building blocks of a total cost goal (or budget). Budgets, in effect, are standard costs multiplied by the volume or activity level expected.

Product Pricing

The selling price of a unit and the cost per unit are usually closely related. In most cases, a change in the selling price of a unit will result in a change in the number of units sold and, accordingly, the number of units that should be produced. As the number of units produced changes, so will the unit cost as fixed overhead costs will be spread over a different number of units. For example, a decrease in the price of a unit usually results in more units being sold. As more units are sold, unit costs decrease because fixed overhead is spread over a larger number of units. Management attempts to achieve the best combination of price and volume for a particular time period, thereby maximizing profits. Standard costs aid management in the decision process by providing standard unit costs for various levels of activity.

Record Keeping

Detailed record keeping may be reduced when standard costs are used in conjunction with actual costs. For example, when materials are kept at standard cost, the materials ledgers need only keep track of quantities.

TYPES OF STANDARDS

Standard costs are also known as *planned costs, predicted costs, scheduled costs,* and *specification costs.* Estimated costs were purposely omitted from this list because the word "estimated" should not be used interchangeably with the word "standard." *Estimated costs* have historically been used as projections of what per unit costs *will be* for a period, while *standard costs* are what a unit cost of a product *should be.* Therefore, while estimated costs are merely an anticipation of actual results, standard costs are objectives set by management which function as controls for monitoring the actual result. Generally standard costs are built into the cost system while estimated costs are not.

ESTABLISHMENT OF STANDARDS

An integral part of any standard cost system is the setting of standards for direct materials, direct labor, and factory overhead. Establishment of standards for direct materials and direct labor will be discussed in this chapter, along with variance analysis.

Direct Materials Standards

Direct materials cost standards may be divided into:

1 Quantity (usage) standards
2 Price standards

Quantity (Usage) Standards. Predetermined specifications of the quantity of direct materials that should go into the production of one finished unit under normal conditions. If more than one direct material is required to complete a unit, individual standards must be computed for each direct material. The number of direct materials required to complete one unit can be developed from engineering studies, analyses of past experiences, and/or test runs under controlled conditions.

The engineering department is normally responsible for setting quantity standards because it is generally responsible for designing production processes for making a product. Many manufacturing companies have separate departments which are assigned the responsibiity for setting standards.

Price Standards. Prices at which direct materials should be purchased. The cost accounting department and/or the purchasing department are normally responsible for setting materials price standards because they have ready access to price data and should have knowledge of market conditions. If more than one direct material is used in a production process, a standard unit price must be computed for each one.

Direct Labor Standards

Direct labor cost standards may be divided into:

1 Efficiency standards
2 Rate standards

Efficiency Standards. Predetermined performance standards of the cost of direct labor that should go into the production, under normal conditions, of one finished unit. Time-and-motion studies are very helpful in developing direct labor efficiency standards. In these studies, an analysis is made of procedures to be followed by workers, and the conditions (space, temperature, equipment, tools, lighting, etc.) under which the worker must perform assigned tasks. Procedures and conditions are closely related; and therefore, a change in one is usually accompanied by a change in the other. For example, the introduction of an additional piece of equipment to an assembly line would require a change in the procedures followed by workers. When either the situations or procedures are changed, a new standard should be developed. Time-and-motion studies must be performed for all steps in the production process.

Staff specialists are usually given the responsibility for setting direct labor efficiency standards. A staff specialist should have a thorough knowledge of the production process used by the factory in addition to a knowledge of the techniques of time-and-motion studies. Many companies have departments devoted solely to the establishment of direct labor efficiency standards.

Rate Standards. Predetermined wage rates for a period. The cost accounting, engineering, or personnel departments are normally responsible for setting direct labor rate standards, because they usually have access to the data required to set the standards.

VARIANCE ANALYSIS

Variances are the differences arising when actual results do not equal the standards because of either external or internal factors. Management has little control over the external factors but should have a significant control over internal factors. Therefore, external factors (uncontrollable variances) should be separated from internal factors (controllable variances). Variance analysis is a valuable technique for separating the two; it aids management in dealing with the "accountability function" (employee reports to their supervisors). Before accountability can be required of employees, responsibility for costs must be assigned. The latter (responsibility) should be assigned only to the department or cost center having the authority to incur the cost. When authority is delegated by top management, accountability should also be delegated. Accountability is required from those individuals who have been delegated the authority and assigned the responsibility for specific costs. These procedures may be diagrammed as follows:

Direct Materials Variances

Direct materials variances may be divided into:

1 Quantity (usage) variance
2 Price variance

Quantity Variance. The difference between actual quantities used of direct materials and standard quantities allowed, multiplied by the standard unit cost.

Standard quantities allowed is equal to the predetermined quantity of direct materials that should go into one finished unit multiplied by the number of units produced. By eliminating the effect of price changes (by using a standard unit cost), any variance that develops can be attributed to differences in the quantity of input. The equation for the direct materials quantity variance is

$$\begin{array}{c}\text{Direct}\\\text{materials}\\\text{quantity}\\\text{variance}\end{array} = \begin{bmatrix}\text{actual} & \text{standard}\\\text{quantity} - \text{quantity}\\\text{used} & \text{allowed}\end{bmatrix} \begin{array}{c}\text{standard}\\\times\text{ unit}\\\text{cost}\end{array}$$

The production department or cost center that controls the input of direct materials into the production process is usually assigned the responsibility for this variance.

Price Variance. The difference between actual unit cost and standard unit cost of direct materials purchased, multiplied by the actual quantity purchased. During periods of rising prices, the actual unit cost may be computed by taking a weighted average of all the purchases made during the week, month, or period under analysis. Actual quantity purchased is used instead of standard quantity allowed because we are seeking the price difference resulting from purchases, not usage. The equation for the direct materials price variance is

$$\begin{array}{c}\text{Direct}\\\text{materials}\\\text{price}\\\text{variance}\end{array} = \begin{bmatrix}\text{actual} & \text{standard}\\\text{unit} - \text{unit}\\\text{cost} & \text{cost}\end{bmatrix} \begin{array}{c}\text{actual}\\\times\text{ quantity}\\\text{purchased}\end{array}$$

Management has very little control over price variances, especially when they result from rising prices. However, the purchasing department may have some control over prices by ordering in economical quantities, and/or finding suppliers who offer the same quality of goods at lower prices. Often the season's needs are contracted for at a fixed price and drawn upon as required. Some companies therefore assign the responsibility of price variances to the purchasing department.

The following example relates to direct materials quantity and price variances:

Units produced (finished product)	10,000
Direct materials quantity standard	4 units of direct materials per unit of finished product
Direct materials used in production	39,000 units
Direct materials purchased	50,000 units
Direct materials standard cost	$2.00 each
Actual direct materials cost	$2.10 each

The two materials variances would be computed as follows:

Direct Materials Quantity Variance:

$$\begin{matrix} \text{Standard} \\ \text{quantity} \\ \text{allowed} \end{matrix} = \begin{matrix} \text{units} \\ \text{produced} \end{matrix} \times \begin{matrix} \text{direct} \\ \text{materials} \\ \text{quantity} \\ \text{standard} \end{matrix}$$

$$40,000 = 10,000 \times 4$$

$$\begin{matrix} \text{Direct} \\ \text{materials} \\ \text{quantity} \\ \text{variance} \end{matrix} = \begin{bmatrix} \text{actual} & \text{standard} \\ \text{quantity} - \text{quantity} \\ \text{used} & \text{allowed} \end{bmatrix} \begin{matrix} \text{standard} \\ \times \text{unit} \\ \text{cost} \end{matrix}$$

$$\begin{matrix} \$2,000 \\ \text{favorable} \end{matrix} = (39,000 - 40,000) \times \$2.00$$

A favorable direct materials quantity variance resulted because the actual quantity used was less than the standard quantity allowed.

Direct Materials Price Variance:

$$\begin{matrix} \text{Direct} \\ \text{materials} \\ \text{price} \\ \text{variance} \end{matrix} = \begin{bmatrix} \text{actual} & \text{standard} \\ \text{unit} - \text{unit} \\ \text{cost} & \text{cost} \end{bmatrix} \begin{matrix} \text{actual} \\ \times \text{quantity} \\ \text{purchased} \end{matrix}$$

$$\begin{matrix} \$5,000 \\ \text{unfavorable} \end{matrix} = (\$2.10 - \$2.00) \times 50,000$$

An unfavorable direct materials price variance resulted because the actual unit cost was greater than the standard unit cost.

Journal Entries for Direct Materials

In most standard cost systems, only the standard cost of direct materials is charged to work-in-process. The recording of direct materials variances, however, may be handled in many different ways.

Two of the most common methods of journalizing direct materials variances in a standard cost system are

1 Maintaining the Materials account at *standard cost*, and recording price variances as materials are received. This method reduces clerical steps by enabling the materials ledger sheet to be kept in quantities only.
2 Maintain the Materials account at *actual cost* and recording price variances when materials are put into production. Under this method, the materials ledger sheet must show both quantities and dollars.

The first method is preferred for control purposes because direct materials prices variances should be computed and recorded when they are incurred in order to notify management of changes that may be necessary. The following sets of journal entries relate to our previous example and show the recording of direct materials variances under the two methods described above:

Method 1

a *To record the purchase of direct materials:*

Materials ($2.00 × 50,000 units) ....*at standard*.	100,000	
Direct materials price variance ($.10 × 50,000 units)	5,000	
Vouchers payable		105,000

b *To record the use of direct materials:*

Work-in-process ($2.00 × 40,000 units) *Standard units × standard cost*	80,000	
Materials ($2.00 × 39,000 units) *Standard cost × actual units used*		78,000
Direct materials quantity variance		2,000

Method 2

a *To record the purchase of direct materials:*

Materials ($2.10 × 50,000 units) ....*at cost*.........	105,000	
Vouchers payable		105,000

b *To record the use of direct materials:*

Work-in-process ($2.00 × 40,000 units) *Std qty at std price*	80,000	
Direct materials price usage variance ($.10 × 39,000 units) .	3,900	
Materials ($2.10 × 39,000 units)		81,900
Direct materials quantity variance		2,000

In the second method, a direct materials price *usage* variance must be computed when the direct materials are placed into production. The direct materials price variance was $5,000 [($2.10 − $2.00) × 50,000] and the direct materials usage variance was $3,900 [($2.10 − $2.00) × 39,000]. The difference of $1,100 ($5,000 − $3,900) belongs to the direct materials that have not yet been put into production and can be computed as follows:

Total direct materials units purchased	50,000
Units of direct materials put into process	39,000
Units of direct materials in ending inventory	11,000

The 11,000 units of direct materials still in ending inventory multiplied by the difference between the standard unit cost and the actual unit cost ($2.10 − $2.00 = $.10) equals the direct materials price variance ($1,100) that has not yet been put into production.

Direct Labor Variances

Direct labor variances may be divided into:

1 Efficiency variance
2 Rate variance

Efficiency Variance. The efficiency variance is the difference between the number of actual direct labor hours worked and the number of standard direct labor hours allowed, multiplied by the standard labor wage rate. "Standard hours allowed" is equal to the number of direct labor hours that should be worked in the production of one finished unit multiplied by the number of units produced. By eliminating the effect of price changes (by using a standard labor rate), any variance that develops can be attributed to the amount of worker efficiency (or inefficiency). The equation for the direct labor efficiency variance is

$$
\begin{array}{c}
\text{Direct} \\
\text{labor} \\
\text{efficiency} \\
\text{variance}
\end{array}
=
\left[
\begin{array}{cc}
\text{number of} & \text{number of} \\
\text{actual} & \text{standard} \\
\text{hours} & \text{hours} \\
\text{worked} & \text{allowed}
\end{array}
\right]
\times
\begin{array}{c}
\text{standard} \\
\text{wage} \\
\text{rate}
\end{array}
$$

The supervisor of the department or cost center in which the work is performed is usually held responsible for direct labor efficiency variances if procedures and conditions remain constant (for example, if no new procedures or equipment were introduced during the period).

Rate Variance. The rate variance is the difference between the actual labor wage rate and the standard labor wage rate, multiplied by actual hours worked. The number of actual hours worked is used instead of the number of standard hours allowed because we are seeking the cost difference that resulted from changes in labor wage rates, not hours worked. The equation for the direct labor rate variance is

$$
\begin{array}{c}
\text{Direct} \\
\text{labor} \\
\text{rate} \\
\text{variance}
\end{array}
=
\left[
\begin{array}{cc}
\text{actual} & \text{standard} \\
\text{wage} - & \text{wage} \\
\text{rate} & \text{rate}
\end{array}
\right]
\times
\begin{array}{c}
\text{actual} \\
\text{number of} \\
\text{hours} \\
\text{worked}
\end{array}
$$

As in the case of the direct materials price variances, management has very little control over rate variances. However, some companies hold the supervisor of the department or cost center where the work is performed responsible if, for example, workers with a higher rate were used in a particular process and as a result, the greatest worker cost efficiency was not achieved.

The following example relates to the direct labor efficiency and rate variances:

Units produced	10,000
Direct labor efficiency standard	2 hours per unit
Actual direct labor hours worked	20,500 hours
Direct labor standard wage rate	$5.00 per hour
Direct labor actual wage rate	$5.20 per hour

The two direct labor variances would be computed as follows:

Direct Labor Efficiency Variances:

$$\begin{matrix} \text{Standard} \\ \text{hours} \\ \text{allowed} \end{matrix} = \begin{matrix} \text{units} \\ \text{pro-} \\ \text{duced} \end{matrix} \times \begin{matrix} \text{number of} \\ \text{direct labor} \\ \text{efficiency} \\ \text{standard hours} \end{matrix}$$

$$20,000 = 10,000 \times 2 \text{ hours}$$

$$\begin{matrix} \text{Direct labor} \\ \text{efficiency} \\ \text{variance} \end{matrix} = \begin{bmatrix} \text{number of} \\ \text{actual hours} - \begin{matrix} \text{number of} \\ \text{standard hours} \\ \text{allowed} \end{matrix} \end{bmatrix} \times \begin{matrix} \text{standard} \\ \text{wage} \\ \text{rate} \end{matrix}$$

$$\underset{\text{unfavorable}}{\$2,500} = (20,500 - 20,000) \times \$5.00$$

An unfavorable direct labor efficiency variance resulted because the number of actual hours worked exceeded the number of standard hours allowed.

Direct Labor Rate Variance:

$$\begin{matrix} \text{Direct labor} \\ \text{rate variance} \end{matrix} = \begin{bmatrix} \text{actual} \\ \text{wage rate} - \begin{matrix} \text{standard} \\ \text{wage rate} \end{matrix} \end{bmatrix} \times \begin{matrix} \text{actual hours} \\ \text{worked} \end{matrix}$$

$$\underset{\text{unfavorable}}{\$4,100} = (\$5.20 - \$5.00) \times 20,500$$

In the above instance, an unfavorable direct labor rate variance resulted because the actual rate exceeded the standard rate.

Journal Entries for Direct Labor

In a standard cost system, direct labor costs are charged to work-in-process, using standard hours allowed and standard rates. Variances result from the difference between payroll (actual hours × actual rates) and standard charges. Labor variances are recognized at the time they are incurred. The following payroll entries relate to the previous example:

a *To record the payroll (payroll taxes were ignored):*

Payroll (20,500 hours × $5.20)	106,600	
Various payables		106,600

b *To allocate payroll and variances:*

Work-in-process (20,000 hours × $5.00)	100,000	
Direct labor efficiency variance	2,500	
Direct labor rate variance	4,100	
Payroll		106,600

DIAGRAM COMPUTATION OF VARIANCES

The following diagram technique shown in Figure 11-1 may be used to compute direct materials and direct labor variances (based on our previous example).

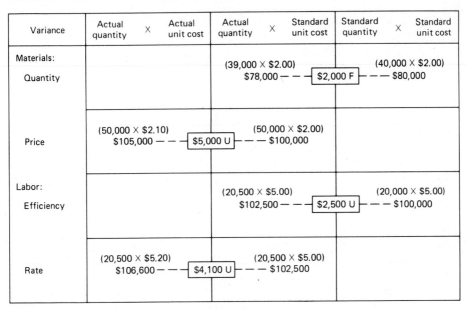

Variance	Actual quantity	X	Actual unit cost	Actual quantity	X	Standard unit cost	Standard quantity	X	Standard unit cost
Materials: Quantity				(39,000 × $2.00) $78,000 — — — $2,000 F — — — $80,000			(40,000 × $2.00) $80,000		
Price	(50,000 × $2.10) $105,000 — — — $5,000 U — — — $100,000			(50,000 × $2.00) $100,000					
Labor: Efficiency				(20,500 × $5.00) $102,500 — — — $2,500 U — — — $100,000			(20,000 × $5.00) $100,000		
Rate	(20,500 × $5.20) $106,600 — — — $4,100 U — — — $102,500			(20,500 × $5.00) $102,500					

FIGURE 11-1 **Diagram Computation of Variances**

CHAPTER REVIEW

Standard costs provide management with goals to attain and bases for comparison of actual results. Standard costing serves basically the same purpose as a budget. However, standard costing is concerned with cost *per unit* while budgets generally provide cost goals in *total* cost figures.

Standard costs do not replace actual costs; they complement each other. According to generally accepted accounting principles, inventory and cost of goods sold must be shown at actual cost. Therefore, standard costs are used by management to determine the effectiveness of operations by comparing them with actual costs.

Cost information may be used for many purposes. Since cost information which serves one purpose may not be appropriate for another, it is important to clearly define the purpose for which the information is needed before developing procedures to accumulate cost data. Standard costs may be used for cost control, for inventory costing, for budgetary planning, for product pricing, and to facilitate record keeping.

Standard costs are also known as "planned costs," "predicted costs," "scheduled costs," and "specification costs." The setting of standards for direct labor, direct materials, and factory overhead is an important part of any standard cost system.

Direct materials cost standards may be divided into quantity (usage) standards and price standards.

Direct labor cost standards may be divided into efficiency standards and rate standards.

Variance analysis is a valuable technique for separating the external factors (uncontrollable variances) and the internal factors (controllable variances).

Direct materials variances may be divided into a quantity (usage) variance and price variance. An unfavorable variance occurs when actual costs exceed standard costs, and a favorable variance occurs when actual costs are less than standard.

The recording of direct materials variances may be handled in a number of ways. Two of the most common methods of journalizing direct materials variances are (1) maintaining the account Materials at standard cost, and recording price variances as materials are received; (2) maintaining the account Materials at actual cost, and recording price variances when materials are put into production. For control purposes, the first method is preferred, because direct materials price variances should be computed and recorded when incurred in order to notify management of changes that may be necessary.

Direct labor variances may be divided into an efficiency variance and a rate variance.

Direct labor costs are charged to work-in-process, using standard hours allowed and standard rates. Variances result from the difference between actual payroll costs and standard costs. Such variances should be recognized when they are incurred.

GLOSSARY

Efficiency Standards—predetermined performance standards of the cost of direct labor that should go into the production, under normal conditions, of one finished unit.

Efficiency Variance—equal to the difference between the number of actual hours worked for direct labor and the number of standard hours allowed, multiplied by the standard labor wage rate.

Favorable Variance—results when actual costs are less than standard costs.

Price Standards—prices at which direct materials should be purchased.

Price Variance—equal to the difference between actual unit cost and standard unit cost of direct materials

purchased, multiplied by the actual quantity purchased.

Quantity (Usage) Standards—predetermined specifications of the quantity of direct materials that should go into the production of one finished unit under normal conditions.

Quantity Variance—equal to the difference between actual quantities used for direct materials and standard quantities allowed, multiplied by the standard unit cost.

Rate Standards—predetermined wage rates for a specific period.

Rate Variance—the difference between the actual labor wage rate and the standard labor wage rate, multiplied by actual hours worked.

Standard Costing—concerned with

cost *per unit*, this serves basically the same purpose as a budget.

Standard Costs—costs that are expected to be achieved in a particular production process under normal conditions.

Unfavorable Variance—results when actual costs are greater than standard costs.

Variance—the difference arising when actual results do not equal standards, due to either external or internal factors.

SUMMARY PROBLEM

The following information, for 19X1, was given for the Ken-Glo Company which manufactures fluorescent light bulbs:

Units of finished product produced	15,000 units
Direct materials quantity standards	3 units of direct materials per unit of finished product
Direct materials used in production	50,000 units
Direct materials purchased	60,000 units
Direct materials standard cost per unit	$1.25 each
Actual direct materials cost per unit	$1.10 each
Direct labor efficiency standard	2 hours per unit
Actual direct labor hours worked	30,250 hours
Direct labor standard wage rate	$4.20 per hour
Direct labor actual wage rate	$4.50 per hour

REQUIRED:

a Calculate the following variances:
 1 Direct materials price variance
 2 Direct materials quantity variance
 3 Direct labor efficiency variance
 4 Direct labor rate variance
b Journal entries to record payroll and allocate payroll variances. Ignore payroll taxes.

SOLUTION TO SUMMARY PROBLEM

a. 1 Direct Materials Price Variance:

$$\begin{bmatrix} \text{Actual} & \text{standard} \\ \text{unit} & - \text{unit} \\ \text{cost} & \text{cost} \end{bmatrix} \times \begin{array}{l} \text{actual} \\ \text{quantity} \\ \text{purchased} \end{array}$$

($1.10 − $1.25) × 60,000 = $9,000 favorable

2 Direct Materials Quantity Variance:

Standard quantity allowed = units produced × direct materials quantity standard

45,000 = 15,000 × 3

$$
\begin{bmatrix} \text{Actual} & \text{standard} \\ \text{quantity} = \text{quantity} \\ \text{used} & \text{allowed} \end{bmatrix} \times \begin{matrix} \text{standard} \\ \text{unit} \\ \text{cost} \end{matrix}
$$

(50,000 − 45,000) × $1.25 = $6,250 unfavorable

3 Direct Labor Efficiency Variance:

$$
\begin{bmatrix} \text{Standard} \\ \text{hours} = \text{produced} \\ \text{allowed} \end{bmatrix} \begin{matrix}\text{units}\end{matrix} \times \begin{matrix} \text{direct} \\ \text{labor} \\ \text{efficiency} \\ \text{standard} \end{matrix}
$$

30,000 = 15,000 × 2 hours

$$
\begin{bmatrix} \text{Actual} & \text{standard} \\ \text{hours} & - \text{hours} \\ \text{worked} & \text{allowed} \end{bmatrix} \times \begin{matrix} \text{standard} \\ \text{wage} \\ \text{rate} \end{matrix}
$$

(30,250 − 30,000) × $4.20 = $1,050 unfavorable

4 Direct Labor Rate Variance:

$$
\begin{bmatrix} \text{Actual} & \text{standard} \\ \text{wage} & - \text{wage} \\ \text{rate} & \text{rate} \end{bmatrix} \times \begin{matrix} \text{actual} \\ \text{hours} \\ \text{worked} \end{matrix}
$$

($4.50 − $4.20) × 30,250 = $9,075 unfavorable

b *To record payroll:*

Payroll ($4.50 × 30,250)	136,125	
Various payables		136,125

To allocate payroll and variances:

Work-in-process (30,000 × $4.20)	126,000	
Direct labor efficiency variance	1,050	
Direct labor rate variance	9,075	
Payroll		136,125

QUESTIONS

1 What does the establishment of standards provide?
2 What is standard costing concerned with, and how does it differ from a budget?
3 What must every cost accumulation system record?

4 What purposes may standard costs be used for?

5 Differentiate between standard costs and estimated costs.

6 What are the two methods of journalizing direct materials variances in a standard cost system?

7 How can a cost accumulation system benefit a company?

8 State whether the following are true or false:

a Standard costs and actual costs complement each other.

b Cost information which serves one purpose may be inappropriate for another.

c Standards enable management to make periodic comparisons of estimated costs with standard costs in order to measure performance and correct inefficiencies.

d Standard costs and budgets are similar because they both represent planned costs for a period.

e The selling price of a unit and the cost per unit are usually entirely separate items.

f An integral part of any standard cost system is the setting of standards for direct materials, direct labor, and factory overhead used in production.

9 What departments are responsible for setting the quantity and the price standards?

10 Discuss the importance of staff specialists.

11 Why is variance analysis important?

12 Why is the standard unit cost of direct materials used instead of the actual unit cost?

13 Differentiate between historical costs and standard costs.

EXERCISES

EXERCISE 1

Direct Materials Variances

Ha-Ha Company produced 7,600 comic books for the year. The direct materials quantity standard was 6 units of direct material per unit. The amount of direct materials used in production was 46,500 units. Direct materials purchased amounted to 36,000 units. The actual direct materials cost was $3.25 each while the standard direct materials cost was $3.30 each.

REQUIRED:

Compute the direct materials price (at time of purchase) and quantity variances and state whether they are favorable or unfavorable.

EXERCISE 2

Direct Labor Variances

Useless Company produced 16,000 widgets for the year. The direct labor efficiency standard was 3 hours per unit. The actual direct labor hours worked was 47,750. The company employs a direct labor standard wage rate of $7.25 per hour; $7.18 was the actual direct labor wage rate.

REQUIRED:

Compute the direct labor efficiency and rate variances and state whether they are favorable or unfavorable.

EXERCISE 3

Material and Labor Variances

Baker Company employs a standard cost system. The standard product costs for materials were 6 pieces at $6.25 per piece; for direct labor were 12 hours at $4.50 per hour; and for factory overhead were 12 hours at $2.00 per hour. During the month of May, production amounted to 400 sets. The raw materials used for the 400 sets amounted to 2,200 pieces for a total cost of $15,400. The direct labor cost for 5,000 actual hours was $23,750. Actual factory overhead was $9,500.

REQUIRED:

a Compute the direct materials quantity and price variances and state whether they are favorable or unfavorable.
b Compute the direct labor efficiency and rate variances and state whether they are favorable or unfavorable.

EXERCISE 4

Entries for Direct Materials

The Babyplay Company had finished goods totaling 5,600 play pens. Six units of direct materials were required for each unit of finished product. The amount of materials used in production totaled 34,000 units; 42,000 units of direct materials were purchased. The direct materials standard cost was $1.75 each. The actual direct materials cost was $1.70 each. Assume no beginning inventories exist.

REQUIRED:

a Prepare the entries for the direct materials variances assuming
   1 The account Materials is maintained at standard costs.
   2 The account Materials is maintained at actual cost.
b Calculate the number of units of direct materials in ending inventory.

EXERCISE 5

Entries for Direct Labor Variances

The G & G Company produced 26,000 units. The direct labor efficiency standard was 2.5 hours per unit. The actual direct labor hours worked was 63,000 hours; $4.25 per hour was the direct labor standard wage rate. The direct labor actual wage rate was $4.30 per hour.

REQUIRED:

Prepare the journal entries for direct labor.

EXERCISE 6

Entries for Direct Materials and Direct Labor

Hope Company uses a standard cost system. The company estimated that the standard cost of materials would be $7,600. However, the actual cost of materials purchased was $7,800. Raw materials of $3,900 were requisitioned from inventory; $200 worth of materials, in excess of the standard allowed, was requisitioned. The standard hours allowed for the company were 5,300 hours. The actual hours worked were 5,400. The direct labor standard rate was $2.75, and the actual rate was $2.70.

REQUIRED:

Prepare the journal entries to record the above transactions. Isolate the direct materials price variance at the time of purchase.

EXERCISE 7

Variances and Entries for Direct Materials

Salvatore Company showed the following standards data for its single product: direct materials—2 yards at $.52 per yard; direct labor—2 hours at $3.25 per hour; and factory overhead—2 hours at $1.75 per hour. The company produced 7,600 units. The material purchases amounted to 25,000 yards at $.50 per yard; 12,000 yards of materials were requisitioned.

REQUIRED:

a Calculate the price and usage variances for materials
  1 At the time of purchase.
  2 At the time of requisition.
b Prepare the necessary journal entries for materials
  1 At the time of purchase.
  2 At the time of requisition.

EXERCISE 8

Variances for Direct Materials and Direct Labor

The Vince Manufacturing Company has a cost accounting department to control and analyze production costs. This department accumulated the following data for the current period:

Actual Data

Production:	55,000 units
Materials: Purchased	160,000 pieces at $.24 per piece
	125,000 pieces at $.32 per piece
Requisitioned	250,000 pieces
Labor: Actual hours worked	46,700
Standard hours allowed	47,000
Average actual labor cost	$7.25 per hour

The company set the following standards for each unit: direct materials—4 pieces at $.25 per piece; direct labor—5 hours at $7.10 per hour; and factory overhead—5 hours at $3.50 per hour. (Use weighted average to figure the price for materials purchased.)

REQUIRED:

a Compute the direct materials price (isolated at time of purchase) and quantity variances and state whether they are favorable or unfavorable.

b Compute the direct labor efficiency and rate variances and state whether they are favorable or unfavorable.

EXERCISE 9

Variances and Entries for Direct Materials and Direct Labor

The Teddy Bear Toy Company accumulated the following data from its books:

Purchased	2,300 yards at $1.25 per yard
Requisitioned	1,500 yards
Materials allowed	1,200 yards per standard production order
Standard materials price	$1.35 per yard
Actual hours worked	975
Actual rate paid	$3.10 per hour
Standard hours allowed	982
Standard rate	$3.05 per hour

REQUIRED:

a 1 Compute the materials price (isolated at time of purchase) and quantity variances and state whether they are favorable or unfavorable.

2 Compute the labor efficiency and rate variances and state whether they are favorable or unfavorable.

b Prepare the necessary journal entries.

EXERCISE 10

Direct Materials Variances: Price and Quantity

The ABC Chair Company uses a standard cost system. To produce its chairs, three raw materials are placed into production at different points during the operations. Below is data pertaining to the standard materials cost of one unit:

Wood (2 planks at $5.07 each)   = $10.14
Vinyl (1 yard at $.75 per yard)   =   .75
Foam (1 pound at $.39 per lb)   =   .39
Total standard materials cost = $11.28

Wood enters production at the beginning of the process, vinyl enters when units are 60% complete, and foam enters when units are 90% complete.

During September, the following activity occurred:

Purchases: Wood   50,000 planks at $5.00 each
Vinyl   9,000 yards at $1.00 per yard
Foam   7,500 pounds at $ .43 per pound

Materials requisitions: Wood   11,100 planks
Vinyl   5,015 yards
Foam   4,905 pounds

Beginning units in process (Sept. 1)		0
Actual units produced and completed		4,825
Ending units in process:		
45% complete	300	
75% complete	150	
92% complete	50	500

The company follows the policy of stating raw materials inventory at standard costs.

REQUIRED:

a Compute the materials price variances for each raw materials purchase during September.

b Compute the standard materials cost of
   1 Units completed during September.
   2 Units still in process, September 30.

c Compute September's materials quantity variances for each of the raw materials.

PROBLEMS

PROBLEM 1

Variances and Entries for Direct Materials and Direct Labor

The following information was given for the Frances Company, which manufactures dolls:

Units of finished product produced	26,000
Direct materials quantity standard	6 units of direct materials per unit of finished product
Direct materials used in production	156,500 units
Direct materials purchased	160,000 units
Direct materials standard cost	$8.10 each
Actual direct materials cost...................	$8.07 each
Direct labor efficiency standard	3 hours per unit
Actual direct labor hours worked	77,600 hours
Direct labor standard wage rate	$6.25 per hour
Direct labor actual wage rate	$6.30 per hour

REQUIRED:

a Calculate the following variances:
   1 Direct materials quantity variance
   2 Direct materials price variance (isolated at purchase)
   3 Direct labor efficiency variance
   4 Direct labor rate variance
b Prepare journal entries for direct materials assuming:
   1 The account Materials is maintained at standard cost.
   2 The account Materials is maintained at actual cost.
c Prepare journal entries for direct labor to record the payroll and allocate the payroll variances. Ignore any payroll taxes.

PROBLEM 2

Entries for Direct Materials and Direct Labor

The Sleepie Company produces several types of beds. The one that produces the most sales is called "El Snoozer." The standard product costs for materials are 4 pieces of metal at $4.25 each, for labor 5 hours at $6.10 per hour; and for factory overhead 5 hours at $3.00 per hour. During the month of April, Sleepie Company purchased 28,000 pieces of material at a total cost of $125,000. The number of beds produced were 4,000 for the month of April. The amount of materials requisitioned amounted to 18,000 pieces of metal. The total direct labor cost for April amounted to $139,150 for 23,000 actual hours.

REQUIRED:

Prepare the necessary journal entries to record direct materials, direct labor, and any related variances. Assume price variance is isolated at time of purchase.

PROBLEM 3

Variances and Entries for Direct Materials and Direct Labor

The P and B Company produces a single product. The standard cost per unit is set by the cost accounting department and is as follows:

Direct materials (3 pints at $1.25/pint)	$ 3.75
Direct labor (5 hours at $1.75/hour)	8.75
Factory overhead (5 hours at $.50/hour)	2.50
Total	$15.00

The standard production for the month of February is 3,250 units. The company actually produced 3,350 units. The direct labor standard was 16,750 hours, but the actual hours worked were 15,075 hours at a rate of $1.85 per hour. The company purchased 12,000 pints at a cost of $13,920. The company requisitioned 11,000 pints for production.

REQUIRED:

a Calculate the following variances:
  1 Direct materials quantity variance
  2 Direct materials price variance
  3 Direct labor efficiency variance
  4 Direct labor rate variance
b Prepare journal entries for direct materials assuming:
  1 The account Materials is maintained at standard cost.
  2 The account Materials is maintained at actual cost.
c Prepare journal entries for direct labor to record the payroll and allocate the payroll variances. Ignore payroll taxes.

PROBLEM 4

T Accounts and Journal Entries

The Painful Surgical Supply Company operates a cost accounting system based on standard costs. The differences between standard costs and actual costs are shown in the following variance accounts—materials quantity variance, materials price variance, labor efficiency variance, and labor rate variance. The company's inventory on July 1 showed raw materials at $36,500, materials in process at $5,700, labor in process at $2,600, and finished goods at $16,500. Budgeted purchases during July were $23,500; however, actual purchases for the same quantity were $24,700. The standard materials cost amounted to $22,600, and the standard labor cost amounted to $14,400. Materials put into production amounted to $30,800. The company's inventories on August 1 showed raw materials at $29,200, materials in process at $6,300, labor in process at $2,600, and finished goods at $6,900. The cost of goods sold for the company (which consists of materials costs plus standard labor) amounted to $46,000. The payroll for the company was $12,750. Direct labor efficiency variance was unfavorable by $400. For simplicity, assume no factory overhead was incurred.

REQUIRED:

a Prepare journal entries to record the above information.
b Use T accounts to record the above information.

PROBLEM 5

Materials and Labor Variance: Job Order Costing

The Crumbly Cake Company manufactures ready-made cakes for large institutions. A job order cost system under standard costing is used by the company. While the cakes ordered may be different in appearance (decorations, etc.), the standard cost of each cake is the same. Below are the standard costs for one cake:

Direct materials (2 cups of cake mix at $.68 per cup)	$1.36
Direct labor [$1/5$ hour (12 minutes) at $3.00 per hour]	.60
Factory overhead ($1/5$ hour at $1.50 per labor hour)	.30
Total standard cost per cake	$2.26

Direct materials are added at the beginning of the operation, and conversion costs are added evenly throughout the operation.

During October, the following job orders were put into production.

Job 102: 300 cakes completed
Job 103: 200 cakes completed
Job 104: 175 cakes completed
Job 105: 100 cakes 50% complete

There were no orders that were partially completed during September. At the end of October, only Job 105 was not complete.

Actual materials requirement, cups of cake mix:

Job 102: 615 cups
Job 103: 395 cups
Job 104: 370 cups
Job 105: 207 cups

Actual direct labor hours:

Job 102: 64 hours
Job 103: 39 hours
Job 104: 33 hours
Job 105: 15 hours

Actual payroll expense:

Job 102: $197.76
Job 103: $117.78
Job 104: $ 99.00
Job 105: $ 45.75

Additional Information

Materials price variances are recognized at the time of purchase. During October, 1,500 cups of cake mix were purchased for $1,125.00.

REQUIRED:

a Compute the materials quantity variance for each job.
b Compute the labor variances for each job.
c Compute the materials price variance for October.

PROBLEM 6

Materials and Labor Variances and Journal Entries

The Wooly Sock Company manufactures socks for men. The socks are made so that one size fits all. Since the company's start three years ago, it has been using a standard cost system. Below are the standard costs for 50 pairs:

Direct materials (25 yards of synthetic fabric at $.56 a yard) $14.00
Direct labor (1.5 hours at $5 per hour) 7.50
Factory overhead (1.5 hours at $8 per hour) 12.00
Total standard costs $33.50

Raw materials requisitioned from the storeroom are assumed to be from the most recent purchases (lifo method). Below is an analysis of September activity in the raw materials inventory account.

	UNIT	UNIT COST
Beginning balance 9/1	2,500 yd	$.50 a yard
Purchases:		
9/5	4,000 yd	.54 a yard
9/10	5,000 yd	.58 a yard
Requisitions:		
9/12	8,600 yd	

Inventory is on a perpetual system. Price variances are journalized when the units are used in production.

During September, the factory employees worked 430 hours at a rate of $5.25 per hour.

Production for the month equaled 15,000 pairs of socks.

REQUIRED:

a Compute the materials variances and the labor variances for September.

b Prepare journal entries to record direct materials, direct labor, and related variances for September. (Ignore payroll taxes.)

PROBLEM 7

Materials and Labor Variances

The XYZ Company manufactures its main product under a process cost system. Costs are applied to work-in-process and finished goods based on standard costs. In Department 2, half of the materials are added at the beginning of the process and half are added at the end of the process. Standard costs for work performed in Department 2 are shown below:

Direct materials (6 parts at $.40 a part)	$2.40
Direct labor (1 hour at $4.25)	4.25
Factory overhead (1 hour at $1.10)	1.10
Total standard costs added	$7.75

Department 2 had the following activity during May:

Beginning units in process	300 60% complete
Units transferred in	2,800
Units transferred out	2,500
Ending units in process	600 20% complete

Actual costs for May: Labor = $11,124.10 for 2,587 direct labor hours

Requisitions: Materials: 16,010 parts

Additional Information:
Beginning work-in-process is costed by means of fifo. Conversion costs are added evenly throughout the process.

REQUIRED:

a Compute the materials quantity variance.

b Compute the labor rate and the labor efficiency variances.

PROBLEM 8

Variance Analysis under Process Costing

The Eversore Shoe Company manufactures leather shoes for infants. A process cost system using standard costs is employed. The company has three processing departments—tanning, forming, and finishing. All raw materials are added at the beginning in the tanning department. Conversion costs are added evenly throughout all three departments. A schedule of the standard costs per pair of shoes is shown on page 415:

	TANNING	FORMING	FINISHING
Direct materials	$ 9.50 (1 yd of leather)		
Direct labor	6.00 (2 hr at $3)	$2.75 (1 hr)	$2.35 (1 hr)
Factory overhead	3.00 (2 hr at $1.50)	1.50 (1 hr)	1.20 (1 hr)
Totals	$18.50	$4.25	$3.55

Quantity information pertaining to November activity is shown below.

	TANNING	FORMING	FINISHING
Beginning units in process	0	0	0
Units started in process	50,000		
Units received during the period		43,000	39,000
Units transferred to next department	43,000	39,000	
Units transferred to finished goods			31,000
Ending units in process	7,000	4,000	8,000
Percent of completion	50%	25%	75%

During November actual costs incurred were as follows:

Materials purchases: 65,000 yards of leather at $9.80 per yard
Materials requisitions: 47,200 yards

Direct labor hours:

	TANNING	FORMING	FINISHING
Actual hours worked	93,750	38,250	37,565
Actual rate	$3.10	$2.95	$2.25

REQUIRED:

a Calculate the materials price variance (isolated at purchase).
b Calculate the materials quantity variance.
c Calculate for each department and in total, the labor rate variance and the labor efficiency variance.
d What is the debit to finished goods to record November's production?

PROBLEM 9

Materials Price and Quantity Variance; Labor Efficiency Variance

The Longhorn Manufacturing Corporation produces only one product, Bevo, and accounts for the production of Bevo using a standard cost system.

At the end of each year, Longhorn prorates all variances among the various inventories and cost of sales. Because Longhorn prices the inventories on the first-in, first-out basis and all the beginning inventories are used during the year, the variances which had been allocated to the ending inventories are immediately charged to cost of sales at the beginning of the following year. This allows only the current year's variances to be recorded in the variance accounts in any given year.

Following are the standards for the production of one unit of Bevo: 3 units of Item A at $1.00 per unit; 1 unit of Item B at $.50 per unit; 4 units of Item C at $.30 per unit; and 20 minutes of direct labor at $4.50 per hour. Separate variance accounts are maintained for each type of raw material and for direct labor. Raw materials purchases are recorded initially at standard.

After proration of the variances, the various inventories at December 31, 19X2, were priced as follows:

Raw Materials

ITEM	NUMBER OF UNITS	UNIT COST	AMOUNT
A	15,000	$1.10	$16,500
B	4,000	.52	2,080
C	20,000	.32	6,400
			$24,980

Work-in-Process

9,000 units of Bevo which were 100% complete as to Items A and B, 50% complete as to Item C, and 30% complete as to labor. The composition and valuation of the inventory follows:

ITEM	AMOUNT
A	$28,600
B	4,940
C	6,240
Direct labor	6,175
Overhead	11,700
	$57,655

Finished Goods

Composed of 4,800 units of Bevo valued as follows:

ITEM	AMOUNT
A	$15,180
B	2,704
C	6,368
Direct labor	8,540
Overhead	16,200
	$48,992

Following is a schedule of raw materials purchased and direct labor incurred for the year ended December 31, 19X3. Unit cost of raw materials and direct labor remained constant throughout the year.

Purchases:

ITEM	NUMBER OF UNITS OR HOURS	UNIT COST	AMOUNT
A	290,000	$1.15	$333,500
B	101,000	.55	55,550
C	367,000	.35	128,450
Direct labor	34,100	4.60	156,860

During the year ended December 31, 19X3, Longhorn sold 90,000 units of Bevo and had ending physical inventories as follows:

Raw Materials:

ITEM	NUMBER OF UNITS
A	28,300
B	2,100
C	28,900

Work-in-Process

7,500 units A and B 100% complete, C 50% complete, direct labor 20% complete.

ITEM	NUMBER OF UNITS OR HOURS
A	22,900
B	8,300
C	15,800
Direct labor	800

Finished Goods

5,100 units of Bevo, as follows:

ITEM	NUMBER OF UNITS OR HOURS
A	15,600
B	6,300
C	21,700
Direct labor	2,050

REQUIRED:

a What was the total charge or credit to the three materials price variance accounts for Items A, B, and C for the year ended December 31, 19X3?

b What was the total charge or credit to the three materials quantity variance accounts for Items A, B, and C for the year ended December 31, 19X3?

c What was the total charge or credit to the direct labor efficiency variance account for the year ended December 31, 19X3?

(AICPA Adapted)

CHAPTER TWELVE

STANDARD COSTS–FACTORY OVERHEAD AND RELATED VARIANCES

The control of factory overhead costs under standard costing is similar to the control of direct materials and direct labor costs, discussed in the preceding chapter. Predetermined standard costs are compared with actual costs as a means of evaluating performance. However, while the basic concept is similar, the procedures used to compute and to apply the standard costs and variances of factory overhead are quite different.

One reason for the different procedures is the variety of items included in "overhead costs." Factory overhead may include indirect materials, indirect labor, factory rent, and depreciation of factory equipment. The individual costs that make up total factory overhead are affected differently by increases or decreases in plant activity. Depending on the cost item, plant activity may cause a direct or a proportional change in total overhead costs (variable factory overhead costs), a disproportionate change in total overhead costs (semivariable factory overhead costs), or no change in the total overhead costs (fixed factory overhead costs). Standard costs, which are compared with the actual costs, must therefore be adjusted for changes in activity levels. This is handled through the use of flexible budgets, which show costs at different levels of activity.

Because of the different items included in factory overhead, the control of costs involves many individuals in the company. For example, a service manager may be responsible for cleaning costs, a plant supervisor may be responsible for indirect materials costs, and a maintenance supervisor may be responsible for repair costs. Costs which are not usually affected by production, such as factory rent, require different methods of control. Since these are fixed costs, they are normally determined by management policy. Here the major emphasis is placed not on the comparison between standard and actual costs, but on the proper and full utilization of the facilities that are directly associated with the fixed costs. The latter should be shown along with the variable costs in the budget, because management should be aware of both kinds of information for purposes of making any necessary changes.

BUDGETS AND
FACTORY OVERHEAD

Budgets are commonly used in controlling factory overhead costs. Prior to the period in question, a budget that shows anticipated costs is prepared. Actual costs are later compared with those budgeted as a means of evaluating cost controls. Two commonly used budgeting approaches are "static budgets" and "flexible budgets."

Static budgets show anticipated costs at one level of activity. Their preparers assume that production will be near the level selected. When all factory overhead costs are unaffected by activity, or when production level is stationary, the static budget will be an appropriate tool. However, such a situation is rare. As we pointed out earlier, factory overhead contains many variable costs, such as indirect labor, indirect materials, and supplies. Also, production levels usually fluctuate. If a static budget is used, and actual production differs from planned production, an accurate cost comparison cannot be made because part of the difference between actual and standard costs is the result of a change in the production activity level.

Flexible budgets show anticipated costs at different activity levels. This eliminates the problems associated with static budgets in terms of production fluctuation. Actual costs are compared with budgeted costs that would be incurred at the activity level. Therefore, they are a more realistic form of budgeting.

Table 12-1 (page 420) is an example of a flexible budget.

SETTING THE STANDARDS

Factory overhead budgets may be prepared by the accounting department or by a separate department set up for the purpose. Accounting departments are usually involved in budget preparation for two reasons: first, they have access to the necessary cost information; and second, those who set the standards should be separate from those responsible for meeting those standards.

Factory overhead budgets are based on expected costs to be incurred during production. This depends in part on experience and in part on knowledge of influences that will affect future costs (such as price increases). Management then will have the final decision on whether to increase or decrease the budgeted costs based on the judgments of those involved.

TABLE 12-1
FLEXIBLE BUDGET

	PRODUCTION LEVEL			ESTIMATED RATE PER DIRECT LABOR HOUR
	700	1,000	1,300	
Estimated direct labor hours	2,450	3,500	4,550	
Variable factory overhead costs:				
Indirect labor	$1,470 (A)	$2,100 (D)	$2,730 (G)	$ .60
Indirect materials	637 (B)	910 (E)	1,183 (H)	.26
Supplies	441 (C)	630 (F)	819 (I)	.18
Total variable factory overhead	$2,548	$3,640	$4,732	$1.04
Fixed factory overhead costs:				
Rent	$1,100	$1,100	$1,100	
Property taxes	200	200	200	
Depreciation of equipment	800	800	800	
Total fixed factory overhead	$2,100	$2,100	$2,100	
Total factory overhead	$4,648	$5,740	$6,832	

Computations:
(A) 2,450 × $.60	(D) 3,500 × $.60	(G) 4,550 × $.60
(B) 2,450 × $.26	(E) 3,500 × $.26	(H) 4,550 × $.26
(C) 2,450 × $.18	(F) 3,500 × $.18	(I) 4,550 × $.18

Budget figures are usually expressed in dollar amounts only. If the cost item is important and is based on some quantity such as the number of labor hours, the additional quantity information is also shown.

When determining a standard product cost, the amount representing factory overhead cost is separated into "variable" and "fixed" costs. A *variable cost* can be assigned to products over a wide range of activity levels. Although the total variable costs will vary directly with the production level, the variable unit cost will remain constant. The total fixed factory overhead cost will remain relatively constant over different activity levels. Fixed unit costs vary inversely; as more items are produced, fixed factory overhead costs are being spread over more units, so that unit cost decreases. Because of this characteristic, assignment of a standard fixed factory overhead cost for each product becomes a problem when production levels vary each month. Standard costing establishes one standard cost which can be applied to products despite fluctuation in production. In order to achieve this, fixed factory overhead unit costs are determined by using a predetermined production capacity level. Four production capacity levels may be used:

1 *Theoretical or ideal capacity*—Standards are based on the maximum capacity that a department or factory is capable of producing under perfect conditions. This is generally considered a standard that cannot be easily, if ever, attained.
2 *Practical or realistic capacity*—Standards are based on theoretical capacity, minus practical constraints such as estimated breakdowns, strikes, delays, and supply shortages.

3 *Normal or long-run capacity*—Standards are based on a constant, average level of utilization of plant and workers over a period of time which is sufficient to even out the high and low levels of production.

4 *Expected actual or short-run capacity*—Standards are based on capacity for the next period.

Normal or long-run capacity is the most appropriate level of production from which to develop standards, because it is based on normal operations; and it is inherent in our concept that standard costs for a particular production process must be calculated under normal conditions.

VARIANCE ANALYSIS

This is a means of determining the effectiveness of the controls over factory overhead costs. Actual factory overhead costs are compared with standard costs applied to production to determine the amount of the variance. In order for the analysis to be effective, responsibility for the variance should be assigned as close to the point of incurrence as possible. When an overall variance is calculated, control responsibility cannot be properly assigned because the figure is too general.

Analysis of factory overhead variance requires more detail than variance analysis used for direct costs (materials and labor). A volume variance must now be considered, in addition to the price and quantity variances that were associated with direct cost analysis.

One-Variance Analysis Method

The single variance is the result of the interrelationship of several of the components previously mentioned. Included in the total figure is a volume variance which is usually beyond the control of the supervisory personnel.

Total factory overhead variance is the difference between total factory overhead actually incurred and the standard factory overhead applied to production. The predetermined rate used to allocate factory overhead is generally based on standard or allowed hours (i.e., budgeted hours based on units produced). Variances result when actual hours differ from standard hours, or when costs are greater or less than were budgeted.

The overall or total factory overhead variance is computed as follows:

Actual factory overhead
Less: Overhead applied to production (standard number of hours allowed
     × standard overhead rate)
Total overhead variance

Basic Data for Examples 1 through 4

Actual number of direct labor hours	7,000
Standard number of hours allowed	7,200
Normal capacity	8,000
Actual factory overhead	$40,800

BUDGETED OVERHEAD AT NORMAL CAPACITY	TOTAL	RATE
Variable factory overhead	$20,000 (A)	$2.50
Fixed factory overhead	24,000 (B)	3.00
Totals	$44,000 (C)	$5.50

(A) 8,000 × $2.50; (B) 8,000 × $3.00; (C) 8,000 × $5.50

EXAMPLE 1

Computation of total overhead variance (one-variance method) is as follows:

Actual factory overhead	$40,800
Overhead applied to production (7,200 × $5.50)	39,600
Unfavorable total factory overhead variance	$ 1,200

The variance is unfavorable since actual expenses were greater than those expected and applied to production. Assigning responsibility (or blame) for this variance requires further analysis. The following additional variances are a further analysis of the unfavorable total factory overhead variance.

Two-Variance Analysis Method

Under the two-variance method, the overall variance is broken down into controllable variance and volume variance. The *controllable variance* is the difference between actual factory overhead expenses and those budgeted, based on the number of allowed hours. The *volume variance* is the difference between the amount budgeted, which was based on the number of allowed hours, and the cost applied to production during the period.

The *controllable variance* consists of variable costs only, and its responsibility can be assigned to a department manager or supervisor. *Volume variance* represents the utilization of plant capacity. An unfavorable volume variance indicates an inefficient use of plant capabilities. The responsibility for the volume variance is that of upper or executive management.

Computation of the two variances is as follows:

1 *Controllable Variance:*

	Actual factory overhead
Less:	Budget allowance at standard number of hours (fixed + variable* expenses)
	Controllable variance

Computation: Standard number of hours allowed × variable overhead rate.

2 *Volume Variance:*

	Budget allowance at standard number of hours
Less:	Overhead applied to production (Standard number of hours allowed × standard overhead rate)
	Volume variance

EXAMPLE 2

Assume the same basic data that was given for Example 1.

1 *Controllable Variance:*

Actual factory overhead		$40,800
Less:		
Budget allowance at standard number of hours:		
Variable (7,200 × $2.50)	$18,000	
Fixed	24,000	42,000
Favorable controllable variance		($ 1,200)

2 *Volume Variance:*

Budget allowed at standard number of hours	$42,000
Less: Standard number of hours allowed × standard allowed overhead rate	
(7,200 × $5.50)	39,600
Unfavorable volume variance	$ 2,400

In Example 2, the total $1,200 overall unfavorable variance [($1,200) + $2,400] is shown not to be a result of overspending at the department or cost center level but to be the result of poor utilization of the plant.

Three-Variance Analysis Method

The three variances calculated under the three-variance method are *spending*, *idle capacity*, and *efficiency*. *Spending variances* are the direct responsibility of the manager of the cost center or department in which the costs were incurred. These variances are the result of having spent more or less than was budgeted. The spending variance is similar to the controllable variance in the two-variance method, except that the influence of actual and standard hours is eliminated.

Idle capacity variance is the responsibility of upper management and not of a particular cost center or department. It deals with the utilization of the plant and the effect of such utilization on the fixed overhead costs. The variance is the result of production at an activity level different from that used to calculate the factory overhead base rate. If production falls below (or above) the level used in determining the rate, factory overhead costs are being underabsorbed (or overabsorbed). An unfavorable (or favorable) variance results.

Responsibility for the *efficiency variance* is assigned to the head of the department in which the costs were incurred. When more (or fewer) hours are actually used than were allowed in the cost center or department, an unfavorable (or a favorable) variance occurs. The variance may be caused by labor, by changes in procedures, or by any type of labor-related inefficiency. Whereas the spending variance consists of variable cost only, and idle capacity consists of fixed costs only, the efficiency variance consists of both types of factory overhead costs.

The computations of the three variances are as follows:

1 *Spending Variance:*

        Actual factory overhead
   Less: Budget allowance at actual number of hours (fixed + variable expenses*)
        Spending variance

   Computation: actual number of hours × variable rate.

2 *Idle Capacity Variance:*

        Budget allowance at actual number of hours
   Less: Actual number of hours × standard overhead rate
        Idle capacity variance

3 *Efficiency Variance:*

        Actual number of hours × standard rate
   Less: Overhead applied to production (Standard number of hours allowed ×
          standard rate)
        Efficiency variance

EXAMPLE 3

Using the same basic data as in Examples 1 and 2, the overall unfavorable variance of $1,200 would be analyzed as follows under the three-variance method:

1 *Spending Variance:*

Actual factory overhead		$40,800
Budget allowance at actual number of hours:		
Variable (7,000 × $2.50)	$17,500	
Fixed	24,000	41,500
Favorable spending variance		($ 700)

If budgeted fixed overhead is subtracted from actual factory overhead, a variable total cost of $16,800 ($40,800 − $24,000) remains; the latter results in a $2.40 rate ($16,800 ÷ 7,000) actually spent per hour. Since the budgeted variable rate is $2.50, the department head spent $.10 less than expected per unit and therefore a favorable spending variance of $700 (7,000 × $.10) resulted.

2 *Idle Capacity:*

Budget allowance at actual number of hours	$41,500
Actual number of hours × standard rate (7,000 × $5.50)	38,500
Unfavorable idle capacity variance	$ 3,000

The budget called for a normal capacity of 8,000 hours. Since the plant was utilized for only 7,000 hours, it was used at only 87½% capacity (7,000 ÷ 8,000) or 12½% under capacity. The fixed overhead expenses of $24,000 have to be allocated over a smaller number of units, which results in an underabsorption of these costs and therefore an unfavorable idle capacity variance of $3,000 ($24,000 × 12½%) resulted.

3 *Efficiency Variance:*

Actual number of hours × standard rate (7,000 × $5.50) $38,500
Standard number of hours allowed × standard rate (7,200 × $5.50) 39,600
Favorable efficiency variance .... ($ 1,100)

The department was efficient in that it required 200 fewer hours than were allowed according to the standard and therefore a favorable efficiency variance of $1,100 (200 × $5.50) resulted.

Four-Variance Analysis Method

The four-variance method consists of all the components of the three-variance method, except that the efficiency variance is analyzed further. Spending variance and idle capacity are the same under both methods. The efficiency variance is analyzed in terms of its fixed and variable components. Thus the four variances are *spending, idle capacity, variable efficiency,* and *fixed efficiency.* The responsibility for controlling both efficiency variances is assigned to the head of the department.

Computations of the variable efficiency variance and the fixed efficiency variance are as follows:

1 *Variable Efficiency Variance:*

Actual number of hours × variable standard rate
Less: Standard number of hours allowed × variable standard rate
Variable efficiency variance

2 *Fixed Efficiency Variance:*

Actual number of hours × fixed standard rate
Less: Standard number of hours allowed × fixed standard rate
Fixed efficiency variance

EXAMPLE 4

Continuing with our basic data from Example 1, the overall variance of $1,200 (unfavorable) is shown under the four-variance method.

1 *Spending Variance*—($700) favorable (same as in Example 3)
2 *Idle Capacity*—$3,000 unfavorable (same as in Example 3)
3 *Variable Efficiency Variance:*

Actual hours × variable rate (7,000 × $2.50) $17,500
Standard hours allowed × variable rate (7,200 × $2.50) 18,000
Favorable variable efficiency variance .... ($ 500)

4 *Fixed Efficiency Variance:*

Actual hours × fixed rate (7,000 × $3.00) $21,000
Standard hours allowed × fixed rate (7,200 × $3.00) 21,600
Favorable fixed efficiency variance .... ($ 600)

TABLE 12-2
FOUR-VARIANCE ANALYSIS METHOD

| | FACTORY OVERHEAD | | | |
| | RECORDED ON BOOKS | | PREDETERMINED ESTIMATE | |
ANALYSIS	ACTUALLY INCURRED	ACTUALLY APPLIED	BUDGETED (AT ACTUAL)	STANDARD APPLIED
Spending ($700) F	$40,800		$41,500	
Idle capacity $3000 U		(AH × SR) $38,500	$41,500	
Variable efficiency ($500) F		(AH × VR) $17,500		(SH × VR) $18,000
Fixed efficiency ($600) F		(AH ×FR) $21,000		(SH × FR) $21,600

Terms:

Factory overhead actually incurred—actual factory overhead incurred and recorded during a particular period.

Factory overhead actually applied—estimated factory overhead that was actually recorded, based on a predetermined rate and applied using actual number of hours incurred.

Factory overhead budgeted—factory overhead that was anticipated for a particular period based on actual production achieved.

Factory overhead standard applied—factory overhead that was based on a predetermined rate and standard number of hours allowed for a particular level of production.

AH—actual hours; SH—standard hours; FR—fixed rate; VR—variable rate; SR—standard rate

Table 12-2 is a diagram of the four-variance analysis method.

The one-, two-, or three-variance methods for analyzing factory overhead can be simply and quickly derived from the four-variance analysis method as follows:

Four-Variance Analysis Method:
  Spending variance
  Idle capacity variance
  Variable efficiency variance
  Fixed efficiency variance

Three-Variance Analysis Method:
  Spending variance
  Idle capacity variance
  Efficiency variance (variable efficiency + fixed efficiency)

Two-Variance Analysis Method:
  Controllable variance (spending variance + variable efficiency variance)
  Volume variance (idle capacity variance + fixed efficiency variance)

One-Variance Analysis Method:
  Total overhead variance (spending + idle capacity + variable efficiency + fixed efficiency)

Thus only the computations to arrive at the four-variance method need be memorized, because the other methods can be arrived at by simply combining elements of the four-variance method.

For example, the variance analysis methods in our previous examples may be derived from the four-variance analysis method as in Table 12-3.

The type and the amount of information desired by management are the major factors to be considered in the selection of variance analysis techniques. Whichever one is selected, it should be noted that the calculation of the variances is only the first step in variance analysis. To be of any value, variances, both favorable and unfavorable, must be analyzed as to their cause. Personnel responsible for controlling the specific costs must be identified and held accountable. Reasons for the variances must be determined and a plan for correction begun. It is important that the specific reason or problem be identified. Just knowing that there was an unfavorable spending variance is not enough. It may be the fault of the department head in not keeping costs within limits, or it may be the fault of an outdated standard. Before an evaluation of the manager's ability to control costs can be made, the cause must be identified.

TABLE 12-3
VARIANCE ANALYSIS METHODS

The Four-Variance Analysis Method:

1. Spending	($ 700)	favorable
2. Idle capacity	$3,000	unfavorable
3. Variable efficiency	($ 500)	favorable
4. Fixed efficiency	($ 600)	favorable

The Three-Variance Analysis Method:

Spending		($ 700)	favorable
Idle capacity		$3,000	unfavorable
Efficiency variance:			
Variable efficiency	($ 500)		
Fixed efficiency	(600)	($1,100)	favorable

The Two-Variance Analysis Method:

Controllable:			
Spending	($ 700)		
Variable efficiency	(500)	($1,200)	favorable
Volume:			
Idle capacity	$3,000		
Fixed efficiency	(600)	$2,400	unfavorable

The One-Variance Analysis Method:

Spending	($ 700)	favorable
Idle capacity	3,000	unfavorable
Variable efficiency	(500)	favorable
Fixed efficiency	(600)	favorable
Total	$1,200	unfavorable

Journal Entries for Overhead Variances

Journal entries should be made to record the activities involving factory overhead expenses and any related variances. Total factory overhead variance represents the difference between the amount charged to the Factory Overhead Control account and the amount applied to the Work-in-Process account. Variance accounts are opened to show the particular variance and to close the Factory Overhead Control account.

Table 12-4 shows the journal entries that would be made for the one-variance, two-variance, three-variance, and four-variance analysis "methods," assuming the same facts as were used in Examples 1, 2, 3, and 4.

Note that in all four methods, the Work-in-Process account is debited with the same amount. This is because, in a standard cost system, all product costs (direct materials, direct labor, and factory overhead) are charged to production at standard costs allowed.

DISPOSAL OF
ALL VARIANCES

The pricing of all inventories (raw materials, work-in-process, and finished goods) is a major concern of cost accounting because of its influence on the reporting of income. When standard costing is used, a decision must be made as to whether to price inventories at standard cost or at actual cost. Disposal of the variances will differ according to which inventory costing basis is used. If inventory is to be shown at standard costs, the variances will be charged off as a period cost. If inventory is to be shown at actual costs, the variances will be divided between inventories and cost of goods sold so as to approximate actual costs. In such cases, variances are treated as product costs.

The criteria generally used to determine which method of disposal to use are (1) the characteristics of the standards used, (2) the ability to keep actual costs near standard costs, and (3) the methods of costing the inventories for external financial statements.

Under the first criterion, the determination of standards is important. When pricing standards are based on current standards rather than fixed standards, there tends to be less variance between actual and standard prices. When factory-overhead rates are kept up to date, factory-overhead variances are kept within bounds. In such cases, the variances will generally be treated as period costs. It is reasoned that the standard costs closely resemble actual costs, so that no further adjustment is necessary.

For external financial-statement purposes, inventories must be reported at actual cost, which is defined as the value given up or service rendered to acquire or produce the asset. Therefore, if inventories are maintained at standard costs, they must be adjusted to approximate actual costs, with the individual variances allocated between inventory and cost of goods sold.

If variances are treated as period costs, they will be closed to the income summary account, either directly or through the cost of goods sold account.

TABLE 12-4
JOURNAL ENTRIES FOR VARIANCE ANALYSIS METHODS

One-Variance Method:

Factory overhead control	40,800	
Various credits		40,800
To record actual factory overhead		
Work-in-process	39,600	(7,200 × $5.50)
Factory overhead control		39,600
To apply factory overhead to work-in-process		
Total factory overhead variance	1,200	($40,800 − $39,600)
Factory overhead control		1,200
To close factory overhead control and record variance		

Two-Variance Method:

Factory overhead control	40,800	
Various credits		40,800
To record actual factory overhead		
Work-in-process	39,600	(7,200 × $5.50)
Factory overhead control		39,600
To apply factory overhead to work-in-process		
Factory overhead volume variance	2,400	($42,000 − $39,600)
Factory overhead controllable variance		1,200 ($40,800 − $42,000)
Factory overhead control		1,200 ($40,800 − $39,600)
To close factory overhead control and record variances		

Three-Variance Method:

Factory overhead control	40,800	
Various credits		40,800
To record actual factory overhead		
Work-in-process	39,600	(7,200 × $5.50)
Factory overhead control		39,600
To apply factory overhead to work-in-process		
Factory overhead idle capacity variance	3,000	($41,500 − $38,500)
Factory overhead efficiency variance		1,100 ($38,500 − $39,600)
Factory overhead spending variance		700 ($40,800 − $41,500)
Factory overhead control		1,200 ($40,800 − $39,600)
To close factory overhead control and record variances		

Four-Variance Method:

Factory overhead control	40,800	
Various credits		40,800
To record actual factory overhead		
Work-in-process	39,600	(7,200 × $5.50)
Factory overhead control		39,600
To apply overhead to work-in-process		
Factory overhead idle capacity variance	3,000	($41,500 − $38,500)
Factory overhead variable efficiency variance		500 ($17,500 − $18,000)
Factory overhead fixed efficiency variance		600 ($21,000 − $21,600)
Factory overhead spending variance		700 ($40,800 − $41,500)
Factory overhead control		1,200 ($40,800 − $39,600)
To close factory overhead control and record variances		

If the variances are treated as product costs, they will be closed to the cost of goods sold and inventory accounts based on a ratio of dollars in each account to total dollars in the sum of those accounts. Below are typical journal entries that would be made under both methods, assuming the following data:

Cost of goods sold	$ 7,000
Ending finished goods	2,000
Ending work-in-process	1,000
Total	$10,000

Variances for Period:

Materials:	Quantity	$ 90	unfavorable
	Rate	(40)	favorable
Labor:	Efficiency	(50)	favorable
	Rate	20	unfavorable
Overhead:	Spending	(140)	favorable
	Idle capacity	(60)	favorable
	Efficiency	70	unfavorable
Net variance		($110)	favorable

To Close Variances to Income Summary:

Materials rate variance	40	
Labor efficiency variance	50	
Spending variance	140	
Idle capacity variance	60	
Materials quantity variance		90
Labor rate variance		20
Efficiency variance		70
Income summary		110

To Close Variances to Cost of Goods Sold and Inventories: Net variance must be allocated to cost of goods sold, ending finished goods, and ending work-in-process inventories based on the proportionate dollars in those accounts to the total of all the accounts.

Cost of goods sold	= 7/10 × $110 =	$ 77
Ending finished goods	= 2/10 × 110 =	22
Ending work-in-process	= 1/10 × 110 =	11
Net variance		$110

Materials rate variance	40	
Labor efficiency variance	50	
Spending variance	140	
Idle capacity variance	60	
Materials quantity variance		90
Labor rate variance		20
Efficiency variance		70
Cost of goods sold		77
Finished goods inventory		22
Work-in-process inventory		11

LOCATION OF VARIANCES
ON THE INCOME STATEMENT

Generally, variances appear on the income statement in one of three places: first, they may be shown as a separate deduction (if unfavorable) or addition (if favorable) to the gross profit figure; second, the variances may be charged directly to the cost of goods sold account; third, the appropriate amount of each variance may be divided between the cost of goods sold and the inventory accounts.

Under the first method, which specifically places emphasis on the variances, the variances are considered period costs. The variances are shown in detail on the statement so that management has the needed information for correction. Users of this method feel that the variance is a result of either efficiencies or inefficiencies and should not be included in product costs.

Under the second method, the variances are also considered period costs. However, the variances are buried in cost of goods sold and are therefore not highlighted on the income statement. Many accountants feel that a distortion of gross profit will occur under this method if the variances are large compared with the total cost of goods manufactured.

The final presentation is used by those who believe that the financial statement should be shown at historical cost rather than at standard cost. Variances are distributed to the specific inventories and the cost of goods sold, in order that these figures will represent actual costs as nearly as possible. This is the preferable method if the variances are significant because under generally accepted accounting principles, inventories should be reported at actual cost.

SPOILAGE, DEFECTIVE UNITS,
SCRAP, AND WASTE MATERIALS

The use of standard costs in a job order cost system or a process cost system does not alter the method of handling spoilage, defective units, scrap, and waste materials (see Chapters 7 and 9 for a complete discussion). The only additional considerations when standard costs are used are whether these items have been included in the standards, and whether they should be included in the analysis of variances.

Spoilage. Normal spoilage is commonly provided for when developing standards and is usually added to the factory overhead rate. When normal spoilage is included in the standard, the cost of normal spoilage should be removed from work-in-process (debited to factory overhead) when the spoiled units are removed from production. This would leave in work-in-process the standard costs of producing good units (which includes the cost of normal spoilage because the standard used to apply factory overhead included an additional charge for normal spoilage). When normal spoilage is not provided for in the standard, the cost of any normal spoilage is left in work-in-process at standard cost when the spoiled units are removed.

The cost of abnormal spoilage would not be incorporated into the standard because it represents spoilage above what is considered normal for a production process and, therefore, cannot be anticipated. Any abnormal spoilage should be removed from work-in-process and treated as a period cost by being charged to an abnormal spoilage loss account.

For example, assume the following:

Standard Costs to Produce Product X

Standards not including normal spoilage:

ELEMENTS		COST
Direct materials—1 rod of steel		$ 5
Direct labor—1 hour		3
Factory overhead (per direct labor hour):		
Variable	$1	
Fixed	1	2
Standard unit cost (without spoilage)		$10

Standards including normal spoilage at 10% of standard unit cost:

ELEMENTS			COST
Direct materials—1 rod of steel			$ 5
Direct labor—1 hour			3
Factory overhead (per direct labor hour):			
Variable	$1		
Normal spoilage (10% × $10)	1	$2	
Fixed		1	3
Standard unit cost (including spoilage)			$11
Normal capacity is 10,000 units			

Inspection for spoilage occurs at the end of the production process; normal spoilage is 10% of units produced.

Actual Data

Actual production 11,000 units (9,800 good units resulted)
Actual units spoiled were 1,200 analyzed as follows:

Normal spoilage (11,000 × 10%)	1,100
Abnormal (1,200 − 1,100)	100
Total spoilage in units	1,200

Assumption A: Standards not including normal spoilage was charged to work-in-process.

Entry to record production at standard costs:

Work-in-process (11,000 × $10)	110,000	
Materials (11,000 × $5)		55,000
Payroll (11,000 × $3)		33,000
Factory overhead control (11,000 × $2)		22,000

The total cost of production can be analyzed as follows:

Good units (9,800 × $10)	$ 98,000
Normal spoilage (1,100 × $10)	11,000
Cost to produce good units	$109,000
Abnormal spoilage (100 × $10)	1,000
Total cost of production	$110,000

Abnormal spoilage must be deducted from work-in-process as follows:

Work-in-process (11,000 × $10)	$110,000
Less abnormal spoilage (100 × $10)	1,000
Cost to produce good units	$109,000

Entry to remove abnormal spoilage for work-in-process:

Abnormal spoilage	1,000	
Work-in-process		1,000

Assumption B: Standard including normal spoilage was charged to work-in-process.

Entry to record production at standard costs:

Work-in-process (11,000 × $11)	121,000	
Materials (11,000 × $5)		55,000
Payroll (11,000 × $3)		33,000
Factory overhead control (11,000 × $3)		33,000

The total cost of production can be analyzed as follows:

Total production cost (11,000 × $11)		$121,000
Less spoilage:		
Normal (1,000 × $10)	$11,000	
Abnormal (100 × $10)	1,000	12,000
Cost to produce good units		$109,000

Entry to remove normal and abnormal spoilage from work-in-process:

Factory overhead control (normal spoilage)	11,000	
Abnormal spoilage	1,000	
Work-in-process		12,000

The final unit cost to produce a good unit would be $11.12 under both methods, computed as follows:

$$\frac{\text{Cost to produce good units}}{\text{Good units}} = \frac{\$109,000}{9,800} = \$11.12$$

Defective Units. When the cost of reworking defective units is provided for in the standard costs, any rework cost for a normal number of defective units is charged to factory overhead at standard cost. In the case of an abnormal number of defective units, rework costs are charged to an abnormal defective unit loss account, thereby reflecting this cost as a period cost. If the cost of reworking defective units is not provided for in the standard, the cost of reworking a normal number of defective units should be charged to work-in-process (at standard cost), and the cost of reworking abnormal defective units should again be charged to an abnormal defective units loss account (same under both methods). See Summary Problem 4 for an example.

Scrap. Scrap is usually considered when computing the materials required to produce one unit. The estimated market value of scrap per unit multiplied by the estimated quantity of scrap that results from the production of one unit should be deducted from the standard direct materials cost. For example, assume one sheet of metal is needed to produce one table and that each sheet weighs 25 pounds and costs $100. The scrap metal that is left over from the production of a table is estimated to be 2 pounds. The estimated market value for this scrap is $2 a pound. The computation of standard direct materials unit cost for the above would be as follows:

Production of One Metal Table:

	POUNDS	COST
1 sheet of metal	25	$100
Less: Scrap	2	4 (2 pounds × $2)
Standard direct materials pounds and cost per unit	23	$ 96

If the value of scrap is not considered when computing the standard rate, the proceeds from its sale are usually credited to factory overhead control.

Waste. An allowance for a normal amount of waste is usually included in the standard cost computation, and any amount above normal will be reflected in the materials quantity variance as being unfavorable.

MIX AND YIELD VARIANCES

Manufacturing processes often require the combination of different materials in a predetermined proportion to produce the finished product. Examples of such items are chemical products, processed meat, and woolen goods. A variation from the prescribed mix will cause a *mix variance* to occur. The amount of output that is usually produced from the amount of materials input may also be affected. If the output changes, such a change is known as a *yield variance*. Mix and yield variances are treated as extensions of the analysis of the variances already examined under standard costing. Analysis of the materials quantity variance in terms of a mix and yield variance often results in the production of more profitable products and less waste. Since related expenses for labor and factory overhead are included in the finished product cost, a yield variance is also calculated for these items.

Materials Mix Variance

The materials standard mix is usually determined through laboratory or engineering tests. Specific grades of materials and quantity are determined before production begins. A mix variance will result when materials are not actually placed into production in the same ratio as the standard formula. For example, if *Product A* is produced by adding 300 lb of raw materials X and 700 lb of raw materials Y, the materials mix is 30% X and 70% Y. Actual raw materials used must be in this 3:7 ratio, or a materials mix variance will occur. A mix variance may occur because an attempt is made to achieve cost savings by changing the mix formula or the needed raw materials quantities may not be available at the required time.

Materials mix variance is computed as follows:

> Actual materials used (individual actual quantities used ×
> individual standard unit input cost)
>
> Less: Standard formula (total actual quantity used × total standard
> weighted average unit-input cost)
> _____
> Materials mix variance

The standard weighted average unit-input cost is determined by dividing total standard materials cost by the total number of units of input.

The following data represents *standard product* and *cost specifications* for 20,000 gallons of *Product X:*

	STANDARD GALLONS ALLOWED		STANDARD UNIT-INPUT COST	STANDARD TOTAL COST
Raw materials A	10,000	×	$1.30	$13,000
Raw materials B	15,000	×	.80	12,000
Total unit—input	25,000		$1.00 (1)	$25,000
Total unit—output	20,000		$1.25 (2)	

$$\text{Standard output/input ratio} = \frac{20,000}{25,000} = 80\%$$

(1) $1.00 input $= \dfrac{\$25,000}{25,000}\quad\dfrac{\text{total cost}}{\text{total units of input}}$

(2) $1.25 output $= \dfrac{\$25,000}{20,000}\quad\dfrac{\text{total cost}}{\text{total units of output}}$

Actual raw materials purchased and placed into production:

Material A	= 10,750
Material B	= 16,250
Total gallons	27,000

Actual cost of materials A and B was $1.35 and $.78 per unit, respectively.

Materials mix variance would be computed as follows:

Actual materials mix:

	ACTUAL GALLONS USED		STANDARD UNIT-INPUT COST	ACTUAL TOTAL COST
Raw materials A	10,750	×	$1.30	$13,975
Raw materials B	16,250	×	.80	13,000
Total				$26,975
Less: Standard formula (27,000 × $1.00)				27,000
Favorable mix variance				($ 25)

The favorable mix variance is the result of using less of the more-expensive raw materials A than was called for under the standard formula.

Materials Yield Variance

The material mix specified in the standard formula is expected to provide a given amount of output or yield. When the expected or standard yield differs from the actual yield, a yield variance exists.

The following computation is used to determine the yield variance:

Expected yield (total actual quantity used × total
standard weighted average unit-input cost)
Less: Actual yield (total actual quantity produced ×
standard weighted average unit-output cost)
Materials yield variance

Note that the above equation for expected yield uses the standard weighted average unit-input cost. This is identical with the equation (standard formula) used in the materials mix computation. When both variances are of interest and are being computed, time is saved by using the method shown above. However, the yield can also be computed by using the standard weighted average unit-output cost and the *ratio* of standard output quantity to standard input quantity as follows:

$$\text{Expected yield} = \text{actual input quantity} \times \frac{\text{standard output quantity}}{\text{standard input quantity}} \times \text{standard weighted average output unit cost}$$

The same information that was given above will be used to illustrate the yield variance. Additional information is as follows:

Actual production for the period was 19,800 gallons.

Materials yield variance:
Expected yield (27,000 × $1) $27,000
Less: Actual yield (19,800 × $1.25) 24,750
Unfavorable yield variance .... $ 2,250

The amount of input should have produced 21,600 (27,000 input ÷ 1.25 input/output ratio) gallons of output, but only 19,800 was actually produced. There was an unfavorable yield of 1,800 (21,600 − 19,800) gallons under what was expected.

When the materials mix variance is added to the materials yield variance, the total will equal the materials quantity variance, computed as follows:

Favorable mix variance	($ 25)
Unfavorable yield variance	2,250
Quantity variance	$2,225 unfavorable

The quantity variance may also be independently computed as follows:

Actual materials used (individual actual quantities used × individual standard unit input cost)	$26,975
Less: Actual yield (total actual quantity produced × standard weighted average unit—output cost)	24,750
Quantity variance	$ 2,225 unfavorable

Note that the above independent calculation of the quantity variance is a modification of the direct materials quantity variance presented in Chapter 11. The modification is necessary because there is more than one raw material in the above example and input/output factors are also considered. Computation of the direct materials price variance would not change and is as follows:

$$\begin{bmatrix} \text{Actual} & \text{standard} \\ \text{unit} - \text{unit} \\ \text{cost} & \text{cost} \end{bmatrix} \times \begin{array}{l} \text{actual} \\ \text{quantity} \\ \text{purchased} \end{array}$$

Raw materials A ($1.35 − $1.30) × 10,750 = $537.50 unfavorable
Raw materials B ($ .78 − $ .80) × 16,250 = (325.00) favorable
Direct materials price variance $212.50 unfavorable

The direct materials variances would, therefore, result in three variances:

Price variance	$ 212.50 unfavorable
Mix variance	(25.00) favorable
Yield variance	2,250.00 unfavorable
Total variance	$2,437.50 unfavorable

Labor and Factory Overhead Yields

When the product is transferred to the finished goods inventory, all product costs are included. Actual quantities are multiplied by the total standard product cost. Because of this, both a *labor yield variance* and a *factory overhead yield variance* should be calculated.

The labor variance was previously divided into a rate variance and an efficiency variance. The labor yield variance is a further refinement of the labor efficiency variance and represents that portion of the labor efficiency variance resulting from the actual yield differing from the expected yield. It is computed as follows:

Labor Yield Variance:

Expected yield (total actual input quantity × output/input ratio × standard labor rate per unit)
Less: Actual yield (total actual output quantity × standard labor rate per unit)
Labor yield variance

We will continue our example and assume these additional facts:

Conversion of 25,000 gallons of materials into 20,000 gallons of product X should require 40 direct labor hours at $4.50 an hour or $.009 per gallon [(40 ÷ 20,000) × $4.50]. Standard labor *hours* per gallon is .002 (40 ÷ 20,000 gallons).
Actual number of direct labor hours were 35 at $4.70. The labor yield variance is computed as follows:

Expected yield (27,000 × .80 × $.009)	$194.40
Less: Actual yield (19,800 × $.009)	178.20
Labor yield variance	$ 16.20 unfavorable

The direct labor efficiency variance presented in Chapter 11 must be modified to include the standard hours allowed for *expected yield*. Expected yield is 21,600 gallons (27,000 gallons put into production × .80 output/input ratio); thus the number of standard hours allowed for expected yield is 43.2 hours (21,600 × .002).

Computation of the direct labor efficiency variance is computed as follows:

$$\left[\begin{array}{c} \text{Number of} \\ \text{actual hours} \\ \text{worked} \end{array} - \begin{array}{c} \text{number of} \\ \text{standard hours} \\ \text{allowed for} \\ \text{expected} \\ \text{production} \end{array} \right] \begin{array}{c} \text{standard} \\ \times \text{ wage} \\ \text{rate} \end{array}$$

$(35 - 43.2) \times \$4.50 = (\$36.90)$ favorable

The direct labor rate variance would still be computed as follows:

$$\left[\begin{array}{c} \text{Actual} \\ \text{wage} \\ \text{rate} \end{array} - \begin{array}{c} \text{standard} \\ \text{wage} \\ \text{rate} \end{array} \right] \begin{array}{c} \text{actual} \\ \times \text{ hours} \\ \text{worked} \end{array}$$

$(\$4.70 - \$4.50) \times \$35 = \$7.00$ unfavorable

The direct labor variances would, therefore, result in three variances:

Rate variance	$ 7.00 unfavorable
Efficiency variance	(36.90) favorable
Yield variance	16.20 unfavorable
Total variance	($ 13.70) favorable

The factory overhead variance was previously divided into a one-, two-, three-, and four-variance analysis in this chapter. When an overhead yield variance is included in the three- or four-variance analysis, the spending and idle capacity variances are still computed as previously discussed. The overhead efficiency variance presented in this chapter must be modified to include the standard hours allowed for *expected yield* (43.2 hours)

The factory overhead yield variance represents that portion of the overhead efficiency variance resulting from the actual yield differing from the expected yield and is computed as follows:

Factory Overhead Yield Variance:

Expected yield (total actual input quantity × output/input ratio × standard overhead rate per unit)

Less: Actual yield (total actual output × standard overhead rate per unit)

Overhead yield variance

We continue our example and assume that factory overhead is applied on a direct labor hour basis at $5 per hour, or $.01 per gallon [(40 ÷ 20,000) × $5]. The standard variable overhead rate is $3 per hour and standard fixed overhead is $100. Actual factory overhead was $210.

The factory overhead yield would be computed as follows:

Expected yield (27,000 × .80 × $.01)	= $216.00
Less: Actual yield (19,800 × $.01)	198.00
Factory overhead yield variance	$ 18.00 unfavorable

Computation of the factory overhead efficiency variance is computed as follows:

Actual number of hours × standard rate (35 × $5)	$175.00
Standard number of hours allowed for expected production × standard rate (43.2 × $5)	216.00
Factory overhead efficiency variance	$ (41.00) favorable

The spending and idle capacity variances would still be computed as follows:

Spending

Actual factory overhead		$210
Budget allowance at actual number of hours:		
Variable (35 × $3)	$105	
Fixed	100	205
Factory overhead spending variance		$ 5 unfavorable

Idle Capacity

Budget allowance at actual number of hours	$205
Actual number of hours × standard rate (35 × $5)	175
Factory overhead idle capacity variance	$ 30 unfavorable

The factory overhead variances (under the former three-variance method) would result in the following variances:

Spending	$ 5 unfavorable
Idle capacity	30 unfavorable
Efficiency variance	(41) favorable
Yield variance	18 unfavorable
Total variance	$12 unfavorable

In the journal entries for mix and yield variances, the debit to work-in-process is based on the standard yield for actual input. The yield variances for materials, labor, and factory overhead constitute the difference between the standard yield for actual input and the standard yield for actual output. Table 12-5 shows the appropriate journal entries.

TABLE 12-5
JOURNAL ENTRIES FOR MIX AND YIELD VARIANCES

1. *Direct Materials*		
Materials	26,975.00	
Direct materials price variance	212.50	
Vouchers payable		27,187.50
Work-in-process (27,000 × $1).............................	27,000.00	
Direct materials mix variance		25.00
Materials		26,975.00
Finished goods	24,750.00	
Direct materials yield variance	2,250.00	
Work-in-process		27,000.00
2. *Direct Labor*		
Payroll	164.50	
Various payables		164.50
Work-in-process (43.2 × $4.50)	194.40	
Direct labor rate variance	7.00	
Direct labor efficiency variance		36.90
Payroll		164.50
Finished goods	178.20	
Direct labor yield variance	16.20	
Work-in-process		194.40
3. *Factory Overhead*		
Factory overhead control	210.00	
Various credits		210.00
Work-in-process (43.2 × $5)	216.00	
Factory overhead control		216.00
Factory overhead control	6.00	
Factory overhead spending variance	5.00	
Factory overhead idle capacity variance	30.00	
Factory overhead efficiency variance		41.00
Finished goods	198.00	
Factory overhead yield variance	18.00	
Work-in-process		216.00

CHAPTER REVIEW

Standard costing aims at determining one standard cost which can be applied to products despite fluctuations in production. Procedures used to compute and to apply the standard costs and variances under standard costing are affected by several factors. One is the variety of costs included in overhead. Another is the fact that there are many individuals in the company who control the cost items in factory overhead, and so it is important that each individual have a complete knowledge about controlling these costs. Standard costing is influenced by costs which are usually not affected by production, such as rent and insurance.

In order to help management control factory overhead costs, budgets are prepared. When actual results are obtained, they are compared with those budgeted, as a means of evaluating control. The static budget and the flexible budget are two budget approaches commonly used.

When determining a *standard product cost*, the amount that represents factory overhead cost must be separated into variable and fixed costs. An analysis of the factory overhead is then made. A volume variance, along with a price and quantity variance, must now be considered.

Variance analysis is a means of determining the effectiveness of controls over factory overhead costs. Actual factory overhead expenses are compared with standard expenses and are applied to production to determine the amount of the variance. There are four methods to analyze the variances that occur— the one-variance method, the two-variance method, the three-variance method, and the four-variance method. The method to be used is decided by management on the basis of the type and amount of information desired.

Variances are shown on the income statement in one of three places. They may be shown as a separate deduction (if unfavorable) or an addition (if favorable) to the gross profit figure. They may also be charged directly to the cost of goods sold account, or the appropriate amount of each variance may be applied separately to the cost of goods sold and inventory accounts.

When standard costs are used, one has to determine whether spoilage, defective units, scrap, and waste materials have been included in the standards. If spoilage is included in the standards, the cost of spoilage (both normal and abnormal) should be removed from the Work-in-Process account at standard cost. If it is not included in the standards, the cost of any normal spoilage is left in work-in-process (at standard cost) and the cost of any abnormal spoilage is removed from work-in-process (at standard cost). When the cost of defective units is provided for in the standard, any rework cost of normal defective units is charged to factory overhead at standard cost; if the cost is not provided for in the standard, the cost of reworking normal defective units should be charged to work-in-process (at standard cost), and the cost of reworking abnormal defective units is charged to an abnormal defective units loss account (the same as if it were included). If scrap is included, the estimated market value of scrap per unit, multiplied by the estimated quantity of scrap that results from the production of one unit, should be deducted from the standard direct materials cost. If it is not included, the proceeds from its sale is usually credited to factory overhead control. An allowance for a normal amount of waste is usually included in the standard cost computation, and any amount above normal will be reflected in an unfavorable materials quantity variance.

Manufacturing processes often require the combination of different materials in a predetermined proportion to produce the finished product. Any deviation from the prescribed mix will result in a mix variance. The amount of output that is usually produced from the amount of materials input may also be affected. If the output changes, such a change is known as a yield variance.

GLOSSARY

Basic Standard—a unit of measure used to compare projected with actual results; it usually remains constant from year to year.

Budget Control Component—a variance caused by spending more or less than the amount provided for in the flexible budget for the actual man or machine hours.

Capacity Volume Component—amount and fixed cost underabsorbed (or overabsorbed) because the number of actual man or machine hours varies from the standard or normal capacity, measured in hours.

Controllable Variance—the difference between actual factory overhead expenses and those budgeted, based on the number of allowed hours.

Current Standards—the standard based on one of four levels of production.

Efficiency Variance—a difference between the number of hours allowed and the number of hours actually used.

Excess Hours Controllable Component—variable cost incurred because the actual number of hours exceeds

(or is less than) the number of standard hours.

Flexible Budget—a form of projecting that shows anticipated costs at different activity levels.

Idle Capacity Variance—the result of production at an activity level different from that used to calculate the factory overhead base rate.

Long-Run or Normal Capacity—standards are based on a constant, average level of utilization of plant and workers over a period of time which is sufficient to even out the high and low levels of production.

Materials Mix Variance—a difference from the prescribed mix which occurs when raw materials are not added to production in the proportion originally formulated.

Practical or Realistic Capacity—standards based on theoretical capacity minus practical constraints such as estimated breakdowns, strikes, delays, and supply shortages.

Short-Run or Expected Actual Capacity—standards based on capacity for the next period.

Spending Variance—the difference

caused by spending more or less than was budgeted. It is similar to the controllable variance.

Static Budget—a form of planning that shows anticipated costs at one level of activity.

Theoretical or Ideal Capacity—standards based on the maximum capacity that a department or factory is capable of producing under perfect conditions.

Variance Analysis—a means of determining the effectiveness of the controls.

Volume Variance—the difference between the amount budgeted, which was based on the number of allowed hours, and the cost applied to production during the period.

Yield Variance—the change in the amount of output expected from the amount actually obtained, based on the amount of raw material input.

SUMMARY PROBLEMS

PROBLEM 1

The Herman Manufacturing Corporation uses a standard cost system. Data for the month of March is shown below:

Budgeted overhead (normal capacity) – 50,000 direct labor hours

		STANDARD RATE
Estimated Factory Overhead:		
Fixed	$110,000	$2.20
Variable	75,000	1.50
	$185,000	$3.70

Actual results for March:

Direct labor hours	48,600
Factory overhead:	
Fixed	$110,000
Variable	82,400
Total actual factory overhead	$192,400

Standard hours allowed for March production: 49,500

REQUIRED:

a Determine the overhead variances for the month using the four-variance method.

b What would the variances be if the two-variance method were used?

c Show the journal entries that would have been made to record factory overhead costs and variances assuming the four-variance method was used.

PROBLEM 2

Healy Products Corporation uses a standard cost system. Examination of its records showed the following for the month of June:

	UNITS
Goods sold:	60,000
Ending finished goods	30,000
Ending work-in-process	10,000
Total units	100,000

Normal capacity: 6,000 direct labor hours
Budgeted overhead at normal capacity:

	TOTAL	RATE
Variable overhead	$ 6,600	$1.10
Fixed overhead	11,100	1.85
Total	$17,700	$2.95

Total actual factory overhead	$15,750
Actual direct labor hours	5,500
Standard hours allowed	5,650

Variances calculated to date for end of period:

Materials quantity variance	$1,200 unfavorable
Materials rate variance	300 favorable
Labor efficiency variance	600 favorable
Labor rate variance	1,000 unfavorable

REQUIRED:

a Calculate the factory overhead variances under the three-variance method.
b Calculate the overall factory overhead variance.
c Prepare the journal entries to dispose of all the variances if **(1)** company policy is to close variances to the income summary or **(2)** company policy is to close variances to cost of goods sold and inventories.

PROBLEM 3

The T. M. Iffy Corporation produces Product Z by combining four raw materials during production. Because of evaporation, it requires 100 lb of raw material input to produce 95 lb of Product Z.
Engineering department specifications show the following recommended mix:

INGREDIENTS	POUNDS	UNIT COST	TOTAL COST
Material A	2,000	$.55	$1,100
Material B	4,000	.75	3,000
Material C	3,000	.60	1,800
Material D	1,000	.15	150
Input	10,000	$.605 (wt avg)	$6,050
Output	9,000	$.6722 (wt avg)	

It requires 75 hours at $3 an hour to convert 10,000 lb input into 9,000 lb output. This equals $.025 per lb [(75 × $3) ÷ 9,000].

Factory overhead is applied based on direct labor hours at a rate of $4 per hour. This equals $.0333 per lb [(75 × $4) ÷ 9,000].

At the end of the period, the following information was obtained from the company records.

Actual raw material input:

Material A	2,500 lb
Material B	4,800
Material C	2,750
Material D	1,450
	11,500 lb

Actual pounds of Product Z produced was 11,000.

REQUIRED:

a   Calculate the mix and yield variances.
b   Calculate the labor yield variance and factory overhead yield variance.
c   Make the necessary journal entries to record the variances.

PROBLEM 4

Fran's Fancy Figures, Inc., produces large chocolate candy figures. The standard costs to produce the chocolate figures are as follows:

	COST
Direct materials	$ 6.00
Direct labor	4.00
Factory overhead:	
Variable	2.25
Fixed	1.75
	$14.00

8,000 good figures were produced at the following costs:

ELEMENT	ACTUAL COST	STANDARD ALLOWED FOR GOOD UNITS
Direct Materials		
Actual—8,500 figures	$ 51,000	
Standard allowed—9,000 figures		$ 54,000
Direct Labor		
Actual—8,700 hours	34,800	
Standard allowed—8,000 hours		32,000
Factory Overhead		
Variable	20,500	18,000
Fixed	13,000	14,000
Total costs	$119,300	$118,000

Additional Information:

Spoilage

Normal	30 figures
Abnormal	15 figures

Defective Units

Normal	40 figures
Abnormal	50 figures

Inspection occurs at the end of production.

Cost to rework defective units:

		COST ALLOCATED TO	
ELEMENT	COST	ABNORMAL ($5/9$)	NORMAL ($4/9$)
Direct materials	$180.00	$100.00	$ 80.00
Direct labor	120.00	66.67	53.33
Factory overhead:			
Variable	67.50	37.50	30.00
Fixed	52.50	29.17	23.33
Total costs	$420.00	$233.34	$186.66

Materials prices and wage rates have not changed during the period.

REQUIRED:

a Compute the materials quantity variance, labor efficiency variance, and factory overhead variance using the two-variance method.

b. Assuming normal spoilage and normal rework costs for defective units of $1.00 per unit were considered when standard costs were computed, write the journal entry to record spoilage and rework costs.

c Assuming normal spoilage and normal rework costs for defective units were not considered when standard costs were computed, write the journal entry to record spoilage and rework costs.

SOLUTIONS TO SUMMARY PROBLEMS

PROBLEM 1

a *Spending Variance:*

Actual factory overhead			$192,400
Less: Budgeted at actual variable (48,600 × $1.50)		$ 72,900	
Fixed		110,000	182,900
Unfavorable spending variance			$ 9,500

Idle Capacity Variance:

Budgeted at actual	$182,900
Less: Actual hours × standard rate (48,600 × $3.70)	179,820
Unfavorable idle capacity variance	$ 3,080

Variable Efficiency Variance:

Actual hours × variable rate (48,600 × $1.50)	$ 72,900
Less: Standard hours × variable rate (49,500 × $1.50)	74,250
Favorable variable efficiency variance	($ 1,350)

Fixed Efficiency Variance:

Actual hours × standard fixed rate (48,600 × $2.20)	$106,920
Less: Standard hours × standard fixed rate (49,500 × $2.20)	108,900
Favorable fixed efficiency variance	($ 1,980)

b Controllable variance = spending variance + variable efficiency variance
Controllable variance = $9,500 unfavorable + ($1,350) favorable
Unfavorable controllable variance = $8,150

Volume variance = idle capacity variance + fixed efficiency
Volume variance = $3,080 unfavorable + ($1,980) favorable
Unfavorable volume variance = $1,100

c

Factory overhead control	192,400	
Various credits		192,400
Work-in-process (49,500 × $3.70)	183,150	
Factory overhead control		183,150
Factory overhead idle capacity variance	3,080	
Factory overhead spending variance	9,500	
Factory overhead variable efficiency variance		1,350
Factory overhead fixed efficiency variance		1,980
Factory overhead control		9,250

PROBLEM 2

a *Spending Variance:*

Actual factory overhead		$15,750
Less: Budgeted at actual variable (5,500 × $1.10)	$ 6,050	
Fixed	11,100	17,150
Favorable spending variance		($ 1,400)

Idle Capacity:

Budgeted at actual	$17,150
Less: Actual hours × standard rate (5,500 × $2.95)	16,225
Unfavorable idle capacity variance	$ 925

Efficiency Variance:

Actual hours × standard rate	$16,225.00
Standard hours × standard rate (5,650 × $2.95)	16,667.50
Favorable efficiency variance	($ 442.50)

b *Overall Factory-Overhead Variance:*

	Actual factory overhead	$15,750.00
Less:	Total applied (5,650 × $2.95)	16,667.50
	Overall variance—favorable	$ 917.50

or:	Spending variance	($ 1,400.00) F*
	+ Idle capacity variance	925.00 U*
	+ Efficiency variance	(442.50) F
		($ 917.50) F

* F = favorable, U = unfavorable.

c **(a)**

Materials quantity variance	1,200.00	
Labor rate variance	1,000.00	
Factory overhead idle capacity variance	925.00	
Materials rate variance		300.00
Labor efficiency variance		600.00
Factory overhead spending variance		1,400.00
Factory overhead efficiency variance		442.50
Income summary		382.50

(b) Goods sold: 6/10 × $382.50 = $229.50 ⎫
Ending finished goods: 3/10 ×   382.50 =   114.75 ⎬ computations
Ending work-in-process: 1/10 ×   382.50 =   38.25 ⎭

Materials quantity variance	1,200.00	
Labor rate variance	1,000.00	
Factory overhead idle capacity variance	925.00	
Materials rate variance		300.00
Labor efficiency variance		600.00
Factory overhead spending variance		1,400.00
Factory overhead efficiency variance		442.50
Cost of goods sold		229.50
Finished goods		114.75
Work-in-process		38.25

PROBLEM 3

a *Materials Mix Variance:*

	Actual materials mix
Less:	Standard formula
	Materials mix variance

2,500 × $.55	=	$1,375.00
4,800 × .75	=	3,600.00
2,750 × .60	=	1,650.00
1,450 × .15	=	217.50
		$6,842.50
Less: 11,500 × $.605	=	6,957.50
Favorable materials mix variance		($ 115.00)

Materials Yield Variance:

	Expected yield	
Less:	Actual yield	
	Yield Variance	

$$11,500 \times \$.605 \ = \$6,957.50$$
$$11,000 \times \ .6722 = \ 7,394.20$$

Favorable materials yield variance ($ 436.70)

b *Labor Yield Variance:*

Expected yield ($11,500 \times {}^9/_{10} \times .025$) $258.75

Less: Actual yield ($11,000 \times .025$) 275.00

Favorable labor yield variance . . . . ($ 16.25)

Factory Overhead Variance:

Expected yield ($11,500 \times {}^9/_{10} \times .0333$) $344.65

Less: Actual yield ($11,000 \times .0333$) 366.30

Favorable factory overhead yield variance . . . . ($ 21.65)

c

Work-in-process	6,957.50	
Materials mix variance		115.00
Materials		6,842.50
Finished goods	7,394.20	
Materials yield variance		436.70
Work-in-process		6,957.50
Finished goods	275.00	
Labor yield variance		16.25
Work-in-process		258.75
Finished goods	366.30	
Overhead yield variance		21.65
Work-in-process		344.65

PROBLEM 4

a Direct materials quantity variance [(8,500 − 9,000) × $6.00] . . . . . ($3,000) favorable

Direct labor efficiency variance [(8,700 − 8,000) × $4.00] . . . . 2,800 unfavorable

Overhead (two-variance method):

Controllable ($20,500 − $18,000) . . . . 2,500 unfavorable

Volume ($13,000 − $14,000) . . . . (1,000) favorable

Total variance . . . . $1,300 unfavorable

b *Normal spoilage and normal rework costs included in the standard:*

Factory overhead control		
(30 × $13* = $390 + $186.66)	576.66	
Abnormal spoilage (15 × $13)	195.00	
Abnormal defective unit loss	233.34	
Materials		180.00
Payroll		120.00
Factory overhead control		120.00
Work-in-process (45 × $13)		585.00

* $14 − $1 spoilage per unit

c *Normal spoilage and normal rework costs were not included in the standard:*

Work-in-process (normal rework costs)	186.66	
Abnormal spoilage	210.00	
Abnormal defective unit loss	233.34	
Work-in-process (abnormal spoilage) (15 × $14)		210.00
Materials		180.00
Payroll		120.00
Factory-overhead control		120.00

QUESTIONS

1 What effects may plant activity have on total overhead costs?
2 What are the two commonly used budgeting approaches? What is their main difference?
3 Why are flexible budgets used more often than static budgets?
4 Why is the accounting department usually given the responsibility for preparing factory overhead budgets?
5 What effect does plant activity have on both fixed factory overhead unit costs and variable factory overhead unit costs?
6 What are the four production capacity levels that may be used?
7 Why is the long-run or normal capacity the most appropriate level of production to use?
8 Why is the analysis of factory overhead variances more complex than direct materials and direct labor variances?
9 What are the two different cost assumptions that can be used in the disposal of factory overhead variances?
10 What is the determining factor as to whether normal spoilage costs should be removed from work-in-process?
11 What causes a mix variance? What additional variance may be caused by the mix variance?
12 When will standard costing produce the same financial statement results as actual or conventional costing?
13 Why is the three-variance method a better basis to judge performance than the two-variance method?
14 What relationship does the materials quantity variance have to mix and yield variances?
15 When should rework costs of normal defective units be charged to the factory overhead control account?

EXERCISES

EXERCISE 1

Multiple Choice

a A company uses a two-way analysis for overhead variances: controllable and volume. The volume variance is based on the

1 Total overhead application rate.
2 Volume of total expenses at various activity levels.
3 Variable overhead application rate.
4 Fixed overhead application rate.

b The budget variance for fixed factory overhead for the normal volume, practical capacity, and expected activity levels would be the
1 Same except for normal volume.
2 Same except for practical capacity.
3 Same except for expected activity.
4 Same for all three activity levels.

c What standard cost variance represents the difference between actual factory overhead incurred and budgeted factory overhead based on actual hours worked?
1 Volume variance
2 Spending variance
3 Efficiency variance
4 Quantity variance

The data below relate to the month of April 19X9 for Marilyn, Inc., which uses a standard cost system:

Actual hours used 14,000
Standard hours allowed for good output 15,000
Actual total overhead $32,000
Budgeted fixed costs .... $ 9,000
Normal activity in hours 12,000
Total overhead application rate per standard direct labor hour $2.25

Marilyn uses a two-way analysis of overhead variance: controllable and volume.

d What was Marilyn's controllable variance for April?
1 $500 favorable
2 $500 unfavorable
3 $2,250 favorable
4 $2,250 unfavorable

e What was Marilyn's volume variance for April?
1 $500 favorable
2 $500 unfavorable
3 $2,250 favorable
4 $2,250 unfavorable

f If a company uses a predetermined rate for absorbing manufacturing overhead, the volume variance is the
1 Underapplied or overapplied variable cost element of overhead.
2 Underapplied or overapplied fixed cost element of overhead.
3 Difference in budgeted costs and actual costs of fixed overhead items.
4 Difference in budgeted costs and actual costs of variable overhead items.

(All AICPA Adapted)

EXERCISE 2

Factory Overhead Variance: Three-Variance Method

The Lake Model Boat Company uses a standard cost system. Factory overhead is applied using a predetermined rate that is based on normal capacity. Below is information for March:

Standard hours allowed	26,000
Budgeted variable overhead	$33,000
Budgeted fixed overhead	$27,000
Actual direct labor hours	28,000
Actual factory overhead	$53,250
Normal capacity hours	30,000

REQUIRED:

Determine the factory overhead variances using the three-variance method.

EXERCISE 3

Factory Overhead Variance: One- and Four-Variance Methods

The XYZ Corporation produces one main product. The company employs a standard cost system. Below is October's flexible budget:

	NORMAL CAPACITY		
Direct labor hours:	800	900	1,000
Variable factory overhead:			
Indirect materials	$ 600	$ 675	$ 750
Indirect labor	400	450	500
Supplies	200	225	250
Total variable	$1,200	$1,350	$1,500
Fixed factory overhead			
Factory rent	$ 950	$ 950	$ 950
Depreciation on equipment	700	700	700
Supervisor	240	240	240
Total fixed	$1,890	$1,890	$1,890
Total factory overhead	$3,090	$3,240	$3,390

Factory overhead is applied based on normal capacity. The number of standard hours allowed for October's production is 850 hours. Actual factory overhead costs for October were $3,350. Actual direct labor hours for the month were 910 hours. Normal capacity is 900 direct labor hours.

REQUIRED:

a Determine the overhead variances for the month using the one-variance method.

b Determine the overhead variances for the month using the four-variance method.

EXERCISE 4

Factory Overhead Variances: Three-Variance Method; Journal Entries

The Smith Company uses a process cost system. Costs are applied to production based on standard costs. Information for September is shown below:

Actual factory overhead	$21,700
Standard labor hours	6,200
Actual labor hours	5,900
Normal capacity hours	6,500
Budgeted variable factory overhead	$ 5,525
Budgeted fixed factory overhead	$19,500
Cost of goods sold	$20,000
Ending finished goods	40,000
Ending work-in-process	10,000

The company treats the variances as product costs.

REQUIRED:

a Calculate the factory overhead variances using the three-variance method.

b Give the journal entries to close the variance accounts.

EXERCISE 5

Variance Analysis with Spoilage and Defective Units

A standard cost system is employed by the A. B. Curly Company. Standard costs to produce its products are as follows:

ELEMENTS	COST
Direct materials	$2.50
Direct labor—1 hour	3.50
Factory overhead (per direct labor hour):	
Variable	1.00
Fixed	.50
Standard unit cost	$7.50

During April, the following occurred:

Spoiled units:		Defective units:	
Normal	70	Normal	30
Abnormal	30	Abnormal	20

Cost to Rework Defective Units:

Direct materials	$ 50	Variable overhead	$50
Direct labor	$175	Fixed overhead	$25

Inspection occurs at the end of production

REQUIRED:

Write the journal entry to account for spoilage and rework cost for defective units assuming that normal spoilage and normal rework costs for defective units were not included in the computation of standard costs.

EXERCISE 6

Material Mix Variance

The Bittersweet Chocolate Company manufactures a chocolate syrup product. The engineer has determined the following materials mix formula to produce 40,000 gallons of the chocolate syrup:

	GALLONS
Raw material A	20,000
Raw material B	15,000
Raw material C	10,000
Raw material D	5,000
Total unit input	50,000

The standard costs for the raw materials are as follows:

Raw material A	$1.25 per gallon
Raw material B	1.05 per gallon
Raw material C	.80 per gallon
Raw material D	.50 per gallon

Actual raw materials placed into production were:

	GALLONS
Raw material A	23,000
Raw material B	14,000
Raw material C	13,000
Raw material D	5,000
Total	55,000

Raw material prices did not change during the period.

REQUIRED:

 a Calculate the standard input cost.
 b Calculate the standard output cost.
 c Calculate the mix variance.

EXERCISE 7

Mix and Yield Variances

The JKL Corporation manufactures a petroleum product. A standard cost system is employed by the company. Five raw materials are combined during production. The amount of each raw material used and its standard cost are shown below.

RAW MATERIALS	POUNDS	STANDARD COST	TOTAL STANDARD COST
10X	35,000	$.15	$ 5,250
10Y	45,000	.60	27,000
10Z	26,000	.35	9,100
20X	46,000	.55	25,300
20Y	48,000	.45	21,600
	200,000		$88,250

The standard output/input rate is 90%. Actual production during the period was

RAW MATERIALS	POUNDS
10X	138,000
10Y	185,000
10Z	103,500
20X	192,250
20Y	181,250
Total actual input	800,000

During the period, 700,000 pounds of the finished product were transferred to the finished goods storeroom.

REQUIRED:

a Calculate the mix variance.
b Calculate the yield variance.

EXERCISE 8

Overhead Variance: Two-Variance Method

Milner Manufacturing Company uses a job order costing system and standard costs. It manufactures one product whose standard cost is as follows:

Materials (20 yards at .90 per yard)	$18.00
Direct labor (4 hours at $6 per hour)	24.00
Total factory overhead (applied at $5/6$ of direct labor cost;	
the ratio of variable costs to fixed is 3 to 1)	20.00
Variable selling, general, and administrative expenses	12.00
Fixed selling, general, and administrative expenses	7.00
Total unit cost	$81.00

The standards are set based on "normal" activity of 2,400 direct labor hours. Actual activity for the month of October 19XX was as follows:

Direct labor	2,100 hours at $6.10 per hour	$12,810
Total factory overhead	500 units actually produced	$11,100

REQUIRED:

a   Compute the variable factory overhead rate per direct labor hour and the total fixed factory overhead based on "normal" activity.
b   Compute the following two variances:
   1   Controllable variance
   2   Volume variance

(AICPA Adapted)

EXERCISE 9

Factory Overhead Variance: Four-Variance Method

Ross Shirts, Inc., makes short- and long-sleeved men's shirts in lots to each customer's order and attaches the store's label to each. The standard costs for a dozen long-sleeved shirts are

Direct materials (24 yards at $.55)	$13.20
Direct labor (3 hours at $2.45)	7.35
Manufacturing overhead (3 hours at $2.00)	6.00
Standard cost per dozen	$26.55

During October 19X9, Ross worked on three orders for long-sleeved shirts. Job cost records for the month disclose the following:

LOT	UNITS IN LOT	MATERIALS USED	HOURS WORKED
30	12,000	24,100 yd	2,980
31	20,400	40,440 yd	5,130
32	14,400	28,825 yd	2,890

The following information is also available:
1   Overhead is applied on the basis of direct labor hours. Manufacturing overhead totaling $22,800 was incurred during October.
2   A total of $288,000 was budgeted for overhead for the year 19X9 based on estimated production at the plant's normal capacity of 48,000 dozen shirts per year. At this level of production, overhead is 40% fixed and 60% variable.
3   There was no work-in-process at October 1. During October, lots 30 and 31 were completed, and all materials were issued for lot 32, which was 80% complete regarding labor.

REQUIRED:

a Compute the standard cost for October for Lots 30, 31, and 32.

b Calculate the overhead variances using the four-variance method.

(AICPA Adapted)

PROBLEMS

PROBLEM 1

Factory Overhead Variances: Two- and Four-Variance Methods

The I. C. Clear Glass Company uses a standard cost system. Standard costs to produce one complete unit are shown below:

Materials (1 sheet of glass)		$ 5.00
Labor (1 hour)		3.75
Overhead:		
Fixed	$4.00	
Variable	2.00	6.00
Total standard cost		$14.75

Factory overhead was calculated using normal capacity of 9,700 direct labor hours. There was no beginning work-in-process. All the 9,650 units started in June were completed. Actual factory overhead amounted to $59,160. The payroll clerk reported that the June payroll amounted to $35,625. All factory workers received $3.75 per hour during June.

REQUIRED:

a Calculate the factory overhead variances using the four-variance method.

b What would the variances be if the two-variance method had been used?

PROBLEM 2

Factory Overhead Variances: Three-Variance Method; Journal Entries

The Straightline Ruler Company manufactures 12-inch wooden rulers. Both process and standard costing are used by the company. Units are placed into production in Department 1 and then are transferred to Department 2. Department 2 adds only conversion costs. Below is information pertaining to certain standards and July's activity for Department 2:

Standard cost per 100 rulers		
Labor (2 hours at $4.25)		$ 8.50
Factory overhead:		
Fixed	$10.00	
Variable	2.75	12.75
Standard unit cost, Department 2		$21.25

Normal capacity is 1,000 direct labor hours. Conversion costs are added evenly throughout the process.

Work-in-process—beginning	2,000 units (60% complete)
Units transferred in	55,000 units
Units transferred to finished goods	48,000 units
Ending work-in-process	9,000 units (30% complete)

Fifo costing is used for the beginning work-in-process. Actual hours worked during July = 850 hours. Actual factory overhead incurred during July = $6,000.25.

REQUIRED:

a Calculate the overhead variances under the three-variance method.

b Give the journal entries to record the factory overhead variances.

PROBLEM 3

Factory Overhead Variance with Spoilage and Rework Costs

The Paris Plaster Company manufactures decorative figurines. A standard cost system is used. The standard costs to produce one figure are as follows:

Direct materials (1.5 oz of plaster at $.26 per oz).............	$ .39
Direct labor (1 hour at $3.40)	3.40
Factory overhead:	
Variable (including provisions for normal spoilage and normal rework costs of $.05)....................................	.30
Fixed	.15
Total standard cost	$4.24

Factory overhead was calculated using normal capacity, which was 8,000 direct labor hours.

Actual results for February are as follows:

Total good units produced	7,600
Total materials used	11,000 oz
Total direct labor hours	7,700
Actual factory overhead	$3,630
Spoilage:	
Normal	$100
Abnormal	50
Defective units:	
Normal	75
Abnormal	25
Rework costs (total):	
Direct materials	$ 23
Direct labor	170
Factory overhead:	
Variable........................	20
Fixed	10
Total rework costs	$223

Inspection occurs at the end of production.

REQUIRED:

a Calculate the following variances:
1 Direct materials quantity variance
2 Direct labor efficiency variance
3 Controllable variance
4 Volume variance
b Assuming normal spoilage and normal rework costs for defective units were considered when standard costs were completed, write the journal entry to record spoilage and rework costs.

PROBLEM 4

Overhead Variance Analysis under a Process Cost System

The Sparky Battery Company uses a process cost system. Standard costs are used to apply product costs to the work-in-process accounts. The assembly department is the second processing department in the company's operations. No materials are added and conversion costs are added evenly throughout the process.

Standard costs for a completed unit in the assembly department are as follows:

Labor (1 hour)............................	$2.90
Factory overhead:	
Variable................................	1.25
Fixed	.85
Total standard costs per unit	$5.00

Normal capacity is 10,000 hours.
Information pertaining to August is shown below.

Beginning units in process	=	1,500 (20% complete)
Units transferred in	=	8,800
Units transferred out	=	8,650
Ending units in process	=	1,650 (10% complete)
Actual labor hours	=	8,500
Actual factory overhead	=	$16,980

Fifo costing is used.

REQUIRED:

a Compute the overhead variances under the three-variance method.
b Prepare the necessary journal entries to record the actual factory overhead, to record the factory overhead applied, and to record the factory overhead variances.

PROBLEM 5

Mix and Yield Variances, Labor and Overhead Variances, and Journal Entries

The Hackers Cough Syrup Company manufactures its product by combining three raw materials. In order that competitors do not discover their secret formula, raw materials are given numbers in place of the ingredient's name. Below is the mix formula for their cough syrup.

RAW MATERIALS	NUMBER OF GALLONS
111	6,000
122	7,000
133	9,000
Standard input	22,000
Standard output	20,000

Additional Standard Information:

Standard material costs:

RAW MATERIALS	COST PER GALLON
111	$2.00
122	1.50
133	1.90

Standard hours allowed per 20,000 completed units	900
Standard labor rates per hour	$4.25
Budgeted factory overhead per month:	
Variable...	$16,000
Fixed	$56,000
Normal capacity (direct labor hours)	25,000

Factory overhead is applied based on direct labor hours.

Actual results for January:

RAW MATERIALS INPUT	GALLONS
111	144,200
122	159,000
133	196,800
Total actual input	500,000

Actual purchases were equal to input of raw materials.

ACTUAL RAW MATERIALS COST	PER GALLON
111	$2.00
122	1.60
133	1.90

Actual direct labor hours 21,000
Direct labor rate (actual) $4.35
Actual factory overhead $60,300
Actual units produced .... 460,000 gallons

REQUIRED:

a Compute the following variances:
1 Direct materials price variance
2 Direct materials mix variance
3 Direct materials yield variance
4 Direct labor rate variance
5 Direct labor efficiency variance
6 Direct labor yield variance
7 Factory overhead spending variance
8 Factory overhead idle capacity variance
9 Factory overhead efficiency variance
10 Factory overhead yield variance

b Prepare the necessary journal entries to record production for Hackers Cough Syrup Company (assume materials inventory is kept at standard costs). Round your answers to the nearest dollar.

PROBLEM 6

Factory Overhead Variances: Four-Variance Method and Disposal of Variances

The Sticky Lollipop Corp. manufactures "all-day suckers." A standard cost system is used by the company. Below is listed selected standard cost information:

Direct materials .... $.36
Direct labor .... $.19
Budgeted overhead:
    Variable $2,400
    Fixed $1,350
Normal capacity (direct labor hours) 15,000

During January, the following activities occurred:

Direct materials price variance   0
Direct materials quantity variance ....   ($115) favorable
Direct labor rate variance .... $ 85 unfavorable
Direct labor efficiency variance .... $130 unfavorable
Actual factory overhead $3,520
Actual direct labor hours   12,750
Standard number of hours allowed   13,000

An examination of the company's general ledger on January 31 revealed the following:

Cost of goods sold $477,000
Work-in-process.................. $ 33,000
Finished goods $400,000

REQUIRED:

a   Compute the factory overhead variances under the four-variance method.
b   Assuming variances are treated as product costs, prepare the journal entries to record the disposal of all variances.

PROBLEM 7

Mix Variances and Factory Overhead Variances

Conti Pharmaceutical Company processes a single compound product known as Nulax and uses a standard cost accounting system. The process requires preparation and blending of three materials in large batches, with a variation from the standard mixture sometimes necessary to maintain quality. Conti's cost accountant became ill at the end of October 19XX, and you were engaged to determine standard costs of October production and explain any differences between actual and standard costs for the month. The following information is available for the blending department:

1   The standard cost card for a 500-pound batch shows the following standard costs:

MATERIALS	QUANTITY	PRICE	TOTAL COST
Mucilloid	250 lb	$.14	$35
Dextrose	200 lb	.09	18
Other ingredients	50 lb	.08	4
Total per batch	500		$57
Labor:			
Preparation and blending	10 hr	$3.00	30
Overhead:			
Variable	10 hr	1.00	10
Fixed	10 hr	.30	3
Total standard cost per 500-lb batch			$100

2 During October, 410 batches of 500 pounds each of the finished product were completed and transferred to the packaging department.

3 Blending department inventories totaled 6,000 pounds at the beginning of the month and 9,000 pounds at the end of the month (assume both inventories were completely processed but not transferred and that both consisted of materials in their standard proportions). Inventories are carried in the accounts at standard prices.

4 During the month of October, the following materials were purchased and put into production:

	POUNDS	PRICE	TOTAL COST
Mucilloid	114,400	$.17	$19,448
Dextrose	85,800	.11	9,438
Other ingredients	19,800	.07	1,386
Totals	220,000		$30,272

5 Wages paid for 4,212 hours of direct labor at $3.25 per hour amounted to $13,689.

6 Actual overhead costs for the month totaled $5,519.

7 The standards were established for a normal production volume of 200,000 lb (400 batches) of Nulax per month. At this level of production, variable factory overhead was budgeted at $4,000 and fixed factory overhead was budgeted at $1,200.

REQUIRED:

a Present computations showing:
   1 October production in both pounds and batches
   2 The standard cost of October production itemized by components of materials, labor, and overhead

b Compute the overhead variances under the two-variance method.

c Compute the materials mix variance.

(AICPA Adapted)

PROBLEM 8

Material and Labor Variances

On May 1, 19XX, Bovar Company began the manufacture of a new mechanical device known as "Dandy." The company installed a standard cost system in accounting for manufacturing costs. The standard costs for a unit of "Dandy" are as follows:

Raw materials	6 lb at $1 per lb	$ 6.00
Direct labor	1 hour at $4 per hour	4.00
Overhead	75% of direct labor costs	3.00
		$13.00

The following data were obtained from Bovar's records for the month of May:

	UNITS
Actual production of "Dandy"	4,000
Units sold of "Dandy"	2,500

	DEBIT	CREDIT
Sales		$50,000
Purchases (26,000 lb)	$27,300	
Materials price variance	1,300	
Materials quantity variance	1,000	
Direct labor rate variance	760	
Direct labor efficiency variance		800
Manufacturing overhead total variance	500	

The amount shown above for materials price variance is applicable to raw materials purchased during May.

REQUIRED:

Compute each of the following items for Bovar for the month of May:
- a Standard quantity of raw materials allowed (in pounds)
- b Actual quantity of raw materials used (in pounds)
- c Standard hours allowed
- d Actual hours worked
- e Actual direct labor rate
- f Actual total overhead

(AICPA Adapted)

PROBLEM 9

Four-Variance Overhead Method

The Terry Company manufactures a commercial solvent that is used for industrial maintenance. This solvent is sold by the drum and generally has a stable selling price. Owing to a decrease in demand for this product, Terry produced and sold 60,000 drums in December 19XX, which is 50% of normal capacity.

The following information is available regarding Terry's operations for the month of December:

1 Standard costs per drum of products manufactured were as follows:

Materials	$21
Direct labor (1 hour)	$ 7
Factory overhead (fixed) per direct labor hour	$ 4
Factory overhead (variable) per direct labor hour.............	$ 6

2 Costs incurred during December were as follows:

Direct labor:
65,000 hours were worked at a cost of $470,000

Factory overhead:
Depreciation of building and machinery (fixed).............. $230,000
Supervision and indirect labor (semivariable) 360,000
Other factory overhead (variable) 76,500
Total factory overhead $666,500

3 The fixed overhead budget for the December level of production was $275,000.

4 In November 19XX, at normal capacity of 120,000 drums, supervision and indirect labor costs were $680,000. All cost functions are linear.

REQUIRED:

Compute the factory overhead variance using the four-variance method.

(AICPA Adapted)

PART THREE
BUDGETING

CHAPTER THIRTEEN

BUDGETING I— MASTER BUDGET

In the preceding chapters we have discussed various phases of costing, planning, control, and decision making, such as job order costing, process costing, and standard costing. We have examined the standard cost planning and control aspects and the nature of and responsibility for variances from the allowed standards. Another aspect of planning and control, in which the management decision is to make the best choice among competing projects or actions, is called *project planning*. Where the management decision concerns what is to be accomplished during a specific period of time, this is called *periodic planning*. If the periodic planning concerns sales, production, and inventory levels, we have *operations* planning or budgeting. If the budget encompasses all functions and management levels of the enterprise, we have a comprehensive or *master budget*.

NATURE OF THE BUDGET

The budget is a quantitative expression of management objectives and a means of monitoring progress toward those objectives. To be effective, the budget must be well coordinated with related management and accounting systems. For example, there must be a sound organization chart and chart of accounts. The organization chart shows the responsibilities of each executive for whom a budget is justified. Another important requirement for a good budget is a standard cost system which will accumulate costs and provide data for reports according to responsibility. Executives are responsible for the preparation and management of their own budget segments. To be effective, company officials must participate in planning the budget and must understand their responsibility in making the budget work.

Budgets can cover different periods of time, depending on the type of budget. For example, operations budgets normally cover a period of one year or less (short term). Budgets for plant or product changes can cover a period of 2 to 10 years (long term). The operations budget is frequently broken down by months for the first quarter and in total for the next three quarters. At the end of the first quarter the budgets for the following three quarters are updated, based on the new information. Many companies now use continuous or moving budgets by which 12-month data is always at hand. At the end of each month, that month is dropped and a new month is added at the end so that a 12-month budget will always be available.

RESPONSIBILITY FOR BUDGETING

Generally the budget director is responsible for coordinating all the parts of the budget. The various components, such as sales by product and territory and production by product and month, are prepared by line management. In most large companies the budget director will report directly to the budget committee, which usually consists of the president, the vice-presidents in charge of marketing, production and engineering, the treasurer, and the controller.

The procedural aspects of budgeting, such as what is to be budgeted, when, and by whom, are the responsibility of the budget director, subject to approval by the budget committee. A budget manual should be prepared giving the due date for each segment of the master budget, assigning responsibility for its preparation, and describing the forms and related budgeting policies and procedures.

MASTER BUDGET

The step-by-step preparation of the various segments of the master budget forces careful management consideration and many key decisions concerning pricing, product lines, production scheduling, capital expenditures, research and development, and many others. The initial draft of a budget and its critical budget review always prompt many questions and management decisions leading to further drafts before the final budget is approved.

Table 13-1 (page 470) gives the principal components of a master budget. In actual practice there would be many additional analyses supporting the budgets shown.

DEVELOPING THE MASTER BUDGET

The basic steps in developing the master budget begin with the sales forecast. The process ends with the completion of the budgeted income statement, cash budget, and budgeted balance sheet. The presentation in the final

TABLE 13-1
MASTER BUDGET

	SCHEDULE	EXHIBIT
Operating budgets:		
Sales......................................	1a	
Production	1b	
Direct materials purchases	1c	
Direct materials usage	1d	
Direct labor	1e	
Factory overhead	1f	
Cost of goods sold.......................	1g	
Selling expenses..........................	1h	
Administrative expenses...................	1i	
Budgeted income statement		1
Cash budgets:		
Cash receipts forecast	2a	
Cash disbursements forecast	2b	
Cash budget.............................		2
Balance sheet budgets:		
Ending inventory budget	3	
Budgeted balance sheet...................		3

statements is similar to that in the regular financial statements except that we are dealing with the future rather than the past.

Essentially there are two extremes in developing the master budget: (1) the top management approach and (2) the "grass roots" approach. In the top management approach the chief officers, such as the top executives for sales, production, finance, and administration, forecast sales based on their experience and knowledge of the company and industry. In the grass roots approach the forecasting begins at the bottom with forecasts made by individual salespeople. In most companies the approach is somewhere between the two extremes, probably closer to the grass roots approach, with management utilizing the benefits of both general approaches. The principal advantage of the top management approach is that it is quick and has the support of top management. An important disadvantage is that middle management, lower management, and other key employees do not participate in budgeting decisions and are not likely to give the cooperation and energy needed to make the budget a success. The principal advantage of the grass roots approach is that all levels in the company participate to some extent in developing the budget estimate and are more likely to feel a responsibility to live within the limits established.

Sales Budget

The foundation upon which the sales budget and all other parts of the master budget rest is the sales forecast. If this forecast has been carefully and accurately prepared, the succeeding steps in the budget process will be reliable. For example, the sales forecast provides the data for developing production budgets, purchasing budgets, and selling and administrative expense budgets. If the sales forecast is wrong, the related budgets will be unreliable.

In many companies the forecast of sales begins with the preparation of sales estimates by individual salespeople. These estimates are then forwarded to the appropriate district managers. At this point forecasting procedures vary a great deal. Generally district managers review the estimates and make adjustments based on additional information or their own experience. The estimates are then consolidated and forwarded to the general marketing manager for review and approval. Just prior to the beginning of this process certain basic external and internal data have been developed by the general marketing manager's department or by a separate specialized market research department in a large company. This information will be made available, in some companies, to the district manager and even to the salespeople as an aid in developing the forecast. In other companies the information is made available only to the general sales manager. Generally considered in the data are the following: general economic conditions, industry sales and profits, general inventory conditions, and competitive conditions. Internal information may also be provided in convenient form, such as past company sales and profits by product, salesperson, territory, and channels of distribution. Generally a product will have a seasonal trend pattern that is different from that of any other product. This trend must be kept in mind when the annual forecast is established and the expected sales by months are set. Entire volumes have been devoted to forecasting and budgeting, and we will not attempt to duplicate such detail in a cost accounting text. To keep the illustration simple, we will assume that the Chadwick Company manufactures and sells only one product and uses only one channel of distribution. If there were more products, a separate forecast would be made for each product. If more than one channel of distribution were used, each product forecast would show a breakdown by channels of distribution, for example, wholesalers, jobbers, and retailers. An analysis of sales by channel of distribution will show the amount each type is contributing toward sales and net profits. If the percentage of net profit on sales to wholesalers or jobbers is very low, for example, it may prompt the company to change its channel of distribution. Therefore, instead of selling to wholesalers or jobbers, the company may establish its own outlets and retail its products.

We will assume that the Chadwick Company has completed the forecasting process and budgeted the following amounts for the first quarter, at an average selling price of $33.

Schedule 1a

Information Required

1 Sales budget, units (SB,u)
2 Sales price, unit (SP,u)

Formula:

$$\text{Sales budget (SB)} = \text{SB,u} \times \text{SP,u}$$

SALES BUDGET
FIRST QUARTER 19XX

	TERRITORY	JANUARY	FEBRUARY	MARCH	QUARTER
Units	1	1,000	1,125	1,210	3,335
	2	600	650	675	1,925
	3	925	900	960	2,785
	4	430	450	475	1,355
	Total	2,955	3,125	3,320	9,400
Value	1	$33,000	$ 37,125	$ 39,930	$110,055
	2	19,800	21,450	22,275	63,525
	3	30,525	29,700	31,680	91,905
	4	14,190	14,850	15,675	44,715
	Total	$97,515	$103,125	$109,560	$310,200

PRODUCTION BUDGET

The quantities for the production budget must be closely tied in with the sales budget and the desired inventory levels. Essentially the production budget is the sales budget adjusted for the inventory changes. Before much work is done on the production budget, it must be determined that the factory can produce the quantities estimated in the sales budget. Production should be scheduled at an efficient level so that there are no wide fluctuations in employment. To stabilize employment it is necessary also to maintain inventories at an efficient level. If inventories are too low, production may be interrupted; if too high, the carrying cost will be excessive.

The Chadwick Company desires that the following units of finished goods be on hand at the specified dates next year: January 1, 2,140; January 31, 2,050; February 28, 2,175; March 31, 2,215. Raw materials inventories are to be set at 60% of the following month's requirements.

With the information provided by the sales budget and the inventory estimates, the production budget can be developed. For easier understanding of the budget illustrations we are using only the first 3 months of the year and only one production department. Any additional months or departments would be largely repetitious.

Schedule 1b

Information Required

1   Sales budget, units (SB ,u)

2 Ending inventory, units (EI,u)
3 Beginning inventory, units (BI,u)

Formula:

$$\text{Production budget, units (PB,u)} = \text{SB,u} + \text{EI,u} - \text{BI,u}$$

PRODUCTION BUDGET
FINISHED GOODS
FIRST QUARTER 19XX

UNITS	JANUARY	FEBRUARY	MARCH	QUARTER
Sales budget	2,955	3,125	3,320	9,400
Add—desired ending inventory	2,050	2,175	2,215	2,215
Subtotal	5,005	5,300	5,535	11,615
Deduct—beginning inventory ..	2,140	2,050	2,175	2,140
Production units required	2,865	3,250	3,360	9,475

DIRECT MATERIALS PURCHASES BUDGET

As was stated above, the Chadwick Company is to maintain an inventory of direct materials equal to 60% of the following month's requirements. This is one of the first cost budgets to be prepared, as the purchasing quantities and delivery schedules must be quickly established in order that materials be available when required. Usually there is a specification sheet or formula for each product showing the type and quantity of each direct material for the unit of production.

Based on this list, the purchasing department prepares purchasing and delivery schedules, which must be closely coordinated with the production budget and with the delivery schedules of the supplier. The budget for supplies and indirect materials is usually included in the factory overhead budget. The standard cost sheet for the Chadwick Company shows that for each unit of finished product, one unit of direct materials is required. The contract price for raw materials is $8.50 per unit until March 1, when it will go to $9 per unit.

For the first quarter, the required units to be purchased and the related costs are shown by month and quarter below.

Schedule 1c

Information Required

1 Production budget, units (PB,u)
2 Ending inventory, units (EI,u)
3 Beginning inventory, units (BI,u)
4 Purchase price, unit (PP,u)

Formula:

$$\text{Direct materials purchases cost (DMP,c)} = (\text{PB,u} + \text{EI,u} - \text{BI,u}) \times \text{PP,u}$$

DIRECT MATERIAL PURCHASES BUDGET
FIRST QUARTER 19XX

	JANUARY	FEBRUARY	MARCH	QUARTER
Production required:				
Units	2,865	3,250	3,360	9,475
Add—desired ending				
inventory (1)	1,950	2,016	2,100	2,100
Subtotal	4,815	5,266	5,460	11,575
Deduct—beginning				
inventory (2)	1,719	1,950	2,016	1,719
Purchases required	3,096	3,316	3,444	9,856
Price per unit	$8.50	$8.50	$9.00	$8.67 (4)
Purchases cost (3)	$26,316	$28,186	$30,996	$85,498

(1) The desired ending inventory is 60% of the following month's requirements. For April the budgeted production units are 3,500; therefore, 2,100 units (3,500 × 60%) of material should be in the March ending inventory.

(2) The beginning inventory for January of 1,719 is 60% of that month's production budget (2,865 × 60%), the same as the ending inventory of the previous month.

(3) Rounded to the nearest dollar.

(4) $85,498 ÷ 9,856.

DIRECT MATERIALS USAGE BUDGET

At about the same time the purchases budget is prepared and the needed materials ordered, it is necessary for budget purposes to prepare the direct materials usage budget. The Chadwick Company's standard cost sheet shows that one unit of direct materials is required for each unit of finished product. The unit cost is the same as that used for purchases, that is, $8.50 for January and February and $9 for March. The usage is budgeted as follows:

Schedule 1d

Information Required

1 Direct materials production budget, units (DMP,u)
2 Purchase price, units (PP,u)

Formula:

$$\text{Direct materials usage budget (DMUB)} = \text{DMP,u} \times \text{PP,u}$$

DIRECT MATERIALS USAGE BUDGET
FIRST QUARTER 19XX

	JANUARY	FEBRUARY	MARCH	QUARTER
Direct materials units required	2,865	3,250	3,360	9,475
Materials unit cost	$8.50	$8.50	$9.00	$8.68 (1)
Direct materials usage cost	$24,353	$27,625	$30,240	$82,218

(1) $82,218 ÷ 9,475.

DIRECT LABOR BUDGET

The direct labor requirements are usually developed by engineers based on time studies. The direct labor budget must be coordinated with the production budget, the purchasing budget, and other parts of the general budget plan. Indirect labor will be included in the factory overhead budget. The budgets for both direct and indirect labor will have to be translated by the personnel department into the types and numbers of employees needed, and when needed. If the production schedule calls for more workers than are now employed, the personnel department may have to provide a training program for new workers. If the budget plan for the next year requires fewer workers than presently employed, the personnel department will prepare a list of workers to be laid off after considering each worker's skill and seniority rights, in accordance with company policy or union contract.

The standard cost data for Chadwick Company shows that 2 *hours* of direct labor are required to complete one unit of finished product. The standard rate per hour is $3 as of January 1, but is expected to rise to $3.50 as of February 1. The following is the budget reflecting the direct labor hours and cost required:

Schedule 1e

Information Required

 1 Production budget, units (PB,u)
 2 Direct labor hours budget, units (DLHB,u)
 3 Rate per hour (RH)

Formula:

$$\text{Direct labor budget (DLB)} = \text{DLHB,u} \times \text{RH}$$

DIRECT LABOR BUDGET
FIRST QUARTER 19XX

	JANUARY	FEBRUARY	MARCH	QUARTER
Production units required	2,865	3,250	3,360	9,475
Direct labor hours (2 per unit)	5,730	6,500	6,720	18,950
Rate per hour	$3.00	$3.50	$3.50	$3.35 (2)
Direct labor cost (1)	$17,190	$22,750	$23,520	$63,460

(1) Rounded to the nearest dollar.
(2) $63,460 ÷ 18,950.

FACTORY OVERHEAD BUDGET

Department heads should be held accountable for expenses incurred by their department. Any expenses allocated to the department should be shown separately from those for which the department head is directly responsible. Generally the department head will prepare budgets of the department for the budget period. After review by the budget department, the department head will be asked to review and comment on any revision before it is made final. For better control the fixed and variable expenses are separated as follows: fixed expenses have dollar values assigned, and variable expenses have rates assigned, based on direct labor hours. The budgets for the first 3 months of the year are shown below.

Schedule 1f

Information Required

1 Direct labor hours budget, units (DLHB,u)
2 Fixed expenses, each (FE,e)
3 Variable expenses, each (VE,e)

Formula:

$$\text{Factory overhead budget (FOB)} = \text{FE,e} + (\text{DLHB,u} \times \text{VE,e})$$

FACTORY OVERHEAD BUDGET
JANUARY 19XX
DIRECT LABOR HOURS 5,730

TYPE OF EXPENSE	FIXED	VARIABLE	TOTAL
Indirect materials.....................	$ 1,200		$ 1,200
Indirect labor (variable—$.50)	1,500	$2,865	4,365
Supervision	1,250		1,250
Payroll taxes (variable—$.30)..........		1,719	1,719
Maintenance (variable—$.20)..........	500	1,146	1,646
Heat and light (variable—$.10)	600	573	1,173
Power (variable—$.12)	450	687	1,137
Insurance	650		650
Taxes................................	1,000		1,000
Depreciation	3,000		3,000
Miscellaneous (variable—$.15)		860	860
Total factory overhead	$10,150	$7,850	$18,000

FACTORY OVERHEAD BUDGET
FEBRUARY 19XX
DIRECT LABOR HOURS 6,500

TYPE OF EXPENSE	FIXED	VARIABLE	TOTAL
Indirect materials.....................	$ 1,200		$ 1,200
Indirect labor (variable—$.50)	1,500	$3,250	4,750
Supervision	1,250		1,250
Payroll taxes (variable—$.30)..........		1,950	1,950
Maintenance (variable—$.20)..........	500	1,300	1,800
Heat and light (variable—$.10)	600	650	1,250
Power (variable—$.12)	450	780	1,230
Insurance	650		650
Taxes................................	1,000		1,000
Depreciation	3,000		3,000
Miscellaneous (variable—$.15)		975	975
Total factory overhead	$10,150	$8,905	$19,055

FACTORY OVERHEAD BUDGET
MARCH 19XX
DIRECT LABOR HOURS 6,720

TYPE OF EXPENSE	FIXED	VARIABLE	TOTAL
Indirect materials......................	$ 1,200		$ 1,200
Indirect labor (variable—$.50)	1,500	$3,360	4,860
Supervision	1,250		1,250
Payroll taxes (variables—$.30).........		2,016	2,016
Maintenance (variable—$.20)..........	500	1,344	1,844
Heat and light (variable—$.10)	600	672	1,272
Power (variable—$.12)	450	806	1,256
Insurance	650		650
Taxes................................	1,000		1,000
Depreciation	3,000		3,000
Miscellaneous (variable—$.15)		1,008	1,008
Total factory overhead	$10,150	$9,206	$19,356

COST OF GOODS SOLD BUDGET

The component parts for the cost of goods sold budget can be taken from the individual budgets previously described and adjusted for changes in inventory. Inventory budgets will be presented later in this chapter.

Schedule 1g

Information Required

1 Direct materials usage budget (DMUB)
2 Direct labor budget (DLB)
3 Factory overhead budget (FOB)
4 Beginning inventory (BI)
5 Ending inventory (EI)

Formula:

Cost of goods sold budget (CGSB) = DMUB + DLB + FOB + BI − EI

COST OF GOODS SOLD BUDGET
FIRST QUARTER 19XX

SUPPORTING BUDGETS	SCHED-ULE	JANUARY	FEBRUARY	MARCH	QUARTER
Direct materials	1d	$ 24,353	$ 27,625	$ 30,240	$ 82,218
Direct labor	1e	17,190	22,750	23,520	63,460
Factory overhead	1f	18,000	19,055	19,356	56,411
Total manufacturing cost		$ 59,543	$ 69,430	$ 73,116	$202,089
Add—finished goods, beginning	3	43,035	42,599	46,458	43,035
Goods available		$102,578	$112,029	$119,574	$245,124
Subtract—finished goods, ending	3	42,599	46,458	48,198	48,198
Cost of goods sold		$ 59,979	$ 65,571	$ 71,376	$196,926

SELLING EXPENSES BUDGET

The selling expenses are made up of a number of items, some of which are fixed and some variable. The principal fixed expenses are salaries and depreciation; the principal variable expenses are commissions, travel, advertising, and bad debts. The variable expenses are based on sales dollars and thus vary directly with sales. Shown below are the selling expenses budgets for January, February, and March of the first quarter of the year 19XX.

Schedule 1h

Information Required

1. Sales dollars (SD)
2. Fixed expenses, each (FE,e)
3. Variable expenses, each (VE,e)

Formula:

$$\text{Selling expenses budget (SEB)} = \text{FE,e} + (\text{SD} \times \text{VE,e})$$

SELLING EXPENSES BUDGET
JANUARY 19XX
SALES DOLLARS $97,515

TYPE OF EXPENSE	FIXED	VARIABLE	TOTAL
Salaries	$3,000		$ 3,000
Commissions (3%)		$2,925	2,925
Travel (2%)		1,950	1,950
Advertising (1%)		975	975
Depreciation	1,000		1,000
Bad debts (.5%)		488	488
Miscellaneous	800		800
Total selling expenses	$4,800	$6,338	$11,138

SELLING EXPENSES BUDGET
FEBRUARY 19XX
SALES DOLLARS $103,125

TYPE OF EXPENSE	FIXED	VARIABLE	TOTAL
Salaries	$3,000		$ 3,000
Commissions (3%)		$3,094	3,094
Travel (2%)		2,062	2,062
Advertising (1%)		1,031	1,031
Depreciation	1,000		1,000
Bad debts (.5%)		516	516
Miscellaneous	800		800
Total selling expenses	$4,800	$6,703	$11,503

SELLING EXPENSES BUDGET
MARCH 19XX
SALES DOLLARS $109,560

TYPE OF EXPENSE	FIXED	VARIABLE	TOTAL
Salaries	$3,000		$ 3,000
Commissions (3%)		$3,287	3,287
Travel (2%)		2,191	2,191
Advertising (1%)		1,095	1,095
Depreciation........................	1,000		1,000
Bad debts (.5%).....................		548	548
Miscellaneous	800		800
Total selling expenses	$4,800	$7,121	$11,921

ADMINISTRATIVE EXPENSES BUDGET

The expenses in this category should be classified so that those individuals responsible for incurrence and control of particular expenses can be held accountable. In some instances a portion of some of these expenses may be allocated to such operations as purchasing and research, but for our purposes we will consider all items as fixed expenses. Since they are considered fixed expenses, it will be necessary to have only one budget for each of the 3 months in the first quarter of 19XX.

Schedule 1i

Information Required

   1   Fixed expenses, each (FE,e)

Formula:

$$\text{Administrative expenses budget (AEB)} = \text{sum of FE,e}$$

ADMINISTRATIVE EXPENSES BUDGET PER MONTH
FIRST QUARTER 19XX

TYPE OF EXPENSE	TOTAL
Executive salaries...	$2,800
Office salaries	500
Insurance	400
Taxes	200
Depreciation...	800
Miscellaneous	500
Total administrative expenses per month	$5,200

BUDGETED INCOME STATEMENT

The final result of all the operations budgets such as those for sales, cost of goods sold, selling expenses, and administrative expenses is summarized in the budgeted income statement. Here the net result of the operations for the budget period is presented. As can be seen in the following statement, the sales showed an upward trend beginning with $97,515 for January and $103,125 for February, and increasing to $109,560 for March. However, the net income does not show a proportionate increase. As the company moves into the budget period, the budget director will investigate the continuing rise in cost of goods sold and will endeavor to reduce costs. Possibly a material of lesser cost can be substituted, if quality can be maintained.

Exhibit 1

BUDGETED INCOME STATEMENT
FIRST QUARTER 19XX

SUPPORTING BUDGETS	SCHED-ULE	JANUARY	FEBRUARY	MARCH	QUARTER
Sales........................	1a	$97,515	$103,125	$109,560	$310,200
Cost of goods sold............	1g	59,979	65,571	71,376	196,926
Gross profit		$37,536	$ 37,554	$ 38,184	$113,274
Operating expenses:					
Selling expenses............	1h	$11,138	$ 11,503	$ 11,921	$ 34,562
Administrative expenses.....	1i	5,200	5,200	5,200	15,600
Total operating expenses..		$16,338	$ 16,703	$ 17,121	$ 50,162
Net income before taxes		$21,198	$ 20,851	$ 21,063	$ 63,112
Income taxes (assumed).......		7,183	5,706	6,453	19,342
Net income		$14,015	$ 15,145	$ 14,610	$ 43,770

CASH BUDGET

The cash budget is now recognized as an essential management tool, and careful cash planning is considered a routine factor in efficient management. Good cash budgets help significantly in stabilizing cash balances and keeping these balances reasonably close to continuing cash requirements. Cash budgets generally help in avoiding dangerous changes in cash position that may jeopardize the company's credit standing or possibly violate the provisions of a securities indenture. Careful cash planning must be made especially for large cash outlays such as payments on bank loans, retirement of securities, acquisitions of other companies, capital expenditures, pension contributions, and income tax installments.

In most enterprises, cash receipts are primarily from collections of accounts receivable and cash sales. The estimated amount of cash collections from accounts receivable is based on the cash collection experience of the company. A study of collections for a few months will indicate the general pattern of collections. For example, the study may show that 10% of the current month's credit sales are collected this month, 80% of last month's credit sales are collected this month, and 8% of the credit sales of 2 months ago are collected this month, and that 2% will be bad debts.

As an illustration, we will apply the above percentages to the appropriate sales to arrive at the estimated collections for the first 3 months of the year 19XX. To do this we will need the total sales for December 19XX, and for each month in 19XX. These sales are as follows: December, $95,040; January, $97,515; February, $103,125; March, $109,560. The cash sales included in the total sales were: December, $4,200; January, $5,400; February, $6,200; March, $7,500. There were no other cash receipts during this period. Following is Schedule 2a, the cash receipts forecast, showing the total estimated cash collections for each month in the quarter.

Schedule 2a

CASH RECEIPTS FORECAST
FIRST QUARTER 19XX

	JANUARY	FEBRUARY	MARCH
Collections:			
December sales, $95,040 − $4,200 = $90,840			
80%	$72,672		
8%		$ 7,267	
January sales, $97,515 − $5,400 = $92,115			
10%	9,212		
80%		73,692	
8%			$ 7,369
February sales, $103,125 − $6,200 = $96,925			
10%		9,693	
80%			77,540
March sales, $109,560 − $7,500 = $102,060			
10%			10,206
Total estimated collections	$81,884	$90,652	$95,115
Cash sales	$ 5,400	$ 6,200	$ 7,500

Cash disbursements are based on the individual budgets previously prepared, with the needed adjustments to change from the accrual to the cash basis. For example, materials purchased are not entirely paid for in the same month; payments are 60% in the month of purchase and 40% the next month. Some part of a payroll for the month is generally accrued at the end of the month and is not an outlay for the current month; however, the accrued portion for the previous month is an outlay this month. For simplicity, we will not have payroll accruals. Of course, noncash items such as provisions for depreciation and bad debts do not require cash outlays. These amounts have to be deducted from the schedule totals for cash budget purposes.

Following is Schedule 2b, cash disbursements forecast for direct materials for the first quarter of 19XX.

Schedule 2b

CASH DISBURSEMENTS FORECAST—DIRECT MATERIALS
FIRST QUARTER 19XX

ACCOUNTS PAYABLE	JANUARY	FEBRUARY	MARCH
Balance 1/1/19XX (assumed)	$10,300		
January purchases, $26,316			
60%	15,790		
40%		$10,526	
February purchases, $28,186			
60%		16,912	
40%			$11,274
March purchases, $30,996			
60%			18,598
Total cash disbursements	$26,090	$27,438	$29,872

In preparing the cash budget, the beginning cash balance is added to the estimated cash receipts to show the expected amount of cash available for each month. From this amount the expected cash disbursements are deducted to determine the excess or (deficiency) of cash at the end of the period. If there is an excess, consideration must be given to possible short-term investment. If there is a deficit, the amount must be borrowed from the bank on some prearranged basis. Interest as well as principal must be included in the repayments. Generally, the repayments are made at the end of a period.

To prepare the cash budget, the following information is needed:

Information Required

1 Cash balance, beginning (CB,b)
2 Cash receipts for period (CR)
3 Cash disbursements for period (CD)

Formula:

$$\text{Cash balance, ending (CB,e)} = \text{CB,b} + \text{CR} - \text{CD}$$

In preparing the cash budget, we find that the beginning cash balance is $20,137. Adjustments have been made for direct materials, converting purchases to the cash basis. Depreciation, bad debts, and other noncash items, must be deducted from the schedules for factory overhead, selling expenses, and administrative expenses. Cash outlays not included in expense schedules are income taxes, which are January, $7,183; February, $5,706; and March, $6,453. Also equipment purchases are as follows: January, $22,000; February, $10,000; and March, $7,500. Management desires to maintain for operating purposes a cash balance of $20,000. Any deficiency estimated below that amount at the end of a month is to be borrowed at the beginning of that month from the company bank at the rate of 12%. Interest is to be paid at the end of each month and principal is repaid when cash is available. Borrowings, repayments, and interest are shown in the financing section. The cash budget is shown below.

Exhibit 2

CASH BUDGET
FIRST QUARTER 19XX

	SCHED-ULE	JANUARY	FEBRUARY	MARCH	QUARTER
Cash balance, beginning		$ 20,137	$ 20,758	$ 21,124	$ 20,137
Cash receipts:					
Collections on account	2a	$ 81,884	$ 90,652	$ 95,115	$267,651
Cash sales	2a	5,400	6,200	7,500	19,100
Total cash receipts		$ 87,284	$ 96,852	$102,615	$286,751
Total cash available		$107,421	$117,610	$123,739	$306,888
Cash disbursements:					
Direct materials	2b	$ 26,090	$ 27,438	$ 29,872	$ 83,400
Direct labor	1e	17,190	22,750	23,520	63,460
Factory overhead	1f	15,000	16,055	16,356	47,411
Selling expenses	1h	9,650	9,987	10,373	30,010
Administrative expenses	1i	4,400	4,400	4,400	13,200
Income taxes		7,183	5,706	6,453	19,342
Equipment purchases		22,000	10,000	7,500	39,500
Total cash disbursements ...		$101,513	$ 96,336	$ 98,474	$296,323
Excess (or deficiency)		$ 5,908	$ 21,274	$ 25,265	$ 10,565
Financing:					
Borrowing, beginning of month		$ 15,000			$ 15,000
Repayment, end of month				($ 5,000)	(5,000)
Interest, 12%*		(150)	($ 150)	(150)	(450)
Effect of financing		$ 14,850	($ 150)	($ 5,150)	($ 9,550)
Cash balance, end		$ 20,758	$ 21,124	$ 20,115	$ 20,115

* Interest computations: $15,000 × .12 × $\frac{1}{12}$ = $150.

ENDING INVENTORIES

Budgeted inventory amounts at month end are needed for direct materials and finished goods for balance sheet purposes. The computations for these amounts are shown in schedule 3 (page 484). The opening inventory of direct materials January 1, 19XX, was 1,719 units at $8.50 = $14,612. The opening inventory of finished goods was 2,140 units at $20.11 = $43,035.

Schedule 3

ENDING INVENTORIES BUDGET
FIRST QUARTER 19XX

	UNITS	UNIT COST*	AMOUNT
Direct materials, month end:			
January	1,950	$ 8.50	$16,575
February	2,016	8.50	17,136
March	2,100	9.00	18,900
January 1, 19XX	1,719	8.50	14,612
Finished goods, month end:			
January	2,050 (A)	$20.78	$42,599
February	2,175 (B)	21.36	46,458
March	2,215 (C)	21.76	48,198
January 1, 19XX	2,140	20.11	43,035

* Unit cost:

MONTH	SCHEDULE 1g MFG. COST	SCHEDULE 1b PRODUCTION	UNIT COST
January	$59,543	2,865	$20.78
February	69,430	3,250	21.36
March	73,116	3,360	21.76

(A) $42,599 ÷ $20.78 = 2,050
(B) $46,458 ÷ $21.36 = 2,175
(C) $48,198 ÷ $21.76 = 2,215

The budgeted balance sheet for March 31, 19XX is shown in Exhibit 3.

Exhibit 3

BUDGETED BALANCE SHEET
MARCH 31, 19XX

Assets

Current assets:

Cash		$ 20,115 (Exhibit 2)
Accounts receivable		97,185 (A)
Materials		18,900 (Schedule 3)
Finished goods		48,198 (Schedule 3)
Total current assets		$184,398

Noncurrent assets:

Land		$ 35,000 (B)
Building and equipment	$200,000 (C)	
Less: Accumulated depreciation	50,000 (D)	150,000
Total noncurrent assets		$185,000
Total assets		$369,398

Liabilities and Stockholders' Equity

Current liabilities:

Accounts payable		$ 12,398 (E)

Stockholders' equity:

Common stock $5 par, 20,000 outstanding	$100,000 (F)	
Retained earnings	257,000 (G)	357,000
Total liabilities and stockholders' equity		$369,398

(A) Accounts receivable: assume beginning balance of $73,736 + $291,100 credit sales − $267,651 collections.

(B) Assumed.

(C) Assume beginning balance of $160,500 + purchases of $39,500.

(D) Accumulated depreciation assumed beginning balance of $35,600 + $14,400 accumulated depreciation for first quarter.

(E) Accounts payable beginning balance of $10,300 + $85,498 purchases − $83,400 disbursements.

(F) Common stock assumed balance of $100,000.

(G) Retained earnings assumed beginning balance of $213,230 + $43,770 net income.

Figure 13-1 presents an overview of the budgets shown in this chapter.

FIGURE 13-1   **Master Budget Components**

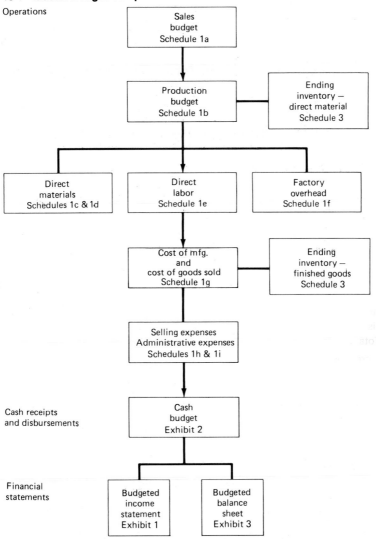

CHAPTER REVIEW

The success of the budget program is primarily the responsibility of line management. If the various levels of line management have participated in determining budget data, they will feel a responsibility to see that the budget program is successful. One of the most important aspects of a budget program is the cooperation of all elements of management and employees and their interest in achieving the company goals.

The budgeting process must be more than a once-a-year exercise. It must be a continuing effort to help the company improve its operations. As problems arise during the progress of the budget period, corrections must be promptly made and the budget projections promptly adjusted.

The master or comprehensive budget is one of the most effective means of planning and control. The company's objectives are built into the overall budget plan, and a reliable yardstick is provided to measure not only the performance of departments but also the performance of many individuals entrusted with carrying out various budget responsibilities.

Budgets may be grouped into two broad categories, (1) budget schedules and (2) budget summaries. Budget schedules include those for sales, production, materials, cash, etc. Budget summaries combine the data in the schedules or supporting information, and include the budgeted income statement and the budgeted balance sheet.

The budgeted income statement shows how profitable operations are expected to be in the following periods and can be used as a reliable measure of what operations should be. Any significant variations should be corrected. The cash budget relates the cash activities from the income statement to the balance sheet. For example, budgeted sales are essential in determining the amount and the timing of cash collections of accounts receivable. Budgets for direct materials, direct labor, and factory overhead are essential in determining the amount and timing of cash disbursements. Selling and administrative expenses budgets must also be considered, as well as taxes and capital disbursements, in establishing budgeted cash disbursements. The budgeted balance sheet incorporates all changes in assets, liabilities, and capital since the last balance sheet, and can indicate critical unfavorable or favorable ratios well ahead of time. For example, unfavorable ratios can cause a reduction in security market prices, or a lower working capital ratio, which may be in violation of an indenture requirement. With advance warning management can take steps to correct the problem.

GLOSSARY

Budget—a quantitative expression of management's objectives and a means of monitoring progress toward these objectives.

Budget Formula—the required information for the particular budget, stated as a formula, or equation.

Budgeted Balance Sheet—a statement

that begins with the current balance sheet adjusted by information in the pertinent budgets. The statement can spotlight serious future financial problems.

Budgeted Income Statement—a statement that summarizes the data developed in the supporting operating budgets such as sales, production, and expense budgets.

Cash Budget—expected cash receipts and disbursements during the budget period adjusted for the opening and closing balances. It can indicate when cash flows are deficient and outside financing is required, or when there is excess cash flow which needs to be invested for higher return.

Continuous Budget — sometimes called a moving budget, in which the month for the next year is added and the same month for the current year is dropped so that a 12-month budget is always available.

Cost of Goods Sold Budget—a budget which summarizes various individual budgets, such as materials usage, direct labor, and factory overhead, adjusted by the beginning and ending inventories.

Expense Budget—generally a list of the individual expenses for selling and administrative expenses, and which may use only fixed expenses or may use fixed and variable expenses.

Grass Roots Budget Approach—a sales forecast that begins from the bottom up, with the individual salespeople preparing budget forecasts.

Long-Range Budget—a long-term plan, usually 2 to 10 years, of sales trends, new products, research and development costs, long-term capital expenditures, financial needs, and profit goals.

Master Budget—a summary of the objectives of all functions of an organization, including sales, production, distribution, and finance.

Operating Budget—a short-term plan of operations, usually 1 year, by quarters or months, or the first quarter by months only, of expected revenues, costs, and profits.

Periodic Planning—when the management decision concerns what is to be accomplished during a specific period of time.

Production Budget—generally an estimate of the production quantity required, based on the sales forecast and the desired inventory levels.

Project Planning—the process of making the best choice among competing projects.

Sales Budget—the starting point, based on product, territory, and customer, in developing the master budget, on which all other operating and financial budgets depend.

Sales Forecast—the estimated volume of sales which is the basis for preparing the sales, production, and financial budgets for the given period.

Top Management Budget Approach—the method in which the sales forecast is made from the top down, with top management making the sales forecast.

SUMMARY PROBLEM

The following information relates to the Atticus Manufacturing Co.:

Average sales price: $56
Sales by territory (units):

	1	2	3	4	5
January	67,500	80,000	35,000	101,000	91,500
February	64,000	89,500	41,000	97,500	87,500
March	70,500	86,000	29,500	112,000	110,500

Desired finished goods inventories (units):

January 1	204,650 (costing $9,618,550)
January 31	201,500
February 28	195,900
March 31	206,100

One unit of direct materials is required to produce one finished unit.
Materials cost per unit: $44
Desired ending raw materials inventory: 55% of next month's production
Production—April: 216,710 (units)

The estimated labor hours and labor cost per hour to complete one unit differ each month due to the different availablility of skilled workers. They are as follows:

	HOURS	COST
January	.834409	$3.595359
February	.830115	3.613957
March	.856078	3.504352

Variable factory overhead rates per direct labor hour:

Indirect labor	.50
Payroll taxes	.20
Maintenance	.25
Heat and light	.05
Power	.10
Miscellaneous	.02

Variable selling expenses as a percentage of total sales dollars:

Commissions	.04%
Travel	.02%
Advertising	.03%
Bad debts	.01%

Fixed expenses per month:

Salaries (sales)	$3,400
Salaries (office)	650
Salaries (executive)	2,800
Depreciation	2,500 (factory)
Taxes	250 (administrative)
Insurance	500 (administative)
Taxes	1,000

Insurance	$ 700
Indirect materials	1,500
Indirect labor	700
Supervision	950
Maintenance	600
Heat and light	400
Power	350

Assume:

All fixed expenses are paid when incurred.

Raw materials are paid when received.

All sales are for cash.

Estimated income taxes are paid monthly.

Cash balance on January 1 is $500,000.

REQUIRED:

Given the above information, prepare the following budgets for the Atticus Manufacturing Company for the first quarter 19X0:

a Sales—in units and dollars
b Production
c Direct materials purchase
d Direct materials usage
e Direct labor
f Factory overhead
g Cost of goods sold
h Selling expenses
i Administrative expenses
j Budgeted income statement, assuming a tax rate of 40%
k Cash budget

SOLUTION TO SUMMARY PROBLEM

a Sales Budget

ATTICUS MANUFACTURING FIRST QUARTER 19X0

	TERRITORY	JANUARY	FEBRUARY	MARCH	QUARTER
Units	1	67,500	64,000	70,500	202,000
	2	80,000	89,500	86,000	255,500
	3	35,000	41,000	29,500	105,500
	4	101,000	97,500	112,000	310,500
	5	91,500	87,500	110,500	289,500
Total		375,000	379,500	408,500	1,163,000
(Average sales price $56)					
Value	1	$ 3,780,000	$ 3,584,000	$ 3,948,000	$11,312,000
	2	4,480,000	5,012,000	4,816,000	14,308,000
	3	1,960,000	2,296,000	1,652,000	5,908,000
	4	5,656,000	5,460,000	6,272,000	17,388,000
	5	5,124,000	4,900,000	6,188,000	16,212,000
Total		$21,000,000	$21,252,000	$22,876,000	$65,128,000

b Production Budget

UNITS	JANUARY	FEBRUARY	MARCH	TOTAL
Sales budget	375,000	379,500	408,500	1,163,000
Add—desired ending inventory	201,500	195,900	206,100	206,100
Subtotal	576,500	575,400	614,600	1,369,100
Less—opening inventory	204,650	201,500	195,900	204,650
Production units required	371,850	373,900	418,700	1,164,450

c Direct Materials Purchase Budget

PRODUCTION REQUIRED	JANUARY	FEBRUARY	MARCH	TOTAL
Units	371,850	373,900	418,700	1,164,450
Add—desired ending inventory	205,645 (A)	230,285 (B)	119,191 (C)	119,191
Subtotal	577,495	604,185	537,891	1,283,641
Deduct—beginning inventory	204,518 (D)	205,645	230,285	204,518
Purchase required	372,977	398,540	307,606	1,079,123
Price per unit	$44	$44	$44	$44
Purchase cost	$16,410,988	$17,535,760	$13,534,664	$47,481,412

(A) 373,900 × 55% = 205,645
(B) 418,700 × 55% = 230,285
(C) 216,710 × 55% = 119,191
(D) 371,850 × 55% = 204,518

d Direct Materials Usage Budget

	JANUARY	FEBRUARY	MARCH	TOTAL
Required units	371,850	373,900	418,700	1,164,450
Unit cost	$44	$44	$44	$44
Usage cost	$16,361,400	$16,451,600	$18,422,800	$51,235,800

e Direct Labor Budget

	JANUARY	FEBRUARY	MARCH	TOTAL
Required units	371,850	373,900	418,700	1,164,450
Labor hours,				
(.834409 × 371,850)	310,275			
(.830115 × 373,900)		310,380		
(.856078 × 418,700)			358,440	
Rate per hour	$3.595359	$3.613957	$3.504352	
Direct labor cost	$1,115,550	$1,121,700	$1,256,100	$3,493,350

f Factory Overhead Budget

	JANUARY (DIRECT LABOR HOURS: 310,275)		
	FIXED	VARIABLE	TOTAL
Indirect materials	$1,500		$ 1,500
Indirect labor	700	$155,138	155,838
Supervision	950		950
Payroll taxes		62,055	62,055
Maintenance	600	77,569	78,169
Heat and light	400	15,514	15,914
Power	350	31,028	31,378
Insurance	700		700
Taxes...............................	1,000		1,000
Depreciation	2,500		2,500
Miscellaneous........................		6,206	6,206
Total	$8,700	$347,510	$356,210

	FEBRUARY (DIRECT LABOR HOURS: 310,380)		
	FIXED	VARIABLE	TOTAL
Indirect materials	$1,500		$ 1,500
Indirect labor	700	$155,190	155,890
Supervision	950		950
Payroll taxes		62,076	62,076
Maintenance	600	77,595	78,195
Heat and light	400	15,519	15,919
Power	350	31,038	31,388
Insurance	700		700
Taxes...............................	1,000		1,000
Depreciation	2,500		2,500
Miscellaneous........................		6,208	6,208
Total	$8,700	$347,626	$356,326

	MARCH (DIRECT LABOR HOURS: 358,440)		
	FIXED	VARIABLE	TOTAL
Indirect materials	$1,500		$ 1,500
Indirect labor	700	$179,220	179,920
Supervision	950		950
Payroll taxes		71,688	71,688
Maintenance	600	89,610	90,210
Heat and light	400	17,922	18,322
Power	350	35,844	36,194
Insurance	700		700
Taxes...............................	1,000		1,000
Depreciation	2,500		2,500
Miscellaneous........................		7,169	7,169
Total	$8,700	$401,453	$410,153

g Cost of Goods Sold Budget

FIRST QUARTER 19X0

SUPPORTING BUDGETS	JANUARY	FEBRUARY	MARCH	QUARTER
Direct materials.........	$16,361,400	$16,451,600	$18,422,800	$51,235,800
Direct labor	1,115,550	1,121,700	1,256,100	3,493,350
Factory overhead	356,210	356,326	410,153	1,122,689
Total manufacturing costs..............	$17,833,160	$17,929,626	$20,089,053	$55,851,839
Add—finished goods beginning	9,618,550	9,663,940	9,393,405	9,618,550
Goods available	$27,451,710	$27,593,566	$29,482,458	$65,470,389
Subtract—finished goods ending.........	9,663,940 (A)	9,393,405 (B)	9,888,678 (C)	9,888,678
Cost of goods sold	$17,787,770	$18,200,161	$19,593,780	$55,581,711

(A) $17,833,160 ÷ 371,850 = $47.96 × 201,500 = $9,663,940
(B) $17,929,626 ÷ 373,900 = $47.95 × 195,900 = $9,393,405
(C) $20,089,053 ÷ 418,700 = $47.98 × 206,100 = $9,888,678

h Selling Expenses Budget

JANUARY 19X0 ($21,000,000 SALES)

TYPE OF EXPENSE	FIXED	VARIABLE	TOTAL
Salaries............................	$3,400		$ 3,400
Commissions		$ 8,400	8,400
Travel		4,200	4,200
Advertising		6,300	6,300
Bad debts		2,100	2,100
Total selling expenses	$3,400	$21,000	$24,400

FEBRUARY 19X0 ($21,252,000 SALES)

TYPE OF EXPENSE	FIXED	VARIABLE	TOTAL
Salaries............................	$3,400		$ 3,400
Commissions		$ 8,501	8,501
Travel		4,250	4,250
Advertising		6,376	6,376
Bad debts		2,125	2,125
Total selling expenses	$3,400	$21,252	$24,652

MARCH 19X0 ($22,876,000 SALES)

TYPE OF EXPENSE	FIXED	VARIABLE	TOTAL
Salaries............................	$3,400		$ 3,400
Commissions		$ 9,150	9,150
Travel		4,575	4,575
Advertising		6,863	6,863
Bad debts		2,288	2,288
Total selling expenses	$3,400	$22,876	$26,276

i Administrative Expenses Budget

PER MONTH

TYPE OF EXPENSE	TOTAL
Executive salaries	$2,800
Office salaries	650
Insurance	500
Taxes	250
Total administrative expenses	$4,200

j Budgeted Income Statement

SUPPORTING BUDGETS	JANUARY	FEBRUARY	MARCH	QUARTER
Sales	$21,000,000	$21,252,000	$22,876,000	$65,128,000
Cost of goods sold	17,787,770	18,200,161	19,593,780	55,581,711
Gross profit	$ 3,212,230	$ 3,051,839	$ 3,282,220	$ 9,546,289
Operating expenses:				
Selling expenses	$ 24,400	$ 24,652	$ 26,276	$ 75,328
Administrative expenses	4,200	4,200	4,200	12,600
Total operating expenses	$ 28,600	$ 28,852	$ 30,476	$ 87,928
Net income before taxes	$ 3,183,630	$ 3,022,987	$ 3,251,744	$ 9,458,361
Income taxes (40%)	1,273,452	1,209,195	1,300,698	3,783,345
Net income	$ 1,910,178	$ 1,813,792	$ 1,951,046	$ 5,675,016

k Cash Budget

	JANUARY	FEBRUARY	MARCH	TOTAL
Cash balance, beginning	$ 500,000	$ 2,319,800	$ 3,324,592	$ 500,000
Cash receipts:				
Cash sales	21,000,000	21,252,000	22,876,000	65,128,000
Total cash available . . .	$21,500,000	$23,571,800	$26,200,592	$65,628,000
Cash disbursements				
Direct materials	$16,410,988	$17,535,760	$13,534,664	$47,481,412
Direct labor	1,115,550	1,121,700	1,256,100	3,493,350
Factory overhead	353,710 (A)	353,826 (B)	407,653 (C)	1,115,189
Selling expenses	22,300 (D)	22,527 (E)	23,988 (F)	68,815
Administrative				
expenses	4,200	4,200	4,200	12,600
Income taxes	1,273,452	1,209,195	1,300,698	3,783,345
Total cash				
disbursements	$19,180,200	$20,247,208	$16,527,303	$55,954,711
Excess	$ 2,319,800	$ 3,324,592	$ 9,673,289	$ 9,673,289

(A) Schedule f; January; $356,210 − $2,500 depreciation = $353,710
(B) Schedule f; February; $356,326 − $2,500 depreciation = $353,826
(C) Schedule f; March; $410,153 − $2,500 depreciation = $407,653
(D) Schedule h; January; $24,400 − $2,100 bad debts = $22,300
(E) Schedule h; February; $24,652 − $2,125 bad debts = $22,527
(F) Schedule h; March; $26,276 − $2,288 bad debts $= $23,988

QUESTIONS

1 Contrast the top management approach with the grass roots approach of budget preparation. Which appears to be the better approach?
2 Name some key decisions necessary in budget preparation.
3 Name two requirements for a successful budget.
4 What is a continuous budget?
5 What essential information is included in the initial step in the preparation of a master budget?
6 Distinguish between a fixed and a flexible budget.
7 Explain why an accurate sales forecast is essential for the preparation of a master budget.
8 List the principal information needed in preparing the sales forecast.
9 Explain why it is unprofitable to carry inventories that are too large or too small.
10 What information is required in preparing the following quantity budgets: (a) production and (b) direct materials purchases?
11 What information is required in preparing the direct labor dollar budgets?
12 Give the formula for the (a) production quantity and (b) direct materials dollar usage budgets.
13 On what bases are budgeted selling expenses and administrative expenses generally presented?
14 What are the principal sections of the cash budget?
15 What does the budgeted income statement show?
16 What does the budgeted balance sheet show?

EXERCISES

EXERCISE 1

Budgeted Income Statement

Rhodes Corporation expects its sales for the current year to be $795,000. In previous years the percentage of gross profit to sales has been 45%. Their operating expenses are expected to be $260,000, of which 40% are administrative, and 60% selling.

REQUIRED:

Assuming a tax rate of 50%, prepare a budgeted income statement for Rhodes Corporation for 19X1.

EXERCISE 2

Sales Budget

Griffin Manufacturing Company has four sales territories in this state. Each salesperson is expected to sell the following number of *units* this quarter:

TERRITORY	1	2	3	4
January	750	790	910	820
February	640	670	870	785
March	810	805	895	805

REQUIRED:

Assuming an average sales price of $33, prepare a first quarter sales forecast in units and dollars for the Griffin Manufacturing Company for 19X2.

EXERCISE 3

Production Budget

In the first quarter of 19X3 Griffin Corporation projects their sales in units to be as follows:

January	3,270
February	2,965
March.....................	3,315

In addition, they desire to have the following units of inventory on hand:

January 1	2,975
January 31	2,705
February 28	2,650
March 31	3,000

REQUIRED:

Prepare a production budget for the first quarter of 19X3.

EXERCISE 4

Direct Materials Purchase Budget

Union Company intends to produce the following units during the third quarter of 19X4:

July	3,685
August	4,450
September	4,175

One unit of direct materials is required for each unit of finished product. Ending inventory is expected to be 70% of the following month's production requirements.

REQUIRED:

Prepare a direct materials purchase budget for Union Company, assuming a purchase price of $6.25. Round calculations to the nearest dollar. Production for October is expected to be 4,000 units.

EXERCISE 5

Direct Materials Purchase Budget

Alshe Manufacturing Company projected the following unit production requirements:

January	7,850
February	9,275
March	8,900
April	8,625

Ending inventory is expected to be 55% of the following month's production
requirements.

REQUIRED:

Prepare a direct materials purchase budget for the first quarter of 19X5 for Alshe
Manufacturing Company, assuming a unit purchase price of $8.75.

EXERCISE 6

Direct and Indirect Labor Cost

Prince Corporation required 3.5 hours of direct labor to complete one unit. Labor
cost is $4.45 per hour. Fixed indirect labor costs amount to $4,500 per week.
Supervision accounts for 55% of this cost; the remaining is allocated to maintenance. The variable portion of indirect labor is applied at $.50 per direct labor
hour. Supervision accounts for 55% of this cost; the remaining is allocated to
maintenance.

REQUIRED:

Assuming 2,750 units are produced each week, prepare a direct labor budget,
and compute the fixed and variable amounts of factory overhead for indirect labor
for the year 19X6.

EXERCISE 7

Factory Overhead Budget

Overton Corporation incurred 4,650 hours of direct labor in July. The following are
the fixed components of factory overhead:

Indirect materials	$1,150
Indirect labor	1,400
Supervision	1,650
Maintenance	700
Heat and light	850
Power	320
Insurance	500
Taxes	1,310
Depreciation	3,200

Variable overhead is based on direct labor hours:

Indirect labor	$.50
Payroll taxes	.35
Maintenance	.17
Heat and light	.12
Power	.16
Miscellaneous	.15

REQUIRED:

Prepare the factory overhead budget for July 19X7.

EXERCISE 8

Factory Overhead Budgets

Overton Corporation incurred 4,920 direct labor hours in August and 4,580 direct labor hours in September. The fixed overhead costs and the variable overhead rates are given in Exercise 7.

REQUIRED:

Prepare factory overhead budgets for August and September 19X8.

PROBLEMS

PROBLEM 1

Selling Expenses Budget

For the months of July, August, and September, Andlyn Company projects its sales to be $167,250, $171,875, and $159,625, respectively.

Salaries are fixed at $9,500 per month and are allocated as follows:

Sales	50%
Executives	30%
Office	20%

The following variable expenses are determined as a percentage of sales dollars:

Commissions	4%
Travel	1%
Advertising	1.5%
Bad debts	1%

The remaining expenses are fixed each month; assume a 50% income tax rate:

Depreciation: $1,600; allocate half each to selling and administrative
Payroll taxes: $300
Miscellaneous: $1,500; allocate 65% to selling and remainder to administrative
Insurance: $750

REQUIRED:

Based on the above information and assuming a gross profit percentage of 40%, prepare selling expenses budgets for July, August, and September 19X1, and for the third quarter of 19X1, and determine the budgeted net income for that quarter. Round answers to the nearest dollar.

PROBLEM 2

Half-Year Sales Report

Choates Company has three sales territories in this state. For the last half of 19X2 each reported selling the following number of items:

	TERRITORY		
MONTH	1	2	3
July	65	71	61
August	48	68	53
September	54	59	47
October	61	76	59
November	57	58	64
December	51	63	56

From July through September, the sales price per item was $14. In October and November, it was $16, and in December it was $15.25.

REQUIRED:

Prepare a sales report in units and dollars for the last half of 19X2.

PROBLEM 3

Production and Direct Materials Budgets in Units

Tivel Company projected its sales in units to be the following for the second quarter of 19X3: April, 2,445; May, 2,310; June, 2,390. They desire to have the following units of finished goods on hand: April 1, 2,100; May 1, 2,235; June 1, 2,250; June 30, 2,190. One unit of direct materials is required for each unit of finished product.

Production for July is expected to be 2,475. They desire an ending raw materials inventory of 70% of the following month's production requirements. Raw materials cost $6.50 per unit in April and $7.50 per unit in May and June.

REQUIRED:

Prepare a production budget, a direct materials purchase budget, and a direct materials usage budget for Tivel Company. Round calculations to the nearest dollar.

PROBLEM 4

Direct Labor and Factory Overhead Budgets

General Corporation requires 3.5 hours of direct labor to produce one unit of product. Direct labor rate is $5.25 per hour. They require production at the following numbers of units: October, 1,675; November, 1,740; December, 1,510.

Fixed factory overhead comprises the following amounts:

Indirect materials	$1,000
Indirect labor	1,600
Supervision	1,175
Maintenance	675
Heat and light	400
Power	700
Insurance	500
Taxes	1,000
Depreciation	2,500

Variable overhead has the following rates, based on direct labor hours:

Indirect labor	$.50
Payroll taxes	.35
Maintenance	.20
Heat and light	.15
Power	.14
Miscellaneous	.10

REQUIRED:

Prepare a direct labor budget for the last quarter of 19X4 and factory overhead budget for October, November, and December 19X4.

PROBLEM 5

Cost of Goods Sold Budget and Selling Expenses Budget

Scott Company discovered that on its quarterly cost of goods sold budget, the percentage of total manufacturing cost for each month was as follows:

January	35%
February	40%
March	25%

The following total costs were incurred during the quarter:

Direct materials	$25,000
Direct labor	37,500
Factory overhead	20,000

Ending inventories of finished goods were as follows:

December 31	$26,700
January 31	24,300
February 28	25,800
March 31	26,650

Sales dollars for the 3 months were as follows:

> January .... $ 97,670
> February 101,895
> March 107,700

The following selling expenses remain fixed each month: salaries $3,600; depreciation $1,400; miscellaneous $575. Variable expenses are assigned a rate based on sales dollars:

> Commissions .... 3 %
> Travel .... 4 %
> Advertising .... 2 %
> Bad debts 1.5%

REQUIRED:

Prepare a quarterly cost of goods sold budget and monthly selling expenses budgets for Scott Company for 19X5.

PROBLEM 6

Sales Budget, Production Budget, Direct Materials and Labor Budget

Hardesty Company expects to sell the following units in each of its five sales territories during the second quarter of 19X6:

| | TERRITORY | | | | |
MONTH	1	2	3	4	5
April	750	785	330	1,095	1,005
May	695	710	305	990	950
June	660	830	390	1,065	935

Sales price is $56 per unit.

Raw materials ending inventory is desired to be 55% of the following month's production. Raw materials inventory on April 1 is 2,400 units. July's production is expected to be 3,600 units. Raw materials purchase price is $41 in April and $47 in May and June. Desired ending finished goods inventory in units for April, May, and June is 3,615, 3,587, and 3,632 respectively. April 1 finished goods inventory is 3,680 units.

It takes 1.5 hours of direct labor to complete one unit, at a cost of $8 per hour. One unit of direct materials is required for each unit of finished product.

REQUIRED:

Prepare the sales budget, production budget, direct materials purchase budget, direct materials usage budget, and direct labor budget for the second quarter for Hardesty Company.

PROBLEM 7

Sales, Production, Raw Materials, Direct Labor, Finished Goods, and Cash Budgets

The Scarborough Corporation manufactures and sells two products, Thingone and Thingtwo. In July 19X7, Scarborough's budget department gathered the following data in order to project sales and budget requirements for 19X8:

19X8 PROJECTED SALES		
PRODUCT	UNITS	PRICE
Thingone	60,000	$ 70
Thingtwo	40,000	$100

	19X8 INVENTORIES—IN UNITS	
	EXPECTED	DESIRED
PRODUCT	JANUARY 1, 19X8	DECEMBER 31, 19X8
Thingone	20,000	25,000
Thingtwo	8,000	9,000

In order to produce one unit of Thingone and Thingtwo, the following raw materials are used:

		AMOUNT USED PER UNIT	
RAW MATERIAL	UNIT	THINGONE	THINGTWO
A	lb	4	5
B	lb	2	3
C	Each		1

Projected data for 19X8 with respect to raw materials is as follows:

RAW MATERIAL	ANTICIPATED PURCHASE PRICE	EXPECTED INVENTORIES JANUARY 1, 19X8	DESIRED INVENTORIES DECEMBER 31, 19X8
A	$8	32,000 lb	36,000 lb
B	$5	29,000 lb	32,000 lb
C	$3	6,000 each	7,000 each

Projected direct labor requirements for 19X8 and rates are as follows:

PRODUCT	HOURS PER UNIT	RATE PER HOUR
Thingone	2	$3
Thingtwo	3	$4

Overhead is applied at the rate of $2 per direct labor hour. Cash balance on January 1, 19X8 is estimated to be $750,000. Raw materials are paid for in the year they are ordered. Factory overhead is estimated at $950,000 and includes $100,000 of depreciation. Factory overhead costs are paid in the year incurred. All sales are for cash. Selling, general, and administrative expenses are estimated at 10% of sales of the period and are paid when incurred. Income taxes for the year are estimated at $500,000 and will be paid in 19X8.

REQUIRED:

Based upon the above projections and budget requirements for 19X8 for Thingone and Thingtwo, prepare the following budgets for 19X8:

    a Sales budget (in dollars)
    b Production budget (in units)
    c Raw materials purchase budget (in quantities)
    d Raw materials purchase budget (in dollars)
    e Direct labor budget (in dollars)
    f Budgeted finished goods inventory at December 31, 19X8 (in dollars)
    g Cash budget for entire year

                                      (AICPA Adapted)

CHAPTER FOURTEEN
BUDGETING II— FLEXIBLE BUDGET

In other chapters we have discussed in some detail the various aspects of developing and implementing budgets. We compared the budgeted operations for the period with actual operations and costs. Most were fixed or static budgets; that is, they were based on a fixed level of operations. When a company has relatively stable operations or when the production volume and production employees remain about the same from period to period, the static budget may seem adequate to use for the purpose. However, operations are seldom as stable as they may appear, and often the fixed type of budget obscures important variances, such as compensatory differences, which should be set forth. For example, actual costs may exceed the budget by only $300, which appears very good. However, if actual labor hours were excessive, causing an unfavorable labor efficiency variance of $1,200, and at the same time the department, by careful spending, kept the actual cost low, resulting in a favorable spending variance of $900, the story is quite different. A suitable flexible budget would readily show these compensatory differences, and corrective steps could then be promptly taken. Flexible budgeting can also be applied to marketing expenses, administrative expenses, and a wide variety of commercial operations, such as those in insurance companies, banks, finance companies, and other companies that have high-volume repetitive operations.

NATURE OF FLEXIBLE BUDGETING

A flexible budget is one in which the budget allowance varies according to the attained level of activity. In developing the flexible budget the cost behavior patterns of numerous cost items are carefully studied and a budget is developed that is suitable for any level of activity.

The development of a flexible budget for variable costs such as direct labor and direct materials is fairly simple because these costs increase in proportion to volume. A different approach is required, however, for factory overhead. Here we have a number of different items, some variable, some semivariable, and some fixed. Their behavior must be analyzed in relation to varying volumes and measuring bases.

For an illustration we will consider the operations of the Hillside Pharmaceutical Company. Following are the individual factory overhead costs at a planned volume of 10,000 units per month for the manufacturing plant.

COMPONENT	AMOUNT
Indirect materials	$12,000
Indirect labor	24,000
Supplies	10,500
Repairs	7,500
Heat, light, and power	8,000
Supervision	10,000
Equipment depreciation	3,000
Factory rent	5,000
Total factory overhead	$80,000
Overhead per unit ($80,000 ÷ 10,000)	$ 8.00

We know that the above items include variable, semivariable, and fixed costs. In this example, assume the first four items change with volume and are considered variable. The next item, heat, light, and power, has both variable and fixed portions. The fixed portion includes a specified minimum charge payable to a public utility and also a minimum cost for operating the boilers when the plant is open, totaling $2,000 per month. The last three items, supervision (assumed to be fixed for this example), equipment depreciation, and factory rent, are the fixed costs.

For flexible budgeting purposes we have the following cost information which can be used for any volume level:

COMPONENT	VARIABLE COST PER UNIT	FIXED COST AMOUNT
Indirect materials ($12,000 ÷ 10,000)	$1.20	
Indirect labor ($24,000 ÷ 10,000)	2.40	
Supplies ($10,500 ÷ 10,000)	1.05	
Repairs ($7,500 ÷ 10,000)	.75	
Heat, light, and power [($8,000 − $2,000) ÷ 10,000] ...	.60	$ 2,000
Supervision		10,000
Equipment depreciation		3,000
Factory rent		5,000
Total factory overhead	$6.00	$20,000

BUDGET ALLOWANCE FORMULA

From the preceding data a formula can be developed and used for any volume of production as follows:

Budget allowance = (unit variable cost × quantity) + fixed costs

$$BA = (UVC \times Q) + FC$$

For the planned volume of 10,000 units, the flexible budget allowance would be:

$$BA = (\$6.00 \times 10,000) + \$20,000$$
$$BA = \$60,000 + \$20,000$$
$$BA = \$80,000$$

RELEVANT RANGE TABLE

In developing a flexible budget, many companies prepare a relevant range table showing the costs for the expected range of activity. The relevant range for the monthly production of the Hillside Pharmaceutical Company is established as between 4,000 and 12,000 units. The variations in cost are usually shown as in Table 14-1 (page 506).

From Table 14-1 we see that the total cost ranges from $44,000 at 4,000 units up to $92,000 at 12,000 units. However, the total unit cost drops, from $11.00 at 4,000 units to $7.67 at 12,000 units, a drop of 30 percent. The cause is the fixed costs, which do not change with the increase in volume. As can be seen the total fixed costs per unit were $5.00 at 4,000 units and only $1.67 at 12,000 units, a drop of 67 percent.

While Table 14-1 is helpful in obtaining a quick view of costs at various levels of activities, a more precise computation using the formula would be used for monthly or other reports or special analyses. Thus, if we wanted to know the cost of producing 9,750 units, we would know the total cost would be just below $80,000, according to Table 41-1.

The cost could be computed more precisely using the formula as follows:

$$\text{Budget allowance} = (UVC \times Q) + FC$$
$$\text{Budget allowance} = (\$6.00 \times 9,750) + \$20,000$$
$$\text{Budget allowance} = \$58,500 + \$20,000$$
$$\text{Budget allowance} = \$78,500$$

BASES OF MEASUREMENT

In Table 14-1 the flexible budget allowances were based on several volumes of production. Four bases of measurement, or levels of capacity, have already been discussed; they are:

TABLE 14-1
HILLSIDE PHARMACEUTICAL COMPANY
RELEVANT RANGE TABLE
AMOUNT PER MONTH, YEAR 19X0

COMPONENTS—UNITS	COST PER UNIT	4,000	6,000	8,000	10,000	12,000
Variable costs:						
Indirect materials	$1.20	$ 4,800	$ 7,200	$ 9,600	$12,000	$14,400
Indirect labor	2.40	9,600	14,400	19,200	24,000	28,800
Supplies	1.05	4,200	6,300	8,400	10,500	12,600
Repairs	.75	3,000	4,500	6,000	7,500	9,000
Heat, light, and power	.60	2,400	3,600	4,800	6,000	7,200
Total variable costs	$6.00	$24,000	$36,000	$48,000	$60,000	$72,000
Fixed costs:						
Heat, light, and power		$ 2,000	$ 2,000	$ 2,000	$ 2,000	$ 2,000
Supervision		10,000	10,000	10,000	10,000	10,000
Equipment depreciation		3,000	3,000	3,000	3,000	3,000
Factory rent		5,000	5,000	5,000	5,000	5,000
Total fixed costs		$20,000	$20,000	$20,000	$20,000	$20,000
Total costs		$44,000	$56,000	$68,000	$80,000	$92,000
Unit cost		$11.00	$9.33	$8.50	$8.00	$7.67

	UNIT COST				
COSTS—UNITS	4,000	6,000	8,000	10,000	12,000
Total variable costs	$ 6.00	$6.00	$6.00	$6.00	$6.00
Total fixed costs	5.00	3.33	2.50	2.00	1.67
Total costs	$11.00	$9.33	$8.50	$8.00	$7.67

Theoretical or Ideal Capacity. The maximum capacity that a department or factory is capable of producing under perfect conditions.

Practical or Realistic Capacity. The theoretical capacity, less practical constraints, such as estimated breakdowns, strikes, and delays.

Normal or Long-Run Capacity. The constant, average level of utilization of plant and workers over a long period of time sufficient to even out the high and low levels of production.

Expected Actual or Short-Run Capacity. The expected actual capacity for the next period or operation.

Generally, the measurement of the levels of activity in a particular department may be more complex. For example, there may be more than one cost center in a department when more than one product is produced by a department. Thus the basis of measurement should be related to the whole department. Typical common bases are labor hours, machine hours, materials weight, miles traveled, and number of calls by salespeople.

Care should be exercised to be sure that extraneous variations are not introduced when the basis is determined. For example, if direct labor dollars are used, the extraneous variations may be the wide differences in the labor rates. Standard costs should be used rather than actual costs, because an inefficient department should not receive a more generous overhead allowance than an efficient one. This will occur if the budget is based upon actual hours rather than upon standard hours allowed.

DEPARTMENTAL OPERATIONS

Cost Control

In the preceding data we were concerned with the production of the entire plant. However, for control and evaluation purposes we will also be concerned with departmental and cost center operations. In the following illustration we will use the standard rate based upon direct labor hours, the same as was used for product costing. Since the standards were based upon one level of production, we will have to give effect to the efficiency variance for any changes in production volume. There will also be a spending variance representing the difference between actual results and the flexible budget at actual production volume. For our example we will use the filling department of Hillside Pharmaceutical Company. The composition of the expenses will vary from department to department and will differ from the costs for the entire plant shown earlier in the chapter.

Unit Costs

The standard rates per direct labor hour have been established for the filling department controllable overhead costs as follows:

CONTROLLABLE OVERHEAD	RATE PER DIRECT LABOR HOUR
Indirect materials	$ .45
Indirect labor	1.05
Supplies	.75
Repairs	.45
Heat, light, and power..................	.30
Total controllable overhead	$3.00

Controllable costs are those over which the departmental supervisor can exert influence over the amount spent. Noncontrollable costs are assigned to a department or cost center by upper management and are therefore not under the control of the departmental supervisor. Service department costs are examples of noncontrollable costs.

Flexible Budget

With the above unit costs available, we can construct the flexible budget for the controllable costs in the filling department (Table 14-2) (page 508). The range is between 3,000 and 7,000 direct labor hours. The standard costs used in product costing are based upon a planned volume of 5,000 direct labor

TABLE 14-2
FLEXIBLE BUDGET
FILLING DEPARTMENT
PER MONTH, YEAR 19X0

CONTROLLABLE OVERHEAD	STANDARD RATE	STANDARD HOURS				
		3,000	4,000	5,000	6,000	7,000
Indirect materials	$ .45	$1,350	$ 1,800	$ 2,250	$ 2,700	$ 3,150
Indirect labor	1.05	3,150	4,200	5,250	6,300	7,350
Supplies	.75	2,250	3,000	3,750	4,500	5,250
Repairs	.45	1,350	1,800	2,250	2,700	3,150
Heat, light, and power	.30	900	1,200	1,500	1,800	2,100
Total controllable overhead	$3.00	$9,000	$12,000	$15,000	$18,000	$21,000

hours per month. At the standard rate of $3 per direct labor hour the controllable overhead budget is $15,000 per month for 5,000 direct labor hours.

Reporting of Costs

The reporting of costs depends upon the needs and desires of management. Generally companies will compare the budget with actual costs for all controllable costs. It is understood that the department head is seldom able to influence the price paid for materials or the wage rate paid to workers. For factory overhead, the supervisor may influence indirect materials, indirect labor, supplies, repairs, and heat, light, and power by the way production is scheduled and by the quality of production. The assignment of noncontrollable costs to production departments may be useful for product costing purposes, but they often obscure significant cost control factors. Therefore, a clear distinction should be made between those costs for which the supervisor is held responsible and those costs clearly beyond supervisory control. A performance report may present variances between actual cost and budget only for those costs under the supervisor's control.

Some companies feel there is a certain psychological benefit in including noncontrollable costs in the performance report. These costs remind supervisors of the total cost entrusted to them. While supervisors may not directly influence noncontrollable costs, they could, through negligence in handling certain items, cause considerable loss. In any case, noncontrollable costs should be shown separately, similar to the manner in which the costs are presented in Table 14-3. Note that the controllable costs are actual, $15,300 and budget, $15,000. Note that the variance associated with the controllable cost was only $300, unfavorable, even though the actual hours were 5,400 compared with 5,000 budgeted. This calls for further analysis.

Evaluation of Performance

The net difference between actual and budget of $300 is a compensatory difference between an unfavorable efficiency variance (due to excess hours used) and a favorable spending variance (because of savings made in dollar

TABLE 14-3
BUDGET REPORT
FILLING DEPARTMENT
JANUARY 19X0

	ACTUAL COST*	BUDGET AT STANDARD†	VARIANCE AMOUNT‡
Controllable costs:			
Indirect materials	$ 2,350	$ 2,250	$100 U
Indirect labor	5,150	5,250	100 F
Supplies	4,100	3,750	350 U
Repairs	2,300	2,250	50 U
Heat, light, and power..................	1,400	1,500	100 F
Total controllable costs	$15,300	$15,000	$300 U
Noncontrollable costs:			
Supervision	$ 2,000	$ 2,000	
Equipment depreciation	1,000	1,000	
Service department allocation	2,500	2,500	
Total noncontrollable costs...........	$ 5,500	$ 5,500	
Total departmental costs	$20,800	$20,500	$300 (U)

Actual hours 5,400, standard hours 5,000.

* Actual cost = 5,400 actual direct labor hours × actual rate per direct labor hour.

† Budget at standard = 5,000 standard direct labor hours × standard rate per direct labor hour.

‡ U = unfavorable, F = favorable.

amounts spent during the month). In order to evaluate the supervisor's performance in this department, we would have to develop a flexible budget based upon actual hours incurred. The flexible budget will first be compared with actual results to determine the spending variance associated with the controllable costs (Table 14-4, page 510).

Next, compare the flexible budget at actual to the budget at standard in order to determine the efficiency variance associated with the controllable costs (Table 14-5, page 510).

In effect, the unfavorable variance amount of $300 can be broken down into a favorable spending variance of $900 and an unfavorable efficiency variance of $1,200. Through the use of a flexible budget, the compensatory differences can be easily seen.

For a more detailed discussion of standard costing and variance analysis, refer to Chapters 11 and 12.

Costs at Varying Capacity Levels

Table 14-6 (page 511) shows the effect of varying capacity levels on factory overhead rates for Chaykin Manufacturing Corp. The theoretical capacity level is 100%, practical capacity 85%, and normal capacity 75%. A decrease in capacity from 100% to 85% causes the total unit cost to increase from $1.20 to $1.33, or 11%; and a decreasing capacity from 100% to 75% causes the total unit cost to increase from $1.20 to $1.44, an increase of 20%. If only fixed overhead is considered, the change from 100% to 85% increases the cost from $.72 to $.85, an increase of 18%; and a change from 100% to 75% increases the

TABLE 14-4
BUDGET REPORT
CONTROLLABLE COSTS
FILLING DEPARTMENT
JANUARY 19X0

| | | FLEXIBLE BUDGET | |
CONTROLLABLE COSTS	ACTUAL COSTS	BUDGET AT ACTUAL*	SPENDING VARIANCE†
Indirect materials	$ 2,350	$ 2,430	$ 80 F
Indirect labor	5,150	5,670	520 F
Supplies	4,100	4,050	50 U
Repairs	2,300	2,430	130 F
Heat, light, and power	1,400	1,620	220 F
Total controllable costs	$15,300	$16,200	$900 F

* Flexible budget at actual = 5,400 actual direct labor hours × standard rate per direct labor hour.
† U = unfavorable, F = favorable.

cost from $.72 to $.96, an increase of 33%. Operations will usually be close to normal capacity, but it is well to know the savings if short-term operations can move close to 100%.

Idle Capacity and Excess Capacity

A distinction should be made between idle capacity and excess capacity. *Idle capacity* is due to a temporary slowdown because of lack of orders. *Excess capacity* is due to greater capacity than can reasonably be used. In other words, idle capacity is a short-term condition that will be corrected as soon as orders are received, while excess capacity will not be corrected in the near future. Idle capacity costs are included in factory overhead but are shown separately

TABLE 14-5
BUDGET REPORT
CONTROLLABLE COSTS
FILLING DEPARTMENT
JANUARY 19X0

| | | FLEXIBLE BUDGET | |
CONTROLLABLE COSTS	BUDGET AT ACTUAL	BUDGET AT STANDARD	EFFICIENCY VARIANCE*
Indirect materials	$ 2,430	$ 2,250	$ 180 U
Indirect labor	5,670	5,250	420 U
Supplies	4,050	3,750	300 U
Repairs	2,430	2,250	180 U
Heat, light, and power	1,620	1,500	120 U
Total controllable costs	$16,200	$15,000	$1,200 U

* U = unfavorable.

TABLE 14-6
CHAYKIN MANUFACTURING CORP.
COSTS AT VARYING CAPACITY LEVELS
FACTORY OVERHEAD RATES

COST COMPONENTS	NORMAL CAPACITY	PRACTICAL CAPACITY	THEORETICAL CAPACITY
Production capacity.....................	75%	85%	100%
Direct labor hours	37,500	42,500	50,000
Factory overhead budget:			
Variable costs	$18,000	$20,400	$24,000
Fixed costs	36,000	36,000	36,000
Total	$54,000	$56,400	$60,000
Unit costs per direct labor hour:			
Variable overhead rate	$ .48	$ .48	$ .48
Fixed overhead rate	.96	.85	.72
Total	$ 1.44	$ 1.33	$ 1.20

for control purposes. Excess capacity costs are excluded from factory overhead and from product costs. Generally this cost is considered a period cost.

NONMANUFACTURING

There are a great many flexible budget applications other than those used in manufacturing and production departments. First, there are the service departments which provide the needed services in the company such as the maintenance department that repairs the equipment in a manufacturing plant. Second, there are the marketing and administrative functions in manufacturing and nonmanufacturing companies. Third, there are the high-volume repetitive operations in all businesses (such as billing operations) and many types of operations in insurance companies, banks, finance companies, and others which handle a large volume of customer paperwork.

Although flexible budgeting has not been as well publicized in these areas as in the production sphere, there has been a steady growth and acceptability of the concept of work measurement in evaluating performance in these areas.

Service Departments

The maintenance department is a good example of a service department in a manufacturing plant. This department has to keep the production machines functioning and may be set up to service the equipment merely on a critical-need basis. The department may also have a program of preventive mainte-nance which can anticipate equipment breakdowns. The plant will have make-ready fixed costs (such as supervision, rent, and tools) and variable unit costs (for mechanics' wages, factory supplies, etc.) which will be used in the flexible budget for the maintenance department. Table 14-7 (page 512) is an example of a flexible budget for a maintenance department.

TABLE 14-7
MAINTENANCE DEPARTMENT
FLEXIBLE BUDGET
PER MONTH

Maintenance hours	3,000	4,000	5,000	5,500
Percentage of plant capacity	60%	80%	100%	110%
Supervision	$ 1,900	$ 2,200	$ 2,500	$ 2,650
Craftspeople	21,000	28,000	35,000	38,500
Supplies	9,000	12,000	15,000	16,500
Tools	2,100	2,800	3,500	3,850
Depreciation	3,000	3,000	3,000	3,000
Rent	1,000	1,000	1,000	1,000
Total expenses	$38,000	$49,000	$60,000	$65,500
Summary:				
Fixed expenses*	$ 5,000	$ 5,000	$ 5,000	$ 5,000
Variable expenses	33,000	44,000	55,000	60,500
	$38,000	$49,000	$60,000	$65,500
Variable rate per maintenance hour	$11.00	$11.00	$11.00	$11.00

* Assume the fixed expenses are $1,000 of supervision, $3,000 of depreciation, and $1,000 of rent.

Marketing Departments

There are many published materials and many different types of time studies relating to marketing or distribution costs. These have ranged from cost standards developed for the cost of a salesperson's call to cost standards for packing a shipping container. For our purposes, however, we are considering controls for the whole marketing department. The flexible budget is based upon the relevant range of net sales.

One type of such a flexible budget is shown in Table 14-8.

Administrative Department

Even though most of the administrative expenses are fixed, it is still necessary for top management to know these costs at varying sales levels as well as they know the flexible costs in the other business functions discussed. As shown in Table 14-9 (page 514), there is a greater rise in costs between the different levels at the upper range. Since the chief executive has the ultimate responsibility for results, many companies have some form of incentive plan or bonus for keeping sales above a given level. Sales level is a very important factor where significant fixed costs are involved.

OTHER OPERATIONS

Practically every business has high-volume repetitive operations. These include not only bookkeeping and accounting functions but also customer billing operations, selling activities, factory packing, office mailing, and various other functions. The standard used for these operations may be engineered (that is, time-studied) or may be a quota per hour or per day based upon experience.

TABLE 14-8
MARKETING DEPARTMENT
FLEXIBLE BUDGET
PER MONTH

NET SALES	% OF NET SALES	$1,600,000	$1,800,000	$2,000,000	$2,200,000
Marketing costs:					
Sales salaries	6.0%	$ 96,000	$108,000	$120,000	$132,000
Advertising	2.0%	32,000	36,000	40,000	44,000
Selling expenses	1.5%	24,000	27,000	30,000	33,000
Other expenses	.5%	8,000	9,000	10,000	11,000
Depreciation	Fixed	25,000	25,000	25,000	25,000
Total monthly costs		$185,000	$205,000	$225,000	$245,000
% of sales		11.6%	11.4%	11.3%	11.1%

The unit of measure varies from operation to operation and may be product units, pounds, tons, or other applicable units, for example:

WORK	UNITS OF MEASURE
Bookkeeping:	
Entering receipts	Lines per hour
Preparing vouchers	Vouchers per hour
Drawing checks	Lines per hour
Sales:	
Billing	Lines per hour
Salespeople's calls	Calls per day
Factory:	
Packing cartons	Pieces per hour
Mailing	Pieces per hour

COMPUTER PROCESSING

Flexible budgeting requires a great many computations and analyses in determining the variable and fixed costs in each department. Performing these computations manually or by a small calculator is a time-consuming and tedious job. A considerable amount of work is also required on a day-by-day or week-by-week basis when revisions are needed because of price changes, processing changes, new products, or other changes. When necessary, the standards should be updated. Computers have the ability to make high-speed computations and are therefore a valuable tool in the preparation and updating of flexible budgets.

STEP CHARTS

Since the flexible budget requires computations for various levels of production, the factory overhead amounts are adjusted along with the pertinent materials or labor costs. Some companies use step charts in budgeting factory overhead costs. The step chart is a convenient device for showing, in minimum space,

TABLE 14-9
ADMINISTRATIVE DEPARTMENT
FLEXIBLE BUDGET
PER MONTH

NET SALES	% OF NET SALES	$1,600,000	$1,800,000	$2,000,000	$2,200,000
Administrative costs:					
Executive salaries	Fixed	$ 40,000	$ 40,000	$ 50,000*	$ 65,000*
Depreciation	Fixed	10,000	10,000	10,000	10,000
Taxes	Fixed	8,000	8,000	8,000	8,000
Insurance	Fixed	5,000	5,000	5,000	5,000
General expenses	4%	64,000	72,000	80,000	88,000
Total administrative costs		$127,000	$135,000	$153,000	$176,000
% of sales		7.9%	7.5%	7.7%	8.0%

* Includes incentive for keeping sales above a given level.

the departmental allowance for nonproduction personnel. It shows the departmental allowance for the relevant range of production and can be used for service departments as well as production departments.

CHAPTER REVIEW

An important advantage of the flexible budget is that it can be made applicable to any volume of activity. Thus it is free of the main fault of a static budget, which usually is not suitable for comparison with actual costs related to significantly different volume levels. Flexible budgets are established for a relevant range, or reasonable range of activity, and the behavior of each cost is carefully studied at each volume level. Thus the budget allowance shows how much cost should be incurred for any volume level, which may be expressed in product units or standard direct labor hours.

The standard unit cost used for product costing is not suitable entirely for flexible budgeting, since it is based generally on a normal level of activity. Flexible budgeting is more suitable for performance reporting, decision making, and management control.

GLOSSARY

Budget Allowance—the dollar amount based on the variable rate plus the fixed dollar amount for any given level in the relevant range.

Controllable Cost—a cost for which the departmental supervisor is able to exert influence over the amount spent.

Excess Capacity—the superfluous amount of productive capacity in the company or the imbalance of machinery or equipment within departments.

Favorable Variance—a variance for which the actual cost is less than the budgeted or standard cost.

Fixed Budget—a budget based on a single volume level, primarily for planning or product costing rather than for cost control.

Flexible Budget—a method of budgeting in which the budget allowance varies according to the attained volume level.

Idle Capacity—temporarily unused production or distribution facilities. An example of a cause is the lack of sales orders.

Noncontrollable Cost—costs assigned to a department or cost center that are not incurred or controlled by the department head. Examples are service department costs, or others controlled at higher management levels.

Service Department—a department that is not engaged in production but renders a special service to other departments. Examples are receiving, maintenance, and accounting.

Volume—the general term for expressing different levels of business activity. Examples are sales volume, production volume, and shipping volume.

Volume Base—the element used in measuring business activity. Examples are units of products manufactured or sold, direct labor hours worked, or machine hours used.

SUMMARY PROBLEMS

PROBLEM 1

Comparison of Static and Flexible Budgets

The M.A.U.R. Corporation uses a static budget for its variable overhead. The 19X0 planned level of capacity for Department L is 30,000 units.

DEPARTMENT L

	ACTUAL	19X0 STATIC BUDGET
Units produced	27,000	30,000
Variable overhead:		
Indirect materials.....................	$25,000	$24,900
Indirect labor	15,000	15,300
Storage costs	9,100	9,000
Maintenance of machinery	11,200	11,100
Total	$60,300	$60,300

REQUIRED:

a Prepare a performance report comparing the 19X0 static budget with the actual results for Department L. Include variances, and indicate whether they are favorable or unfavorable.

b Develop a flexible budget for 19X0. Use the following levels of production: 24,000, 27,000, 30,000, 33,000, 36,000.

c Prepare a performance report to compare the flexible budget for 19X0 with the actual results. Include variances, and indicate whether they are favorable or unfavorable.

PROBLEM 2

Fixed, Variable, and Semivariable Overhead Expenses

FACTORY OVERHEAD

DESCRIPTION	VARIABLE COST PER DIRECT LABOR HOUR	FIXED AMOUNT
Variable overhead:		
Supplies	$1.50	
Indirect labor	.70	
Receiving costs	.54	
Fixed overhead:		
Depreciation (straight-line)		$ 5,500
Property insurance		2,000
Real estate taxes		450
Semivariable overhead:		
Supervisors' salaries.........................	2.60	9,600
Factory employees' insurance	.46	1,700
Heat, light, and power	.70	750
Total	$6.50	$20,000

Relevant range: 10,000 to 60,000 direct labor hours

REQUIRED:

Using the budget allowance formula, prepare a graph showing variable and fixed elements of total factory overhead expense. Indicate the relevant range on your graph.

PROBLEM 3

Spending and Efficiency Variance

Jeff Palermo, Inc., manufactures tennis balls to sell to several sporting goods stores located in New Jersey. The following information was used by Jeff in order to determine spending and efficiency variances for variable overhead:

Standard machine hours: 15,000
Actual machine hours: 18,000

VARIABLE FACTORY OVERHEAD	ACTUAL COSTS	BUDGET PER STANDARD MACHINE HOUR
Indirect materials	$19,500	$1.10
Indirect labor	17,950	.95
Supplies	4,000	.30
Lubricants	4,750	.25
Repairs	6,700	.35
Miscellaneous	1,200	.10
	$54,100	$3.05

REQUIRED:

Prepare a schedule showing spending and efficiency variances. Indicate whether the variances are favorable or unfavorable.

SOLUTIONS TO SUMMARY PROBLEMS

PROBLEM 1

a Performance Report:

DEPARTMENT L	ACTUAL	19X0 STATIC BUDGET	VARIANCE*
Units produced	27,000	30,000	3,000 U
Variable overhead:			
Indirect materials	$25,000	$24,900	$100 U
Indirect labor	15,000	15,300	300 F
Storage costs	9,100	9,000	100 U
Maintenance of machinery	11,200	11,100	100 U
Total	$60,300	$60,300	0

* U = unfavorable, F = favorable.

b Flexible Budget for 19X0:

DEPARTMENT L VARIABLE OVERHEAD	BUDGET FORMULA* PER UNIT	UNITS PRODUCED				
		24,000	27,000	30,000	33,000	36,000
Indirect materials	$ .83	$19,920	$22,410	$24,900	$27,390	$29,880
Indirect labor	.51	12,240	13,770	15,300	16,830	18,360
Storage cost	.30	7,200	8,100	9,000	9,900	10,800
Maintenance	.37	8,880	9,990	11,100	12,210	13,320
Total	$2.01	$48,240	$54,270	$60,300	$66,330	$72,360

$$* \quad \frac{\text{Amount of overhead at static budget}}{\text{Planned level of overhead at static budget}} \text{, e.g., } \frac{\$24,900}{30,000} = \$.83$$

c Performance Report:

DEPARTMENT L	ACTUAL	FLEXIBLE BUDGET FOR 19X0	VARIANCE*
Flexible budget units: 27,000			
Variable overhead:			
Indirect materials	$25,000	$22,410	$2,590 U
Indirect labor	15,000	13,770	1,230 U
Storage costs	9,100	8,100	1,000 U
Maintenance	11,200	9,990	1,210 U
Total	$60,300	$54,270	$6,030 U

* U = unfavorable, F = favorable.

PROBLEM 2

Budget allowance formula: Let x = direct labor hours and y = total overhead cost (budget allowance).

$$y = \$6.50\,x + \$20,000$$

Graphic Solution of Summary Problem 2

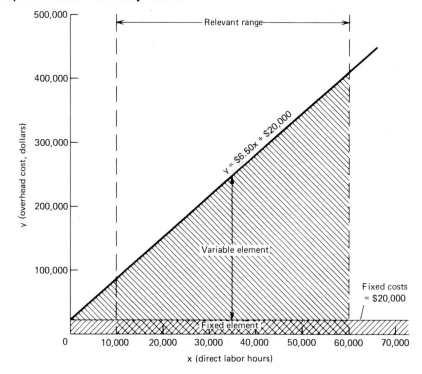

PROBLEM 3

VARIABLE OVERHEAD	ACTUAL COSTS (AQ × AR)	BUDGET BASED UPON 18,000 ACTUAL HOURS (AQ × SR)	BUDGET BASED UPON 15,000 STANDARD HOURS (SQ × SR)	(1) TOTAL VARIANCE*	(2) SPENDING VARIANCE*	(3) EFFICIENCY VARIANCE*
Indirect materials	$19,500	$19,800	$16,500	$3,000 U	$ 300 F	$3,300 U
Indirect labor	17,950	17,100	14,250	3,700 U	850 U	2,850 U
Supplies	4,000	5,400	4,500	500 F	1,400 F	900 U
Lubricants	4,750	4,500	3,750	1,000 U	250 U	750 U
Repairs	6,700	6,300	5,250	1,450 U	400 U	1,050 U
Miscellaneous	1,200	1,800	1,500	300 F	600 F	300 U
Total	$54,100	$54,900	$45,750	$8,350 U	$ 800 F	$9,150 U

*U = unfavorable, F = favorable.

(1) Total variance = actual costs − budget based upon standard hours

(2) Spending variance = actual costs − budget based upon actual hours
   = (AQ × AR) − (AQ × SR)
   = AQ × (AR − SR) = actual quantity of hours × (actual rate − standard rate)

(3) Overhead efficiency variance = budget based upon actual hours − budget based upon standard hours
   = (AQ × SR) − (SQ × SR)
   = (AQ − SQ) × SR = (actual quantity of hours − standard quantity of hours) × standard rate

QUESTIONS

1 When is it appropriate to use a fixed budget? What is the disadvantage of using a fixed budget?
2 What is the advantage of flexible budgeting? In what circumstances can a flexible budget be used?
3 Define a flexible budget and how it is developed.
4 How is factory overhead treated differently from direct materials in flexible budgeting?
5 How is the basis of measurement chosen for a department? Name the bases most commonly used by departments.
6 What is the budget allowance formula used in the flexible budgeting of factory overhead? Can this budget be used for selling expenses, administrative expenses, and other manufacturing costs? Explain your answer.
7 Describe a relevant range table and how it is used with flexible budgets. Explain why total unit cost drops as the amount of units increases.
8 Discuss how a company should present controllable costs and noncontrollable costs in a performance report.
9 Explain the compensatory difference which comprises the total variance between actual variable costs and standard variable costs. How are these compensatory differences determined?
10 Define theoretical capacity, idle capacity, and excess capacity. How are these capacities shown on the income statement?
11 Describe a maintenance department and its functions in a manufacturing plant. How is a budget for the maintenance department usually developed?
12 Why are the costs very high for the departments that operate at or above theoretical capacity? Why would the departments want to operate at these capacities?
13 Discuss the reasons why computer processing is a useful tool for budgeting purposes. Explain the work that would be done manually if the company had no access to computers.

EXERCISES

EXERCISE 1

Performance Reports for Static and Flexible Budgets

The Exfibble Corporation developed a flexible budget for its one product called reflex. If the company could produce 18,000 units, the manufacturing costs would be budgeted for:

Direct labor	$22,140
Direct materials	21,420
Factory overhead:	
Indirect labor	13,680
Indirect materials	10,080
Supervision	1,000
Rent	450
Depreciation	680
Total manufacturing costs	$69,450

Exfibble planned on producing 16,000 reflexes but produced only 15,000. The actual costs were

Direct labor	$18,000
Direct materials	17,700
Factory overhead:	
Indirect labor	11,400
Indirect materials	8,700
Supervision	1,000
Rent	450
Depreciation	680
Total manufacturing costs	$57,930

The fixed noncontrollable costs are supervision, rent, and depreciation.

REQUIRED:

a   Prepare a performance report comparing the static budget with actual results. Include variances, and indicate whether the variances are favorable or unfavorable.

b   Prepare a performance report comparing the flexible budget with actual results. Include variances, and indicate whether the variances are favorable or unfavorable.

EXERCISE 2

Graphs of Factory Overhead

BUDGET—LIST OF EXPENSES

DESCRIPTION	AMOUNT	FIXED PERCENTAGE
Sales salaries	$43,290	
Craftspeople, service department		
(manufacturing overhead)	13,400	100
Factory tools expense	8,750	40
Factory equipment depreciation	4,250	100
Heat, light, and power—factory	10,000	65
Factory supervision	10,845	100
Direct labor	33,250	

DESCRIPTION	AMOUNT	FIXED PERCENTAGE
Indirect materials	$10,500	
Advertising	28,860	
Repairs on factory machines	875	20
Factory rent	1,330	100
Sales commissions	7,215	
Office equipment depreciation	6,000	100
Indirect labor	525	
Office supplies	1,443	
Direct materials	28,000	
Insurance expense—administrative	4,810	40
Miscellaneous office expense	5,772	75
Other marketing expense........................	555	35
Factory supplies	175	
Rent expenses—marketing	2,100	100
Idle capacity	700	

The budget for administrative and marketing expenses was based upon $360,750 net sales. The budget for manufacturing expenses was based upon 35,000 units of production.

REQUIRED:

Prepare a graph showing variable and fixed elements of total factory overhead expense. Include the relevant range of 15,000 to 55,000 on your graph.

EXERCISE 3

Budget Allowance Formulas

Use the data given in Exercise 2 to solve this problem.

REQUIRED:

Determine the budget allowance formulas for each of the following:
  a Administrative expenses   c Manufacturing expenses
  b Marketing expenses

EXERCISE 4

Flexible Budget

Art Lorraine and Sons, Inc., have developed the following budget for one of its products, the Suzie.

	FIXED	VARIABLE COST PER MACHINE HOUR
Direct labor	—	$4.55
Indirect labor..................	—	1.65
Direct materials	—	5.60
Indirect materials	—	2.05

	FIXED	VARIABLE COST PER MACHINE HOUR
Rent	$ 4,500	
Depreciation	$10,000	
Utilities	1,755	$ .70
Maintenance	5,680	.25
Miscellaneous	430	.05

Supervision costs for the product are

MACHINE HOURS	COSTS
0–9,999	$1,000
10,000–29,999	2,200
30,000–59,999	4,500
60,000 and above	6,000

Overtime costs for the product are

MACHINE HOURS	COSTS
20,000–49,999	$4,000
50,000 and above	9,000

REQUIRED:

Develop a flexible budget for the following machine hours: 5,000, 10,000, 20,000, 40,000, and 60,000. Include the total unit cost for factory overhead.

EXERCISE 5

Flexible Budget with Capacity Levels

The Trish June Company manufactures footballs that it sells to sporting goods stores throughout Ryan County. Using 85% capacity, the Trish June Company budgeted the following costs:

Fixed expenses:	
Heat, light, and power	$ 36,000
Supervision	15,000
Indirect labor	21,000
Factory rent....................................	10,000
Equipment depreciation	66,000
Variable expenses (based upon footballs produced):	
Direct labor	196,350
Indirect materials	157,080
Direct materials	207,570
Repairs	48,620
Indirect labor	140,250
Heat, light, and power	90,695
Supervision	34,595

The Trish June Company maintains a maximum capacity of 110,000 footballs.

REQUIRED:

Determine total costs and total unit costs for each of the following capacity levels: 80, 90, and 100%. Also prepare a flexible budget.

EXERCISE 6

Flexible Budget for Service Departments

The Nofix Corp. has one service department, the maintenance department, which services all other production departments in the building. The budgeted costs for this department were

	VARIABLE	FIXED
Craftspeople	$27,060	
Supervision	5,500	$15,760
Supplies	3,300	
Tools	1,452	2,000
Depreciation	—	7,780
Rent	—	3,600
Total	$37,312	$29,140

The above costs were based upon 22,000 direct labor hours. The fixed expenses were allocated to the other departments in the ratio of 4:3:2:1 for Departments A, B, C, D, respectively. The variable expenses were allocated using the total variable rate per direct labor hour. During the year, the actual direct labor hours for the departments were

A	4,375
B	3,500
C	5,725
D	6,400

REQUIRED:

a Prepare a budget (at actual direct labor hours) for the maintenance department.

b Determine how much overhead will be applied to Departments A, B, C, and D.

EXERCISE 7

Flexible Budget for Marketing and Administrative Expenses

The Artsfoh Corp. has decided to set up a flexible budget for its marketing department and its administrative department. The static budget is as follows:

525

MARKETING DEPARTMENT		ADMINISTRATIVE DEPARTMENT	
Fixed:		Fixed:	
Depreciation	$ 4,556	Executive salaries	$15,750
Rent	2,000	Depreciation	2,100
Insurance	1,044	Rent	1,500
Miscellaneous	500	Insurance	500
Variable:		Miscellaneous	150
Insurance	1,250	Variable:	
Sales salaries	50,000	Office salaries	37,500
Advertising	12,500	Insurance	1,250
Miscellaneous	250	Miscellaneous	500
Total	$72,100	Total	$59,250

Marketing and administrative expenses are based on budgeted sales of 250,000 units.

REQUIRED:

Set up a flexible budget for 150,000, 200,000, 250,000, and 300,000 units sold. Include total unit costs for both marketing and administrative expenses.

EXERCISE 8

Departmental Budgets at Different Capacity Levels

DESCRIPTION	DEPARTMENT A	DEPARTMENT B	DEPARTMENT C	TOTAL
Capacity	100%	100%	100%	
Units produced	20,000	15,000	18,000	53,000
Direct labor hours	19,000	16,000	18,000	53,000
Machine hours	11,000	18,000	24,000	53,000
Factory overhead:				
Storage costs	$ 400	$ 1,200	$ 1,100	$ 2,700
Indirect materials	4,400	5,280	6,000	15,680
Indirect labor	3,200	6,000	2,640	11,840
Maintenance	1,000	1,200	1,400	3,600
Repairs	1,000	900	750	2,650
Supplies	200	400	720	1,320
Depreciation	1,550	2,200	1,455	5,205
Rent	400	650	375	1,425
Supervision	8,900	7,755	8,100	24,755
Utilities	1,600	2,000	600	4,200
Total	$22,650	$27,585	$23,140	$73,375

Depreciation, rent, and supervision are fixed expenses. Storage costs and repairs are 40% fixed, while maintenance and utilities are 55% fixed.

Department A uses units produced as a base for calculating its overhead. Department B uses direct labor hours as a base for its overhead, and Department C uses machine hours as the base.

REQUIRED:

Prepare the same chart as the one on page 525 for a capacity of 90%.

EXERCISE 9

Standard Costing

The following information was collected by analysts for the Dono Co.:

	BUDGET PER STANDARD DIRECT LABOR HOUR	ACTUAL COSTS
Direct labor	$1.55	$37,200
Direct materials	1.40	32,400
Controllable overhead costs:		
Indirect materials	.90	21,360
Indirect labor	.75	18,240
Supplies	.20	4,800
Lubricants....................	.16	4,800
Maintenance	.14	3,120
Repairs	.21	4,800
Other	.09	2,160

Normal capacity: 25,750 direct labor hours
Standard direct labor hours: 25,000
Actual direct labor hours: 24,000

REQUIRED:

Prepare a schedule showing efficiency and spending variances. Indicate whether the variances are favorable or unfavorable.

PROBLEMS

PROBLEM 1

Flexible Budget for Factory Overhead Costs

Carol and Brian are the production managers at Mariani, Ltd. Lately they have been disagreeing about the quantity of components to produce. The current budget of production is for 75,000 components, and the overhead costs associated with this budget are

Factory rent (fixed)	$ 1,500
Factory equipment depreciation (fixed)	2,750
Supervision (80% fixed)	37,500
Heat, light, and power (60% fixed)	9,375
Indirect materials (variable)	112,500
Indirect labor (variable)	75,000
Supplies (variable)	750
Repairs (50% fixed)	750
Miscellaneous overhead expenses (75% fixed)	6,000

REQUIRED:

a Develop a relevant range table for the following amounts: 50,000, 60,000, 70,000, 80,000, and 90,000. Include a complete unit cost analysis for total variable costs, total fixed costs, and total costs.

b Determine the budget allowance formula for total factory overhead.

PROBLEM 2

Developing Graphs

O. Sewtlick Co. manufactures hair tonic for men who prefer their hair to have the "wet look." The production manager wants to find out the behavior of variable and fixed costs. You are asked to develop graphs for variable and fixed costs based on the following data:

FACTORY OVERHEAD	DEPARTMENT A	DEPARTMENT B	DEPARTMENT C
Indirect labor	$1,550	$2,000	$1,500
Indirect materials	2,700	3,150	2,500
Depreciation	1,050	2,000	1,000
Power and electricity	475	555	470
Other utilities	125	50	25
Maintenance	900	1,100	950
Taxes	40	55	30
Building occupancy	850	900	800
Supervision	1,175	2,450	1,775
Factory supplies	600	750	450
General expenses	150	200	250

The variable expenses above are based upon 5,000 direct labor hours. The fixed and semivariable expenses are

DESCRIPTION	% FIXED
Depreciation	100
Power and electricity	65
Other utilities	70
Maintenance	40
Taxes	100
Building occupancy	100
Supervision	85
General expenses	50

The relevant range of activity is 2,000 to 8,000 direct labor hours.

REQUIRED:

Develop graphs for the following overhead expenses:
- **a** 100 percent variable overhead expenses
- **b** 100 percent fixed overhead expenses
- **c** Semivariable overhead expenses
- **d** Total overhead expenses

In all the graphs show the relevant range. In (**c**) and (**d**) show variable and fixed elements.

PROBLEM 3

Comparison of Static and Flexible Budgets

NEVER CHANGING, INC.
STATIC BUDGET
FOR YEAR ENDED DECEMBER 31, 19XX

Selling and administrative expenses:	
Sales salaries (100% variable)	$ 82,500
Advertising (100% variable)	11,000
Sales expenses (80% variable)	6,875
Depreciation (0% variable)	2,300
Executive salaries (0% variable)	40,000
Taxes (0% variable)	54,100
Insurance (0% variable)	4,000
General expenses (40% variable)	20,625
Total selling and administrative expenses	$221,400
Manufacturing expenses:	
Direct labor (100% variable)	$ 45,000
Direct materials (100% variable)	49,500
Factory overhead:	
Indirect labor (100% variable)	4,500
Indirect materials (100% variable)	900
Supervision (0% variable)	13,500
Rent (0% variable)	1,000
Maintenance (60% variable)	7,500
Utilities (20% variable)	11,250
Total manufacturing expenses	$133,150
Total expenses	$354,550

Selling and administrative expenses are based upon $550,000 sales dollars, and manufacturing expenses are based upon direct labor dollars.

NEVER CHANGING, INC.
ACTUAL RESULTS—$500,000 SALES DOLLARS
FOR YEAR ENDED DECEMBER 31, 19XX

Sales salaries	$ 75,000
Advertising	15,000
Sales expenses	6,000
Depreciation	2,300
Executive salaries	41,000
Taxes...........................	54,000
Insurance	4,000
General expenses	21,000
Direct labor	50,000
Direct materials	49,500
Indirect labor	5,100
Indirect materials	1,000
Supervision	13,500
Rent............................	1,000
Maintenance	8,600
Utilities	11,750
Total expenses	$358,750

REQUIRED:

a Prepare a performance report comparing actual costs with the static budget. Include variances, and indicate whether they are favorable or unfavorable. (Assume Never Changing, Inc., does not distinguish between controllable and noncontrollable costs.)

b Prepare a budget at actual cost, using the information obtained from the static budget.

PROBLEM 4

Controllable and Noncontrollable Costs

Secretaries, Unlimited, prepare tests to sell to colleges throughout the United States. Eva, Nan, Silvia, and Rejeanne have been asked to develop a flexible budget for the company's overhead. The company usually operates at 120% capacity to produce 60,000 tests. Eva expects capacity to drop to 80% in the near future because of summer vacation.

The following data pertains only to budgeted overhead costs at 80% capacity:

Total budgeted factory overhead: $120,000
Ratio of controllable costs to noncontrollable costs: 7:5

Controllable costs are based upon units of production.

BREAKDOWN—80% CAPACITY

VARIABLE CONTROLLABLE COSTS	%	FIXED NONCONTROLLABLE COSTS	%
Materials handling	45	Rent expense	15
Supplies	30	Maintenance	20
Depreciation	10	Insurance	5
Idle time	2	Taxes	3
Clerical expenses	5	Supervision	55
Other indirect labor	8	Other expenses	2
Total percentage of controllable costs........................	100%	Total percentage of noncontrollable costs	100%

REQUIRED:

Prepare a flexible budget using capacity levels: 80, 90, 100, 110, and 120%. Include for each capacity level the factory overhead rate per unit of production.

PROBLEM 5

Flexible Budget for Yacht Expenses

Nathan Slavin has decided to develop a flexible budget in order to control his yacht expenses. The following budget was established for 20,000 miles operated for the year 19X0:

	FIXED EXPENSES	VARIABLE EXPENSES
Gasoline		$ 5,600
Oil		2,400
Other lubricating expenses	$1,100	1,300
Repairs	950	1,450
Dock expenses	2,400	
Registration costs	500	
Tax expenses..	275	
Insurance expenses	1,200	
Depreciation (motor and other equipment)	900	
Depreciation (yacht)		2,600
Miscellaneous expenses................................	150	300
Total	$7,475	$13,650

Variable expenses are based upon miles operated for the year 19X0:

During 19X0, Nathan Slavin operated his boat 22,000 miles and incurred the following expenses:

	FIXED EXPENSES	VARIABLE EXPENSES
Gasoline		$ 6,160
Oil		2,420
Other lubricating expenses	$1,100	1,320
Repairs	900	1,760
Dock expenses	2,450	
Registration costs	500	
Tax expenses	280	
Insurance expenses	1,200	
Depreciation (motor and other equipment)	900	
Depreciation (yacht)		2,860
Miscellaneous expenses	175	220
Total	$7,505	$14,740

REQUIRED:

a Develop a flexible budget for the relevant range of 16,000, 18,000, 20,000, and 22,000 miles.

b Determine the budget allowance formula for Nathan Slavin's expenses.

c Prepare a performance report comparing actual results with the flexible budget developed for 19X0. Include variances in your report, and indicate whether they are favorable or unfavorable. Assume *all* costs are controllable by Nathan Slavin.

PROBLEM 6

Flexible Budgets for Departments

Erentsen Army and Navy Supplies, Inc., has three departments: two production departments and one service department.

BUDGET FOR THE MONTH OF APRIL

	PRODUCTION DEPARTMENTS*		SERVICE DEPARTMENT
	1	2	REPAIR SHOP
Machine hours	1,800	1,700	
Direct labor hours	3,500	2,500	
Percentage of plant capacity	100%	100%	100%
Manufacturing costs:			
Direct labor	$ 9,275	$ 6,000	
Direct materials	7,350	4,975	
Factory overhead:			
Craftspeople	6,650	5,025	$ 6,650
Supervision	4,750	3,000	6,125
Supplies	2,625	1,650	2,975
Depreciation (straight-line)	2,050	1,990	850
Rent expense	1,000	875	900
Miscellaneous	875	825	700
Total manufacturing costs	$34,575	$24,340	$18,200

* Production department costs do not include the service department costs.

ACTUAL DATA FOR THE MONTH OF APRIL

| | PRODUCTION DEPARTMENTS* | | SERVICE DEPARTMENT |
	1	2	REPAIR SHOP
Machine hours	1,500	1,300	
Direct labor hours	3,150	1,750	
Manufacturing costs:			
Direct labor	$ 8,190	$ 4,200	
Direct materials	6,930	3,325	
Factory overhead:			
Craftspeople	5,985	3,675	$ 5,320
Supervision	4,700	3,000	4,760
Supplies	2,331	1,050	2,408
Depreciation (straight-line)	2,000	1,900	850
Rent expense	1,000	875	900
Miscellaneous	945	525	560
Total manufacturing costs	$32,081	$18,550	$14,798

* Production department costs do not include service department costs.

Fixed expenses are supervision, depreciation, and rent expense. Variable expenses in the production departments are based on direct labor hours. Variable expenses in the service department are based on machine hours.

REQUIRED:

a   Prepare a flexible budget for the service department using the following capacity levels: 80 and 90%. Distinguish between variable and fixed expenses. Determine the rates per machine hour for variable, fixed, and total expenses in the service department. Machine hours at 100% capacity for Department 1 and 2 is 1,800 and 1,700 respectively.

b   Prepare a performance report for each of the three departments. Include variances, and indicate whether they are favorable or unfavorable. All variable costs and supervision are considered controllable costs. (Assume the company does not allocate any service department costs to the production departments until the end of year.)

PROBLEM 7

Performance Reports

The Dynamic Corp. developed the following budget for the company's expenses; 35,000 units were budgeted to be sold, but only 30,000 units were sold:

FEBRUARY

EXPENSES	BUDGET FIXED COSTS	BUDGET VARIABLE COST PER UNIT	ACTUAL COSTS
Salaries of factory supervisors	$10,000	$ .30	$ 20,000
Depreciation of factory equipment	1,200	—	1,200
Salespeople's insurance	750	—	740
Maintenance of factory machinery and tools	1,750	.10	4,500
Factory rent	400	—	400
Rework on factory perishable tools	50	.25	7,500
Advertising expense	—	.90	27,500
Idle capacity	—	.35	9,200
Sales salaries	—	1.20	33,000
Miscellaneous overhead	45	.15	3,100
Depreciation on office equipment	2,000	—	2,000
Direct labor	—	1.15	43,000
Rent—sales office	560	—	560
Excess capacity	—	.10	3,100
Administrative salaries	4,000	—	3,950
Direct materials	—	1.30	48,500
Indirect materials	—	.95	38,500
Other administrative expenses	100	.05	1,700
Total	$20,855	$6.80	$248,450

Management of the Dynamic Corporation feels the budget is inaccurate. The sales and administrative expenses are based upon units sold. The manufacturing expenses are based upon units produced; 40,000 units were budgeted to be produced, but only 38,000 were produced.

REQUIRED:

a Develop a budget allowance formula for:
  1 Sales expenses
  2 Administrative expenses
  3 Direct labor
  4 Direct materials
  5 Factory overhead

b Prepare a separate performance report for each of the following:
  1 Sales expenses
  2 Administrative expenses
  3 Manufacturing expenses
Determine the variances, and indicate whether they are favorable or unfavorable. Assume all costs are controllable.

PROBLEM 8

Flexible Budgets for Income Statement Items

The Rich Sluggo Company planned to sell 310,000 shogs during 19X0 at a price of $5.50 per shog. The variable marketing and administrative expenses were budgeted using percentages of net sales:

Office salaries	3.5%
General administrative expenses	2.0%
Sales salaries	6.2%
Advertising	5.0%
Miscellaneous marketing expenses...........	.5%
Office supplies.............................	.3%

The fixed marketing and administrative expenses were budgeted at

Office equipment depreciation	$18,000
Office supervisor	23,500
Rent expense (60% marketing)	44,000
Insurance expense (75% marketing)	60,000
Depreciation of marketing department equipment	6,000

Total purchases for the year were budgeted for 350,000 shogs at a cost of $1.60 per shog. There was no beginning inventory. The management estimated sales returns and allowances to be 1% of total sales.

REQUIRED:

a   Prepare a budgeted income statement in good form (ignoring taxes) assuming the Rich Sluggo Company sells 310,000 shogs as planned. Determine the percentage of net sales for total marketing costs and the percentage of net sales for total administrative costs.

b   Prepare the same as in (a), except Rich Sluggo Company sells 350,000 shogs.

PROBLEM 9

Standard Costs and Flexible Budgets

Larry Petri, production manager for Worldwide Bank Corp., evaluates the performance of the production departments by comparing budget and standard costs with actual costs. The following data was collected for Production Department 79 during 19XX:

DESCRIPTION	BUDGET DATA		ACTUAL DATA	
FACTORY OVERHEAD	VARIABLE	FIXED	VARIABLE	FIXED
Indirect labor	$15,750		$16,500	
Indirect materials	11,200		12,650	
Supplies	955		1,100	
Maintenance	1,010	$ 400	1,100	$ 400
Repairs	870	600	990	600
Depreciation......................		2,400		2,400
Supervision		9,900		9,900
Rent		755		750
Miscellaneous	215	445	220	450
Total	$30,000	$14,500	$32,560	$14,500

The overhead rate, used to apply the above overhead budget to work-in-process, is computed by using a base equivalent to the 80% capacity level.

Theoretical capacity for Department 79 is 12,500 direct labor hours, and the standard number of direct labor hours allowed is 10,500. Department 79 actually incurred 11,000 direct labor hours during the year.

REQUIRED:

a Develop a flexible budget for the following capacity levels: 80, 90, and 100%. Include unit costs for variable overhead, fixed overhead, and total overhead.

b Assuming fixed costs are not controllable, prepare a performance report comparing the flexible budget with actual results for Department 79. Include variances, and indicate whether they are favorable or unfavorable.

c Since the company maintains a standard cost system, determine the following variance *only* for total overhead costs (not for each overhead item):
  1 Spending variance
  2 Idle capacity variance
  3 Variable efficiency variance
  4 Fixed efficiency variance

CHAPTER FIFTEEN
BUDGETING III— CAPITAL BUDGETING

The preceding budgeting chapters were concerned primarily with planning the short-term income and expenses of an enterprise. In this chapter we will be concerned with the longer-range aspects of investing in property, plant, and equipment, which will affect the well-being of the enterprise for many years.

Capital assets represent the largest single item on the balance sheets of most industrial companies. While the chances of improper conversion are not as great as with cash or inventories, there is a greater danger that company resources may be haphazardly committed and that the financial condition of the company may be endangered in later years.

PLANNING CAPITAL COMMITMENTS

Capital expenditures involve the long-term commitments of a firm's resources. Some examples of capital expenditures are the purchase of a building or equipment, creation of new processes or products, or the revision of existing projects.

In recent years three factors have been important in causing management to feel the need for an objective systematic review of capital expenditures: (1) the magnitude of capital expenditures involved with new products and processes, (2) the continued uptrend of capital asset costs, and (3) the limited amount of capital funds available. It has become important to emphasize the need for a greater study of expenditures *before* rather than *after* commitments are made. Increased recognition is now being given to internal controls, particularly budgetary controls, in managing capital expenditures. Continued inflation has caused capital projects to cost far more than they would have only a few years ago. With lower depreciation charges based on historical cost and resulting higher taxes, many companies have not been able to finance capital asset expansion out of profits. These factors have tended to decrease the amount of capital funds available.

CAPITAL BUDGET PROGRAM

Capital budgeting is the program for determining that capital expenditures represent the most profitable outlay of funds, that they are in accordance with company policy, and that they do not endanger the financial well-being of the company. The principal problem of capital budgeting in most companies is the allocation of available funds to the most worthwhile projects. In a small company the amount of funds to be allotted and the particular projects to be approved are determined fairly quickly by top management. As the company becomes larger and top management is further removed from detailed operations, a need develops for a method of evaluating each project in relation to all others.

In order for a capital budget program to function properly, three basic controls should be implemented in varying degrees in most companies:

1 Authorization policy and procedures
2 Capital budgets
3 Authorization for expenditure

Authorization Policy and Procedures

Before a budget program is put into effect, there should be careful planning for the essential controls of a successful program. One of the first steps is to prepare a general policy relating to capital expenditures. When a company has a number of subsidiaries, manufacturing plants, and divisions, it is fundamental to the success of the capital budget program that a list of authorization levels be established at the outset. For example, the president or principal officer of the parent or subsidiary company may have unlimited authority to approve capital expenditures. At the next level, a plant manager or division head may approve capital expenditures up to $50,000 for any project; and assistant plant managers may approve capital expenditures up to $25,000 per project. At the last level are engineers, analysts, and others specifically delegated by plant managers or division managers to authorize projects at a lower cost. The amount may vary with size of the plant or responsibility of the individual.

Closely related to the authorization policy are the written procedures outlining the program and describing the preparation of the authorization forms.

Capital Budgets

The key to control of all capital expenditures is the capital budget. Generally, it is prepared for a 1-year period; however, many companies use long-range capital budgeting for 5- or 10-year periods to plan ahead for funds needed in the future. In preparing a particular budget for a location, it is generally necessary for the budget to pass through several management levels for approval. For example, in a manufacturing plant there will generally be a budget committee to formulate the local budget. Later, the various individual budgets are reviewed and a consolidated budget is prepared. Since more is generally requested in the total budget than there are funds available, it is necessary to reduce the requests to the total amount available. This usually entails sending the budget back to the source with a request that the total amount be reduced by a certain amount or certain percentage. Remember, the capital budget is not an authorization to commit funds. It is merely an efficient means of consolidating all requests for funds and comparing the consolidated budget against the funds made available by management.

It is understood by the budget committees that some requests will be turned down and others possibly deferred. Therefore, the budget procedures generally provide a means of ranking projects in order of priority. Procedures vary widely among companies. Some may divide projects into two broad categories: those that improve the return on capital, and those that merely maintain the existing return. Where many individual capital budgets are prepared, as in a medium-sized or large company, it is desirable to have specific priority codes established so that projects with low priorities can be quickly deleted or deferred. Often there are categories which supersede cost reduction or quality improvement, for example, a new legal requirement, such as equipment to reduce pollution, or employee safety requirements such as a guard bar or other device to prevent accidents.

The following is an example of the priority codes used by some companies to rank capital projects:

1 Legal and safety needs
2 Employee health and welfare
3 New products or processes
4 Improved products or processes
5 Cost reduction
6 Replacement

Authorization for Expenditure

In most companies the capital budget does not provide automatic approval of capital expenditures. Often there is a period of many months between the time the budget was prepared and the expected commencement of work on a project. During this time business conditions change, so that a significant change in total capital expenditures may be required. Individual projects are reevaluated by preparing an authorization for expenditure (AFE) form when work is to begin. The AFE is actually the request to expend capital funds. However, if a project has been approved in a budget, the subsequent AFE approval is more routine than the request for approval of a job which was not in a budget. Provision must also be made for emergency projects. For example, when a machine that was expected to last for several years suddenly breaks down and must be replaced, funds must be available to remedy the situation.

METHODS OF EVALUATION

Until recently there was little planning and control of capital expenditures. When funds were limited, projects were accepted or rejected based on the degree of urgency. Since inadequate planning was done, most projects were urgent and most decisions were based on subjective judgment. Later it became apparent that it would be preferable to measure the profitability of projects objectively and rank them according to some logical priority basis. Quantitative methods that could be used in evaluating proposed projects were developed. The six principal methods of evaluation are (1) payback, (2) average annual return on investment, (3) internal rate of return, (4) net present value, (5) index of profitability, and (6) discounted payback. Each of these methods will be described, and the advantages and disadvantages of each method indicated.

Payback Method

This method, sometimes called the payout or payoff method, determines the length of time required to recover the initial outlay of a project. It was one of the first methods used when objective procedures began to replace the subjective manner of capital budgeting decision making. Because of its simplicity it is still a widely used evaluation method. Following is an example of the payback method: A company is considering the purchase of a machine, Project L, costing $10,000, with an estimated service life of 10 years. It is expected to return cash savings of $2,500 a year, that is, *cash flow from operations*. Cash flow from operations is equal to net income after taxes plus depreciation (a detailed discussion of how cash flow from operations is computed occurs later in this chapter). The computation of the payback period is as follows:

$$\text{Payback period } (P) = \frac{\text{investment } (I)}{\text{annual cash flow from operations } (C)}$$

$$P = \frac{\$10,000}{\$\ 2,500} = 4 \text{ years}$$

At the same time a competitive machine, Project M, costing $8,000, with a service life of 5 years and the same cash flow, is also considered. What is the payback period for this machine?

$$P = \frac{\$8,000}{\$2,500} = 3.2 \text{ years}$$

Under the payback method, Project M would be favored, since its payback period would be 3.2 years, instead of the 4 years for Project L. However, the useful life of Project M is only 5 years and it would have zero profits at the end of that time, whereas Project L would yield profits for 5 years beyond its payback period. The payback method does not take these factors into consideration. Because total profitability of a project is not considered in the payback method, it should be used only in conjunction with the other methods described later.

If cash flow from operations is not constant each year, the payback period is computed by adding the cash flow from operations each year until the amount invested is reached. The total number of years it takes to reach the amount invested is the payback period. For example, an $18,000 investment is expected to generate the following cash flow from operations:

YEAR	CASH FLOW FROM OPERATIONS
1	$6,000
2	5,000
3	5,000
4	4,000
5	3,000
6	2,000

Payback is 3½ years computed as follows:

YEAR	CASH FLOW FROM OPERATIONS	PAYBACK YEARS
1	$ 6,000	1.0
2	5,000	1.0
3	5,000	1.0
4	2,000 (a)	.5 (b)
	Total $18,000	3.5

(a) $18,000 − $16,000 ($6,000 + $5,000 + $5,000) = $2,000
(b) $2,000 ÷ $4,000 = .5

Advantages of the payback method are: (1) it is simple to compute, (2) it is easily understood, and (3) it is superior to the rule-of-thumb method.

Disadvantages of this method are (1) the time value of money is ignored, and (2) it ignores the cash flow from operations that may be returned beyond the payback period.

Average Annual Return on Investment Method

This method is sometimes referred to as the accounting method because it uses net income after taxes to compute the return. The average annual return-on-investment method provides a measure of profitability that is not provided by the payback method. However, this method, like the payback method, has a serious fault in that it ignores the time value (interest) of money. A number of variations of the method are used, with the principal types using either the initial outlay (the original investment) or the average investment as the denominator. The numerator in *both* variations is net income after taxes (on the accrual basis), which is the same as cash flow from operations less depreciation.

Again we consider Project L, costing $10,000, with an estimated service life of 10 years. The annual cash flow from operations is $2,500. Depreciation on the straight-line basis, assuming no salvage value, is $1,000 ($10,000 ÷ 10 years) per year. The two variations of the method are illustrated below. The first variation uses the *original* investment as the denominator and is computed as follows:

$$\text{Return (R)} = \frac{\text{net income after taxes}}{\text{original investment (I)}}$$

$$R = \frac{\$1,500^*}{\$10,000} = 15\%$$

* $2,500 cash flow from operations − $1,000 depreciation

The higher the resulting percentage the better, because it represents a higher return on the money invested.

The second variation uses the *average* of the undepreciated value of the asset over its service life as the denominator because each year the investment is decreased by $1,000 through depreciation. The average investment may be computed as one-half the original cost (or outlay), which for Project L is equal to $5,000 ($10,000 ÷ 2). The second variation would be computed as follows:

$$\text{Return (R)} = \frac{\text{net income after taxes}}{\text{original investment} \div 2}$$

$$R = \frac{\$1,500}{\$5,000} = 30\%$$

The advantage of the average annual return-on-investment method is that it considers income over the life of the project. Disadvantages of this method are (1) it ignores the time value of money as did the payback method, and (2) it is not applicable if any investment is made after the project begins.

Discounted Cash Flow Methods

Discounted cash flow methods reflect the fact that money has a time value and that a cost (interest) results when money is used. The payback and the average annual return-on-investment methods that were previously discussed did not consider the time value of money, and this was noted as being a major drawback of these methods (see the appendix of this chapter for a review of present-value concepts). The following four discounted cash flow methods will be presented:

1 Internal rate of return
2 Net present value
3 Index of profitability
4 Discounted payback

Internal Rate of Return Method.   The internal rate of return (also known as the time-adjusted rate of return or yield) method computes the yield that is expected to be earned on an investment. The internal rate of return (IRR) for an investment is defined as the discount rate (or interest rate) that will make the present (or discounted) value of the cash flow from operations equal to the initial outlay.

To illustrate the computation of the internal rate of return, assume we are considering Project A, which requires an initial outlay of $13,450 and has an economic life of 4 years. The cash flow from operations is $5,000 per year. Remember, we want to find a discount rate such that when we discount the $5,000 cash flow from operations each year for the next 4 years it will be equal to the initial outlay of $13,450. In this example, we have a special case of a cash flow that is equal each year. As explained in the appendix, this cash flow pattern is called an annuity. To find the present value of an annuity, all that is necessary is to find the annuity factor from Table 15-2 [Present Value (PV) of $1 Received Annually for N Years] in the appendix (page 559), and multiply that annuity factor by the value to be received in 1 year. In our case, we want to find a value from Table 15-2 so that when we multiply $5,000 by this value we obtain $13,450. The value we are looking for, therefore, is 2.690 ($13,450 ÷ $5,000).

If we look at Table 15-2 and limit our examination of the table to 4 years (since this is the number of years of expected cash flow), we find 2.690 under the column representing 18%. This discount or interest rate of 18% is the internal rate of return for Project A. To summarize, since a discount rate of 18% makes the cash flow from operations equal to the initial outlay of $13,450, it is the IRR.

We started the illustration of the IRR with a very simple case. In most real-world problems, however, the cash flow from operations will not follow the pattern of an annuity. In such cases, the computation to determine the IRR will be more time-consuming, although the same principles are followed. To illustrate a case in which the cash flow from operations is different in each year, consider a second investment, Project B, with an initial outlay of $15,408 and an economic life of 4 years. The expected cash flow from operations is $4,000 in each of the first 2 years, $5,000 in the third year, and $8,000 in the fourth year.

The IRR is the discount rate that discounts the cash flow from operations of $4,000, $4,000, $5,000 and $8,000 for years 1 through 4, respectively, so that its present value is equal to $15,408. The present value of an annuity (Table 15-2) cannot be used because this table assumes an equal cash flow each year. Instead, the present value of $1 (Table 15-1 in the appendix, page 558) is used because the present value of the cash flow for each year must be independently computed.

The discount rate that will make the cash flow from operations equal the initial outlay is found by trial and error when cash flows are not equal each year. Let us start with 10%. The present value of the cash flow from operations using a discount rate of 10% is shown below.

YEAR	CASH FLOW FROM OPERATIONS	×	10% DISCOUNT RATE PV OF $1 (Table 15-1)	=	PRESENT VALUE
1	$4,000		.909		$ 3,636
2	4,000		.826		3,304
3	5,000		.751		3,755
4	8,000		.683		5,464
			Total		$16,159

The total present value is $16,159. Since this is not equal to the initial outlay of $15,408, 10% is *not* the IRR. We must try a different discount rate. Should a higher or lower discount rate be used? Remember that the higher the discount rate, the lower the present value. Since the 10% discount rate resulted in a present value greater than the initial outlay, we must use a higher discount rate so that a lower present value is obtained. The present value using a rate of 14% is shown below.

YEAR	CASH FLOW FROM OPERATIONS	×	14% DISCOUNT RATE PV OF $1	=	PRESENT VALUE
1	$4,000		.877		$ 3,508
2	4,000		.769		3,076
3	5,000		.675		3,375
4	8,000		.592		4,736
			Total		$14,695

The present value using a discount rate of 14% is $14,695. This value is less than the initial outlay of $15,408. From our previous computation using a discount rate of 10%, we know that the discount rate we are seeking must be between 10% and 14%. At 12% the present value is exactly equal to the initial outlay as shown below.

YEAR	CASH FLOW FROM OPERATIONS	×	12% DISCOUNT RATE PV OF $1	=	PRESENT VALUE
1	$4,000		.893		$ 3,572
2	4,000		.797		3,188
3	5,000		.712		3,560
4	8,000		.636		5,088
			Total		$15,408

Since the discount rate that makes the cash flow from operations equal the initial outlay is 12%, this rate is the IRR for Project B.

The trial-and-error procedure must be employed to determine the IRR when the cash flow from operations is not the same in each year. There are no short-cut procedures to find the exact rate. Some firms have developed or have access to a computer program that computes the IRR. Some pocket calculators have a built-in feature that will determine the IRR.

When hand calculations are used, we may not find a discount rate that gives us the exact initial outlay. Assume the initial outlay for the second investment project analyzed was $15,315. The 12% discount rate would give a present value of $15,408. There are two ways to determine a more exact IRR. First, an approximation method based on interpolating values from the present value table can be used. The more precise method, however, is to use a more detailed present-value table, which provides present values for discount rates between 12% and 13%. For example, a discount rate of 12.2% would provide a present value for the cash flows from operations in our second example of precisely $15,315.

Once we have computed the IRR for a project, we can then determine whether it is an attractive project. Management has to decide upon a minimum rate of return that a project must earn (or yield) in order to be attractive. For example, if management specified a minimum rate of return of 10%, then both the investment projects previously analyzed (Project A's IRR was 18% and Project B's IRR was 12%) will be attractive since the IRR for each project is greater than 10%. However, if the minimum rate of return is 15%, then Project A would be acceptable (IRR of 18%) while Project B would be unacceptable (IRR of 12%).

The minimum rate of return specified by management is commonly referred to as the *hurdle rate*. This rate is based on the firm's cost of capital. Estimating the firm's cost of capital is an extremely difficult task. In general, one can define the cost of capital as the rate of return required by those who supply capital to the firm. The rates of return required by the different suppliers of capital—debt holders, preferred stockholders, and common stockholders—are determined in the market by the actions of investors competing against one another.

Once it has been determined that a project is attractive, mutually exclusive projects must be compared. Mutually exclusive projects are those that essentially do the same job. For example, suppose a trucking company is considering the construction of a terminal in either Hempstead, Long Island, or an alternative site 5 miles away in Mineola, Long Island. Only one terminal is needed by the trucking firm. The two site proposals for the construction of a terminal represent mutually exclusive projects. As another example, suppose a firm is considering the acquisition of either an IBM computer or a Honeywell computer. These two investment proposals represent mutually exclusive investments.

It is possible to find that all mutually exclusive proposals are attractive, that is, have an IRR greater than the hurdle rate. From the mutually exclusive projects we would select the one with the highest IRR.

Firms also have projects that are independent of each other. For example, the purchase of a new truck and the purchase of a minicomputer by a trucking firm represent independent projects. How are priorities assigned to such projects? Under the IRR criterion, projects are ranked according to their IRR. The higher the IRR, the higher the priority.

The advantage of the internal rate of return is that it takes into consideration the time value of money. It is also easily understood by management. Management frequently discusses projects in terms of yield. There are, however, several disadvantages of this method. First, some might argue that the lengthy computations might make it unattractive. This is a disadvantage we dismiss. Sound capital budgeting practices should not be cast aside simply because the decision maker does not want to go through the necessary computations. Also, as previously indicated, some pocket calculators that currently cost less than $50 provide the internal rate of return. A second disadvantage is that the internal rate of return is affected by the size of the investment. For example, consider a $100 investment that has a 100% IRR and a $100,000 investment that has an 18% IRR for a firm that has specified a 10% hurdle rate. Which investment is more attractive? We shall return to this point later in the chapter. A third disadvantage is that the internal rate of return calculation assumes that the cash flow from operations can be reinvested at the internal rate of return. Thus, for example, if a project is expected to have an IRR of 25%, it is assumed that each time a cash flow from operations is received, the firm will have the opportunity to reinvest the cash flow and earn a 25% return over the life of the investment. A fourth disadvantage is that an investment proposal may not have an internal rate of return or may have multiple rates of return.

Whether a project has none, one, or multiple internal rates of return depends upon the pattern of cash flow from operations. In real-world problems, cash flow patterns can be either conventional or nonconventional. A conventional cash flow pattern starts with an outlay in the first few years followed by cash flow from operations. For example, the following three patterns represent conventional cash flow patterns for three capital investment proposals (C, D, and E) with an expected life of 7 years:

				YEARS				
PROPOSAL	0	1	2	3	4	5	6	7
C	−$50	$10	$ 5	$15	$20	$10	$20	$10
D	− 50	−10	20	18	9	40	60	20
E	− 50	−10	−5	−5	60	90	80	40

The negative figures denote outflows. Year 0 is the initial investment required at the start of each proposal. Proposal C requires only one initial outlay at the beginning of the project. Proposal D requires two outlays of cash and proposal E requires four outlays of cash.

Notice that in the conventional pattern the sign changes from negative to positive only once. When we have a conventional cash flow pattern, there is only one IRR.

A nonconventional cash flow pattern occurs when the sign changes from negative to positive and back to negative at least one time in the future. The following three cash flow patterns are nonconventional cash flow patterns for proposals F, G, and H:

PROPOSAL	YEARS							
	0	1	2	3	4	5	6	7
F	−$50	$10	$25	−$20	$10	$20	$20	$25
G	−50	−10	−10	80	60	100	45	−40
H	−50	−10	40	60	25	−40	120	−10

A nonconventional cash flow pattern can have either no internal rate of return, one internal rate of return, or multiple internal rates of return. (The reason that a nonconventional cash flow pattern can produce such unusual results is beyond the scope of this book.)

Net Present Value Method. The net present value (NPV) method, like the internal rate of return method, takes account of the time value of money. In the IRR method, the computed IRR is compared to the firm's required rate of return to determine whether the project is profitable. Under the NPV method, the cash flow from operations is discounted at the required rate of return. The discounted value of the cash flow from operations is then compared with the initial outlay. If the discounted value of the cash flow exceeds the initial outlay, it means the project investigated is attractive, since it is expected to earn more than the required rate of return. If the initial outlay is greater than the discounted cash flow using the required rate of return, then the project is not profitable.

To illustrate the NPV method, consider Project B analyzed in the previous section. The initial outlay was $15,408, and the cash flow from operations was $4,000, $4,000, $5,000 and $8,000 in years 1 through 4, respectively. Assume that the required rate of return specified by management is 8%. The NPV is computed as follows:

YEAR	CASH FLOW FROM OPERATIONS	×	8% DISCOUNT RATE PV of $1	=	PRESENT VALUE
1	$4,000		.926		$ 3,704
2	4,000		.857		3,428
3	5,000		.794		3,970
4	8,000		.735		5,880
	Discounted value of cash flow				$16,982
	Less: Initial outlay				15,408
	NPV				$ 1,574

The NPV is $1,574. Since this value is positive, the project is profitable.

Although the project is profitable, that does not mean it will be chosen from alternative mutually exclusive projects. The NPV criterion requires that the firm select the project with the highest NPV. Thus, if the above project was one of two mutually exclusive projects, it would be selected if the alternative project had an NPV less than $1,574. Independent projects are ranked based on the magnitude of the NPV. The higher the NPV, the higher the priority assigned to the project.

It should be noted that a project could be attractive under one required rate of return but unprofitable under another. For example, we supposed the above project was analyzed at a time when management specified a required rate of return of 8%. However, assume external conditions have forced management to change its required rate of return to 14%. The discounted value or present value of the cash flow is $14,695 computed as follows:

YEAR	CASH FLOW FROM OPERATIONS	×	14% DISCOUNT RATE PV OF $1	=	PRESENT VALUE
1	$4,000		.877		$ 3,508
2	4,000		.769		3,076
3	5,000		.675		3,375
4	8,000		.592		4,736
	Discounted value of cash flow				$14,695
	Less: Initial outlay				15,408
	NPV				$ − 713

Therefore, the NPV is −$713 and the project is now unprofitable.

Although decision makers are accustomed to talking about yields, they find it more difficult to comprehend the concept of net present value. How does one interpret, for example, an NPV of $1,574? The NPV of $1,574 represents the unrealized profit that the project will generate immediately after the expenditure of $15,408 if the cash flow from operations is realized.

The advantage of the NPV technique is that it is easy to compute given the cash flow from operations and the required rate of return. Unlike the IRR, the NPV can always be calculated, and there is a unique NPV for a given required rate of return.

Sometimes a conflict will arise between the NPV and the IRR techniques for mutually exclusive projects. This conflict arises because the NPV technique assumes the opportunity of reinvestment of the cash flow from operations at the required rate of return, while the IRR method assumes the opportunity of reinvestment at the IRR. Also, the IRR is sensitive to the size of the investment. The way this conflict is resolved will be discussed later in this chapter.

Index of Profitability Method. The index of profitability (IP) method is a variant of the NPV technique. It is also known as the profitability index or the benefit-cost ratio. The latter terminology is common in government agencies.

The IP is computed with the data obtained from the NPV computation. However, instead of subtracting the initial outlay from the discounted value of the cash flow from operations, we compute the ratio of the two values. The numerator is the discounted value of the cash flow from operations and the denominator is the initial outlay. For example, for Project B analyzed in the previous section, the initial outlay was $15,408 and the discounted value of the cash flow from operations, given an 8% required rate of return, was found to be $16,982. The IP is therefore 1.102 ($16,982 ÷ $15,408).

The decision rule for determining whether a project is attractive is simply that the IP must be greater than 1. Notice that this is equivalent to having an NPV greater than zero. The decision rule for selecting from profitable mutually exclusive projects using the IP criterion requires us to select the project with the highest IP. Independent projects are ranked in order of priority from the highest (most desirable) IP to the lowest (least desirable) IP.

The IP, like the IRR, is affected by the size of the investment. As a result, conflicts in selecting from among mutually exclusive projects can arise.

Discounted Payback Method.   The payback method presented earlier can be reworked, taking into consideration the time value of money and the firm's required rate of return, thereby overcoming one of the disadvantages of the undiscounted payback method. The discounted payback method will be illustrated for Project M, which has an estimated cash flow from operations of $1,078 each year, and Project N, which has a different cash flow each year as follows:

Year 1	....	$1,590
Year 2	....	1,800
Year 3	....	1,760
Year 4	....	1,720

Both projects will be discounted at a required rate of return of 10% and call for an initial investment of $5,000.

PROJECT M

YEAR	CASH FLOW FROM OPERATIONS	PRESENT VALUE OF $1 AT 10% (TABLE 15-1)	PRESENT VALUE	DISCOUNTED PAYBACK YEARS
1	$1,078	.909	$ 980	1.0
2	1,078	.826	890	1.0
3	1,078	.751	810	1.0
4	1,078	.683	736	1.0
5	1,078	.621	669	1.0
6	1,078	.564	608	1.0
7	598 (b)	.513	307 (a)	.6 (c)
	Total		$5,000	6.6

(a) $5,000 − $4,693 ($980 + $890 + $810 + $736 + $669 + $608) = $307
(b) $307 ÷ .513 = $598
(c) $598 ÷ $1,078 = .55 or .6

In year 7 only $307 is needed to reach the $5,000 initial investment. The payback period for year 7 is .6 ($598 ÷ $1,078). It would therefore take 6.6 years to recover the initial investment of $5,000 for Project M.

PROJECT N

YEAR	CASH FLOW FROM OPERATIONS	PRESENT VALUE OF $1 AT 10% (TABLE 15-1)	PRESENT VALUE	DISCOUNTED PAYBACK YEARS
1	$1,590	.909	$1,445	1.0
2	1,800	.826	1,487	1.0
3	1,760	.751	1,322	1.0
4	1,092 (b)	.683	746 (a)	.6 (c)
Total			$5,000	3.6

(a) $5,000 − $4,254 ($1,445 + $1,487 + $1,322) = $746
(b) $746 ÷ .683 = $1,092
(c) $1,092 ÷ $1,720 = .63 or .6

In year 4 only $746 is needed to reach the $5,000 initial investment. The payback period for year 4 is .6 ($1,092 ÷ $1,720 full amount for year). It would therefore take 3.6 years to pay back the initial investment of $5,000 for Project N.

The discounted payback is sometimes used in conjunction with the NPV or IRR to determine the relative attractiveness of projects. Keep in mind that if you compute a discounted payback but never get to recover the initial outlay, the project is unprofitable at the required rate of return.

Conflict among NPV, IRR, and IP. Because of the reinvestment assumption and the effect of size on the IRR, a conflict can arise between the NPV and the IRR in selecting among mutually exclusive projects. To illustrate a conflict, consider two mutually exclusive investment projects, X and Y. The NPVs for each project for various required rates of return are shown on Figure 15-1 (page 550).

To construct Figure 15-1 (which depicts the way a conflict can arise between NPV and IRR), label the vertical axis NPV in dollars and the horizontal axis Required Rate of Return (RRR) in percentages. Assume the following:

	PROJECT	
	X	Y
Initial investment	$343,300	$450,625
Cash flow from operations per year (assume equal for 5 years)	100,000	125,000

To plot the graph, we must compute the NPVs for each project for various RRRs. Since the cash flow is even for each year, the present value of $1 received annually for N years (Table 15-2) is used to discount the cash flows as follows:

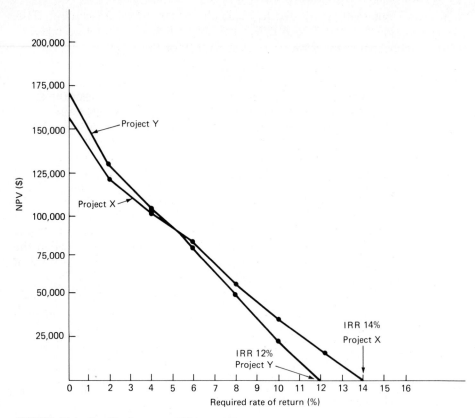

FIGURE 15-1 **Conflict between NPV and IRR**

PROJECT X

IRR %	CASH FLOW	PV OF ORDINARY ANNUITY[1]		INITIAL OUTLAY		NPV
0	($100,000 × 5.000)	–		$343,300	=	$156,700
2	(100,000 × 4.646)	–		343,300	–	121,300
4	(100,000 × 4.452)	–		343,300	=	101,900
6	(100,000 × 4.212)	–		343,300	=	77,900
8	(100,000 × 3.993)	–		343,300	=	56,000
10	(100,000 × 3.791)	–		343,300	=	35,800
12	(100,000 × 3.605)	–		343,300	=	17,200
14	(100,000 × 3.433)	–		343,300	=	0

[1] PV of 0% to 4% not in Table 15-2.

		PROJECT Y		
		PV OF		
	CASH	ORDINARY	INITIAL	
IRR %	FLOW	ANNUITY[1]	OUTLAY	NPV
0	($125,000 × 5.000)	–	$450,625 =	$174,375
2	(125,000 × 4.646)	–	450,625 =	130,125
4	(125,000 × 4.452)	–	450,625 =	105,875
6	(125,000 × 4.212)	–	450,625 =	75,875
8	(125,000 × 3.993)	–	450,625 =	48,500
10	(125,000 × 3.791)	–	450,625 =	23,250
12	(125,000 × 3.605)	–	450,625 =	0

[1] PV of 0% to 4% not in Table 15-2.

Now all the points can be plotted in Figure 15-1. For example, for Project X, when the RRR is 0% the NPV is $156,700, and for Project Y, when the RRR is 0% the NPV is $174,375. At an 8% RRR, Project X has an NPV of $56,000, while Project Y has an NPV of $48,500.

Notice that the NPV decreases as the required rate of return increases. Where is the IRR on Figure 15-1? Recall that the IRR is the discount rate such that the discounted value of the cash flow from operations will be equal to the initial outlay. This is precisely where the NPV is equal to zero, since the NPV is the difference between the discounted value of the cash flow from operations and the initial outlay. Thus, the IRR for each project is where the NPV curve intersects the horizontal axis. For Project X the IRR is 14%, and for Project Y the IRR is 12%.

Let us now look at the decision rules if the required rate of return is 10%. First, the NPV criterion states that the project with the highest NPV should be selected. At a 10% required rate of return, Projects X and Y are profitable since the NPV is positive (that is, above the horizontal axis—see Figure 15-1). Yet at 10% the NPV for Project X is greater than that for Project Y. Hence, Project X is preferred to Project Y using the NPV criterion with a required rate of return of 10%. Both projects have an IRR greater than the required rate of return and are therefore profitable under the IRR criterion. Again, as in the NPV analysis, X is preferred to Y because it has a higher IRR. Thus there is no conflict.

Now let us change one assumption. Assume the required rate of return is 4%. Notice that the change in the required rate of return does not affect the preference based on the IRR criterion, since the IRR is still 14% for Project X and 12% for Project Y. Therefore, Project X is still preferred to Project Y. Using the NPV criterion, both projects are still profitable since they have an NPV greater than zero. However, now the NPV of Project Y is greater than that for Project X. Hence, Project Y is preferred to Project X according to NPV. We now have a conflict. In fact, as can be seen from Figure 15-1, there will only be a conflict if the required rate of return is lower than the point at which the two NPV curves intercept.

552

When a conflict arises, the net present value method should be used if future reinvestment rates are expected to be closer to the required rate of return than to the IRR. A conflict can also arise between the NPV and the IP because of the impact on the size of the investment on the IP. In such cases, the conflict should be resolved by using the NPV.[1]

Replacement Chains

Because the IRR and NPV have different implicit assumptions for the reinvestment of the cash flow from operations, mutually exclusive projects with different lives may result in conflicts. Thus, it is common to set up what is known as replacement chains. For example, assume two mutually exclusive projects have cash flows from operations as shown below:

END OF YEAR	PROJECT 1	PROJECT 2
0	$-4,000	$-4,000
1	2,000	1,000
2	4,500	2,000
3	–	3,000
4	–	2,500

A replacement chain is set up for Project 1 that simply repeats the initial outlay and cash flow from operations, starting at the end of year 2 (in order not to break the investment chain). The replacement chain for Project 1 follows:

END OF YEAR	ORIGINAL CASH FLOW, PROJECT 1	REPLACEMENT CHAIN	PROJECT 1, ASSUMING REPLACEMENT CHAIN
0	$-4,000	–	$-4,000
1	2,000	–	2,000
2	4,500	$-4,000	500
3	–	2,000	2,000
4	–	4,500	4,500

The cash flow from operations at the *end* of the second year represents the inflow of $4,500 less the initial outlay that is assumed *repeated* for analysis purposes at the beginning of the third (or equivalently the end of the second year) of $4,000.

Had Project 2 lasted 3 years instead of 4, a common denominator year would have been established. In this case it would have been 6 years. A replacement chain for both projects would then be constructed and used in the analysis. Once the replacement chain has been developed, the revised cash flows are used as the cash flow for computing IRR and NPV.

[1] For a more detailed discussion see Eugene F. Brigham, *Financial Management: Theory and Practice*, The Dryden Press, 1979, Appendix 11B.

Keep in mind that replacement chains are *only* established for mutually exclusive projects, not independent projects with unequal lives. Moreover, replacement chains are simply a convenience. A more precise analysis would require an investigation of how, for example, the operations of Project 1 would actually be continued in years 3 and 4 after Project 1 was terminated.

Computation of Cash Flow from Operations and Initial Outlay

The cash flow from operations represents the net income after taxes expected to be generated from the project, plus depreciation. Depreciation is added back, since it is not an out-of-pocket cash outlay. For example, suppose that a $5,000 piece of equipment the firm is considering has the following associated revenue and expenses:

YEAR	ADDITIONAL REVENUE	ADDITIONAL EXPENSES	NET INCOME BEFORE DEPRECIATION AND TAXES
1	$5,475	$3,000	$2,475
2	7,000	4,000	3,000
3	8,900	6,000	2,900
4	9,800	7,000	2,800
5	9,100	7,000	2,100

Assume that the firm intends to depreciate the asset on a straight-line basis with no salvage value and that the marginal tax bracket of the firm is 60% (federal plus state). The cash flow from operations is shown below:

	YEARS				
	1	2	3	4	5
Net income before depreciation and taxes	$2,475	$3,000	$2,900	$2,800	$2,100
Less depreciation	1,000	1,000	1,000	1,000	1,000
Income subject to tax	$1,475	$2,000	$1,900	$1,800	$1,100
Less income taxes (60%)	885	1,200	1,140	1,080	660
Net income	$ 590	$ 800	$ 760	$ 720	$ 440
Plus depreciation	1,000	1,000	1,000	1,000	1,000
Cash flow from operations	$1,590	$1,800	$1,760	$1,720	$1,440

If a salvage value is expected at the end of the useful life of an asset, it should be considered in the analysis of cash flow. The salvage value is considered a lump sum payment to be received at the *end* of the investment. A separate computation is necessary to discount to present value the cash flow from the salvage value. For example, assume an investment of $35,000 will result in an equal cash flow of $10,000 for 5 years and that at the end of the project a salvage value of $2,000 is expected to be received. The net present value of the above investment, assuming a required rate of return of 10%, is computed as follows:

Cash flow from operations:
$10,000 × 3.791 (Table 15-2 at 10%) $37,910
Salvage value:
$2,000 × .621 (Table 15-1 at 10%)   1,242
Discounted value of cash flow $39,152
Less: Initial outlay 35,000
NPV .... $ 4,152

It is important that the revenues and expenses be the incremental (additional) revenues and expenses associated with the investment proposal. For example, assume a company manufactures one line of tennis racquets called ADV. The company expects to have sales of 30,000 units per year for the next 4 years. Each unit will sell for $20. The company's engineers have designed an improved tennis racquet that they are contemplating manufacturing. The new racquet will be called SW ("Sure Winner"). The marketing department believes the company will sell 30,000 units of the SW racquet at $30 per unit for the next 4 years. However, of the 30,000 units, 10,000 will represent sales that will be lost from the ADV racquets. That is, the company will reduce its own sales of ADV to the extent of 10,000 units per year. Is the relevant revenue for the SW racquets $900,000 (30,000 times $30 per unit) or is it $700,000 due to the loss of sales of ADV? The incremental revenue of introducing SW is computed as follows:

Manufacture SW:
Revenue from ADV
$20 × 20,000 (30,000 before SW − 10,000 decrease) .... $ 400,000
Revenue from SW
($30 × 30,000) 900,000
Total revenue if SW is manufactured $1,300,000

Don't Manufacture SW:
Revenue from ADV ($20 × 30,000) 600,000
Additional (incremental) revenue .... $ 700,000

Therefore the relevant revenue is the incremental revenue of $700,000, which results from adopting a new product.

A common question is how inflation should be incorporated into the analysis of the cash flow from operations. The additional revenue and expenses should include the impact of inflation. The reason for incorporating changing prices is that the required rate of return embodies the impact of inflation. Recall that the required rate of return will be based on the company's cost of capital. The cost of capital, in turn, is based on the required return demanded by suppliers of capital. Inflationary expectations are incorporated into the return required by suppliers of capital. Hence, failure to incorporate inflation into the cash flow from operations could result in the rejection of projects that would in fact be attractive to the firm.[1]

We have concentrated thus far on the cash flow from operations. It should

[1] See James C. Van Horne, "A Note on Biases in Capital Budgeting Introduced by Inflation," *Journal of Financial and Quantitative Analysis*, January 1971.

be kept in mind that the initial outlay for a project may not always be obvious. For example, if a firm purchases a piece of equipment that qualifies for the investment tax credit, the initial outlay must be reduced by the amount of the credit. Suppose also that the piece of equipment under consideration will be replacing an existing wornout piece of equipment that has a scrap value. Then the cash proceeds that are expected to be received from the sale of the old equipment should be used to reduce the initial outlay. Moreover, the effect on taxes of the sale of the old equipment must be considered.

Sometimes an increase in working capital is required as an outlay for a project. Outlays of working capital should be considered when made, even though they may be recovered at some future time. For example, suppose additional materials of $10,000 are necessary for an investment project, but they are expected to be recouped when the project terminates in five years. In such a case, $10,000 is considered as part of the *initial outlay*, but the recovery is part of the cash inflow from operations at the *end* of the fifth year. It is a common error to believe that the outlay and recovery are simply a wash. Although in terms of undiscounted dollars they are a wash, the time value of money indicates that the two flows are not equal.

Also be aware of different terminology used for the cash flow from operations. Some authors, as well as the AICPA, use terms such as "cash inflows," "cash outflows," "cash savings," and "net benefits." These terms are all synonymous with cash flow and are sometimes modified further as "pretax" or "after-tax." When "after-tax" is used to describe the cash flow from operations, it is the same as the cash flow from operations used in this chapter. When the cash flow is defined as pretax, it is probably equivalent to the net income from operations before depreciation and taxes. Hence, taxes must be considered to determine the cash flow from operations.

Risk Analysis

In the economic analysis techniques discussed thus far, it was implicitly assumed that the risk of the projects being compared is the same. However, in real-world problems, risk must be considered. Several techniques can be employed to take risk into consideration. The two techniques that will be discussed here are the risk-adjusted discount rate and the sensitivity analysis.

Risk-Adjusted Discount Rate. The required rate of return used to discount the cash flow from operations in the NPV analysis or used as the hurdle rate in the IRR analysis assumes that projects have the same risk. Management can require a premium over the required rate of return to account for additional risk. For example, management might specify a minimum required rate of return of 10% for projects with low risk. Other projects are then classified as either medium- or high-risk. For medium-risk projects management may decide that a 2 percent premium should be added to the minimum required rate of return, while a 5 percent premium should be added for high-risk projects. Hence, the hurdle or required rate of return for medium- and high-risk projects would be 12% and 15%, respectively.

There are three problems with this approach. First, criteria must be specified for management to classify the degree of risk of a project. This sounds easier than it is in actual situations. Second is the problem of determining the risk premium. Again, in practice this is an extremely difficult task. Third, a criticism of this approach is that it heavily penalizes projects for which the risk is in the initial outlay as opposed to the cash flow from operations after the initial year. For example, a firm may have a government contract to produce a product for the next 10 years at a predetermined price. The product will be manufactured in a factory that the firm must build. The risk the firm faces is in incurring the cost of building the factory. The high discount rate would penalize the less risky cash flows from operations when in fact the real risk lies in the initial outlay, which is not affected by the discount rate used.

Sensitivity Analysis. In most business decisions, the factors that affect the decisions are subject to variations from the value expected. Sensitivity analysis is essentially a determination of how a change in key factors in the analysis will affect the decision. For example, Figure 15-1 (page 550) is a form of sensitivity analysis since it shows how sensitive the NPV of two projects, X and Y, are with respect to the required rate of return.

The firm may choose to perform the analysis based on the most optimistic and the most pessimistic conditions for the cash flow from operations and the initial outlay. If the investment project is profitable under the most pessimistic conditions, the decision makers will have more confidence in their decision.

POSTCOMPLETION REVIEW

The postcompletion review or postaudit involves comparing the cash flow from operations for the project with the projected values used to justify the project. Generally, it is desirable periodically to find out how close the projections are to the results. It is usually better for a centralized group such as the internal audit department to make the review and render the report. In most cases only jobs above a predetermined dollar amount are compared. Also, the review can be considered routine rather than a special undertaking. Sometimes a general pattern is found, and certain locations have a consistent record of overstating the cash flows. An audit report showing actual cash flows against claimed cash flows on representative projects can bring about a reappraisal of the economic value of a project to determine whether the company should continue the project or abandon it. Many companies making postcompletion audits find that the knowledge that the claimed yield will be reviewed is enough to cause those computing it to be more careful before endorsing the project.

CHAPTER REVIEW

One of the most important functions of management is the evaluation of long-term capital requirements. Unlike expenditures for inventory or other current assets, expenditures for capital investments are committed for a long time and may have a lasting unfavorable impact on company progress. Therefore, it is essential that long-term objectives be established early and a capital budget program be set up to assure adherence to capital investment objectives of the firm. For example, a company may have plans to expand, to bring out new products, and to improve production processes. Therefore, management must make sure that capital expenditures conform with the long-term objectives. The most effective means of doing this is by means of a capital budget program.

Generally the amount requested for capital expenditures is far greater than the available funds. Scarce funds must therefore be carefully rationed. Sufficient analyses must be made for each project to make sure that the particular project is more profitable than various alternate uses of the funds. Outside of emergency or essential jobs all other requests must show at least a desirable rate of return. The most common methods for evaluation of projects are the payback period, the average annual return on investment, the internal rate of return, the net present value, the index of profitability, and the discounted payback. The first two techniques are simple to compute but do not give consideration to the time value of money. The last four techniques are known as discounted cash flow techniques since the time value of money is considered. Sometimes conflicts can occur between the internal rate of return and the net present value when selecting mutually exclusive projects. The conflict arises because the opportunity for reinvestment of funds from operations is different for the two techniques and, in addition, the internal rate of return is influenced by the size of the investment. A conflict may also arise between the net present value and the index of profitability, because the latter measure is also affected by the size of the investment. Not all investment proposals have the same degree of risk. Two techniques for incorporating risk into the analysis discussed in this chapter are risk-adjusted discount rates and sensitivity analysis.

APPENDIX: TIME VALUE OF MONEY AND PRESENT-VALUE CONCEPTS

Money is valuable not only because it can be exchanged for goods and services but because by itself it can earn more money. Over a period of time, money can be invested to earn additional money, called interest. This concept of money earning more money over time is known as the time value of money.

Because it has the ability to earn more money over a period of time, money received today is worth more than money to be received at a future date. Present value equates what a sum of money is worth today if it will not be received until some future date. The longer one must wait to receive money, the less value it has in the present. For example, $1 received today and invested in a savings bank for 1 year at a 6% interest rate would be worth $.06 (6% interest rate × $1 principal × 1 year time) *more* in 1 year. Thus the total value of $1 invested at 6% for 1 year is $1.06 ($1 original investment or principal + .06 interest). Put another way, assuming a 6% interest rate, if a person had to *wait* for 1 year to receive $1.06, it is worth only $1 *today*. Thus the present value of $1.06 to be received in 1 year (assuming a 6% interest rate) is $1. Present-value tables like Tables 15-1 and 15-2 are available for the computation of the present value of $1 for different periods (N) at different interest rates.

TABLE 15-1
PRESENT VALUE OF $1

YEARS	5%	6%	8%	10%	12%	14%	16%	18%	20%	22%	24%	25%
1	.952	.943	.926	.909	.893	.877	.862	.847	.833	.820	.806	.800
2	.907	.890	.857	.826	.797	.769	.743	.718	.694	.672	.650	.640
3	.864	.840	.794	.751	.712	.675	.641	.609	.579	.551	.524	.512
4	.823	.792	.735	.683	.636	.592	.552	.516	.482	.451	.423	.410
5	.784	.747	.681	.621	.567	.519	.476	.437	.402	.370	.341	.328
6	.746	.705	.630	.564	.507	.456	.410	.370	.335	.303	.275	.262
7	.711	.665	.583	.513	.452	.400	.354	.314	.279	.249	.222	.210
8	.677	.627	.540	.467	.404	.351	.305	.266	.233	.204	.179	.168
9	.645	.592	.500	.424	.361	.308	.263	.225	.194	.167	.144	.134
10	.614	.558	.463	.386	.322	.270	.227	.191	.162	.137	.116	.107
11	.585	.527	.429	.350	.287	.237	.195	.162	.135	.112	.094	.086
12	.557	.497	.397	.319	.257	.208	.168	.137	.112	.092	.076	.069
13	.530	.469	.368	.290	.229	.182	.145	.116	.093	.075	.061	.055
14	.505	.442	.340	.263	.205	.160	.125	.099	.078	.062	.049	.044
15	.481	.417	.315	.239	.183	.140	.108	.084	.065	.051	.040	.035
16	.458	.394	.292	.218	.163	.123	.093	.071	.054	.042	.032	.028
17	.436	.371	.270	.198	.146	.108	.080	.060	.045	.034	.026	.023
18	.416	.350	.250	.180	.130	.095	.069	.051	.038	.028	.021	.018
19	.396	.331	.232	.164	.116	.083	.060	.043	.031	.023	.017	.014
20	.377	.312	.215	.149	.104	.073	.051	.037	.026	.019	.014	.012

TABLE 15-2
PRESENT VALUE OF $1 RECEIVED ANNUALLY FOR N YEARS

YEARS N	5%	6%	8%	10%	12%	14%	16%	18%	20%	22%	24%	25%
1	.952	.943	.926	.909	.893	.877	.862	.847	.833	.820	.806	.800
2	1.859	1.833	1.783	1.736	1.690	1.647	1.605	1.566	1.528	1.492	1.457	1.440
3	2.723	2.673	2.577	2.487	2.402	2.322	2.246	2.174	2.106	2.042	1.981	1.952
4	3.546	3.465	3.312	3.169	3.037	2.914	2.798	2.690	2.589	2.494	2.404	2.362
5	4.330	4.212	3.993	3.791	3.605	3.433	3.274	3.127	2.991	2.864	2.745	2.689
6	5.076	4.917	4.623	4.355	4.111	3.889	3.685	3.498	3.326	3.167	3.020	2.951
7	5.786	5.582	5.206	4.868	4.564	4.288	4.039	3.812	3.605	3.416	3.242	3.161
8	6.463	6.210	5.747	5.335	4.968	4.639	4.344	4.078	3.837	3.619	3.421	3.329
9	7.108	6.802	6.247	5.759	5.328	4.946	4.607	4.303	4.031	3.786	3.566	3.463
10	7.722	7.360	6.710	6.145	5.650	5.216	4.833	4.494	4.192	3.923	3.682	3.571
11	8.306	7.887	7.139	6.495	5.937	5.453	5.029	4.656	4.327	4.035	3.776	3.656
12	8.863	8.384	7.536	6.814	6.194	5.660	5.197	4.793	4.439	4.127	3.851	3.725
13	9.394	8.853	7.904	7.103	6.424	5.842	5.342	4.910	4.533	4.203	3.912	3.780
14	9.899	9.295	8.244	7.367	6.628	6.002	5.468	5.008	4.611	4.265	3.962	3.824
15	10.380	9.712	8.559	7.606	6.811	6.142	5.575	5.092	4.675	4.315	4.001	3.859
16	10.838	10.106	8.851	7.824	6.974	6.265	5.669	5.162	4.730	4.357	4.033	3.887
17	11.274	10.477	9.122	8.022	7.120	6.373	5.749	5.222	4.775	4.391	4.059	3.910
18	11.690	10.828	9.372	8.201	7.250	6.467	5.818	5.273	4.812	4.419	4.080	3.928
19	12.085	11.158	9.604	8.365	7.366	6.550	5.877	5.316	4.844	4.442	4.097	3.942
20	12.462	11.470	9.818	8.514	7.469	6.623	5.929	5.353	4.870	4.460	4.110	3.954

Table 15-1 can be used to compute the present value of $1 at various interest rates and years. For example, to compute the present value of $1.06 to be received in 1 year at 6% interest, simply go to the column that has 6% at the top and move down the column to the row listing 1 year. The figure at this point is .943. When .943 is multiplied by $1.06, the resulting figure is $.995 or $1.

If a *series* of equal payments are to be received, we have an annuity. Table 15-2 should be used to compute present value. It presents the present value of $1 received annually for N years. For example, assuming a 6% interest rate, if $1 is to be received at the *end* of each year for 5 years, we can determine the present value of the series of payments. Using Table 15-2, go to the column with 6% interest at the top and move down the column to the row that has 5 years in the first column; the number at this point is 4.212. Multiply $1 × 4.212 to get $4.21, which is the present value of $1 received annually for 5 years at a 6% interest rate.

Additional Examples:

1 Compute the present value of $20,000 to be received at the end of 11 years assuming an 8% interest rate.
   Solution: The present value of $1 (Table 15-1) at 8% for 11 years is .429; thus for $20,000 simply multiply $20,000 × .429 = $8,580.

2 Compute the present value of $7,000 to be received at the *end* of each year for 8 years at 10% interest a year.
   Solution: The present value of $1 received annually for 8 years (Table 15-2) at 10% is 5.335; thus $7,000 × 5.335 = $37,345.

3 Recompute Example 2 if the $7,000 was to be received at the *beginning* of each year.
   Solution:

	AMOUNT
The first payment will be received immediately; therefore, the present value of the first $7,000 is equal to $7,000 because no time has passed	$ 7,000
The remaining 7 payments will be received over 7 years at 10% per year; using Table 15-2 we get 4.868 × $7,000	34,076
Total	$41,076

GLOSSARY

Accounting Method—see average annual return on investment.

Authorization for Expenditure—a form that requests approval to make capital expenditures.

Authorization Policy and Procedures—levels for approval of capital expenditures, and the related procedures to prepare the forms.

Average Annual Return on Investment—evaluation process that uses accrual accounting data (net income) in determining the profitability of a project.

Average Investment—sum of the original investment amount divided by 2.

Capital Budgeting—program for determining which capital expenditures represent the most profitable outlay of funds, that they are in accordance with company policy, and that they do not endanger the financial well-being of the company.

Cost of Capital—rate a corporation pays to suppliers of capital.

Discounted Cash Flow—evaluation process that uses present value concepts to measure the profitability of a project.

Discounted Payback Method—computes the time required for the discounted cash flow from operations to recover the initial outlay.

Evaluation of Projects—economic techniques for the appraisal of capital projects for investment.

Hurdle Rate—the cutoff rate, determined by the cost of capital or the required rate of return, against which the profitability of the capital projects may be measured.

Index of Profitability Method—the discounted cash flow from operations (at the required rate of return) is divided by the initial outlay. A project is attractive if the result is greater than the number one (1.0).

Initial Outlay—the original investment for a capital project.

Internal Rate of Return Method—computes the yield that is expected to be earned on an investment.

Net Present Value Method—cash flow from operations is discounted at the required rate of return. The discounted value of the cash flow from operations is then compared with the initial outlay. If the discounted value of the cash flow exceeds the initial outlay the project is considered attractive.

Payback Method—evaluation process that measures the length of time required to recover the initial outlay.

Postcompletion Audit—followup review to compare the claimed benefits at the time of approval to the operating results actually experienced.

Present Value—what a sum of money is worth today (at an assumed interest rate) if it will not be received until some future date.

Present Value of $1 Table—listing of the present worth of future amounts of $1, based on specified interest rates and time periods.

Present Value of Annuity of $1 Table—listing of the present worth of future annuities, or series of payments based on specified interest rates and time periods.

Project—particular job or investment that is subject to evaluation.

Time Value of Money—ability of money to earn more money over time periods.

SUMMARY PROBLEMS

PROBLEM 1

Laurie's Computer Manufacturing, Inc., is planning to buy a new piece of machinery. The cost is $7,500, and the expected useful life is 5 years. Net income before depreciation and taxes is expected to be $3,500 per year. The machine will be depreciated on a straight-line basis and no salvage value is anticipated.

REQUIRED:

Assuming a tax rate of 40%, compute the payback period and average annual return on the original investment for Laurie's Computer Manufacturing.

PROBLEM 2

Maureen's Fashion Jeans is going to buy a new sewing machine to increase productivity. The machine will cost $11,560 and will be depreciated over a 5-year life on a straight-line basis. Net income before depreciation and taxes associated with the new sewing machine for the 5 years is expected to be:

YEAR	NET INCOME BEFORE DEPRECIATION AND TAXES
1	$7,059
2	6,059
3	5,059
4	4,059
5	3,059

Assume a tax rate of 40%.

REQUIRED:

a   Determine the internal rate of return.
b   Assuming a desired rate of 10%, compute the net present value.
c   Compute the discounted payback period.
d   Compute the index of profitability.

PROBLEM 3

Paul and Maggie Lobster Company is considering the purchase of equipment that will enable it to raise its own lobsters. The following information about the investment is available:

Annual cash flow from operations each year (for next 15 years)	$20,000
Additional working capital requirements (expected to be recovered in full at the end of the investment)	10,000
Initial cash outlay	150,000
Investment tax credit	10,500
Estimated salvage value	8,000
Required rate of return	8%

REQUIRED:

Compute the net present value of the investment if the equipment is expected to last 15 years.

SOLUTIONS TO SUMMARY PROBLEMS

PROBLEM 1

$$\text{Payback period} = \frac{\text{investment}}{\text{annual cash flow from operations}}$$

$$= \frac{\$7,500}{\$2,700} = 2.78 \text{ years}$$

Net income before depreciation and taxes	$3,500
Less depreciation ($7,500 ÷ 5 years)	1,500
Balance	$2,000
Less taxes	800
Net profit after taxes	$1,200
Plus depreciation	1,500
Annual cash flow from operations	$2,700

$$\text{Return on investment} = \frac{\text{Net profit after taxes}}{\text{investment}}$$

$$= \frac{\$1,200}{\$7,500} = 16\%$$

PROBLEM 2

Cash Flow from Operations:

	YEARS				
	1	2	3	4	5
Net income before depreciation and taxes	$7,059	$6,059	$5,059	$4,059	$3,059
Less depreciation	2,312	2,312	2,312	2,312	2,312
Income subject to tax	$4,747	$3,747	$2,747	$1,747	$ 747
Less taxes	1,899	1,499	1,099	699	299
Net profit after taxes	$2,848	$2,248	$1,648	$1,048	$ 448
Plus depreciation	2,312	2,312	2,312	2,312	2,312
Cash flow from operations	$5,160	$4,560	$3,960	$3,360	$2,760

a Internal rate of return

YEAR	CASH FLOW FROM OPERATIONS ×	PRESENT VALUE OF $1 (24%)	PRESENT VALUE
1	$5,160	.806	$ 4,159
2	4,560	.650	2,964
3	3,960	.524	2,075
4	3,360	.423	1,421
5	2,760	.341	941
			$11,560

b Net Present Value

YEAR	CASH FLOW FROM OPERATIONS ×	10% DISCOUNT RATE PV OF $1	PRESENT VALUE
1	$5,160	.909	$ 4,690
2	4,560	.826	3,767
3	3,960	.751	2,974
4	3,360	.683	2,295
5	2,760	.621	1,714
Discounted value of cash flow			$15,440
Initial outlay			11,560
NPV			$ 3,880

c Discounted Payback Period

YEAR	CASH FLOW FROM OPERATIONS	10% DISCOUNT RATE PV OF $1	PRESENT VALUE	DISCOUNTED PAYBACK YEARS
1	$5,160	.909	$ 4,690	1.0
2	4,560	.826	3,767	1.0
3	3,960	.751	2,974	1.0
4	189 (B)	.683	129 (A)	.1 (C)
			$11,560	3.1

(A) $11,560 − $11,431 = $129
(B) 129 ÷ .683 = 189
(C) 189 ÷ $3,360 = .06 or .1

d Index of Profitability

$$\frac{\$15,440}{\$11,560} = 1.34$$

Problem 3

Cash flow from operations:	
$20,000 × 8.559 (Table 15-2 at 8%)	$171,180
Salvage value:	
$8,000 × .315 (Table 15-1 at 8%)	2,520
Recovery of working capital	
$10,000 × .315 (Table 15-1 at 8%)	3,150
Discounted value of cash flow	$176,850

Less: Initial cash outlay	$150,000	
Additional working capital necessary	10,000	
Total	$160,000	
Investment credit	10,500	149,500
NPV		$ 27,350

QUESTIONS

1 Why is it necessary to plan capital budget projects carefully?
2 What are the three factors that necessitate having an objective review of capital expenditures?
3 What is capital budgeting?
4 What three controls should be instituted in order to have a sound capital budgeting program?
5 True or false:
   a A capital budget is an authorization to commit funds.
   b All companies should begin a capital budget program by preparing a general policy relating to capital expenditures.
   c Capital budgets provide automatic approval for expenditures.
6 How does a company prepare a capital budget?
7 In what case would a capital expenditure project be implemented if it does not reduce costs or improve quality?
8 Why were quantitative measures developed to evaluate capital expenditure projects?
9 What are the disadvantages of the payback method of evaluation?
10 Under the net present value method, how is the feasibility of a project determined?
11 What is a postcompletion review?

EXERCISES

EXERCISE 1

Multiple choice

1 The method of project selection which considers the time value of money in a capital budgeting decision is accomplished by computing the:
   a Accounting rate of return on initial investment.
   b Accounting rate of return on average investment.
   c Internal rate of return.
   d Payback period.
2 A capital budgeting method that explicitly incorporates a required rate of return into the basic computations is the:
   a Accounting book value method.
   b Payback method.
   c Net-present-value method.
   d Average-rate-of-return method.
3 The payback method measures:
   a How quickly investment dollars may be recovered.
   b The cash flow from an investment.

   c   The economic life of an investment.

   d   The profitability of an investment.

EXERCISE 2

Payback Method

Beth's and Mike's Stereo Manufacturing is considering purchasing new equipment. Beth and Mike have two alternatives:

$$X = \$12{,}500 \text{ cost, } 10\text{-year life, } \$2{,}500 \text{ return each year}$$
$$Y = \$ \ 8{,}000 \text{ cost, } \ 4\text{-year life, } \$3{,}000 \text{ return each year}$$

REQUIRED:

Assuming a tax rate of 40%, determine which piece of equipment is more desirable, using the payback method.

EXERCISE 3

Average Annual Return on the Original Investment

Joan and Mary's Hamburger House plans to purchase a new oven in order to meet a rapidly increasing demand. The oven will cost $24,000 and will have a useful life of 8 years. The income tax rate is 40%. Assume straight-line depreciation and no salvage value.

REQUIRED:

Assuming a net income before depreciation and taxes generated from the oven of $9,000 per year, compute the return on the original investment and the average annual return on average investment.

EXERCISE 4

Payback and Average Annual Return on the Original Investment

Betty and Ray's Catering Supplies are evaluating a capital budget proposal. The initial cost of the equipment is $16,000. It is expected to have an 8-year life, with no salvage value. Cash flow from operations before depreciation and taxes from implementing the project will be $5,000 per year.

REQUIRED:

Assuming straight-line depreciation and an income tax rate of 30%, compute the payback period and average annual return on average investment.

EXERCISE 5

Internal Rate of Return

Project X initially cost $31,341 and has an estimated life of 5 years. Cash flow from operations for the 5 years are as follows:

YEAR	CASH FLOW
1	$13,000
2	12,000
3	11,000
4	10,000
5	9,000

REQUIRED:

Compute the internal rate of return for Project X.

EXERCISE 6

Net Present Value, Discounted Payback Period, and Index of Profitability

A capital budget proposal has an estimated useful life of 7 years and an initial investment of $21,000. The cash flow from operations for the life of the project is

YEAR	CASH FLOW
1	$18,000
2	17,500
3	17,000
4	16,500
5	16,000
6	15,500
7	14,000

A hurdle rate of 12% is desired.

REQUIRED:

Compute the net present value, discounted payback period, and index of profitability.

EXERCISE 7

Conflict between NPV and IRR

Consider Projects A and B with cash flows from operations shown below.

PROJECT	INITIAL OUTLAY	CASH FLOW FROM OPERATIONS IN YEAR	
		1	2
A	−$3,000	$ 603	$3,600
B	− 3,000	3,000	937

REQUIRED:

a What is the NPV for both projects if the required rate of return is 5%?
b What is the IRR for both projects?
c If A and B are mutually exclusive projects is there a conflict?

EXERCISE 8

Multiple Choice

1 Which of the following statements is correct?
   a An investment project with a conventional cash flow pattern can have more than one internal rate of return.
   b For all investment proposals for which a cash flow from operations can be provided an internal rate of return can be computed.
   c The required rate of return must be known before the internal rate of return can be computed.
   d The ranking of two mutually exclusive projects is not affected by a change in the required rate of return.

2 Which of the following statements is correct?
   a The net present value decreases as the required rate of return increases.
   b Replacement chains should be established for independent investment projects with unequal lives.
   c A conflict can not arise between the internal rate of return and net present value methods.
   d The index of profitability will always rank projects the same as the payback method.

3 The net present value for a project with an initial outlay of $2,000 is $5,000. Which of the following is correct?
   a The index of profitability is 3.5.
   b The discounted value of the cash flow from operations is $7,000.
   c The project is profitable at the required rate of return.
   d All of the above are correct statements.

4 The accounting area in which the only objective of depreciation accounting relates to the effect of depreciation charges upon tax payments is
   a Capital budgeting.
   b Cost-volume-profit analysis.
   c Income determination.
   d Responsibility accounting.

5 The method of project selection which considers the time value of money in a capital budgeting decision is accomplished by computing the
   a Accounting rate of return on initial investment.
   b Accounting rate of return on average investment.
   c Discounted cash flow.
   d Payback period.

6 The effectiveness of the net present value method has been questioned as an evaluation technique for capital budgeting decisions on the basis that:
   a Predicting future cash flows is often difficult and clouded with uncertainties.
   b The accounting rate of return is usually more accurate and useful.
   c The payback technique is theoretically more reliable.
   d The computation involves some difficult mathematical applications that most accountants *cannot* perform.

7 Which of the following best identifies the reason for using probabilities in capital budgeting decisions?

    a Uncertainty or risk

    b Cost of capital

    c Time value of money

    d Projects with unequal lives

8 Which of the following capital expenditure planning and control techniques has been criticized because it fails to consider investment profitability?

    a Payback method

    b Average return on investment method

    c Present-value method

    d Time-adjusted rate-of-return method

(Questions 4 to 8 AICPA Adapted)

EXERCISE 9

Salvage Value, Working Capital, and Investment Tax Credit Considerations

Jeff & Terry's Real Estate Corporation is considering the following investment in a building:

Initial cash outlay	$200,000
Estimated salvage value	10,000
Annual cash flow from operations *each* year (for next 10 years)	30,000
Additional working capital requirements (which are expected to be recovered in full at the end of the investment)	25,000
Investment credit	20,000
Life of the investment	10 years

REQUIRED:

Compute the net present value of the investment if the required rate of return for Jeff & Terry's Real Estate Corporation is 12%.

EXERCISE 10

Capital Budgeting

Capital budgeting has received increased attention in recent years. The quantitative techniques employed for capital budgeting decisions depend largely upon accounting data.

REQUIRED:

    a Distinguish between capital budgeting and budgeting for operations.

    b Three quantitative methods used in making capital budgeting decisions are **(1)** payback period, **(2)** unadjusted accounting rate of return, and **(3)** discounted cash flow. Discuss the merits of each of these methods.

    c Two variations of the discounted cash flow method are **(1)** time-adjusted rate of return and **(2)** net present value (sometimes referred to as excess present value). Explain and compare these two variations of the discounted cash flow method.

d Cost of capital is an important concept in capital budgeting. Define the term "cost of capital" and explain how it is used in capital budgeting.

(AICPA Adapted)

PROBLEMS

PROBLEM 1

Incremental Revenue

Mike and Helen's (M & H) Bicycle shop manufactures a 3-speed bicycle. The owners are now considering introducing an additional new 10-speed bicycle. The following information has been developed:

	3-SPEED BICYCLE	10-SPEED BICYCLE
Selling price (each)	$110	$150

If the new 10-speed bicycle is produced in addition to the existing 3-speed bicycle, it is anticipated that the number of 3-speed bicycles sold will decrease by 20% because some customers will switch to the 10-speed bicycle.

Annual sales of the 3-speed bicycle is expected to be 1,000 if the new 10-speed bicycle is not introduced. Annual sales of the 10-speed bicycle is expected to be 450 bicycles.

REQUIRED:

Compute the incremental (additional) revenue from introducing the 10-speed bicycle.

PROBLEM 2

Internal Rate of Return

Villani's Distillery is considering a capital budget project. The initial investment is $4,710. The cash flow from operations is as follows:

YEAR	AMOUNT
1	$1,750
2	1,500
3	1,250
4	1,000
5	750

REQUIRED:

Compute the internal rate of return for the project.

PROBLEM 3

Net Present Value and Index of Profitability

Loebeck Company is evaluating two capital expenditure proposals. Project Q initially costs $15,000, has no salvage value, and has an estimated life of 5 years. Project T has an initial cost of $25,000, no salvage value, and an estimated life of 5 years. Net income before depreciation and taxes for each project is as follows:

YEAR	PROJECT Q	PROJECT T
1	$5,800	$7,800
2	5,400	7,600
3	5,000	7,400
4	4,600	7,000
5	4,200	6,800

Loebeck desires a straight hurdle rate of 8%. Assume a tax rate of 30%. Assume straight-line depreciation for both projects.

REQUIRED:

Determine which project is more desirable using the net present value method and index of profitability method.

PROBLEM 4

Payback and Average Annual Return on the Original Investment

Knox Corporation has just purchased a new piece of equipment and wishes to compute its payback period and average annual return on original investment. The equipment costs $26,000 and has an estimated life of 13 years. Net income before depreciation and taxes from the project are expected to be $4,600 annually. The income tax rate is 40%.

REQUIRED:

Compute the payback period and average annual return on original investment for Knox Corporation. Assume straight-line depreciation and no salvage value.

PROBLEM 5

Capital Budgeting Proposal

The Apex Company is evaluating a capital budgeting proposal for the current year. The relevant data follow:

YEAR	PRESENT VALUE OF AN ANNUITY OF $1 AT 15%
1	.870
2	1.626
3	2.284
4	2.856
5	3.353
6	3.785

The initial investment would be $30,000. It would be depreciated on a straight-line basis over 6 years with no salvage. The before-tax annual cash inflow due to this investment is $10,000, and the income tax rate is 40% paid the same year as incurred. The desired rate of return is 15%. All cash inflows occur at year end.

1 What is the after-tax accounting rate of return on Apex's capital budgeting proposal?

   a 10%

   b $16^{2}/_{3}\%$

   c $26^{2}/_{3}\%$

   d $33^{1}/_{3}\%$

2 What is the after-tax payback reciprocal for Apex's capital budgeting proposal?

   a 20%

   b $26^{2}/_{3}\%$

   c $33^{1}/_{3}\%$

   d 50%

3 What is the net present value of Apex's capital budgeting proposal?

   a $(7,290)

   b $280

   c $7,850

   d $11,760

4 How much would Apex have had to invest 5 years ago at 15% compounded annually to have $30,000 now?

   a $12,960

   b $14,910

   c $17,160

   d Cannot be determined from the information given.

(AICPA Adapted)

PROBLEM 6

Risk-Adjusted Net Present Value and Discounted Payback

Thoroughbred Dog Food Company is considering the following two mutually exclusive projects:

	PROJECT A	PROJECT B
Initial investment	$200,000	$280,000
Cash flow from operations:		
Year 1	60,000	100,000
Year 2	60,000	80,000
Year 3	60,000	70,000
Year 4	60,000	60,000
Year 5	60,000	40,000

The management of Thoroughbred Company feels the required rate of return for Project A is 8%, but a 2% premium is added to the required rate of return for Project B because it is considered to be a higher risk.

REQUIRED:

Compute the risk-adjusted net present value and discounted payback period for Projects A and B and determine which project should be accepted.

PROBLEM 7

Replacement Chains and Net Present Value

Gemini Corporation is considering two mutually exclusive projects (R and P). The following cash flow data is available:

END OF YEAR	PROJECT R	PROJECT P
0	−$20,000	−$30,000
1	15,000	12,000
2	11,000	10,000
3	21,000	10,000
4	—	5,000
5	—	4,000
6	—	3,000

REQUIRED:

Set up a replacement chain for Project R and compute the net present value for both Projects R and P assuming a required rate of return of 8%.

PROBLEM 8

Comprehensive Capital Budgeting Problem

Pescow Dairy Corporation is considering the following two mutually exclusive projects:

	PROJECT T	PROJECT S
Initial outlay	$141,530	$156,680
Cash flow from operations (after deducting taxes and adding back depreciation)		
Year 1	60,000	90,000
Year 2	20,000	30,000
Year 3	30,000	20,000
Year 4	90,000	60,000
Life of asset	4 years	4 years
Salvage value	0	0
Depreciation method	Straight line	Straight line

Management desires a minimum required rate of return on any project of 10%.

REQUIRED:

a Compute the following for Projects T and S:
    1 Payback years
    2 Average annual return on original investments
    3 Internal rate of return
    4 Net present value
    5 Index of profitability
    6 Discounted payback
b Determine which project should be selected.

PROBLEM 9

Capital Budgeting

The management of McAngus, Inc. has never used formal planning techniques in the operation of its business. The president of McAngus has expressed interest in the recommendation of its accountants that the company investigate various techniques it may use to manage the business more effectively.

McAngus, a medium-sized manufacturer, has grown steadily. It recently acquired another company located approximately 1,000 miles away. The new company manufactures a line of products which complements the present product line. Both manufacturing plants have significant investments in land, buildings, machinery, and equipment. Each plant is to be operated as a separate division headed by a division manager. Each division manager is to have virtually complete authority for the management of his division; i.e., each will be responsible primarily for the profit contribution of his division. A complete set of financial statements is to be prepared for each division as well as for the company.

The president and his immediate management team intend to concentrate their efforts on coordinating the activities of the two divisions and investigating and evaluating such things as new markets, new product lines, and new business acquisition possibilities. Because of the cash required for the recent acquisition and the cash needs for desired future expansion, the president is particularly concerned about cash flow and the effective management of cash.

REQUIRED:

Construct your answer to each of the following requirements to consider known facts about McAngus, Inc., as presented in the question. Confine your answer to the accounting techniques and processes involved.
    a Explain the objectives and describe the process which McAngus can use to plan for and evaluate the long-term commitment of its resources including cash.

b Describe three techniques including one which considers the time value of money that McAngus can use to help evaluate various alternatives in its long-range plan. Explain the advantages and disadvantages of each.

(AICPA Adapted)

PART FOUR

ANALYSIS AND CONTROL

CHAPTER SIXTEEN

BREAK-EVEN ANALYSIS AND COST-VOLUME- PROFIT PLANNING

In the study of management, the decision maker should understand the relationship between the cost of doing business and the revenue generated from the sales of the firm. This relationship is important because in the simplest way it is the definition of profit. Accountants are uniquely qualified to develop and use this relationship.

The study of break-even analysis appeals to accountants because it gives a concise picture of the cost and revenue behavior of the firm. It is an easy tool for management to understand and interpret, and it is valuable in the planning process. Decision makers are always faced with decisions concerning price, variable costs of production, and fixed costs. These decisions can be for day-to-day activities or over a longer period of time.

INTRODUCTORY TERMS

While most cost accounting students may be familiar with the terms used in this chapter, they will be defined as follows:

Total Sales Revenue. Total sales revenue can be calculated in more than one way. In any calculation it is the number of units sold, multiplied by some measure of price. The price measure could be actual price, average price, or some other useful price measure. Sales revenue is price times units sold and does not include income from nonoperating activities or any fixed income not associated with production.

Variable Costs. Variable costs are those which vary in direct proportion to changes in volume; if the volume is doubled, the variable costs are doubled. Examples are raw materials, labor on a piecework basis, and power costs based on consumption.

Fixed Costs. Fixed costs are those which are not directly associated with production but are incurred in providing the *capacity to do business*. They are assumed to be constant for any relevant range of production. Average fixed cost per unit decreases as the level of production increases, since the constant total fixed costs are spread over more units of output. Examples are property taxes and rent.

Contribution Margin or Profit. Contribution margin is measured on a per unit basis. For example, assume a product sells for $2 and has an average variable cost of $1.50. Contribution margin (CM) per unit would be computed as follows:

Selling price (per unit)	$2.00
Variable costs (per unit)	1.50
CM per unit	$ .50

Each unit sold would generate $.50 above the variable costs of producing the unit. Total contribution margin is applied first towards covering total fixed costs. Any excess of total contribution margin above fixed costs is considered income. If total contribution margin is less than total fixed costs, a loss will result. For example, if the selling price were still $2 per unit and sales were 500,000 units with the same variable cost of $1.50 per unit and total fixed costs of $150,000, profit would be equal to:

Total sales revenue (500,000 × $2)	$1,000,000
Total variable costs (500,000 × $1.50)	750,000
Contribution margin	$ 250,000
Total fixed costs	150,000
Profit	$ 100,000

Break-Even Point. The break-even point is defined as that point where

$$\text{Total sales revenue} = \text{total variable costs} + \text{total fixed costs}$$

and thus there is no profit. The break-even point can be computed in terms of dollar profit or units. The computation of the break-even point is commonly performed under one of the following analytical techniques:

1 Break-even equations (algebraic technique)
2 Graphic presentation
3 Simplified income statement approach

BREAK-EVEN EQUATIONS (ALGEBRAIC TECHNIQUE)

Let us incorporate the following terms into our discussion of break-even analysis:

TSR = total sales revenue in dollars
TC = total cost in dollars
TVC = total variable costs
TFC = total fixed costs
u   = volume or output in units
AVC = average variable cost per unit in dollars
P   = selling price per unit in dollars
BEP = break-even point
RR = relevant range, the range of volume over which the amount of fixed costs and rate of variable costs remains unchanged

The BEP in units and dollars is given as

$$BEP_u = \frac{TFC}{P - AVC}$$

$$BEP_\$ = \frac{TFC}{1 - AVC/P}$$

Thus from our earlier figures, we see that if

$$TFC = \$150,000$$
$$P = \$2$$
$$AVC = \$1.50$$

then

$$BEP_u = \frac{\$150,000}{\$2 - \$1.50} = 300,000 \text{ units}$$

$$BEP_\$ = \frac{\$150,000}{1 - \dfrac{\$1.50}{\$2.00}} = \$600,000$$

Note that for a break-even point (BEP) of 300,000 units, at $2 per unit, we need total sales revenue (TSR) of $600,000.

The break-even point can also be computed by using the following format:

BEPu

BEPu = TSR (unit selling price × units sold)
             = TVC (variable unit cost × units sold) + TFC

The unknown factor is the number of units sold and is represented as x.

$$\$2x = \$1.5x + \$150,000$$
$$\$.5x = \$150,000$$
$$x = 300,000 \text{ units}$$

BEP$_\$$

$$BEP_\$ = \text{unit selling price} \times BEP_u$$

$$\$2 \times 300{,}000 = \$600{,}000$$

GRAPHIC PRESENTATION

Graphic presentations or charts will be developed based on the information given in the previous example. For our purposes we may group the charts into two general types: (1) the basic charts and (2) the break-even chart.

Basic Charts. Figures 16-1 to 16-4 (pages 581 to 583) are called basic or single-line charts, since they depict simple relationships. The information needed for the basic charts is as follows:

REQUIRED INFORMATION	FORMULA
Figure 16-1—total sales revenue (TSR)	TSR = $2(u)
Figure 16-2—total variable costs (TVC)	TVC = $1.50(u)
Figure 16-3—total fixed costs (TFC)	TFC = $150,000
Figure 16-4—total costs (TC)	TC = TVC + TFC

Break-Even Chart. To help in further understanding the various relationships, we will describe the information required, the break-even formula, and the steps in constructing the chart. The data in the previous equations will be used in constructing Figure 16-5 (page 583).

Information required:

1 Total sales revenue in dollars (TSR)
2 Total variable costs (TVC)

FIGURE 16-1 **Total Sales Revenue (TSR)**

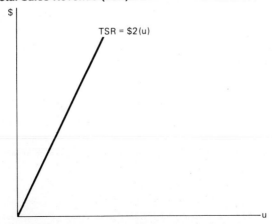

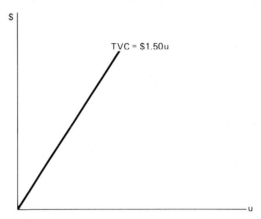

FIGURE 16-2   **Total Variable Costs (TVC)**

3 Total fixed costs (TFC)
4 Total costs (TC)

Breakeven formula:

$$BEP: \quad TSR = TC$$

Steps in Constructing the Breakeven Chart in Figure 16-5

1 *Vertical line.* Draw a vertical line (*y* axis) to show the number of dollars (in thousands).
2 *Horizontal line.* Draw a horizontal line (*x* axis) to show the number of units (in thousands). It should intersect the vertical line at point 0.
3 *Total sales revenue line.* Choose any number of units (greater than zero) on the hoizontal line (*x* axis) and multiply by $2 (selling price per unit). The result will equal total sales revenue (TSR) for that number of units. Choosing 450,000 units will result in $900,000 TSR (450,000 × $2). Next plot the point on the chart where 450,000 units on the *x* axis intercepts the $900,000 on the *y* axis. A straight line representing TSR can now be drawn from point 0 to $900 ($900,000).

FIGURE 16-3   **Total Fixed Costs (TFC)**

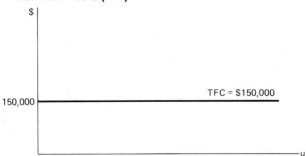

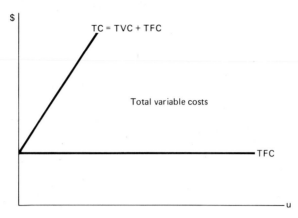

FIGURE 16-4 **Total Costs (TC)**

4 *Total costs line.* The total costs (TC) line is the total of fixed costs and variable costs at any particular point on the chart. Fixed costs of $150,000 in this example are assumed to remain unchanged from 150,000 to 450,000 units (the relevant range—a range of volume over which fixed costs and the per unit rate of variable costs remain unchanged). Variable costs (VC) are $1.50 per unit. Choosing 450,000 units and multiplying

FIGURE 16-5 **Break-Even Chart**

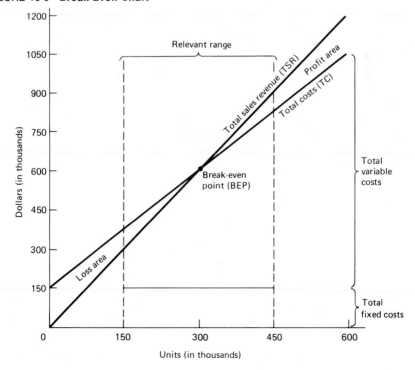

it by $1.50 will result in total variable costs of $675,000 at 450,000 units of production. Total costs at 450,000 units is therefore $825,000 ($150,000 FC + $675,000 VC). Next, plot the point on the chart where 450,000 units on the x axis intercepts the $825,000 on the y axis. A straight line representing TC can now be drawn from $150 ($150,000) on the y axis (fixed cost portion) to $825 ($825,000).

5 *Break-even point.* The total costs line (TC) intersects the total sales revenue line (TSR) at the break-even point. Sales are $600,000 and total costs are $600,000, for 300,000 units.

SIMPLIFIED INCOME STATEMENT APPROACH

With the simplified income statement approach, pro forma income statements are set up at various levels of production to determine the break-even point, profit, or loss at each level. For example, the simplified income statement for 200,000 units, 300,000 units, and 400,000 units was prepared as follows (from our previous example):

	LEVELS OF PRODUCTION		
Units	200,000	300,000	400,000
Sales	$400,000	$600,000	$800,000
Less variable expenses	300,000	450,000	600,000
Contribution margin.................	$100,000	$150,000	$200,000
Fixed expenses	150,000	150,000	150,000
Profit (loss)	($ 50,000)	$ 0	$ 50,000

Note that with this method, the break-even point is at 300,000 units or $600,000 in sales. This result is consistent with the results determined under the equations (algebraic) method and graphic presentation method.

EQUATIONS, GRAPHS, OR INCOME STATEMENTS

When should the accountant or manager use one or another approach to break-even analysis, since the three methods yield the same result? An exhaustive answer to this question is not possible here, but some general guidelines can be given. If you refer to Chapter 22, you will find a discussion on the problems of giving the manager too much data.

The break-even point is that position where revenue and costs are equal and the profit or loss is zero. Break-even analysis, cost-volume-profit analysis, profit-volume studies, and similar analyses are an important tool in present-day profit planning and decision making. Break-even charts provide management with an efficient, easily understood device which takes the place of many volumes of hard-to-read statistical or financial reports. The information as to total sales, total costs, variable and fixed costs, and profit at any given volume can be easily read from the chart.

The graphic method is especially helpful in reports to nonaccountants or in presentations to groups such as a middle management company group. The equation method is very precise and easily computed. However, computations must be made for each level of volume. It is most useful for decision makers who are familiar with fairly sophisticated quantitative techniques. The income statement method is generally limited in use to those individuals who understand the concepts being presented. For example, the distinction between contribution margin and profit may be very technical and confusing to a group which does not understand the concepts involved. An accountant must pay particular attention to the audience when using one presentation method as opposed to another.

It should be mentioned that the break-even point is ordinarily not the most important information on a break-even chart. Management is usually more interested in reading on the chart the revenue, costs, and profit for various volume levels. Also it should be mentioned that there are limitations to the use of break-even analysis. For example, a change in selling price, volume, sales mix, or costs may distort the chart data. These factors must be taken into account when using a break-even chart.

PLANNING WITH COST-VOLUME-PROFIT DATA

In the preceding sections of this chapter we have discussed the concept and the advantages of break-even analysis. Many companies fail to derive the most important benefit of break-even analysis, which is an understanding of the interrelationships of all factors affecting profits, particularly the behavior of costs as volume changes. This knowledge is essential when management is planning future operations, such as the operations budget for the next year. Management may want to know, for example, what effect on net income the following expected changes will have: a 15% increase in price, a 10% increase in volume, and a $300 increase in fixed costs. Similar questions are discussed in the following paragraphs.

COST-VOLUME-PROFIT FACTORS

The principal factors in the cost-volume-profit (CVP) relationship are

1 Sales price
2 Sales volume
3 Variable costs
4 Fixed costs

The interrelationship of the above factors is the major consideration for management decisions as to product prices, production quantity, advertising plans, and introduction of new products. The interrelationship in some way affects practically all the decisions of management. It has a most important impact on the profit potential and even on the success of the company.

The cost-volume-profit ratio (CVP) is as follows:

Sales = variable costs + fixed costs + profit

The basic difference between the cost-volume-profit equation and the break-even equation is the addition of profit. In order to illustrate the effects of changes in the above factors we may use the practical example below.

The Englewood High School Key Club has the concession for selling hot dogs at high school affairs. The net proceeds are used for various school and community service and charitable projects. The club has the following unit cost data for a typical school affair:

ITEM		UNIT COST	%
Price of hot dog		$.60	100
Variable costs:			
Hot dog	$.22		
Roll	.07		
Mustard and supplies	.04	.33	55
Contribution margin		$.27	45
Fixed costs:			
Wages of clerks (10 at $19)	$190		
Rental of stand	100		
Liability insurance	7		
Total	$297		

The first step is to compute the break-even point. How many hot dogs have to be sold to break even; that is, where is the profit zero? This can be computed by use of the CVP equation:

$$\text{Sales} = \text{variable costs} + \text{fixed costs} + \text{profit}$$
$$\$.60x = \$.33x + \$297 + 0$$
$$\$.27x = \$297$$
$$x = 1,100 \text{ hot dogs}$$

As can be seen above, 1,100 hot dogs have to be sold to cover the total costs. To find the *sales dollars* required to break even, the following computation can be made:

$$1,100 \text{ hot dogs} \times \$.60 = \$660$$

In some cases the percentage relationship may be known but not the dollar relationship. In that case the percentage relationship shown in the above table can be used as follows:

$$x = .55x + \$297 + 0$$
$$.45x = \$297$$
$$x = \$660$$

The income summary will appear as follows:

	AMOUNT	%
Sales (1,100 at $.60)	$660	100
Variable costs at $.33	363	55
Contribution margin	$297	45
Fixed costs	297	45
Profit	$ 0	0

Business people who are planning for a future period must provide for more than merely breaking even. They must also earn a return or profit on operations or they will not be in business very long. They must therefore price the product high enough to cover all costs and provide for a profit. How many hot dogs will have to be sold to earn a profit of $300? We can use the same CVP equation as before and add $300 as the profit:

$$\$.60x = \$.33x + \$297 + \$300$$
$$.27x = \$297 + \$300$$
$$.27x = \$597$$
$$x = 2,211 \text{ hot dogs}$$

To break even, it was necessary to sell 1,100 hot dogs. However, to earn a profit of $300, it is necessary to sell 2,211 hot dogs.

The income summary will now appear as follows:

	AMOUNT	%
Sales (2,211 at $.60)	$1,327	100
Variable costs at $.33	730	55
Contribution margin	$ 597	45
Fixed costs	297	22
Profit	$ 300	23

UNIT CONTRIBUTION MARGIN AND PROFIT/VOLUME RATIO OR CONTRIBUTION MARGIN RATIO

The *total* contribution margin procedure is a vital tool for every business person. To make an even more effective analysis, the *unit* contribution margin can also be used. The equation is as follows:

Unit contribution margin = unit sales price − unit variable cost

The unit contribution margin for the Englewood High School Key Club is $.27 ($.60 sales price − $.33 variable cost). Since the contribution margin is the excess of sales over variable costs, the break-even point is where the excess, or contribution margin, equals fixed costs. The break-even point in units can therefore be computed by dividing total fixed costs by the unit contribution margin. The equation is as follows:

$$\text{Break-even (BEP}_u) = \frac{\text{total fixed costs (TFC)}}{\text{unit contribution margin (UCM)}}$$

This equation can be used to determine the break-even point for the Key Club:

$$BEP_u = \frac{\$297}{\$.27} = 1,100 \text{ hot dogs}$$

Often the unit contribution margin is shown as a percentage, which is commonly called the profit/volume (P/V) ratio, or the contribution margin (CM) ratio. The equation is

$$P/V = \frac{\text{total contribution margin (TCM)}}{\text{total sales revenue (TSR)}}$$

The Key Club has a 45% P/V ratio (computed at 1,100 hot dogs sold):

$$P/V = \frac{\$297}{\$660} = 45\%$$

While the unit contribution margin can be used to determine the break-even point in units, the P/V (or CM) ratio can be used to determine the break-even point in dollars.

$$BEP_\$ = \frac{\text{total fixed costs (TFC)}}{\text{P/V ratio}}$$

For the Key Club the break-even in dollars is now computed as follows:

$$BEP_\$ = \frac{\$297}{.45} = \$660$$

PLANNING FOR CHANGES

In planning for next year's operations, or for any period, business people must provide for expected changes. Changes in sales prices, sales volume, variable costs, and fixed costs are a way of life in business, and plans must be made accordingly. Following are a discussion and examples of the effect on profit of changes in the various factors.

Change in Sales Price

This is one of the most common changes encountered, especially in times of rising costs. The Key Club (continuation of previous example) is considering raising the hot dog price to $.70. With a sales volume of 2,211 hot dogs, the income summary will be as follows:

	AMOUNT	%
Sales (2,211 × $.70)	$1,548	100
Variable costs at $.33	730	47
Contribution margin	$ 818	53
Fixed costs	297	19
Profit	$ 521	34

Often there is sales resistance to a price increase and sales volume tends to decrease. The Key Club estimates there will be a decrease of 10% in the number of hot dogs sold. Thus 1,990 (2,211 − 221) hot dogs will be sold at the increased price. The income summary will then show the following:

	AMOUNT	%
Sales (1,990 × $.70)	$1,393	100
Variable costs at $.33	657	47
Contribution margin	$ 736	53
Fixed costs	297	21
Profit	$ 439	32

The difference between the profits shown in the two income summaries above is $82. It is the difference between the $521 profit projected after the price increase and the $439 profit projected after the 10% volume decline.

Business people often want to know how much the sales can decline, after a price increase, without affecting existing profits. This can be answered by using the same CVP equation as before (assuming a desired profit of $300):

$$\text{Sales} = \text{variable costs} + \text{fixed costs} + \text{profit}$$
$$\$.70x = \$.33x + \$297 + \$300$$
$$\$.37x = \$597$$
$$x = 1,614 \text{ hot dogs}$$

Therefore, if the selling price of hot dogs is raised from $.60 to $.70, the total sales volume can decline from the present 2,211 to 1,614 and the Key Club will still earn the profit of $300. The income summaries for the old price of $.60 and the new price of $.70 are shown below:

PRICE OF $.60		PRICE OF $.70	
Sales (2,211 at $.60)	$1,327	Sales (1,614 at $.70)	$1,130
Variable costs at $.33	730	Variable costs at $.33	533
Contribution margin	$ 597	Contribution margin	$ 597
Fixed costs	297	Fixed costs	297
Profit	$ 300	Profit	$ 300

Change in Sales Volume

The Key Club concession has been successful so far, and it appears the operation will soon expand. The school has just added 25% more seating capacity at the football field and it is expected that sales volume will increase proportionately. The number of hot dogs sold is expected to increase by 25% from 2,211 to 2,764, or an increase of 553. The price increase to $.70 will not be needed. Following is an income summary showing the increase in sales volume.

	AMOUNT	%
Sales (2,764 at $.60)	$1,658	100
Variable costs at $.33	912	55
Contribution margin	$ 746	45
Fixed costs	297	18
Profit	$ 449	27

With the additional seating capacity there is a suggestion that three students be hired to sell in the bleachers at $21 each per game. It is estimated that the students would sell 700 additional hot dogs each game. In addition to the income summary analysis used in preceding examples, we may use the P/V ratio or incremental analysis, as described below.

P/V Ratio

The profit/volume ratio of 45% (computed earlier), can be multiplied by the increase in sales to determine the increase in contribution margin. The additional fixed costs must then be deducted because the P/V ratio does not take into consideration fixed costs (remember that the P/V ratio is calculated based on the excess of sales over variable costs). The Calculation of the additional profit is as follows:

Increased profit margin		
700 hot dogs at $.60	$420	
P/V ratio	45%	
Increase in contribution margin		
($420 × 45%)	$189	
Increase in fixed costs:		
3 students at $21 each	63	
Additional profit	$126	

Incremental Analysis

By the incremental analysis method the total sales figure is used, and the *normal* variable costs and the *additional* fixed costs are deducted, as follows:

Incremental revenue:		
700 hot dogs at $.60		$420
Incremental costs:		
Variable: 700 hot dogs at $.33	$231	
Fixed: 3 students at $21	63	294
Additional profit		$126

Change in Variable Costs

When there is a change in variable costs, the contribution margin and the break-even point are changed. For example, if the cost of a hot dog, included in our original cost data, changes from $.22 to $.30, what effect will it have on the break-even point and the number of hot dogs which have to be sold to break even? An increase of $.08 in hot dog cost would *increase* the total variable cost to $.41 ($.33 + $.08). At the same time it would *decrease* the contribution margin from $.27 to $.19 at a selling price of $.60.

The break-even point in sales would change from 1,100 ($297 fixed cost ÷ $.27 contribution margin) to 1,563 ($297 ÷ $.19). Thus an additional 463 hot dogs have to be sold to break even. If, by some rare happening, the cost of a hot dog were to decrease by $.08, the contribution margin would *increase* by the same amount to $.35. The break-even point would decrease from 1,100 sales to only 849 ($297 ÷ $.35).

If it is desired to maintain the $300 in profit, as described earlier, how many hot dogs will now have to be sold assuming an $.08 increase in variable costs? Let us use the same CVP equation as before:

$$\text{Sales} = \text{variable costs} + \text{fixed costs} + \text{profit}$$
$$\$.60x = \$.41x + \$297 + \$300$$
$$\$.19x = \$597$$
$$x = 3,142 \text{ hot dogs}$$

In order to produce $300 in profit, 3,142 hot dogs must now be sold, rather than the 2,211 needed before. Thus an additional 931 hot dogs must be sold at the $.60 price. At this point consideration may be given to increasing the price to $.70.

Change in Fixed Costs

With the enlargement of the seating capacity of the football stadium it was desirable also to enlarge the hot dog stand to take care of the increased sales. The cost of enlarging the hot dog stand will cause an estimated increase in rent of $60, to $160 per game. What will be the effect on the break-even point of an increase in hot dog stand rental? How many hot dogs will have to be sold to maintain the $300 in profit?

The fixed costs would change from $297 to $357. The change in fixed costs would have no effect on the break-even contribution margin of $.27. Thus we will divide the new fixed costs of $357 by $.27 to determine that 1,322 hot dogs will now have to be sold to break even. This is an increase of 222 additional hot dogs to be sold over the original requirement of 1,100.

How many hot dogs will now have to be sold to still produce the $300 profit? We will use the original data, and therefore disregard the changes illustrated in preceding examples. We will use the same CVP equation as before:

$$\text{Sales} = \text{variable costs} + \text{fixed costs} + \text{profit}$$
$$\$.60x = \$.33x + \$357 + \$300$$
$$\$.27x = \$657$$
$$x = 2,433 \text{ hot dogs}$$

In order to produce $300 in profit, 2,433 hot dogs must now be sold, rather than the 2,211 sales needed before the fixed costs increased.

Profit Planning and Income Taxes

When a firm desires to determine the sales volume that will achieve a specific profit *after* taxes, consideration must also be given to income taxes. In our previous examples we were computing profit before taxes. When an *after*-tax profit is desired we must first adjust the after-tax profit to a before-tax profit by dividing the after-tax profit by 1 minus the tax rate $(1 - t)$. Once this adjustment has been made, the analysis is the same as with the previous examples. Income taxes are not considered in break-even analysis because there is no income tax at zero income.

For example, assume a company wishes to achieve a desired after-tax profit of $60,000. The contribution margin per unit is $20, fixed costs are $200,000, and the corporate income tax rate is 40%. The number of units that must be sold to produce an after-tax profit of $60,000 is computed as follows:

$$\text{Desired before-tax profit} = \frac{\text{desired after-tax profit}}{1 - \text{tax rate}} = \frac{\$60,000}{1 - 40\%} = \$100,000$$

Units necessary to achieve after-tax profit of $60,000:

$$\frac{\$200,000 + \$100,000}{\$20} = 15,000 \text{ units}$$

Therefore, at a volume of 15,000 units, the desired after-tax profit of $60,000 would result as follows:

Contribution margin ($20 per unit × 15,000)	$300,000
Fixed costs	200,000
Before-tax profit	$100,000
Income taxes (40% × $100,000)	40,000
After-tax profit	$ 60,000

PRODUCT MIX

In the preceding examples we used totals for sales, costs, and contribution margins. These totals, as for single products, were useful for illustrative purposes, but generally a company will have more than one product to consider in its cost-volume-profit (CVP) computations. When more than one product is involved, it is highly desirable that the CVP ratios be computed for each product, as there may be wide variations in the contribution margins of the products.

In order to explain the impact on the CVP, we will assume that the Key Club will now sell hamburgers and soda in addition to the hot dogs sold previously. As we saw before, the contribution margin for 1,100 hot dogs in the original break-even example was $.27, or a contribution margin (CM) ratio of 45%. The CM ratios for hamburgers and sodas will be somewhat lower, as seen below. Let us assume that 875 hamburgers will sell for $.80 each, with variable costs of $.56 and contribution margin of $.24 ($.80 − $.56), or a CM ratio of 30%. Let us assume also that 1,600 cups of soda will sell for $.25 a cup, with variable costs of $.20 and contribution margin of $.05 ($.25 − $.20), or a CM ratio of 20%.

The cost data for the three products is summarized below:

COST DATA	HOT DOGS	HAMBURGERS	SODA	TOTAL
Sales......................	$660	$700	$400	$1,760
Variable costs	363	490	320	1,173
Contribution margin	$297	$210	$ 80	$ 587
CM ratio	45%	30%	20%	33.4%

We can see above that the total contribution margin is now $587, which provides $290 ($587 − $297) above the fixed costs previously mentioned. The average CM ratio for the three products was 33.4%.

Now let us see what will be the effect on the average CM ratio of 33.4% if there is a 50% decrease in sales of hot dogs, the most profitable item, and an 80% increase in sales of soda, the least profitable item. The new data is summarized below:

COST DATA	HOT DOGS	HAMBURGERS	SODA	TOTAL
Sales......................	$330	$700	$720	$1,750
Variable costs	182	490	576	1,248
Contribution margin	$148	$210	$144	$ 502
CM ratio	45%	30%	20%	28.7%

As can be seen, the average CM ratio dropped from 33.4% to 28.7% and the contribution amount dropped from $587 to $502. It can be seen that the total sales decreased only $10, but the contribution margin dropped considerably.

CHAPTER REVIEW

The study of break-even analysis is used by accountants because it gives a concise picture of the cost and revenue behavior of the firm. The break-even point is defined as that point where total sales revenue equals total variable costs plus total fixed costs and thus there is no profit or loss. It can be computed in terms of dollars or units, and can be presented in either equation or graphic form. It can also be viewed as a simplified presentation of the income statement.

The equation (algebraic) approach to break-even analysis is appealing because it is precise and easy to compute. It is most useful to decision makers who have had some training in the subject.

The graphic approach allows the audience to see pictorially the results of the analysis, and is very helpful when the accountant is called upon to make a presentation before a group of peers or managers.

The income statement approach is useful when presented to other accountants or managers who understand the concepts being presented.

The most important benefit of break-even analysis is an understanding of the interrelationships of all factors affecting profits, particularly the behavior of costs as volume changes. This knowledge is essential when management is planning future operations, such as the operations budget for the next year.

GLOSSARY

Break-Even Chart—a graphic presentation showing the cost-volume-profit relationships and the point at which the total costs equal total sales revenue.

Break-Even Point—the point in terms of dollars or units at which total costs equal total revenue and profit equals zero.

Contribution Margin—total sales revenue less variable expenses.

Cost-Volume-Profit Relationship—the relationship that volume has with costs and profits.

Equation Approach—a method that provides easily computable answers to given volume levels and is often favored by those unfamiliar with more advanced quantitative techniques.

Fixed Costs—costs which are not directly associated with production and

which remain constant for any relevant range of production.

Product Mix—preferably called sales mix, this refers to the composition of the sales of various products relative to total sales.

Relevant Range—the extent of volume over which the amount of fixed costs and unit rate of variable costs remain unchanged.

Total Costs—the sum of the fixed costs plus the variable costs at a given volume.

Total Sales Revenue—a measure of revenue derived by multiplying units sold by the price per unit.

Variable costs—costs which are directly associated with producing the product and which vary in proportion to volume.

SUMMARY PROBLEMS

PROBLEM 1

RGC has asked you to determine the level of sales they must attain to cover their fixed and variable costs. The sales price is $5, fixed costs are $160,000, and the contribution margin is 40% of sales.

REQUIRED:

Determine RGC's break-even point in units and dollars using the algebraic and graphical approaches.

PROBLEM 2

Maur-Shei Bakery sells only chocolate chip cookies. Each cookie sells for $.20. Variable costs are

Flour and sugar	$.02
Butter and eggs	.02
Chocolate chips	.04

Fixed costs per week are

Wages—2 salespeople × $25	$ 50
Store rent.....................................	100
	$150

REQUIRED:

Compute the level of sales in units necessary per week (1) to break even and (2) to earn a profit of $250 under the following assumptions (ignore income taxes):
  a   Assume the information above is held constant.
  b   The sales price is increased to $.25.
  c   The cost of flour and sugar is doubled.
  d   The rent is increased to $150.
  e   The sales price drops to $.15.
  f   The cost of chocolate chips doubles.

SOLUTIONS TO SUMMARY PROBLEMS

PROBLEM 1

Algebraic solution:
  Sales price: $5 per unit
  Variable costs: $3 per unit
  Fixed costs: $160,000

$$\text{Break-even point} = \frac{\text{fixed costs}}{\text{sales price} - \text{variable costs}}$$

$$BEP_u = \frac{\$160,000}{\$5 - \$3}$$

$$BEP_u = \frac{\$160,000}{\$2}$$

$$BEP_u = \underline{\underline{80,000}}$$

$$\$80,000 \times \$5 = \underline{\underline{\$400,000}}$$

or

$$\text{Break-even point} = \cfrac{\text{fixed costs}}{1 - \cfrac{\text{variable costs}}{\text{sales}}}$$

$$\$80,000 \times \$5 = \underline{\underline{\$400,000}}$$

$$BEP_\$ = \cfrac{\$160,000}{1 - \cfrac{\$3}{\$5}}$$

$$BEP_\$ = \frac{\$160,000}{1 - .6}$$

$$BEP_\$ = \frac{\$160,000}{.4}$$

$$BEP_\$ = \underline{\underline{\$400,000}}$$

$$BEP_u = \underline{\underline{80,000}} \ (\$40,000 \div \$5)$$

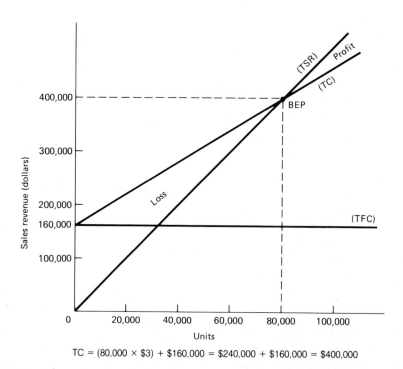

$$TC = (80,000 \times \$3) + \$160,000 = \$240,000 + \$160,000 = \$400,000$$

Graphic Solution of Summary Problem 1

PROBLEM 2

Sales = variable costs + fixed costs + profit

a 1 $.20x = .08x + 150 + 0$
$.12x = 150$
$x = 1,250$

2 $.20x = .08x + 150 + 250$
$.12x = 400$
$x = 3,333$

b 1 $.25x = .08x + 150 + 0$
$.17x = 150$
$x = 882$

2 $.25x = .08x + 150 + 250$
$.17x = 400$
$x = 2,353$

c 1 $.20x = .10x + 150 + 0$
$.10x = 150$
$x = 1,500$

2 $.20x = .10x + 150 + 250$
$.10x = 400$
$x = 4,000$

d 1 $.20x = .08x + 200 + 0$
$.12x = 200$
$x = 1,667$

2 $.20x = .08x + 200 + 250$
$.12x = 450$
$x = 3,750$

e 1 $.15x = .08x + 150 + 0$
$.07x = 150$
$x = 2,143$

2 $.15x = .08x + 150 + 250$
$.07x = 400$
$x = 5,714$

f 1 $.20x = .12x + 150 + 0$
$.08x = 150$
$x = 1,875$

2 $.20x = .12x + 150 + 250$
$.08x = 400$
$x = 5,000$

QUESTIONS

1 What is the break-even point?
2 When is graphical break-even analysis most useful to accountants?
3 What information does a break-even chart show?
4 In what ways is break-even analysis useful?

5 What is meant by the term contribution margin?
6 How does product mix affect break-even analysis?
7 What are the three approaches to break-even analysis?
8 What are the principal factors in the cost-volume-profit relationship?
9 What is the incremental analysis method?
10 Explain the difference between fixed and variable costs.
11 If variable costs are $.50 per unit, fixed costs are $75, and the contribution margin percentage is 25%, what is the break-even point in units?
12 If the sales price is $2.50 per unit, variable costs are $.75 per unit, and the break-even point in units is 500, what are the fixed costs?

EXERCISES

EXERCISE 1

Break-Even Point in Units and Dollars

A company knows its variable cost per unit is $0.10 and its selling price is $0.50. If total fixed costs are $50,000, **(a)** What is the break-even point in units? **(b)** What is the break-even point in dollars?

EXERCISE 2

Income Statement

Construct an income statement for Exercise 1 when sales are $31,250 and $93,750 (ignore income taxes).

EXERCISE 3

Break-Even Point in Units and Dollars

Total fixed costs are given at $100,000, average variable cost per unit is $2, price of the product is $8. **(a)** What is the break-even point in units? **(b)** What is the break-even point in dollars?

EXERCISE 4

Equations

The ABC Company knows its total fixed cost is $50,000, its variable cost is $0.20 per unit, and its selling price is $1 per unit. What are the equations that will yield the results for total cost, total revenue, total fixed cost, and total variable cost?

EXERCISE 5

Computation of Total Revenue

If a firm sells 100 units at $5, 100 units at $4, and 100 units at $2 of the same product, what value should it use for its total revenue?

EXERCISE 6

Computation of Average Selling Price

If the firm in Exercise 5 decides to use the average price per unit to determine its total revenue calculations for all sales of units in the future, what should the average selling price be?

EXERCISE 7

Cost-Volume-Profit Analysis

LaSalle Company currently has a sales price of $8 and fixed costs of $600. Variable costs are 55% of sales.

REQUIRED:

Consider each independently. Compute the

a   Break-even point in units
b   Level of dollar sales needed to earn a profit before income tax of $200
c   Break-even point in units assuming an increase in price to $11
d   Break-even point in units if variable costs increase to 60% of sales

EXERCISE 8

Break-Even Point

EJC Company currently sells its main product at $25. Fixed costs are $750 and variable costs are $10 per unit.

REQUIRED:

Compute the break-even point in units and dollars.

EXERCISE 9

Graphical Determination of Break-Even Point

EJC Company wishes to show its break-even point graphically in units and dollars. Fixed costs are $750, variable costs are $10 per unit, and the sales price is $25 per unit.

REQUIRED:

Graphically determine the break-even point.

EXERCISE 10

Analysis of Selling Prices Using a Contribution Margin Approach

E. Berg and Sons build custom-made pleasure boats which range in price from $10,000 to $250,000. For the past 30 years, Mr. Berg, Sr. has determined the selling price of each boat by estimating the costs of material, labor, a prorated portion of overhead, and adding 20% to these estimated costs.

For example, a recent price quotation was determined as follows:

Direct materials	$5,000
Direct labor	8,000
Overhead	2,000
	$15,000
Plus 20%	3,000
Selling price	$18,000

The overhead figure was determined by estimating total overhead costs for the year and allocating them at 25% of direct labor cost.

If a customer rejected the price and business was slack, Mr. Berg, Sr. would often be willing to reduce his markup to as little as 5% over estimated costs. Thus, average markup for the year is estimated at 15%.

Mr. Ed Berg, Jr. has just completed a course on pricing and believes the firm could use some of the techniques discussed in the course. The course emphasized the contribution margin approach to pricing and Mr. Berg, Jr. feels such an approach would be helpful in determining the selling prices of their custom-made boats.

Total overhead which includes selling and administrative expenses for the year has been estimated at $150,000 of which $90,000 is fixed and the remainder is variable in direct proportion to direct labor cost.

REQUIRED:

Assume the customer in the example rejected the $18,000 quotation and also rejected a $15,750 quotation (5% markup) during a slack period. The customer countered with a $15,000 offer.

1 What is the difference in net income for the year between accepting or rejecting the customer's offer?

2 What is the minimum selling price Mr. Berg, Jr. could have quoted without reducing or increasing net income?

(CMA Adapted)

PROBLEMS

PROBLEM 1

Cost-Volume-Profit Analysis Concepts and Computations

Cost-volume-profit analysis (break-even analysis) is used to determine and express the interrelationships of different volumes of activity (sales), costs, sales prices, and sales mix with earnings. More specifically, the analysis is concerned with the effect on earnings of changes in sales volume, sales prices, sales mix, and costs.

REQUIRED:

a   Certain terms are fundamental to cost-volume-profit analysis. Explain the meaning of each of the following terms:
   1   Fixed costs
   2   Variable costs
   3   Relevant range
   4   Break-even point
   5   Sales (product) mix

b   In a recent period Zero Company had the following experience:
Sales (10,000 units at $200): $2,000,000

	FIXED	VARIABLE
Costs:		
Direct materials		$ 200,000
Direct labor		400,000
Factory overhead	$160,000	600,000
Administrative expenses	180,000	80,000
Other expenses	200,000	120,000
Total costs	$540,000	$1,400,000
Grand total		$1,940,000
Net income		$ 60,000

Each item below is independent.
1   Calculate the break-even point for Zero in terms of units and sales dollars.
2   What sales volume would be required to generate a net income of $96,000 (ignore income taxes)?
3   What is the break-even point if management makes a decision which increases fixed costs by $18,000?

(AICPA Adapted)

PROBLEM 2

Multiple Choice

Carey Company sold 100,000 units of its product at $20 per unit. Variable costs are $14 per unit (manufacturing costs of $11 and selling costs of $3). Fixed costs are incurred uniformly throughout the year and amount to $792,000 (manufacturing costs of $500,000 and selling costs of $292,000). There are no beginning or ending inventories.

1   The break-even point for this product is
   a $3,640,000 or 182,000 units
   b $2,600,000 or 130,000 units
   c $1,800,000 or 90,000 units
   d $1,760,000 or 88,000 units
   e   None of the above
2   The number of units that must be sold to earn a net income of $60,000 for the year before income taxes would be

  a   142,000
  b   132,000
  c   100,000
  d   88,000
  e   None of the above

3   If the income tax rate is 40%, the number of units that must be sold to earn an after-tax income of $90,000 would be
  a   169,500
  b   157,000
  c   144,500
  d   104,777
  e   None of the above

4   If labor costs are 50% of variable costs and 20% of fixed costs, a 10% increase in wages and salaries would increase the number of units required to break even (in fraction form) to
  a   807,840/5.3
  b   831,600/5.78
  c   807,840/14.7
  d   831,600/14.28
  e   None of the above

(AICPA Adapted)

PROBLEM 3

Break-Even Computations

A client has recently leased manufacturing facilities for production of a new product. Based on studies made by the staff, the following data have been made available to you (estimated annual sales 24,000 units):

	AMOUNT	PER UNIT
Estimated costs:		
Materials	$ 96,000	$4.00
Direct labor	44,400	.60
Overhead	24,000	1.00
Administrative expense	28,800	1.20
Total	$163,200	$6.80

Selling expenses are expected to be 15% of sales, and profit is to amount to $1.02 per unit.

REQUIRED:

1   Compute the selling price per unit.
2   Project a profit and loss statement for the year (ignore income taxes).
3   Compute a break-even point expressed in dollars and in units, assuming that overhead and administrative expenses are fixed but that other costs are fully variable.

(AICPA Adapted)

PROBLEM 4

Multiple Choice

Select the best response to the following:

1 The cost-volume-profit analysis underlying the conventional break-even chart does not assume that
   a Prices will remain fixed.
   b Production will equal sales.
   c Some costs vary inversely with volume.
   d Costs are linear and continuous over the relevant range.
2 The most useful information derived from a break-even chart is the
   a Amount of sales revenue needed to cover enterprise variable costs.
   b Amount of sales revenue needed to cover enterprise fixed costs.
   c Relationship among revenues, variable costs, and fixed costs at various levels of activity.
   d Volume or output level at which the enterprise breaks even.
3 The major assumption as to cost and revenue behavior underlying conventional cost-volume-profit calculations is the
   a Constancy of fixed costs.
   b Variability of unit prices and efficiency.
   c Curvilinearity of relationships.
   d Linearity of relationships.
4 Given the following notations, what is the break-even sales level in units?

$$SP = \text{selling price}$$
$$FC = \text{total fixed cost}$$
$$VC = \text{variable cost per unit}$$

a $\dfrac{SP}{FC \div VC}$ b $\dfrac{VC}{SP - FC}$

c $\dfrac{FC}{VC \div SP}$ d $\dfrac{FC}{SP - VC}$

PROBLEM 5

Break-Even Concepts

After reading an article you recommended on cost behavior, your client asks you to explain the following excerpts from it:

"Fixed costs are variable per unit of output and variable costs are fixed per unit of output (though in the long run all costs are variable)."

"Depreciation may be either a fixed cost or a variable cost, depending on the method used to compute it."

REQUIRED:

For each excerpt:
   a Define the *underscored* terms. Give examples where appropriate.
   b Explain the meaning of each excerpt to your client.

PROBLEM 6

Multiple Choice

Select the best response to the following:

1 Which of the following best describes a fixed cost?

a It may change in total where such change is unrelated to changes in production.

b It may change in total where such change is related to changes in production.

c It is constant per unit of change in production.

d It may change in total where such change depends on production within the relevant range.

2 If a company's variable costs are 70% of sales, which formula represents the computation of dollar sales that will yield a profit equal to 10% of the contribution margin, where S equals sales in dollars for the period and FC equals total fixed costs for the period?

a $S = \dfrac{.2}{FC}$ **b** $S = \dfrac{.27}{FC}$

c $S = \dfrac{FC}{.2}$ **d** $S = \dfrac{FC}{.27}$

3 The following data apply to Freim Corporation for a given period:

Total variable cost per unit	$3.50
Contribution margin ÷ sales	30%
Break-even sales (present volume)	$1,000,000

Freim wants to sell an additional 50,000 units at the same selling price and contribution margin. By how much can fixed costs increase to generate a gross margin equal to 10% of the sales value of the additional 50,000 units to be sold?

a $50,000

b $57,500

c $67,500

d $125,000

4 The contribution margin per unit is the difference between the selling price and the variable cost per unit, and the contribution margin ratio is the ratio of the contribution margin to the selling price per unit. If the selling price and the variable cost per unit both increase 10% and fixed costs do not change, what is the effect on the contribution margin per unit and the contribution margin ratio?

a Contribution margin per unit and the contribution margin ratio both remain unchanged.

b Contribution margin per unit and the contribution margin ratio both increase.

c Contribution margin per unit increases and the contribution margin ratio remains unchanged.

d Contribution margin per unit increases and the contribution margin ratio decreases.

(AICPA Adapted)

PROBLEM 7

Decisions Using Break-Even Concepts

The management of the Southern Cottonseed Company has engaged you to assist in the development of information to be used for managerial decisions. The company has the capacity to process 20,000 tons of cottonseed per year. The yield of a ton of cottonseed is as follows:

PRODUCT	AVERAGE YIELD PER TON OF COTTONSEED	AVERAGE SELLING PRICE PER TRADE UNIT
Oil	300 lb	$ .15 per lb
Meal	600 lb	50.00 per ton
Hulls	800 lb	20.00 per ton
Lint	100 lb	3.00 per cwt
Waste	200 lb	

A special marketing study revealed that the company can expect to sell its entire output for the coming year at the listed average selling prices. You have determined the company's cost to be as follows:

Processing costs:
Variable .... $9 per ton of cottonseed put into process
Fixed .... $108,000 per year
Marketing costs:
All variable .... $20 per ton sold
Administrative costs:
All fixed .... $90,000 per year

From the above information you prepared and submitted to management a detailed report on the company's break-even point. In view of conditions in the cottonseed market, management told you that they would also like to know the average maximum amount that the company can afford to pay for a ton of cottonseed.

Management has defined the average maximum amount that the company can afford to pay for a ton of cottonseed as the amount that would result in the company's having losses no greater when operating than when closed down under the existing cost and revenue structure. Management states that you are to assume that the fixed costs shown in your break-even point report will continue unchanged even when the operations are shut down.

REQUIRED:

a   Compute the average maximum amount that the company can afford to pay for a ton of cottonseed.

b   You also plan to mention to management that the factors, other than the costs that entered into your computation, that they should consider in deciding whether to shut down the plant. Discuss these additional factors.

c   The stockholders consider the minimum satisfactory return on their invest-ment in the business to be 25% before corporate income taxes. The stockholders' equity in the company is $968,000. Compute the maximum average amount that the company can pay for a ton of cottonseed to realize the minimum satisfactory return on the stockholders' investment in the business.

(AICPA Adapted)

PROBLEM 8

Contribution Margin

a The Wing Manufacturing Corporation produces a chemical compound, Product X, which deteriorates and must be discarded if it is not sold by the end of the month during which it is produced. The total variable cost of the manufactured compound, Product X, is $50 per unit, and its selling price is $80 per unit. Wing can purchase the same compound from a competing company at $80 per unit plus $10 freight per unit. Management has estimated that failure to fill orders would result in the loss of 80 percent of customers placing orders for the compound. Wing has manufactured and sold Product X for the past 20 months. Demand for Product X has been irregular and at present there is no consistent sales trend. During this period monthly sales have been as follows:

UNITS SOLD PER MONTH	NUMBER OF MONTHS
8,000	5
9,000	12
10,000	3

REQUIRED:

1 Compute the probability of sales of Product X of 8,000, 9,000, or 10,000 units in any month.
2 Compute what the contribution margin would be if 9,000 units of Product X were ordered and either 8,000, 9,000, or 10,000 units were manufactured in that same month (with additional units, if necessary, being purchased).
3 Compute the average monthly contribution margin that Wing can expect if 9,000 units of Product X are manufactured every month and all sales orders are filled.

b In the production of Product X, Wing uses a primary ingredient, K-1. This ingredient is purchased from an outside supplier at a cost of $24 per unit of compound. It is estimated that there is a 70 % chance that the supplier of K-1 may be shut down by a strike for an indefinite period. A substitute ingredient, K-2, is available at $36 per unit of compound, but Wing must contact this alternative source immediately to secure sufficient quantities. A firm purchase contract for either material must now be made for production of the primary ingredient next month. If an order were placed for K-1 and a strike occurred, Wing would be released from the contract and management would purchase the chemical compound from its competitor. Assume that 9,000 units are to be manufactured and all sales orders are to be filled.

REQUIRED:

1 Compute the monthly contribution margin from sales of 8,000, 9,000, and 10,000 units if the substitute ingredient, K-2 is ordered.
2 Prepare a schedule computing the average monthly contribution margin that Wing should expect if the primary ingredient, K-1, is ordered with the existing probability of a strike at the supplier. Assume that the expected average monthly contribution margin from manufacturing will be $130,000 using the primary ingredient, and the expected average monthly loss from purchasing Product X from the competitor (in case of a strike) will be $45,000.

(AICPA Adapted)

PROBLEM 9

Decision Using Contribution Margins

The Justa Corporation produces and sells three products. The three products, A, B, and C, are sold in a local market and in a regional market. At the end of the first quarter of the current year, the following income statement has been prepared:

	TOTAL	LOCAL	REGIONAL
Sales	$1,300,000	$1,000,000	$300,000
Cost of goods sold	1,010,000	775,000	235,000
Gross margin	$ 290,000	$ 225,000	$ 65,000
Selling expenses	$ 105,000	$ 60,000	$ 45,000
Administrative expenses	52,000	40,000	12,000
	$ 157,000	$ 100,000	$ 57,000
Net income	$ 133,000	$ 125,000	$ 8,000

Management has expressed special concern with the regional market because of the extremely poor return on sales. This market was entered a year ago because of excess capacity. It was originally believed that the return on sales would improve with time, but after a year no noticeable improvement can be seen from the results as reported in the above quarterly statement.

In attempting to decide whether to eliminate the regional market, the following information has been gathered:

	PRODUCTS		
	A	B	C
Sales...	$500,000	$400,000	$400,000
Variable manufacturing expenses as a percentage of sales	60%	70%	60%
Variable selling expenses as a percentage of sales	3%	2%	2%

	SALES BY MARKETS	
PRODUCT	LOCAL	REGIONAL
A	$400,000	$100,000
B	300,000	100,000
C	300,000	100,000

All administrative expenses and fixed manufacturing expenses are common to the three products and the two markets and are fixed for the period. Remaining selling expenses are fixed for the period and separable by market. All fixed expenses are based upon a prorated yearly amount.

REQUIRED:

a Prepare the quarterly income statement showing contribution margins by markets.

b Assuming there are no alternative uses for the Justa Corporation's present capacity, would you recommend dropping the regional market? Why or why not?

c Prepare the quarterly income statement showing contribution margins by products.

d It is believed that a new product can be ready for sale next year if the Justa Corporation decides to go ahead with continued research. The new product can be produced by simply converting equipment presently used in producing Product C. This conversion will increase fixed costs by $10,000 per quarter. What must be the minimum contribution margin per quarter for the new product to make the changeover financially feasible?

(CMA Adapted)

PROBLEM 10

Break-Even Analysis

R. A. Ro and Company, maker of quality handmade pipes, has experienced a steady growth in sales for the past five years. However, increased competition has led Mr. Ro, the president, to believe that an aggressive advertising campaign will be necessary next year to maintain the company's present growth.

To prepare for next year's advertising campaign, the company's accountant has prepared and presented Mr. Ro with the following data for the current year, 19X2:

COST SCHEDULE	
Variable costs:	
Direct labor	$ 8.00/pipe
Direct materials	3.25/pipe
Variable overhead	2.50/pipe
Total variable costs	$13.75/pipe

Fixed costs:
Manufacturing	$ 25,000
Selling	40,000
Administrative	70,000
Total fixed costs	$135,000
Selling price, per pipe	$25.00
Expected sales, 19X2 (20,000 units)	$500,000

Tax rate: 40%

Mr. Ro has set the sales target for 19X3 at a level of $550,000 (or 22,000 pipes).

REQUIRED:

a What is the projected after-tax net income for 19X2?

b What is the break-even point in units for 19X2?

c Mr. Ro believes an additional selling expense of $11,250 for advertising in 19X3, with all other costs remaining constant, will be necessary to attain the sales target. What will be the after-tax net income for 19X3 if the additional $11,250 is spent?

d What will be the break-even point in dollar sales for 19X3 if the additional $11,250 is spent for advertising?

e If the additional $11,250 is spent for advertising in 19X3, what is the required sales level in dollar sales to equal 19X2's after-tax net income?

f At a sales level of 22,000 units, what is the maximum amount which can be spent on advertising if an after-tax net income of $60,000 is desired?

(CMA Adapted)

PROBLEM 11

Analysis of Changes Using Break-Even and Contribution Margin Techniques

All-Day Candy Company is a wholesale distributor of candy. The company services grocery, convenience, and drug stores in a large metropolitan area.

Small but steady growth in sales has been achieved by the All-Day Candy Company over the past few years while candy prices have been increasing. The company is formulating its plans for the coming fiscal year. Presented below are the data used to project the current year's after-tax net income of $110,400.

Average selling price	$4.00 per box
Average variable costs:	
Cost of candy	$2.00 per box
Selling expenses	.40 per box
Total	$2.40 per box
Annual fixed costs:	
Selling	$160,000
Administrative	280,000
Total	$440,000
Expected annual sales volume (390,000 boxes)	$1,560,000
Tax rate	40%

Manufacturers of candy have announced that they will increase prices of their products an average of 15 percent in the coming year due to increases in raw material (sugar, cocoa, peanuts, etc.) and labor costs. All-Day Candy Company expects that all other costs will remain at the same rates or levels as the current year.

REQUIRED:

a What is All-Day Candy Company's break-even point in boxes of candy for the current year?

b What selling price per box must All-Day Candy Company charge to cover the 15% increase in the cost of candy and still maintain the current contribution margin ratio?

c What volume of sales in dollars must the All-Day Candy Company achieve in the coming year to maintain the same net income after taxes as projected for the current year, if the selling price of candy remains at $4.00 per box and the cost of candy increases 15%?

(CMA Adapted)

PROBLEM 12

Analysis of Changes Using Break-Even Analysis Techniques

Hewtex Electronics manufactures two products—tape recorders and electronic calculators—and sells them nationally to wholesalers and retailers. The Hewtex management is very pleased with the company's performance for the current fiscal year. Projected sales through December 31, 19X7, indicate that 70,000 tape recorders and 140,000 electronic calculators will be sold this year. The projected earnings statement, which appears on page 611, shows that Hewtex will exceed its earnings goal of 9% on sales after taxes.

The tape recorder business has been fairly stable the last few years, and the company does not intend to change the tape recorder price. However, the competition among manufacturers of electronic calculators has been increasing. Hewtex's calculators have been very popular with consumers. In order to sustain this interest in their calculators and to meet the price reductions expected from competitors, management has decided to reduce the wholesale price of its calculator from $22.50 to $20.00 per unit effective January 1, 19X8. At the same time the company plans to spend an additional $57,000 on advertising during fiscal year 19X8. As a consequence of these actions, management estimates that 80% of its total revenue will be derived from calculator sales as compared to 75% in 19X7. As in prior years, the sales mix is assumed to be the same at all volume levels.

The total fixed overhead costs will not change in 19X8, nor will the variable overhead cost rates (applied on a direct labor hour base). However, the cost of materials and direct labor is expected to change. The cost of solid state electronic components will be cheaper in 19X8. Hewtex estimates that material costs will drop 10% for the tape recorders and 20% for the calculators in 19X8. However, direct labor costs for both products will increase 10% in the coming year.

HEWTEX ELECTRONICS
PROJECTED EARNINGS STATEMENT
FOR THE YEAR ENDED DECEMBER 31, 19X7

	TAPE RECORDERS		ELECTRONIC CALCULATORS		
	TOTAL AMOUNT (000 OMITTED)	PER UNIT	TOTAL AMOUNT (000 OMITTED)	PER UNIT	TOTAL (000 OMITTED)
Sales	$1,050	$15.00	$3,150	$22.50	$4,200.0
Production costs:					
Materials	$ 280	$ 4.00	$ 630	$ 4.50	$ 910.0
Direct labor	140	2.00	420	3.00	560.0
Variable overhead	140	2.00	280	2.00	420.0
Fixed overhead	70	1.00	210	1.50	280.0
Total production costs	$ 630	$ 9.00	$1,540	$11.00	$2,170.0
Gross margin	$ 420	$ 6.00	$1,610	$11.50	$2,030.0
Fixed selling and administrative					1,040.0
Net income before income taxes					$ 990.0
Income taxes (55%)					544.5
Net income					$ 445.5

REQUIRED:

a How many tape recorder and electronic calculator units did Hewtex Electronics have to sell in 19X7 to break even?

b What volume of sales is required if Hewtex Electronics is to earn a profit in 19X8 equal to 9% on sales after taxes?

c How many tape recorder and electronic calculator units will Hewtex have to sell in 19X8 to break even?

(CMA Adapted)

CHAPTER SEVENTEEN
DIRECT COSTING

The cost of manufactured products is generally determined by *absorption costing*, the full costing concept, or by *direct costing*, the variable costing concept. In the preceding chapters of this book we have discussed absorption costing in detail, since it is more widely used than direct costing. In this chapter we will define and illustrate direct costing, discuss its advantages and disadvantages, and compare it with absorption costing.

MEANING OF DIRECT COSTING

Under absorption costing, sometimes called full or conventional costing, all factory overhead costs, both variable and fixed, are charged to product costs. Under direct costing, only factory overhead costs that tend to vary with volume are charged to product costs. That is, only direct materials, direct labor, and variable factory overhead are included in inventory and hence are considered as products costs.

Fixed factory overhead under direct costing is not included in inventory and, therefore, is considered a period cost. In direct costing, fixed costs are differentiated from variable costs not only in cost statements but in the various cost accounts as well.

The use of direct costing has grown in the last few years because it is more suitable for management's needs for planning, control, and decision making. Since profit under direct costing moves in the same direction as sales volume, the operating statements can be more readily understood by general management, by marketing and production executives, and by the various departmental supervisors. Direct costing is useful in evaluating performance, and provides ready information for the important cost-volume-profit computations.

DIRECT COSTING
VERSUS ABSORPTION COSTING

Under direct costing product costs include only those manufacturing costs which are closely related to the product and vary with production volume. Under absorption costing all manufacturing costs, direct and indirect, are included as product costs. Thus under absorption costing all expenses are charged to product costs except those applicable to selling and general administration. Therefore, costs of goods manufactured includes executive salaries, depreciation, rent, insurance, property taxes, etc. Some part of fixed factory overhead is carried forward in work-in-process and finished goods inventories until the product is sold.

In direct costing, fixed factory overhead is not carried forward because it is not included in product costs. It is classified as a period cost and charged against revenue when incurred.

The principal differences between income statements prepared under direct costing and absorption costing follows.

Gross Contribution Margin and Gross Profit.   In direct costing, gross contribution margin is the difference between sales and variable manufacturing costs. It is similar to the gross profit figure for absorption costing after fixed factory overhead costs are excluded from inventory and cost of goods sold. Gross contribution margin will always be greater than gross profit because fixed costs are excluded from the contribution margin. Under direct costing the cost of goods sold varies directly with sales.

For example, assume the following:

Sales		$120,000
Variable costs:		
Direct materials	$20,000	
Direct labor	15,000	
Variable manufacturing overhead	10,000	
Variable selling and administrative costs ...	5,000	50,000
Fixed costs:		
Fixed manufacturing overhead	$25,000	
Fixed selling and administrative costs	30,000	55,000

Assume no beginning or ending inventories. The gross contribution margin (direct costing) and gross profit (absorption costing) would be computed as follows:

	GROSS CONTRIBUTION MARGIN		GROSS PROFIT	
Sales		$120,000		$120,000
Cost of goods sold:				
Direct materials	$20,000		$20,000	
Direct labor	15,000		15,000	
Variable manufacturing overhead	10,000		10,000	
Fixed manufacturing overhead	—	45,000	25,000	70,000
Gross contribution margin		$75,000		
Gross profit				$ 50,000

Contribution Margin. This is sometimes called marginal income and reflects the excess of sales over total variable costs, including variable manufacturing, selling, and administrative costs. This is an important feature of the direct costing income statement and is especially useful in profit planning for short-run and long-run operations.

Contribution margin for the previous example would be computed as follows:

Sales		$120,000
Total variable costs:		
Direct materials	$20,000	
Direct labor	15,000	
Variable manufacturing overhead	10,000	
Variable selling and administrative costs	5,000	50,000
Contribution margin		$70,000

Inventory Costs. Under direct costing, fixed factory overhead is not included in inventories and unit product costs. This procedure is not considered as being in accordance with "generally accepted accounting principles" and therefore cannot be used for costing inventories on external financial statements. Neither the Internal Revenue Service nor the Securities and Exchange Commission will accept direct costing. Of course, the opposition of these agencies is only related to *external* reports. Firms using direct costing in internal reports for managerial control merely add back applicable fixed factory overhead costs to inventories to conform with absorption costing procedures for reports issued to stockholders and those filed with the IRS and SEC.

For example, assume the following per unit costs:

Direct materials	$4
Direct labor	$3
Variable factory overhead	$2
Fixed factory overhead	$1
Units in ending inventory	
(assume no beginning inventory)	10,000

Ending inventory under absorption costing and direct costing would be computed as follows:

	ABSORPTION COSTING	DIRECT COSTING
Direct materials ($4 × 10,000)	$ 40,000	$40,000
Direct labor ($3 × 10,000)	30,000	30,000
Variable factory overhead ($2 × 10,000)	20,000	20,000
Fixed factory overhead ($1 × 10,000)	10,000	
	$100,000	$90,000

Net Operating Profit. The difference in net operating profit under direct costing and absorption costing is due to the amount of fixed factory overhead charges included in inventories. Where there are no beginning or ending inventories, the net operating profit would be the same.

Assume the following basic data for the Englewood Company for April and May of 19X2:

Produced	10,000 units
Sold	8,000 units
Selling price per unit	$15
Direct materials	$.20 per unit
Direct labor	$.10 per unit
Fixed overhead	60% of total factory overhead

For the 2-month period, fixed expenses were as follows:

Factory:	
Heat	$2,000
Light	2,000
Equipment	2,000
Depreciation	3,000
Maintenance	1,500
Rent	5,000
Insurance	1,500
Indirect labor..............................	2,000
Repairs	2,500
Taxes	2,500
Other:	
Selling and administrative expenses	5,000

Income statements using (1) full or absorption costing and (2) direct costing follow.

1 Full or Absorption Costing:

ENGLEWOOD COMPANY
INCOME STATEMENT
FOR MONTHS OF APRIL AND MAY 19X2

Sales (8,000 units at $15)		$120,000
Direct materials (10,000 units at $.20)	$ 2,000	
Direct labor (10,000 units at $.10)	1,000	
Variable factory overhead ($40,000* − $24,000)	16,000	
Fixed factory overhead	24,000	
Cost of goods manufactured		$ 43,000
Beginning inventory		0
Cost of goods available for sale		$ 43,000
Ending inventory (2,000 units at $4.30†)		8,600
Cost of goods sold		$ 34,400
Gross profit on sales		$ 85,600
Selling and administrative expenses		5,000
Net operating profit		$ 80,600

* Total factory overhead = $24,000 (fixed factory overhead) ÷ 60% = $40,000.

† Total cost per unit = $43,000 ÷ 10,000 units produced = $4.30 per unit.

2 Direct Costing:

ENGLEWOOD COMPANY
INCOME STATEMENT
FOR MONTHS OF APRIL AND MAY 19X2

Sales (8,000 units at $15)		$120,000
Direct materials (10,000 units at $.20)	$ 2,000	
Direct labor (10,000 units at $.10)	1,000	
Variable factory overhead ($40,000 − $24,000)	16,000	
Cost of goods manufactured		$ 19,000
Beginning inventory		0
Cost of goods available for sale		$ 19,000
Ending inventory (2,000 at $1.90)*		3,800
Cost of goods sold		$ 15,200
Contribution margin		$104,800
Less fixed expenses:		
Factory overhead	$24,000	
Selling and administrative expenses	5,000	
Total fixed expenses		29,000
Net operating profit		$ 75,800

Note: The difference in net operating profit under the two methods results from the different unit cost applied to the ending inventory in each case.

* Total cost per unit = $19,000 ÷ 10,000 units produced = $1.90 per unit.

The difference in net operating profit under the two methods can be explained as follows.

Net operating profit under:	
Absorption costing	$80,600
Direct costing	75,800
Difference	$ 4,800
Ending inventory under:	
Absorption costing	$ 8,600
Direct costing	3,800
Difference	$ 4,800

The $4,800 difference is due to the difference in unit cost applied to the ending inventory in each method. If the $1.90 unit cost used in the direct costing method is deducted from the $4.30 unit cost used in the absorption costing method, a $2.40 difference results. When the $2.40 is multiplied by the 2,000 units of ending inventory, the $4,800 difference results.

ADVANTAGES OF DIRECT COSTING

The National Association of Accountants has long favored the use of direct costing and as far back as 1936 issued research reports and other publications pointing out the advantages of that cost method. Older versions of direct costing were used many years before that. The Financial Executives Institute through its Financial Executives Foundation reports a growing number of companies using direct costing. The rapid expansion of the work of many CPA firms' management services divisions is due in significant part to the installation of direct costing systems. Much of this work had long been carried out by specialized management consulting firms. It might be pointed out that the advantages or disadvantages do not actually relate to internal use or external use, but rather to the method itself. For many years companies using absorption costing have made analyses of direct and indirect costs and have prepared break-even charts. However, this data required special studies because the information was not readily available in the accounts as it is in direct costing.

The advantages of direct costing have generally been well recognized by top executives, production managers, marketing executives, and cost analysts. Direct costing overcomes the principal problem of absorption costing, that is, the distortion of the time relationship of sales, cost of goods sold, and net income.

Following are the principal advantages of direct costing.

Operations Planning. The plan of operations, or budget plan, covers all aspects of future operations designed to reach an established profit goal. Direct costing facilitates the compilation of profit-planning data which cost departments have always developed—often at great expense of time and effort, long before the advent of the present direct costing structures. The readily available data on variable cost and contribution margin permits quick answers to the scores of cost decisions which management must make each day, such as, the installation of a new machine or special cost center. Reliable estimates of the variable costs and total fixed costs can readily be provided by direct costing. If variable costs are $14 per unit, which is expected to be 70% of the unit sales price of $20, in line with similar products, and the total fixed costs are $45,000, the following quick feasibility computation can be made. The sales units are projected at 20,000 per year.

	PER UNIT	TOTAL AMOUNT	%
Sales, 20,000 units	$20	$400,000	100.0
Variable costs	14	280,000	70.0
Contribution margin	$ 6	$120,000	30.0
Fixed costs		45,000	11.2
Net operating income		$ 75,000	18.8

The key to the above computation is the variable cost of $14. The product would have to sell at $20, in accordance with the general pricing policy of cost being 70% of selling price ($14 ÷ 70% = $20). The marketing department estimates that annual sales would be approximately 20,000 units. With $400,000 sales, the net operating income would be $75,000, or 18.8% of sales. The project would be worth exploring further, since the net operating income percentage comfortably exceeds the break-even point, described below, under cost-volume-profit analysis.

Cost-Volume-Profit or Break-Even Analysis. A great many applications of this type of analysis are used continually by management in the day-to-day operations of a manufacturing company. Most managerial decisions are cost-related, and an understanding of these relationships is essential.

There are simple computations to determine the break-even point after the contribution margin and fixed costs are known. *The break-even point is the sales volume at which there will be neither a profit nor a loss.* Below this level a loss will occur; above this level a profit will be earned. This will be at the point where the *contribution margin is equal to the fixed expenses.* In the above example the contribution margin was 30% of sales or $6 per unit. Therefore, if we divide $45,000 by 30%, we have $150,000 sales.

To arrive at the number of units which have to be sold to break even, we could either divide the fixed cost by the contribution margin per unit or divide the sales by the unit selling price. The number of units which must be sold to break even:

$$\frac{\$45,000 \text{ fixed cost}}{\$6 \text{ unit contribution margin}} = 7,500 \text{ units}$$

$$\frac{\$150,000 \text{ sales}}{\$20 \text{ unit selling price}} = 7,500 \text{ units}$$

Based on the break-even sales computed above, the following summary can now be prepared:

	PER UNIT	TOTAL AMOUNT	%
Sales, 7,500 units	$20	$150,000	100
Variable costs (7,500 units)	14	105,000	70
Contribution margin	$ 6	$ 45,000	30

It can be seen the break-even sales point would be at $150,000, or 7,500 units. At this point the contribution margin and the fixed costs are equal.

Management Decisions. An adequate direct cost system will provide for the proper separation of fixed and variable costs. Semivariable costs will have been separated into fixed and variable components, and thus a convenient system is provided for the accumulation and evaluation of costs. Forecasting of costs and contribution margins, flexible volume analysis, relationship of costs to sales volume and price, and many other cost relationships can be readily studied. The direct cost income statement will enable management to see and understand the effect that period costs have on profits and will facilitate better decision making.

Product Pricing. Business people have been using variable costing in setting prices for a great many years. The understanding of contribution margin and pricing is one of the first things they must learn if they are to stay in business. Retailers know they must add a given percentage to the cost to arrive at the selling price. The contribution margin added (sales minus variable costs) must be large enough to cover all fixed expenses such as salaries, rent, and taxes and also provide a living income, or adequate return on investment.

Of course they cannot arrive at unreasonable selling prices because they have competitors who may have a lower selling price. The law of supply and demand will come into operation. If the price is too high, customers will not buy and the inventory will not move. Therefore, retailers will have to lower the selling price by reducing the rate of markup, and if the final return is to be maintained, they will have to reduce fixed costs.

Management Control. The reports based on direct costing are far more effective for management control than those based on absorption costing. First of all, the reports can be more directly related to the profit objective or budget for the period. Deviations from standards are more readily apparent and can be corrected more quickly. The variable cost of sales changes in direct proportion with volume. The distorting effect of production on profit is avoided, especially in the month following a high production month when substantial amounts of fixed costs are carried in inventory over to the next month. A substantial change in sales in the month after high production under absorption costing can result in a significant change in the net operating profit or loss.

Direct costing can pinpoint responsibility according to organizational lines;

individual performance can be evaluated on reliable data based on the current period. Operating reports can be prepared for all segments of the company, with costs separated into fixed and variable and the nature of any variance clearly shown. The responsibility for costs and variances can be attributed to specific individuals and functions, from top management down.

DISADVANTAGES OF DIRECT COSTING

External Reporting. The principal disadvantage of direct costing is its lack of acceptance for external reporting by the American Institute of Certified Public Accountants (predecessor of the Financial Accounting Standards Board), the Internal Revenue Service, and the Securities and Exchange Commission. Their opposition is highlighted as follows:

American Institute of Certified Public Accountants. According to the AICPA Professional Standards, Volume 3, AC Section 5.21, Inventory Pricing, formerly Accounting Research Bulletin 43, "The primary basis of accounting for inventories is cost, which has been defined generally as the price paid or consideration given to acquire an asset. As applied to inventories, cost means in principle the sum of the applicable expenditures and charges directly or indirectly incurred in bringing an article to its existing condition and location." This section also states that "It should also be recognized that the exclusion of all overheads from inventory does not constitute an accepted accounting procedure." The Financial Accounting Standards Board in its Interpretation No. 1 has supported the AICPA position.

Internal Revenue Service. Under IRS Regulation 1.471 certain costs must be included or excluded from inventory for income tax reporting *depending upon* their treatment for financial reporting, "but only if such treatment is not inconsistent with generally accepted accounting principles." Therefore, firms using direct costing must adjust inventories and net income to what they would have been under absorption costing.

Securities and Exchange Commission. The SEC also does not accept financial reports prepared under the direct costing method. Primarily this lack of acceptance is because direct costing is not a "generally accepted accounting procedure." It is also an SEC policy to encourage consistency in financial reporting. The reports of firms using direct costing must also be adjusted for inventories and net income to what they would have been if absorption costing had been used.

Separation of Variable and Nonvariable Costs. The opponents of direct costing argue that while direct costing appears theoretically attractive, it cannot be reliably achieved in practice. For example, there are a number of semivariable items which cannot readily be separated into variable and nonvariable costs. However, in a further step the variable and nonvariable components can be reasonably distinguished. These separations are equally as or more reliable than a large number of the arbitrary distributions of many indirect costs made in absorption costing that are only slightly related to manufacturing.

ADJUSTING FINANCIAL
STATEMENTS FOR EXTERNAL REPORTS

Companies using direct costing may obtain all the benefits of that method for managerial control and internal reporting and at the end of the period make a simple journal entry to adjust the data for external reports. A reconciliation of direct costing to absorption costing will be required as long as the direct costing procedure is not accepted by the AICPA, IRS, and SEC.

The only items to be adjusted are inventories and cost of goods sold for the amount of fixed factory overhead which was excluded from product costs under the direct costing method.

CHAPTER REVIEW

Direct costing has now come of age and is proving to be an extremely valuable tool in planning and controlling operations in many large industrial companies. Though still not as widely used as absorption costing, it is steadily gaining in use. The principal point of difference between the two costing methods is the treatment of fixed factory overhead costs. Absorption cost proponents contend that all factory costs, whether variable or fixed, are part of product costs and should be included in unit product costs in inventory. The proponents of direct costing maintain that fixed or nonvariable costs, whether in factory overhead or selling or administrative costs, are period costs related to time and have no future benefit, and are thus not acceptable as inventory costs. At present there is disagreement among accountants on the use of direct costing for external reports because of the exclusion of fixed overhead costs from inventories and its effect on net income. However, there is little doubt among accountants that direct costing is better suited for internal management purposes in planning, control, and decision making. A large number of companies now keep their records for both internal and external reporting needs. The records are maintained on the direct costing basis for management's daily needs, and at the end of the year when tax returns and formal financial statements are prepared for regulatory agencies and stockholders, a simple adjustment is made. The fixed factory overhead costs which were excluded under direct costing are added back to inventories, and the net income is adjusted to what it would have been if absorption costing had been used. Under absorption costing net income will tend to *vary with production* because of the deferred fixed costs included in inventory, whereas under direct costing net income will *vary with sales*.

GLOSSARY

Absorption Costing—the costing method under which all direct and indirect costs, including fixed factory overhead, are charged to product costs.

Contribution Margin—sales less variable manufacturing, selling, and administrative costs.

Direct Costing—the costing method under which only costs which tend to vary with the volume of production are charged to product costs.

External Reports—primarily formal financial statements such as the income statement, balance sheet, and statement of changes in financial position, filed with government regulatory agencies as required, or to stockholders.

Fixed Factory Overhead—period costs, such as rent, insurance, and taxes, required to *provide* or *maintain* facilities in condition for manufacturing.

Gross Profit—under absorption costing the sales, less cost of goods sold.

Internal Reports—the various cost, operating, and financial reports that are prepared daily, weekly, monthly, etc., for internal management in planning and controlling operations.

Variable Factory Overhead—the variable costs, such as indirect materials and payroll fringe benefits, which are *additional* costs needed to produce the particular product.

SUMMARY PROBLEM

Direct Cost and Absorption Cost

Stacey Manufacturing Co. is interested in comparing net earnings for two periods. The company's operating data is as follows:

	PERIOD 1	PERIOD 2
Standard production (units)	30,000	30,000
Actual production (units)	30,000	25,000
Sales (units)	25,000	30,000
Selling price per unit.............................	$15.00	$15.00
Variable manufacturing costs per unit:		
Direct materials $1.50		
Direct labor 2.50		
Variable overhead 2.00		
Total variable manufacturing costs per unit	$6.00	$6.00
Fixed overhead ($4 per unit)......................	$120,000	$120,000
Selling and administrative expenses	$ 50,000	$ 60,000

REQUIRED:

a Prepare a statement of earnings for both periods under the **(1)** absorption costing method, **(2)** direct costing method.

b Account for the difference in net earnings between the two methods.

c Explain why net earnings are equal under the two methods for the two periods combined.

d If the firm used direct costing in its formal accounting records, what adjustment is necessary for external reports?

(AICPA Adapted)

SOLUTION TO SUMMARY PROBLEM

a Statement of Earnings, Period 1

Absorption Costing

Sales (25,000 × $15)	$375,000
Cost of goods sold:	
Current manufacturing costs (30,000 × $10)*	$300,000
Less ending inventory (5,000 × $10)	50,000
Cost of goods sold	$250,000
Gross profit	$125,000
Selling and administrative expenses	50,000
Net earnings	$ 75,000

* Variable manufacturing cost ($6) + fixed overhead per unit ($4) = $10

Direct Costing

Sales (25,000 × $15)	$375,000
Cost of goods sold:	
Variable manufacturing costs (30,000 × $6)	$180,000
Less ending inventory (5,000 × $6)	30,000
Variable cost of goods sold	$150,000
Gross contribution margin	$225,000
Less fixed manufacturing overhead	120,000
	$105,000
Less selling and administrative expenses	50,000
Net earnings	$ 55,000

Statement of Earnings, Period 2

Absorption Costing

Sales (30,000 × $15)	$450,000
Cost of goods sold:	
Beginning inventory (5,000 × $10)	$ 50,000
Current manufacturing costs (25,000 × $10)	250,000
Less ending inventory	0
Cost of goods sold	$300,000
Gross profit	$150,000
Less underabsorbed overhead*	20,000
	$130,000
Less selling and administrative expenses	60,000
Net earnings	$ 70,000

*Actual overhead	$120,000	
Absorbed (25,000 × $4)	100,000	
Underabsorbed overhead	$ 20,000	

Direct Costing

Sales (30,000 × $15)	$450,000
Cost of goods sold:	
Beginning inventory (5,000 × $6)	$ 30,000
Variable manufacturing costs—variable (25,000 × $6)	150,000
Less ending inventory	0
Variable cost of goods sold	$180,000
Gross contribution margin	$270,000
Less fixed manufacturing overhead	120,000
	$150,000
Less selling and administrative expenses	60,000
Net earnings	$ 90,000

b The difference between the net earnings of period 1 of $75,000 (absorption costing) and $55,000 (direct costing) is attributable to the $20,000 of fixed overhead ($4 × 5,000 units) in the ending inventory under absorption costing which will not be charged to the statement of earnings until the next period when the units are sold.

c Sales equals production for the two periods combined (30,000 + 25,000 = 55,000 units); therefore, the net earnings are equal under the two methods for the two periods combined ($145,000) because there were no beginning inventories in period 1 and no ending inventories in period 2.

d If the firm uses direct costing in its formal accounting records, the cost of goods sold on the statement of earnings and the ending inventory on the statement of financial position would have to be adjusted to an absorption costing basis for external reporting to stockholders.

QUESTIONS

1 Discuss the difference between product costs and period costs.
2 An income statement prepared by direct costing is more helpful to management than an income statement prepared by the absorption costing method. Explain.
3 Describe direct costing. Explain how direct costing differs from absorption costing.
4 What would be the effect on net income reported under direct costing compared with absorption costing if sales exceed production?
5 What kind of cost figures are most likely to be helpful in determining a proper sales price?
6 Explain what factor, related to manufacturing costs, will cause a difference in net earnings computed using absorption costing, and net earnings computed using direct costing.

(AICPA adapted)

7 If the ending inventory increases with respect to the beginning inventory in terms of units, what will be the difference in net earnings computed using direct costing as opposed to absorption costing?

(AICPA adapted)

8 A basic tenet of direct costing is that period costs should be currently expensed. Explain the rationale behind this procedure.
9 Explain why direct costing is not in accordance with generally accepted accounting principles.
10 Discuss the principal differences between income statements prepared under direct costing and under absorption costing.
11 List two other terms for direct costing.
12 Discuss the principal disadvantage of direct costing.

EXERCISES

EXERCISE 1

Direct Costing Net Income

CS Company began its operations on January 1, 19X0, and produces a single product that sells for $7 per unit. Standard capacity is 100,000 units per year: 100,000 units were produced and 80,000 units were sold in 19X0.

Manufacturing costs and selling and administrative costs were as follows:

	VARIABLE COSTS
Raw materials	$1.50 per unit produced
Direct labor	1.00 per unit produced
Factory overhead ($150,000 fixed)	.50 per unit produced
Selling and administrative costs ($80,000 fixed)	.50 per unit sold

There were no variances from the standard variable costs. Any under- or over-applied overhead is written off directly at year end as an adjustment to cost of goods sold.

REQUIRED:

a In presenting inventory on the balance sheet at December 31, 19X0, what is the unit cost under absorption costing?

b What is net income in 19X0 under direct costing?

(AICPA Adapted)

EXERCISE 2

Multiple Choice

Select the best answer for each of the following:

1 Net profit under absorption costing may differ from net profit determined under direct costing. Is the difference calculated as a:
   a Change in the quantity of all units in inventory times the relevant fixed cost per unit?
   b Change in the quantity of units in inventory times the relevant variable cost per unit?
   c Change in the quantity of all units produced times the relevant fixed cost per unit?
   d Change in the quantity of all units produced times the relevant variable cost per unit?

2 Absorption costing differs from direct costing in the:
   a Fact that standard costs can be used with absorption costing but not with direct costing.
   b Amount of costs assigned to individual units of product.
   c Kinds of activities for which each can be used to report.
   d Amount of fixed costs that will be incurred.

3 Income computed by the absorption costing method will tend to exceed income computed by the direct costing method if:
   a Units produced exceed units sold.
   b Fixed manufacturing costs decrease.
   c Variable manufacturing costs decrease.
   d Units sold exceed units produced.

4 What is the term that means that all manufacturing costs (direct and indirect, variable and fixed) which contribute to the production of the product are traced to output and inventories?
   a Job order costing
   b Process costing
   c Full or absorption costing
   d Variable or direct costing

(AICPA Adapted)

EXERCISE 3

Multiple Choice

Select the best answer for each of the following:

1 A basic cost accounting method in which the fixed factory overhead is added to inventory is:
   a Absorption costing.
   b Direct costing.
   c Variable costing.
   d Process costing.

2 Reporting under the direct costing concept is accomplished by:
   a Including only direct costs in the income statement.
   b Eliminating the work-in-process inventory account.
   c Matching variable costs against revenues and treating fixed costs as period costs.
   d Treating all costs as period costs.

3 Which of the following is a more descriptive term for the type of cost accounting often called "direct costing"?
   a Out-of-pocket costing
   b Variable costing
   c Relevant costing
   d Prime costing

4 Product costs under direct costing include:
   a Prime costs only.
   b Prime costs and variable overhead.
   c Prime costs and fixed overhead.

5 The contribution margin is also known as:
   a Marginal income.
   b Net income.
   c Net operating profit.

(AICPA Adapted)

EXERCISE 4

Multiple Choice

Select the best answer for each of the following:

1 Why is direct costing not in accordance with generally accepted accounting principles?
   a Fixed manufacturing costs are assumed to be period costs.
   b Direct costing procedures are not too well known in industry.
   c When direct costing procedures are used, net earnings are always overstated.
   d Direct costing ignores the concept of lower of cost or market when valuing inventory.

2 The basic assumption made in a direct costing system concerning fixed costs is that fixed costs are:
  a A sunk cost.
  b A product cost.
  c Fixed as to total cost.
  d A period cost.
3 Net earnings using full absorption costing can be reconciled to net earnings determined using direct costing by computing the difference between:
  a Inventoried fixed costs in the beginning and ending inventories and any deferred over- or underapplied fixed factory overhead.
  b Inventoried discretionary costs in the beginning and ending inventories.
  c Gross margin (absorption costing method) and contribution margin (direct costing method).
  d Sales as recorded under the direct costing method and sales as recorded under the absorption costing method.
4 What will be the difference in net earnings computed using direct costing as opposed to absorption costing if the ending inventory increases with respect to the beginning inventory in terms of units?
  a There will be no difference in net earnings.
  b Net earnings computed using direct costing will be higher.
  c The difference in net earnings cannot be determined from the information given.
  d Net earnings computed using direct costing will be lower.

(AICPA Adapted)

EXERCISE 5

Absorption Costing—Net Income

James Engine Co. manufactures parts for small motors. The income using direct costing was $50,000 for a given period. Beginning and ending inventories for that period were 13,000 and 18,000 units, respectively. Ignore income taxes. The fixed overhead application rate was $2 per unit.

REQUIRED:

  What was the income using absorption costing?

(AICPA Adapted)

EXERCISE 6

Inventory Valuation—Direct Costing

Baldwin, Inc., manufactured 700 units of its new product, Whiz Ball, in 19X1. Whiz Ball's variable and fixed manufacturing costs per unit were $6 and $2, respectively. The inventory on December 31, 19X1, consisted of 100 Whiz Balls. There was no inventory of Whiz Balls on January 1, 19X1.

REQUIRED:

Calculate the change in the dollar amount of inventory on December 31, 19X1, if the direct costing method was used instead of the absorption costing method.

(AICPA Adapted)

EXERCISE 7

Inventory Valuation, Direct Costing

The accounting firm of Smith, Melodia, Soldano, and Michaels was asked by Daniel, Incorporated, to determine the value of its inventory. The company produces a line of two-piece bathing suits. In the month of July the company made 90,000 suits. It was a warm month; so sales increased 20% from June (June sales 50,000). Costs per suit for the 90,000 suits were

Direct materials	$4.00
Direct labor	2.00
Variable overhead	1.00
Fixed overhead	1.50

The ending inventory was 30,000 suits. The CPA firm used direct costing to value the inventory.

REQUIRED:

Compute the value of the ending inventory.

(AICPA Adapted)

EXERCISE 8

Inventory Costs—Absorption Costing vs. Direct Costing

The Stratford Manufacturing Co. is considering adopting a direct costing system. The management of The Stratford Manufacturing Co. has asked the controller what effect adopting the direct costing system would have on inventories. In answering the questions, the following figures, representing last year's operations, are used:

Units produced, 50,000 of which 15,000 were not sold:

Direct materials	$250,000
Direct labor	285,000
Factory overhead:	
Variable expenses	175,000
Fixed expenses	85,000

REQUIRED:

a The cost to be assigned the 15,000 units in inventory using absorption costing.

b The cost to be assigned the 15,000 units in inventory using direct costing.

EXERCISE 9

Direct Costing Income Statement

Danny's Sporting Goods Co. has prepared the following information and would like an income statement prepared using the direct costing (variable costing) approach. There were no beginning inventories of work-in-process or finished goods and no ending inventories of work-in-process.

Production: 550,000 units, of which 450,000 were sold for $32 each. Unit direct materials cost was $8, unit direct labor cost was $8.50, variable manufacturing cost was $1 per unit, and fixed manufacturing cost was $1,500,000. Variable selling and administrative cost was $1.25 per unit sold; fixed selling and administrative cost was $850,000.

REQUIRED:

Prepare an income statement using the direct costing approach.

EXERCISE 10

Unit Cost—Direct Costing

The Gary Tool Company produces a special saw for cutting plastic. Each saw sells for $25, and the company sells approximately 300,000 saws each year. Unit cost data for 19X1 are presented below:

Direct materials $5.00
Direct labor 4.00

	VARIABLE	FIXED
Other costs:		
Manufacturing	$2.00	$6.00
Distribution	3.00	2.00

REQUIRED:

Find the unit cost per saw for inventory using the direct costing approach.

(AICPA Adapted)

PROBLEMS

PROBLEM 1

Direct Costing vs. Absorption Costing

Supporters of direct costing have contended that it provides management with more useful accounting information. Critics of direct costing believe that its negative features outweigh its contributions.

REQUIRED:

a Describe direct costing. How does it differ from conventional absorption costing?

b List the arguments for and against the use of direct costing.

c Indicate how each of the following conditions would affect the amounts of net profit reported under conventional absorption costing and direct costing:

    1 Sales and production are in balance at standard volume.

    2 Sales exceed production.

    3 Production exceeds sales.

(AICPA Adapted)

PROBLEM 2

Direct Costing vs. Absorption Costing

Smith and David Fabricating Co. is considering changing its method of inventory valuation from absorption costing to direct costing. You are to determine the effects of the proposed change on the 19X0 financial statements.

The company manufactures fishing poles made from Marsh plastic. The Marsh plastic is added before processing starts, and labor and overhead are added evenly during the manufacturing process. Production capacity is 110,000 fishing poles annually. The standard costs per pole are

Marsh plastic, 2 pounds	$3.00
Labor	6.00
Variable manufacturing overhead ...	1.00
Fixed manufacturing overhead	1.10

A process cost system is used employing standard costs. Variances from standard costs are now charged or credited to cost of goods sold. If direct costing were adopted, only variances resulting from variable costs would be charged or credited to cost of goods sold. Inventory information for 19X0 follows:

	UNITS	
	JANUARY 1	DECEMBER 31
Marsh plastic (pounds)	50,000	40,000
Work-in-process:		
2/5 processed	10,000	
1/3 processed		15,000
Finished goods	20,000	12,000

During 19X0, 220,000 pounds of Marsh plastic were purchased and 230,000 pounds were transferred to work-in-process. Also 110,000 fishing poles were transferred to finished goods. Actual fixed manufacturing overhead during the year was $121,000. There were no variances between standard variable costs and actual variable costs during the year.

REQUIRED:

a Prepare schedules which present the computation of
    1 Equivalent units of production for materials, labor, and overhead
    2 Number of units sold.
    3 Standard unit cost under direct costing and absorption costing.
    4 Amount, if any, of over- or underapplied fixed manufacturing overhead.
b Prepare a comparative statement of cost of goods sold using standard direct costing and standard absorption costing.

(AICPA Adapted)

PROBLEM 3

Direct Costing: Net Operating Profit

The C.M.S. Corporation sells review books to accounting students. The company noticed a decline in sales for the months of May, June, and July, presumably due to the reduced number of students attending the summer session.

The variable costs to produce each book are as follows:

Direct materials	$2.00
Direct labor	1.00
Variable overhead	1.00
Total	$4.00

Fixed overhead is $12,000 per year; selling and administrative expenses are $6,000 per year. The selling price per book is $5. Actual data relating to inventories and sales are as follows:

QUANTITY	MAY	JUNE	JULY
Inventory (beginning)	0	1,000	3,000
Books produced	5,000	4,000	2,000
Books sold	4,000	2,000	1,000
Inventory (ending)	1,000	3,000	4,000

REQUIRED:

Find the net operating profit for May, June, and July, using direct costing.

PROBLEM 4

Income Statements: Direct Costing, Absorption Costing

The financial data for the Winsor Corporation are shown on page 634.

	19X8	19X9
Sales (in units)	125,000	95,000
Selling price (per unit)	$2.00	$2.00
Beginning inventory (units)	15,000	10,000
Ending inventory (units)	10,000	15,000
Production (units)	120,000	100,000
Direct materials (per unit)	$.10	$.05
Direct labor (per unit)	$.10	$.05
Variable overhead (per unit)	$.10	$.05
Fixed overhead (per unit)	$.20	$.10
Selling and administrative expenses total	$5,000	$3,000

Assume there was no under- or overapplied overhead

REQUIRED:

a Using the direct costing method, prepare an income statement for 19X9.

b Using the absorption costing method, prepare an income statement for 19X8.

c What is the effect on retained earnings in 19X8 if direct costing is used instead of absorption costing?

(AICPA Adapted)

PROBLEM 5

Direct Costing—Profit and Break-Even Analysis

The cost department of G. Smith and Sons, Inc., has established the following standards for manufacturing.

Normal capacity (units)	200,000
Maximum capacity (units)	250,000
Standard variable manufacturing cost per unit	$15
Variable marketing expenses per unit sold	$5
Fixed factory overhead	$400,000
Fixed marketing expenses	$250,000
Sales price per unit	$30

Operating units for the year ended 19X8 were as follows:

Beginning inventory	20,000
Sales	175,000
Production	180,000

REQUIRED:

a Prepare an income statement using direct costing.

b What is the break-even point expressed in dollars?

c How many units are to be sold to earn $80,000 in net operating income?

(AICPA Adapted)

PROBLEM 6

Direct Costing—Break-Even/Net Income

The following data relates to a year's budgeted activity for the Collins Corporation, a single-product company:

	UNITS
Beginning inventory	50,000
Production	100,000
Available	150,000
Sales	110,000
Ending inventory	40,000

	PER UNIT
Selling price	$5.00
Variable manufacturing costs	1.00
Variable selling costs	2.00
Fixed manufacturing costs (based on 100,000 units)	.25
Fixed selling costs (based on 100,000 units)	.65

Total fixed costs remain unchanged within the relevant range of 25,000 units to total capacity of 160,000 units.

REQUIRED:

a Break-even point in sales units for the Collins Corporation.
b Break-even in sales dollars.
c Projected net income for the Collins Corporation for the year under the direct (variable) costing approach.

(AICPA Adapted)

PROBLEM 7

Income Statements: Direct Costing and Absorption Costing

The Carpenter Manufacturing Co. provided the following data pertaining to its operations for the current calendar year:

Product units:

Beginning inventory	10,000
Produced	90,000
Sold	85,000
Ending inventory	15,000

Standard costs per product unit:

Direct materials	$3.25	
Direct labor	4.25	
Variable overhead	1.50	$ 9.00
Fixed overhead		2.00
Total		$11.00

Selling and administrative expenses:

Variable	$200,000
Fixed	80,000
Selling price per unit........................	$16.00

Assume there was no under- or overapplied overhead

REQUIRED:

a Construct two independent income statements using standard production costs for inventories and cost of goods manufactured. Construct one income statement using the absorption costing method and another using the direct costing method. Ignore income taxes.

b Reconcile the difference in net incomes shown by the two methods.

(AICPA Adapted)

PROBLEM 8

Computing Unit Costs, Contribution Margins, and Break-Even Point

Island Industries, Inc., operates its production department only when orders are received for one or both of its two products, two sizes of metal disks. The manufacturing process begins with the cutting of doughnut-shaped rings from rectangular strips of sheet metal; these rings are then pressed into disks. The metal sheets, each 4 feet long and weighing 32 ounces, are purchased at $1.36 per running foot. The department has been operating at a loss for the past year, as shown in the following table:

Sales for the year....................	$172,000
Expenses	177,200
Net loss for the department	($5,200)

The following information is available:

1 Ten thousand 4-foot pieces of metal yielded 40,000 large disks, each weighing 4 ounces and selling for $2.90, and 40,000 small disks, each weighing 2.4 ounces and selling for $1.40.

2 The corporation has been producing at less than "normal capacity" and has had no spoilage in the cutting step of the process. The skeletons remaining after the pieces have been cut are sold for scrap at $.80 per pound.

3 The variable conversion cost of each large disk is 80% of the disk's direct materials cost, and the variable conversion cost of each small disk is 75% of the disk's direct materials cost. Variable conversion costs are the sum of direct labor and variable overhead.

REQUIRED:

a For each of the parts manufactured, prepare a schedule computing:

1 Unit materials cost after deducting the value of salvage (or scrap value).

    2 Unit variable conversion cost.
    3 Unit contribution margin.
    4 Total contribution margin for all units sold.
  b Assuming you computed the materials cost for large disks at $.85 each and for small disks at $.51 each, compute the number of units the corporation must sell to break even based on a normal production capacity of 50,000 units. Assume no spoiled units and a product mix of one large disk to each small disk.

(AICPA Adapted)

PROBLEM 9

Net Income, Income Statements, Break-Even Point

Zullo Company has a maximum productive capacity of 180,000 units per year. Standard variable manufacturing costs are $11 per unit. Fixed factory overhead is $360,000 per year. Variable selling expenses are $3 per unit sold, and fixed selling expenses are $252,000 per year. The unit sales price is $20.
  The operating results for 19X9 are

Sales.........................	150,000 units
Production	160,000 units
Beginning inventory	10,000 units

  Net unfavorable variance for standard variable manufacturing cost is $40,000. All variances are written off as additions to (or deductions from) standard cost of sales.

REQUIRED:

  (For parts **a** and **b** assume no variances from standards for manufacturing costs.)
  a How many units must be sold to have net earnings of $60,000 per year?
  b What is the break-even point expressed in dollar sales?
  c Prepare a formal statement of earnings for 19X9 under
    1 Conventional (absorption) costing
    2 "Direct" costing
  d Briefly account for the difference in net earnings between the two statements of earnings.

(AICPA Adapted)

PROBLEM 10

Income Statements under Direct and Absorption Costing

The S. T. Shire Company uses direct costing for internal management purposes and absorption costing for external reporting purposes. Thus, at the end of each year financial information must be converted from direct costing to absorption costing in order to satisfy external requirements.
  At the end of 19X1 it was anticipated that sales would rise 20% the next year.

Therefore, production was increased from 20,000 units to 24,000 units to meet this expected demand. However, economic conditions kept the sales level at 20,000 units for both years.

The following data pertain to 19X1 and 19X2:

	19X1	19X2
Selling price per unit	$30	$30
Sales (units)	20,000	20,000
Beginning inventory (units)	2,000	2,000
Production (units)	20,000	24,000
Ending inventory (units)	2,000	6,000
Unfavorable labor, materials, and		
variable overhead variances (total)	$5,000	$4,000

STANDARD VARIABLE COSTS PER UNIT FOR 19X1 AND 19X2

Labor	$ 7.50
Materials	4.50
Variable overhead	3.00
	$ 15.00

ANNUAL FIXED COSTS FOR 19X1 AND 19X2 (BUDGETED AND ACTUAL)

Production ....:...............................	$ 90,000
Selling and administrative	100,000
	$190,000

The overhead rate under absorption costing is based upon practical plant capacity, which is 30,000 units per year. All variances and under- or overabsorbed overhead are taken to cost of goods sold. All taxes are to be ignored.

REQUIRED:

a Present the income statement based on direct costing for 19X2.
b Present the income statement based on absorption costing for 19X2.
c Explain the difference, if any, in the net income figures. Give the entry necessary to adjust the book figures to the financial statement figure, if one is necessary.

(CMA Adapted)

CHAPTER EIGHTEEN

DECENTRALIZED OPERATIONS AND RESPONSIBILITY ACCOUNTING

In this chapter we will discuss the effect of decentralized operations on the cost accounting function and the relationship of responsibility accounting to cost accounting. The question of how much decentralization is desirable in a company has been a controversial subject for many years. As a company grows, top management must continually rearrange responsibilities among the various managers. At the point where it is desirable or necessary to separate physical units of the organization, top management must decide first how to divide the responsibilities and the activities, and second how to coordinate the decentralized segments.

In recent years greater attention has been focused on responsibility accounting and the development of reports which measure how the assigned responsibility is being carried out. These factors will be discussed in this chapter.

CONCEPTS OF ORGANIZATION

A business organization is a combination of people, money, and machines brought together to fulfill an economic objective. Organization planning is essentially determining how these elements will be coordinated to achieve the specific company objectives. A few years ago the emphasis was on economic resources and company objectives. However, in recent years it has been shown that greater recognition should be given to human resources and that the need for personal motivation should be considered in any definition of organization planning. Therefore, we might broaden the conventional definition to give effect to human resources as follows: "Organization planning is

the process of logically grouping activities, delineating authority and responsibility, and establishing working relationships that will enable both the
company and the employee to realize their mutual objectives."[1]

This definition recognizes that corporate objectives are accomplished only
through people. Employees, particularly professional employees, identify
themselves with company objectives only to the extent that their own objectives
are also achieved. Therefore, in any organizational arrangement the needs
and aspirations of employees must be carefully considered.

GROUPING OF ACTIVITIES

The first consideration in developing organization structures is to decide which
way and to what extent the activities shall be grouped. The major approaches
usually are functional, product, and geographical.

Functional Approach

In the functional approach the company is organized according to such major
functions as production, marketing, personnel, and finance. Generally the
control is centralized at the vice president level. The production employees
report upward from the lowest operating level to the vice president level. The
disadvantage is that key decisions must be made at the top, which is usually
a long process.

Product Approach

In the product approach the functional responsibilities are combined according
to products or groups of products and responsibilities are fixed in terms of the
product. The principal advantage is the more effective coordination of activities
relating to the product.

Geographical Approach

In the geographical approach the responsibilities are grouped according to
geographical areas. The managerial responsibility will encompass all functions
and all products in a particular geographical area. The benefits here lie in the
better coordination of all operations in a particular geographical area.

The choice of approaches depends upon the nature of the activities involved
and upon which may need to be more centralized. In most cases there will be
some overlap; some functions will be organized on one level, some on another.
The sales function may be established at the top on a functional basis, but at
the field level it may be organized on a geographical basis, with district and
regional offices, or it may be set up at some levels on a customer basis (retail
users, industrial users, etc.). In practice the problem is to find the best
combination of approaches.

[1] Corporate Organization Structures, Studies in Personnel Policy No. 158, National Industrial
Conference Board.

EXAMPLES OF TYPES OF ORGANIZATION
STRUCTURE AND RESPONSIBILITY REPORTING

The principal approaches, functional, product, and geographical or regional, to grouping organization activities and the related reporting of responsibilities are illustrated below. For each approach we include an organization chart to show the arrangement of activities, and cost reports to illustrate the manner of reporting costs at each level. Generally the higher the level the more condensed the report would be. For example, the report to the president would show the expenses of the office according to category of expense and then the total for each division or group that reports directly. The president would direct any questions concerning the costs of a particular group to the vice president responsible for that division.

In presenting charts or reports for responsibility accounting, generally one of two methods is used: method 1, starting from the top and going down, that is, with level 1 as the president, down to level 4, the department supervisor; or method 2, starting from the bottom and going up, that is, with level 1 as the department supervisor, up to level 4, the president. For the following charts and reports we will use method 1, with level 1 as the president. Later in the chapter method 2 will be presented in the discussion of responsibility accounting.

The levels of responsibility should be well defined and should be consistent for all levels. At *level 1* we have the office of the *president*, who is responsible for all operations, assuming that the president is the chief executive officer. In some companies the chairperson of the board is the chief executive officer and receives the report. At *level 2* we have the *vice presidents*, each of whom is responsible for a division. They report to the president. At *level 3* we have the *plant managers*, each of whom is responsible for a plant in one of the divisions. They report to a vice president. At *level 4* we have the *supervisors*, each of whom is responsible for a department of a plant. They report to the manager of the plant. We could carry it further to another level, such as a cost center in a department, but that is not needed for our purpose. The costs may be classified in a number of ways, depending on the desires of the company. If there are many divisions and plants in a company, it is important that there be a uniform system of accounts so that the cost classifications among units are comparable and the cost of an individual item in one plant can be compared with the cost in another plant. In some cases only controllable costs are detailed; in others, the company may include noncontrollable costs in the report. The exact arrangement of costs in reports will vary greatly among companies.

For each approach the relationships of the various levels and the reporting responsibilities of those levels are as shown below.

Functional Approach

As can be seen in Figure 18-1 (page 642), all vice presidents, level 2, report to the president, level 1. For easier understanding we use only three divisions: marketing, manufacturing, and finance. In practice there would ordinarily be

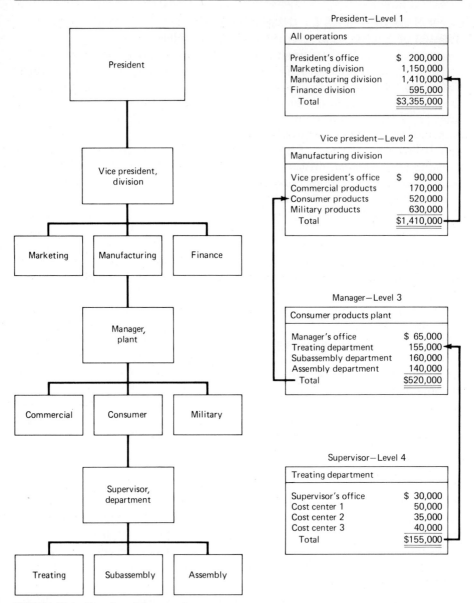

FIGURE 18-1 **Functional Approach**

more than three divisions, but the principle is the same. On the reporting side
we see the operations of all divisions of the company condensed in the
president's report. Shown are the costs of the president's office, including the
president's salary, that of the president's secretary, and various other expenses.
Following are shown the totals only of the divisions, which are: marketing,
$1,150,000; manufacturing, $1,410,000; and finance, $595,000.

For illustrating level 2 we will use the operations of the manufacturing division. As can be seen, the total for the manufacturing division agrees with the total shown in level 1. We see that the manufacturing plants in this division produce three distinct products, commercial products, consumer products, and military products. The costs of running the manufacturing vice president's office amount to $90,000, and the costs for the individual plants are: commercial, $170,000; consumer, $520,000; and military, $630,000. The total is $1,410,000. The other plants would report similarly.

The next level would be manager—level 3. For illustration we will use the consumer products plant, although any other plant would do as well. Here we see that the total is $520,000, which agrees with the amount shown on the next higher level. The manager's office cost is $65,000, and the department costs are as follows: treating, $155,000; subassembly, $160,000; and assembly, $140,000.

The next level would be supervisor—level 4. For illustration we will use the treating department, which has a total cost of $155,000 and agrees with the amount shown in level 3. The cost of the supervisor's office is $30,000, and the amounts for the cost centers are: cost center 1, $50,000; cost center 2, $35,000; and cost center 3, $40,000.

In addition to the summary statements shown above for the various levels, there would be a cost statement for each unit or cost center according to the nature of the cost, such as supervision or fringe benefits. For example, if we showed such costs for level 5, cost center 1, for controllable costs, it would appear somewhat as follows:

Cost center 1 — Level 5

Controllable costs	
Supervision	$20,000
Fringe benefits	5,000
Machine setup	3,000
Rework	8,000
Supplies	5,000
Other costs	9,000
Total	$50,000

FIGURE 18-A **Cost Center**

Product Approach

Under this approach (Figure 18-2, page 644) we see that the total for all operations, level 1, is the same as before but that the organizational grouping is entirely different from that under the functional approach. All the activities of the company can be related to either chemical, drug, or paint operations. Here we see that the drug division total, level 2, is $1,430,000 and that it is the largest division shown on the president's report, level 1. In the report for the vice president—level 2, we see that the drug division is responsible for three

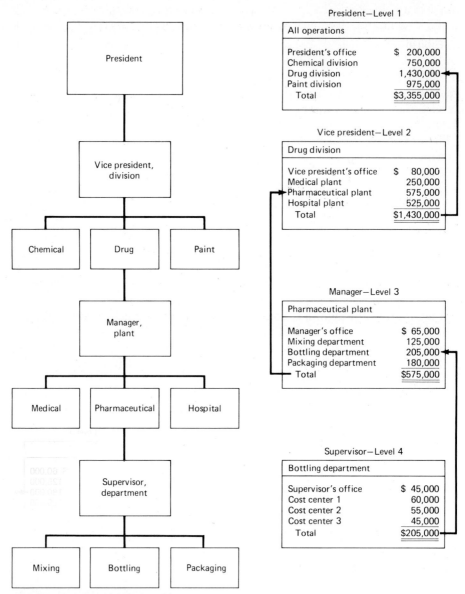

FIGURE 18-2 **Product Approach**

manufacturing plants which make the following distinct professional supplies: medical, pharmaceutical, and hospital. As can be seen, the level 2 report shows a total cost for the pharmaceutical plant as $575,000. The other two plants would present similar reports. The manager's report, level 3, shows that there are also three separate departments in the pharmaceutical plant: mixing, bottling, and packaging. The total for the level 3 report of $575,000 agrees with the amount shown on the level 2 report. In the level 4 supervisor's report, it can be seen that there are three separate cost centers in the bottling department, making up the total of $205,000, which is shown on the level 3 report. We could go on to the next level to show one of the cost centers, but the principle should now be apparent.

Geographical Approach

Under this approach, sometimes called the regional approach (Figure 18-3), the total for all operations is the same as in the functional approach and the

FIGURE 18-3 **Geographical Approach**

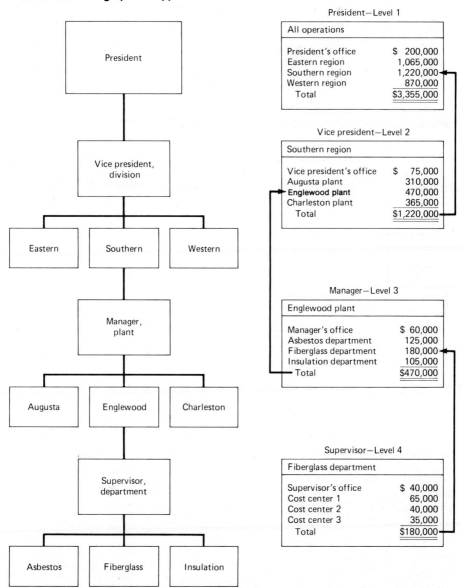

President—Level 1

All operations	
President's office	$ 200,000
Eastern region	1,065,000
Southern region	1,220,000
Western region	870,000
Total	$3,355,000

Vice president—Level 2

Southern region	
Vice president's office	$ 75,000
Augusta plant	310,000
Englewood plant	470,000
Charleston plant	365,000
Total	$1,220,000

Manager—Level 3

Englewood plant	
Manager's office	$ 60,000
Asbestos department	125,000
Fiberglass department	180,000
Insulation department	105,000
Total	$470,000

Supervisor—Level 4

Fiberglass department	
Supervisor's office	$ 40,000
Cost center 1	65,000
Cost center 2	40,000
Cost center 3	35,000
Total	$180,000

product approach, but the subsidiary levels vary considerably. Instead of being arranged according to function or product, the structure is arranged according to geographic region. Companies that have products which are very bulky and costly to transport may have manufacturing and warehousing facilities in the same region to minimize shipping costs. Thus, a company may have an Eastern division, a Southern division, and a Western division. This arrangement could serve customers in the respective regions much more efficiently. In the Southern region, level 2, there are three plants: Augusta, Ga., Englewood, Fla., and Charleston, S.C. Each plant may have its own warehouse, or there may be a large warehouse, centrally located, from which all divisional shipments may be made.

In level 3 we see that the total of $470,000 for the Englewood plant ties in to the amount for that plant shown in the level 2 report. The Englewood plant has three departments making distinct products composed of the following materials: asbestos materials, fiberglass materials, and insulation materials. We can see that the total for the fiberglass department of $180,000 ties in to the applicable amount shown in the level 3 report.

DECENTRALIZATION PROBLEMS

Determining the extent of authority and responsibility that should be decentralized is a problem that is common to all the approaches to grouping of activities. Generally the degree of decentralization will be greater under the product approach, and in many instances it will be a practical requirement, as in cases of foreign locations. The extent of decentralization will depend somewhat on the ability of the individuals to be responsible for the lower-level decisions, the feasibility of coordinating the various operations, and the impact of the decentralized decisions on other units of the company.

Advantages of Decentralization

The principal advantages of decentralization are:

1 Top managers will have more time to devote to general planning instead of being burdened with routine daily decisions.
2 The decision-making task is distributed among more personnel so that each person will have enough time to give matters sufficient attention.
3 Better control can be achieved, as the manager can move quickly to make needed corrections.
4 Managers are more motivated, as they have more control over the matters that measure their performance.
5 Managers are more likely to exercise initiative such as "comparison shopping" of outside materials costs. This comparison of internal and external costs tends to keep internal costs, such as transfer pricing of intracompany goods, in line.
6 As managers become more proficient in decision making, they become more qualified for higher management positions.

The greater the independence, the greater the need for coordination in order to obtain benefits for the company as a whole. Where the operating units have substantial independence, there may actually be competition among the units for certain limited materials. The costs of decentralization are minimized when the decentralized unit:

1 Can establish its own goals without coordination with other units.
2 Does not depend on other units for its raw materials.
3 Does not depend on other units for its sales.
4 Does not compete externally with other units for limited raw materials, supplies, etc.
5 Does not compete internally for limited capital or research appropriations.

Cost of Decentralization

The principal cost of decentralization is probably the very thing that is also the most beneficial, that is, the delegation of responsibility. The decentralization concept can be carried too far, and the goals of the corporation as a whole and the good of the decentralized unit may not conform. For example, the manager of a unit may take certain actions that benefit the unit but may not be beneficial to the company as a whole.

In some instances there may be a bonus plan for the operating units based on volume of sales. Where the incentive plan is based on sales rather than gross profit, it is advantageous for the manager of an operating unit to concentrate on selling those products which have a high sales price but a low gross profit and which often have a slightly lower price than competitors' products. Therefore, the particular unit would have a high proportion of sales but a low proportion of gross profit. In most companies some effect is given to gross profit to offset any effort to benefit the unit or manager to the detriment of the company as a whole.

PROFIT CENTER

A *profit center* is a segment of the organization that has been assigned control over both *revenues* and *costs*. A *cost center*, on the other hand, is a segment of the organization that has been assigned control only over the incurrence of *costs*. A cost center has no control over sales or marketing activities. Therefore, the manager of a unit or division that has control over both income and costs will attempt to maximize the profit on their assigned investment. Generally, the profit center is the principal means of implementing decentralization. However, we must keep in mind that it is possible to have profit centers in highly centralized companies and cost centers in highly decentralized companies. In fact, it is common to have both centralized sections and decentralized sections in one company. Generally, certain limitations are placed on a profit center by corporate headquarters. For example, while profit center managers may have control over sales and costs, they often do not have control over the amount of investment or final approval over individual projects, above a designated maximum amount. Decisions on investment projects are generally made by a top management committee which includes corporate officers.

An example of a profit center would be a division under a vice president who has responsibility for sales and costs. For example, in Figure 18-2, the vice president for the drug division would generally have control over sales and costs. In Figure 18-3, the vice president of the Southern division would also have control over sales and costs.

An *investment center* differs from a profit center in that it has control not only over *revenues* and *costs* but also over *invested funds*.

RESPONSIBILITY ACCOUNTING

Most cost accounting systems were originally designed to accumulate and distribute costs for product or inventory cost and for general cost control. The accounts were set up to gather product costs and period costs in accordance with the needs of the income statement and balance sheet. This system worked well in showing where the money was spent but not so well in determining who was responsible for incurring the cost and how to take prompt corrective action if necessary. In the balance of this chapter we will be concerned with an accounting system directed toward individuals, that is, *who* spent the money rather than *what* the expense was. It is not necessary to change the generally accepted accounting principles used for many of the accounting statements prepared. However, this is definitely a different approach to cost accumulation, with emphasis shifting from product costing to responsibility accounting.

Responsibility Accounting Defined

Before proceeding further, we should define what we mean by the term "responsibility accounting." Various definitions are given in leading accounting texts, but they all contain the essential points included in the following definition: "Responsibility accounting is a system designed to accumulate and report costs by individual levels of responsibility. . . . Each supervisory area is charged only with the cost for which it is responsible and over which it has control."[1] The responsibility accounting system should also provide costs for establishing policies and for making daily decisions.

Essentials of Control

No matter how well designed a system is, it will not be successful unless it has the support of the people who operate the system. The system must be based on people responsibility, as it is people who incur costs and should be held accountable for each expenditure. The principal controls in the incurrence of costs are:

[1] John A. Higgins, "Responsibility Accounting," *The Arthur Andersen Chronicle*, Vol. C.

1 An organization plan which establishes objectives and goals to be achieved.
2 The delegation of authority and responsibility for cost incurrence through a system of policies and procedures.
3 Motivation of individuals by developing standards of performance together with incentives.
4 Timely reporting and analysis of exceptions between goals and performance by means of a system of records and reports.
5 A system of appraisal or internal auditing to assure that unfavorable variances are clearly shown and that corrective action and follow-up are applied.

Organization Structure

Before a responsibility accounting system is designed, there must be a thorough study of the organization. The lines of authority must be clarified before the responsibility system is completed. Where authorities and responsibilities have been properly established, there will be a structure of management levels each of which will have a responsibility center or sphere of responsibility and the authority to make decisions within the established sphere. Responsibility accounting will provide the means of tracing costs to individual managers primarily responsible for incurring the particular costs. Generally, the system should be set up so that costs can be automatically traced to the individual at the lowest organization level responsible for the item. Managers are not subject to day-to-day monitoring of their decisions but are held accountable by means of responsibility accounting.

Responsibility Accounting System

One of the first requirements in developing a good responsibility accounting system is a sound organization structure, which is usually shown by means of an organization chart. In some cases the installation of a responsibility accounting system has uncovered weaknesses in the organization structure which had to be corrected before the accounting system could be established. The next step is to develop a chart of accounts which will collect costs, not by products or types of expense, but by responsibility centers.

For illustration, we will use the Columbia Manufacturing Company, which produces and sells appliance parts. Costs are gathered for each responsibility center as needed; some are reported daily, others weekly and monthly. There are four levels of responsibility in the Columbia Manufacturing Company, designated as in Figure 18-4 (page 650).

Level 1—Departments. In this plant there are three production departments, machining, assembly, and finishing. There are also service departments such as engineering and purchasing whose costs are prorated back to the production departments as indirect costs. However, they do not need to be shown on the chart for our purposes.

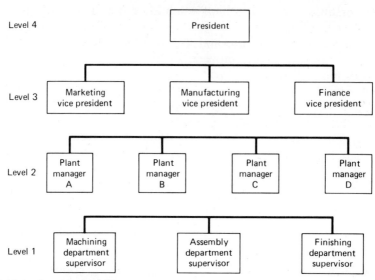

FIGURE 18-4 **Organization Chart**

Level 2—Plants.   The company has four manufacturing plants, A, B, C, and D, which are all located within a radius of 20 miles of headquarters. The headquarters for the company is located in Plant C.

Level 3—Vice Presidents.   The company has three vice presidents for the functions of marketing, manufacturing, and finance. There are staff assistant vice presidents but they are not needed on the chart for our purposes.

Level 4—President.   The company president is also the chief executive officer. There are four staff assistants, but they are not needed on the chart for our purpose.

Responsibility Accounting Reports

Responsibility accounting reports are prepared according to responsibility levels shown in the organization chart. At each level the direct costs incurred by the unit manager are listed, and then the costs incurred by each of the subordinate unit managers are shown. Thus, at level 4 the report would include the total cost for the company, that is, the cost of the president's office plus the costs of the immediate subordinates, the vice presidents.

As can be seen in Table 18-1 the performance reports for the month of March 19X0 have been presented on four levels—Level 1 for the assembly department supervisor, level 2 for the plant manager, Plant C, level 3 for the vice president—manufacturing, and level 4 for the president. These reports are discussed in detail below.

Level 1—Assembly Department Supervisor.   The detailed costs listed are those directly controllable by the supervisor. Materials and direct labor are charged

TABLE 18-1
RESPONSIBILITY REPORTS, CONTROLLABLE COSTS, MARCH 19X0

| | CURRENT MONTH | | |
	BUDGET	ACTUAL	VARIANCE
Level 4—President:			
President's office	$ 25,000	$ 24,000	($1,000)
Vice president—marketing	125,000	128,000	3,000
Vice president—manufacturing	165,000	164,800	(200)
Vice president—finance	50,000	49,000	(1,000)
Total controllable cost	$365,000	$365,800	$ 800
Level 3—Vice President—Manufacturing:			
Vice president—manufacturing office	$ 10,000	$ 8,000	($2,000)
Plant A	20,000	21,000	1,000
Plant B	25,000	23,500	(1,500)
Plant C	70,000	71,300	1,300
Plant D	40,000	41,000	1,000
Total controllable cost	$165,000	$164,800	($ 200)
Level 2—Plant Manager—Plant C:			
Plant manager's office	$20,000	$20,500	$ 500
Machining department	10,000	9,400	(600)
Assembly department	15,000	15,400	400
Finishing department..................	25,000	26,000	1,000
Total controllable cost	$70,000	$71,300	$1,300
Level 1—Assembly Department Supervisor:			
Direct materials	$ 8,000	$ 8,500	$ 500
Direct labor	5,000	4,400	(600)
Machine setup	1,000	1,300	300
Rework	500	700	200
Supplies	200	100	(100)
Other.................................	300	400	100
Total controllable costs	$15,000	$15,400	$ 400

( ) = Variance favorable.

to the department at standard cost. The materials price variance is charged to purchasing, and the labor rate variance is charged to personnel. The variances attributable to the department are analyzed and investigated where they are significant. The budget cost for the department was $15,000 for the month, with a total unfavorable variance of $400. These amounts are shown in a year-to-date report, similar to the current-month report.

Level 2—Plant Manager—Plant C. In the report, the plant manager's office cost is shown first, then the totals for each of the departments of that plant. These totals are taken from the reports prepared by the departments for which the plant manager is responsible. Note that the amounts for the assembly department as described above are listed in the plant manager's report. The budget cost for the plant was $70,000 for the month with a total unfavorable variance of $1,300.

Level 3—Vice President—Manufacturing. The cost of the office of the vice president—manufacturing is shown first on the report, then the totals for each of the plants for which the vice president is responsible. These totals are taken from the reports prepared for the plants reporting to the vice president—manufacturing. The total amounts for Plant C, as described above, are listed in the vice president—manufacturing report. The budget cost for all plants and for the headquarters office was $165,000 for the month, with a favorable variance of $200. These amounts are carried to the president's report as described below.

Level 4—President. In the president's report the cost of the office is shown first, then the totals for each of the subordinate vice presidents. The totals are taken from the reports of the various plants for which the vice president is responsible. The amounts for the vice president—manufacturing as described above are listed in the presidents report. The budget cost for all operations of the company was $365,000 for the month, with a total unfavorable variance of $800.

THE ESSENTIALS OF
GOOD PERFORMANCE REPORTS

Performance reports answer a wide variety of needs and are as diverse as the desires and needs of differing managements. However, certain essentials should govern the design and distribution of performance reports. The following is adapted from "How to Set Up Internal Reports for Managerial Purposes" by James A. Cashin, in *Accountant's Encyclopedia*, Prentice-Hall:

1 *Fit report to recipient*—Find out what the manager wants and what he can use. Provide more detail for lower levels, more summarized data for upper levels.
2 *Fit report to organization chart*—Have individual reports for each organization level.
3 *Keep number of reports to a minimum*—Make sure each report is used and serves a specific purpose.
4 *Make reports timely*—Determine if the report should be made daily, weekly, or monthly.
5 *Use action reports*—Use action techniques that motivate management to take corrective action.
6 *Include only essential data*—Emphasize important elements; group less important items into significant totals.
7 *Issue reports earlier*—Make flash reports when practical; organize accounting system to expedite reports; make earlier cutoffs.
8 *Pinpoint responsibility*—Fit data to responsibility. Individual responsibility should be apparent.
9 *Standardize presentation, forms, etc.*—Style of presentation should be consistent. Use conventional form, size, paper, etc.

10 *Simplify and clarify*—State facts concisely; arrange data in logical sequence; interpret significant data; use short titles; use physical units as well as dollars.

11 *Show comparisons, ratios, trends, etc.*—Compare current and cumulative data to budget and to last year; use principle of exception; show variances as favorable or unfavorable.

12 *Make system flexible*—Revise reports as conditions warrant; change emphasis as needed; issue special reports, if needed.

13 *Consider cost*—Avoid duplication of data; obtain data from regular accounting process; investigate alternate methods of presentation, reproduction, etc., to reduce costs.

14 *Use visual aids*—Visual presentation conserves management time; relationships and trends are clearer than statistical presentation; consider advantages of each chart type; use trend indicators, daily, weekly, etc.

15 *Control distribution*—Make sure the individual responsible gets report; fix responsibility for distribution of reports; keep distribution list up to date.

CONTROLLABLE COSTS

In the reports presented in Table 18-1 the only costs shown are those which can be controlled by the responsibility unit managers. That approach is a matter of preference, which is based on the premise that managers should not be charged with costs over which they have no control. However, many companies look at it another way and show separately the costs allocated from other departments. They point out that while managers are not charged with control of these allocated costs, they should be aware of the total cost of the responsibility unit for which they are responsible.

Controllable costs are those that may be directly influenced by unit managers in a given time period. Where managers have both the acquisition right and the use right, the cost may be considered as controllable by them. However, in most cases, controllability generally is not the complete responsibility of one person; there are varying degrees of influence by other individuals in most companies. It may be said that all costs are controllable at some level at some time. The unit manager does not have complete control over direct materials costs. Thus the price at which materials are purchased is controllable by the purchasing department. If the price variance is excluded, the unit manager then has control primarily over usage. However, there may be excess usage or spoilage in a particular period which cannot be charged to the manager. For example, in a period of scarcity the purchasing agent could not get materials from the regular supplier and had to get the goods from a new supplier. During production it was found that the goods were of inferior quality in certain respects such as tensile strength, and excess spoilage resulted. The reports showed the manager had excess spoilage, but it should not end there. Such problems could probably have been averted if independent tests had been ordered by the purchasing department or if a test had been made by the company value analysis unit or the laboratory.

COSTS OF SERVICE DEPARTMENTS

The costs incurred by service departments generally will have to be allocated to production departments in order to arrive at proper product costs. We must keep in mind that responsibility accounting must also be applied to service departments as well as to producing departments. The purchasing department, for example, must be as cost-conscious as the production department, and only costs properly chargeable as purchasing expenditures should be included. The next question is how the costs of the service departments are to be allocated. There may be one or more suballocations before the principal allocation is made to the producing departments. The allocation may be considered as a purchase by the recipient, in the same manner as a purchase of direct materials or labor. Thus when a maintenance department employee repairs a machine in a producing department it may be looked on as incurring the cost of a repair from an outside repair company. The overhead of the maintenance department may be allocated to maintenance jobs on the basis of maintenance labor hours. For example, if maintenance Job 150 called for the repair of a machine in the drill press department requiring 4 hours, the allocated cost would be 4 hours times the rate per maintenance labor hour. Assuming the maintenance labor is $5 per hour and maintenance overhead is 100% of labor, the total rate per hour would be $10. The total to be allocated to the drill press department for that job would be $40 ($20 labor + $20 overhead).

CHAPTER REVIEW

As organizations have grown in size and are more widespread in operations, the burden on central management has greatly increased. In order to help lessen the pressure, the decision-making responsibility in many cases has been decentralized in line with the decentralization of the physical properties of the company. The decision making is thus located closer to the operations and has more information than is generally available at headquarters. This allows the decisions to be made at a lower level and helps in training local managers for higher responsibilities. It also gives the top executives more time to concentrate on the higher policy-making decisions.

A change to a responsibility accounting system does not require any significant change in accounting theory or generally accepted accounting principles. It involves primarily a change in emphasis, from product costing to responsibility costing. Thus, revenues and expenses are accumulated and reported by levels of responsibility in order that actual costs can be controlled by the responsible manager and compared with budgeted performance data. An important advantage of responsibility accounting is that a built-in means for evaluating a manager's performance is readily available. Also, information is readily available to act promptly to correct deviations from the established company objectives.

GLOSSARY

Decentralized Operations — the spreading of responsibility and decision making over a wider range of managers, generally of a lower level.

Functional Approach—the organization structure in which responsibilities are grouped based on specific functions such as sales and production.

Geographic Approach—the organization structure in which responsibilities are grouped according to geographical area.

Levels of Responsibility—the responsibility structure from the lowest level, level 1, the supervisor, to the highest responsibility level, the president or chairperson of the board.

Organization Planning—the process of logically grouping activity, authority, and responsibility to enable both the company and the employee to realize their objectives.

Product Approach—the organization structure in which the functions and activities are grouped according to products or groups of products.

Profit Center—a unit in which performance is measured in terms of budgeted profit and has responsibility for both income and expenses.

Responsibility Accounting—an accounting system designed to accumulate and report costs by individual levels of responsibility.

Responsibility Center—a unit in which the manager has the responsibility and authority to make decisions for that unit.

Responsibility Reports—the performance reports showing the performance of managers accountable for specific responsibility units.

SUMMARY PROBLEMS

PROBLEM 1

In the Sunny Company, every level of management reports to the president. Four vice presidents oversee the following activities: marketing, manufacturing, finance, and sales. Products are fabricated at five plants A, B, C, D, and E, each with three departments. Each plant is run by a manager, and each department, forming, cleaning, and packing, is headed by a supervisor.

There are three sales territories, each headed by sales managers X, Y, and Z. One department in the firm takes care of all its advertising.

In the accounting area, there are three major divisions: accounts payable, accounts receivable, and payroll. Accounting is part of the finance activity.

REQUIRED:

Prepare an organization chart for Sunny Corporation.

PROBLEM 2

Sunny Company has five plants, A, B, C, D and E. Each plant has a forming, cleaning and packing department. Each level of management at Sunny Company has responsibility over costs incurred at its level.

The budget for the current year has been set up as follows:

PLANT	BUDGETED COST
A	$135,000
B	122,500
C	108,400
D	135,000
E	135,000

Budgeted information for Plant C is as follows:

Plant manager's office	$ 2,350
Forming department	30,000
Cleaning department	55,450
Packing department	20,600

Budgeted information for Plant C forming department is as follows:

Direct materials	$ 8,333
Direct labor	15,000
Factory overhead	6,667

The following additional budgeted costs are available:

President's office	$16,250
Vice president—marketing	20,000
Vice president—manufacturing office	4,167

The following actual costs were incurred during the year:

PLANT	ACTUAL COST
A	$127,650
B	124,300
C	108,475
D	131,100
E	136,800

Actual costs for Plant C—forming department were as follows:

Direct materials	$ 333 under budget
Direct labor	4,000 under budget
Factory overhead	333 over budget

Actual costs for Plant C—plant manager were

Plant manager's office	$ 2,475
Cleaning department	57,500
Packing department...................	22,500
Forming department	?

Actual costs for the president's level were

President's office	$ 16,375
Vice president—marketing	29,800
Vice president—manufacturing	633,315

REQUIRED:

Prepare a responsibility report for the year showing the details of the budgeted, actual, and variance amounts for levels 1 through 4 for the following areas:

Level 1—Forming department—Plant C

Level 2—Plant manager—Plant C

Level 3—Vice president—manufacturing

Level 4—President

SOLUTIONS TO SUMMARY PROBLEMS

PROBLEM 1

Sunny Corporation Organization Chart

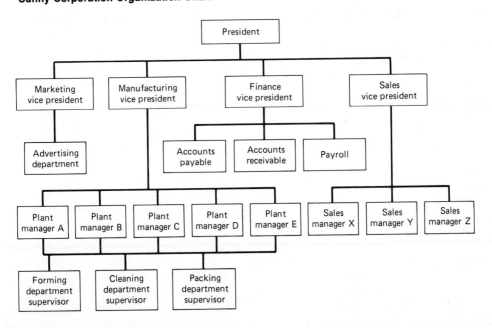

PROBLEM 2

SUNNY COMPANY
RESPONSIBILITY REPORT
FOR THE YEAR ENDED 19X0

	BUDGETED	ACTUAL	VARIANCE
Level 4—President:			
President's office:	$ 16,250	$ 16,375	$ 125
Vice president—marketing	20,000	29,800	9,800
Vice president—manufacturing	640,067	633,315	(6,752)
Total controllable costs	$676,317	$679,490	$3,173
Level 3—Vice President—Manufacturing:			
Vice president—manufacturing office	$ 4,167	$ 4,990	$ 823
Plant A	135,000	127,650	(7,350)
Plant B	122,500	124,300	1,800
Plant C	108,400	108,475	75
Plant D	135,000	131,100	(3,900)
Plant E	135,000	136,800	1,800
Total controllable costs	$640,067	$633,315	($6,752)
Level 2—Plant Manager—Plant C:			
Plant manager's office	$ 2,350	$ 2,475	$ 125
Forming department	30,000	26,000	(4,000)
Cleaning department	55,450	57,500	2,050
Packing department	20,600	22,500	1,900
Total controllable costs	$108,400	$108,475	$ 75
Level 1—Forming Department—Plant C:			
Direct materials	$ 8,333	$ 8,000	($ 333)
Direct labor	15,000	11,000	(4,000)
Factory overhead	6,667	7,000	333
Total controllable costs	$ 30,000	$ 26,000	($4,000)

( ) = Variance favorable

QUESTIONS

1 What is meant by the term "responsibility accounting?"
2 What is a major consideration in developing an organization structure?
3 List several advantages of having an organization that is decentralized.
4 Although decentralization is advantageous in certain organizations, other organizations would not benefit from it. What are some of the costs or disadvantages of decentralization?
5 How can the costs of decentralization be minimized?
6 Define controllable costs.
7 Describe the three major approaches for grouping an organization.
8 How is the use of profit centers related to decentralization?

9   How does responsibility accounting differ from most accounting systems?
10   What role does an organization chart play in the formation of responsibility accounting reports?

EXERCISES

EXERCISE 1

Centralization versus Decentralization

The Massillon Paper Company, which has its headquarters and manufacturing operations in the midwest, has as its principal product kraft wrapping paper. The company recently increased its production substantially and, for product outlets, acquired three corrugated box plants located in Canton, Akron, and Springfield, Ohio. Two bag manufacturing plants, located in Hempstead and Locust Valley, Long Island, were also acquired. This expansion required decentralization of much of the manufacturing operations, and there has been considerable discussion of decentralization of the accounting operations as well. As the chief cost accountant you have been asked to make a study and prepare a report covering the following points; (a) What are the principal advantages of decentralization? (b) Should the accounting and cost functions be decentralized? (c) If decentralized, to whom should the local accountant report? Should the local accountant have line, staff, or functional responsibilities?

EXERCISE 2

Cost Controls

Describe briefly the principal types of controls a parent unit may establish over subsidiary units for the incurrence of costs.

EXERCISE 3

Organization Chart

Marketing division vice president   Purchasing department supervisor
Box plant manager   Manufacturing division vice president
Finance division vice president   Shipping department supervisor
President   Pulpwood plant manager
Paper plant manager   Production department supervisor

REQUIRED

Based on the above data, draw an organization chart using the functional approach.

EXERCISE 4

Responsibility Reports

From the information in Exercise 3 prepare responsibility reports for the president and a vice president. Provide your own figures.

EXERCISE 5

Allocation of Office Costs

The Regent Company sells products manufactured at its three subsidiaries, Companies X, Y, and Z. An executive office is maintained in New York. The cost of the office is allocated to the companies on the basis of income, which for the year 19X0 was as follows:

COMPANY	SALES	COSTS
X	$500,000	$395,000
Y	300,000	180,000
Z	200,000	125,000

The cost of the executive office for 19X0 was $150,000.

REQUIRED:

Compute the amount of executive office cost to be allocated to each company.

(AICPA Adapted)

EXERCISE 6

Multiple Choice

1 What term identifies an accounting system in which the operations of the business are broken down into cost centers and the control function of a foreman, sales manager, or supervisor is emphasized?
 a Responsibility accounting
 b Operations-research accounting
 c Control accounting
 d Budgetary accounting

2 Periodic internal performance reports based upon a responsibility accounting system should not:
 a Distinguish between controllable and uncontrollable costs.
 b Be related to the organization chart.
 c Include allocated fixed overhead in determining performance evaluation.
 d Include variances between actual and budgeted controllable costs.

3 Which of the following statements best describes a characteristic of a factory-overhead control report prepared for use by a production-line department head?
 a It is more important that the report be precise than timely.
 b The report should include information on all costs chargeable to the department, regardless of their origin or control.
 c The report should be stated in dollars rather than in physical units so the department head knows the financial magnitude of any variances.
 d The costs in the report should include only those controllable by the department head.

4 Internal reports prepared under the responsibility accounting approach should be limited to which of the following costs?

    a Only variable costs of production

    b Only conversion costs

    c Only controllable costs

    d Only costs properly allocable to the cost center under generally accepted accounting principles

5 Which of the following items of cost would be least likely to appear in a performance report based on responsibility accounting techniques for the supervisor of an assembly line in a large manufacturing situation?

    a Supervisor's salary

    b Materials

    c Repairs and maintenance

    d Direct labor

(AICPA Adapted)

EXERCISE 7

Responsibility Accounting

An important concept in management accounting is that of "responsibility accounting."

REQUIRED:

    a Define the term "responsibility accounting."

    b What are the conditions that must exist for there to be effective "responsibility accounting?"

    c What benefits are said to result from "responsibility accounting?"

(CMA Adapted)

PROBLEMS

PROBLEM 1

Organization Chart

Satin Company wishes to change its levels of responsibility in order to have better control over costs. The president is ultimately responsible for every department in the firm. Each of the three vice presidents oversees the function of a division. The vice president—marketing controls the advertising budget. The vice president—sales controls the two sales territories in this region. The vice president—finance is also the treasurer of the company and controls the accounting department.

    The advertising department reports directly to the vice president—marketing. Each sales territory has three salespeople. Within the accounting department are the purchasing, billing, and payroll functions.

REQUIRED:

Prepare an organization chart for Satin Company.

PROBLEM 2

Responsibility Report

Chris Corporation requests that you prepare a responsibility report to help determine if they are adequately controlling costs in every department. All production is completed in one department, under a supervisor. Total manufacturing costs for the year were budgeted at $360,000, divided 2:1:1 into materials, labor, and overhead, respectively. Office expenses were budgeted as follows: president, $300,000; vice president—manufacturing, $180,000; and plant manager, $90,000.

Actual manufacturing costs for January of this year were

Materials	$16,200
Labor	6,900
Overhead	8,100

Actual office expenses for the same period were

President	$23,400
Vice president—manufacturing	16,700
Plant manager	8,300

REQUIRED:

Prepare a responsibility report for January showing budgeted and actual costs, and the variances for each item. Assume that costs are incurred evenly throughout the year.

PROBLEM 3

Responsibility Reports

Vince's Insulation Corp. has two plants, A and B. Each plant has a forming and packing department.

The current year standard costs per unit produced in the forming department of Plant B was estimated as follows:

Direct materials	$10
Direct labor	16
Factory overhead	6
Standard cost per unit	$32

Production for the forming department of Plant B is estimated at 1,000 units. Total budgeted costs for the packing department in Plant B are estimated at $30,000. Budgeted costs for the plant manager's office in Plant B are $58,000.

Budgeted costs for the entire Plant A are estimated at $63,000. The vice president of manufacturing oversees the operations of both plants and has a budgeted cost of $85,000. Budgeted expenses for the vice president of marketing's office is $125,000, and for the president's office, $150,000.

Actual expenses were as follows:

President's office	$146,100
Vice president—marketing	123,400
Vice president—manufacturing office	84,800
Total cost for Plant A	61,700
Plant B:	
Plant manager's office	58,300
Packing department	38,000
Forming department:	
Direct materials	8,000
Direct labor	17,000
Factory overhead	5,500
Units produced	1,000

REQUIRED:

Prepare a responsibility report showing the details of the budgeted, actual, and variance amounts for levels 1 through 4 for the following:

Level 1—Forming department, Plant B
Level 2—Plant manager, Plant B
Level 3—Vice president—manufacturing
Level 4—President's office

PROBLEM 4

Functional versus Product Chart

You are given the following information for the Gander Company.

Level 1—President
Level 2—Vice president responsible for a division
Level 3—Manager of a plant
Level 4—Supervisor of department in a plant

The major functions of the company can be divided into marketing and production divisions. The manufacturing plants of the production division produce two types of products, industrial products and military products. The industrial products plant can be divided into three departments: melting, fabricating, and cutting.

All the activities of the company can be related to metal or plastic operations. The manufacturing plants of the plastics division produce materials for the auto industry and the construction industry. There are three departments in the manufacturing plant for the auto industry: mixing, weighing, and molding.

REQUIRED:

Using the above information, develop two organizational charts. One chart should utilize the product approach and the other the functional approach.

PROBLEM 5

Functional versus Product Approach

The following information is in reference to Gander Company of Problem 4.

FUNCTIONAL APPROACH

RESPONSIBILITY LEVEL AND TITLE OF REPORT	TOTAL EXPENSE FOR EACH LEVEL	COMPONENTS MAKING UP THE VARIOUS REPORTS	
Level 1: All operations	$1,736,000	President's office	$133,000
Level 2: Production division	826,000	Vice president's office	60,000
Level 3: Industrial products plant	346,000	Manager's office	43,000
		Melting department	107,000
Level 4: Fabricating department	103,000	Supervisor's office	20,000
		Cost center 1	33,000
		Cost center 2	50,000

PRODUCT APPROACH

RESPONSIBILITY LEVEL AND TITLE OF REPORT	TOTAL EXPENSE FOR EACH LEVEL	COMPONENTS MAKING UP THE VARIOUS REPORTS	
Level 1: All operations	$1,736,000	President's office	$133,000
Level 2: Plastics division	573,000	Vice president's office	53,000
Level 3: Auto products plant	353,000	Manager's office	43,000
		Mixing department	83,000
Level 4: Weighing department	107,000	Supervisor's office	30,000
		Cost center A	40,000
		Cost center B	37,000

REQUIRED:

a Develop a report under the functional approach for each level of Gander Company and show the dollar flow from level 4 to level 1.

b Repeat the requirement for a utilizing the product approach.

PROBLEM 6

Organization Chart of Profit Centers

You are given the following information for the Star Company:

Level 1—President
Level 2—Vice president responsible for a profit center
Level 3—Manager of a plant
Level 4—Supervisor of a department in a plant

The Star Company is divided into three profit centers: the Northeastern coastal area, the Mid-Atlantic coastal area, and the Southern coastal area. In the Northeastern coastal area (level 2) there are three plants: Long Island City, N.Y.; Bridgeport, Conn.; and Providence, R.I. The Bridgeport plant has three departments making distinct products containing the following materials: petroleum, steel, and synthetics.

REQUIRED:

Develop an organizational chart utilizing the above information.

PROBLEM 7

Reports for Profit Centers

The following information is in reference to the chart developed in Problem 6.

Level 1—President
Level 2—Vice president responsible for a division
Level 3—Manager of a plant
Level 4—Supervisor of a department in a plant

RESPONSIBILITY LEVEL AND TITLE OF REPORT	TOTAL EXPENSE FOR EACH LEVEL	COMPONENTS MAKING UP THE VARIOUS REPORTS	
Level 1: All operations	$1,830,000	President's office	$170,000
		Mid-Atlantic profit center	300,000
Level 2: Northeastern division	1,110,000	Vice president's office	110,000
		L. I., N. Y. plant	250,000
Level 3: Bridgeport plant	450,000	Manager's office	55,000
		Petroleum department	190,000
Level 4: Steel department	115,000	Supervisor's office	45,000
		Cost Center 1:	30,000
		Cost Center 2:	40,000

REQUIRED:

Develop a report for each level and show the dollar flow from level 4 to level 1.

PROBLEM 8

Responsibility Accounting

George Johnson was hired on July 1, 19X1 as assistant general manager of the Botel Division of Staple, Inc. It was understood that he would be elevated to general manager of the division on January 1, 19X3, when the incumbent general manager retired and this was duly done. In addition to becoming acquainted with the division and the general manager's duties, Mr. Johnson was specifically charged with the responsibility for development of the 19X2 and 19X3 budgets. As general manager in 19X3, he was, obviously, responsible for the 19X4 budget.

Staple, Inc., is a multiproduct company that is highly decentralized. Each division is quite autonomous. The corporation staff approves division-prepared operating budgets but seldom makes major changes in them. The corporate staff actively participates in decisions requiring capital investment (for expansion or replacement) and makes the final decisions. The division management is responsible for implementing the capital program. The major method used by Staple, Inc., to measure division performance is contribution return on division net investment. The budgets presented below were approved by the corporation. Revision of the 19X4 budget is not considered necessary even though 19X3 actual departed from the approved 19X3 budget.

BOTEL DIVISION (000 Omitted)

ACCOUNTS	ACTUAL			BUDGET	
	19X1	19X2	19X3	19X3	19X4
Sales........................	$1,000	$1,500	$1,800	$2,000	$2,400
Less division variable costs:					
Material and labor	$ 250	$ 375	$ 450	$ 500	$ 600
Repairs	50	75	50	100	120
Supplies	20	30	36	40	48
Less division managed costs:					
Employee training	30	35	25	40	45
Maintenance	50	55	40	60	70
Less division committed costs:					
Depreciation	120	160	160	200	200
Rent	80	100	110	140	140
Total	$ 600	$ 830	$ 871	$1,080	$1,223
Division net contribution	$ 400	$ 670	$ 929	$ 920	$1,177
Division investment:					
Accounts receivable	$ 100	$ 150	$ 180	$ 200	$ 240
Inventory	200	300	270	400	480
Fixed assets	1,590	2,565	2,800	3,380	4,000
Less accounts and wages payable	(150)	(225)	(350)	(300)	(360)
Net investment	$1,740	$2,790	$2,900	$3,680	$4,360
Contribution return on net investment	23%	24%	32%	25%	27%

REQUIRED:

a Identify Mr. Johnson's responsibilities under the management and measurement program described above.

b Appraise the performance of Mr. Johnson in 19X3.

c Recommend to the president any changes in the responsibilities assigned to managers or in the measurement methods used to evaluate division management based upon your analysis.

(CMA Adapted)

PROBLEM 9

Geographical Analysis

The Scent Company sells men's toiletries to retail stores throughout the United States. For planning and control purposes the Scent Company is organized into 12 geographic regions with two to six territories within each region. One salesperson is assigned to each territory and has exclusive rights to all sales made in that territory. Merchandise is shipped from the manufacturing plant to the twelve regional warehouses, and the sales in each territory are shipped from the regional warehouse. National headquarters allocates a specific amount at the beginning of the year for regional advertising.

The net sales for the Scent Company for the year ended September 30, 19X4 totaled $10 million. Costs incurred by national headquarters for national administration, advertising, and warehousing are summarized as follows:

National administration	$250,000
National advertising	125,000
National warehousing	175,000
	$550,000

The results of operations for the South Atlantic region for the year ended September 30, 19X4 are presented at the top of page 669.

The South Atlantic Region consists of two territories—Green and Purple. The salaries and employee benefits consist of the following items:

Regional vice president	$24,000
Regional marketing manager	15,000
Regional warehouse manager	13,400
Salesmen (one for each territory with all receiving the same salary base)	15,600
Employee benefits (20%)	13,600
	$81,600

The salespeople receive a base salary plus 4% commission on all items sold in their territory. Bad debt expense has averaged 0.4% of net sales in the past. Travel and entertainment costs are incurred by the salespeople calling upon their

SCENT COMPANY
STATEMENT OF OPERATIONS FOR SOUTH ATLANTIC REGION
FOR THE YEAR ENDED SEPTEMBER 30, 19X4

Net sales		$900,000
Costs and expenses:		
Advertising fees	$ 54,700	
Bad debt expense	3,600	
Cost of sales	460,000	
Freight-out	22,600	
Insurance	10,000	
Salaries and employee benefits	81,600	
Sales commissions	36,000	
Supplies	12,000	
Travel and entertainment	14,100	
Wages and employee benefits	36,000	
Warehouse depreciation	8,000	
Warehouse operating costs..............................	15,000	
Total costs and expenses		753,600
Territory contribution		$146,400

customers. Freight-out is a function of the quantity of goods shipped and the distance shipped. About 30% of the insurance is expended for protection of the inventory while it is in the regional warehouse, and the remainder is incurred for protection of the warehouse. Supplies are used in the warehouse for packing the merchandise that is shipped. Wages relate to the hourly paid employees who fill orders in the warehouse. The warehouse operating costs account contains such costs as heat, light, and maintenance.

The following cost analyses and statistics by territory for the current year are representative of past experience and are representative of expected future operations.

	GREEN	PURPLE	TOTAL
Sales.....................................	$300,000	$600,000	$900,000
Cost of sales	$184,000	$276,000	$460,000
Advertising fees	$21,800	$32,900	$54,700
Travel and entertainment	$6,300	$7,800	$14,100
Freight-out	$9,000	$13,600	$22,600
Units sold	150,000	350,000	500,000
Pounds shipped	210,000	390,000	600,000
Salespeople miles traveled	21,600	38,400	60,000

REQUIRED:

a The top management of Scent Company wants the regional vice presidents to present their operating data in a more meaningful manner. Therefore, management has requested the regions separate their operating costs into the fixed and variable components of order-getting, order-filling and admin-istration. The data are to be presented in the following format:

	TERRITORY COSTS		REGIONAL	TOTAL
	GREEN	PURPLE	COSTS	COSTS
Order-getting				
Order-filling				
Administration				

Using management's suggested format, prepare a schedule that presents the costs for the region by territory with the costs separated into variable and fixed categories by order-getting, order-filling, and administrative functions.

b Suppose the top management of Scent Company is considering splitting the Purple territory into two separate territories (Red and Blue). From the data that has been presented, identify what data would be relevant to this decision (either for or against), and indicate what other data you would collect to aid top management in its decision.

c If Scent Company keeps its records in accordance with the classification required in **a**, can standards and flexible budgets be employed by the company in planning and controlling marketing costs? Give reasons for your answer.

(CMA Adapted)

CHAPTER NINETEEN
PERFORMANCE MEASUREMENT

All enterprises, regardless of nature, size, or organization, are vitally concerned with performance measurement. In a private enterprise, one way the investors measure management's performance is by the dividend on the investment in securities. In a governmental agency the results accomplished and the effectiveness in utilizing the assigned resources are measured by the General Accounting Office or the agency internal audit staff. In most enterprises, particularly large industrial companies, it is necessary to develop a sound basis for measuring many different segments or divisions of the company, since they are primarily responsible for the performance of the company as a whole. In this chapter we will be concerned with the problems involved in establishing and administering an adequate program of performance measurement.

BASIS OF MEASUREMENT

A substantial number of factors must be considered in developing an effective performance measurement program. Should the principal figure be the percentage of net income to net sales or should it be net income to investment, or capital employed? Should some other income figure be used, such as income from operations or income before income taxes? Should the investment amount be the total assets or should it be net investment, or net assets, after liabilities are deducted? Does the basis used for the individual affiliates, divisions, or departments have to be the same as that for the company as a whole? There is no one answer for all companies. Manufacturing companies will differ from service companies, such as banks or insurance companies, and retail stores will differ from utilities or government agencies. There will be differences even within the particular industry. The method of performance measurement for a particular company will depend on company needs and management preference. The most common method of performance measurement is called the return on investment method (ROI).

RETURN ON INVESTMENT (ROI)

The return on investment is usually computed by dividing net income by total assets employed. Total assets employed is equal to a company's total assets appearing on the balance sheet. Total assets employed is also commonly referred to as investment, invested capital, or capital employed. These terms will be used interchangeably in this chapter.

The return on investment, or return on capital method, has been used for many years in banking and other financial activities to measure performance. However, the ROI method did not come into general use in industry until the 1960s, when the concept was developed and publicized by some of the leading industrial companies. While the method does have some limitations, such as the determination of invested capital, it also has many advantages over most other methods. For example, the ROI can be compared with internal or external activities. A company may wish to compare the internal return on a capital investment, such as purchasing a $25,000 machine, as opposed to the external ROI of investing $25,000 in industrial securities with a guaranteed return of 11%. Comparison can be made between the ROI on competing projects to determine which is the most favorable investment. For some time investors have been making comparisons among companies, using as a measurement the net income percentage to sales, or earnings per share. Such comparisons can be very misleading where there is a significant difference in the amount invested in the companies. For example, Company A and Company B may each have sales of $5,000,000 and net income of $500,000, or 10% ($500,000 ÷ $5,000,000) return on sales. However, Company A may be employing $4,000,000 in assets to earn that net income, while Company B may be employing only $2,000,000 in assets to earn the same amount.

Table 19-1 clearly shows the difference in return based on assets employed. As can be seen above, Company B, while making the same return on sales as Company A, is making twice the return of Company A, based on total assets employed.

TABLE 19-1
RETURN ON INVESTMENT

	COMPANY A	COMPANY B
Sales	$5,000,000	$5,000,000
Net income	500,000	500,000
Total assets employed	4,000,000	2,000,000
Return on sales	10%	10%
Return on investment	$12^1/_2$% (A)	25% (B)

(A) $500,000 ÷ $4,000,000
(B) $500,000 ÷ $2,000,000

INVESTMENT TURNOVER AND EARNINGS RATIO

A somewhat different approach is to use an equation to express the return on investment. The ROI equation is generally shown in two distinct parts, the *investment turnover* and the *earnings ratio*. The investment turnover indicates management's efficiency in using assets at its disposal to generate sales volume and earnings and is computed as follows:

$$\text{Investment turnover} = \frac{\text{sales}}{\text{total assets employed}}$$

The investment turnover is the percentage of sales generated in relation to the amount of total assets employed. The higher the investment turnover the better, because this means that a larger percentage of sales is generated in relation to the amount invested. For example, assume sales of $500,000 and an investment (total assets employed) of $2,000,000. The investment turnover would be 25% ($500,000 ÷ $2,000,000). If $600,000 in sales were generated the investment turnover would increase to 30% ($600,000 ÷ $2,000,000). Note that the investment turnover does not give any indication of the amount of profit or loss from the sales, and therefore, a high investment turnover does not necessarily mean that a corporation will have a high net income; in fact, a loss could result. Investment turnover is primarily used to compare one firm to another, within an industry, to determine how efficiently the firms are using their invested capital (total assets employed). A corporation's management may also compute the investment turnover to compare the current turnover with prior periods to determine whether any change in the turnover is developing.

The earnings ratio shows the sales/expense relationship and is computed as follows:

$$\text{Earnings ratio} = \frac{\text{net income}}{\text{sales}}$$

The earnings ratio depicts the relationship of net income to sales and the percentage of profit in each dollar of sales. The earnings ratio can be favorably increased by increasing sales or decreasing expenses. The higher the earnings ratio the better, because this indicates that a larger percentage of each sale is made up of profit as compared to a return of cost. For example, sales of $500,000 that generated a net income of $100,000 would result in a 20% ($100,000 ÷ $500,000) earnings ratio. Therefore, 20% of sales represents profit and 80% cost. If profit were to increase to $150,000 the earnings ratio would increase to 30% ($150,000 ÷ $500,000). Management would be interested in any change in the earnings ratio because it means that a shift has developed in the sales/expense relationship.

Total Company Evaluation

Generally, the data for the total company would be obtained from published reports such as the annual report to stockholders. Only the final results, such as net income and net sales, would be used. The invested capital would be the total assets used in the business. The ROI is an easy method of performance measurement, but there are differences of opinion as to what is to be included in some of the factors. The equation is generally stated as follows:

$$\text{ROI} = \text{investment turnover} \times \text{earnings ratio}$$

or

$$\text{ROI} = \frac{\text{sales}}{\text{total assets employed}} \times \frac{\text{net income}}{\text{sales}}$$

As can be seen, the equation could be shortened by canceling out sales in the two fractions. If this were done, however, the primary objective of the two independent variables, investment turnover and earnings ratio, would be lost.

Divisional Evaluation

In order that the maximum potential advantage be obtained from decentralization, it is essential that management systematically measure and control the performance of its separate divisions. In many cases management is unduly concerned with dollar sales, dollar earnings, and profit margins. A far more meaningful measure of managerial effectiveness could be obtained by combining investment and earnings into a single ROI equation. The figures used in the divisional computations are a little different from those used in the total company computations. The preferred profit figure to be used for a specific division is *operating income*. Nonoperating items are usually the responsibility of general management and should be excluded. The investment base would be the total assets made available to the division. The division manager would be expected to produce a return on total assets employed greater than might be obtained on any alternate choice, such as investment in securities. The divisional ROI equation is generally stated as follows:

$$\text{ROI} = \text{divisional investment turnover} \times \text{divisional earnings ratio}$$

or

$$\text{ROI} = \frac{\text{divisional sales}}{\text{divisional total assets employed}} \times \frac{\text{divisional operating income}}{\text{divisional sales}}$$

Here we are relating divisional investment (total assets employed) to divisional operating income in order to measure performance. This is a valid method of comparing the performance of a division manager with the performance of other managers, assuming the underlying investment and sales data are comparable. As division managers understand more about performance measurement, they can act to influence the data favorably. For example, they may work the invested capital (total assets employed) more by converting part of the plant to other product lines or by reducing or transferring part of the investment base. Sales would be improved by increasing the sales volume or increasing the selling price, thereby improving the earnings ratio. Expenses could be reduced or held stable at the same time that sales are increased to augment the earnings ratio further. Therefore, to measure divisional operating performance properly, it is necessary to combine both the investment turnover and the earnings ratio.

In most companies today divisional ROI has largely replaced profit as the basis used for measuring the performance of division managers. Surveys in recent years have shown that two-thirds of the major United States industrial companies are using some variation of the return on investment method.

STRENGTHS AND WEAKNESSES OF ROI

The principal strengths of ROI in performance measurement are that it can:

1 Act as a comprehensive measure, sensitive to every influence affecting the financial status of a company.
2 Center management's attention upon maximizing earnings on invested capital (total assets employed).
3 Serve as a basis for measuring management's performance in utilizing total assets as well as divisional resources.
4 Help make the goals of the division manager coincide with those of corporate management.
5 Provide an objective comparison of various internal performance results among divisions and also with projected external performance results.
6 Help division managers evaluate and improve their own performance.
7 Provide an incentive to use existing assets to their fullest and to acquire only those additional resources that will increase the return on investment ratio.

The principal weaknesses of ROI in performance measurement are:

1 It focuses on maximization of a ratio rather than an improvement in absolute profit amounts.
2 The established rate of return may be too high and could discourage divisional incentive.
3 It is not used where the divisional ROI is higher than the corporate ROI and the division manager is reluctant to acquire additional investments that might lower the ROI.
4 Division managers may make decisions that help the divisional ROI to look good but that are not good for the long-term interest of the company.
5 It may oversimplify a complex decision process.

RESIDUAL INCOME

The residual income concept was developed to overcome one of the principal shortcomings of ROI, the focus on maximization of the *rate* of return rather than on absolute dollars. This important refinement of the ROI concept was developed by General Electric Company for its own performance measurement. Under this method divisional performance is measured by the *amount* of residual income rather than by the *rate* of return. The residual income of a division is its net income minus a prescribed percentage charge ("imputed" interest) on the investment, used by the division manager. Following is an example of residual income (RI):

DIVISION X	CURRENT PERIOD
Invested capital (total assets employed)	$50,000
Net income	$10,000
Return on investment (ROI), ($10,000 ÷ $50,000)	20%
Charge (imputed interest) 12% ($50,000 × 12%)	$6,000
Residual income (RI) ($10,000 − $6,000)	$4,000

One of the advantages of the residual income concept is that the particular division should expand as long as it earns a rate above the charge for invested capital. Thus any division earning over 12% on its invested capital could continue to expand. Under this method division managers will focus on increasing dollars rather than a percentage rate. Thus, a division manager using ROI may reject projects with a return of less than 20%, as shown above. However, a manager who is charged only 12% would be likely to accept all projects that would have a return above that rate.

ALLOCATING ASSETS AND EXPENSES

In using return on capital in divisional performance measurement, certain complications arise in determining the amount of capital employed and the amount of income returned. For direct divisional items of asset and expense there are no particular problems. However, in most companies there are many items such as cash and receivables which may be maintained at corporate headquarters. Also there may be corporate expenses or services rendered by headquarters which are distributed to the divisions. In ROI computations should these items be left unallocated, or should they be allocated to the divisions? Generally it is better to allocate assets and expenses to the divisions whenever it is reasonable to do so.

In determining the amount of capital invested or capital employed, the problem is much easier for the company as a whole than for the particular division. For the total company evaluation no allocation is needed for such items as cash, accounts receivable, inventory, and plant and equipment. In companies where these assets are carried on the corporate books rather than the divisional books some means of allocation is needed when computing divisional evaluations. Many accountants feel that the capital invested should be measured not at one date or two dates but as frequently as possible. For example, the balances at the end of each month may be averaged, or the amounts needed, as shown by a cash budget, may be used. Another consideration is that today most corporate headquarters for a company of any size would have a computer. It is simple then to obtain data as to the number and amount of various transactions made by the division. Following are the allocation bases suggested for specific assets.

Cash

The cash needs for a division will generally be shown in a cash budget, or an analysis may be obtained from the corporate interoffice transactions at headquarters.

Accounts Receivable

Many companies maintain all accounts receivable at headquarters for greater control and convenience. Thus, instead of having a number of different divisions dealing with a large general supplier, such as General Electric, there would be one account maintained on the computer at corporate headquarters. Of course, underlying information such as the divisional code number would be readily available. Again budget data could also be used, particularly the detailed cash budget, which would probably be available.

Inventory

Unlike cash or accounts receivable, some important valuation problems may be involved with inventory. Comparisons may be distorted between companies where one company uses fifo and the other company uses average cost, or lifo. Generally most companies would use the same inventory method for all divisions. In most cases inventories would be maintained on the divisional books rather than at headquarters, as would be the case with cash and accounts receivable. The needed ROI data could also be obtained from budgeted data for sales, or cost of sales.

Plant and Equipment

Generally plant and equipment will be valued according to one of the three following methods: original cost, book value, or replacement cost.

Proponents of original cost valuation point out that the particular assets of one plant can more reasonably be compared with the same assets at another plant. Proponents of book value valuation or depreciated cost basis point out that such costs should not be overstated, that the net recorded book value should be used. Proponents of replacement cost valuation argue that realistic values should be used rather than original costs of some years ago. In some cases the net book value of plant and equipment has worked out best, along with other asset values at a specific date.

DIVISIONAL TRANSFERS

Many companies today are structured on some variation of vertical integration in which the finished products of some divisions become the raw materials of other divisions.

For example, in a paper manufacturing company the output of the paper division may be sold to outside customers or may be transferred to other company plants which make paper bags or corrugated boxes. Here the problem of interdivisional pricing arises. Several different pricing bases are in use, each with its own advantages and disadvantages, including (1) cost, full cost, or marginal cost; (2) established price or cost plus, which includes cost plus handling charges; (3) market price, less selling and administrative expenses; and (4) negotiated price.

The cost basis is not theoretically sound, since the producing division is assured of cost recovery and there is little incentive for cost control. The established price basis is commonly used in most companies. Here a price is fixed periodically for all divisions, which generally includes cost, on the basis used, plus about 15 or 20%. The market price is often used, less selling and administrative expenses which are not incurred on divisional transfers.

Frequently a negotiated price is used which is generally based on periodic negotiation between representatives of the producing and buying divisions. Often some very troublesome problems arise in performance measurement where there are a number of divisions. In comparing performance it has been found that Division A may sell all its output to outsiders at the market price. Division B, producing the same product in about the same quantity, sells about three-fourths of its production to outsiders and about one-fourth to other company divisions at the established transfer price of $60 a ton, about half the selling price to outsiders. Division C sells only one-fourth to outsiders and transfers three-fourths to other divisions. Division D sells all its production to outsiders at market prices and buys all its raw material from company divisions. Division E, producing the same product in about the same quantity, sells all its production to outsiders and buys all its raw material from outsiders.

It is obvious that there will be substantial distortions in the operating income of the various divisions. Sales of Division B will be understated for the one-fourth of its total to interdivision sales, and sales of Division C will be severely understated for the three-fourths of its total to interdivision sales. Division D will show a high operating income, since it sells all its production at the highest price and buys all its raw material at the lowest price.

Obviously it is necessary to adjust prices to a common denominator if meaningful comparisons are to be made. It is a very difficult problem, and many division managers are often unhappy and feel that they are not being fairly evaluated, especially if a bonus plan is in use.

A more detailed discussion of transfer pricing will be presented in Chapter 21.

CHAPTER REVIEW

Successful company operations result from careful planning and control of all company activities. An important factor is the balancing of invested capital among all divisions and the planned return on invested capital for all segments of the company. The success of company operations as a whole depends on the success of its divisional components. The most effective tools yet devised for measuring divisional performance are return on investment (ROI) and residual income (RI). Residual income is a further refinement of ROI and represents the amount of divisional return less the imputed interest for the invested capital. Formerly most performance measures were based on net income or operating income in relation to sales. This was not a very reliable measure, as no recognition was given to the amount of capital invested (total assets employed) in the particular unit. Today most companies use the return on investment or residual income to measure the performance of divisions or departments—a far more reliable measure.

GLOSSARY

Division or Department—a segment of a business.

Earnings Ratio—the percentage of earnings to sales; net income ÷ sales.

Employed Capital—same as total assets employed.

Interdivision or Interplant—transactions between units within the same company. It may be between divisions or between individual plants.

Invested Capital—same as total assets employed.

Investment Turnover Rate—the relationship of sales to total assets employed; sales ÷ total assets employed.

Residual Income—net income, less imputed interest on the invested capital.

Return on Investment (ROI)—the investment turnover rate times the earnings ratio.

ROI Equation

$$\frac{\text{Net income}}{\text{Sales}} \times \frac{\text{sales}}{\text{total assets employed}}$$
$$= \text{return on investment}$$

Total Assets Employed—total assets appearing on the balance sheet.

SUMMARY PROBLEM

Keller Company has two divisions, M and N. Total sales for the year are $1,000,000. It is estimated that division M will account for 65% of the total sales.

Pertinent data for each division is as follows:

	M	N
Cost of goods sold..........................	$400,000	$150,000
Selling and administrative expenses	100,000	100,000
Plant investment (total assets employed)	700,000	350,000

Keller wishes to earn at least 15% on its plant investment.

REQUIRED:

Compute the following for Divisions M and N of the Keller Company:

a   Investment turnover
b   Earnings ratio
c   Return on investment
d   Residual income

SOLUTION TO SUMMARY PROBLEM

	M	N
Sales.......................................	$650,000	$350,000
Cost of goods sold	400,000	150,000
Gross profit	$250,000	$200,000
Selling and administrative expenses	100,000	100,000
Net income	$150,000	$100,000

a   Investment turnover $= \dfrac{\text{sales}}{\text{total assets employed}}$

$$\text{Division M} = \frac{\$650,000}{\$700,000} = 92.9\%$$

$$\text{Division N} = \frac{\$350,000}{\$350,000} = 100\%$$

b   Earnings ratio $= \dfrac{\text{net income}}{\text{sales}}$

$$\text{Division M} = \frac{\$150,000}{\$650,000} = 23.1\%$$

$$\text{Division N} = \frac{\$100,000}{\$350,000} = 28.6\%$$

c   Return on investment $= \dfrac{\text{sales}}{\text{total assets employed}} \times \dfrac{\text{net income}}{\text{sales}}$

$$\text{Division M, ROI} = \frac{\$650,000}{\$700,000} \times \frac{\$150,000}{\$650,000} = 21.4\%$$

$$\text{Division N, ROI} = \frac{\$350,000}{\$350,000} \times \frac{\$100,000}{\$350,000} = 28.6\%$$

d

RESIDUAL INCOME	M	N
Net income	$150,000	$100,000
Charge (15%)	105,000	52,500
Residual income	$ 45,000	$ 47,500

QUESTIONS

1 Name some of the groups that will be concerned with the performance of various enterprises.
2 List some of the factors that must be considered when measuring the performance of a company.
3 What are the two components of the return on investment equation?
4 Why is operating income preferred over net income when measuring divisional performance?
5 Why is it beneficial for division managers to understand performance measurement?
6 List the strengths and weaknesses of ROI in performance measurement.
7 What is residual income? What is one of the advantages of its use in performance measurement?
8 What problems may arise from the use of return on capital in divisional performance measurement.
9 What are the three principal methods of valuing plant and equipment?
10 Why do proponents of each method of valuing plant and equipment prefer that method?
11 List the different pricing bases that a company might use.
12 Why would problems arise when there are a number of divisions within a company?

EXERCISES

EXERCISE 1

Return on Investment

Hurdle Company wishes to know its return on investment. This year their plant investment (total assets employed) was $400,000, net income was $16,000, and earnings ratio was 8%.

REQUIRED:

Compute the ROI for Hurdle Company.

EXERCISE 2

Residual Income

Jay Company wishes to earn 14% on $210,000, its total assets employed. Its net income is $42,000 and its ROI is 20%.

REQUIRED:

Compute Jay Company's residual income.

EXERCISE 3

Return on Investment

Joe Corporation wants to know whether it is more profitable to continue operations or invest the capital to earn a rate of 9%.

Net income	$15,000
Sales	60,000
Investment (total assets employed)	75,000

REQUIRED:

Compute the ROI for Joe Corporation, and show if it is more profitable to continue operations or invest its capital.

EXERCISE 4

Residual Income of Two Divisions

Checker Company has two divisions, A and B, and wants to determine which one is more profitable.

Division A has net income of $10,000, sales of $50,000, and plant investment (total assets employed) of $75,000.

Division B has net income of $15,000, sales of $75,000, and plant investment of $100,000. Checker Company has an imputed interest charge of 10%.

REQUIRED:

Determine which division of Checker Company has a higher residual income.

EXERCISE 5

Multiple Choice

1 The most desirable measure of departmental performance for evaluating the performance of the department manager is departmental:
   a Net income
   b Contribution to indirect expenses
   c Revenue, less departmental variable expenses
   d Revenue, less controllable departmental expenses

2   With other variables remaining constant, the rate of return on capital employed
    by a merchandising company will increase with a decrease in:
    a   Sales
    b   Inventory turnover
    c   Profit margin
    d   Investment in inventory

(AICPA Adapted)

EXERCISE 6

ROI and Residual Income

Angel Company has asked you to determine how profitable its operations are. It
hopes to earn 12% on its investment. Angel Company invested $600,000 in its
plant (total assets employed). Sales were $350,000 and the earnings ratio was 17%.

REQUIRED:

Compute the ROI and residual income for Angel Company.

PROBLEMS

PROBLEM 1

Return on Investment and Residual Income

Winthrop Company wishes to know how profitable its operations are this year. Its
plant investment (total assets employed) is $750,000, sales are $485,000, and
selling and administrative expenses are $44,000. Their gross profit is 40% of sales.
Winthrop Company wishes to have an imputed interest rate of 12%.

REQUIRED:

Compute the return on investment and residual income for Winthrop Company.

PROBLEM 2

ROI Divisional Income of Two Divisions

Blank Company has decided that it must close one of its two divisions.
    Division 1 has a plant investment (total assets employed) of $325,000, and
Division 2 has a plant investment of $270,000.
    Blank Company had sales of $500,000, with each division accounting for one-
half of the sales. However, owing to differences in costs, Division 1 has net income
of $125,000, and Division 2 has net income of $60,000.

REQUIRED:

Determine which division should be kept, based upon ROI and residual income.
Blank Company wishes to earn 15% on its investment.

PROBLEM 3

Return on Investment

Maxwell Company wants to measure its profitability by determining its return on investment. This year sales were $480,000. A partial income statement for Maxwell Company follows:

> Sales: 100%
> Gross profit: 40% of sales
> Selling and administrative expenses: 10% of sales

Maxwell invested (total assets employed) $1,200,000 in plant and equipment.

REQUIRED:

Compute the ROI for Maxwell Company.

PROBLEM 4

Residual Income for Two Divisions

Chuck Company's two divisions are competing for a year-end bonus. The division with a higher residual income at the end of the year will split the bonus among its employees.

Financial data for Chuck Company follows:

	TOTAL	DIVISION S	DIVISION T
Plant investment (total assets employed)	$650,000	60%	40%
Sales	400,000	50%	50%
Earnings ratio		30%	35%

REQUIRED:

Determine which division of Chuck Company will earn the bonus. Assume an imputed interest charge of 16%.

PROBLEM 5

Comparing Divisional Performance Using ROI

Minute Company wants to determine which of its four divisions is the most profitable. Following is the pertinent information for each division:

Division A: Sales, $200,000; net income, $30,000; investment turnover, 40%
Division B: Sales, $150,000; net income, $10,000; plant investment, $220,000.
Division C: Net income, $25,000; earnings ratio, 20%; plant investment, $300,000.
Division D: Investment, $450,000; sales, $150,000; earnings ratio, 25%.

REQUIRED:

Compute the ROI for each division, showing which is the most profitable.

PROBLEM 6

Investment Turnover, Earnings Ratio, Return on Investment, and Residual Income for Two Corporations.

Veri Slick, the president of Shyster Corporation, bets Ima Goodbody, the president of Wholesome Corporation, that Shyster Corporation is more profitable than Wholesome Corporation.

Relevant financial data for both corporations appears as follows:

	CORPORATION	
	SHYSTER	WHOLESOME
Gross sales	$2,000,000	$1,200,000
Sales returns and allowances	1,200,000	0
Bad debt expenses	400,000	0
Losses from lawsuits	150,000	0
Cost of goods sold	75,000	600,000
Selling and administrative expenses	80,000	1,000,000
Total assets employed	100,000	1,000,000

Both corporations inpute interest at 10%.

REQUIRED:

Prepare the following performance measures to determine who wins the bet if the two corporations agree to determine the winner based on the following:
  a   Investment turnover
  b   Earnings ratio
  c   Return on investment
  d   Residual income

PROBLEM 7

Divisional ROI

The Texon Co. is organized into autonomous divisions along regional market lines. Each division manager is responsible for sales, cost of operations, acquisition and financing of divisional assets, and working capital management.

The vice president of general operations for the company will retire in September 19X5. A review of the performance, attitudes, and skills of several management employees has been undertaken. Interviews with qualified outside candidates also have been held. The selection committee has narrowed the choice to the managers of divisions A and F.

Both candidates were appointed division managers in late 19X1. The manager of division A had been the assistant manager of that division for the prior five years. The manager of division F had served as assistant division manager of division B before being appointed to his present post. He took over division F, a division newly formed in 19X0, when its first manager left to join a competitor. The financial results of their performance in the past three years appear on page 684.

	DIVISION A			DIVISION F		
	19X2	19X3	19X4	19X2	19X3	19X4
			(000 omitted)			
Estimated industry sales—market area	$10,000	$12,000	$13,000	$5,000	$6,000	$6,500
Division sales	$ 1,000	$ 1,100	$ 1,210	$ 450	$ 600	$ 750
Variable costs	$ 300	$ 320	$ 345	$ 135	$ 175	$ 210
Managed costs	400	405	420	170	200	230
Committed costs	275	325	350	140	200	250
Total costs	$ 975	$ 1,050	$ 1,115	$ 445	$ 575	$ 690
Net income	$ 25	$ 50	$ 95	$ 5	$ 25	$ 60
Assets employed	$ 330	$ 340	$ 360	$ 170	$ 240	$ 300
Liabilities incurred	103	105	115	47	100	130
Net investment	227	235	245	123	140	170
Return on investment	11%	21%	39%	04%	18%	35%

REQUIRED:

a Texon Co. measures the performance of the divisions and the division managers on the basis of their return on investment (ROI). Is this an appropriate measurement for the division managers? Explain.

b Many believe that a single measure, such as ROI, is inadequate to fully evaluate performance. What additional measure(s) could be used for performance evaluation? Give reasons for each measure listed.

c On the basis of the information given, which manager would you recommend for vice president of general operations? Present reasons to support your answer.

(CMA Adapted)

CHAPTER TWENTY
GROSS PROFIT ANALYSIS

In order for operations to be profitable, they must be carefully planned and executed as planned. The execution of the plan must be closely monitored. Any variation from the plan should be promptly recognized and corrective action taken. Management should be informed immediately of any variances which affect gross profit. Analysis of gross profit is a continuous and intensive process. Analysis of gross profit can be made in a manner similar to the analysis of standard cost variances, as described in an earlier chapter. It is possible to analyze gross profit whether standard costs are used or not. We touched on aspects of gross profit analysis in describing the behavior of cost-volume-profit relationships also in an earlier chapter, but the emphasis was different. In this chapter we will be discussing the factors that directly affect gross profit. Gross profit, sometimes called gross margin, is the excess of sales over the cost of goods sold. This differs from contribution margin, which is the excess of sales over *all* variable costs, including variable manufacturing, selling, and administrative costs.

CHANGE IN GROSS PROFIT

In analyzing the change in gross profit, a comparison can be made between budgeted and actual operations for the current year or between actual operations for the prior year and for the current year. Where a budget has been carefully prepared, it is usually preferable to compare actual with budget. The amounts attributable to different causes of change can be determined and management action taken for corrections. The principal causes for a difference in gross profit are changes in sales price, sales volume, costs, and product mix.

ANALYZING CHANGE
IN GROSS PROFIT

In analyzing the change in gross profit, we will compare the actual for the current year with that of the prior year. To make the comparison simple, we will assume that the Englewood Company manufactures and sells a single product.

As can be seen in Table 20-1, sales increased by $2,998, or 6.0% ($2,998 ÷ $50,000). However, cost of goods sold also increased, in an amount of $2,120 or 7.1% ($2,120 ÷ $30,000), which was greater than the increase in sales. *Therefore, the gross profit ratio decreased to 39.4%.* The $878 represented an increase of only 4.4% ($878 ÷ $20,000) over the amount of gross profit for the prior year. The amount of gross profit must be high enough to provide for selling, administrative, and all other costs, including income taxes. In addition it must also be high enough to provide a return, or profit, on assets invested. Thus, business people must be aware of the change and the causes of any significant change in gross profit so that correction can be promptly made.

In most companies two other very important ratios are the cost of sales ratio (CSR) and the gross profit ratio (GPR). The cost of sales ratio is the relationship of cost of sales to sales. The gross profit ratio is the relationship of gross profit to sales. In the comparison in Table 20-1 there was a GPR of 40.0% ($20,000 ÷ $50,000) in 19X1 and a GPR of 39.4% ($20,878 ÷ $52,998) in 19X2. The CSR in Table 20-1 was 60.0% ($30,000 ÷ $50,000) in 19X1 and 60.6% ($32,120 ÷ $52,998) in 19X2. The CSR plus the GPR for any one period must always equal 100% (sales for the period). An unfavorable situation was developing from 19X1 to 19X2 because the GPR decreased while the CSR increased. This means that in 19X2 it cost more to produce the units sold in relation to the selling price of units sold. Any change in CSR over GPR should be further analyzed into the following three possible causes:

Volume changes — When volume changes, total sales and total cost of sales will change and therefore, gross profit will change.

TABLE 20-1
ENGLEWOOD COMPANY
COMPARATIVE INCOME STATEMENT
19X1 AND 19X2

	19X1	19X2	CHANGE	%
Sales	$50,000	$52,998	+$2,998	6.0
Cost of sales	30,000	32,120	−2,120	7.1
Gross profit	$20,000	$20,878	+$ 878	4.4
Cost of sales ratio	60.0%	60.6%		
Gross profit ratio	40.0%	39.4%		
Total	100.0%	100.0%		

Price changes — When selling price per unit changes, total sales will change and therefore, gross profit will change.

Cost changes — When cost per unit changes, total cost of sales will change and therefore, gross profit will change.

Unit Data Known

In some cases the quantities and unit prices are available. If such is the case, the analysis of gross profit is simplified. Assume, for example, that the unit information in Table 20-2 is available for the income statement in Table 20-1.

In order to analyze volume and price changes, one of the elements must be kept constant. Thus:

Computing Volume Change. The price factor must be kept constant.

Computing Price Change. The volume factor must be kept constant.

Effect of Volume Change. As can be seen in Table 20-2, there was a volume decrease of 182 units. Therefore, $182 \times \$4.00$ (19X1 gross profit per unit) equals a *decrease* in gross profit of $728.

Effect of Price Change. There was a change in price of $1.00 ($11 − $10). Therefore, 4,818 units times $1.00 equals an *increase* in gross profit of $4,818.

Effect of Cost Change. This is the increase in cost per unit times the number of units sold. Thus $.6666 × 4,818 equals a *decrease* in gross profit of $3,212.

The total change in gross profit of $878 can now be summarized as follows:

Volume decrease	$ 728	unfavorable
Price increase	(4,818)	favorable
Cost increase	3,212	unfavorable
Change in gross profit	$(878)	favorable

Unit Data Unknown

In many cases the number of units sold is not maintained, only the dollar amount of sales. Generally, however, the amount of any price change would be known.

Effect of Volume Change. In computing the volume change, the price factor must be kept constant, which for the Englewood Company means that we

TABLE 20-2
COST DATA PER UNIT

	19X1	19X2	CHANGE
Volume	5,000	4,818	−182
Sales price	$10.00	$11.00	+$1.00
Cost	6.00	6.6666	+.6666
Gross profit	4.00	4.3333	+.3333

must eliminate any increase in sales due to price change. Thus, the Englewood Company had a price change of 10% ($1 ÷ $10), which must be eliminated. This is accomplished by dividing 19X2 sales by 110%. This gives 19X2 sales at 19X1 prices (19X2 sales $52,998 ÷ 110% = $48,180).

19X1 sales at 19X1 prices	$50,000	
19X2 sales at 19X1 prices	48,180	
Decrease in revenue	$ 1,820	
Gross profit 19X1	40%	
Unfavorable decrease in sales volume		$ 728

Effect of Price Change. The sales volume must be kept constant in order to compute the effect of a price change.

19X2 sales at 19X2 prices	$52,998	
19X2 sales at 19X1 prices	48,180	
Favorable increase in sales prices		(4,818)

Effect of Cost Change. The volume must be kept constant in order to compute the effect of a cost change.

19X2 volume at 19X2 cost	$32,120	
19X2 volume at 19X1 cost		
($48,180 × 60%)	28,908	
Unfavorable increase in cost price		3,212
Increase in gross profit		($ 878)

MULTIPRODUCTS

In the preceding examples we used cost data for the Englewood Company, which manufactured only one product. Today most manufacturing companies make more than one product, and the sales, cost, and gross profit vary widely among the products. For purposes of illustration we will use the cost data for the Egan Manufacturing Company which makes and sells three products, X, Y, and Z. We will compare the actual income data with the budgeted income data for the year 19X0. The analysis can be approached in the same way as is the computation of standard cost variances in earlier chapters. The cost data used is in Tables 20-3 and 20-4 (page 692).

As can be seen in Table 20-3, the Egan Company had expected to make a gross profit of $45,000 on estimated sales of 60,000 units, for an average gross profit of $.75 per unit, or 17.3% on sales. The actual results showed sales of 62,000 units, or 103.3% (62,000 ÷ 60,000) of the target. However, the actual gross profit was only $33,230, or only 73.8% ($33,230 ÷ 45,000) of the budgeted gross profit, and the gross profit per unit was only $.54, compared to the

TABLE 20-3
EGAN MANUFACTURING COMPANY
BUDGETED INCOME SUMMARY,
YEAR 19X0

PRODUCT NAME	UNITS SOLD	SALES		COST		GROSS PROFIT		
		PRICE	AMOUNT	UNIT	AMOUNT	UNIT	AMOUNT	%
X	30,000	$5.00	$150,000	$4.00	$120,000	$1.00	$30,000	20.0
Y	20,000	4.00	80,000	3.40	68,000	.60	12,000	15.0
Z	10,000	3.00	30,000	2.70	27,000	.30	3,000	10.0
Total	60,000	$4.33 (A)	$260,000	$3.58 (B)	$215,000	$ .75 (C)	$45,000	17.3 (D)

(A) $260,000 ÷ 60,000
(B) $215,000 ÷ 60,000
(C) $45,000 ÷ 60,000
(D) $45,000 ÷ $260,000

TABLE 20-4
EGAN MANUFACTURING COMPANY
ACTUAL INCOME SUMMARY
YEAR 19X0

PRODUCT NAME	UNITS SOLD	SALES		COST		GROSS PROFIT		
		PRICE	AMOUNT	UNIT	AMOUNT	UNIT	AMOUNT	%
X	23,000	$5.50	$126,500	$4.94	$113,620	$.56	$12,880	10.2
Y	26,500	3.50	92,750	2.85	75,525	.65	17,225	18.6
Z	12,500	3.25	40,625	3.00	37,500	.25	3,125	7.7
Total	62,000	$4.19 (A)	$259,875	$3.65 (B)	$226,645	$.54 (C)	$33,230	12.8 (D)

(A) $259,875 ÷ 62,000
(B) $226,645 ÷ 62,000
(C) $33,230 ÷ 62,000
(D) $33,230 ÷ $259,875

budgeted gross profit per unit of $.75. The average actual GPR was 12.8% on sales, as compared with 17.3% budgeted.

There were wide differences between budget and actual results for the individual products. Product X, according to the budget, was the most profitable, with a GPR of 20% (Table 20-3, $30,000 ÷ $150,000) would contribute $30,000 in gross profit. However, assume raw materials shortages reduced the sales volume by 23% [($30,000 − $23,000) ÷ $30,000], resulting in gross profit of only $12,880, or only about 43% ($12,880 ÷ $30,000) of the budgeted amount. The actual GPR was only 10.2% (Table 20-4) instead of the estimated 20.0%. Product Y contributed $17,225 (Table 20-4) as compared with a budgeted amount of only $12,000. Product Z also improved upon the budget in the amount contributed, $3,125 to $3,000, but the GPR was less, 10.0% (Table 20-3) as compared to 7.7% (Table 20-4), despite a price increase.

As described previously, in order to compute the effect of volume, it is necessary to hold the prices constant. Thus in Table 20-5 (page 694), we use the actual quantities for 19X0 but the budgeted prices, as shown in Table 20-5.

If prices, volume, and costs had been the same as budgeted, the gross profit would have been $45,000. However, as shown in Table 20-4, the gross profit was only $33,230. What factors caused the decrease in gross profit of $11,770, ($45,000 − $33,230) or 26.2% [($45,000 − $33,230) ÷ $45,000]? The factors which caused this decrease are illustrated and discussed below.

Effect of Price Changes

This data can be taken directly from Tables 20-4 and 20-5.

Sales:
Actual sales (Table 20-4)	$259,875	
Actual units sold at budgeted prices (Table 20-5)	258,500	
Favorable sales price variance		($ 1,375)

Cost:
Actual cost of goods sold (Table 20-4)	$226,645	
Actual units sold at budgeted costs (Table 20-5)	215,850	
Unfavorable cost price variance		10,795
Net unfavorable price variance		$ 9,420

Effect of Volume and Mix

To determine the effect of volume change, we keep the prices constant.

Sales:
Budgeted sales (Table 20-3)	$260,000	
Actual units sold at budgeted prices (Table 20-5)	258,500	
Unfavorable sales volume variance		$ 1,500

Cost:
Actual units sold at budgeted costs (Table 20-5)	$215,850	
Budgeted costs (Table 20-3)	215,000	
Unfavorable cost volume variance		850
Net unfavorable volume variance		$ 2,350

TABLE 20-5
EGAN MANUFACTURING COMPANY
ACTUAL AT BUDGETED PRICES INCOME SUMMARY
YEAR 19X0

PRODUCT NAME	UNITS SOLD	SALES			COST			GROSS PROFIT		
		PRICE	AMOUNT	UNIT	AMOUNT	UNIT		AMOUNT	%	
X	23,000	$5.00	$115,000	$4.00	$ 92,000	$1.00		$23,000	20.0	
Y	26,500	4.00	106,000	3.40	90,100	.60		15,900	15.0	
Z	12,500	3.00	37,500	2.70	33,750	.30		3,750	10.0	
Total	62,000	$4.17 (A)	$258,500	$3.48 (B)	$215,850	$ .69 (C)		$42,650	16.5 (D)	

(A) $258,500 ÷ 62,000
(B) $215,850 ÷ 62,000
(C) $42,650 ÷ 62,000
(D) $42,650 ÷ $258,500

The volume variance should be further broken down into sales mix and final sales volume variance, as shown below.

Sales mix:

Actual units sold times budgeted gross profit, 62,000 × $.75	$46,500	
Actual quantities at budgeted prices gross profit (Table 20-5)	42,650	
Unfavorable sales mix		$ 3,850
Sales volume variance:		
Actual units sold times budgeted gross profit..............	$46,500	
Budgeted gross profit (Table 20-3)	45,000	
Favorable volume variance		(1,500)
Net unfavorable volume variance		$ 2,350

	FAVORABLE	UNFAVORABLE
Summary:		
Increased sales prices...................	$1,375	
Increased cost		$10,795
Change in sales mix		3,850
Decrease in units sold	1,500	
Total	$2,875	$14,645
Minus		2,875
Net decrease in gross profit		$11,770

The total change in gross profit of $11,770 can also be summarized as follows:

Increased sales price	($ 1,375)
Increased cost	10,795
Change in sales mix	3,850
Decrease in units sold	(1,500)
Net decrease in gross profit..............	$11,770

SALES MIX

Often it is desirable to present the change in gross profit according to individual products, especially where there has been a significant change in the sales mix, as is the case with the Egan Manufacturing Company. The sales mix is the ratio of individual product's sales to the total sales. Generally this is based on sales units rather than dollars so that the information is not affected by sales price changes. As can be seen in Table 20-6 (page 696), the sales of product X, which had the highest gross profit per unit, was expected to have 50% ($30,000 ÷ $60,000) of the total sales volume. However, product X amounted to only 37.1% ($23,000 ÷ $62,000) of the actual total sales. Product Y, which was expected to have 33% of total sales volume, increased its proportion to 42.7% of total actual sales. Product Z was expected to have 17% of sales but had 20.2% of total actual sales. Unfortunately, product X had $1.00 budgeted gross profit per unit, but Y and Z had only $.60 and $.30 gross profit per unit, as shown by Table 20-3. The product with the highest margin decreased, while the two products with much lower margins increased. The sales mix by products is shown in Table 20-6.

TABLE 20-6
EGAN MANUFACTURING COMPANY
SALES MIX BY PRODUCTS
YEAR 19X0

PRODUCTS	BUDGET	ACTUAL	INCREASE OR (DECREASE)	MIX % BUDGET	ACTUAL
X	$30,000	$23,000	($7,000)	50	37.1
Y	20,000	26,500	6,500	33	42.7
Z	10,000	12,500	2,500	17	20.2
Total	$60,000	$62,000	$2,000	100	100.0

MANAGEMENT ANALYSIS

The preceding summaries and analyses provide ample information for management to take corrective action, especially those analyses which show the differences between budgeted and actual operations. For example, if there has been a drop from expected sales of the product with the highest gross profit per unit, it may be advisable to increase the advertising budget for succeeding periods to recoup the sales for that product.

As can be seen, product X units sold were 7,000 (30,000 per Table 20-3 less 23,000 per Table 20-4) below the budgeted quantity, which had a significant effect on gross profit. Product Y had an increase of 6,500 units over budget and product Z had an increase of 2,500 units over the budget.

The marketing department should be called on to explain the reasons for these changes, especially the increase in sales of the less profitable products. Sometimes a bonus plan may be set up in such a way that the earnings are based on quantities sold rather than on higher rates for higher gross profit items. Perhaps the bonus plan should be revised to consider the sale of higher gross profit items. As can be seen, prices for products X and Z were increased by $.50 and $.25, respectively (Table 20-4). Product Y was decreased by $.50 per unit (Table 20-4). The control of prices is usually also under the control of the marketing department. The net favorable effect of price increases of $1,375 was more than offset by the unfavorable effect of the sales mix of $3,850.

CHAPTER REVIEW

Gross profit analysis is one of the most fruitful areas for management to look for improving operations. In-depth analysis of the changes in sales, costs, and gross profit provides a thorough understanding of the steps needed to bring actual operations more in line with budgeted expectations.

The net change in gross profit is usually a combination of changes in selling prices, volume, cost, and sales mix. Each of these factors can be isolated, and the amount which each factor has contributed to the net change in gross profit can be identified. Different departments will be responsible for the various factors and should explain the reason for changes in a specific factor. For example, the marketing department should explain the changes in sales prices, the shift in product mix, and the decrease in units sold, and the production department should explain the increase in cost.

GLOSSARY

Average Gross Profit Per Unit—the total gross profit divided by the total units sold.

Contribution Margin—excess of sales over all variable costs, including those in cost of goods sold, selling and administrative costs, etc.

Favorable Variance—one that increases the amount of gross profit.

Gross Profit—excess of sales over cost of goods sold.

Gross Profit Analysis—determination of the causes for the increase or decrease in gross profit.

Income Summary—condensed income data for sales, cost of goods sold, and gross profit.

Price Change—the difference between the unit selling or cost figure of one period compared with similar data for another period.

Product Mix—same as sales mix, the preferable term. Not to be confused with product mixture, the ingredients of the formula used in manufacturing.

Sales—as used here for simplicity, the term is net sales, that is, gross sales less sales returns and allowances, cash discounts, etc.

Sales Mix—sometimes called product mix, this is the proportion of individual product sales to total sales.

Sales Volume Variance—the changes in sales, cost, or gross profit due to the change in quantity.

Unfavorable Variance—a change that causes a decrease in the amount of gross profit.

Volume Change—a variance due to a difference in quantity.

SUMMARY PROBLEMS

PROBLEM 1

DAIKER COMPANY
COMPARATIVE INCOME STATEMENT
YEARS 19X1 AND 19X2

	19X1	19X2	CHANGE	%
Sales	$75,000	$78,000	+$3,000	4.0
Cost of goods sold	45,000	39,780	+ 5,220	11.6
Gross profit	$30,000	$38,220	$8,220	27.4
Gross profit ratio	40%	49%		

Additional Information:

COST DATA PER UNIT

	19X1	19X2	CHANGE
Quantity	5,000 units	6,240 units	+1,240
Sales price	$15.00	$12.500	−2.500
Cost	9.00	6.375	−2.625
Gross profit	6.00	6.125	+ .125

REQUIRED:

Compute the effects of volume change, price change, and cost change on gross profit. Show details.

PROBLEM 2

FLOWER COMPANY
COMPARATIVE INCOME STATEMENT
YEARS 19X3 AND 19X4

	19X3	19X4
Sales.........................	$40,000	$38,000
Cost of goods sold............	28,000	25,000
Gross profit	$12,000	$13,000

Selling prices were 5% lower in 19X4 than in 19X3.

REQUIRED:

Compute the effect of change in selling price, change in unit cost prices, and change in volume on gross profit.

PROBLEM 3

Big Al, Inc., is a manufacturer of Product B and Product F. The following information is for the month of January.

BUDGETED

	SALES		COST	
PRODUCT	UNIT	AMOUNT	UNIT	AMOUNT
B	$3.00	$30,000	$2.50	$25,000
F	4.50	45,000	3.75	37,500
Total		$75,000		$62,500

ACTUAL RESULTS FOR JANUARY

	SALES	
PRODUCT	UNIT	AMOUNT
B	$4.00	$28,000
F	4.00	52,000
Total		$80,000
Cost of sales		61,750
Gross profit		$18,250

REQUIRED:

Compute the effect of price change, cost change, and volume change on gross profit.

SOLUTIONS TO SUMMARY PROBLEMS

PROBLEM 1

Effect of Volume Increase:

1,240 (6,240 − 5,000) units × $6 (19X1 gross profit per unit) = ($7,440)
Favorable increase in sales volume

Effect of Price Decrease:

($15 − $12.50) = $2.50 price decrease
$2.50 × 6,240 units (19 × 2) = $15,600
Unfavorable decrease in sales prices

Effect of Cost Decrease:

($9 − 6.375) = $2.625 × 6,240 units (19X2) = ($16,380)
Favorable decrease in cost prices
Net increase in gross profit = ($8,220)

SUMMARY

	INCREASE	DECREASE
Volume change	$ 7,440	
Price change		$15,600
Cost change	16,380	
Total	$23,820	$15,600
Minus	15,600	
Net increase in gross profit	$ 8,220	

PROBLEM 2

First, 19X4 sales at 19X3 prices must be computed.

$38,000 (19X4 sales) ÷ 95% = $40,000 (19X4 sales at 19X3 prices)

Computing Price Change Effect:

19X4 sales at 19X3 prices	$40,000	
19X4 sales at 19X4 prices	38,000	
Unfavorable decrease in sales prices		$2,000

Computing Cost Change Effect:

19X4 volume at 19X3 cost		
$40,000 × 70% CSR	$28,000	
19X4 volume at 19X4 cost	25,000	
Favorable decrease in cost prices		($3,000)

Computing Volume Change Effect:

19X3 sales at 19X3 price	$40,000	
19X4 sales at 19X3 price	40,000	
No change in volume		0
Net increase in gross profit		($1,000)

PROBLEM 3

Increase in gross profit between actual and budgeted was $5,750 [($75,000 − 62,500) − $18,250]. The first step is to determine the budgeted amount of units to be sold and the actual amount of units sold.

Budgeted:
- Product B .... $30,000 ÷ $3 = 10,000 units
- Product F .... $45,000 ÷ $4.50 = 10,000 units

Actual results:
- Product B .... $28,000 ÷ $4 = 7,000 units
- Product F .... $52,000 ÷ $4 = 13,000 units

The next step is to develop an actual at budgeted price schedule. This is shown below.

ACTUAL AT BUDGETED PRICES

PRODUCT	PRICE	AMOUNT	UNIT	AMOUNT
		SALES		COST
B	$3.00	$21,000	$2.50	$17,500
F	$4.50	58,500	$3.75	48,750
Total		$79,500		$66,250

Effect of Price Change:

Actual sales	$80,000	
Actual units sold at budgeted prices	79,500	
Favorable increase in sales prices		($500)

Effect of Cost Change:

Actual units sold at budgeted prices	$66,250	
Actual costs	61,750	
Favorable decrease in cost prices		($4,500)

Effect of Sales Volume Change:

Actual units sold at budgeted prices	$79,500	
Budgeted sales	75,000	
Favorable increase in sales volume ...		($4,500)

Effect of Cost Volume Change:

Actual units sold at budgeted price	$66,250	
Budgeted costs	62,500	
Unfavorable increase in cost volume ..		$3,750
Net increase in gross profit		($5,750)

QUESTIONS

1 What is the difference between gross profit and contribution margin?
2 What are the principal causes of changes in gross profit?
3 Why is gross profit analysis important?
4 Name the two types of comparisons that can be used in analyzing the change in gross profit. Which is preferable? Why?
5 Name two important ratios used in connection with gross profit analysis. Define each.
6 When computing volume change, what must be kept constant? When computing price change, what must be kept constant?
7 After *net* volume variance is computed, it should be further broken down into _____ and _____ _____ .
8 When there is a *significant change* in sales mix, what may be necessary for a company to do?
9 Changes in prices are generally the responsibility of what department? What else should this department be able to explain?
10 Define final sales volume variance, sales mix variance, and sales volume variance.

EXERCISES

EXERCISE 1

Volume, Price, and Cost Changes

The Kong Company is a manufacturer of bugle parts. Below is information pertaining to a valve spring it manufactures.

	19X3	19X4
Sales	$50,000	$62,500
Cost of goods sold	40,000	45,000
Gross profit...................	$10,000	$17,500

Cost data per unit (4 springs per unit):

	19X3	19X4
Quantity	200,000 units	250,000 units
Sales price	$.25	$.25
Cost	.20	.18
Gross profit	$.05	$.07

REQUIRED:

Compute the effects of volume change, price change, and cost change. State whether each change is favorable or unfavorable.

EXERCISE 2

Volume, Price, and Cost Changes

The Adler Manufacturing Company produces airplane parts. The following information pertains to part 11577:

	19X3	19X4
Sales	$200,000	$180,000
Cost of goods sold	125,000	135,000
Gross profit...................	$ 75,000	$ 45,000

Additional data: The company had a sales price *increase* of $10, making the sales price $60 per unit.

REQUIRED:

Computate the effects of volume change, price change, and cost change. State whether each is favorable or unfavorable.

EXERCISE 3

Volume, Price, and Cost Changes and Summary

The Wes Manufacturing Company produces two products, Product A and Product P. The following information pertains to these products:

	19X2	19X3
Product A:		
Sales	$60,000	$68,000
Cost of sales	$45,000	$46,000
Quantity sold	10,000 units	12,500 units
Sales price per unit	$6.00	$5.44
Cost	$4.50	$3.68
Product P:		
Sales	$75,000	$72,000
Cost of sales	$65,000	$66,000
Sales price per unit	$3.00	$4.00

REQUIRED:

a Compute volume change effect, price change effect, and effect of cost change for each product.

b In summary form give a breakdown of the total change in gross profit for the Wes Manufacturing Company.

EXERCISE 4

Analysis of Changes in Gross Profit

You have received the following information for 19X1 and 19X2 for J. V., Inc.:

	19X1		19X2		DOLLAR INCREASE
Sales	$750,000	100%	$840,000	100%	$90,000
Cost of sales	495,000	66%	560,000	$66^2/_3$%	65,000
Gross profit	$255,000	34%	$280,000	$33^1/_3$%	$25,000
Unit selling price	$10		$12		

REQUIRED:

Develop an analysis showing the reasons for the change in gross profit.

(AICPA Adapted)

EXERCISE 5

Multiple Choice

Select the *best* answer to each of the following questions:

1 An increase in cost of sales *greater* than an increase in sales will cause the gross profit percentage to:
  a Decrease.
  b Increase.
  c Remain the same.
2 The Fitz Company's sales increased by 6%. At the same time its cost of sales increased by 7%. Gross profit therefore increased (decreased) by
  a 3%
  b 1%
  c Not determinable from information given
3 The Stamp Co. had sales of $40,000 and a GPR of 20%. Its cost of sales was therefore:
  a $4,000
  b $36,000
  c $32,000
  d $8,000
4 A volume decrease will have what kind of effect on gross profit?
  a Favorable
  b Unfavorable
5 What type of change in sales price will have a favorable effect on gross profit?
  a Increase
  b Decrease

The following information pertains to questions 6 to 10: The J. F. Company is a multiproduct company and is analyzing its gross profit for the year 19X1. This is accomplished by comparing budgeted figures with actual figures. In order to aid in the company's analysis, an "actual at budgeted prices" schedule was made.

6 In computing the sales price variance, actual sales at actual prices were *greater* than actual sales at budgeted prices. This represents a (an), (a) favorable, (b) unfavorable change in gross profit.
7 In computing the cost price variance, the actual cost of sales was *less* than the budgeted cost of actual goods sold. This is a (an) (a) favorable, (b) unfavorable change in gross profit.
8 In computing the sales volume variance, the budgeted sales were *greater* than the actual sales at budgeted prices. This has a (an) (a) favorable (b) unfavorable effect on gross profit.
9 In computing the cost volume variance, the budgeted cost of actual goods sold was *less* than budgeted costs. This represents a (an) (a) favorable (b) unfavorable change in gross profit.

10 The sales mix for the J. F. Company changed significantly from the budgeted amount. In such a situation the president of the company should
   a Call on the marketing department for an explanation.
   b Develop a product analysis of each product.
   c Ask the production department for an explanation.
   d Both a and b.
   e None of the above.

EXERCISE 6

Volume, Price, Cost, and Mix Changes

1 Solve for the unknowns in each case:

	19X1	19X2
Sales	$100,000	$120,000
Cost of sales	B	C
Gross profit	A	D
	GPR = 30%	CSR = $66^2/_3$%

2 The Yale Company manufactures product C in five different colors. The color does not affect sales price or cost. The company compares actual figures with budgeted figures in analyzing its gross profit. You receive the following information:

   Actual sales were 200,000 units at a gross profit of $.4 per unit. GPR per unit = 40%.

   Budgeted sales were 180,000 units at a gross profit of $.375 per unit. GPR per unit = $41^2/_3$%.

REQUIRED:

   a Compute the sales price variance and sales volume variance.
   b Is the sales mix of the Yale Company important? Why?
   c Using the information from part b:
     1 Compute the cost price variance and cost volume variance.
     2 Compute the net change in gross profit for the Yale Company.
     3 Prepare in summary form the effect of the variances on gross profit.

EXERCISE 7

Volume, Price, and Cost Changes

Actual and budgeted figures for 19X1 for the China Company are as follows:

	PRODUCT K		PRODUCT F		
	UNIT PRICE	NO. OF UNITS	UNIT PRICE	NO. OF UNITS	TOTAL
Budgeted sales	$1.50	100,000	$1.00	25,000	$175,000
Budgeted cost of sales	1.00	100,000	.60	25,000	115,000
Actual sales	1.20	110,000	1.20	20,000	156,000
Actual cost of sales	.90	110,000	.70	20,000	113,000

REQUIRED:

a Compute the sales price variance, cost price variance, sales volume variance, and cost volume variance.

b Compute the net change in gross profit between budgeted and actual amounts. List results in part **a** in summary form.

EXERCISE 8

Mix and Sales Volume Variances

REQUIRED:

Using the data from Exercise 7 for the China Company:

1 Develop an analysis of the net volume variance into sales mix and final sales volume.

2 Develop an analysis of sales mix and volume by product.

PROBLEMS

PROBLEM 1

Analysis of Changes in Gross Profit

The 19X1 income statement of the Vanatta Company is given below.

Sales (90,500 units)	$760,200
Cost of sales	452,500
Gross profit	$307,700

For 19X2 it has been estimated that sales volume will be 100,000 units at a price of $8.30 per unit. For 100,000 level activity, variable costs have been predicted to be $4.90 per unit. There are no fixed costs in the cost of sales.

REQUIRED:

Prepare an analysis of the difference in gross profit between the two years. The following should be included: sales price variance, cost price variance, sales volume variance, cost volume variance.

PROBLEM 2

Analysis of Changes in Gross Profit

The president of the Farmbrook Manufacturing Company is concerned because his gross profit has decreased from $130,000 in 19X3 to $87,960 in 19X4. He asks you to prepare an analysis of the causes of change.

You find that the company operates two plants, each as a separate unit. Investigation reveals the following information:

Plant No. 1 (makes a variety of products):

	19X4	19X3
Sales..................	$200,000	$300,000
Cost of sales	160,000	210,000
Gross profit	$ 40,000	$ 90,000

Plant No. 2 (makes only one product):

	19X4		19X3	
	AMOUNT	PER UNIT	AMOUNT	PER UNIT
Sales..................	$112,200	$10.20	$100,000	$10.00
Cost of sales	64,240	5.84	60,000	6.00
Gross profit	$ 47,960	$ 4.36	$ 40,000	$ 4.00

REQUIRED:

Prepare a detailed analysis of the causes of the change in gross profit for each of the plants to the extent that the above data permit such an analysis. Critical comment on the analysis is not required.

PROBLEM 3

Price, Volume, Cost, and Sales Mix

The following information is taken from the income statement of the Screech Company:

	19X1	19X2
Sales..................	$200,000	$220,000
Cost of sales	150,000	154,000
Gross profit	$ 50,000	$ 66,000

In addition the following information was taken from various accounting records of the company:

PRODUCT	19X1 SALES			19X1 COST OF SALES	
	UNITS	PRICE	AMOUNT	UNIT	AMOUNT
G	15,000	$8.00	$120,000	$6.00	$ 90,000
L	10,000	3.00	30,000	2.00	20,000
O	25,000	2.00	50,000	1.60	40,000
Total	50,000		$200,000		$150,000

| PRODUCT | 19X2 SALES | | | 19X2 COST OF SALES | |
	UNITS	PRICE	AMOUNT	UNIT	AMOUNT
G	12,000	$10.00	$120,000	$7.00	$84,000
L	9,000	4.00	36,000	2.80	25,200
O	25,600	2.50	64,000	1.75	44,800
Total	46,600		$220,000		$154,000

REQUIRED:

a Compute the sales price variance, sales volume variance, cost price variance, and cost volume variance.

b Prepare an analysis of net volume variance broken down into sales mix and final sales volume variance. Show all details.

PROBLEM 4

Analysis of Gross Profit

Fred Williams has been an accountant for a large candy company for 5 years. Seeing the opportunity to make more money, Mr. Williams decided to leave his present job and start his own company. After all the financial details were worked out, Mr. Williams' company started producing candy at the beginning of July. The company produces three different candies, G, M, and F. Below is budgeted data for the month of July for the three candies. Unit = case of candy.

| CANDY | SALES | | COST OF GOODS SOLD | |
	PRICE	AMOUNT	UNIT	AMOUNT
G	$10	$ 100	$5	$ 50
M	15	1,500	8	800
F	12	600	8	400
Total		$2,200		$1,250

At the end of the month, actual results were as follows:

| CANDY | SALES | | COST OF GOODS SOLD | |
	PRICE	AMOUNT	UNIT	AMOUNT
G	$ 8	$ 96	$5	$ 60
M	15	1,350	9	810
F	13	780	7	420
Total		$2,226		$1,290

Mr. Williams had been doing all the accounting work for the company, but because of the large volume it was taking too much of his time. He decided to hire an accountant to help with the work.

Two college graduates applied for the position. Both were found to be qualified. Mr. Williams decided to test them by having them make a report of the difference in budgeted to actual gross profit for July.

The following was submitted by the two applicants:

	APPLICANT 1		APPLICANT 2	
	FAVORABLE	UNFAVOR-ABLE	FAVORABLE	UNFAVOR-ABLE
Change in sales price	$36		$36	
Change in cost		$30		$30
Sales mix		32		
Change in volume	12			20
Total	$48	$62	$36	$50
Minus		48		36
Net decrease in gross profit		$14		$14

REQUIRED:

a Show how the applicants arrived at the various effects on gross profit.
b Which report is preferable? Why?

PROBLEM 5

Analysis of Variances from a Budget

The following information is for the month of May for a small manufacturing firm:

Budgeted:

	SALES		COST OF GOODS SOLD	
PRODUCT	PRICE	AMOUNT	UNIT	AMOUNT
X	$10.00	$10,000	$9.00	$ 9,000
Y	8.00	20,000	6.00	15,000
Z	4.00	12,000	3.50	10,500
Total		$42,000		$34,500

Actual:

	SALES		COST OF GOODS SOLD	
PRODUCT	PRICE	AMOUNT	UNIT	AMOUNT
X	$10.00	$ 9,000	$9.00	$ 8,100
Y	7.50	22,500	6.50	19,500
Z	4.00	10,000	3.25	8,125
Total		$41,500		$35,725

REQUIRED:

As the accountant for the firm, you have been asked to show why the budget was not met for the month of May. Show all details.

PROBLEM 6

Analysis of Increase in Gross Profit

The Golden Corporation sells a special suntan lotion. The company's 19X1 and 19X2 income reports showed the following:

	19X1	19X2
Sales........................	$840,000	$891,000
Cost of sales	945,000	688,500
Gross profit (loss)............	($105,000)	$202,500

Sales price increased from $8 to $11 per bottle. Costs were reduced from $9.00 to $8.50 per bottle.

REQUIRED:

Prepare an analysis showing the reasons for the increase in gross profit in 19X2. Show all detail work.

(AICPA Adapted)

PROBLEM 7

Analysis of Gross Profit for Two Plans

Actual results of Sports, Inc., for the month of August were as follows:

PRODUCT	UNITS	SALES PRICE	SALES AMOUNT	COST OF SALES UNIT	COST OF SALES AMOUNT
A	10,000	$3.00	$30,000	$2.50	$25,000
B	12,000	2.50	30,000	2.00	24,000
C	8,000	4.00	32,000	3.75	30,000
Total	30,000		$92,000		$79,000

At the marketing department's weekly meeting, two plans were suggested to raise the gross profit of the firm. In each case a maximum of 30,000 units can be produced. Plan A calls for eliminating product C and replacing it with product D. Plan B calls for the elimination of products A, B, and C and replacing them with products E, F, and D, respectively. Projected data for both plans are given below:

	UNITS	SALES PRICE	SALES AMOUNT	COST OF SALES UNIT	COST OF SALES AMOUNT
Plan A:					
A	10,000	$3.00	$ 30,000	$2.50	$25,000
B	12,000	2.50	30,000	2.00	24,000
D	8,000	5.00	40,000	4.00	32,000
Total	30,000		$100,000		$81,000

		SALES		COST OF SALES	
	UNITS	PRICE	AMOUNT	UNIT	AMOUNT
Plan B:					
E	8,000	$5.00	$ 40,000	$4.00	$32,000
F	8,000	2.00	16,000	1.75	14,000
D	14,000	3.50	49,000	2.50	35,000
Total	30,000		$105,000		$81,000

REQUIRED:

a Prepare an analysis of Plan A and Plan B with respect to the actual data for the month of August.

b Are there sales mix variances for Plan A and Plan B? If so, what are the variances?

c Which plan will produce the greater increase in gross profit because of a sales price increase?

PROBLEM 8

Analysis of Changes in Gross Profit Using a Flexible Budget

1 The following information was taken from the flexible budget of the Oscar Company:

Sales (units)	100,000	150,000	200,000	250,000
Total cost of goods sold				
($50,000 fixed costs)	$350,000	$500,000	$650,000	$800,000

Sales price per unit is budgeted at all levels to be $5.

Actual data for July and August:

July:
Sales .... 100,000 units
Cost of goods sold $400,000
Sales price per unit $5.10

August:
Sales .... 200,000 units
Cost of goods sold $655,000
Sales price per unit $4.90

REQUIRED:

Prepare an analysis of the deviation from budgeted data for July and August.

2 At the beginning of September new machinery was put into operation. The machinery was expected to increase production and lower costs. The following budget was formulated for September, taking into consideration the new machinery:

Sales ($4.50 per unit) $900,000
Cost of goods sold 500,000
Gross profit $400,000

Because of unforeseen raw materials shortages, production was limited to 150,000 units for the month of September. All the units produced were sold at $4.75 per unit, with total costs of goods sold being $400,000.

REQUIRED:

Prepare an analysis accounting for the causes for the variation of actual results from budgeted data.

PART FIVE

SPECIAL TOPICS

CHAPTER TWENTY-ONE TRANSFER PRICING

Transfer pricing is the dollar basis used for transferring goods or services from one affiliated unit to another. A few years ago transfer pricing was a relatively unimportant factor in cost accounting. However, with the substantial expansion in most companies along with the trend toward decentralization, there are a number of significant factors to be considered in establishing transfer prices. First, the nature of the business is an important factor; that is, is the intermediate product commercial and is there a competing product with a known market price? If the product is specialized or customized, there may be no ready outside market or competing product. If the company is heavily integrated, the finished product of one division becomes the raw materials of the next stage of production.

Whatever transfer prices are established can have an important impact on the profit of each division or segment. The transfer price can directly affect how much is transferred among company divisions and how much may be purchased outside the company. For example, a company may have large holdings of timberland and each year may sell timber output on the open market at a higher price than the transfer price, or it may use some of the output as pulpwood in its own operations. Therefore, the timber division may show a high profit, a low profit, or no profit at all, depending on the level at which the transfer price is set. Another factor is the degree of control of the market price. If general timber operations are not good, the price per cord may be high and the company may decide to cut its own timber, thereby reducing the demand, which will tend to reduce the market price. If the market price is low, possibly even lower than the company cutting costs, the company will buy most of its requirements outside, which will increase demand and tend to drive prices upward.

Companies may also use transfer pricing to manipulate the impact of taxes. For example, if a company has foreign operations where tax rates are low, the transfer prices for raw materials to this country may be set high so as to show greater profits abroad at the lower tax rate. In another case a company may have a warehouse in a state which has an inventory tax. Here, it is desirable to have lower transfer prices in order to keep the tax expense lower. Of course, it is desirable to watch the quantity as well, especially at the dates when the tax liability is established.

As can be seen above, there are a number of complex factors which affect transfer prices which can have an important bearing on the well-being of a company.

SHORT-TERM PROBLEMS

Much has been written in the management area concerning the motivation and the autonomy of the divisional manager. Most companies today give careful consideration to these factors in establishing separate divisions and in selecting managers for those divisions. There is a possibility that at times the interests of the division may conflict with the interests of the total company. In such a case top management must act to ensure that the division's interests are made congruent or brought into line with total company interests. We may restate the objectives of transfer prices as (1) goal congruence, (2) motivation, and (3) autonomy. An example where divisional goals and company goals were not congruent occurred in a situation where the divisional manager's performance record was based on sales. However, it was later found that the largest volumes of sales were for products with a low profit margin, which was not to the benefit of the company as a whole. Such problems are generally short-term and are usually corrected as comparative divisional analyses are evaluated.

TRANSFER PRICING METHODS

The transfer price method used must be the one most suitable for company operations. Five general methods are used to arrive at transfer prices. These are (1) cost, (2) cost plus, (3) market price, (4) negotiated price, and (5) dual price. These are described below:

Cost

According to a study, "Interdivisional Transfer Pricing," made by the National Industrial Conference Board, most companies use the cost or cost plus methods for determining transfer prices. The cost used may be based on actual, budgeted, standard, variable, or any other reasonable estimate of cost. Where actual or full costs are used, there may not be enough incentive for the selling division to reduce inefficiencies. Standard costs or budgeted costs may help to lessen the problem of inefficiencies or fluctuations in production because variations from the standard or budget should be accounted for. A transfer price based on variable costs may cause some difficulty for a decentralized company which must determine the profitability of each of the autonomous units. Difficulties in using a cost basis can also occur when comparing divisional profits. For example, Division A may sell three-fourths of its output to outside sources at a 60% markup and one-fourth to other divisions at no markup. Division B may sell only one-third of its output outside at a 60% markup and two-thirds to other divisions at no markup. At the end of the year when the company is considering divisional profits and evaluating the operating performance of divisional managers, Division B will be severely penalized through no fault of its own. Its contribution to profits will generally be less than that of Division A, even though it may be more efficient. Companies have attempted to equalize such operations by dual pricing and making adjustments to bring sales to an equitable basis.

Cost Plus

In a cost plus transfer price there would be an increment, usually 20 to 40% of cost, added onto the cost of the product. This interdivisional profit would have to be eliminated when financial statements are prepared, as described later on under accounting entries.

A large number of companies use the cost plus method, which gives some approximation to market prices. Often this is considered a practical approach to the problem of divisional and corporate interests. The base cost used in determining the transfer price varies with different companies. In some cases top management may want to base transfer prices on variable costs or perhaps on outlay costs. Fixed costs and idle capacity costs may also be included.

Even though a transfer price may be higher than an actual cost, it may be in the general company interest to transfer the product within the company. For example, the Chadwick Company is an integrated manufacturing company with a number of autonomous divisions. The entire output of Division X is transferred to Division Y at a standard cost of $25 a unit. Division Y has additional processing and marketing costs of $5 a unit. Division Y has complained to top management that the transfer price is too high, since it can sell its completed product outside for only $28 a unit. The standard cost of Division X consists of $18 variable cost and $10 fixed cost, at normal capacity. The division has some idle capacity at present.

	DIVISION Y COSTS	COMPANY COSTS
Outside price	$28	$28
Costs:		
Transfer price from division X	$25	$15*
Cost in Division Y	5	5
Total cost	$30	$20
Profit or (loss)	($ 2)	$ 8

* $25 − $10 fixed costs.

The preceding summary shows that for divisional operating performance there is a loss of $2 per unit. However, for the company as a whole there is a profit of $8. The difference is the fixed cost per unit of $10. Since Division X has idle capacity at this time, it is desirable to transfer the materials within the company.

Market Price

Where the competitive market price is determinable for the output of a division, such as the price charged to outside customers, the market price is generally satisfactory. It is expected that the market price is one obtained through arm's length transactions, based on representative quantities. Generally internal transfers will be made where the selling division's product is equal to that of outsiders in quality and price. Often a lower price may be justified, since there will be less selling and administrative expenses, larger purchases will be made, and there is practically a guaranteed market. The buying division also has assurance of continuing good quality and dependable delivery.

There are certain factors that have to be considered in using the market price. There may be no market price for the exact product, or there may not be a market for the intermediate product. A quoted price must be equal in quality, delivery, credit terms, etc. In some cases prices obtained may not be reliable; they may be distress prices for excess inventory or defective goods and would not be a long-term source.

Another point is that a bidder who has consistently lost to internal transfer of goods may possibly make an unreliable bid or deliberately submit a low price. It is desirable to maintain contact with more than one seller or buyer so that a reasonable market price, based on the stated factors, can be obtained.

For example, the Panda Company is a medium-sized manufacturing company with two large plants, Plant A, the processing unit, and Plant B, the finishing unit. The finished product of Plant A becomes the raw materials of Plant B. Plant A has the option of selling its finished product to Plant B or to outside customers at $14 per unit. Manufacturing costs for Plant A are variable costs of $8 per unit and fixed costs of $4 per unit.

Manufacturing costs for Plant B are transfer costs of $14 per unit and added variable costs of $4 per unit. Plant B has the option of buying its raw materials either from Plant A or from outside suppliers, which presently have the same price as Plant A. Plant B sells its product to outsiders for $22 per unit.

The total company contribution margin is now $6 ($2 for Plant A and $4 for Plant B). Future management problems include the need for Plant B to purchase more goods from outside customers, as Plant A is at near capacity and also may have an opportunity to produce a slightly different product for sale to outsiders at $25 a unit. It is probable that Plant B will be able to negotiate a lower price from outsiders with a promised higher quantity of purchases. Figure 21-1 (page 720) is an illustration of transfer pricing when market prices are used.

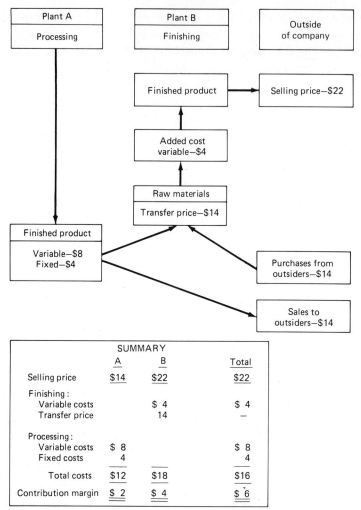

FIGURE 21-1   **The Panda Company, Transfer Pricing, Year 19X0**

Negotiated Price

Generally a negotiated price arrived at between the buying and selling divisions gives division managers the greatest control over divisional profit. One of the serious difficulties with this method is that it takes time and a great deal of analysis and data must be developed. Also there may be frequent requests for revisions. Possible overemphasis on divisional welfare rather than company welfare may result. Sometimes stalemates may occur and top management has to step in and resolve the issues. At times ill feeling may develop between the involved division managers that more than offsets the benefits gained.

Dual Price

As can be seen, it is not always effective to have a single transfer price. The buying division and the selling division have different interests in the transfer price. In one case the price is used to make a decision to buy; in the other case the price may be an important factor in evaluating the performance of the selling division. In a dual-price situation Division Y may be charged $10, the variable cost, for a unit, while Division X is given credit for an estimated market price of $14. The profit for the total company will be less than the total of the divisional profits. In preparing financial statements, interdivisional eliminations would have to be made for these differences. Any amount transferred in excess of company costs would have to be eliminated. This method has not been in common use, as it has a basic weakness. Since both the buying division and the selling division get what they want, there is a tendency to become careless and disregard needed cost controls.

PERFORMANCE EVALUATION

As can be seen above, a competitive market price is one of the best transfer prices that can be used. Where there is no competitive price for an intermediate product, the variable cost may be used. As stated previously in this chapter, there are wide variations among divisions in the percentage of their output transferred to other divisions. A division manager with about the same volume of operations and profit potential as another division will not be happy to be directed by top management to transfer most of the output at no profit, while the other division sells most of its output outside at about a 50% markup. When comparative divisional evaluations are made, the first division may have a poor record of profit relative to the second division. Generally management must make some compromise, such as allowing a markup close to outside markup, and also must make some allowance for fixed costs. In effect, a trade-off has to be made in order to retain the benefits of decentralization.

ACCOUNTING ENTRIES

Most companies which have a significant volume of interdivisional or interplant transfers will make these transfers at some transfer price above cost. Therefore, some portion of interdivisional profit will be in inventories at any given time. In accordance with generally accepted accounting principles, profit can be made only on sales outside the company. Therefore, it is necessary to make elimination entries when financial statements are prepared. Unless elimination entries are made for transfers, the total sales amount will be substantially overstated, as will the accounts receivable, the cost of goods sold, and the inventory amounts. The internal reports for divisional operations are ordinarily designed for management purposes, while financial reports must be prepared for investors, the SEC, the IRS, and other external users. Thus interdivisional profits must be eliminated periodically when financial statements are prepared. This can be difficult where a company is fully integrated and there are a large number of transfers. It is necessary to maintain interdivisional gross profit accounts. A number of these accounts may be needed in a large company. One mill in a division may sell to another mill in the same division creating an *intermill gross profit* or to a mill in another division creating an *interdivision gross profit*. Often companies will use only one account, *interdivision gross profit*, with details being shown on the working papers. Generally, the financial statements will be prepared at company headquarters. In some cases divisional statements may be prepared at divisional headquarters. In any case the divisional statements will show separately the interdivision amounts for sales, cost of goods sold, accounts receivable, and accounts payable, plus any other related accounts such as "interdivision loans." Generally certain reconciliations will be needed, for example, when one location has made a transfer and recorded the sales, and the buying location has not received the goods. Entries will then be made to eliminate the amount of interdivision gross profit.

We may use the following example of the Chadwick Company, an integrated company with many locations. There are a large number of transfers each month which are made at cost plus, that is, standard cost plus 25% of cost. During the month of October, Division X transferred materials with a cost of $1,000 to Division Y at a transfer price of $1,250. Following are the entries on the books of each division and on the combined working papers:

Division Records

Division X:
Accounts receivable—Division Y 1,250
    Interdivision sales 1,250
Interdivision cost of goods sold 1,000
    Inventory 1,000
Division Y:
Inventory 1,250
    Accounts payable—Division X 1,250

Working Papers

Accounts payable—Division X 1,250
    Accounts receivable—Division Y 1,250
To eliminate interdivision receivables and payables.
Interdivision sales 1,250
    Interdivision cost of goods sold 1,000
    Interdivision gross profit 250
To close accounts and show gross profit.
Interdivision gross profit 250
    Inventory 250
To eliminate interdivision gross profit.

Another method of eliminating interdivision gross profit where there are many transfers is based on balances at the end of the period. Realistically, there would be interdivision balances in receivables, payables, inventory, etc., at the end of each period, and it would not be necessary to make gross profit entries for the transactions of the month. It is simpler to eliminate whatever interdivision gross profit remains in inventory at the end of the period. One method of accounting for transferred goods is to have each division prepare a report, at the end of the period, listing the description, quantity, and value of interdivision products on hand. Thus, if a percentage is added to cost, the amount of interdivision profit included can be computed as follows:

$$\frac{\text{Percent above cost}}{100\% + \text{percent above cost}} \times \text{amount of interdivision inventory}$$

For example, if only $600 of interdivision inventory was on hand at the end of the month, assuming the inventory was originally purchased from another division at cost (100%) plus a 25% markup above cost, the amount of interdivision gross profit not realized at the end of the month is $120 [(25%/125%) × $600].

The entry to be made is

```
Interdivision gross profit  .................  120
    Inventory ............................         120
```

CHAPTER REVIEW

In a decentralized company there will generally be a substantial amount of interdivision transfer of materials. The transfer price policy adopted by a company must be carefully monitored to determine that it is operating as intended and is meeting the needs of division managers and the company as a whole. The established transfer price must be high enough to motivate the division manager to produce quality goods while controlling costs.

There are five methods commonly used to arrive at a transfer price. They are (1) cost, (2) cost plus, (3) market price, (4) negotiated price, and (5) dual price. The most satisfactory transfer price will usually be the competitive market price, if one exists. Unfortunately, often no such market price is readily available. If a satisfactory market price is not available, the variable cost, plus some portion of fixed costs of the selling unit, should be used.

There is danger in having the transfer price so low that the selling unit will show losses on interdivision transfers. Such losses may lead to a poor performance evaluation which will tend to cancel all the benefits of decentralization.

GLOSSARY

Autonomy—the right of division managers to self-govern their divisions.

Cost—when used in transfer pricing, it may mean full cost, standard, or variable cost.

Cost Plus—the established cost plus a percentage of cost.

Dual Prices—A method of transfer pricing where the transferor division uses one price, and transferee division uses another price.

Goal Congruence—when the interests of both the division and the total company coincide.

Interdivision Gross Profit—the excess amount over cost a producing division uses in billing materials to another division.

Market Price—the price at which a division may buy or sell materials outside and which is based on an arm's length transaction in an open market.

Motivation—the incentive for a division manager to act in the best interest of the division and the company.

Negotiated Price—the transfer price arrived at in negotiations between the buying and selling divisions.

Performance Evaluation—the review and appraisal by management of the performance of a division or a division manager.

Transfer Price—the price at which materials or services are exchanged among units of a combined entity.

SUMMARY PROBLEMS

PROBLEM 1

The Fisher Corporation has two divisions, A and B. Division A produces a computer circuit that is used in the finished product of Division B.

The costs of producing the circuit are variable costs of $4 per circuit and fixed costs of $1 per circuit. The part is sold in the highly competitive computer market for $7 per circuit.

Up until now Division B bought 60% of the output of Division A at a negotiated price of $6.50 per circuit. But because of overemphasis on divisional welfare rather than company welfare, a new transfer pricing method must be developed. The suggestion was to add 35% to the total cost of the circuit when transferring to Division B. Another suggestion was to use the variable costs of $4 per circuit in arriving at a transfer price.

REQUIRED;

Using the above information and suggestions, determine the gross profit per finished unit for Division B according to the five principal transfer pricing methods.

Pertinent data of Division B: In addition to the transfer price of the circuit, there are additional processing and marketing costs of $10 per unit. The selling price of the finished product of Division B is $20 per unit.

PROBLEM 2

The Tiger Company has two divisions, X and Y. Parts that are manufactured in Division X are transferred to Division Y, where they are assembled into Product A.

For the month of May, parts having a total manufacturing cost of $15,000 were transferred to Divison Y at a selling price of $17,500. All purchases were made on credit.

REQUIRED:

a Prepare entries on the books of Division X and Division Y for the transfer of goods. Assume a perpetual inventory.

b Combined financial statements must be prepared for the month of May. Prepare all elimination entries required for the Tiger Company.

SOLUTIONS TO SUMMARY PROBLEMS

PROBLEM 1

1 *Negotiated transfer price*

Selling price per finished unit of Division B		$20.00
Transfer price (given)	$ 6.50	
Additional costs in Division B	10.00	16.50
Gross profit per unit		$ 3.50

2 *Cost transfer price*

Selling price per finished unit of Division B		$20.00
Transfer price (variable costs of Division A)	$ 4.00	
Additional costs in Division B	10.00	14.00
Gross profit per unit		$ 6.00

3 *Cost plus transfer price*

Selling price per finished unit of Division B		$20.00
Transfer price (total cost + 35% of total cost; $5 + $1.75)	$ 6.75	
Additional costs in Division B	10.00	16.75
Gross profit per unit		$ 3.25

4 *Market transfer price*

Selling price per finished unit of Division B		$20.00
Transfer price ($7 market price)	$ 7.00	
Additional costs in Division B	10.00	17.00
Gross profit per unit		$ 3.00

5 *Dual transfer pricing*

Selling price per finished unit of Division B		$20.00
Transfer price (variable costs of Division A)	$ 4.00	
Additional costs in Division B................................	10.00	14.00
Gross profit per unit		$ 6.00

Under dual pricing, one possibility is that Division A would be credited with a transfer price of $7 per circuit, which represents the market price it could receive.

PROBLEM 2

a   Entries on Division X's Books:

Accounts receivable—Division Y	17,500	
Interdivision sales		17,500
Interdivision cost of goods sold	15,000	
Inventory...		15,000

Entries on Division Y's Books:

Inventory...	17,500	
Accounts payable—Division X		17,500

b   Entries on Elimination Worksheet:

1 Accounts payable—Division X 17,500

      Accounts receivable—Division Y 17,500

    To eliminate interdivision receivables and payables.

2 Interdivision sales 17,500

      Interdivision cost of goods sold 15,000

      Interdivision gross profit 2,500

    To close accounts and show gross profit.

3 Interdivision gross profit 2,500

      Inventory 2,500

    To eliminate interdivision gross profit.

QUESTIONS

1   What are some of the factors that must be considered when establishing a system of transfer pricing?

2   Name the three objectives of transfer prices.

3   What are the principal methods used to arrive at transfer prices?

4   Explain how transfer prices are determined under each method.

5   Why may a company eliminate entries made for transfers within the company?

6 How is interdivision profit in ending inventory computed?
7 Name a weakness in using the cost method and the dual price method.
8 The gross profit of an interdivision sale cannot be realized until when?

EXERCISES

EXERCISE 1

Multiple Choice

1 In order to evaluate the performance of each department, interdepartmental transfer of a product preferably should be made at prices:
   a Equal to the market price of the product.
   b Set by the receiving department.
   c Equal to fully allocated costs to the producing department.
   d Equal to variable costs to the producing department.
2 In a decentralized company in which divisions may buy goods from one another, the transfer pricing system should be designed primarily to:
   a Increase the consolidated value of inventory.
   b Prevent division managers from buying from outsiders.
   c Minimize the degree of autonomy of division managers.
   d Aid in the approval and motivation of managerial performance.

(AICPA Adapted)

EXERCISE 2

Transfer Pricing and Idle Capacity

The Knoebel Company had two decentralized divisions, A and B. Division A has always purchased certain units from Division B at $75 per unit. Because Division B plans to raise the price to $100 per unit, Division A desired to purchase these units from outside suppliers for $75 per unit. Division B's costs follow:

B's variable costs per unit	$70
B's annual fixed costs	$15,000
B's annual production of these units for A	1,000 units

REQUIRED:

If Division A buys from an outside supplier, the facilities Division B uses to manufacture these units would remain idle. Would it be more profitable for the company to enforce the $100 transfer price than to allow A to buy from outside suppliers at $75 per unit?

(AICPA Adapted)

EXERCISE 3

Market Price and Cost Method

Divisions C and D are two decentralized divisions of the Color TV Corporation. Division C produces a picture tube used in the console TVs produced in Division D.

The following information pertains to the two divisions for the month of June:

Division C:

Sales to outsiders	500 tubes at $15 per tube
Sales to Division D	300 tubes at $_____
Variable costs per tube	$7.00
Fixed costs (annual)	$24,000

Division D:

Sales ($250 each)	300 console TVs
Transfer price	(300 tubes) $_____
Variable costs of producing TV	$150 per TV
Fixed costs (annual)	$54,000

REQUIRED:

a Calculate the gross profit of each division using the market price method of transfer pricing.

b Calculate the gross profit of each division assuming variable costs are used in transfer pricing.

EXERCISE 4

Fill-In

1 According to a study made by the National Industrial Conference Board, most companies use the _____ or _____ method for determining transfer prices.

2 Where there is a determinable competitive _____ for the output of a division, the _____ is generally satisfactory as a transfer price.

3 A _____ arrived at between the buying and selling divisions gives division managers the greatest control over divisional profit.

4 The _____ transfer method recognizes that the buying division and selling divisions have different interests in the transfer price.

5 The profit for the total company will be less than the total of the divisional profits using the _____ transfer method.

6 One problem using the _____ method is that a division may show no profit at all because it transferred all its goods at _____.

7 The _____ method gives some approximation to market prices.

8 Two serious difficulties of the _____ method are the great deal of time it takes to develop it and the possibility of overemphasis on divisional welfare rather than company welfare.

9 When obtaining a _____, one must make sure the price obtained is reliable and not a distress price or a price for defective goods.

10 A basic problem of the _____ method is that both the selling and buying divisions get what they want and there may be a tendency to become careless and disregard needed cost controls.

REQUIRED:

Fill in the blanks using the following:
   a Cost
   b Cost plus
   c Market price
   d Negotiated price
   e Dual price

EXERCISE 5

Market Price and Cost Plus Method

The Dial Corporation has two divisions, X and Y. Sixty percent of the output of Division X is transferred to Division Y. The remainder is sold to outside firms at a competitive price of $20 per unit.

At the beginning of 19X1 obsolete machinery of Division X was replaced with new equipment. The result of this was huge savings on operating costs for 19X1.

Although the division was operating at a high efficiency level, the corporation informed the manager of Division X that the division was of low profitability for 19X1.

The manager of Division X argued that the low profit for 19X1 was the result of the transfer pricing method currently being used and suggested that a market or cost plus method of transfer pricing would be more appropriate.

The following information pertains to Division X for 19X1:

Sales to outside firms (4,000 units)	$80,000
Sales to Division Y (6,000 units)	40,000
Variable costs per unit	4
Fixed costs	60,000

REQUIRED:

a Compute the gross profit for Division X using the market price method for transfer pricing.

b Compute the gross profit for Division X using the cost plus method. Assume a plus of 50% of cost. Show all work.

c State whether you agree with the manager of Division X. Why?

EXERCISE 6

Negotiated Price and Dual Price Methods

The Appeal Company has decided that its manufacturing division will no longer buy raw material X from outside firms. Starting this coming year, the company plans to start its own extracting division. It is estimated that the company will utilize 60% of the output of the new division. The remainder will be sold on the open market.

The following are the estimated revenue and expenses for the manufacturing division and the extracting division for the coming year:

MANUFACTURING		EXTRACTING	
Sales	$5,000,000	Sales to outside firms (10,000 tons)	$1,400,000
Cost of raw material X (15,000 tons)	_____	Sales to manufacturing division (15,000 tons)	_____
Other variable costs	$750,000	Variable costs (per ton)	$40
Fixed costs (annual)	$750,000	Fixed costs (annual)	$1,000,000

The final meeting between the manager assigned to the new division and company officials was held last week. A negotiated transfer price of $100 per ton was agreed upon. But the manager assigned to the new division feels pressured into accepting the negotiated price.

REQUIRED:

As an accountant for the company you have been asked to submit a report showing the following:

1 Gross profit of each division using the negotiated transfer price established.
2 Gross profit of each division using the dual price method. Assume the Manufacturing Division uses a standard cost of $90 for raw materials X and the Extracting Division uses $140 as a sales price for raw materials X.

EXERCISE 7

Worksheet Elimination Entries

a. Computer, Inc., has two divisions, C and M. Materials having a cost of $500 were transferred from Division C to Division M at a price of $700.

REQUIRED:

Assume a perpetual inventory system. Prepare the elimination entries required, assuming financial statements must be prepared immediately.

b. At the end of the accounting period the records of the Rogers Company indicated that $1,000 of interdivision inventory was still on hand. Interdivision goods are transferred at total cost plus 30% of total cost.

REQUIRED:

Compute the interdivision profit *not* realized and prepare the accompanying elimination entry. Round to nearest dollar.

EXERCISE 8

Performance Evaluation

The Wheel and Tire Company has a new division that produces a special ball bearing. For the past 4 months, about two-thirds of the output has been sold to Division Y, another division of the company. The remainder of the output has been sold to outside firms. Last month's operating data follow:

TO DIVISION Y		TO OUTSIDE FIRMS	
Sales, 10,000 units at $17.50 ...	$175,000	Sales, 5,000 units at $25	$125,000
Variable costs at $12.50	$125,000	Variable costs at $12.50	$ 62,500
Fixed costs	37,500	Fixed costs	18,750
Total costs	$162,500	Total costs	$ 81,250
Gross margin	$ 12,500	Gross margin	$ 43,750

An outside supplier has offered the manager of Division Y the opportunity to purchase the special ball bearing at $16.25 per unit. The manager of the ball bearing division says the price cannot be matched because no margin can be earned.

REQUIRED:

Assume that you are the manager of Division Y. Show the manager of the ball bearing division that the division and the company as a whole will benefit if the $16.25 price is met. Assume that the 10,000 units cannot be sold by the ball bearing division to outside firms.

PROBLEMS

PROBLEM 1

Five Methods of Transfer Pricing

Divisions X and Y are two decentralized divisions of the T. O. Company. Seventy percent of the output of Division X is transferred to Division Y at a negotiated price of $9 per unit. The following are the estimated revenues and expenses for X and Y for 19X1:

DIVISION X		DIVISION Y	
Sales (3,000 units)	$30,000	Sales	$175,000
Sales to Division Y		Cost of units from	
(7,000 units)	_____	Division X	_____
Variable costs	$2 per unit	Other variable costs	
		($4 per unit)	$28,000
Fixed costs (annual)	$60,000	Fixed costs	$75,000

REQUIRED:

Determine profitability for each division under the five different methods of transfer pricing. Assume a plus of 25% of total cost when using the cost plus method. Use variable costs and estimated market price (total cost plus 25% of total cost) when using the dual price method.

PROBLEM 2

Analysis Using Transfer Prices

The Smilay Corporation is considering closing Division X because of low profitability. The corporation currently calculates transfer prices using the *cost* method. Division X sells 80% of its production to other divisions of the corporation. The following information pertains to Division X for the year just ended:

Sales to outside firms (40,000 units)	$ 400,000
Sales to other divisions of the corporation (160,000 units)	1,280,000
Variable costs per unit	5
Fixed costs per unit	3

REQUIRED:

Develop an analysis that should be made before closing Division X. Any assumptions made in the analysis should be realistic and in conformance with the contents of the chapter.

PROBLEM 3

Analysis of Transfer Price Methods

Management would like to know which transfer pricing method will generate the highest gross profit for their new division based on the following estimated data:

Total sales	200,000 units
70% of sales will be interdivision sales	
Market price	$10 per unit
Total operating costs ($7 per unit)	$1,400,000

REQUIRED:

Prepare a comparison of transfer pricing techniques using the above information. Assume 20% plus total costs when using the cost plus method. Also assume a negotiated price of $8.50 per unit.

PROBLEM 4

Entries on Books and Worksheet

Refer to Problem 3. Assume the figures in Problem 3 to be actual data for the last quarter for the new division. All interdivision sales were made to Division X, another division of the same company.

REQUIRED:

a Prepare journal entries for the interdivision sales of the new division for each of the five different transfer pricing methods. Assume all sales were made on credit and are still outstanding. Also the divisions use a perpetual inventory system.

b Assume financial statements for the last quarter must be prepared for the division. Give the worksheet elimination entries that would be required for each of the five different transfer pricing methods.

PROBLEM 5

Analysis of Sales between Divisions

The Ajax division of Gunnco Corp., operating at capacity, has been asked by the Defco division of Gunnco Corp. to supply it with electrical fitting number 1726. Ajax sells this part to its regular customers for $7.50 each. Defco, which is operating at 50% capacity, is willing to pay $5.00 each for the fitting. Defco will put the fitting into a brake unit that it is manufacturing on essentially a cost plus basis for a commercial airplane manufacturer.

Ajax has a variable cost of producing fitting number 1726 of $4.25. The cost of the brake unit being built by Defco is as follows:

Purchased parts—outside vendors	$22.50
Ajax fitting—1726	5.00
Other variable costs	14.00
Fixed overhead and administration	8.00
	$49.50

Defco believes the price concession is necessary to get the job.

The company uses return on investment and dollar profits in the measurement of division and division manager performance.

REQUIRED:

a Consider that you are the division controller of Ajax. Would you recommend that Ajax supply fitting 1726 to Defco? (Ignore any income tax issues.) Why or why not?

b Would it be to the short-run economic advantage of the Gunnco Corp. for the Ajax division to supply Defco division with fitting 1726 at $5.00 each? (Ignore any income tax issues.) Explain your answer.

(CMA Adapted)

PROBLEM 6

Analysis Using Market Method

The Marcus Company has two divisions, X and Y. Division X produces an engine used in the finished product of Division Y. The intermediate product produced by Division X has a known market price of $100. Currently, Division X is running at 60% capacity.

The following data pertains to the two divisions:

DIVISION X	DIVISION Y
Transfer price of engine (market price) $100	Selling price of finished product $150
Cost to produce one engine (fixed and variable costs) $60	Cost to complete intermediate product (fixed and variable costs) $75

REQUIRED:

a Show the contribution to company profit per unit for each division using the transfer pricing method of the company.

b Show whether the final product produced by the company has a positive or negative contribution to the firm as a whole.

c Assume the remaining capacity of Division X will be adequate to meet the demands of Division Y. If Division X had the opportunity to sell its current output to an outside firm, should it do so?

PROBLEM 7

Cost and Cost Plus Transfer Price Methods

The Urban Corporation has three divisions, A, B, and C. Division A produces parts used in the subassembly manufactured by Division B. There is no intermediate market for these parts. The subassembly produced in Division B is used in the final product produced by Division C. The market price for the subassembly is $35 per unit.

Transfer prices between Divisions A and B are calculated using the cost method. Transfer prices between Divisions B and C are calculated using the cost plus method (cost plus 20% of cost). Pertinent information for the divisions is as follows:

Division A:
Sales to Division B	10,000 units
Variable costs per unit	$7
Fixed costs (annual)	$30,000

Division B:
Sales to Division C	10,000 units
Transfer costs from Division A	$_____
Variable costs to produce subassembly	$10
Fixed costs (annual)	$50,000

Division C:
Sales at $42 per unit .... 10,000 units
Transfer costs from Division B .... $_____
Variable costs to produce finished product $2/unit
Fixed costs (annual) $30,000

REQUIRED:

a   Calculate the gross profit of each division using the transfer price methods utilized by the corporation.

b   Suppose the cost plus method used between Divisions B and C has not fairly represented the potential market price of the subassembly. The manager of Division B insists on transferring at the market price of the subassembly. But the manager of Division C refuses because transferring at market price would have a huge adverse effect on the division's performance evaluation. So after 2 weeks of intensive negotiating, a transfer price of $32.50 per unit was agreed upon.
    Calculate the gross profit of each division using the new transfer price.

c   Assume all three divisions are evaluated the same way; that is, the gross profit of each division is used as a basis for performance evaluation. Does this seem fair to Division A? If not, give some possible solutions.

PROBLEM 8

Entries on Books and Worksheet

Refer to Problem 7. Assume the information from Problem 7 is for a 1-month period. All interdivision sales were made for cash and are still outstanding. There is no ending inventory for any division. The perpetual inventory system is used in all three divisions.

REQUIRED:

Prepare journal entries on books of each division and elimination entries for each division.

PROBLEM 9

Calculation of Division Income under Transfer Pricing

A.R. Oma, Inc. manufactures a line of men's perfumes and after-shaving lotions. The manufacturing process is basically a series of mixing operations with the addition of certain aromatic and coloring ingredients; the finished product is packaged in a company-produced glass bottle and packed in cases containing six bottles.

A. R. Oma feels that the sale of its product is heavily influenced by the appearance and appeal of the bottle and has, therefore, devoted considerable managerial effort to the bottle production process. This has resulted in the development of certain unique bottle production processes in which management takes considerable pride.

The two areas (i.e., perfume production and bottle manufacture) have evolved over the years in an almost independent manner; in fact, a rivalry has developed between management personnel as to "which division is the more important" to A. R. Oma. This attitude is probably intensified because the bottle manufacturing plant was purchased intact 10 years ago and no real interchange of management personnel or ideas (except at the top corporate level) has taken place.

Since the acquisition, all bottle production has been absorbed by the perfume manufacturing plant. Each area is considered a separate profit center and evaluated as such. As the new corporate controller you are responsible for the definition of a proper transfer value to use in crediting the bottle production profit center and in debiting the packaging profit center.

At your request, the bottle division general manager has asked certain other bottle manufacturers to quote a price for the quantity and sizes demanded by the perfume division. These competitive prices are

VOLUME	TOTAL PRICE	PRICE PER CASE
2,000,000 eq. cases*	$ 4,000,000	$2.00
4,000,000	7,000,000	1.75
6,000,000	10,000,000	1.67

*An "equivalent case" represents six bottles each.

A cost analysis of the internal bottle plant indicates that they can produce bottles at these costs:

VOLUME	TOTAL PRICE	COST PER CASE
2,000,000 eq. cases	$3,200,000	$1.60
4,000,000	5,200,000	1.30
6,000,000	7,200,000	1.20

(Your cost analysts point out that these costs represent fixed costs of $1,200,000 and variable costs of $1.00 per equivalent case.)

These figures have given rise to considerable corporate discussion as to the proper value to use in the transfer of bottles to the perfume division. This interest is heightened because a significant portion of a division manager's income is an incentive bonus based on profit center results.

The perfume production division has the following costs in addition to the bottle costs:

VOLUME	TOTAL COST	COST PER CASE
2,000,000 cases	$16,400,000	$8.20
4,000,000	32,400,000	8.10
6,000,000	48,400,000	8.07

After considerable analysis, the marketing research department has furnished you with the following price-demand relationship for the finished product:

SALES VOLUME	TOTAL SALES REVENUE	SALES PRICE PER CASE
2,000,000 cases	$25,000,000	$12.50
4,000,000	45,600,000	11.40
6,000,000	63,900,000	10.65

REQUIRED:

a   The A. R. Oma Company has used market price transfer prices in the past. Using the current market prices and costs, and assuming a volume of 6,000,000 cases, calculate the income for:
   1   The bottle division.
   2   The perfume division.
   3   The corporation.
b   Is this production and sales level the most profitable volume for:
   1   The bottle division?
   2   The perfume division?
   3   The corporation?

(CMA Adapted)

PROBLEM 10

Economic Effect of Transfer Pricing on Entire Company

The Lorax Electric Company manufactures a large variety of systems and individual components for the electronics industry. The firm is organized into several divisions with division managers given the authority to make virtually all operating decisions. Management control over divisional operations is maintained by a system of divisional profit and return on investment measures which are reviewed regularly by top management. The top management of Lorax has been quite pleased with the effectiveness of the system they have been using and believe that it is responsible for the company's improved profitability over the last few years.

The devices division manufactures solid-state devices and is operating at capacity. The systems division has asked the devices division to supply a large quantity of integrated circuits IC378. The devices division currently is selling this component to its regular customers at $40 per hundred.

The systems division, which is operating at about 60% capacity, wants this particular component for a digital clock system. It has an opportunity to supply large quantities of these digital clock systems to Centonic Electric, a major producer of clock radios and other popular electronic home entertainment equipment. This is the first opportunity any of the Lorax divisions have had to do business with Centonic Electric. Centonic Electric has offered to pay $7.50 per clock system.

The systems division prepared an analysis of the probable costs to produce the clock systems. The amount that could be paid to the devices division for the integrated circuits was determined by working backward from the selling price. The cost estimates employed by the division reflected the highest per unit cost the systems division could incur for each cost component and still leave a sufficient margin so that the division's income statement could show reasonable improvement. The cost estimates are summarized on page 738.

Proposed selling price		$7.50
Costs excluding required integrated circuits IC378		
Components purchased from outside suppliers	$2.75	
Circuit board etching—labor and variable overhead	.40	
Assembly, testing, packaging—labor and variable overhead	1.35	
Fixed overhead allocations	1.50	
Profit margin	.50	6.50
Amount which can be paid for integrated circuits IC378		
(5 @ $20 per hundred)		$1.00

As a result of this analysis, the systems division offered the devices division a price of $20 per hundred for the integrated circuit. This bid was refused by the manager of the devices division because he felt the systems division should at least meet the price of $40 per hundred which regular customers pay. When the systems division found that it could not obtain a comparable integrated circuit from outside vendors, the situation was brought to an arbitration committee which had been set up to review such problems.

The arbitration committee prepared an analysis which showed that $.15 would cover variable costs of producing the integrated circuit, $.28 would cover the full cost including fixed overhead, and $.35 would provide a gross margin equal to the average gross margin on all of the products sold by the devices division. The manager of the systems division reacted by stating, "They could sell us that integrated circuit for $.20 and still earn a positive contribution toward profit. In fact, they should be required to sell at their variable cost—$.15—and not be allowed to take advantage of us."

Lou Belcher, manager of devices, countered by arguing that, "It doesn't make sense to sell to the systems division at $20 per hundred when we can get $40 per hundred outside on all we can produce. In fact, systems could pay us up to almost $60 per hundred and they would still have a positive contribution to profit."

The recommendation of the committee, to set the price at $.35 per unit ($35 per hundred), so that devices could earn a "fair" gross margin, was rejected by both division managers. Consequently, the problem was brought to the attention of the vice president of operations and his staff.

REQUIRED:

What will be the immediate economic effect on the Lorax Company as a whole if the devices division were required to supply IC378 to the systems division at $.35 per unit—the price recommended by the arbitration committee? Explain your answer.

(CMA Adapted)

CHAPTER TWENTY-TWO

ECONOMIC ORDER QUANTITY AND LINEAR PROGRAMMING

This chapter deals with two decision-making techniques applied in two unrelated and distinct situations. One technique involves minimizing the total inventory costs using the "economic order quantity" theory. The other technique permits management to make the optimal use of the available resources and therefore increase profits by utilizing linear programming methods. As today's managers move into the complex world of decision making, they are often called upon to attempt to optimize the use of the firm's resources. In every case, the firm is faced with limited resources in terms of time, money, materials, personnel, etc. The economic order quantity and linear programming theories are very valuable tools for management, as they provide logical and systematic procedures in establishing guidelines for use in the decision-making process.

DETERMINING THE ECONOMIC ORDER QUANTITY

Inventories are a necessity of any manufacturing operation. It is impossible to estimate precisely the quantity of raw materials that will be needed for production during a given period. Inventories are a means of safeguarding against shortages caused by planning errors, by supply-and-demand variations or by delays in orders. They provide for the continual, even flow of production.

Specific costs associated with inventory decisions are total ordering costs, total carrying costs, and total acquisition costs. These three costs comprise the total cost of an inventory policy.

Total ordering costs are those costs incurred by the company in the purchasing of raw materials. Included in these costs are the processing and receiving costs incurred for each purchase order. The ordering costs are expressed as a cost-per-order figure.

Total carrying costs are those costs incurred because the raw materials are in a company's possession. These costs generally include insurance, personal property taxes, cost of storage space, breakage, obsolescence, and the rate of return on the investment in inventory desired by the company. The carrying costs may be expressed as a cost per unit per year or as a percentage of the unit inventory value.

Total acquisition costs are the actual prices paid to suppliers. Usually, total acquisition costs are not a major concern in planning inventory policy. Except where a quantity discount is available, these costs do not change with the way in which inventory is purchased. For example, if a company requires 6,000 units which cost $2 per unit, the total acquisition costs will be $12,000. It does not matter whether the 6,000 units are purchased together or in 20 different purchase-order groups of 300 each.

Total carrying costs and total ordering costs vary inversely. The greater the inventory on hand, the greater the total carrying costs but the lower the total ordering cost. If a small inventory is on hand, total carrying costs will be lower; but more orders will be placed, thus increasing the total ordering costs. It is the responsibility of management to find the proper inventory policy that keeps the total inventory cost (total carrying costs + total ordering costs + total acquisition costs) to a minimum. In calculating both ordering and carrying costs, only those costs that vary because of a change in inventory level or a change in purchasing activity should be considered. Fixed costs should not be included in the decision process.

PROCUREMENT OF MATERIALS

Because inventory policy aims at minimizing total inventory costs, one of the main decisions of an inventory policy is the quantity of raw materials to be ordered per purchase order. The decision must properly balance two costs—total carrying costs and total ordering costs. A small number of items per order will produce high ordering costs but low carrying costs, while a large number of items per order will produce high carrying costs but low ordering costs. The purchase order which results in the minimum total inventory cost is called the "economic order quantity."

The economic order quantity, or EOQ, may be determined by using one of three methods: (1) tabular, (2) graphic, or (3) formula. Each of the methods will be explained using the following data:

Estimated annual required inventory	3,000 units
Materials cost per unit	$2.50
Ordering costs per order	$5.00
Inventory carrying cost—per unit per year	$.20
Or percentage of unit inventory value	8%

The Tabular Method

With the tabular method, several purchase-order quantity alternatives are listed in separate columns. Total inventory costs, showing both carrying and ordering costs, are calculated for each alternative. The column with the lowest cost will be the economic order quantity. A tabulation using the previously mentioned data is shown in Table 22-1. According to the tabulation, the economic order quantity is 400 units, or a placement of an order every 48 days (360 days ÷ 7.5 orders). Because not every possible order quantity was calculated, it is possible that the EOQ may fall between 300 and 400 units or between 400 and 600 units. The tabulation gives a very close *approximation* of the economic order quantity. Further analysis may be done to learn whether a quantity falling between these two ranges produces a smaller annual inventory cost. For example, order quantities of 350 and 500 could be used to determine whether they produce a total cost of less than $77.50.

The Graphic Method

The graphic method determines the EOQ by plotting the annual carrying costs, annual ordering costs, and total inventory costs on a graph. Order

TABLE 22-1
TABULAR METHOD FOR COMPUTING EOQ

	ORDER SIZE							
	50	100	150	200	300	400	600	800
Quantity data:								
Number of orders (estimated annual requirement ÷ order size)	60	30	20	15	10	7.5	5	3.75
Average inventory (order size ÷ 2)*	25	50	75	100	150	200	300	400
Cost data:								
Annual carrying costs (average inventory, units† × $.20)	$ 5	$ 10	$ 15	$20	$30	$40.00	$60	$80.00
Annual ordering costs (number of orders × $5)	300	150	100	75	50	37.50	25	18.75
Total annual inventory costs	$305	$160	$115	$95	$80	$77.50	$85	$98.75

*The assumption is that stock is zero when each order is received. An inventory balance may be present and still will not influence the decision as long as the inventory balance is the same for each alternative.

†Or: Average inventory (units) × cost per unit ($2.50) × % of average inventory (8%)

quantity is shown on the x axis (horizontal line), and cost is shown on the y axis (vertical line). The point at which the ordering-cost line intersects the carrying-cost line represents the economic order quantity. It is at this point that total ordering costs equal total carrying costs, and the total inventory cost is at a minimum.

The first step in preparing a graph is to compute information about the annual carrying costs, the annual ordering costs, and the total annual inventory costs at various order sizes (quantity). Information compiled in Table 22-1 will be used to draw the graph in Figure 22-1. The order size at 200 units will be plotted for explanation purposes. For all three lines (annual carrying costs, annual ordering costs, and total annual inventory costs), start at the horizontal axis (x) at 200 units. To plot annual carrying costs, move up vertically from 200 units, stop when you parallel $20 on the vertical axis (y), and plot the point. To plot annual ordering costs, move up vertically from 200 units, and stop when you parallel $75 on the vertical axis (y). To plot total annual inventory costs, move up vertically from 200 units, and stop when you parallel $95 on the vertical axis (y). Continue this procedure until all the points relating to the order sizes have been plotted. After the other order sizes have been plotted, draw a line connecting the points relating to each line. The EOQ in Figure 22-1 is at 387 units (where annual carrying costs equal annual ordering costs). At EOQ the total annual inventory costs will equal $77 (the minimum level on the total annual inventory cost line).

Both of the previous methods suffer from two shortcomings. First, the

FIGURE 22-1 **Graphic Method for Computing EOQ**

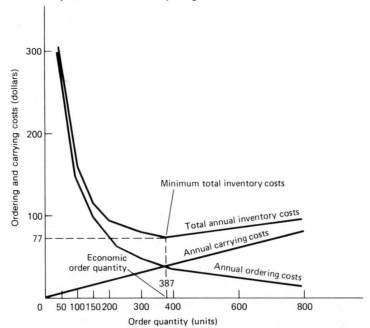

calculations are time-consuming. Second, they are inexact and are only close estimates.

The Formula Method

The formula method is easy to calculate, and it produces a reliable figure. It is based on a formula derived through the use of calculus. To determine the economic order quantity in terms of *units*, the following standard equation is used:

$$EOQ = \sqrt{\frac{2 \times RU \times CO}{CU \times CC}} \quad \text{or} \quad \sqrt{\frac{2 \times RU \times CO}{S}}$$

where   EOQ = economic order quantity
RU = annual required inventory, in units
CO = ordering costs per order
CU = materials cost per unit
CC = carrying cost expressed as a percentage of unit inventory value
S = carrying cost per unit per year

The economic order quantity for the previous example is calculated below:

$$EOQ = \sqrt{\frac{2 \times RU \times CO}{CU \times CC}}$$

$$= \sqrt{\frac{2 \times 3,000 \times \$5}{\$2.50 \times .08}}$$

$$= \sqrt{\frac{30,000}{.20}}$$

$$= \sqrt{150,000}$$

$$= \underline{387 \text{ units}}$$

If the economic order quantity is desired in *dollars* rather than units, the following equation can be used:

$$EOQ = \sqrt{\frac{2 \times A \times B}{I}}$$

where   A = annual required inventory, in dollars
B = ordering cost per order (same as CO in EOQ in units equation)
I = carrying costs expressed as a percentage of unit inventory value (same as CC in EOQ in units equation)

Our example, calculated for economic order quantity in dollars, is shown below:

$$EOQ = \sqrt{\frac{2 \times A \times B}{I}}$$

$$EOQ = \sqrt{\frac{2 \times 7,500 \times \$5}{.08}}$$

$$= \sqrt{\$937,500}$$

$$= \$968 \quad \text{or} \quad 387 \text{ units} \left(\frac{\$968}{\$2.50}\right)$$

where A = 3,000 × \$2.50 = \$7,500
       B = \$5
       I = 8% = .08

When needed items are manufactured rather than purchased, the economic order quantity formula can be used to determine the most economical size of the production run. The formula is as follows:

$$\text{Optimum size of production run} = \sqrt{\frac{2 \times RU \times SC}{VC \times CC}}$$

where VC = variable manufacturing costs
       SC = setup costs

If a quantity discount is offered, the economic order quantity may be affected. An acquisition cost saving caused by the discount may counteract the increased carrying cost of the additional units. Economic order quantity should then be recalculated, with the quantity discount taken into consideration.

Once the economic order quantity has been determined, management must decide *when* to place the order; that is, the order point must be established. If the lead time and the inventory usage rate are known, determination of the order point is very simple. *Lead time* is the period between the placement of an order and the receipt of the materials. *Inventory usage rate* is the quantity of materials used in production over a period of time. *The order point* should be where the inventory level reaches the number of units that would be consumed during the lead time. Using the following data, an equation and a graphic representation of the order point are shown:

Economic order quantity	387 units
Lead time	3 weeks
Average inventory usage rate	75 units a week

Equation for Inventory Order Point

Inventory order point = lead time × average inventory usage rate

where lead time is in days, weeks, or months and usage rate is in units per day, week, or month.

Example:

Order point = 3 weeks × 75 units a week
            = 225 units (normal usage for a 3-week period)

When the inventory level of materials is reduced to 225 units, an order should be placed for 387 units (the EOQ).

Graphic Presentation of Inventory Order Point

In Figure 22-2, the order point is determined by first plotting the EOQ (387) on the y axis (inventory, units) and the total number of weeks supplied by each order (387 EOQ ÷ 75 units consumed per week = 5.16) on the x axis (weeks). A straight line is then drawn from the EOQ (387) point on the y axis to the point on the x axis (5.16) that shows the number of weeks supplied by each order. Next the lead time per order (3 weeks) is subtracted from the total number of weeks supplied by each order (5.16 weeks) to arrive at 2.16 weeks [5.16 − 3.00 weeks or 387 (EOQ) − 225 (units used during lead time) ÷ 75 usage per week]. The 2.16 weeks is plotted on the x axis and a vertical line is drawn up from the 2.16 on the x axis until it intercepts point A on the first line drawn. At point A on the illustration a horizontal line is drawn to the y axis; the point of interception is equal to the order point.

In the order-point calculation in Figure 22-2 it is important that the lead time and the inventory usage rate be precisely known. If the lead time should be more than expected or usage greater than anticipated, a stockout (when a company runs out of raw materials) will occur. Costs will be increased as the result of possible extra transportation costs (e.g., air freight), loss of possible orders, or costs incurred because of the disruption of the production schedule. If the lead time is shorter than expected or the demand for the materials is less than estimated, additional inventories will be accumulated. This will increase the carrying costs.

FIGURE 22-2 Graphic Presentation of Order Point

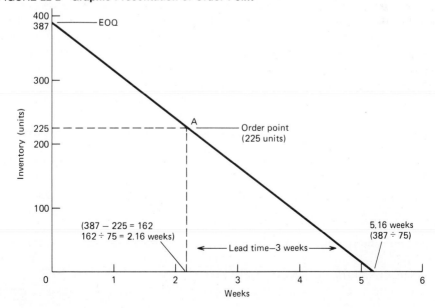

SAFETY STOCK

Since it is almost impossible to estimate lead time and average usage rate with certainty, many companies prefer to carry a *safety stock* (or additional inventory) as a cushion against possible stockouts. In such a case, the order point is computed by adding the safety stock to the estimated usage during the lead time. A safety-stock calculation should arrive at a figure which properly balances the risk of a stockout against the additional carrying costs incurred by the extra inventory. One method is to determine safety stock based on experience or traditional rules of thumb. While this method is less involved, it does not ensure that the optimum amount will be chosen.

Another method of calculating safety stock is to provide for the extreme boundaries of lead time and usage variance. Estimates are made for the longest possible time for delivery and the greatest possible usage rate. "Safety stock" is the number of additional units needed above the order point if the lead time and usage rate should increase to the estimated maximum. For example, using the same information as in the previous examples, let us assume that delivery could take 7 weeks and the usage rate could be as much as 100 units per week; the order point and safety stock would be calculated as follows:

Normal order point (units)		225
Safety stock:		
Usage for additional 4-week delay (75 units × 4)	300	
Usage rate variance [(100 maximum usage − 75 average		
usage) × 7 lead time]	175	
Safety stock		475
Revised order point		700 units

The maximum materials inventory should be 862 units, which is the economic order quantity of 387 units plus the safety stock of 475 units. A graphic representation showing the effects of safety stock is shown in Figure 22-3.

The construction of a graphic presentation of safety stock is almost identical to the construction of the order point. The only additional step necessary to develop Figure 22-3 is to add safety stock to the EOQ before plotting the EOQ on the y axis.

The disadvantage of this method is that calculation for safety stock uses the extreme variance rather than the optimum amount. If the variance never again reaches the maximum, the company is carrying unnecessary inventory and thus incurring unnecessary costs.

Additional methods of computing safety stock appear in Chapter 23. These methods attempt to calculate the optimum safety stock size using statistical probabilities.

It should be noted that the formula presented for EOQ is only a tool to be used by management and that one simple formula and a hand calculator cannot solve all the inventory problems of a company. EOQ is part of a model building concept used to derive at a decision rule and normally requires much

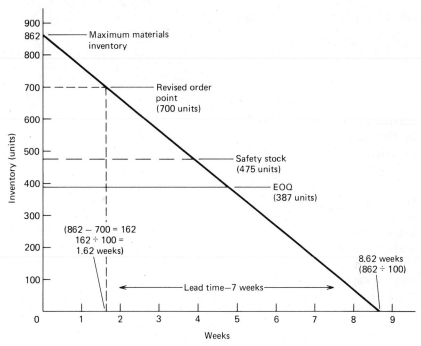

FIGURE 22-3 **Graphic Presentation of Safety Stock**

greater sophistication levels for application in the vast majority of real world situations.

The following sections of this chapter will discuss another problem faced by management which entails maximizing profit given the constraints of producing a number of different products. As we shall see, each problem analyzed by management must be attempted by using the appropriate problem-solving technique.

LINEAR PROGRAMMING

Linear programming is a mathematical programming technique that is used in solving a general class of linear optimization models. The technique permits management to make the optimal use of available resources. The explanation of linear programming will be presented by providing an illustration. Consider a small manufacturing firm producing two products, X and Y, Product X being a small frame and Product Y being a small gate. Both products are fabricated from steel and require cutting and welding. Product X requires 1 hour of cutting time and 1 hour of welding time. Product Y requires 1 hour of cutting time and 2 hours of welding time. The company owns two cutting machines and two welding machines. Because of maintenance problems, each cutting machine is scheduled to be out of operation 10 hours per week. Therefore, in a standard 40-hour week, the cutting machines are available for only 60 hours and the welding machines are available for 80 hours. The contribution margin for Product X is $3 and for Product Y is $5.

Management must decide how much of each product to produce, given the available resources, so as to maximize the total contribution margin from both products. The contribution margin is defined as the selling price minus the variable cost for each product. The total contribution margin per product is the contribution margin times the number of units sold.

The Equation

To state this problem in linear programming terminology, it is best to lay it out in tabular form and then relate the data in the table to mathematical equations.

PRODUCT	CUTTING TIME (HR)	WELDING TIME (HR)	CONTRIBUTION MARGIN
X	1	1	$3
Y	1	2	5
Machine capacity	60	80	

The equations derived from the above data are as follows:

$$CM = 3X + 5Y$$
$$\text{Cutting constraint} = X + Y \leqslant 60$$
$$\text{Welding constraint} = X + 2Y \leqslant 80$$
$$\text{General constraints} = X \geqslant 0$$
$$Y \geqslant 0$$

In linear programming terminology the cutting and welding times are called activity coefficients, the machine capacities are called the production requirements vectors, and the contribution margin figures are called the objective functions. The purpose of linear programming solutions is to maximize the objective functions value within the general constraints. Also X and Y must both be positive.

Two linear programming solution methods will be considered in this chapter, the graphic solution and the simplex algorithm.

Graphic Solution Method

To begin the graphic solution to this problem, the constraint equations are drawn on a standard X, Y coordinate graph. To accomplish this, the constraints are examined as follows:

$$\text{Cutting constraint} = X + Y \leqslant 60$$
$$\text{Welding constraint} = X + 2Y \leqslant 80$$

If X = 0

$$Y \leqslant 60 \text{ in cutting constraint}$$
$$Y \leqslant 40 \text{ in welding constraint}$$

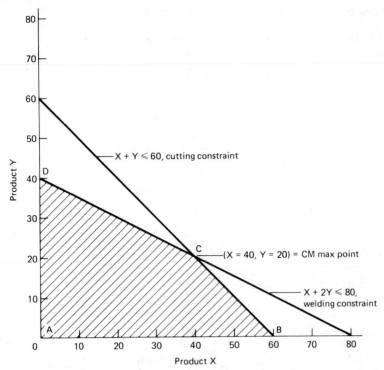

FIGURE 22-4 **Graphic Presentation of the Solution Space for the Linear Programming Problem**

If $Y = 0$

$$X \leqslant 60 \text{ in cutting constraint}$$
$$X \leqslant 80 \text{ in welding constraint}$$

These values determine the limits of the constraint equations depicted on the graph in Figure 22-4; when plotted on the graph they constitute the corner points.

The solution space is defined by the shaded area on the graph and is limited by the corner points A, B, C, and D. Actually, any point on or inside the solution space can provide a solution to the linear programming problem. There is a theorem of linear programming, whose mathematical proof[1] is beyond the scope or intention of this book, which states that the optimal solution to the problem will occur at one of the corner points. Therefore, to find the optimal solution using the graphic method, only the corner points A, B, C, and D must be examined. Point A is at the origin, and therefore, its values are (0, 0). Point B likewise has its Y value at 0, and its coordinates are (60, 0). Point D has its X value at 0; so its coordinates are (0, 40). The coordinates of point C are listed on the graph as (40, 20) and are obtained by solving the two constraint equations simultaneously.

$$X + \ Y = 60$$
$$X + 2Y = 80$$

---

[1] G. Hadley, *Linear Programming*, Addison-Wesley, Reading, Mass., 1963, pp. 61–66, 76.

First take one of the equations and isolate X:

$$X + Y = 60$$
$$X = 60 - Y$$

Then substitute the X value (where $X = 60 - Y$) into the second equation and solve for Y:

$$X + 2Y = 80$$
$$60 - Y + 2Y = 80$$
$$60 + \ Y = 80$$
$$Y = 20$$

Then substitute the value of Y in either of the constraint equations to determine the value of X:

$$X + Y \ = 60$$
$$X + 20 = 60$$
$$X = 40$$

Since it is now known that the optimal solution lies at one of the corner points on the graph, these constraints can be stated as equalities instead of inequalities. Thus we have the coordinates of all the corner points, which are summarized in Table 22-2.

These contribution margin values are obtained by inserting the X and Y values in the objective function and performing the necessary additions. For example, the CM value of $180 is obtained from

$$CM = 3X + 5Y$$
$$CM = 3(60) + 5(0)$$
$$CM \text{ (point B)} = 180$$

Thus it can be seen from the table that at point C, 40 of Product X should be produced and 20 of Product Y should be produced. This production combination will then yield a CM that is maximized at $220. In other words, this is the optimum contribution margin that the company is seeking.

A few final comments are in order concerning the graphic solution method of solving linear programming problems. For all practical purposes, this method is limited to use with only two products. More than two equations can be used, but seldom more than two variables. This method cannot be used with more than three variables, and even with three the process of solution

TABLE 22-2
CORNER POINT CONTRIBUTION MARGIN VALUES

CORNER POINT	PRODUCT X VALUE	PRODUCT Y VALUE	CONTRIBUTION MARGIN
A	0	0	$ 0
B	60	0	180
C	40	20	220
D	0	40	200

is very difficult. The graphic method is useful in understanding the logic behind the solutions by other methods, which is the subject of the next section.

Simplex Algorithm Method

The simplex algorithm method can be used to solve problems of a general nature; that is, there is practically no limit on the number of variables or on the number of equations. Also, while the examples in this chapter are restricted to maximization problems, the simplex algorithm method can as easily solve a general class of cost minimization problems. Students interested in a more complete examination of the simplex algorithm method should consult the references at the end of the next chapter.

The simplex algorithm method is a repetitious procedure that moves one step at a time to examine the corner points of the solution space. It is even more effective than the graphic method, as it assures us of an optimal solution, if one exists, in a finite number of steps. This means that it will be unnecessary to examine all the corner points in the solution space. This is true because the simplex algorithm will identify those corner points that are pertinent to the solution and will eliminate those that are not feasible. This process will become apparent as the simplex method unfolds.

Contribution Margin Problem Revisited. The simplex algorithm method is based on the principles of linear algebra. Previously, a contribution margin problem was solved graphically (see Figure 22-4) and the optimal solution was found as CM = $220, X = 40, Y = 20. In this section, that problem will be solved by the simplex method, and the solution will be related to the graph in Figure 22-4.

The problem is restated as

$$CM = 3X + 5Y \qquad \text{objective function}$$
$$X + Y \leqslant 60 \qquad \text{cutting constraint}$$
$$X + 2Y \leqslant 80 \qquad \text{welding constraint}$$
$$Y \geqslant 0 \qquad \text{general constraints}$$
$$X \geqslant 0$$

Step 1. The simplex algorithm uses a matrix array (a rectangular arrangement of quantities in rows and columns) as the basis of the solution procedure. This matrix array is called a tableau and consists of equations instead of inequalities. (The theorem presented earlier limited solutions to the corner point. Since the corner points are on the constraint equations, they are now effective equalities.) To convert the inequalities into equalities in the simplex algorithm, it is necessary to add one slack variable to each constraint. A slack variable is an arbitrary amount that is used in linear programming models to convert the inequality sign to an equality sign. The addition of the slack variable to each constraint simply means that the slack is removed from the constraint. Since the slack variable is a helping variable, its contribution margin is zero. In other words, a unit of slack will never be produced and whatever slack is left over is worth nothing. Adding the slack variables, the problem appears as follows:

$$CM = 3X + 5Y + 0(S1) + 0(S2)$$

or

$$CM - 3X - 5Y - 0(S1) - 0(S2) = 0$$

$$X + Y + S1 + 0(S2) = 60$$
$$X + 2Y + 0(S1) + S2 = 80$$
$$Y \geqslant 0$$
$$X \geqslant 0$$

Step 2. Many forms of the tableau are in use. The one used here is a common format. The initial version is shown in Table 22-3.

Note that all values from the problem are included in the initial tableau. The product column initially contains CM or the slack variables (S1 and S2). This is because all situations are considered to begin with no production taking place. The value of the objective function is therefore equal to zero and is obtained as follows:

$$CM = 3X + 5Y + 0(S1) + 0(S2)$$
$$CM = 3(0) + 5(0) + 0(60) + 0(80) = 0$$

This is the same as point A on the graph (Figure 22-4). In other words, production is ready to begin but the product mix must first be determined.

Moving from the Initial Solution to the First Tableau: An Improved Solution.

Step 3. The purpose of the simplex algorithm is to provide a solution to maximize the CM. To do this, two decision rules must be established.

1 Which variable, X or Y, should be considered for production first?
2 In the product column, which slack variable should be eliminated from the initial tableau?

Decision Rule 1. Choose the variable in the objective function row (row CM in Table 22-3) that has the highest absolute value as the variable to be

TABLE 22-3
FIRST TABLEAU
COLUMNS

	PRODUCT	X	Y	S1	S2	REQUIREMENTS VECTOR
	CM	−3	−5	0	0	0
Rows	S1	1	1	1	0	60
	S2	1	2	0	1	80

considered for production first. This variable will enter the product column. In this case choose Y because 5 is larger than 3.

Decision Rule 2. Select the variable in the product column to be eliminated (either S1 or S2) by computing the ratio of the requirements vector to the activity coefficients of the variable picked to enter, and choose the minimum positive ratio.

Example of the Computations. Since Y is the variable to enter, the two ratio coefficients necessary are

$$\frac{60}{1} = 60 \qquad \text{and} \qquad \frac{80}{2} = 40$$

Variable S2 should therefore be replaced by Y to complete the second tableau.
    Once the variable has been chosen to enter and the slack variable chosen to be replaced, the solution procedure can continue.

Step 4. Identify the pivot element. The pivot element lies at the intersection of the variable column entering and the row leaving. In this case Y enters and S2 leaves; so the pivot element is 2. The pivot element must be converted to a value of 1; therefore, row S2, which is being replaced by Y, must be multiplied by ½. The new tableau will then look as follows:

PRODUCT	X	Y	S1	S2	REQUIREMENTS VECTOR
CM					
S1					
Y	½	1	0	½	40

Step 5. All other values in the Y column must now be converted to zero. This is accomplished by using the new pivot element just created and multiplying it by the element in column Y, row S1 and column Y, and row CM with the opposite sign. Then add it to every element in row S1 and row CM.

Example of the Computations. The 1 in column Y, row S1 must be converted to 0 as well as the −5 in column Y, row CM. To eliminate the 1, multiply every element in row Y in the new tableau by −1 and add it to row S1 in the first tableau. Row Y and old S1 row are as follows:

PRODUCT	X	Y	S1	S2	REQUIREMENTS VECTOR
CM					
Old S1	1	1	1	0	60
Y	½	1	0	½	40

Conversion of column Y, row S1:

(-1)	$\times$	(ELEMENT IN Y ROW)	$+$	(ELEMENT IN S1 ROW)	$=$	(NEW VALUE IN S1 ROW)
-1	$\times$	$\frac{1}{2}$	$+$	1	$=$	$\frac{1}{2}$
-1	$\times$	1	$+$	1	$=$	0
-1	$\times$	0	$+$	1	$=$	1
-1	$\times$	$\frac{1}{2}$	$+$	0	$=$	$-\frac{1}{2}$
-1	$\times$	40	$+$	60	$=$	20

The next stage of the second tableau looks as follows:

PRODUCT	X	Y	S1	S2	REQUIREMENTS VECTOR
CM					
S1	$\frac{1}{2}$	0	1	$-\frac{1}{2}$	20
Y	$\frac{1}{2}$	1	0	$\frac{1}{2}$	40

The old CM row and the Y row are as follow:

PRODUCT	X	Y	S1	S2	REQUIREMENTS VECTOR
Old CM	-3	-5	0	0	0
S1					
Y	$\frac{1}{2}$	1	0	$\frac{1}{2}$	40

Conversion of column Y, row CM:

5	$\times$	(ELEMENT IN Y ROW)	$+$	(ELEMENT IN CM ROW)	$=$	(NEW VALUE IN CM ROW)
5	$\times$	$\frac{1}{2}$	$+$	-3	$=$	$-\frac{1}{2}$
5	$\times$	1	$+$	-5	$=$	0
5	$\times$	0	$+$	0	$=$	0
5	$\times$	$\frac{1}{2}$	$+$	0	$=$	$\frac{5}{2}$
5	$\times$	40	$+$	0	$=$	200

The completed second tableau now appears as in Table 22-4.

If you refer to Figure 22-4 in an earlier section of this chapter, you can determine that we have moved from point A to point D. The simplex algorithm now says to produce 40 units of Product Y and gain a contribution margin of $200.

TABLE 22-4
SECOND TABLEAU

PRODUCT	X	Y	S1	S2	REQUIREMENTS VECTOR
CM	$-\frac{1}{2}$	0	0	$\frac{5}{2}$	200
S1	$\frac{1}{2}$	0	1	$-\frac{1}{2}$	20
Y	$\frac{1}{2}$	1	0	$\frac{1}{2}$	40

TABLE 22-5
THIRD TABLEAU

PRODUCT	X	Y	S1	S2	REQUIREMENTS VECTOR
CM					
X	1	0	2	−1	40
Y					

It is known by referring to the graphical solution that the second tableau (Table 22-4) does not yield the optimal solution to the problem. The method for determining when the optimal solution has been reached requires that the CM row be reexamined to see if a negative number remains in it. If one does, at least one more iteration must be performed. Upon reexamination of the CM row in the second tableau, a −½ is found in the X column. This indicates that the CM value can be improved if X is entered into the problem solution.

To do this steps 3 through 5 must be reapplied. In step 3, Decision Rule 1 indicates that X is to enter and Decision Rule 2 indicates that variable S1 is to leave. The new pivot element is ½, the intersection of column X and row S1. Performing the same sequence of calculations as was done to construct the second tableau will yield the third tableau (Table 22-5).

Solution Procedure.   The new pivot element (step 4) must be converted to 1. This is accomplished by multiplying the S1 row in the second tableau (Table 22-4) by 2. This stage of the new tableau will appear as in Table 22-5.

Observing the second tableau, the ½ in column X, row Y and the −½ in column X, row CM must be converted to 0. Conversion of column X, row Y:

	(ELEMENT IN ROW X)		(ELEMENT IN ROW Y)		(NEW ELEMENT IN ROW Y)
−½ ×	1	+	½	=	0
−½ ×	0	+	1	=	1
−½ ×	2	+	0	=	−1
−½ ×	−1	+	½	=	1
−½ ×	40	+	40	=	20

The third tableau now appears as in Table 22-6.

The final step necessary to complete the third tableau is to convert the −½ in column X, row CM to zero. This is accomplished by the calculations presented on the top of page 756.

TABLE 22-6
THIRD TABLEAU

PRODUCT	X	Y	S1	S2	REQUIREMENTS VECTOR
CM					
X	1	0	2	−1	40
Y	0	1	−1	1	20

	(ELEMENT IN ROW X)		(ELEMENT IN CM ROW)		(NEW ELEMENT IN CM ROW)
$\frac{1}{2}$ ×	1	+	$-\frac{1}{2}$	=	0
$\frac{1}{2}$ ×	0	+	0	=	0
$\frac{1}{2}$ ×	2	+	0	=	1
$\frac{1}{2}$ ×	-1	+	$\frac{5}{2}$	=	2
$\frac{1}{2}$ ×	40	+	200	=	220

The completed third and optimal tableau appears as in Table 22-7.

If you refer to the graphical solution method presented earlier, you will find that the third tableau is consistent with point C on the graph in Figure 22-4. The simplex algorithm indicates this is the optimal solution to the problem because an examination of the CM row in the third tableau (Table 22-7) reveals no negative numbers.

This is the requirement for optimality. If any further substitution were tried, the contribution margin would be reduced. Thus the optimal production strategy is to make 40 units of Product X and 20 units of Product Y and to maximize the contribution margin at $220. No other strategy can yield as great a contribution margin as this one.

SHADOW PRICES

In linear programming, the terms "shadow price" and "sensitivity analysis" are often encountered with respect to the optimal solutions. Sensitivity analysis is a term used to describe how sensitive the linear programming optimal solution is to a change in any one number in it. It is possible to test to find out how sensitive the solution is, whether the number is an activity coefficient, a production requirements vector, or an objective function coefficient. Such a comprehensive treatment of sensitivity analysis is beyond the scope or intent of this book, but a discussion of shadow prices is in order here.

Our contribution margin maximization problem solved earlier in this chapter was a problem having two products and two constraints. Each constraint was controlled by the number of labor hours available to perform the activities of cutting and welding. In our problem, all the labor hours were used in the process of manufacturing the two products.

The shadow price is similar to the concept of marginalism in economics. The question one must ask concerning shadow prices is as follows: What would

TABLE 22-7
THIRD TABLEAU

PRODUCT	X	Y	S1	S2	REQUIREMENTS VECTOR
CM	0	0	1	2	220
X	1	0	2	-1	40
Y	0	1	-1	1	20

the firm be willing to pay to obtain one more hour of cutting time or welding time? If the firm can buy more of either resource, it can produce more of Product X and/or Product Y and therefore increase the contribution margin.

Return to the third and optimal tableau (Table 22-7) for the contribution margin maximization problem. Examine the coefficients in the objective function row (the CM row). Notice the two variables we are producing are X and Y and that their coefficients in that row are zero. The coefficients of the slack variables are 1 and 2, respectively. These are the shadow prices of cutting and welding time. Remember slack variable S1 was used with the cutting constraint; so $1 is the shadow price of 1 hour of cutting time. Similarly, $2 is the shadow price of welding time. So, every hour of cutting time increases CM by $1. Similar reasoning can be applied to the welding shadow price of $2. Total cutting time for production is 60 hours valued at $1 per hour. Total welding time for production is 80 hours valued at $2 per hour. The maximum contribution margin of $220 is composed of $60 from cutting and $160 from welding.

At this point one might say that the coefficients are called shadow prices and yet all that has been referred to is contribution margin. This is because the shadow price has yet another interpretation referred to earlier as being very close to marginalism in economics. The shadow price is the actual price the firm would be willing to pay to gain one more unit of cutting or welding time. Thus the firm would be willing to pay up to $1 more per hour of cutting time and $2 more per hour of welding time and not have the total contribution margin change. Examined on a per unit basis, the per unit variable cost could increase by up to $1 and $2, respectively, for cutting and welding hours, until it reaches the point where the per unit contribution margin would become zero.

This section has been geared toward a clear and concise presentation of shadow prices. The whole area of sensitivity analysis and shadow prices is very important and has many applications to management decision making. Most colleges and universities have advanced courses in management science that deal with these subjects. As the world becomes more quantitatively oriented, students seeking knowledge in highly technical areas such as cost accounting should investigate the possibility of including such training in their backgrounds.

LINEAR PROGRAMMING
—CONCLUDING COMMENTS

It is beyond the scope or intent of this book to present a comprehensive and detailed account of linear programming technology. Let us say that it is a general and powerful tool for solving a class of linear optimization problems where the objective is to allocate scarce resources to production.

This chapter has dealt primarily with problems concerning the maximization of contribution margin. Linear programming is certainly not restricted to such applications. There are a host of minimization applications concerning cost, blending problems, scheduling, personnel allocation, and many others. These are treated in more advanced management science textbooks such as those listed at the end of the next chapter.

Minimization problems have been excluded from this chapter because they can be solved more readily by computer. Most organizations today either have their own computer or have access to one. These computers can be mathematically programmed to solve linear programming problems much faster, more efficiently, and more accurately than by hand calculations.

Linear programming then becomes a steppingstone to other quantitative techniques available to the cost accountant. These other techniques include inventory models, queuing theory, and cost-volume-profit analysis, to name only a few. As more and more applications are developed, cost accountants will have to become more familiar with these decision-making tools.

The cost accountant in today's complex world must be able to recognize when these mathematical models will aid in the planning and decision making of the manager or client. The cost accountant must coordinate the generation of the data and its effective use in the decision-making process. Linear programming gives the cost accountant another set of tools to help accomplish this goal.

CHAPTER REVIEW

The chapter begins with a discussion of the "economic order quantity" and its use in inventory analysis. Inventories are a necessity of any manufacturing operation. They are a means of safeguarding against shortages which could disrupt production. Management has the responsibility of making inventory decisions. Specific costs associated with an inventory policy are total carrying costs, total ordering costs, and total acquisition costs. Together they comprise the total cost of keeping a company's inventory. Management usually attempts to arrive at the optimum inventory cost. Because ordering costs and carrying costs have a direct opposite relationship, the optimum point is where the two costs are balanced. Acquisition costs are usually fixed, unless a quantity discount is offered.

The normal purchase order which incurs the minimum total inventory cost is called the "economic order quantity" or the "EOQ." It may be calculated using the tabular, the graphic, or the formula method. The formula method is preferred because of its accuracy and ease of calculation.

Once the economic order quantity has been determined, management must decide when to place an order. If the lead time and the usage rate are known, the order point is determined by multiplying the lead time by the usage rate, or it may be determined graphically.

Estimates are seldom exact or correct. Companies operate in fluctuating environments. To prevent stockouts, safety stock is maintained. It is important that safety stock be calculated correctly. Too little safety stock may lead to a stockout, while too much safety stock will cause unnecessary carrying costs to be incurred. Safety stock may be determined by (1) tradition or judgment, (2) calculations based on the extreme possible variances, (3) probability and statistics with the use of standard deviations (this will be discussed in Chapter 23).

Another section of this chapter presented an integrated approach to linear programming as it applies to resource allocation problems that face the cost accountant in the areas of time, money, materials, personnel, etc. Linear programming provides the decision maker with a powerful and diverse tool for solving a general class of resource allocation problems where the primary objective is one of optimization. The mathematical techniques presented in this chapter are precise enough to solve most problems that today's cost accountant is likely to encounter in the real job situation.

In the complex decision-making framework now facing management, tools such as the economic order quantity and linear programming have become practically indispensable in business and industry. Today, the cost accountant has the capability of integrating the conceptual thought processes (the mathematics) with the available technology (the computer). These sophisticated problems would have been practically insolvable only a few years ago. This capability readily establishes the cost accountant as a key partner in the decision-making process faced by current management.

It appears that in the future the accounting profession will become more and more involved with linear programming, the economic order quantity theory, and other mathematical techniques. These tools are gaining wide acceptance by management, and their implementation by the decision makers is a certainty. Since the cost accountant plays a decisive role in this planning and decision-making process, the application of quantitative techniques to accounting problems will continue to expand.

GLOSSARY

Acquisition Costs—the costs of buying materials from the supplier.

Activity Coefficient—the amount of time necessary to perform a manufacturing operation.

Carrying Costs—the costs associated with having materials in the company's possession.

Economic Order Quantity (EOQ)—the normal purchase order which incurs the minimum total inventory cost.

Inventory Usage Rate—the amount of materials that is expected to be consumed over a period of time.

Lead Time—the period between the placing of the order and the receipt of the order.

Linear Programming—a mathematical programming technique used in solving a general class of linear optimization models.

Objective Function—the equation in a linear programming model that is to be optimized.

Order Point—predetermined inventory level at which an order should be placed.

Ordering Cost—cost associated with processing and receiving a purchase order.

Production Requirements Vector—total number of units of resources available for performing a complete process operation.

Safety Stock—additional units of materials inventory which act as a safeguard against stockouts.

Shadow Price—the marginal value of one additional unit of a resource to be entered into production.

Simplex Algorithm—a matrix algebra-based technique for solving linear programming problems.

Slack Variable—a variable used with a ≤ constraint in linear programming models to convert the inequality sign to an equality sign.

Solution Space—geometric space described by the constraint equations in a linear programming model that will contain the optimal solution, if one exists.

Stockout—situation that exists when there is no available inventory to meet demand.

SUMMARY PROBLEMS

PROBLEM 1

FMC Corporation produces Product X. The estimated annual materials requirement per finished goods is 2,500 units. The cost of materials per unit is $4.50. The order cost per purchase order is $6.75. The annual inventory carrying cost per unit is $.40, or the percent of average inventory cost is 11%.

REQUIRED:

   a   Calculate the economic order quantity (EOQ) using the tabular method for order sizes of 50, 75, 100, 150, 250, 400, and 600.
   b   Calculate the EOQ using the graphical method.
   c   Calculate the EOQ using the formula method in both units and dollars.

PROBLEM 2

The BOF Company has in the past ordered raw material X in quantities of 3,250 units, which is a 26 weeks' supply. Management has decided to change over to an ordering system based on economic order quantities. Assume the following information pertaining to the company's purchasing and production activity:

Inventory usage rate: 125 units per week
Lead time: 3 weeks
Unit price: $1.50
Annual requirement: 6,500 units
Order cost: $7.50 per order
Carrying cost: $.30 per unit per year

REQUIRED:

a   Calculate the economic order quantity using the EOQ formula.
b   Calculate the order point.
c   Calculate the order point if safety stock is desired to cover a possible lead time of 5 weeks and a usage increase to 200 units a week.
d   How much would the company save by using this new method? (Assume the order point calculated in part **b** is used).

PROBLEM 3

The EOQ for KMVP Company is 325. The lead time is 5 weeks and the average inventory usage rate is 55 units a week.

REQUIRED:

Calculate the safety stock and revised order point assuming maximum usage of 75 units a week and possible delivery could take 8 weeks.

PROBLEM 4

The Random Company manufactures two products, Zeta and Beta. Each product must pass through two processing operations. All materials are introduced at the start of Process 1. There are no work-in process inventories. Random may produce either one product exclusively or various combinations of both products subject to the following constraints:

	PROCESS 1	PROCESS 2	CONTRIBUTION MARGIN PER UNIT
Hours required to produce one unit of			
Zeta	1 hour	1 hour	$4.00
Beta	2 hours	3 hours	$5.25
Total capacity, hours per day	1,000	1,275	

A shortage of technical labor has limited Beta production to 400 units per day. There are no constraints on the production of Zeta other than the hour constraints in the above schedule. Assume that all relationships between capacity and production are linear, and that all the above data and relationships are deterministic rather than probabilistic.

REQUIRED:

a   Given the objective to maximize total contribution margin, what are the production constraints for Process 1 and Process 2?
b   Given the objective to maximize total contribution margin, what is the labor constraint for production of Beta?
c   What is the objective function of the data presented?

(AICPA Adapted)

PROBLEM 5

Roy Campaign, Inc., produces two products, Bull and Puff. The management wishes to maximize the contribution margin by using linear programming techniques. The following set of equations were determined by the company (assuming B is the amount of Bull produced and P is the amount of Puff produced):

$$CM = 4B + 9P$$
$$2B + 3P \leq 30$$
$$P \leq 8$$
$$B + P \leq 12$$
$$P \geq 0$$
$$B \geq 0$$

REQUIRED:

Solve the linear equations by using the following methods:
  a   Graphical method
  b   Simplex method

SOLUTIONS TO SUMMARY PROBLEMS

PROBLEM 1

a

	ORDER SIZE						
	50	75	100	150	250	400	600
Quantity data:							
Number of orders	50	33.33	25	16.67	10	6.25	4.17
Average inventory	25	37.5	50	75	125	200	300
Cost data:							
Annual carrying costs	$ 10.00	$ 15.00	$ 20.00	$ 30.00	$ 50.00	$ 80.00	$120.00
Annual ordering costs	337.50	225.00	168.75	112.52	67.50	42.19	28.15
Total annual inventory costs	$347.50	$240.00	$188.75	$142.52	$117.50	$122.19	$148.15

The EOQ is 250 units, or a placement of an order every 36 days (360 days ÷ 10 orders). The EOQ may fall between 150 and 250 units or between 250 and 400 units.

b

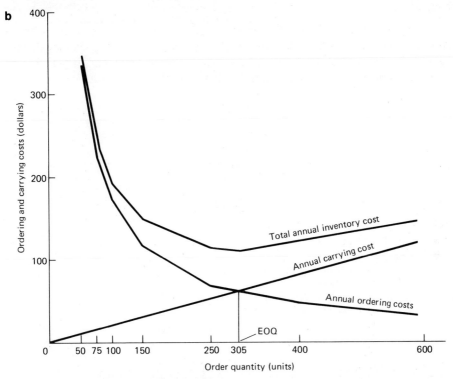

Graphic Solution of Summary Problem 1b

c

$$EOQ = \sqrt{\frac{2 \times RU \times CO}{CU \times CC}} = \sqrt{\frac{2 \times 2,500 \times \$6.75}{\$4.50 \times .11}}$$

$$= \sqrt{\frac{33,750}{.495}}$$

$$= \sqrt{68,182}$$

$$= 261 \text{ units}$$

To calculate EOQ in dollars:

$$EOQ = \sqrt{\frac{2 \times A \times B}{I}}$$

where   A = 2,500 × $4.50 = $11,250
         B = $6.75
         I = 11%

$$EOQ = \sqrt{\frac{2 \times \$11,250 \times \$6.75}{.11}}$$

$$= \sqrt{1,380,682}$$

$$= \$1,175 \quad \text{or} \quad 261 \text{ units} \left(\frac{\$1,175}{\$4.50}\right)$$

PROBLEM 2

a
$$EOQ = \sqrt{\frac{2 \times RU \times CO}{S}}$$

$$= \sqrt{\frac{2 \times 6,500 \times \$7.50}{\$.30}}$$

$$= \sqrt{\frac{97,500}{.30}}$$

$$= \sqrt{325,000}$$

$$= 570.09 \text{ or } 570 \text{ units}$$

b   Order point = lead time × inventory usage rate
$$= 3 \text{ weeks} \times 125 \text{ units a week}$$
$$= 375 \text{ units}$$

c Normal order point .... 375 units
Safety stock:
  Usage over increased lead time (3 to 5 weeks)
    (125 units × 2 weeks) 250
  Usage increase (125 to 200 units)
    (200 − 125) units × 5 weeks 375
  Safety stock 625
  Revised order point .... 1,000 units

d Old inventory costs:
  Total carrying costs = $.30 × 1,625*   = $487.50
  Total ordering costs = $7.50 × 2   =   15.00
    Total inventory cost $502.50

  New method:
  Total carrying costs = $.30 × 285*   = $ 85.50
  Total ordering costs = $7.50 × 11†   =   82.50
                                        $168.00

      Cost saving = $334.50

*Average inventory = order size ÷ 2 (3,250 ÷ 2 = 1,625; 570 ÷ 2 = 285)
†6,500 (annual requirement) ÷ 570 (EOQ) = 11.4 = 11 times a year

PROBLEM 3
  Normal order point (units) .... 275(a)
  Safety stock:
    Usage for 3-week delay (55 units × 3) 165
    Usage rate variance (75 maximum usage −
    55 average usage × 8) 160
  Safety stock 325
  Revised order point .... 600 units

(a) Normal order point = lead time × average inventory usage rate
               = 5 weeks × 55 units a week
               = 275 units

PROBLEM 4

a Production constraints:
   Process 1

$$Z + 2B \leqslant 1{,}000 \text{ hours}$$

   Process 2

$$Z + 3B \leqslant 1{,}275 \text{ hours}$$

where Z represents the amount of Zeta produced and B represents the amount of Beta produced (both Z and B $\geqslant$ 0).

b Labor constraints for production of Beta:

$$B \leqslant 400 \text{ units}$$

c Objective function:

$$CM = \$4.00Z + \$5.25B$$

where CM is the contribution margin.

PROBLEM 5

a **Graphic Method:**

PRODUCT	ACTIVITY COEFFICIENT			CONTRIBUTION MARGIN
	(1)	(2)	(3)	
B (amount of Bull)	2	0	1	$4
P (amount of Puff)	3	1	1	$9
Capacities	30	8	12	

Examine the constraints:

(1) $2B + 3P \leqslant 30$
(2) $\quad\quad P \leqslant 8$
(3) $B + \ P \leqslant 12$

If B = 0

(1) $3P \leqslant 30$
     $P \leqslant 10$
(2) $P \leqslant \ 8$
(3) $P \leqslant 12$

If P = 0

(1) $2B \leqslant 30$
     $B \leqslant 15$
(3) $B \leqslant 12$

Graphic Solution of Summary Problem 5a

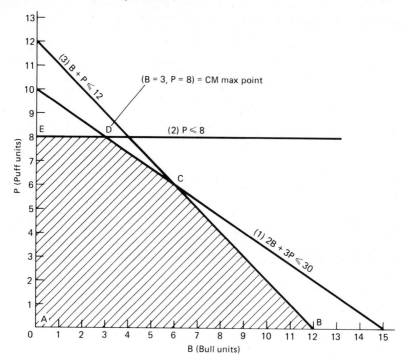

These values determine the limits of the constraint equations depicted on the graph.

Determine the contribution margin for each corner point using the equation

$$CM = \$4B + \$9P$$

CORNER POINT CONTRIBUTION MARGIN VALUES

CORNER POINT	B VALUE	P VALUE	CONTRIBUTION MARGIN
A	0	0	$ 0
B	12	0	48
C	6	6	78
D	3	8	84
E	0	8	72

It can be seen from the table that 3 units of Bull should be produced and 8 units of Puff should be produced. This production combination will then yield a contribution margin that is maximized at $84.

b Simplex Algorithm Method:

Step 1: Restate the problem by adding slack variables to the inequalities to convert them into equalities:

$$CM = 4B + 9P + 0(S1) + 0(S2) + 0(S3)$$
$$2B + 3P + S1 + 0(S2) + 0(S3) = 30$$
$$0(B) + P + 0(S1) + S2 + 0(S3) = 8$$
$$B + P + 0(S1) = 0(S2) + S3 = 12$$
$$P \geqslant 0$$
$$B \geqslant 0$$

Step 2: Set up the first tableau.

PRODUCT	B	P	S1	S2	S3	REQUIREMENTS VECTOR
CM	−4	−9	0	0	0	0
S1	2	3	1	0	0	30
S2	0	1	0	1	0	8
S3	1	1	0	0	1	12

Step 3: Use the decision rules on page 752. Determine which variable (B or P) should be considered first (rule 1), and determine which slack variable (S1, S2, or S3) should be eliminated from the initial tableau (rule 2):

Rule 1. P is considered for production first, since P has the highest *absolute* value of 9 in the CM row.

Rule 2. The remaining rows (S1, S2, and S3) have P values which will be compared with the requirements vector of each row. Determine the ratio of the requirements vector to the P of each row:

$$\text{Ratio} = \frac{\text{requirements vector of row}}{\text{P value of row}}$$

$$S1 \quad \frac{30}{3} = 10$$

$$S2 \quad \frac{8}{1} = 8$$

$$S3 \quad \frac{12}{1} = 12$$

Eliminate S2, since this is the lowest *positive* ratio.

The first tableau will now appear as follows:

PRODUCT	B	P	S1	S2	S3	REQUIREMENTS VECTOR
CM	−4	−9	0	0	0	0
S1	2	3	1	0	0	30
P	0	1*	0	1	0	8
S3	1	1	0	0	1	12

*This variable has a pivot element already equal to 1.

Step 4: Identify the pivot element and convert this value to 1.

Step 5: Convert all other values in the P column to zero: Eliminate the −9 in row CM. Multiply the P row by 9, and add each column of row P to the corresponding column of row CM. Use the same procedure for row S1 (eliminating the 3) and row S3 (eliminating the 1).

The completed second tableau is

PRODUCT	B	P	S1	S2	S3	REQUIREMENTS VECTOR
CM	−4	0	0	9	0	72
S1	2	0	1	−3	0	6
P	0	1	0	1	0	8
S3	1	0	0	−1	1	4

Observation: Since a negative value remains in the CM row, the optimal solution to the problem has not been determined. B must enter into the solution in order to determine maximum CM. To do this, steps 3 to 5 must be reapplied to B using the second tableau.

Step 3 reapplied to B:
  Rule 1. B is now considered for production (there are no other variables).
  Rule 2.

$$\text{Ratio} = \frac{\text{requirements vector in row}}{\text{B value in row}}$$

$$S1 \quad \frac{6}{2} = 3$$

$$S3 \quad \frac{4}{1} = 4$$

Eliminate S1 since this is the lowest *positive* ratio.
  The second tableau will now appear as follows:

PRODUCT	B	P	S1	S2	S3	REQUIREMENTS VECTOR
CM	−4	0	0	9	0	72
B	2*	0	1	−3	0	6
P	0	1	0	1	0	8
S3	1	0	0	−1	1	4

Step 4 reapplied to B: The variable marked * in the second tableau above has a pivot element equal to 2. Therefore, divide row B by 2 to convert this value to 1. The tableau will now appear as follows:

PRODUCT	B	P	S1	S2	S3	REQUIREMENTS VECTOR
CM	−4	0	0	9	0	72
B	1	0	½	−³/₂	0	3
P	0	1	0	1	0	8
S3	1	0	0	−1	1	4

Step 5 reapplied to B: Convert all other values in the B column to zero.
1 Eliminate the −4 in row CM.

Multiply the B row by 4, and add each column of row B to the corresponding column of row CM.

2 Eliminate the 1 in row S3.

Multiply the B row by −1 and add each column of row B to the corresponding column of row S3.

The completed third tableau will be

PRODUCT	B	P	S1	S2	S3	REQUIREMENTS VECTOR
CM	0	0	2	3	0	84
B	1	0	½	−³⁄₂	0	3
P	0	1	0	1	0	8
S3	0	0	−½	½	1	1

Conclusion: An examination of the CM row reveals that it contains no negative numbers. This indicates that the third tableau is the optimal solution. Thus the optimal production strategy is to make 3 units of Bull and 8 units of Puff to yield a contribution margin of $84.

QUESTIONS

1 In what ways do inventories benefit production and the manufacturing operation?
2 Describe the three costs which comprise the total cost of an inventory policy. Do these costs fluctuate with how inventory is purchased?
3 What is the relationship between total carrying costs and total ordering costs? What does the proper inventory policy try to do? Are total acquisition costs relevant in determining the proper inventory policy?
4 What is the tabular method for determining the economic order quantity? What are the disadvantages of this method?
5 Answer the following in reference to the graphic method for determining EOQ.

Graphic Diagram of Economic Order Quantity

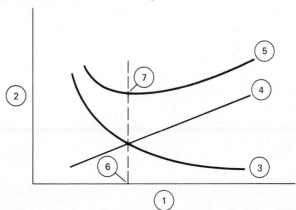

    a Identify 1 through 7 in the above graph.
    b What is the relationship between 6 and 7?
    c What is the relationship between 4 and 3?
    d How is 5 influenced by 4 and 3?

6 What is the equation used in the formula method of determining EOQ? Identify each term. What costs must be minimized in determining the optimum size of a production run? Do quantity discounts have an effect upon the EOQ? Why?

7 "It is important that the lead time and the inventory usage rate be precisely known." Explain.

8 Describe the two methods which are not statistical that are used to calculate the optimum amount of safety stock. Include the advantages and disadvantages of each.

9 Select the best answer to each of the following multiple choice questions:
In a linear programming problem, the purpose of a slack variable is to:
    a Find one corner point.
    b Start at the origin.
    c Convert the inequality sign on a $\leqslant$ constraint to an equality sign.
    d Make the problem more complex.
A method that may be helpful in allocating scarce resources when all the constraints are linear is called:
    a Linear regression.
    b Linear programming.
    c Linear algebra.
    d Linear queues.
Which of the following is *not* true of a linear programming technique?
    a It is used to maximize contribution margin.
    b It is used to minimize costs.
    c It is used to analyze waiting lines.
    d It is used to solve blending problems.
In a system of equations for a linear programming model, what can be done to equalize an inequality such as $3X + 2Y \leqslant 15$?
    a Nothing.
    b Add a slack variable.
    c Add a tableau.
    d Multiple each element by -1.

10 In the graphic solution method of linear programming, how is the optimal solution to the problem determined?

11 What are the limitations of the graphic solution method of linear programming? Does the simplex algorithm method have these limitations? Explain.

12 Describe the two interpretations of shadow pricing.

13 The Golden Hawk Manufacturing Company wants to maximize the profits on Products A, B, and C. The contribution margin for each product follows:

PRODUCT	CONTRIBUTION MARGIN
A	$2
B	5
C	4

The production requirements and departmental capacities are as follows:

	PRODUCTION REQUIREMENTS BY PRODUCTS (HOURS)			CAPACITIES (TOTAL HOURS)
	A	B	C	
Assembling	2	3	2	30,000
Painting	1	2	2	38,000
Finishing	2	3	1	28,000

What is the profit-maximization formula for the Golden Hawk Company?
a $2A + $5B + $4C = X$ (where X = profits)
b $5A + $8B + $5C \leqslant 96,000$
c $2A + $5B + $4C \leqslant X$ (where X = profits)
d $2A + $5B + $4C = 96,000$
What is the constraint for the painting department?
a $1A + 2B + 2C \geqslant 38,000$
b $2A + 5B + 4C \geqslant 38,000$
c $1A + 2B + 2C \leqslant 38,000$
d $2A + 3B + 2C \leqslant 30,000$

EXERCISES

EXERCISE 1

Economic Order Quantity—Tabular Method

The Michelebob Company manufactures various household appliances. The company found that it required 2,000 units of Material A each year. The inventory carrying cost was 8% of the average inventory value, and the cost of the item per unit was $1.75. The order cost per purchase order for Material A is $5.

REQUIRED:

Calculate the economic order quantity (EOQ) using the tabular method for the following order sizes: 100, 200, 400, 600, 800, 1,000.

EXERCISE 2

Economic Order Quantity—Graphic Method

MOD Corporation manufactures furniture. The ordering costs and carrying cost of the materials for the following order sizes are

ORDER SIZE (UNITS)	ANNUAL CARRYING COSTS	ANNUAL ORDERING COSTS
50	$ 18.75	$468.75
100	37.50	234.38
175	65.63	133.93
275	103.13	85.23
400	150.00	58.59
550	206.25	42.61

The ordering cost per purchase order is $3.

REQUIRED:

Calculate the EOQ using the graphic method.

EXERCISE 3

Economic Order Quantity—Formula Method

The Sikki-Nikki Company manufactures aspirin to sell to the opera houses of Loudsville, N.Y. In order to analyze the costs of carrying and ordering the aspirin goods, the management collected the following data:

Clerical costs	$2.60 per purchase order
Stationery	$4.80 for four purchase orders
Desired annual rate of return on investment	8%
Postage	$.25 per purchase order
Personal property taxes	$.03 per bottle per month
Depreciation on clerical machines	$115 per year
Warehousing or storage	$60 per 6 months
Insurance	$.50 per bottle per year
Telephone bill	$.40 per purchase order
Storeroom supervisor	$400 every two weeks
Material cost per bottle	$3.00
Annual required bottles	8,000

REQUIRED:

Determine the economic order quantity using the formula method.

EXERCISE 4

EOQ

The Atias Atlas Company has a good system of materials inventory control. The schedule on page 773 is used to calculate the optimum order quantity necessary to keep costs at a minimum.

ITEM NUMBER	ANNUAL REQUIREMENTS (UNITS)	UNIT COST	ORDERING COST PER ORDER	CARRYING COST PERCENTAGES
X-2	4,000	$4.00	$10.00	15
X-3	2,500	6.50	8.00	20
X-4	15,000	2.75	7.50	25
X-5	11,500	3.30	5.00	19
X-6	9,150	5.05	9.75	11

REQUIRED:

Calculate the economic order quantity in dollars for each item.

EXERCISE 5

Optimum Size of the Production Run

The McCarthy Corp. uses the following information in order to determine the optimum size of the production run:

Fixed cost of producing $14.80
Labor cost of rearranging .... $2.50 per production run
Adjusting machines .... $1.05 per production run
Variable cost of producing .... $6.00 per unit
Cost of carrying one unit in inventory $2.25

Management usually produces 1,000 units a run and has 70 runs a year.
Labor costs of rearranging and adjusting the machine are considered setup costs.

REQUIRED:

Find the optimum size of the production run in units.

EXERCISE 6

Optimum Size of Production Run—Multiple Choice

The Laurette P. J. Corp. produces flannel pajamas. The annual requirement for these pajamas is 4,000 and the setup cost per run is $12.50. The carrying cost is 15% and the production cost per pajama is $6.75. In order to determine the optimum quantity of pajamas to produce in each run, this company uses the following formula:

$$X = \sqrt{\frac{2 \times RU \times SC}{VC \times CC}}$$

where X is the quantity of pajamas produced in each production run.

1 The average number of pajamas in inventory at any time is
   a $4,000 - (X/2)$
   b $4,000/X$
   c $\sqrt{(RU \times SC)/2 \times (VC \times CC)}$
   d $2X$
   e None of the above

2 The number of production runs annually are
   a $X/2$
   b RU/X
   c $4,000/X$
   d Both **b** and **c**
   e All of the above

3 The total annual cost of inventory is
   a $VC \times CC \times (X/2)$
   b $RU \times (SC/2) \times X$
   c $(2 \times RU \times SC) + (X \times VC \times CC)$
   d $RU \times SC \times X$
   e $[(2 \times RU \times SC) + (VC \times CC \times X^2)]/(2 \times X)$

4 The annual setup cost is
   a $(RU \times SC)/X$
   b $50,000/X$
   c $27,000/X$
   d Both **a** and **c**
   e Both **a** and **b**

5 The annual carrying cost is
   a $(4,000/X) \times VC$
   b $VC \times CC \times X$
   c $(VC/2) \times CC \times X$
   d Both **a** and **c**
   e None of the above

EXERCISE 7

EOQ and the Order Point

S. Patak and Smelley Co. manufactures foot devices for athletes and dancers. They usually have to wait 4 weeks for delivery of materials, and the usage rate is normally 25 devices a week. The ordering cost per order is $4.80 and the carrying cost per device per year is $.80.

REQUIRED:

   a Calculate the economic order quantity using the EOQ formula.
   b Calculate the order point.
   c When should S. Patak place the next order if the lead time happened to be 5 weeks and the inventory contains an amount equivalent to the economic order quantity?

EXERCISE 8

EOQ, Order Point, and Safety Stock

	1	2	3
Beginning inventory (units)	1,500	1,500	(m)
Units in inventory at order point	(a)	465	3,750
Usage to order point (units)	820	(h)	3,750
Usage during normal lead time (units)	(b)	(i)	(n)
Maximum inventory at date of delivery (units)	0	(j)	2,250
Normal lead time (weeks)	4	2	5
EOQ units received	(c)	(k)	(o)
Average inventory assuming normal lead time			
and usage (units)	(d)	1,105	6,250
Maximum inventory (units)	2,050	2,050	(p)
Usage variance (units)	0	(l)	2,250
Normal usage (units per week)	(e)	155	300
Maximum usage (units per week)	(f)	155	(q)
Maximum lead time (weeks)	(g)	3	5

The Maureen Machine Co. utilizes the economic order quantity theory when it orders materials. Since a constant usage rate is unlikely to occur and the lead time tends to vary, this company maintains a safety stock large enough to safeguard against any stockouts.

REQUIRED:

For each of the above unrelated items (1 through 3) find the missing values (a through q).

EXERCISE 9

Linear Programming—Simplex Algorithm Method

The Camille Corp. derived the following equations from the linear programming information collected during the year. Two products manufactured by Camille Corp. are represented by the variables X and Y.

$$CM = 8X + 6Y$$
$$4X + 2Y \leqslant 60$$
$$2X + 4Y \leqslant 48$$
$$Y \geqslant 0$$
$$X \geqslant 0$$

REQUIRED:

Solve the linear equations by using the simplex method.

EXERCISE 10

Linear Programming—Graphic Solution Method

A firm can produce one or both of two products, A or B. The contribution margin for Product A is $2.50, and for Product B it is $1.25. Production of both products requires the consumption of a scarce raw material which is limited in supply to 18,000 pounds. One unit of A requires 2 pounds and one unit of B requires 1½ pounds. In addition, one unit of A requires 2 hours of machining time and one unit of B requires 5 hours. There are no more than 30,000 hours of machining time available. Each unit requires assembly time of 1.25 hours for A or B. There are a maximum of 10,000 hours of assembly time available.

REQUIRED:

If the firm's goal is to maximize contribution margin by use of linear programming techniques, determine maximum CM by utilizing the graphic solution method. (Round all your values to the nearest dollar.)

(AICPA Adapted)

EXERCISE 11

Linear Programming Techniques

The cost accountant of the Stangren Corporation, your client, wants your opinion of a technique suggested to him by a young accounting graduate he employed as a cost analyst. The following information was furnished for the corporation's two products, trinkets and gadgets:

1

	DAILY CAPACITIES IN UNITS		SALES PRICE PER UNIT	VARIABLE COST PER UNIT
	CUTTING DEPARTMENT	FINISHING DEPARTMENT		
Trinkets	400	240	$50	$30
Gadgets	200	320	70	40

2 The daily capacities of each department represent the maximum production for either trinkets or gadgets. However, any combination of trinkets and gadgets can be produced as long as the maximum capacity of the department is not exceeded. For example, two trinkets can be produced in the cutting department for each gadget not produced and three trinkets can be produced in the finishing department for every four gadgets not produced.
3 Materials shortages prohibit the production of more than 180 gadgets per day.
4 The figure shown on page 777 is a graphic expression of simultaneous linear equations developed from the production information above.

REQUIRED:

a Comparing the information in the table with the graph in the figure, identify and list the graphic location (coordinates) of the:
   1 Cutting department's capacity.
   2 Production limitation for gadgets because of the materials shortage.
   3 Area of feasible (possible) production combinations.
b 1 Compute the contribution margin per unit for trinkets and gadgets.
   2 Compute the total contribution margin of each of the points of intersections of lines bounding the feasible (possible) production area.
   3 Identify the best production alternative.

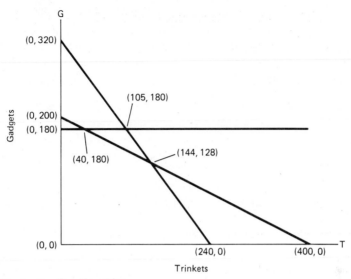

Graph of Production Relationships

PROBLEMS

PROBLEM 1

Economic Order Quantity—Tabular, Graphic, and Formula Methods

The Small Company manufactures an assortment of menswear. The annual requirement is usually 35,000 units, and the ordering cost is $8.33 per order. The average inventory is $10.50 per unit, and carrying costs are $4.66 per unit. This company never used the EOQ formula and is debating whether to use the graphic or tabular methods. In order to choose the proper method, they relied upon the analysts' decisions.

REQUIRED:

a Calculate the economic order quantity using the tabular method for order sizes of 50, 150, 250, 350, 450, 550, and 650.
b Calculate the EOQ using the graphic method.
c Calculate the EOQ using the formula method.
d If you were the analyst, which method would you suggest the Small Company use?

PROBLEM 2

Economic Order Quantity and Quantity Discounts

The Meeruam Manufacturing Company has always used the economic order quantity formula when determining the best quantity to order. Recently they were given the opportunity to receive quantity discounts for various materials. The managers assembled the schedule of discounts as follows:

UNITS PURCHASED	DISCOUNT
1–98	None
99–449	$.10 per unit
450–999	.30 per unit
1,000 up	.40 per unit

This company normally uses 3,000 units each year and pays $10.50 for each purchase order. The carrying cost is 10% of average inventory value and each unit costs $15.

REQUIRED:

a Using the formula method and ignoring the discounts, calculate the EOQ.
b The management has decided to determine the economic order quantity for order sizes of 50, 150, 300, 450, 600, 900, 1,500, and 2,500. Show tabulations which include the expense of the foregoing quantity discounts.

PROBLEM 3

EOQ—Tabular, Graphic, and Formula Methods

Corona's Mad Machine, Inc., sells very sophisticated electrical equipment to the United States government. They aim at minimizing their total inventory costs by using the graphic method of determining EOQ. The carrying cost is 15% of the average inventory value, and the ordering cost is $35 per order. The cost of each item is $81, and if management were to order 125 units at each purchase, 30 orders a year would be required to satisfy their needs.

REQUIRED:

a Calculate the EOQ using the tabular method and the graphic method. Use the following order sizes for your answer: 50, 75, 100, 150, 200, 300, 500, 750.
b Calculate the EOQ in both units and dollars using the formula method.

PROBLEM 4

EOQ, the Order Point, and Safety Stock

The O'Donnell Bottling Company distributes a wide selection of soda pop to the surrounding local communities. The lemon-lime soda pop is sold in crates containing 24 medium-sized bottles. The selling price of one crate is $15. It has been determined that the materials cost per crate of soda is $8. The ordering cost for the raw materials used to manufacture the soda pop is $2.60 per order, and the carrying cost is $1.60 per crate per year. The monthly requirement for the soda pop is 52 crates, and lead time is 3 weeks before delivery of the materials.

REQUIRED:

a Calculate the economic order quantity using crates as the unit of measurement. The management prefers to use the formula method of determining EOQ.

b The weekly usage of materials is equivalent to 288 bottles. Calculate the order point and present it on a graph. (Use the same units as in part **a**.)

c What would the safety stock be if the weekly usage rate became 16 crates and the materials are delayed for 7 weeks?

PROBLEM 5

Safety Stock and Graph

The beginning inventory of Nan Corporation consisted of 860 machines. This company maintains an inventory that never exceeds 940 units and, assuming normal lead time and usage, averages about 740 units. Normally the company uses 180 units during the usual lead time of 3 weeks. When usage reaches the maximum of 80 units per week, management orders the economic order quantity at a time when inventory is at the level of 720 machines.

REQUIRED:

a Assuming that management maintains a safety stock adequate enough to safeguard against maximum usage and maximum lead time, calculate the following:

1 The usage to order point.
2 The amount of safety stock.
3 The EOQ received.
4 The normal usage rate.
5 The estimated maximum lead time.
6 The usage variance.

b Draw a graphic representation showing the effects of safety stock.

PROBLEM 6

Simplex Algorithm and Graphic Methods of Linear Programming

The Simplex Graphic Firm manufactures two products, Simply A and Simply B, both of which require drilling and tapping. The firm's production and contribution margin data are presented below:

PER UNIT DATA	A	B	MAXIMUM TIME
Drilling time (hours)	25	25	1,800
Tapping time (hours)	20	40	2,400
Contribution margin (dollars)	4	6	

REQUIRED:

Assume the firm's goals are to maximize contribution margins by using linear programming techniques. Determine maximum CM by using:

a The simplex algorithm method.
b The graphic method.

PROBLEM 7

Linear Programming Using the Graphic Solution Method and Simplex Algorithm Method

Equations derived from linear programming data:

$$2A + B \leqslant 1{,}000$$
$$A + B \leqslant 800$$
$$B \geqslant 0$$
$$A \geqslant 0$$

The Robert Emmet Ryan Company wants to maximize its total contribution margin given the above production constraints. A has a per unit contribution margin of $4 and B has a per unit contribution margin of $3.

REQUIRED:

Solve the linear equations by using:
a The graphic method.
b The simplex algorithm method.

PROBLEM 8

Linear Programming Methods—Graphic and Simplex

Patsy, Inc., manufactures two products, X and Y. Each product must be processed in each of three departments: machining, assembling, and finishing. The hours needed to produce one unit per department and the maximum possible hours per department follow:

	PRODUCTION HOURS PER UNIT		MAXIMUM
	DEPART-MENT X	DEPART-MENT Y	CAPACITY, HOURS
Machining	4	1	420
Assembling	2	2	500
Finishing	2	3	600

Other restrictions follow:

$$X \geqslant 20$$
$$Y \geqslant 20$$

The objective is to maximize profits where profits = $4X + $2Y.

REQUIRED:

a Given the objective and constraints, what is the most profitable number of units of X and units of Y to manufacture? Determine your answer by utilizing the graphic solution method.

b What would your answer be to part **a** if there were no restrictions on X and Y? Use the simplex algorithm method to obtain your answer.

(AICPA Adapted)

PROBLEM 9

Simplex Linear Programming

Watch Corporation manufactures Products A, B, and C. The daily production requirements are shown below:

		HOURS REQUIRED PER UNIT PER DEPARTMENT		
PRODUCT	PROFIT PER UNIT	MACHINING	PLATING	POLISHING
A	$10	1	1	$1/5$
B	20	3	1	1
C	30	2	3	2
Total hours per day per department		16	12	6

REQUIRED:

a Determine:
  1 The activity coefficients.
  2 The production requirements vectors.
  3 The objective functions.
b Set the problem into linear equations.
c Solve the linear equations by using the simplex algorithm method. (Assume the products can be broken down into any fractional amount.)
d Determine the shadow prices of machining. plating, and polishing time.

(AICPA Adapted)

PROBLEM 10

Linear Programming Terminology and Graphs

Jean Radcliffe, Inc., produces two products, tables and chairs. The contribution margins for these products are $4 per chair and $12 per table. Tables require 5 board feet of oak and 1 board foot of pine. Chairs require 2 board feet of oak and 3 board feet of pine. There are a total of 1,000 board feet of oak and 700 board feet of pine available for production. It takes 3 hours to make a table and 2 hours to make a chair and 500 labor hours are available for production. Demand projections indicate that no more than 150 tables and 300 chairs should be made.

REQUIRED:

a Indicate:
  1 Activity coefficients.
  2 Production requirements vectors.
  3 Objective functions.

b Use the above data to derive the linear equations.

c Set the problem in simplex tableau format (do not solve).

d Solve the linear equations by using the graphic solution method.

PROBLEM 11

Maximizing a Production Schedule

a The Witchell Corporation manufactures and sells three grades, A, B, and C, of a single wood product. Each grade must be processed through three phases—cutting, fitting, and finishing—before it is sold.

    The following unit information is provided:

	A	B	C
Selling price	$10.00	$15.00	$20.00
Direct labor	$5.00	$6.00	$9.00
Direct materials	$.70	$.70	$1.00
Variable overhead	$1.00	$1.20	$1.80
Fixed overhead	$.60	$.72	$1.08
Materials requirements in board feet	7	7	10
Labor requirements in hours			
Cutting	$3/6$	$3/6$	$4/6$
Fitting	$1/6$	$1/6$	$2/6$
Finishing	$1/6$	$2/6$	$3/6$

    Only 5,000 board feet per week can be obtained. The cutting department has 180 hours of labor available each week. The fitting and finishing departments each have 120 hours of labor available each week. No overtime is allowed.

    Contract commitments require the company to make 50 units of A per week. In addition, company policy is to produce at least 50 additional units of A and 50 units of B and 50 units of C each week to actively remain in each of the three markets. Because of competition only 130 units of C can be sold each week.

REQUIRED:

    Formulate and label the linear objective function and the constraint functions necessary to maximize the contribution margin.

b The graph provided on page 783 presents the constraint functions for a chair manufacturing company whose production problem can be solved by linear programming. The company earns $8.00 for each kitchen chair sold and $5.00 for each office chair sold.

REQUIRED:

    1 What is the profit maximizing production schedule?

    2 How did you select this production schedule?

                                                                     (CMA Adapted)

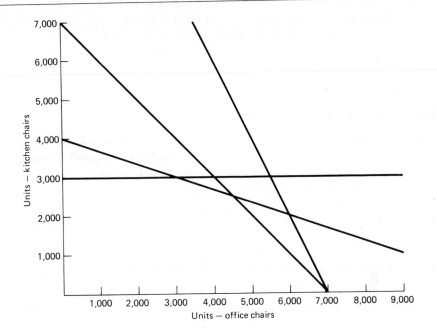

PROBLEM 12

Economic Order Quantity

The Robney Company is a restaurant supplier that sells a number of products to various restaurants in the area. One of its products is a special meat cutter with a disposable blade.

The blades are sold in packages of 12 blades for $20.00 per package. After a number of years, it has been determined that the demand for the replacement blades is at a constant rate of 2,000 packages per month. The packages cost the Robney Company $10.00 each from the manufacturer and require a 3-day lead time from date of order to date of delivery. The ordering cost is $1.20 per order, and the carrying cost is 10% per year.

Robney is going to use the economic order quantity formula:

$$EOQ = \sqrt{\frac{2(\text{annual requirements})(\text{cost per order})}{(\text{price per unit})(\text{carrying cost})}}$$

REQUIRED:

a Calculate:
1 The economic order quantity.
2 The number of orders needed per year.
3 The total cost of buying and carrying blades for the year.
b Assuming there is no reserve (safety stock) and that the present inventory

level is 200 packages, when should the next order be placed? (Use 360 days = 1 year.)

(CMA Adapted)

PROBLEM 13

Maximizing Daily Profits

Girth, Inc., makes two kinds of men's suede leather belts. Belt A is a high-quality belt, while Belt B is of somewhat lower quality. The company earns $7.00 for each unit of Belt A that is sold, and $2.00 for each unit sold of Belt B. Each unit (belt) of type A requires twice as much manufacturing time as is required for a unit of type B. Further, if only Belt type B is made, Girth has the capacity to manufacture 1,000 units per day. Suede leather is purchased by Girth under a long-term contract which makes available to Girth enough leather to make 800 belts per day (A and B combined). Belt A requires a fancy buckle, of which only 400 per day are available. Belt B requires a different (plain) buckle, of which 700 per day are available. The demand for the suede leather belts (A or B) is such that Girth can sell all that it produces.

The graph below displays the constraint functions based upon the facts presented above.

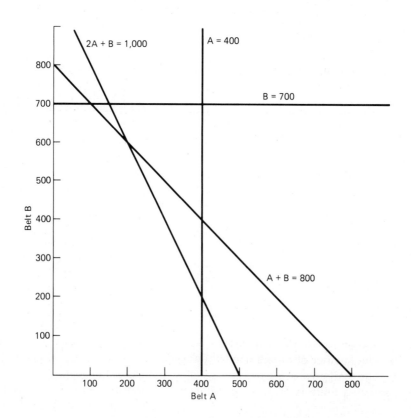

REQUIRED:

a Using the graph, determine how many units of Belt A and Belt B should be produced to maximize daily profits.

b Assume the same facts above except that the sole supplier of buckles for Belt A informs Girth, Inc., that it will be unable to supply more than 100 fancy buckles per day. How many units of each of the two belts should be produced each day to maximize profits?

c Assume the same facts as in b except that Texas Buckles, Inc., could supply Girth, Inc., with the additional fancy buckles it needs. The price would be $3.50 more than Girth, Inc., is paying for such buckles. How many, if any, fancy buckles should Girth, Inc., buy from Texas Buckles, Inc.? Explain how you determined your answer.

(CMA Adapted)

PROBLEM 14

Product Mix and Shadow Prices

The Frey Company manufactures and sells two products—a toddler bike and a toy high chair. Linear programming is employed to determine the best production and sales mix of bikes and chairs. This approach also allows Frey to speculate on economic changes. For example, management is often interested in knowing how variations in selling prices, resource costs, resource availabilities and marketing strategies would affect the company's performance.

The demand for bikes and chairs is relatively constant throughout the year. The following economic data pertain to the two products:

	BIKE (B)	CHAIR (C)
Selling price for unit	$12	$10
Variable cost per unit	8	7
Contribution margin per unit	$ 4	$ 3
Raw materials required:		
Wood	1 bd ft	2 bd ft
Plastic	2 lb	1 lb
Direct labor required	2 hr	2 hr

Estimates of the resource quantities available in a nonvacation month during the year are

Wood	10,000 bd ft
Plastic	10,000 lb
Direct labor	12,000 hr

The graphic formulation of the constraints of the linear programming model that Frey Company has developed for nonvacation months is presented on page 786. The algebraic formulation of the model for the nonvacation months is as follows:

Objective function: MAX Z = 4B + 3C

Constraints:

$$B + 2C \leqslant 10,000 \text{ board feet}$$
$$2B + C \leqslant 10,000 \text{ pounds}$$
$$2B + 2C \leqslant 12,000 \text{ direct labor hours}$$
$$C \geqslant 0$$
$$B \leqslant 0$$

The results from the linear programming model indicate that Frey Company can maximize its contribution margin (and thus profits) for a nonvacation month by producing and selling 4,000 toddler bikes and 2,000 toy high chairs. This sales mix will yield a total contribution margin of $22,000 in a month.

REQUIRED:

a   During the months of June, July, and August, the total direct labor hours available are reduced from 12,000 to 10,000 hours per month due to vacations.
1   What would be the best product mix and maximum total contribution margin when only 10,000 direct labor hours are available during a month?
2   The "shadow price" of a resource is defined as the marginal contribution of a resource or the rate at which profit would increase (decrease) if the

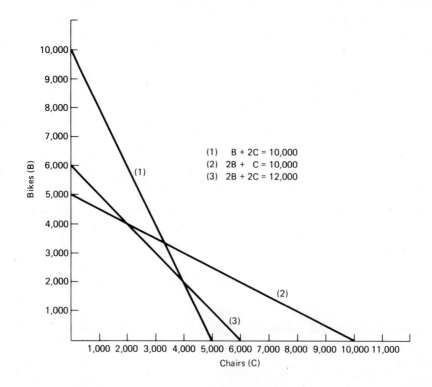

(1)   B + 2C = 10,000
(2)   2B + C = 10,000
(3)   2B + 2C = 12,000

amount of resource were increased (decreased). Based upon your solution for **1** what is the shadow price on direct labor hours in the original model for a nonvacation month?

b Competition in the toy market is very strong. Consequently, the prices of the two products tend to fluctuate. Can analysis of data from the linear programming model provide information to management which will indicate when price changes made to meet market conditions will alter the optimum product mix? Explain your answer.

(CMA Adapted)

PROBLEM 15

Cost Savings under EOQ

Hermit Company manufactures a line of walnut office products. Hermit executives estimate the demand for the double walnut letter tray, one of the company's products, at 6,000 units. The letter tray sells for $80 per unit. The costs relating to the letter tray are estimated to be as follows for 19X7:

1. Standard manufacturing cost per letter tray unit—$50.00.
2. Costs to initiate a production run—$300.00.
3. Annual cost of carrying the letter tray in inventory—20 percent of standard manufacturing cost.

In prior years, Hermit Company has scheduled the production for the letter tray in two equal production runs. The company is aware that the economic order quantity (EOQ) model can be employed to determine optimum size for production runs. The EOQ formula as it applies to inventories for determining the optimum order quantity is shown below.

$$EOQ = \sqrt{\frac{2\,(\text{annual demand})(\text{cost per order})}{(\text{cost per unit})(\text{carrying cost})}}$$

REQUIRED:

Calculate the expected annual cost savings Hermit Company could experience if it employed the economic order quantity model to determine the number of production runs which should be initiated during the year for the manufacture of the double walnut letter trays.

(CMA Adapted)

CHAPTER TWENTY-THREE
DECISION THEORY

In recent years a new branch of problem solving has evolved called *decision theory*. Decision theory is concerned with real-world situations and is characterized by data that is uncertain, incomplete, almost nonexistent, or suspect. This branch of problem solving falls into the area of statistics and is utilized with various management techniques and in many situations. Probability concepts are useful for network methods such as PERT (program evaluation and review technique), and aid in calculating the optimum safety stock size for the company's inventory. This chapter will examine a number of ways decision theory can be applied.

AN OUTLINE OF THE DECISION THEORY METHOD

Decision theory specifically evaluates different courses of action open to the manager when the various actions can be measured in terms of monetary outcomes. When a manager must choose from among several different types of machines that might be purchased, the various alternatives should reflect the profit or loss that might be expected, given each course of action. Decision theory allows the examination of all the available alternatives to enable managers to make a decision with the knowledge of the monetary consequences of each action.

The decision theory method can be applied to various problems encompassing any time span. Most applications of decision theory contain a fairly common set of factors. Thus, most problem solvers take a consistent approach to seeking a solution to the problem at hand. The decision theory method is usually stated mathematically. Therefore, the model, used to explain the consequences of the various alternatives, contains the following elements:

1 A *quantifiable objective* that the manager is seeking. Most of the time the objective will be to maximize or minimize a particular monetary value such as to maximize profit or to minimize the stockout of inventories. This sounds similar to the objective of a linear programming problem, but the decision theory method is based on uncertainty and the linear programming model is not.

2 A set of *decision variables or actions* are available to the decision maker. These actions must be completely defined and mutually exclusive.

3 Each decision variable can be described by a monetary reward, either positive or negative, called the *payoff*.

4 The model will have a set of *uncontrollable variables or events*. These events are completely defined and mutually exclusive where only one can occur at a time.

5 The set of events must be described by a group of *probabilities* that indicate the likelihood of the occurrence of each event.

All examples in the remainder of this chapter will contain the essential ideas of the decision theory method. The following general approach to uncertainty will illustrate this decision theory model.

A GENERAL APPROACH TO UNCERTAINTY

Assume that a firm deals in a highly perishable product that has a shelf life of 1 day. The product is purchased each morning at a cost of $3 per unit and a selling price of $5 per unit, yielding a profit of $2 per unit. If at the end of the day the product is still on the shelf, it must be thrown away. Therefore, the loss on an unsold unit is its cost of $3. The problem is to determine how many units to order each morning to maximize expected profits.

The firm has studied its daily demand pattern and determined the following probability distribution (the likelihood of each event occurring as determined by management):

DEMAND (EVENTS)	PROBABILITY OF EVENTS P(E)
E1: 0 units	.10
E2: 1 unit	.20
E3: 2 units	.40
E4: 3 units	.30

The firm must be able to compute the expected profit of each of the following potential decisions:

A1:   Action 1—order 0 units
A2:   Action 2—order 1 unit
A3:   Action 3—order 2 units
A4:   Action 4—order 3 units

In summary, the elements in the decision model are

1   The quantifiable objective is to maximize expected profits.
2   The decision variable or action is the number of units to order.
3   The payoff is the expected profit from each order decision.
4   Demand is the uncontrollable variable or the event.
5   Each variable of demand has been assigned a probability as seen in the probability distribution above.

The consequences of the ordering process are given in the payoff table (Table 23-1).

Thus, based on the expected profit for each action, the optimal strategy under uncertainty is to order two units, since this yields the highest expected payoff. Since accountants often compute the information used in such models, they should keep in mind the consequences that the data may have on the design and implementation of these models.

What if the firm knew in advance exactly what its demand would be? Then it would know exactly how many units to order each morning and exactly what the expected value of such consequences would be. The expected value of having such perfect information about the daily demand is simply the demand times the probability of that demand occurring:

DEMAND (EVENTS)	P(E)	ACTUAL PROFIT	EXPECTED PROFIT
E1: 0 units	.10	$0	$0
E2: 1 unit	.20	2.00	.40
E3: 2 units	.40	4.00	1.60
E4: 3 units	.30	6.00	1.80
	1.00		$3.80

Thus the expected value of the profit under perfect conditions is $3.80.

The difference between the expected value of the profit with perfect information and the optimal expected value of the profit under uncertain information is $1.80 (or $3.80 − $2.00). This $1.80 difference is called the expected value of perfect information (EVPI) and is the top price which the decision maker should be willing to pay for having perfect demand information in advance. In fact, the firm is not likely to pay the $1.80, because no matter how much additional information it obtains it will never attain perfection.

In the real world, perfect information is usually not available. However, it may be possible to obtain additional information that may increase the expected value of the profit. In this example, this may occur if better probabilities of the demand could be estimated.

The expected value of additional information (EVAI) is a complex area, and

TABLE 23-1
PAYOFF TABLE

DEMAND (EVENTS)	P(E)	A1: ORDER 0 ACTUAL PROFIT**	EXPECTED PROFIT*	A2: ORDER 1 ACTUAL PROFIT**	EXPECTED PROFIT*	A3: ORDER 2 ACTUAL PROFIT**	EXPECTED PROFIT*	A4: ORDER 3 ACTUAL PROFIT**	EXPECTED PROFIT*
E1: 0 units	.10	0	0	−$3.00 (A)	−$ .30 (C)	−$6.00	−$ .60	−$9.00	−$ .90
E2: 1 unit	.20	0	0	2.00 (B)	.40 (D)	− 1.00	− .20	− 4.00	− .80
E3: 2 units	.40	0	0	2.00 (B)	.80 (E)	4.00	1.60	1.00	.40
E4: 3 units	.30	0	0	2.00 (B)	.60 (F)	4.00	1.20	6.00	1.80
Expected profit for each action†			0		$1.50		$2.00 (Optimal)		$ .50

All negative values are losses.

*Expected profit = actual profit × probability of events P(E).

†Expected profit for each action = Σ expected profit for E1, E2, E3, and E4.

**Actual profit = (units sold × selling price) − cost

(A) (0 × $5) − $3.00 = −$3.00
(B) (1 × $5) − $3.00 = $2.00
(C) −$3.00 × .10 = −$.30
(D) $2.00 × .20 = $.40
(E) $2.00 × .40 = $.80
(F) $2.00 × .30 = $.60

a precise treatment of it is beyond the scope of this book. In general, we can say that it involves such concepts as sampling, estimates of range values, the revision of probabilities, and the introduction of both discrete and continuous probability distributions. The list of references at the end of this chapter will indicate some sources where complete treatments of EVAI are given.

PROJECT PROPOSALS AND UNCERTAINTY

The idea of uncertainty can be demonstrated by examining three projects under consideration by a firm. The cash flows generated by these three projects, each having a 1-year "use" period, and their assigned discrete probabilities are listed below.

PROJECT 1		PROJECT 2		PROJECT 3	
PROBA-BILITY	CASH FLOW	PROBA-BILITY	CASH FLOW	PROBA-BILITY	CASH FLOW
.15	$1,000	.05	$1,500	.2	$1,500
.20	2,000	.20	2,000	.2	2,000
.30	3,000	.50	3,000	.2	3,000
.20	4,000	.20	4,000	.2	4,000
.15	5,000	.05	4,500	.2	4,500

One way to examine the three projects is to compute their expected value and then choose the one that yields the highest expected cash flow of the three. The expected value is simply the arithmetic mean where the probabilities are assigned as weights. The formula for computing the expected value of each project is given as:

$$\overline{X} = \sum_{i=1}^{n} X_i P_i$$

For example, $\overline{X}_1$ would mean the expected value of Project 1, $\overline{X}_2$ would mean the expected value of Project 2, etc.

At this point, note the difference between Projects 2 and 3. Both projects have identical cash flows, but the probabilities assigned to each are different. This situation could be considered as the case where the decision makers could not agree as to the probabilities to be assigned to the cash flows and therefore two sets have been chosen. The consequences of these two different sets of probabilities will be demonstrated in the rest of this section.

The expected value of the cash flow for Project 1 is given as

$\overline{X}_1 = [.15(\$1,000) + .20(\$2,000) + .30(\$3,000) + .20(\$4,000) + .15(\$5,000)]$
$= \$3,000$

For Project 2 it is

$\overline{X}_2 = [.05(\$1,500) + .20(\$2,000) + .50(\$3,000) + .20(\$4,000) + .05(\$4,500)]$
$= \$3,000$

For Project 3 it is

$\overline{X}_3 = [.2(\$1,500) + .2(\$2,000) + .2(\$3,000) + .2(\$4,000) + .2(\$4,500)]$
$= \$3,000$

Therefore, the expected values for each of the three projects are all the same. It seems that the decision maker who must choose among the three proposals is left in a quandary, realizing that the information used to make a decision is based on probability and that the use of only one number, the expected value, may not lead to the proper decision.

One way out of the quandary is to derive a summary measure that describes the dispersion of the probabilities assigned to the events. The summary measure of the dispersion is called the *standard deviation*, and the formula for the standard deviation of each project is given as

$$S = \sqrt{\sum_{i=1}^{n} (X_i - \overline{X})^2 P_i}$$

where X_i = individual cash flows
$\overline{X}$ = expected value of all cash flows
P_i = probabilities assigned to each cash flow

The standard deviations for the three projects under consideration are given below.

Project 1:

$$S_1 = [.15(\$1,000 - \$3,000)^2 + .20(\$2,000 - \$3,000)^2$$
$$+ .30(\$3,000 - \$3,000)^2 + .20(\$4,000 - \$3,000)^2$$
$$+ .15(\$5,000 - \$3,000)^2]^{1/2} = \$1,265$$

Project 2:

$$S_2 = [.05(\$1,500 - \$3,000)^2 + .20(\$2,000 - \$3,000)^2$$
$$+ .5(\$3,000 - \$3,000)^2 + .20(\$4,000 - \$3,000)^2$$
$$+ .05(\$4,500 - \$3,000)^2]^{1/2} = \$791$$

Project 3:

$$S_3 = [.2(\$1,500 - \$3,000)^2 + .2(\$2,000 - \$3,000)^2$$
$$+ .2(\$3,000 - \$3,000)^2 + .2(\$4,000 - \$3,000)^2$$
$$+ .2(\$4,500 - \$3,000)^2]^{1/2} = \$1,140$$

Since the expected values of the projects were all equal to $3,000, the standard deviation can be considered as a relative measure of risk or uncertainty. Thus, it can be seen that Project 2 is the least risky of the three because it has the lowest standard deviation. Since the cash flows were the same for Project 2 and Project 3, the only differences between these projects were the probabilities assigned to the cash flows. The implication of this situation is that managers must now decide which set of probabilities is closer to a correct estimate of the real state of affairs. Also note that in this example, regardless of which set of probabilities is chosen for Project 2 or Project 3, both projects are less risky than Project 1.

When the expected values of the projects under consideration are not equal, the standard deviation is not an appropriate measure of the risk or uncertainty.

In this new situation the appropriate measure of risk or uncertainty is the coefficient of variation, which is the standard deviation divided by the expected value. The higher the coefficient of variation the more risky is the project. Consider the following new example to illustrate this concept.

A firm is considering three projects with the following data associated with each project:

	PROJECT 1	PROJECT 2	PROJECT 3
Expected value	$3,000	$4,000	$5,000
Standard deviation	600	860	900
Coefficient of variation	.20	.215	.18

Although Project 3 has the greatest standard deviation, it has the lowest coefficient of variation and therefore is considered the least risky of the three projects.

Thus it has been shown that the accountant, through either the standard deviation or the coefficient of variation, is able to supply useful data to the decision maker under conditions of risk or uncertainty. The use of subjective probabilities often enters this area of decision making. While some may rebel at the thought of such practices, the use of subjectivity in the managerial role is really only an attempt to formalize the procedures that managers often use when playing hunches or guessing games. It certainly allows managers to examine the outcomes of their hunches, especially when they are in an "either/ or" situation.

In any event, practically all data, including data generated by generally accepted accounting principles, are subject to uncertainty. Thus, instead of exact numbers, what is left for us to use are estimates as to what really happened in the real-world situation. Uncertainty is a fact of life in the real world, and the accountant should utilize the best estimates available.

PERT AND UNCERTAINTY

The following section concerns another technique used for planning and control of projects. Called PERT (program evaluation and review technique), it is concerned with management planning and control and involves the theory of CPM (critical path method). PERT and CPM were originally used as evaluations of special projects for both the industrial and military sectors of the country.

PERT may be used to schedule a research and development program, minimize production delays, forecast future progress, or coordinate the various parts of the overall job. Our main focus will be upon PERT as an outstanding approach to achieving completion of projects on time. The objectives will be to determine the probability of meeting specified deadlines, to identify the activities which will have the most likely delays, and to study the results of changes in the program.

The following new terms are introduced:

Activity—one step in the production process necessary to complete a project

Event—the stage or location in a production process where an activity will begin and end

Assume, for example, that a company wishes to produce Widgets. The engineering department prepares the following schedule of activities and events necessary to produce Widgets.

PRODUCTION SCHEDULE TO PRODUCE WIDGETS

Activity

A	(Assembling)—setting up various parts for production
B	(Bolting)—bolting together various pieces of raw materials
C	(Cleaning)—cleaning of certain raw materials
D	(Drilling)—drilling holes into parts assembled in Activity A
E	(Enameling)—painting enamel on certain parts bolted together in Activity B
F	(Forging)—forging (shaping) certain sections bolted in Activity B
G	(Grinding)—grinding of certain raw materials cleaned in Activity C and forged parts from Activity F
H	(Hammering)—hammering together certain raw materials cleaned in Activity C to forged parts from Activity F
I	(Integrating)—putting together the various sections received from Activity D, E, and G.

All the above activities must be completed to produce Widgets. Notice that some activities cannot be started until others are completed. For example, Activity D cannot begin until Activity A is completed. Therefore, in scheduling production of a Widget the location (or event) of an activity in the production process is very important. The following schedule depicts activities and events necessary to produce Widgets:

ACTIVITY	PREDECESSOR ACTIVITY	NETWORK REPRESENTATION FOR ACTIVITY	BEGINNING EVENT	ENDING EVENT
A	—	1-2	1	2
B	—	1-3	1	3
C	—	1-4	1	4
D	A	2-5	2	5
E	B	3-5	3	5
F	B	3-4	3	4
G	C,F	4-5	4	5
H	C,F	4-6	4	6
I	D,E,G	5-6	5	6

As can be seen above, the events do not require any work but specify when the activities will begin and end.

It is necessary to develop a graphic representation of the project's activities and events called the PERT *network*. Activities are depicted as arrows → and events are depicted as circles or nodes ○. Remember that all activities preceding another activity must be completed before the next activity occurs. The network for producing Widgets is depicted in Figure 23-1 (page 797).

Once the PERT network has been drawn, the next step is to determine the time necessary to complete each activity. This is especially important when the start of one activity is dependent upon the completion of another activity. The engineering department, together with the production department, must estimate the time necessary to complete an activity. The letters t_e will denote the time necessary to complete an activity.

Because of the uncertainty associated with projects which were never done before, estimated time t_e is **better described** by a probability distribution than by a single estimate. These variable time estimates allow for the fact that we cannot perfectly predict the duration of an activity. We obtain the three estimates (from a beta distribution) as follows:

> a: Optimistic estimate (shortest time)
> m: Most likely estimate
> b: Pessimistic estimate (longest time)

Each estimate is individually weighted, since it is more likely that the project will be completed near the m estimate than near either the a or b estimates. Both a and b are given the same weight in the algebraic formula and m is given a weight of 4. Therefore, we compute the expected elapsed time of an activity using the following *standard* formula:

$$t_e = \frac{a + 4m + b}{6}$$

Consider the following additional information (a,m,b) for the illustration. Using the weighted average formula, we come up with the expected durations t_e for activities A through I as follows:

	CALENDAR WEEKS			
ACTIVITY	a	m	b	t_e
A	14.0	22.0	30.0	22.0 (A)
B	7.0	9.0	17.0	10.0
C	4.0	18.5	30.0	18.0
D	.5	8.0	9.5	7.0
E	10.0	12.0	26.0	14.0
F	10.0	15.0	20.0	15.0
G	8.0	8.5	12.0	9.0
H	8.0	21.0	28.0	20.0
I	5.5	7.0	14.5	8.0

(A) $a = 14$, $m = 22$, and $b = 30$ (weeks),
$$t_e = \frac{14 + 4(22) + 30}{6} = 22 \text{ weeks}$$

Critical Path. It is always desirable to shorten the time required to complete the entire project and thereby lower costs and minimize inefficiencies. Shortening of total time can be accomplished only by shortening the critical path, which is the longest path through the network. A path is a sequence of

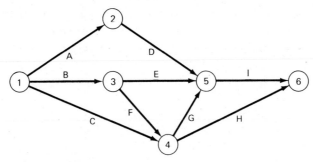

FIGURE 23-1 **PERT Network**

activities (or events) leading from the start event (No. 1) to the end event (No. 6). By the time the longest path is completed all the other paths would have also been completed. The time to complete a path is the sum of the activity durations (Σt_e) along the path. For our network, we have:

PATH	DURATION (WEEKS), Σt_e
A-D-I	22 + 7 + 8 = 37
B-E-I	10 + 14 + 8 = 32
B-F-G-I	10 + 15 + 9 + 8 = 42
B-F-H	10 + 15 + 20 = 45
C-G-I	18 + 9 + 8 = 35
C-H	18 + 20 = 38

The longest path (B-F-H with Σt_e = 45 weeks) determines the overall duration of the project and is called the *critical path*.

Another method available to determine the critical path uses the following new terms:

T_E—the earliest expected time to complete an activity
T_L—the *latest* expected (or allowable) time to complete an activity before delays occur
S—slack time for an activity equals $T_L - T_E$

The earliest expected completion time (T_E) is the earliest "point in time" at which an activity is completed. The term "point in time" is used, since this is different from duration. A point in time is, for example, 7:00 A.M., July 11, 19X9. For our computations we shall use a "clock" which starts at zero when the project begins and is measured in whatever units are used to specify t_e values (days or weeks). The latest allowable time (T_L) is the latest point in time at which an activity can be completed so as not to delay the project beyond its expected completion time. As determined in the path analysis, the T^9 for this problem is 45 weeks. If activity I is completed later than 45 weeks, the project is delayed beyond the expected completion date.

The T_E for each activity is found by adding the t_e of the preceding activities to the t_e for the current activity. Thus the T_E for the previous example is computed as follows:

ACTIVITY t_e	T_E WEEKS
A = 0 + 22 (A)	22
B = 0 + 10 (B)	10
C = 0 + 18 (C)	18
D = 0 + 22 (A) + 7 (D)	29
E = 0 + 10 (B) + 14 (E)	24
F = 0 + 10 (B) + 15 (F)	25
G = 0 + 10 (B) + 15 (F) + 9 (G)	34
H = 0 + 10 (B) + 15 (F) + 20 (H)	45
I = 0 + 10 (B) + 15 (F) + 8 (I)	42

Note that T_E for activities G, H, and I is the time it takes the longest series of activities to reach that activity. In other words, T_E for each activity is found by examining all the activities terminating at that activity and taking the largest T_E value of those activities. The largest value is used since the current activity cannot occur until all the activities terminating at that point are completed. For example, the T_E to reach activity G or H is the larger of the T_E for activity C (18 weeks) or the T_E for activity F (25 weeks); therefore the T_E to reach activities G and H is 25 weeks.

The T_L for each activity requires working backward. For example, if activity I can be completed no later than T_L = 45 weeks (critical path) then the T_L for activities D, E, and G (activities that must be completed before activity I begins) is 37 weeks (45 less $8t_e$ for activity I). The T_L for the remaining activities are computed as follows:

ACTIVITY	T_L	COMPUTATIONS
A	30	45 − [7 (t_eD) + 8 (t_eI)]
B	10	45 − [15 (t_eF) + 20 (t_eH)]
C	25	45 − 20 (t_eH)
F	25	45 − 20 (t_eH)
H	45	

Note that in computing the T_L for activities B, C, and F that the *longest* path to completion after the activity must be deducted from the critical path.

FIGURE 23-2 The PERT Chart

Activity	t_e	T_E	T_L	S
A	22	22	30	8
B	10	10	10	0 *
C	18	18	25	7
D	7	29	37	8
E	14	24	37	13
F	15	25	25	0 *
G	9	34	37	3
H	20	45	45	0 *
I	8	42	45	3

*Critical activities that make up the critical path

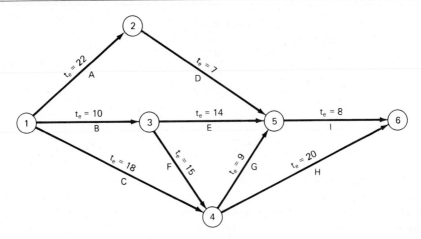

FIGURE 23-3   **PERT Network**

Slack time (S) for an activity equals $T_L - T_E$ (the latest allowable time less the earliest expected completion time). This is the amount of time that the activity completion or occurrence may be delayed and still not delay the project completion beyond the expected point in time of 45 weeks. The critical path may be found as those activities with zero slack (B, F, and H) which will join those events (events 1, 3, 4, and 6). Any delay along the critical path B-F-H will delay the project completion beyond the expected date of 45 weeks. Figures 23-2 and 23-3 present a completed PERT chart and network for the example given.

PERT is not a stagnant method of evaluating projects but must be revised for each change in resources, for every relaxation of technical specification, and for any change in the arrangement of activities. Standard deviation could also be used to allow for the fact that an activity may take longer or shorter to complete than its expected time. In essence, PERT as well as any evaluation method must be continually reexamined and replanned in order to achieve the best performance in light of changing conditions and newly introduced factors.

INVENTORY STOCKOUTS AND UNCERTAINTY

The basic concepts behind the computation of safety stock were discussed in the previous chapter. This section will present two decision theory methods that utilize statistical probabilities to calculate the optimum safety stock size for the company's inventory. Probability is a useful means of preventing stockout and minimizing unnecessary costs. One method develops a probability distribution for various levels of inventory usage and compares these usage levels to normal usage. The safety stock amount with the least costs involved

TABLE 23-2
TOTAL USAGE AND PROBABILITY OF STOCKOUT
(3-WEEK PERIOD)

Total actual usage	150	175	200	225*	250	275	300
Probability of stockout ..	.25	.10	.15	.45	.15	.10	.025

*Normal usage.

is considered the optimal safety stock level. Another method utilizes past performance with estimated performance to obtain standard deviations and average variances. This information is combined with the desired probability, chosen by management, to arrive at the best level of safety stock. Both methods in this section strive for more accurate and economical levels of safety stock needed to prevent stockouts in the future. The following will demonstrate how probability, standard deviation, and average variance are helpful tools for inventory budgeting and control.

First Method. The probability that an event will happen is an estimate of the "chance" that something will happen. It is easily calculated by dividing "the number of favorable outcomes desired" by the "total number of possible outcomes."

$$P = \frac{\text{number of favorable outcomes desired}}{\text{number of possible outcomes}}$$

Statistical probabilities can be assigned to different levels of total inventory usage. An illustration is shown in Table 23-2.

The probability of having a stockout using different levels of safety stock can be calculated. Stockouts will occur when total usage exceeds what is considered normal usage. Assume normal usage for this period to be 225 units. Thus the total usage figures that exceed the normal (225 units) are used to calculate stockouts in terms of units. This can be seen in Tables 23-3 and 23-4.

In this illustration, safety stock of 50 units should be maintained because it produces the lowest total cost of $11.94.

A difficulty in the first method is the determination of stockout costs. While the loss in sales revenue from stockouts is usually simple to estimate, the loss

TABLE 23-3
STOCKOUT IN TERMS OF UNITS

	USAGE ABOVE 225 UNITS		
Probability	.15	.10	.025
Total actual usage	250	275	300
Less normal usage	225	225	225
Excess usage	25	50	75
Stockout if safety stock is:			
0 units	25 (25 − 0)	50 (50 − 0)	75 (75 − 0)
25 units	0 (25 − 25)	25 (50 − 25)	50 (75 − 25)
50 units	0	0 (50 − 50)	25 (75 − 50)
75 units	0	0	0 (75 − 75)

TABLE 23-4
STOCKOUT IN TERMS OF UNITS AND COST

SAFETY STOCK LEVEL IN UNITS	NO. OF ORDERS PER YEAR*	PROBA- BILITY OF STOCKOUT	STOCKOUTS IN UNITS	STOCKOUT COST†	EXPECTED STOCKOUT COSTS‡	CARRYING COSTS§	TOTAL COSTS
0	7.75	.150	25	$10	$11.63		
0	7.75	.100	50	20	15.50		
0	7.75	.025	75	30	5.81		
					$32.94	$ 0	$32.94
25	7.75	.100	25	$10	$ 7.75		
25	7.75	.025	50	20	3.88		
					$11.63	$ 5	$16.63
50	7.75	.025	25	$10	$ 1.94	$10	$11.94
75	7.75	0	0	0	0	$15	$15.00

*Annual requirement ÷ EOQ

3,000 ÷ 387 = 7.75 orders per year

†Assume a stockout cost of $.40 per unit. Stockout in units × $.40.

‡Number of orders per year × probability × stockout cost.

§Safety stock × carrying costs per unit per year. Assume carrying costs of $.20 per unit, per year.

of goodwill caused by not having enough inventory is very difficult to measure in dollar amounts. An alternative to the first method is to base safety stock on a desired probability rather than on cost. For example, the manager may decide to have only a .025% probability of suffering a stockout and so will carry a safety stock level of 50 units.

Other statistical methods can be used to calculate the safety stock amount. An advantage of using statistical procedures is their allowance for reasonable protection against a stockout at a lower cost.

Second Method. Below is an illustration of a statistical method which uses standard deviation as a means of determining the level of safety stock that will ensure against a stockout at different percentages of assurance. Standard deviation is a measure of the distance from the mean (or average) of the population (total number of items being tested).

Step 1. The previous months' estimated usage values are compared with their actual usage values. The individual differences are calculated and totaled (Table 23-5).

Step 2. An additional column shows the results of squaring the individual differences. The squares are totaled:

	4
January	25
February	100
March	64
April	49
May	25
June	361
	624

Step 3. The first step in calculating the standard deviation is to take the total of the squared difference (column 4) and reduce it by the result of taking the

TABLE 23-5
ACTUAL COMPARED WITH ESTIMATED USAGE

	1	2	3
			DIFFER-ENCE
	ESTIMATED USAGE	ACTUAL USAGE	ESTIMATED ACTUAL
January	225	230	− 5
February	210	200	+10
March	245	253	− 8
April	208	215	− 7
May	235	230	+ 5
June	220	239	−19
			−24

square of the sum of individual differences (column 3) divided by the number of time periods (6 months):

$$624 - \frac{(-24)^2}{6} = 624 - \frac{576}{6}$$
$$= 624 - 96$$
$$= \underline{528}$$

Step 4. The *standard deviation* is now computed by taking the result in step 3 and dividing it by the number of time periods (6 months) minus 1 and then taking the square root of that calculation:

$$\sqrt{\frac{528}{6-1}} = \sqrt{\frac{528}{5}} = \sqrt{105.6}$$

Standard deviation = $\underline{10.28}$

Step 5. Once the standard deviation is determined, the next procedure is to calculate the *average variance* between estimated usage and actual usage. Since the total difference has already been determined in step 1, all that is needed is to divide the total difference (column 3) by the number of time periods (6 months):

$$\text{Average variance} = \frac{-24}{6} = \underline{-4}$$

Step 6. If a stockout is to be avoided 97.5% of the time, the following formula is used to calculate the necessary safety stock:

(2 × standard deviation) − average variance = safety stock

In the example, it would be

$$2 \times 10.28 - (-4) = 24.56 = 25 \text{ units}$$

Because the average variance is a negative figure, which indicates that on the average the actual usage is greater than was estimated, the safety stock is increased by the above figure. A positive average variance will decrease the amount of safety stock needed. The example assumes a 1-month lead time. If the period is different, the following formula should be used to calculate safety stock:

$$\text{Safety stock} = \left(2 \times \text{standard deviation} \times \sqrt{\substack{\text{number of lead time measures} \\ \text{(days, months, etc.)}}} \right)$$

$$- \left(\substack{\text{average} \\ \text{variance}} \times \substack{\text{number of lead} \\ \text{time measures}} \right)$$

For example, if lead time was 4 months,

$$\text{Safety stock} = (2 \times 10.28 \times \sqrt{4}) - (-4 \times 4)$$
$$= 41.12 + 16$$
$$= \underline{\underline{57 \text{ units}}}$$

Step 7. If a 99.5% assurance against a stockout is desired, the formula for safety stock would be

$$(3 \times \text{standard deviation}) - \text{average variance} = \text{safety stock}$$

Using the data from our previous example,

$$3 \times 10.28 - (-4) = 34.84 = 35 \text{ units}$$

In order to use the above formula, the lead time units and the units used in computing the standard deviation must be the same (e.g., days, weeks, months).

EXPECTED VALUE OF PROFIT AND UTILITY

In most accounting and business situations, the most common concept used in decision making under uncertainty is the expected value of the various alternatives measured in monetary units. There are cases where pure monetary value will not be the prime consideration. The actions of firms and managers may be psychological rather than purely monetary.

For example, consider the case where two people have the opportunity to start a new firm. The incorporation fees, inventory, leases, and all other associated costs come to $5,000. There is a slightly better than even chance that the firm will succeed, 60-40. If it does succeed, the realizable profit after all costs will be $12,500. The relative monetary consequences of starting the firm are presented as follows:

	EVENT	
	SUCCESS	FAILURE
Probability	.6	.4
Action:		
Start the firm	$12,500	−$5,000
Do not start	0	0

$\overline{X}$(Start the firm) = .6($12,500) + .4(−$5,000) = $5,500
$\overline{X}$(do not start) = 0

Because of different psychological assessments, the two people may have completely different attitudes toward the proposal. The decision to be made is whether it is worth a 40% risk of losing $5,000 to gain a 60% chance of making $12,500. The decision between the two individuals may depend upon whether one has ample capital and the other does not. It may depend on security needs of being employed by an established firm. In any event, the decision will ultimately depend on either individual's personal preference.

This expression of personal preference is referred to as an "expected utility value." For example, after the accumulation of a certain amount of dollars, the expected utility value of a dollar may only be $0.50. In other words, the risks involved with the dollar may make it worth only half its monetary value. This is surely one expression of personal preference and as such will vary highly among individuals. In such cases expected monetary value is not valid for decision making. The expected utility value must then be used to establish the decision-making criteria.

Accountants have not, in general, incorporated utility into their practices but rather have used expected monetary value as their decision standard. When expected utility values are considered, the attempt to optimize expected utility as opposed to expected monetary value will incorporate the trade-offs between the person's perception of risk and returns.

UNCERTAINTY, RISK, AND THE ACCOUNTANT

In the past, writers attempted to make a great distinction between the terms "risk" and "uncertainty." Generally, the debate centered around the ability to assign the set of probabilities to the events discussed in this chapter. Some probabilities were known with a high degree of accuracy, while others were not known at all.

The term "risk" was reserved for the situation where the decision maker knew the probabilities with a high degree of certainty or even with absolute certainty. Firms may be able to assign highly accurate probabilities to events (such as the percentage of defective parts based on the production records from several thousands of those parts).

The term "uncertainty" was reserved for the situation where decision makers had no information from mathematical probability or from data based on their production records. In this case, the person responsible for making the decision must use subjective probabilities. A subjective probability is one that is assigned to an event when there is no prior evidence about the likelihood of the occurrence of that event. The probability is subjective also because persons assessing the event may not agree as to what the actual probability is.

If one were to attempt precise definitions for the terms "risk" and "uncertainty," it is likely that no decisions would ever be made. In today's business world the terms are used interchangeably. However, when you use the terms synonymously, you should be prepared to make some statement as to how confident you are of the probabilities you use. One approach to the problem of having no evidence on which to base the probabilities is to use a range of numbers instead of one number. This approach may gain consensus among the decision makers while still allowing individual differences within that range.

CHAPTER REVIEW

This chapter has presented some of the basic concepts of decision making under risk and uncertainty. In the complex world in which we live today, the accountant should be aware of all the elements of the decision process. With uncertainty and risk occurring in the real world, the accountant must constantly be aware of ever-changing probabilities and the outcomes that occur as a result.

More and more use is being made of decision theory because it forces the decision maker to replace the guesses, hunches, and intuition of the past with well-designed and more objective approaches to decision making. Decision theory causes the accountant to almost demand that managers be more explicit in the output they need. This reveals what data will be necessary to collect, what decision model to use to evaluate the data, and how much information must be presented so that the decision will be made in a rational manner.

Concepts such as expected value, standard deviation, coefficient of variation, and utility are important to the manager and to the accountant. Both groups should be on guard to protect against the situation where they rely on the preciseness of these numbers. The numbers are only estimates, and a completely different set may be derived by a different person. Even the data available at any point in time is subject to uncertainty. However, the proper understanding, interpretation, and implementation of the concepts presented in this chapter will help the accountant to cope with the uncertainty that prevails in the real world.

REFERENCES

Bierman, Harold, Charles Bonini, and Warren Hausman: *Quantitative Analysis for Business Decisions*, Richard D. Irwin, Homewood, Ill., 1977, chapters 4–10, 17–19.

Budnick, Frank, Richard Mojena, and Thomas Vollmann: *Principles of Operations Research for Management*, Richard D. Irwin, Homewood, Ill., 1977, chapters 11, 17, 18.

Levin, Richard I.: *Statistics for Management*, Prentice-Hall, Englewood Cliffs, N.J., 1978.

Levin, R. I., and C. A. Kirkpatrick: *Quantitative Approaches to Management*, McGraw-Hill, New York, 1978.

GLOSSARY

Activity—one step in the production process necessary to complete a project.

Coefficient of Variation—a relative measure of risk relating the standard deviation to the expected value.

CPM (Critical Path Method)— PERT utilizes CPM theory to evaluate special projects for management planning and control.

Critical Path—longest path in the PERT network; determines the overall duration of the project.

Decision Model—a formal model, usually mathematical, that explains the consequences of various alternatives.

Decision Theory—a body of knowledge that allows the evaluation of different courses of action when these actions can be measured.

Decision Variables—completely defined and mutually exclusive actions which are available to the decision maker for making decisions.

Earliest Expected Completion Time—earliest "point in time" at which an activity is completed and an event occurs in the PERT network.

EVAI (Expected Value of Additional Information)—the top dollar the firm is willing to pay for additional information at the time when the decision is to be made.

Event—the stage or location in a production process where an activity will begin and end.

EVPI (Expected Value of Perfect Information)—top price the decision maker should be willing to pay for having perfect demand information in advance.

Expected Value—the arithmetic mean of a probability distribution.

Latest Allowable Time—latest "point in time" in the PERT network at which an activity can be completed or an event occur so as not to delay the project beyond its expected completion time.

Mathematical Probability—estimate of the "chance" that something will occur; derived from mathematical proofs and statistical studies.

Payoff—positive or negative monetary reward derived from a decision variable.

PERT (Program Evaluation and Review Technique)—technique used for planning and control of special projects. One main objective of PERT is to achieve completion of projects on time.

PERT Network—graphic representation of the project's activities and events using PERT theory.

Quantifiable Objective—an objective that will maximize or minimize a particular monetary value.

Slack Time—amount of time that the activity completion or event occurrence may be delayed and still not delay the project completion beyond the expected point in time.

Standard Deviation—measure of the dispersion of individual observations about the mean (or average) of the population (number of items under study).

Subjective Probabilities—probabilities that depend on the best judgment or intuition of the decision maker.

Uncertainty and Risk—terms used to describe events that are controlled by probabilities.

Uncontrollable Variables—completely defined and mutually exclusive states of nature or events which must be considered in the decision-making process.

Utility—a personal preference measure used as a substitute for monetary value in uncertain situations.

SUMMARY PROBLEMS

PROBLEM 1

A firm has surveyed the quantity sold of its product for 100 days. The results are as follows:

DAILY UNITS SOLD	NUMBER OF SALE DAYS
30	15
40	20
50	30
60	30
70	5
	100

REQUIRED:

Construct a probability distribution reflecting the probability that each number will be sold.

PROBLEM 2

A firm is considering two investment projects. It has capital available to do only one project.

PROJECT 1		PROJECT 2	
PROBA-BILITY	CASH FLOW	PROBA-BILITY	CASH FLOW
.15	$ 2,000	.05	$3,000
.20	4,000	.20	4,000
.30	6,000	.50	6,000
.20	8,000	.20	8,000
.15	10,000	.05	9,000

REQUIRED:

Given the above data, which project would you recommend to management?

PROBLEM 3

Another firm is considering two projects. The firm faces the same capital constraints as the firm in Problem 2. The results from Project 1 are

$$\overline{X} = 2,700$$
$$S = 1,005$$
$$C_v = .372$$

REQUIRED:

What would you recommend given the following data for Project 2:

PROBABILITY	CASH FLOW
.10	$1,500
.40	2,000
.40	2,000
.10	4,500

PROBLEM 4

Cosmo Corporation estimates its total usage and probability of stockout for a 5-week period as follows:

	5-WEEK PERIOD						
Total usage	125	150	175	200	225	250	300
Probability of stockout ..	.10	.15	.20	.35	.20	.15	.10

REQUIRED:

Calculate the probability of having a stockout at different levels of safety stock. Assume a stockout cost of $.30 per unit, expected usage of 220, annual requirement of 2,000, EOQ of 250, and carrying cost per unit of $.30.

SOLUTIONS TO SUMMARY PROBLEMS

PROBLEM 1

NUMBER SOLD	PROBABILITY THAT EACH NUMBER WILL BE SOLD
30	.15
40	.20
50	.30
60	.30
70	.05
	1.00

PROBLEM 2

Compute the expected value of both projects:

$$\bar{X}_1 = [.15(\$2,000) + .20(\$4,000) + .30(\$6,000) + .20(\$8,000) + .15(\$10,000)] = \$6,000$$
$$\bar{X}_2 = [.05(\$3,000) + .20(\$4,000) + .50(\$6,000) + .20(\$8,000) + .05(\$9,000)] = \$6,000$$

Since the means are equal, compute the standard deviation on both projects.

$$S_1 = [(\$2,000 - \$6,000)^2 .15 + (\$4,000 - \$6,000)^2 .20 + (\$6,000 - \$6,000)^2 .3$$
$$+ (\$8,000 - \$6,000)^2 .20 + (\$10,000 - \$6,000)^2 .15]^{1/2} = \$2,530$$
$$S_2 = [(\$3,000 - \$6,000)^2 .05 + (\$4,000 - \$6,000)^2 .20 + (\$6,000 - \$6,000)^2 .5$$
$$+ (\$8,000 - \$6,000)^2 .20 + (\$9,000 - \$6,000)^2 .05]^{1/2} = \$1,581$$

$$S_1 = \$2,530$$
$$S_2 = \$1,581$$

Since the means are equal, the standard deviation can be used as a measure of risk; therefore, choose Project 2 over Project 1.

PROBLEM 3

Compute expected value, standard deviation, and coefficient of variation.

$$\overline{X} = [.1(1,500) + .4(2,000) + .4(2,000) + .1(1,500)] = \$2,200$$

$$S = [.1(1,500 - 2,200)^2 + .4(2,000 - 2,200)^2 + .4(2,000 - 2,200)^2$$
$$+ .1(4,500 - 2,200)^2]^{\frac{1}{2}} = \$781$$

$$C_V = \frac{781}{2,200} = .355$$

In this case choose Project 2 because of the lower coefficient of variation.

PROBLEM 4

Probability	.20	.15	.10
Total actual usage	225	250	300
Less expected usage	220	220	220
Excess usage	5	30	80

Stockout if safety stock is:				
0 units	5	(5 − 0)	30 (30 − 0)	80 (80 − 0)
5 units	0	(5 − 5)	25 (30 − 5)	75 (80 − 5)
30 units	0		0 (30 − 30)	50 (80 − 30)
80 units	0		0	0 (80 − 80)

STOCKOUT IN TERMS OF UNITS AND COST

SAFETY STOCK LEVEL IN UNITS	NO. OF ORDERS PER YEAR*	PROBA-BILITY OF STOCKOUT	STOCKOUT IN UNITS	STOCKOUT COST	EXPECTED STOCKOUT COST†	CARRYING COSTS‡	TOTAL COSTS
0	8	.20	5	$ 1.50	$ 2.40		
0	8	.15	30	9.00	10.80		
0	8	.10	80	24.00	19.20		
					$32.40	$ 0	$32.40
5	8	.15	25	7.50	$ 9.00		
5	8	.10	75	22.50	18.00		
					$27.00	$ 1.50	$28.50
30	8	.10	50	15.00	$12.00	$ 9.00	$21.00
80	8	0	0	0	0	$24.00	$24.00

*Annual requirement
 EOQ

†Number of orders per year × probability × stockout cost.
‡Safety stock × carrying costs per unit per year.

QUESTIONS

1 What are the five elements contained in the decision theory model? How does the decision theory model differ from the linear programming model?

2 What is the mathematical equation for the expected value of the profit with perfect information? Describe the concepts that pertain to the expected value of additional information.

3 What is the measure of risk for comparing projects with the same expected value? What is the measure of risk for comparing projects with different expected values? Explain the relationship between these measures and the amounts of risk involved.

4 Discuss the role of subjective probabilities as they are used in the area of decision making.

5 List four uses of PERT. What are the objectives associated with achieving completion of projects on time?

6 How is an event related to an activity? Do all activities begin at once? Explain.

7 What role does CPM play in the theory of PERT? How is the "latest allowable time" related to CPM?

8 Why is probability used in developing the PERT network? Describe the algebraic formula used for computing the expected elapsed time.

9 How is "slack time" related to the "latest allowable time," the "earliest expected completion time," and the "critical path"? Give a complete explanation.

10 What are the advantages and disadvantages of using statistical probabilities for determining the safety stock amount? In the statistical methods that utilize standard deviation as a means of determining the safety stock, what is the relationship between the average variance and the amount of safety stock?

11 Describe situations in which utility, as opposed to expected monetary value, is a prime consideration for making decisions.

12 How do the meanings of risk and uncertainty differ?

13 Answer true or false for the following statements:

a A payoff is the maximum or minimum monetary value of the decision theory method.

b In the PERT network, an event must be completed before the activity occurs.

c Shortening of total time can be accomplished by shortening the latest allowable time of the PERT network.

d The probability of an event is calculated by dividing "the number of possible outcomes" by "the number of favorable outcomes."

e To reduce the amount of risk involved in decision making, the firm utilizes subjective probabilities.

EXERCISES

EXERCISE 1

Expected Value

The VYZ Corp. must choose between two projects with the following information:

PROJECT 1		PROJECT 2	
PROBA-BILITY	CASH FLOW	PROBA-BILITY	CASH FLOW
.10	$1,500	.15	$1,500
.25	2,000	.20	2,000
.40	2,500	.35	3,000
.25	4,000	.30	3,500

REQUIRED:

Given the above data, compute the expected value of each project. Which project would you recommend to the management?

EXERCISE 2

Expected Value

The local florist sells carnations in bunches of six. The following costs are related to one flower:

Fertilizer	$.15
Utilities	.50
Miscellaneous	.10

Selling price of each bunch is $7.50. If the flowers are not sold at the end of each day, they are sent to the local hospital.

The probability of selling the following number of bunches was determined to be

NUMBER	PROBABILITY
0	.03
1	.05
2	.08
3	.12
4	.15
5	.20
6	.17
7	.10
8	.08
9	.02

REQUIRED:

Determine the expected profit under perfect information.

EXERCISE 3

PERT Network

ACTIVITY	DAYS			PREDECESSOR ACTIVITIES
	a	m	b	
Cutting	40	45	50	
Assembling	38	39	42	Cutting
Welding	32	36	40	Assembling
Painting	27	30	33	Cutting
Polishing	42	48	50	Welding
Sorting	24	26	30	Painting
Finishing	36	37	38	Polishing, sorting

REQUIRED:

a Prepare an illustration of the PERT network. Include the following in the illustration:
  1 Expected completion time of activity t_e.
  2 Earliest expected completion time for event T_e.
  3 Latest allowable time for event T_L.
b From the above solution, determine the critical path.

EXERCISE 4

PERT

TYPE OF ACTIVITY	PREDECESSOR ACTIVITY	t_e (DAYS)
A	—	40
B	A	36
C	A	24
D	B	48
E	B	54
F	C	30
G	D	33
H	D	25
I	E, F	32
J	G	27
K	H	21
L	I, J, K	38

REQUIRED:

a Draw a representation of the PERT network, identifying the expected duration of each activity.
b Prepare a schedule for the PERT network showing T_E, T_L, and S.

EXERCISE 5

PERT Network

The Neil Corp. has a contract with a large aircraft company and has five tasks to perform before the contract will be completed. The following information was collected by Neil:

ACTIVITY	TIME ESTIMATES (WEEKS)		
	OPTIMISTIC	MOST LIKELY	PESSIMISTIC
Processing	4	6	9
Welding	3	5	6
Reinforcement	5	6	7
Assembling	7	9	11
Finishing	9	10	12

The predecessor activity for welding and reinforcement is processing, and the predecessor activity for assembling is welding. The predecessor activities for finishing are assembling and reinforcement.

REQUIRED:

Prepare an illustration of the PERT cost network showing the critical path.

EXERCISE 6

PERT Network

The S. Rose Construction Company has contracted to complete a new building and has asked for assistance in analyzing the project. Using the program evaluation review technique (PERT), the following network has been developed:

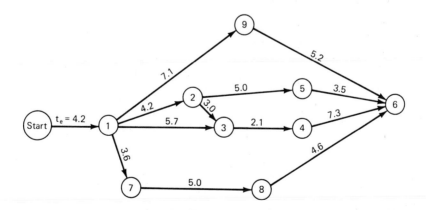

The numbers above the paths represent expected completion times for the activities (measured in days).

REQUIRED:

Select the best multiple choice answer for the following statements:
a The critical path is
1   1-2-5-6
2   1-2-3-4-6
3   1-3-4-6
4   1-7-8-6
5   1-9-6

b Slack time on path 1-9-6 is
1   4.3 days
2   2.8 days
3   .9 day
4   .4 day
5   0 days

c The latest time for reaching event 6 via path 1-2-5-6 is
1   20.8
2   19.3
3   17.4
4   16.5
5   12.7

d The earliest time for reaching event 6 via path 1-2-5-6 is
1   20.8
2   16.9
3   16.5
4   12.7
5   3.5

e If all other paths are operating on schedule but path segment 7-8 has an unfavorable time variance of 1.9,
1   The critical path will be shortened.
2   The critical path will be eliminated.
3   The critical path will be unaffected.
4   Another path will become the critical path.
5   The critical path will have an increased time of 1.9.

(AICPA Adapted)

EXERCISE 7

Safety Stock and Order Point

Jones Manufacturing Company operates in a very competitive market. Management believes that a raw materials stockout would greatly affect their production schedule and sales. Mr. Jones would like to be 99.5 % assured against a stockout. His cost accountant supplied him with the following schedule:

JONES MANUFACTURING COMPANY
RAW MATERIALS USAGE SCHEDULE
FOR THE PERIOD JANUARY–JULY 19X8

	ESTIMATED	ACTUAL
January	200	205
February	200	190
March	210	200
April	225	205
May	200	195
June	215	220
July	185	200
	1,435	1,415

Lead time is 1 month.
Average estimated monthly usage rate = 205.

REQUIRED:

a Calculate the safety stock using the statistical method.
b Calculate the order point.

EXERCISE 8

Safety Stock—Statistical Probabilities

According to McAuley Enterprises, excess usages of 130, 590, and 1,050 units, above the normal usage for a 2-week period, are given 21%, 9.5%, and 2.7% chances of stockout, respectively. The carrying cost for one unit is $2.65, and analysts have calculated stockouts to cost $3.12 per unit. To meet the annual requirement using EOQ, there are six purchases made a year.

REQUIRED:

Determine which level of safety stock should be chosen as the most economical quantity to carry: 0, 130, 590, or 1,050 units.

EXERCISE 9

Safety Stock—Standard Deviations

Standard deviations are utilized by the Jeff Lerman Paper Co. in order to calculate the level of safety stock that is necessary for a 97.5% chance of avoiding stockouts.

The company collected data for 5 weeks and organized it into the following chart:

	WEEKS				
	1	2	3	4	5
Estimated usage (units)	300	286	305	356	301
Actual usage (units)	274	308	315	326	341
Difference (units)	26	−22	−10	30	−40

REQUIRED:

Calculate the level of safety stock desired by the Jeff Lerman Co. if the lead time is 1 month.

EXERCISE 10

PERT

The Dryfus Company specializes in large construction projects. The company management regularly employs the Program Evaluation and Review Technique (PERT) in planning and coordinating its construction projects. The following schedule of separable activities and their expected completion times have been developed for an office building which is to be constructed by Dryfus Company.

ACTIVITY DESCRIPTION	PREDECESSOR ACTIVITY	EXPECTED ACTIVITY COMPLETION TIME (IN WEEKS)
a Excavation	—	2
b Foundation	a	3
c Underground utilities	a	7
d Rough plumbing	b	4
e Framing	b	5
f Roofing	e	3
g Electrical work	f	3
h Interior walls	d,g	4
i Finish plumbing	h	2
j Exterior finishing	f	6
k Landscaping	c,i,j	2

REQUIRED:

a Identify the critical path for this project and determine the expected project completion time in weeks.

b Briefly discuss how the "expected activity completion times" are derived in the PERT method and what the derived value for the expected activity completion time means in the PERT method

(CMA Adapted)

PROBLEMS

PROBLEM 1

Payoff Tables

The Rifkan Rifraf Corporation purchases a highly perishable product on a daily basis at a unit cost of $30. If each product was not sold for $50 and was left over at the end of the day, it would be discarded since it has no salvage value. Because of the occasional and infrequent need for this product, the demand each day never exceeds four units. Andy Rifkan, the purchasing manager, has made a study of the product's demand situation and has determined the following:

DEMAND (UNITS)	PROBABILITY OF DEMAND
0	.05
1	.20
2	.30
3	.25
4	.20

REQUIRED:

a Determine the optimal strategy to yield the highest expected payoff under uncertainty utilizing a payoff table.

b Determine the expected value of perfect information (EVPI).

PROBLEM 2

The Payoff Table

The M & O supermarket has five products; A, B, C, D, and E, which must be sold within 5 days from their arrival date. These products are normally purchased in one combined order from the Bev. Manufacturing Corp. If any of the products are not sold, they will either be discarded or returned to the manufacturer. The following data was collected by the M & O supermarket:

DEMAND PATTERNS

PRODUCTS A AND B		PRODUCTS C AND D		PRODUCT E	
DEMAND	PROBABILITY OF DEMAND	DEMAND	PROBABILITY OF DEMAND	DEMAND	PROBABILITY OF DEMAND
0 units	.05	0 units	.08	0 units	.03
1	.15	1	.12	1	.19
2	.25	2	.20	2	.18
3	.20	3	.30	3	.25
4	.25	4	.15	4	.15
5	.10	5	.15	5	.20

Additional data:

PRODUCT	SALES PRICE PER UNIT	PURCHASE PRICE PER UNIT	SALVAGE VALUE PER UNIT
A	$3.60	$1.70	
B	5.20	3.65	$1.75
C	4.85	3.00	.90
D	2.55	1.40	.65
E	3.95	1.85	

REQUIRED:

a Determine the optimal strategy under uncertainty for the purchase of these five products utilizing a payoff table.

b What would be the expected value of the profit under perfect conditions?

c Calculate the EVPI for this problem.

PROBLEM 3

Expected Value

Vernon Enterprises designs and manufactures toys. Past experience indicates that the product life cycle of a toy is 3 years. Promotional advertising produces large sales in the early years, but there is a substantial sales decline in the final year of a toy's life.

Consumer demand for new toys placed on the market tends to fall into three classes. About 30% of the new toys sell well above expectations, 60% sell as anticipated, and 10% have poor consumer acceptance.

A new toy has been developed. The following sales projections are made by carefully evaluating consumer demand for the new toy:

CONSUMER DEMAND FOR NEW TOY	CHANCE OF OCCURRING	ESTIMATED SALES IN
		YEAR 1
Above average	30%	$1,200,000
Average	60	700,000
Below average	10	200,000
		YEAR 2
Above average	30%	$2,500,000
Average	60	1,700,000
Below average	10	900,000
		YEAR 3
Above average	30%	$ 600,000
Average	60	400,000
Below average	10	150,000

Variable costs are estimated at 30% of selling price. Special machinery must be purchased at a cost of $860,000 and will be installed in an unused portion of the factory which Vernon has unsuccessfully been trying to rent to someone for several years at $50,000 per year; they have no prospects for future utilization.

Fixed expenses (excluding depreciation) of a cash flow nature are estimated at $50,000 per year on the new toy. The new machinery will be depreciated by the sum-of-the-years'-digits method with an estimated salvage value of $110,000 and will be sold at the beginning of the fourth year. Advertising and promotional expenses will be incurred uniformly and will total $100,000 the first year, $150,000 the second year, and $50,000 the third year. These expenses will be deducted as incurred for income tax reporting.

Vernon believes that state and federal income taxes will total 60% of income in the foreseeable future and may be assumed to be paid uniformly over the year income is earned.

REQUIRED:

a Prepare a schedule computing the probable sales of this new toy in each of the 3 years, taking into account the probability of above average sales occurring.

b Assume that the probable sales computed in part **a** are $900,000 in the first year, $1,800,000 in the second year, and $410,000 in the third year. Prepare a schedule computing the probable net income for the new toy in each of the 3 years of life.

c Prepare a schedule for net cash flows from sales of the new toy for each of the years involved and from disposition of the machinery purchased. Use sales data given in **b**.

(AICPA Adapted)

PROBLEM 4

PERT

ACTIVITY	ACTIVITY REPRESENTATIONS	WEEKS a	m	b
A	1-2	2	3	5
B	1-3	4	6	7
D	2-3	3	5	8
G	3-7	8	9	10
C	1-4	6	7	8
F	3-5	2	4	6
H	4-5	5	6	7
E	2-6	7	8	10
J	6-7	1	2	4
I	5-8	5	6	7
K	7-8	3	4	7

REQUIRED:

a Draw a representation of the PERT network, identifying the expected completion with each path.

b Identity the critical path and the time necessary to complete it.

c Identify the predecessor activities for each activity.

PROBLEM 5

PERT

Show Glow, Inc., has signed a contract with the More Poor Corp. to design an apartment complex and construct the buildings within. The following data was collected by the engineers:

ACTIVITY	PREDECESSOR ACTIVITY	DURATION (WEEKS)	COST PER WEEK
A	—	9	$ 1,500
B	—	8	1,400
C	A	11	2,100
D	A	4	1,050
E	B, D	7	3,000
F	B, D	13	5,500
G	C, E	7	2,750
H	C, E	2	9,000
I	F	12	5,000
J	F	3	1,750
K	H, I	5	900
L	H, I	6	2,000
M	G, K	12	4,450
N	G, K	1	10,330
O	J	4	850
P	M	14	1,050
Q	L, N, O	10	7,050

Assume activities A and B begin at the same event and activities P and Q are completed at the same event.

REQUIRED:

a Develop the PERT network. Include the duration of each activity in your diagram.
b Determine the following:
 1 The earliest expected completion time for each event.
 2 The latest allowable time for each event.
 3 The slack time for each event.
c Determine the total cost of completing the critical path.

PROBLEM 6

Safety Stock

The Chipper Manufacturing Company normally requires 600 chippers during 1½ weeks of lead time. Looking back at past records, the following data was assembled in order to determine the level of safety stock desired:

USAGE DURING LEAD TIME	NUMBER OF TIMES THE QUANTITIES WERE USED
480	5
520	11
560	18
600	98
640	21
680	10
720	7

The chippers were ordered 650 in each batch and were carried at a cost of $15 per chipper. The cost of being out of one chipper usually approximated $8.

REQUIRED:

Since management strives to minimize costs, determine the best safety stock to carry. Using the past records, calculate the level which will safeguard against stockouts and losses.

PROBLEM 7

Stockouts and Statistical Probabilities

Dunn Cousins, Inc., sells premium beer to grocery stores throughout Long Island. Management uses the economic order quantity formula when it calculates the optimum number of bushels of barley to order. They gathered the following information in order to determine the best possible level of safety stock to carry:

Cost of a bushel of barley	$3.00
Annual cost of carrying one bushel of barley	$1.65
Annual requirement for barley	5,200 bushels
Inventory order point......................................	330 bushels
EOQ	400 bushels
Cost of being out of stock	$2.25 per bushel

Total usage over a 2-week period is expected to be:

Total usage (bushels)	200	240	280	320	360	400	440
Probability of stockout	.05	.12	.18	.30	.18	.12	.05

REQUIRED:

a   Use statistical probabilities to calculate the safety stock which will incur the least costs.

b   Management wants only a 5% chance of having a stockout; what level should the safety stock be?

c   Determine the ordering costs per order that are incurred when management orders 180 bushels at each purchase. Assume 180 bushels is the economic order quantity.

PROBLEM 8

Safety Stock and Standard Deviations

	FORECAST (UNITS)	UNITS CONSUMED
March	360	375
April	325	310
May	320	295
June	290	270
July	310	315
August	350	330
September	330	300

The Worrywart Manufacturing Company is taking steps to prevent losses due to stockouts. Management desires a 97.5% degree of protection.

REQUIRED:

a   Use the preceding data to compare the previous months' actual usage with the estimated usage. Calculate the desired safety stock by using statistical methods. (Assume a 1-month lead time.)

b   What would the safety stock be if management wanted a 99.5% assurance against stockout?

c   What would the safety stock be if there was a 3-month lead time and management would like to be assured 99.5% of the time against stockouts?

PROBLEM 9

Safety Stock and Reorder Point

The Starr Company manufactures several products. One of its main products requires an electric motor. The management of Starr Company uses the economic order quantity formula (EOQ) to determine the optimum number of motors to order. Management now wants to determine how much safety stock to order.

Starr Company uses 30,000 electric motors annually (300 working days). Using the EOQ formula, the company orders 3,000 motors at a time. The lead time for an order is five days. The annual cost of carrying one motor in safety stock is $10. Management has also estimated that the cost of being out of stock is $20 for each motor they are short.

Starr Company has analyzed the usage during past reorder periods by examining the inventory records. The records indicate the following usage patterns during the past reorder periods:

USAGE DURING LEAD TIME	NUMBER OF TIMES QUANTITY WAS USED
440	6
460	12
480	16
500	130
520	20
540	10
560	6
	200

REQUIRED:

a   Determine the level of safety stock for electric motors that Starr Company should maintain in order to minimize costs.

b   What would be Starr Company's new reorder point?

c   What factors should Starr Company have considered to estimate the out-of-stock costs?

(CMA Adapted)

PROBLEM 10

Pert

Edward Jones is responsible for finding a suitable building and establishing a new convenience grocery store for Thrift-Mart, Inc. Jones enumerated the specific activities which had to be completed and the estimated time to establish each activity. In addition, he prepared a network diagram, which appears below, to aid in the coordination of the activities. The list of activities to locate a building and establish a new store is as follows:

ACTIVITY NUMBER	DESCRIPTION OF ACTIVITY	ESTIMATED TIME REQUIRED IN WEEKS
1–2	Find building	4
2–3	Negotiate rental terms	2
3–4	Draft lease	4
2–5	Prepare store plans	4
5–6	Select and order fixtures	1
6–4	Delivery of fixtures	6
4–8	Install fixtures	3
5–7	Hire staff	5
7–8	Train staff	4
8–9	Receive inventory	2
9–10	Stock shelves	1

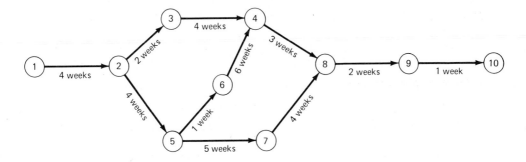

REQUIRED:

a   Identify the critical path for finding and establishing the new convenience store.

b   Edward Jones would like to finish the store 2 weeks earlier than indicated by the schedule, and as a result, he is considering several alternatives. One such alternative is to convince the fixture manufacturer to deliver the fixtures in 4 weeks rather than in 6 weeks. Should Jones arrange for the manufacturer to deliver the fixtures in 4 weeks if the sole advantage of this schedule change is to open the store 2 weeks early? Justify your answer.

c   A program, such as the one illustrated by the network diagram for the new convenience store, cannot be implemented unless the required resources are available at the required dates. What additional information does Jones need to administer the proposed project properly?

(CMA Adapted)

CHAPTER TWENTY-FOUR

HUMAN RESOURCE ACCOUNTING

A new branch of managerial accounting or cost accounting is human resource accounting (HRA). It is concerned with applying accounting concepts and procedures to personnel. Company publications and television commercials often make statements to the effect that "our employees are our most important asset." However, most companies make no attempt to actually determine the value of the human resource asset, and their accounting departments offer little help. While the greatest thrust for recognizing human resource accounting has occurred within the last decade, many leading accountants over the years have advocated such recognition. As far back as 1922, Professor William A. Paton came out strongly for the concept when he wrote: "In the business enterprise, a well organized and loyal personnel may be a more important 'asset' than a stock of merchandise. . . . At present there seems to be no way of measuring such factors in terms of the dollar. . . . But let us, accordingly, admit the serious limitation of the conventional balance sheet as a statement of financial condition."

OBJECTIONS TO CONVENTIONAL ACCOUNTING

In accordance with generally accepted accounting principles, most human resource costs are treated as expenses when incurred. Proponents of HRA have raised objections over the failure of accounting principles to provide management and investors with relevant information. Rensis Likert[1] and

[1] Rensis Likert, *New Patterns of Management*, McGraw-Hill, New York, 1961.

others pointed out in the 1960s that the failure of accounting to recognize human resources properly was causing erroneous conclusions to be drawn concerning long-term profits of companies, the effectiveness of management, and motivation of employees. There was much debate over the principles set forth by the participative school of management advocated by Likert, and what he called the authoritarian school of management advocated by most textbooks on management. Likert states that when managers attempt to decrease production cost they reduce personnel, increase supervision, restrict worker authority, and decrease employee benefits. Profits will rise over the short term because of cost cuts and increased productivity. However, according to the participative school of management, the long-term effect (1 or 2 years) of such authoritarian management techniques may be a net loss to the company. Likert points out that there may be a rise in (1) the level of hostility between labor and management, (2) the desire to restrict production, (3) grievances, (4) absenteeism, and (5) turnover.

The principal failures of conventional accounting, according to HRA advocates, may be summarized as follows:[2]

1 *Human resource costs are expensed.* A great many HRA costs have both asset and expense components. Those that benefit future periods such as acquisition and development costs should be capitalized and spread over the productive life of the particular employee.

2 *Long-term HRA costs are ignored.* Without adequate HRA information, management has little idea of the total investment in human resources. Questions cannot be answered as to: What is the cost of recruiting in engineering? What is the development cost for an accountant? What is the dollar turnover cost?

3 *Lack of data needed for planning and control.* Management needs personnel data as much as data for materials and overhead, for proper planning and control. Present accounting systems do not provide the needed data. For example, HRA would provide the cost information necessary for budgeting, such as the cost of recruiting and training new employees. Human resource control helps assure that human resource objectives are attained.

4 *Lack of social responsibility.* HRA advocates some time ago criticized many large companies for their lack of social responsibility. The effort has been effective in raising the consciousness of American business people. Now profit is not the only goal of most companies. Social and environmental aspects must now be considered. Does the product increase air pollution? Does it harm the health of consumers or neighbors? Does it harm the environment? Many environmental agencies have been established by governmental bodies to measure and report any unfavorable environmental impact.

---

[2] James Fales, *Human Resource Accounting*, vol. 3, p. 254, Current Problems in the Accounting Profession, Hofstra University Yearbook of Business, 1979.

5 *Ignoring employee needs.* HRA advocates state that managers at every level should recognize the abilities, skills, and creativity of employees they direct. Workers want to participate and contribute in the management of the company. Frustration caused by low-level routine work and stifling of initiative leads to a high job turnover rate. Frustration also has been found to be a causative factor in family problems and in alcoholism. Has the company made a conscientious effort to improve the "quality of life" of employees? How does the effort of one company compare with the efforts of other companies in the same industry.

NATURE OF HUMAN RESOURCE ACCOUNTING

Definition

We may define human resource accounting as *the recording, management, and reporting of personnel costs.* The American Accounting Association has defined HRA as *the process of identifying and measuring data about the human resources and communicating this information to interested parties.*[3] Human resource accounting recognizes investments in employees as enterprise resources and facilitates the application of accounting principles to the acquisition and development of human resources.

Objectives of HRA

The objectives of human resource accounting have been stated as follows:

1 *Quantitative information.* To provide quantitative information on an organization's human resources that management and investors can use in decision making
2 *Evaluation methods.* To provide evaluation methods for the utilization of human resources
3 *Theory and model.* To provide a theory and relevant variables to explain the value of people to formal organizations, to identify relevant variables, and to develop an ideal model for management of human resources[4]

Assumptions Underlying HRA

Human resource accounting makes three basic assumptions, as follows:

1 *People are valuable organizational resources.* The first assumption of human resource accounting is that people are valuable enterprise resources. They provide current and future services but they are not owned as are machines or materials. The invested resources can be

---

[3] Report of the Committee on Human Resource Accounting, AAA, *Accounting Review Supplement*, 1973.
[4] Thomas McRae, "Human Resource Accounting as a Management Tool," *Journal of Accounting*, August 1974, p. 32.

accounted for without ownership. For example, we can accumulate the acquisition and development costs as well as the related replacement costs. Human resource accounting data can be presented as supplementary material to the conventional external report. Negative factors such as replacement costs can be shown as an *allowance for turnover* just as we provide an *allowance for uncollectible accounts*.

2   *Influence of management style.* The second assumption of HRA is that the value of human resources can be influenced by the way they are managed. Some attitudes or styles of management may increase employee motivation and increase productivity, while other management styles may decrease motivation and thus decrease productivity.

3   *Need for human resource information.* The third assumption of HRA is that information about human resource cost and value is necessary for effective and efficient management of people as an organization resource. Human resource cost and value are useful in various aspects of the human resource management process, including planning and control of the acquisition, development, allocation, composition, conservation, and utilization of people. In this sense, HRA is intended as a component of the overall managerial accounting information system.[5]

TYPES OF HUMAN RESOURCE COSTS

Most of the cost concepts of conventional accounting are applicable to human resource accounting. Before proceeding, it is desirable to define some of the basic accounting terms. The principal terms used are[6]

Cost.   A sacrifice (cost) incurred to obtain some anticipated benefit or service. It may apply to tangible objects or intangible benefits. Many costs may have asset and expense components.

Asset.   The portion of cost that is expected to provide benefits during future accounting periods.

Expense.   The portion of cost that has been consumed during the current accounting period.

The various types of human resource costs are shown in Figure 24-1 (page 830).

Acquisition Costs

These are the costs incurred in the recruitment, selection, hiring, and induction of employees. Efficient management of human resources is essential in attaining the enterprise's objectives. Costs are capitalized and accumulated under the respective functions. This information is essential in the planning and control of human resources and the budgeting of personnel. Many

[5] S. Davidson and R. Weil, *Handbook of Cost Accounting*, McGraw-Hill, New York, 1978.
[6] *Ibid.*, p. 26-6.

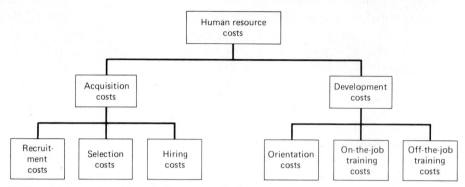

FIGURE 24-1 **Types of Human Resource Costs**

companies have developed standard costs for the acquisition and development related to various company positions.

Recruitment Costs. These are costs incurred in locating and identifying the candidates for a position. Included would be candidates from inside and outside the organization. Costs would include job advertisements, agency fees, recruiters' salaries and benefits, travel and entertainment, materials such as recruiting brochures, administrative costs, etc.

Selection Costs. These costs are incurred in determining those to be offered employment. The selection costs will vary somewhat with the particular job involved. The principal costs are interviewing, testing, evaluating, and any other processing cost. The cost of the extended tests would result in greater costs for managers, accountants, or engineers than for machine workers, secretaries, or bank tellers. Where employment agencies may be used to screen employees, agency fees would generally be higher.

Hiring Costs. These costs are incurred in bringing the employee into the enterprise and placing the person in the particular job. The employee may be transferred or promoted from inside the enterprise or hired from outside. Costs would include relocation costs for new or present employees, such as moving and travel costs and temporary living costs until permanent quarters are established, physical examinations, costs of placing the employee on the books, and any special equipment needed for the job.

Development Costs

These costs are incurred to train a person to the level needed or to enhance the individual's skills. They might be incurred at the beginning of the new job or later, or to develop the employee for a possible supervisory position. There would be a familiarization period when the employee may need to learn company policies and the background and the hierarchy of the enterprise. Learning costs would be those incurred to make the person an effective member of the enterprise. The extent of the training would depend on the level of the position; the higher the position, the higher the cost. Development costs would be accumulated by individual and amortized over the expected employment period of the employee. When an individual resigns or is fired, the enterprise would lose the investment accumulated, and the unamortized cost would be written off as an expense in the period the person leaves the enterprise. This treatment is comparable with the conventional accounting procedure when a physical asset is involved.

Orientation Costs. These costs involve the usual expenditures incurred in the formal orientation of employees. Generally, orientation includes providing information to the new employee concerning personnel policies, enterprise management, products and services, facilities and locations, fringe benefits such as pension and medical benefits, bonus and stock option plans, etc. These costs also include materials such as personnel booklets describing the various employee plans. Also included are salaries and costs of persons providing the training. The orientation period will vary according to the job and may require a few hours, days, or weeks.

On-the-Job Training Costs. These costs are incurred in training an employee while on the specific job, rather than in the more general orientation program which all new employees would take. The period of time may extend from a short period for production workers to several months for the more responsible positions. One of the principal costs during this period is the imputed cost, that is, the difference between the productivity of a trainee and of an experienced employee. Various types of learning curves have been developed to show graphically the reduction in learning cost as the training progresses and productivity increases.

Off-the-Job Training Costs. These costs are incurred generally for advanced technical training or management development programs not directly related to job performance. The programs may be "in house" classes taught by qualified company personnel or by outside instructors. Employees may also attend professional seminars or conferences offered by professional associations of engineers or accountants. Many enterprises also encourage employees to attend nearby colleges or universities. Often as an inducement the enterprise may pay directly for this training or may reimburse the employee if a satisfactory grade is earned. Specific costs for off-the-job training include salaries, travel, tuition, materials, etc.

Replacement Costs

As in Figure 24-2 (page 832), replacement costs include acquisition costs and development costs as well as separation costs. Replacement costs are those incurred in replacing an employee in a given position. The costs are concerned with the *position* rather than the *individual employee*. For example, there may be a number of individuals with various characteristics who are engineers in a company. They all meet the standard specifications established for an engineer. Thus we are concerned with the costs to replace an employee

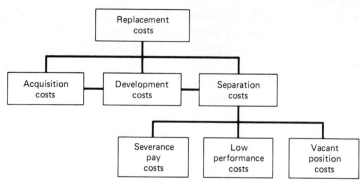

FIGURE 24-2 **Costs Involved in Replacing an Employee**

meeting the standard job specifications. The three components of replacement costs are acquisition costs, development costs, and separation costs. Acquisition and development costs have already been discussed.

Separation Costs. These are the costs involved in the termination of an employee. Included are the outlay costs such as severance pay and often substantial imputed or indirect costs. These costs generally relate to the low performance ordinarily resulting from employee dissatisfaction, and the higher costs and lower productivity of associated employees or departments when a position is vacant. Generally, most employees must depend upon another employee to provide information or material before their work can be completed.

Severance Pay Costs. This is the amount of prepaid compensation given to an employee upon leaving the company. Usually the cost estimated for management control purposes is the average pay for the particular classification. In a given case the amount may range from a small amount for a lower-level position to a very substantial amount for a high-level position. Generally, the amount is based on the compensation for a week or month. For example, the severance pay may come to 3 weeks for a weekly-paid employee or 1 to 3 months for a monthly-paid employee. For an officer or executive the severance pay may be the individual's salary for over a year or more. Often the costs, though very substantial, are not now measured or reported.

Low-Performance Costs. This cost represents the loss of productivity before the employee leaves the company. Generally, employees give low performance before separation. They may be absent having interviews for another job, or even if present, they have lost interest in the current job and thus have a low performance rate.

Vacant Position Costs. When a position is vacant, indirect costs may be incurred in related areas. For example, if the position of cost accountant is vacant in a manufacturing company, others from a higher level such as an office manager may have to fill in temporarily. This may cause a delay in completing the work and a resultant delay in forwarding the financial statements. Also other positions may not receive needed information. Certain imputed costs may be involved, for example, when a sales job is vacant and definite sales have been lost.

ACCOUNTING FOR HUMAN RESOURCE COSTS

Many of the problems that have caused a great deal of discussion over the years with respect to physical assets continue as problems in accounting for human resource costs. These are (1) historical versus replacement costs, and (2) outlay versus imputed costs.

Historical versus Replacement Costs

Before we discuss the two accounting terms mentioned here, it might be well to define what we mean by each term.

Historical or original cost is the cost actually incurred to acquire a resource. In present-day accounting this is the cost that would ordinarily be retained for the life of a physical asset.

Replacement cost is the cost that must be incurred to replace a resource presently owned or employed. The problem of historical versus replacement costs has been widely debated. The SEC and FASB currently require replacement cost as supplementary information, not as an integral part of financial statements. The differences between historical and replacement costs for human resources can be very substantial. When we consider that the service life of an employee may extend to 45 years or more, the costs to acquire and train an employee can vary dramatically. Replacement cost for HRA can be an added part to the historical data or it can be integrated into the accounting system. The two costs, historical and replacement, have separate managerial uses, and it is usually desirable to maintain both historical and replacement costs. There are two separate concepts of replacement cost: (1) positional replacement cost, and (2) personal replacement cost.

Positional replacement cost refers to the cost incurred today to replace satisfactorily a person in a *specified position*. Personal replacement cost refers to the cost incurred today to replace satisfactorily a *particular person*. Generally, personnel managers think in terms of requiring a substitute for a specified position rather than for a particular individual. For managerial decision making, replacement cost is generally more relevant than historical cost. For example, if a company is considering opening a new plant in another location and it will be necessary to replace 13 engineers and 2 cost accountants, which would be sent to the new plant? The replacement cost for these 15 employees could well be a significant factor in the decision to expand or not to expand. Replacement costs would be more useful in this case than would historical cost. It would also be a more accurate method in establishing standard position acquisition costs and for personnel department costing.

Outlay versus Imputed Costs

We have already mentioned how imputed costs may affect human resource accounting. At this point we should distinguish between outlay and imputed costs by defining each term.

Outlay costs are the actual cash expenditures incurred to acquire or replace a resource. It is the cash that must be given up.

Imputed costs do not require actual cash outlays and thus are not shown in the accounting records or reports. For example, if a company has sold out a particular product and orders are received, there is an imputed loss of gross profit on orders not shipped.

FINANCIAL STATEMENTS UTILIZING HUMAN RESOURCE ACCOUNTING

Some firms are now publishing Human Resource Financial Statements as supplemental information in their Annual Reports. Table 24-1 is an actual income statement and balance sheet for a manufacturing firm that capitalizes human resource costs, compared with the firm's conventional income statement and balance sheet.

OUTLOOK FOR HRA

In recent years progress has been made in measuring and quantifying many human resource costs. In fact, human resource accounting installations have been made in recent years in various enterprises, including manufacturing companies, and service organizations such as banks, insurance companies, and CPA firms. Research must still be done on the theoretical aspects of HRA, such as whether such costs are to be accepted as assets and how they are to be valued. Empirical data from companies using HRA must yet be assembled, analyzed, and published. The question at present remains—will this more costly system result in better management decisions that will offset the additional cost?

CHAPTER REVIEW

Human resource accounting is finally coming of age as a new branch of cost accounting. Although the concept has been around for many years, it is only in the last few years that important practical advances have been made. A number of new advocates, accountants rather than economists, have helped to bring the theoretical aspects more in line with accounting theory and practice. Installations of human resource accounting have been made in a number of enterprises, including manufacturing companies and various other industries. There is still much empirical data to gather based on the present installations.

TABLE 24-1

HUMAN RESOURCE ACCOUNTING VERSUS CONVENTIONAL ACCOUNTING

	HUMAN RESOURCE ACCOUNTING	CONVENTIONAL ACCOUNTING
Statement of Income		
Net sales	$28,164,181	$28,164,181
Cost of sales	18,252,181	18,252,181
Gross profit	$ 9,912,000	$ 9,912,000
Selling, general, and administrative expenses ...	7,546,118	7,546,118
Operating income	$ 2,365,882	$ 2,365,882
Other deductions, net	250,412	250,412
Income before federal income taxes	$ 2,115,470	$ 2,115,470
Net increase (decrease) in human resource investment	$ (43,900)	—
Adjusted income before federal income taxes ...	$ 2,071,570	$ 2,115,470
Federal income taxes	1,008,050	1,030,000
Net income	$ 1,063,520	$ 1,085,470
Balance Sheet		
Assets		
Total current assets	$10,944,693	$10,944,693
Net property, plant, and equipment	1,682,357	1,682,357
Excess of purchase price of subsidiaries over net assets acquired	1,188,704	1,188,704
Net investments in human resources	942,194	—
Other assets	166,417	166,417
	$14,924,365	$13,982,171
Liabilities and Stockholders' Equity		
Total current liabilities	$ 3,651,573	$ 3,651,573
Long-term debt, excluding current installments .	2,179,000	2,179,000
Deferred compensation	77,491	77,491
Deferred federal income taxes based upon full tax deduction for human resource costs	471,097	—
Stockholders' equity:		
Capital stock	1,087,211	1,087,211
Additional capital in excess of par value	3,951,843	3,951,843
Retained earnings:		
Financial	3,035,053	3,035,053
Human resources	471,097	—
Total stockholders' equity	$ 8,545,204	$ 8,074,107
	$14,924,365	$13,982,171

The principal failures of conventional accounting, according to HRA advocates are (1) human resources are expensed, (2) long-term HRA costs are ignored, (3) data needed for planning and control is lacking, (4) social responsibility is lacking, and (5) employee needs are ignored. Most of these problems are now being researched by HRA advocates, and research papers concerning results are constantly being published. According to HRA, there are certain basic human resource costs that should be capitalized and spread over the working life of the employee. The principal costs involved are acquisition costs and development costs relating to employees. Management has a great deal of information on which to make management decisions concerning materials and overhead, but very inadequate data to make decisions concerning personnel.

With adequate reports and analyses concerning personnel, HRA advocates believe that many personnel decisions now being made would be entirely different if more personnel data were available. It is expected that with further developments in the field more companies may adopt HRA. However, more studies will have to be made to prove that the additional cost of human resource accounting is justified by improved management decisions concerning personnel.

GLOSSARY

Acquisition Costs—the costs incurred in the recruitment, selection, hiring, and induction of employees.

Development Costs—the costs incurred in training employees to the required performance level, or to enhance their technical, administrative, or general skills.

Hiring Costs—the costs incurred in bringing the employee into the enterprise and into the particular job.

Historical Costs—costs initially incurred to obtain a resource. Sometimes called "original costs."

Human Resource Accounting—the recording, management, and reporting of personnel costs.

Imputed Costs—the costs which do not require actual cash outlays and generally are not shown in the accounting records or reports.

Low Performance Costs—the loss of productivity, usually indirect, prior to the time the employee leaves the company.

Off-the-Job Training—the costs incurred generally for advanced technical training or management development programs not directly related to job performance.

On-the-Job Training—the costs incurred in training an employee while on the specific job.

Orientation Costs—the costs incurred in providing information to new employees concerning personnel policies, employee benefits, enterprise management, products and services, facilities and locations, etc.

Original Costs—same as historical costs.

Outlay Costs—the actual cash expenditures made to acquire or replace a resource.

Recruitment Costs—the costs incurred in locating and identifying candidates for a position.

Replacement Costs—the costs incurred in replacing an employee in a given position.

Selection Costs—the costs incurred, such as interviewing and testing, in determining those to be offered employment.

Separation Costs—the costs involved in the termination of an employee.

Severance Pay Costs—the amount of prepaid compensation given to an employee upon leaving the company.

Vacant Position Costs—the costs incurred, generally indirectly, in related positions which do not receive essential information.

QUESTIONS

1   Define human resource accounting and state its purpose or objective.
2   What are the three basic assumptions of human resource accounting?
3   In terms of HRA, describe what is meant by acquisition costs.
4   What are some of the negative effects of an authoritarian management?
5   What is the difference between outlay costs and imputed costs?
6   There are three major components of replacement costs. State the three components and briefly describe each one.
7   Define the term "separation costs," and describe the costs grouped under that heading.
8   What are the weaknesses in conventional accounting that encourage the acceptance of HRA?
9   Compare on-the-job training costs and off-the-job training costs in terms of their similarities and differences.
10   What is meant by the term "orientation costs"?

INDEX

INDEX